Information, Institutions, and Local Government in England, 1550–1700

Information, Institutions, and Local Government in England, 1550–1700

Turning Inside

PAUL GRIFFITHS

OXFORD
UNIVERSITY PRESS

OXFORD
UNIVERSITY PRESS

Great Clarendon Street, Oxford, OX2 6DP,
United Kingdom

Oxford University Press is a department of the University of Oxford.
It furthers the University's objective of excellence in research, scholarship,
and education by publishing worldwide. Oxford is a registered trade mark of
Oxford University Press in the UK and in certain other countries

Published in the United States of America by Oxford University Press
198 Madison Avenue, New York, NY 10016, United States of America

British Library Cataloguing in Publication Data
Data available

Library of Congress Control Number: 2023942392

ISBN 978-0-19-289626-1

DOI: 10.1093/oso/9780192896261.001.0001

Printed and bound by
CPI Group (UK) Ltd, Croydon, CR0 4YY

For Eva and Keith Wrightson
Thanks for everything since 1988

Preface

This book has been quite long in the making. It goes all the way back to the mid-1990s when, sitting in the long gone and missed Corporation of London Record Office, working on what would eventually become *Lost Londons: Change, Crime, and Control in the Capital City, 1550–1660* (Cambridge, 2008), I began to think more than ever before about how the records I was reading were objects and subjects in themselves.

This had been drummed into me in one talk/chat/paper/drink after another in Cambridge, and the foibles and duplicities of the archive were second nature to me. Perhaps I had given more thought to how they might touch and tinge my own work rather than what it meant for how records were made and used in the first place. This distinction matters. It was an entry in a repertory insisting that records must be kept 'secret' and 'safe' at all costs that got me thinking along these lines. This was hardly a very revealing or memorable moment worthy of recording, but it made me think long and hard about what records meant to the people who made them and to those who were present at their making. As well as being essential elements in retrieving the pieces and people of the past, the records that I was holding in my hands constituted particular processes, constructions of places and events, and cultures of governance that were sunk in time. They included categorization, quantification, the organization and practices of what at the time was called 'knowledge' and 'informaccon' or 'making knowne', and secrecy and security as if nothing else mattered. My first published words on these things appeared in an article on secrecy in *The Historical Journal* (1997); the next were the last chapter in *Lost Londons*: 'Policing: Information'.

We historians have written with archives for so long but not enough about them. Or, to put it another way, the archive is more often thought of as a repository to go to and not as a construction or representation of a particular authority and ideology that was put together in deliberate and calculated ways that continue up to this day. In other words, any archive or record is the creation of categorization, selection, organization, and economics. Our archives today are only the most recent manifestation of a six-century-long evolution for early modern records, and there is a cold and cruel story to tell of Victorian pulping and also of what we lost in the need for paper in World War II.[1] We should probably be grateful for what we have.

[1] P. Thorsheim, *Waste into Weapons: Recycling in Britain During the Second World War* (Cambridge, 2015).

We think about archives as a source, for the most part, not as a subject. But they were not made for us. Their makers had the next generation in mind if they ever spoke of 'posterity'. I decided to write a book about archives and information after *Lost Londons*. This book, I decided, would not be based in and around royal bureaucracies, as that was already well-trodden ground.[2] I wanted to work instead from the bottom up, where I saw lots of great work on particular pieces of information and/or administration but not too much on the valuable aggregate or comprehensive systems of information gathering and use in England's towns and villages. I wanted to work with local judicial and government records that could talk to me about England's scattered particles, not its heavy Whitehall centre. I ended up working in three dozen archives in all parts of the country, although York was as far north as I got on the east side and Kendal on the other side.

Things changed over a decade or more, as they so often do. Fresh finds in archives, handy tips from friends, or new pieces of scholarship made me think twice or more about something that mattered. My agenda grew over the years. It quickly became clear that information and archives should never be studied alone or apart. Information, after all, was brought to archives from the world outside to be sorted and stored. We find a place or idea written or constructed in their records. So, my thoughts turned to the contexts, concepts, and cultures that shaped more widespread and effective local information systems in all corners of the country. The word 'inside' had been on my mind for a long while; 'Inside Government' was the first working title of this book for a few years. This title was deliberately double-edged. The book would be both a close-up study of workaday local government and how I felt that it was turning inside while still pursuing 'manifestaccon' (or representing authority in public). They were clearly related. Little changed in one that did not have knock-on effects for the other. *Information, Institutions, and Local Government in England, 1550–1700* is split fairly evenly between people and events outside ('manifestaccon' and the public punishment of petty crime) and inside (institutions and information). Their relations, tensions, and divergences are its main themes and topics.

A National Humanities Centre Fellowship in 2002–3 which was awarded to write *Lost Londons* also gave me plenty of time to think through many of the issues in this book. A National Endowment of the Humanities Fellowship (FA-57894-14 2014-15) gave me precious time to begin writing *Information, Institutions, and Local Government in England, 1550–1700*. I am also grateful to Iowa State University College of Liberal Arts and Sciences and Center for Excellence in the Arts and Humanities for financial support for trips to England to work in archives.

[2] Nicholas Popper is currently doing some important work on information and central government archives. See his 'An information state for Elizabethan England', *Journal of Modern History*, 90 (2018).

My first debt, as ever, is to the archivists and staff in the many archives I have worked in for this book from the mid-1990s on. Like universities, and especially anything to do with the humanities, their resources get cut and cut again, but their commitment to the records and willingness to help with some fairly basic questions are greatly appreciated. Warm thanks also to Rebecca Ireland at OUP for believing in this book and to Cathryn Steele and Aimee Wright for guiding it home over the finishing line. Many friends and colleagues have given me helping hands over the two decades or so in which this book has been in the making. They include Kevin Amidon, Bernard Capp, Tom Cogswell, Andy Delbanco, Martin Ingram, Trevor Johnson (RIP), Paulina Kewes, Peter King, Randall McGowen, Maggie Pelling, David Porter, Dave Rollison, Ulinka Rublack, Roger Schofield (RIP), Moshe Shuvlosky, and Tim Wales.

I would like to give special thanks to Ian Archer, John Beattie (RIP), Ian Gentles, Mark Jenner, Dave Postles, Jim Sharpe (my first ever mentor at the University of York), and my longest early modern friend since our days at York, Andy (Wood).

Ian Archer and Keith Wrightson both read *Information, Institutions, and Local Government in England, 1550*–1700 in draft, and I am deeply grateful to both of them.

Bob Scribner has been dead for over a quarter of a century, but our many times together in two Cambridges will always be an inspiration to me forever. Only Keith Wrightson matters more for whatever sort of historian I have become over the last three decades or so. This book is for Eva and Keith. Thank you both with all the warmth that words on a page can bring for everything that you have done for me from the house on New Square to this day. Vd'aka!

A Note on References

A large number of documents that I first read in the now gone Corporation of London Records Office (CLRO) and also in the London Guildhall Library, Manuscripts Division, (GL) have been moved to the London Metropolitan Archives (LMA). This book was first drafted using the old CLRO and GL manuscript references and rather than changing every single reference in the footnotes, I have supplied the current LMA references at the end of each entry in the Bibliography at the end of this book.

Contents

List of Illustrations

Figures

Plates

List of Tables

List of Abbreviations

AHR	*American Historical Review*
APC	J. R. Dasent et al., eds., *Acts of the Privy Council*, 46 vols (1890–1964)
BIA	Borthwick Institute for Archives, York
BL	British Library
BMM	Bethlem Museum of the Mind
BRO	Berkshire Record Office
C&C	*Continuity and Change*
CA	Cheshire Archives and Local Studies
CH	Clothworkers' Hall, London
CKS	Centre for Kentish Studies
CSPV	Calendar of State Papers Venetian
CUL	Cambridge University Library
DHC	Dorset History Centre
DRO	Devon Record Office
ECHR	*Economic History Review*
EHR	*English Historical Review*
ERO	Essex Record Office
ESBHRO	East Sussex and Brighton and Hove Record Office
GA	Gloucestershire Archives
GCL	Goldsmiths' Company Library, London
GL	Guildhall Library, London
HA	Hampshire Archives and Local Studies
HEA	Herefordshire Archives and Record Centre
HJ	*Historical Journal*
HL	Huntington Library, San Marino
HOL	House of Lords
HWJ	*History Workshop Journal*
JBS	*Journal of British Studies*
Jour.	*Journal of London Common Council*
KAC	Kendal Archive Centre
LA	Lancashire Archives
LBHC	London Bridewell Hospital Courtbook
LERO	Leicestershire Record Office
LMA	London Metropolitan Archives
NA	Northamptonshire Archives
NDRO	North Devon Record Office
NMCC	Norwich Mayor's Court Courtbook
NOTTA	Nottinghamshire Archives

NRO	Norfolk Record Office
ODNB	*Oxford Dictionary of National Biography*, 60 vols (2004)
OHC	Oxfordshire History Centre
P&P	*Past & Present*
Rep.	Repertory of London Court of Aldermen
SA	Southampton Archives
SAI	Suffolk Archives, Ipswich
SBHA	St Bartholomew's Hospital Archive
SH	*Social History*
SHA	Shropshire Archives
SP	State Papers
SRPJ	J. F. Larkin and P. L. Hughes, eds., *Stuart Royal Proclamations, Vol. 1: Royal Proclamations of King James I, 1603–25* (Oxford, 1973)
STAC	Star Chamber
TNA	The National Archives
TRHS	*Transactions of the Royal Historical Society*
UH	*Urban History*
WAC	Westminster Archive Centre
WRO	Warwickshire Record Office
WSHC	Wiltshire and Swindon History Centre
YCA	York City Archives

Things aren't what they look like, Paul.

Julian Barnes, *The Only Story* (2018)

Introduction

Information, Institutions, and Local Government in England, 1550–1700 investigates shifts of long-lasting significance in local-level government (*c*.1550–*c*.1700). It was in these 150 years that magistrates from Whitehall to Westmorland came to rely much more heavily on developing information systems and cultures in forms and extent that was innovative and a range of institutions that were clearly distinctive, including England's first nationwide system of incarceration inside bridewells for what was called 'better' government. This was 'turning inside'. These shifts were not yet fully realized by the end of the seventeenth century but the groundwork for them was secure. The age-old reliance on public/visual representations of authority or 'manifestaccon' remained, but it was being questioned more sharply than ever before. It would not be long until a fair number of its parts would become museum pieces.

A series of parallel developments, with many things in common and all involving sixteenth-century roots, were powerful enough together to make 'turning inside' possible. Each one was sufficiently significant to make a real difference, but together they changed local government (and England) for good. They include (1) the consequences of far-reaching social, demographic, and economic changes that included much deeper poverty, thinner resources, more movement, and real or imagined crime waves; (2) a more commercial society that required its dedicated members to acquire greater competence in accounting, record-keeping, and using records more effectively in order to compete; (3) reconfigurations of the greater reach of the State across the land in modified reciprocal relations with local governments that put great weight on the shoulders of 'middling-sort' parish officers in towns and villages; (4) the growing prominence and accumulated know-how of 'substantial inhabitants' in work and office acting knowledgeably and confidently; (5) more self-conscious and tightly knit local bodies and government in self-styled associations like the more autonomous 'urban commonwealths' or the vestry in Swallowfield in Berkshire; (6) sharpening concerns with the effectiveness of representing authority in 'publique', including public punishment; (7) the various ways in which information collection and a range of institutions became through the contemporary term 'experience' absolutely indispensable to law and order and governing more generally; and (8) more persuasive insistence on precision and clarity in broad bodies of knowledge, culture, and practice that had lasting impacts on governing England's towns and villages.

Information, Institutions, and Local Government in England, 1550–1700: Turning Inside. Paul Griffiths, Oxford University Press. © Paul Griffiths 2023. DOI: 10.1093/oso/9780192896261.003.0001

I

The key role of 'middling' men in running local government is among the common denominators that link all that follows in this book. The more elevated among them made up the cream of the civic crop taking life-long positions as aldermen and maybe mayor one day if all went well. It was farmers, shopkeepers, traders, and craftworkers who filled the positions of churchwardens, constables, and overseers in England's towns and villages. They had the most to lose whenever the parish peace or purse was at risk and their property and income felt vulnerable. These office-holder(s), employers, and ratepayers made choices about the cost, form, and effectiveness of 'manifestaccon' or the public representation of governing ethics and politics (Chapter 2) and about whom to punish and the best ways to do it (Chapter 3). The records that they made reveal their aspirations to be 'true', 'exact', and 'precyse' in or out of office (Chapters 1 and 5). With the courts that they so often turned to as individual members of a community, they regulated and ran bridewells and chose whether to punish troublemakers inside these 'prysonnes' or outside at whipping posts, for instance, or with the only gender-specific penalty at this time—the waterside ducking/cucking stool (Chapters 3–4). And, crucially, 'middling' men in local office were the driving force behind the organization of more sophisticated systems of information collection and their use for governing England's towns and villages (Chapter 5).

These 'middling' officers thought both practically and conceptually—as we should too—about how government outside and inside related to each other. Looking back, after the fact, it is clear today that the balance has tipped decisively away from articulating authority in open spaces. But this would not have been so apparent to anyone holding local office four centuries ago. There was no grand government scheme at any level to turn increasingly inside, although the 1610 legislation that insisted on at least one bridewell in every town and county points in that direction. I cannot think of a single sustained argument in a book or anywhere else that made a case in full for such fundamental changes in grass-roots government in the sixteenth and seventeenth centuries. There was no road-to-Damascus moment anywhere in England for the 'turn inside' or any contemporary words that catch what this book is about in a crisp sentence. Choices and outcomes were instead pragmatic, accumulative, and long in the making. They were rooted in what governors called 'experience'. The 'turn inside' was a time-consuming manoeuvre driven slowly in low gear over 150 years through experiential decision-making for the most part rather than by design.

Influential 'middling' office-holder(s) are also leading lights in the most recent configuration of the greater administrative presence/reach of the central government in England's parishes on a daily basis. This was not the straightforward outcome of top-heavy interventions from the State. Keith Wrightson made the point forty years ago that this was not aggressive centralization but a growth in governance that touched all parts of the country in which local officers worked hand in hand with Whitehall. Later work by Mike Braddick and Steve Hindle did not add anything substantial to Wrightson's conceptual groundwork. But it did confirm the narrative of state formation as a two-way process of delegation where local government responded to articles and orders from Whitehall that became more intense from the stormy 1590s on. Local governors also took progressively more initiatives of their own to deal with local needs.[1] There was little if any root-and-branch restructuring of institutions from 'above'. The Crown did turn lord lieutenancies into permanent positions to meet military necessities in the Spanish War in 1585, while the number of justices appointed in the provinces soared sevenfold over the course of Elizabeth's long reign, with a parallel growth in commissions. Acting locally, a good number of parishes pruned their vestries to 'select' status and size. But centralization—*pace* Wrightson—was more about expanding regulation with the help of local hands and 'experience'.

Norman Jones writes smartly that central government was in effect a form of local government. Braddick calls this 'a local interaction order'. 'Governmental will', in his words, was carried out by officers who read it with the well-being of their communities in mind. Seeing the State as 'a coordinated and territorially bounded network of agencies', ideas of how it worked must reach down to 'middling' men in the cockpits of local government.[2] They were the 'chieffe inhabitants' of Swallowfield parish (Berkshire) who knew full well their dual charge to their country and community. We meet, they said, 'for the better servynge of her Ma[jes]tie [for] sessments or other [royal] besynes [or] any other mater or cause consernynge the churche, the poore or the parrishe'.[3] This mighty effort needed to come to terms with social, demographic, and economic challenges that pulled the English State and locality together like never before. Many of this period's 'stacks of statutes' were either targeted towards specific local matters or depended for implementation on the goodwill and work of local officers. This by now routine central/local collaboration is clear in local government records. Reading corporation bought 'the booke of statutes made in every parylment since the vii yere of King John' in 1629 ('to be kept in this hall for the service of the companye'). Yarmouth bought the 'statutes att lardge in two volumes [and] Daltons justice of peace in 2 books' in 1630 ('on the backside with Great Yermouth stampt in gould').[4] Oxford council instructed the clerk to 'buy the statutes att lardge [and] all new statutes since the impression and edition of Dalton's justice of the peace'

[1] K. Wrightson, *English Society, 1580–1680* (1982); S. Hindle, *The State and Social Change in Early Modern England, c.1550–1640* (Basingstoke, 2000); M. J. Braddick, *State Formation in Early Modern England* (Cambridge, 2000).

[2] N. Jones, *The English Reformation: Religion and Cultural Adaptation* (Oxford, 2002), 135; Braddick, *State Formation*, 75, 16, 9; Hindle, *State and Social Change*, 23, 20, chap. 8.

[3] HL Ellesmere MS 6162, fo. 35.

[4] BRO R/AC1/1/3, fo. 19; NRO Y/C27/2, 1633.

in 1679.[5] Towns spent varying sums to buy statute books: thirty-nine shillings in Marlborough in 1618, 4s. 6d. (Gloucester), four shillings (Lyme Regis), 3s. 4d. in Kendal in 1598 when the work of the new Poor Law fell on the shoulders of local authorities, and 2s. 2d. (Barnstaple).[6] Leicester forked out twenty-pence 'for the booke of statuts of the last parliament' in 1576 that included legislation on poverty and bridewells. Many towns also spent up to eight shillings 'for a booke called the abridgemente of statutes'.[7] Policies and news also crossed the land in letters, of course. Gloucester's mayor listed 'dyvers bundles of letters from his majesties councell' among his papers in 1613.[8] Messengers carried royal proclamations to all corners of the land to be read aloud in market squares and pinned on posts for people to read. Hereford splashed out £5 'for wine, sugar, and other guifts' for one in 1662. Thetford spent £2 8s. on 'proclamacons and commissions' in 1625.[9] Small South Newington five miles from Banbury paid six-pence in 1684 to buy a copy of 'the proclamation of the kings martherdum'. While a messenger picked up 7s. 6d. from Gloucester's rulers in 1685 for bringing 'proclamacons for a reward of 5000li for the taking Monmouth and one for hindring distribucon of Monmouths declaracon'.[10]

The Poor Law (1598, 1601) was the main legislative building block in the working relationship between Whitehall and local governors. The parish was the core organizational unit for this landmark legislation that stayed on the statute book until 1834. Locally chosen overseers drew up rate assessments of the better-off and collected the money to distribute handouts to deserving resident paupers whose needs they had also calculated. No other single piece of legislation created more records or required more information gathering at local levels. It also insisted on the benefits of bridewells.[11] The 1662 Settlement Act also tightened ties in the 'parish state', calling for extensive documentation of length of residence by local authorities.[12] Other legislation and policies needed the State and locality to work in tandem, but nothing on the scope and scale of the Poor Law. Social policy more generally could only work if local governors played their parts. Privy

[5] OHC C/FC/1/A1/04, fo. 180.

[6] WSHC G22/1/205/2, fos. 54, 61; GA GBR/F/4/3, fos. 78v, 237v; GBR/F/4/7, fo. 97; DHC DC/LR/G/2/2, 1577–8, 1661–2; KAC WSMB/K/1/5, 1597–8, 1616–17.

[7] LERO BRIII/2/43; BRIII/2/45. See also DRO B1/3792; DHC DC/BTB/M2/1625; SHA 3365/511; 365/523; NRO Norwich Chamberlains' Accounts, 1625/48, fos. 14, 104; Clavors Book 1, fos. 54, 98v; CKS FA/AC4, fo. 5; Md/Acm1/3, fo. 3.

[8] GA GBR/G/G3/SO/1, fo. 29.

[9] HEA BG/11/23, fo. 15; NRO T/C1/4, fo. 24.

[10] E. R. C. Brinkworth, ed., *South Newington Churchwardens' Accounts 1553–1684*, Banbury Historical Society, 6 (1964), 72; GA GBR/F/4/7, fo. 355. Cf. C. Kyle, 'Monarchs and marketplace: proclamations as news in early modern England', *Huntington Library Quarterly*, 78 (2015); C. Boswell, *Disaffection and Everyday Life in Interregnum England* (Woodbridge, 2017), 47–52.

[11] P. Slack, *Poverty and Policy in Tudor and Stuart England* (Harlow, 1988).

[12] N. Tadmor, 'The settlement of the poor and the rise of the form in England, c.1662–1780', *P&P*, 236 (2017); N. Landau, 'The laws of settlement and the surveillance of immigration in eighteenth-century Kent', *C&C*, 3 (1988); S. Hindle, *On the Parish: the Micro-Politics of Poor Relief in Rural England, c.1550–1750* (Oxford, 2004), chap. 5.

councillors sent them Books of Orders whenever plague or dearth hit hard from 1578 to 1632 that were guides for how to cope, including surveys.[13] We again see the 'parish state' in local records. Reading governors told 'constables, churchwardens, overseers of the poore, surveyors of the higheswayes and other officers of this burrough' to come to the hall in 1631 to hear the king's 'booke of orders and the counsells letters . . . reade and dirreccons given them'. The 'booke of orders was openly reade' there in the year before and 'audibly reade' in Yarmouth.[14] Local authorities spent a few pennies to get the 'kings book': three-pence in Marlborough in 1623, six-pence for two in Lambeth in 1578, and a shilling 'for 3 books of order for ye plage' in Ipswich in 1585.[15]

This partnering role in helping the Crown with 'points and matters of state' did not devalue local government.[16] Far from it. It was likely to get tighter, more self-conscious, and aware of what needed to be done in testing times. Local worthies tended to become more tightly knit in self-styled associations like the 'companye' in rural Swallowfield and urban Reading (that 'will not fall out one w[i]th another', the rural group said). It is entirely possible that 'middling' men in office who did what was expected of them developed sharper senses of identity and purpose from the challenges of far-reaching changes, a more insistent State, and their own home troubles. These challenges, in other words, created multiple opportunities to rethink government. Communal 'norms of order and self-sufficiency' were foremost in the minds of local governors. Local communities more often than not preferred to deal with local issues 'in-house'. 'And everye of us', Swallowfield's 'chieffe inhabitants' said in the middle of the tough 1590s,

> doth promyse one to another & to the whole company th[a]t whatsoever suyte shall growe or aryse [in the] tythings or in [any] inhabytantes . . . w[hi]ch touchethe the whole tythinges . . . That then we agree to ioyne together in purse, travell & credett in defence of all suche wronges.[17]

[13] P. Slack, 'Books of Orders: the making of English social policy, 1577–1631', *TRHS*, 5th series, 30 (1980).

[14] BRO R/AC1/1/3, fos. 135, 112; NRO Y/C/19/6, fo. 184.

[15] WSHC G22/1/205/2, fo. 59v; C. Drew, ed., *Lambeth Churchwardens' Accounts 1504–1645 and Vestry Book 1610*, Surrey Record Society, 3 volumes, 60, 63–4 (1940, 1941, 1943), III, 133; SAI C/4/3/1/1/2, fo. 23; C/3/4/1/17.

[16] Quoting W. Raleigh, *Maxims of State* (1650), 55.

[17] HL Ellesmere MS 6162, fo. 35. See also Slack, *Poverty and Policy*, 148–61; J. Kent, 'State formation and parish government in England crica 1640–1740', *HJ*, 38 (1995); J. Pitman, 'Tradition and exclusion: parochial officeholding in early modern England, a case study from north Norfolk, 1580–1640', *Rural History*, 15 (2004). Pioneering studies include K. Wrightson, 'Two concepts of order: justices, constables, and jurymen in seventeenth-century England', in J. Brewer and J. Styles, eds., *An Ungovernable People: The English and Their Law in the Seventeenth and Eighteenth Centuries* (1980); J. A. Sharpe, 'Enforcing the law in the seventeenth-century English village', in V. A. C. Gatrell, B. Lenman, and G. Parker, eds., *Crime and the Law: The Social History of Crime in Western Europe Since 1500* (1980).

This 'in-house' first choice came under close scrutiny over the course of the sixteenth and seventeenth centuries. Terling in Essex is the classic case study of power falling into the hands of a group of godly 'middling' men who for considerations that rose above time-honoured concepts of neighbourliness used the full force of law to take action against people they bumped into each day of the week.[18]

But senses of the 'publique affayers of the tythyng [and] inhabytantes' remained.[19] Lawyer Thomas Wilson thought of towns as a 'common-wealth among themselves' in 1600. Yarmouth's one-time clerk and second historian Henry Manship defined this urban 'commonwealth' as a 'community or society [in 1619], which makes a civil body, formed and made of divers members'.[20] Ideas of the urban 'commonwealth' came into their own to signify both 'urbanity' and more cohesive local authority.[21] The most important step was incorporation by royal charter to fully fledged borough status. Incorporation, William Sheppard remarked in 1659, made a town 'in a sort immortal', where 'fraternity' and 'brother-hood' bound governors in one tight body.[22] Incorporation was in effect a muscular strengthening of authority and identity. Robert Tittler has counted incorporations and reincorporations in the 155 years after 1485. There were thirteen in the first fifty-five years; forty-four in 1540–58; and no less than 149 incorporations and seventy-two reincorporations in the century after 1540 when England's population doubled in size and towns paid the price (sixty-five of these six dozen were couched in terms of requests for more authority).[23] Tittler also emphasizes expanding 'autonomous authority' in English towns, that through incorporation became more self-governing and aware, and that this was visually represented in more impressive civic buildings. Almost 200 town halls were built in the century after 1540 and by far the lion's share of them were finished in the years around 1600. Each one stood—often on the edge of market squares in the beating heart of a town—as an iconic symbol of an urban commonwealth that was more unified and certain of itself (this story will be picked up in Chapter 2).[24] As they sat in the hall thinking about their town, governors looked at portraits of their brethren hanging on the walls in numbers that grew at the same time as 'hall

[18] K. Wrightson and D. Levine, *Poverty and Piety in an English Village: Terling 1525–1700* (New York, 1979)—reprinted by Clarendon Press in 1995 with a new 'postscript' written by Wrightson.

[19] HL Ellesmere MS 6162, fo. 36.

[20] T. Wilson, *The State of England anno. Domm. 1600*, ed. F. F. Fisher, Camden Miscellany (1936), 20; H. Manship, *The History of Great Yarmouth*, completed in manuscript in 1619, ed. C. J. Palmer, Kessinger Legacy Reprints (1854), 23.

[21] See P. Withington, *The Politics of Commonwealth: Citizens and Freemen in Early Modern England* (Cambridge, 2005).

[22] Sheppard is quoted in P. Slack, 'Great and good towns 1540–1700', in P. Clark, ed., *The Cambridge Urban history of Britain, Volume II, 1540–1840* (Cambridge, 2000), 364.

[23] R. Tittler, *Reformation and the Towns in England: Politics and Political Culture, c.1540–1640* (Oxford, 1998), 188–93.

[24] R. Tittler, *The Face of the City: Civic Portraiture and Civic Identity in Early Modern England* (Manchester, 2007); Tittler, *Reformation and the Towns*, 133; R. Tittler, *Architecture and Power: The Town Hall and the English Urban Community, c.1500–1640* (Oxford, 1991), 162–8, 158.

building'. This civic portraiture was highly self-conscious to celebrate a more inclusive identity and government. The worthies on the walls were a constant reminder of good works, 'comportment', and 'sage governance'.[25] Printed and manuscript histories also traced towns from a long way back to speak now of a dignified and confident present.[26] More town maps that highlighted tokens of pride were also drawn at this crunch time. A Norwich plumber was paid well 'for castinge the leade that counter-payse [Mr Moore's] map with the citties armes' in 1598. Maps of the city were hung up in the guildhall chamber in yet another rendering of pride and place.[27]

Phil Withington calls this period a time of 'sustained' urbanity that had far-reaching consequences for political culture, nationwide politics, and associative identities and administrative roles of 'middling' men.[28] The significance of these transformations in local government shape what we see in this book. An animated localism that was amplified, not impaired, by the State trained thoughts on the most effective ways to govern. It was a self-conscious commitment that could never lamely accept the status quo. A more questioning eye crossed towns and villages to weigh up more effective options to run local government in challenging times.

II

Our quantification and analysis has shown that crime, vagrancy, and poverty were on the rise, and this was not lost on people at the time. 'Theft, murders, and adulteries are very common' nowadays, Ralph Josselin mused, sitting in his Essex parish in 1667. 'Thieves are having a prosperous time', Thomas Isham noted in Northamptonshire five years later. 'The misery of ye poore and ye thievery yt is abroad' are sure signs of 'sad judgm[ent]s unto us', Henry Newcome brooded in his home not far from Manchester in 1661.[29]

25 Tittler, *Face of the City*, chaps 4–6, quoting 162; R. Tittler, *Portraits, Painters, and Publics in Provincial England, 1540–1640* (Oxford, 2012), esp. chaps 6–7; T. Cooper, *Citizen Portrait: Portrait Painting and the Urban Elite of Tudor and Jacobean England and Wales* (London and Newhaven, 2012); I. W. Archer, 'The arts and acts of memorialization in early modern London', in J. F. Merrit, ed., *Imagining Early Modern London: Perceptions and Portrayals of the City from Stow to Strype* (Cambridge, 2001); F. Williamson, *Social Relations and Urban Space: Norwich 1600–1700* (Woodbridge, 2014), 43–56.

26 On writing history and its uses see D. Woolf, *The Social Circulation of the Past: English Historical Culture 1500–1730* (Oxford, 2003).

27 NRO Norwich Chamberlains Accounts 1589–1602, fo. 235v; 1625–48, fo. 104.

28 Withington, *Politics of Commonwealth*, 7.

29 A. Macfarlane, ed., *The Diary of Ralph Josselin, 1616–1683*, British Academy Records of Social and Economic History, NS, III (Oxford, 1976), 540; *The Diary of Thomas Isham*, ed. Sir G. Isham, trans. N. Marlow (Farnborough, 1971), 177; T. Heywood, ed., *The Diary of the Rev. Henry Newcome From September 30, 1661 to September 29, 1663*, Chetham Society, 18 (Manchester, 1849), 37.

None of these three lived in sizeable towns, although they visited them. Rural areas felt winds of change, but more heated and insistent 'noise' tended to come from towns and cities. Southampton was lurching from one problem to the next in the final quarter of the sixteenth century. Like other towns, it was trying to cope with the consequences of rapid population growth: migrants streaming in through gates or landing on quays; 'newecomers' squeezing into cheap clammy rooms; beggars pestering people on streets and steps; angry locals blaming a surge of 'straungers' for the lack of work; and much else besides. We can put ourselves in the shoes of governors reacting to the shock of mounting pressures by reading records. Sitting on the south coast, Southampton was journey's end for many protestant refugees on the run from Catholic France. They were invited by the Crown but rarely got red-carpet treatment in their new homes. 'Doubting' that all 'straungers' were 'frendes', Southampton governors told officers to cover 'conduitte heddes' in 1569 and lock them when curfew sounded 'for feare' that 'straungers' might poison the water. 'Englishemen' asked governors in the same year to explain why 'straungers' seemed 'more freer' than them to sell 'things in thear [own] howses'. The newly settled French harmed family fortunes. It was rumoured in 1575 (three years after the St Bartholomew's Day Massacre) that 'french people' slipped out of bed after dark to 'defyle' streets. Journeymen fumed that 'strangers' damaged their hopes of becoming householders by taking too many apprentices and, to rub salt into wounds, they gave clear preference to 'french and guernsey children'. To make matters worse, the town also had to deal with down-on-luck people from surrounding areas who saw better opportunities there. 'This towne is marvelously oppressed with under tenants', governors said in 1582, who are poor 'for the most parte' and do little else but beg. The lament three years later was that Southampton was 'greatly overcharged with undertenants w[hi]ch encreaseth povertie much'. There were similar stories from all over England, although Sotonians ranked their town top of the league in 'newecomer' issues in the 1590s. Our 'towne is so comonlie oppressed as no towne in England the like', governors there said, and if nothing changes quickly, they added gloomily, the likely outcome will be 'the utter ruin and overthrowe of ye state of this towne'. The 'manie' shady 'newcomers' were 'pesterous [to] civill government'. Grievous 'abuses' caused by 'inmates and undertenants' were 'intollerable' in 1601. The number of inmates was still 'intollerable' two years later, and it 'dayly' grew. Southampton was 'overmuch increaseinge' just as plague was about to begin its deadly dance through the town.[30]

Southampton was typical with the exception of its 'straunger' issues that were largely limited to the South and East Anglia. These tense times forced local governments to think long and hard about policy and process. Like Southampton,

[30] SA 6/1, fos. 7, 11, 17, 18, 23, 25, 26, 27.

the majority of towns report on record that they were 'dayly' or 'contynually' under greater pressure, with an urgency that we can still feel today. 'Poverty invades us dayly like an armed man', Norwich's clerk wrote in 1670.[31] Magistrates sitting in the heart of towns were genuinely concerned that they were teetering on the brink of collapse. Thetford magistrates fretted that offences 'do dayly increase' in 1598, adding ominously that 'all things runne to ruine and utter decaye'. 'Journeymen strangers' getting cheap room and board along Chester's fringes were 'a dayly hynderance' in 1601 that showed no signs of slowing down.[32] County benches spoke in similar tones of great danger. Leicestershire justices were greatly alarmed by the 'dayly concourse and great increase of rogues, vagabonds and sturdy beggers'.[33] It was often said that problems had accelerated 'of late'. It sometimes seems that governors believed that they were living in the worst of times. A shrill chorus lamented that the terrible twins, poverty and trouble, were 'moche increased' of 'late yeares'. The protest from Tewkesbury in 1632 was that 'the poore of this towne have of late time so greatly increased [and] that the better sort of inhabitants are scarce able to relieve them'. 'The state of this towne is like in shorte tyme to be utterly overthrown', governors there concluded.[34] 'The number of those [needing] reliefe is growne farr greater then in tymes past', Salisbury governors pointed out in 1638, not long after surveying the poor. 'The number of pore people [here has] greatly increased' lately, Norwich magistrates noted uneasily in 1602. Cheshire justices knew by their 'experience' in 1629 that a 'great and groweing evill' was spreading a dark shadow over the county as the number of vagrants 'infesting' it had 'infinitely increased' in recent years.[35]

'Growne farr greater then in tymes past' was a lament for the times. 'Intollerable', 'exceeding', and 'dayly' troubles are another backdrop for this book. These glum perceptions spawned policies that inform what follows. They could not be more different to the imagined well-ordered 'manifestaccons' of urban 'commonwealths' (Chapter 2), and their reverse representations of order drew attention to evident flaws in punishing outside (Chapter 3). Bridewells were tailor-made to deal with vagrants and other 'good-for-nothings' whose numbers, it was felt, were soaring (Chapter 4). And the larger scope and scale of 'credible informacon' gathering that was in large part propelled by urban risk revealed the dimensions of issues like Southampton's 'newecomers' (Chapter 5). Population growth settled down for a century or so after 1630 when numbers hovered around 5.3 million. But problems did not go away. Towns continued to grow. The number of people

[31] R. Hill and G. Holley, eds., *A Miscellany Comprising the Correspondence of Thomas Corie, Town Clerk of Norwich, 1664–1687 and Observations and Comments on the Visitation of Norfolk, 1664*, Norfolk Record Society, 27 (1956), 30.

[32] NRO T/C1/6, fo. 30v; CA Z/AB/1, fo. 265. See also HA W/B1/4, fo. 110; CUL CUR 37.3, fo. 126; CA QJB/15, fos. 232v–4; Z/AB/1, fo. 265.

[33] LERO QS/6/1/2, fo. 58v.

[34] GA TBR/A/1/2, fo. 25.

[35] WSHC G23/1/3, fo. 397; NRO Norwich Assembly Book 5, fo. 273; CA QJB/15, fos. 232v–4.

living in one doubled over the course of the seventeenth century. Urban stresses and strains sharpened over time. The question of the effectiveness of local government would have been food for thought inside town halls and also among village elites who mulled over the state of their community and what they could do to make it better.

III

This might all seem extremely 'Foucauldian' nearly five decades after *Discipline and Punish* first saw the light of day (1975). Foucault still looms large over anyone who turns their attention to the historical development of punishment, institutions, and information. His ideas have shaped agendas in many fields for a long while now. He believes that penal systems for the first time concentrated on reforming the minds of offenders inside prisons in the second quarter of the nineteenth century. Troublemakers had been dealt with in public up to then, and the main aim of magistrates was to inflict pain. The soul in Foucault's narrative took the place of bodies in the understandings of Victorian legal practice and principle. His biggest mistake was not to substitute punishing felony for punishment more generally. As we will see, the timeline of punishing petty crime through time leads to a very different set of interpretations. Foucault's grasp of early modern theology and jurisprudence is thin at best. His rigid division of bodies and souls would have made no sense to early modern magistrates and religious reformers/moralists who made the amendment of minds their leading priority. Nor would it have held any meaning for advocates of spiritual medicine to soothe physical suffering in cultures that induced Edward Heron to write *Physicke for Body and Soule* (1621). Bodies and emotions were irretrievably coupled at this time, and this is made clear in Erasmus's visual-verbal remark that the 'outward honesty of the body cometh of the soul well composed and ordered'.[36]

Far from being something that had to wait until a couple of centuries later to come of age, reforming character/offenders was the spiritual and emotional essence of early modern penal systems. Even whipping was intended to train thoughts and emotions; the whipping post along London's busiest street, Cheapside, was called significantly 'the post of reformation'.[37] The idea of reforming wrongdoers inside walls started with sixteenth-century bridewells, not

[36] Erasmus is quoted in M. Ingram, 'Sexual manners: the other face of civility in early modern England', in P. Burke, B. Harrison, and P. Slack, eds., *Civil Histories: Essays Presented to Sir Keith Thomas* (Oxford, 2000), 93. See also A. R. Jones and P. Stallybrass, *Renaissance Clothing and the Materials of Memory* (Cambridge, 2000), chap. 1; M. Healy, *Fictions of Disease in Early Modern England: Bodies, Plagues and Politics* (Basingstoke, 2001), esp. 28–34; C. Rawcliffe, *Medicine for the Soul: The Life, Death and Resurrection of an English Medieval Hospital* (Stroud, 1999), esp. 161, 170; Macfarlane, *Diary of Ralph Josselin*, 39, 58, 114, 438, 600.

[37] E. Cohen, 'The animated pain of the body', *AHR*, 105 (2000).

nineteenth-century prisons. Edward Coke believed that few are sent 'to the house of correction or working house but they come out better'.[38] Punishment took a new path after England's first bridewell opened its doors in London in 1553. The tight interconnections between punishment, institutions, and surveillance developed from this point on. Many more troublemakers were punished inside walls than outside in the open in England after 1550. Languages and practices of 'private' punishment were well understood (Chapters 3–4). A Westminster parish wanted to build 'a private house of correction' in 1617.[39] But there was no sudden displacement of 'public' by 'private' forms of punishment at any time along the lines set out by Foucault. They coexisted all through the sixteenth and seventeenth centuries.

My chapter sequence expresses 'turning inside', starting with 'precyson' or being 'exact' and the ongoing necessity to quash various forms of 'mysprecyson': disguise, for example, anything or anyone who was unknown, or 'deceit crimes' such as forgery and perjury. 'Precyson' is examined in broader bodies of knowledge and practice in science, for instance, the law, and local government where officers were told to be 'exact' when carrying out their duties. Case studies of the sort of 'middling' men who held office show them doing their level best to be 'precyse' for their own ends at home or work: calculating, recording, checking. This reciprocal 'precyson' in and out of office trained a sharp eye on 'manifestaccon' (or publicly representing authority) and its parts: architecture, ceremonies, street cleaning, civic clothing, gates and walls, and crosses and conduits (Chapter 2). Townscapes were draped with insignia to be read as text. Many of these parts are no longer with us or they have lost their political charge and consequence, becoming in the process honorific and antique. This long-term shift was already evident before 1700 when the problems of 'manifestaccon' were persistently apparent.

Punishing petty crime in the public eye was another component of 'manifestaccon': the stocks, whipping, ducking stools, pillories, carting (Chapter 3). This apparatus was etched in townscapes, markets, main streets, crosses, and riversides. But like 'manifestaccon' more generally, public punishment was scrutinized and questioned; in fact, the scope and scale of these 'open' penalties were cut back over the seventeenth century. The signs would be unmissable if someone was able to travel through time from, say, 1550 to 1700 for a week or so in England's second city, Norwich. This time traveller might have been struck by the fewer whippings in the marketplace. He/she would have wondered why so few troublemakers were getting whipped through the streets tied to the back of a cart. Nor did anyone seem to be shamed standing up in a cart as it rolled along the streets (this would have been improbable in the years after Robert Kett captured the city). The

[38] E. Coke, *The Second Part of the Institutes of the Lawes of England* (1644), 729.
[39] WAC F2201, fo. 114.

stocks were empty all week long and that seemed strange to this mid-Tudor visitor. The ducking stool was perched on the banks of the Wensum ready to go, but nobody could remember when it was last used. And what was this new-fangled bridewell supposed to do?

'Precyson' exposed the risks and unpredictability of 'manifestaccon'. But it was also a factor behind the growing reliance on information and institutions in local government. Hospitals and almshouses played a large part in the lives of medieval people; monasteries were the most important source of charity. But England's first nationwide system of incarceration that was set up by statute in 1610 made the difference, along with more coordinated institutional networks across towns and cities (Chapter 4). Institutions loomed large over the lives of early modern people. So, too, did data that surreptitiously sneaked into their lives to shape and reshape all aspects of their being, often without them knowing. This all at a time when local governors knew far more about the people they governed than ever before (Chapter 5). We tend to date the clear emergence of extensive and sophisticated local information gathering to somewhere deep in the 'long eighteenth century' or even later. But if we go back to around 1600, we are not in a dry backwater before government by information in England's towns and villages was taken seriously. Far from it. Policy and policing by information were routine in local government by then. Elizabethan England has been called an 'information state'—'a government [Nicholas Popper describes] that prioritized the collecting, interpreting, manipulating, and disseminating of information as a primary mode of exercising and maintaining power'.[40] The difference in these pages is that I approach information, or 'making known' in a definition that was shared by a number of lexicographers, from the bottom up.[41] Not in the plush offices, comfy corridors, and handily centralized archives of royal government, but in the chores of churchwardens, constables, overseers, and surveyors in their little part of England that through them have left records in archives everywhere. They got to know their patch and people through the archive and the records that they made which were themselves an embodiment of local place and identity. Local government surveying revealed the dimensions of the people and 'problems' in a

[40] N. Popper, 'An information state for Elizabethan England', *Journal of Modern History*, 90 (2018), quoting 503. See also R. Ahnert and S. E. Ahnert, 'Metadata, surveillance, and the Tudor state', *HWJ*, 87 (2019). And for early modern Europe see P. Burke, *A Social History of Knowledge From Gutenberg to Diderot* (Oxford, 2000), 117–19; B. Dooley and S. Baron, eds., *The Politics of Information in Early Modern Europe* (Abingdon, 2001); J. Soll, *The Information Master: Jean-Baptiste Colbert's Secret State Intelligence System* (Ann Arbor, MI, 2009); J. Rule and B. Trotter, *A World of Paper: Louis XIV, Colbert de Torcy and the Rise of the Information State* (Montreal, 2014); F. de Vivo, *Information and Communication in Venice: Rethinking Early Modern Politics* (Oxford, 2007); R. Head, ed., 'Archival knowledge cultures in Europe, 1400–1900', special issue, *Archival Science*, 10 (2010); F. de Vivo, A. Guidi, and A. Silvestri, eds., 'Archival transformations in early modern European history', special edition, *European History Quarterly*, 46 (2016).

[41] E. Coles, *An English Dictionary* (1673) and E. Phillips, *The New World of Words. Or a General English Dictionary* (4th edition, 1678), s.v. information.

particular place on a scope and scale that were unprecedented for what in Salisbury was called the 'better government of this citie'.[42] Census-taking became standard practice for what in Liverpool in a memorable word was called 'comput[ing]' and in next-door Walton-on-the-Hill in an equally resonant word was called 'particularizing'.[43] This acute attention to administration was developing in socio-economic conditions that were more challenging than anyone alive could remember. And once information techniques were refined, they established a momentum that might well have had setbacks but was never reversed.

Together these five chapters make the case that there was a clear 'turn inside' in English local government in the 150 years after 1550. More emphasis was placed on institutions to deal with troublemakers (and others), and information systems and cultures reached a level of use and finesse that was distinctive. Public representations of authority still mattered in the eighteenth century and after. People still lined streets to watch impressive processions; conduits and crosses still stood in the hearts of towns speaking in symbols; and market squares were still read for their messages. But the writing was on the wall. Looking back over 300 years later, we know in which direction the overall drift in politics, culture, and technology was heading; ever nearer to what we have today, an honorific regard for a procession, crest, or government building that are no longer the vehicles they once were for articulating authority and ethics with all the intensity of a sixteenth- or seventeenth-century panic. The last 'official' punishment staged outdoors was over 150 years ago, and there seems to be an institution for each one of our needs today, but this has been the case for a long time now. And we live for better or for worse nowadays in a fast-evolving information society that can stun us with its latest turn.

But we now need to go back to the early seeds of these things and start with the idea and practice of 'precyson'. This 'precyson' that became a refrain in local government was one of the driving forces behind two related shifts that are the spine of this book. The first of them is the long-drawn-out decline in representing authority in public that began in the early modern period (Chapters 2–3). The second is 'turning inside' (Chapters 4–5). We start with a basic question, but one that every magistrate needed to ask whenever someone unknown walked into the room: 'Who are you?'

[42] WSHC G23/1/3, fos. 231, 291v, 153v.

[43] M. Power, ed., *Liverpool Town Books, 1649–1671*, Records Society of Lancashire and Cheshire, 136 (Dorchester, 1999), 92–3; E. M. E. Ramsey and A. J. Maddock, eds., *The Churchwardens' Accounts of Walton-on-the-Hill, Lancashire, 1627–1667*, Lancashire and Cheshire Record Society, 151 (2005), 90.

1

'(Mys)precyson'

> Improvising is not my thing. When I made *The Magic Flute*, I was like a child at play, it was a game, every day Mozart's music in the wings, but, mind you, all of it was very precisely thought out. Precision. Precision. Precision. Precision.
>
> L. Ullman, *Unquiet* (New York, 2019), 246

'Who are you?' befuddled King Lear asks loyal Kent as Shakespeare's play draws to its harrowing close. 'What are you? Your name, your quality...', a herald with no name asks Edgar in the same scene, the latter disguised for a second time, this time in battledress to fight his bastard brother, double-crossing Edmund. 'What art thou?' dying Edmund asks Edgar after the fatal blow that he knows is his end as he reaches for that last breath (*King Lear*, V.iii, 335–6, 142–3, 197). These might have been the most asked questions in these times. They were certainly among the more fraught.

Maidstone magistrates memorably called anyone sneaking into their town the 'undiscovered'.[1] They were in effect question marks, anonymous, and threatening. These magistrates knew what they had to do in such cloudy moments: 'survey', 'compute', and 'particularize' to find out 'what they be'.

This is 'what I am', Gloucester mercer Richard Cooper told Bridport (Dorset) magistrates in 1650.[2] He was in a spot of bother 100 miles from home, having never set foot in Bridport before. Cooper was a question mark there, with no history, biography, or papers. Governors did not know him from Adam. 'I am not knowne' here, he said, suddenly startled as the true extent of his 'vague' situation dawned on him. The only thing he could do was write home for verification and a place in this new Dorset world. 'This is to certifie to you that I am now in Burpott in prison for want of a certificate', Cooper wrote in a letter to Gloucester officials; 'the bayliefs and justices of this place [will] detaine me til such time that they are satisfied what I am'. 'I have tould them all my condition, trade and commodities', he told governors in his Gloucester that must have seemed very far away. But words were not enough. Cooper needed paper. 'Beinge in a strainge place wherof I am not knowne [he said, I] have no friends to send to nearer than yorselfe'. 'My request' is for you to 'write a satisfactory letter...with as many hands to itt as doe knowe mee there [making clear] what I am and [the] reason of my coming to this

[1] CKS Md/ACm1/3, fo. 173v.

[2] Richard Cooper's story is in DHC DC/BTB/L8.

Information, Institutions, and Local Government in England, 1550–1700: Turning Inside. Paul Griffiths, Oxford University Press. © Paul Griffiths 2023. DOI: 10.1093/oso/9780192896261.003.0002

cuntry'—that 'heare is a good place for the trade I tould you of wher I intend to settle if not in this towne [then] hereaboute the country'. Tell them 'what I am'.

Cooper's predicament got suddenly worse in this nervy dawn of the English republic, when anything suspicious seemed ten times more so. 'They doe take me to bee another [man]', he told folk back home in Gloucester, who 'may bee prejudicial to the state of this kingdome'. He was thought to be suspected royalist malcontent Henry Francis, who had also just arrived in the town where, like Cooper, he had no past. Francis was a Warwickshire mercer who told Bridport's 'examiners' that he had lodged for eleven days three weeks ago at the Star in Southampton before getting on board a boat for the Isle of Wight, where he picked up '5li of tallow' to trade. Cooper sailed back to Southampton, 'where he solde some silke wares'. His next stop was Salisbury with more silk to sell. Customers' names on a piece of paper gave him a ring of credibility. He stayed one day before travelling fifty miles to Weymouth to find out 'whether were fitt to make pott ashes'. He got a tip-off that Bridport and its satellite villages were 'places affordinge manye beanes', and so he rode the fifteen miles there, drawn 'by the plenty of bean straw one of the best materials for pott ashes which is used for London soape'. But Francis was now in prison in a town that he did not know with a stranger who he was told was him.

Cooper hired a messenger and 'I pray you', he urged Gloucester officials, 'hast him away with speede and bee mindfull of me'. He signed his letter 'in all love Henry Francis or Richard Cowper which you please' in a sarcastic swipe at Bridport's governors, who could not read his sealed letter but could see its back where he signed his name only. It was 5 April 1650; the letter from Gloucester arrived nine days later with nine signatures. Cooper could now breathe a long sigh of relief: 'Theise are to certifie that Richard Cooper late of Gloucester, mercer, is and to our knowledge hath bin allwaies reputed a man of honest life and conversacon' and was 'never [in] armes against the parliament'. Quite the reverse. He 'served in armes' against the king, Gloucester's governors confirmed, defending the town that fell to royalists in late summer 1643, and has 'never [been] accompted an enemy to the present government' or 'ever suspected for treason or felony'. Records run dry now and Cooper disappears. But he was no longer in limbo. Maybe he stayed in Bridport or 'hereaboute the country' to make some money from the 'manye beanes' there, or maybe he hurried back to a place where he was known, having learned his lesson the hard way.

Richard Cooper was another victim of 'precyson'. His appearance on that grey day in Bridport made him dangerously imprecise. He belonged with Maidstone's loathed 'undiscovered' as a new face in a new place. The point for the Duke in *Measure for Measure* was to see 'what our seemers be' (I, iii, 59–60); to seek precision not an appearance. 'Seemers' in a single word narrates an entire fear and ideology; much like 'I am' does in two.

This opening chapter examines developing cultures of precision in many walks of life, from the supposed lofty heights of epistemological knowledge to coney-catching. It ends with local government that it was hoped, in a word from both Chester and Cambridge, would be 'certyn'. The chapter shifts from 'mysprecyson' to 'precyson' that together in tension reveal a great deal about the nature and aims of governance. They are two sides of the same coin. We will turn to 'mysprecyson' first in a variety of forms to show the contempt in which it was held and how it was said to obscure civil society, the smooth turnover of the economy, and good government. These forms included disguise, forgery, perjury, weights and measures, impersonation, rogue writing, counterfeiting, cheating, cozening, and other 'like shifting'. Pursuing 'precyson' was in effect a permanent condition that defined governance. The balance between it and 'mysprecyson' was key to the state of local government. This was why magistrates tried to get this balance right through bookkeeping, timekeeping, record-keeping, price-fixing, rate-fixing, and, if necessary, taking matters to the courts.

They did so as part of a broader intellectual, practical, and cultural precision in a variety of overlapping disciplines like surveying, mathematics, law, natural science, medicine, legal protocols, and evolving conceptions of the nature of credibility, plausibility, and facts. This all resulted in prolific and improved observation, classification, and calculation in laboratories, for instance, landholding, workshops, courtrooms, and local government where Walter Raleigh's 'middle sort' of men handled affairs. These office-holder(s) were becoming more adept at managing accounts, information, and records in farms and workshops. Maybe they benefitted from taking lessons in the new 'practical' or 'shop arithmetic' that was meant for them. We will meet some of them putting their administrative skills to work at home, work, and also in office, playing their part, it was hoped, in making local government, in words from by-laws, 'exact', 'true', 'perfect', and 'certyn'. This 'precyson' is the aspiration that guided the actions of local authorities that inform this book. But we will begin with Richard Cooper's kith and kin, who one day turned up somewhere where they were not known.

I

Thomas Dekker's 'inquisitor' asked these questions of women who were caught walking after dark in early Stuart London: 'Where have you been so late? 'Are you married?' 'What's your husband?' 'Where lie you?'[3] 'Who are you?' 'What are you?' 'What art thou?' Questions asked over and over again. Three suspected 'nightwalkers' who were caught on London streets after curfew in 1644 were locked up in Bridewell 'untill Mr Treasurer be satisfied what they are'. Isabell Snell, who was 'taken' on a London street five years earlier 'late at night and would

[3] T. Dekker, *Lanthorne and Candle-Light*, first published in 1608, The English Experience, 585 (Amsterdam and New York, 1973), 42–2v.

have gone with a man' [the constable said], was put to work 'till it is reported by mr leech what she is'. Someone we know only as Toby, 'a mad man', was 'kept' in the same place in 1641 'till' the court 'heare what he is'.[4] Two Dorchester constables went 'at eleven of the clock at night into the George [in 1633 and] going up the stayers [they] heard musick'. Walking into the room, they 'perceyved one standing ther in the dark and enquired what he was 3 or 4 times'. He 'made answer hee was one of the towne and pressing him to tell his name he sayd Gold'. 'Which Gold?' a constable asked. The man in the shadows again said that 'his name was Gold [and] discovered no more than before'. It turned out that Gold was his name, but he made the constables' job harder than it should have been.[5]

'Which Gold?' Magistrates had to assume that someone was not what they seemed and that in fact they were 'seemers'. They needed to get to the bottom of things. Question marks like Cooper turned up in towns all the time. 'It is informed that a strainger whose name is not yett knowne hath layed in [the town] three or fower dayes', Reading governors noted in 1632, 'taking knowledge' that he 'has spent his time from alehowse to alehowse without any busines that was perceaved by his host or any man else'.[6] Also in Reading, Rose Underwood was caught selling 'bruised pewter' on the streets in 1630. She lived in Bishopsgate Street in London, she said, and got the pewter somewhere in Oxfordshire. 'But of whome or in what place' she could not say. Nor could she tell 'whither she was goeinge or what her busines [was] in this cuntrye'. She did say that 'her husband's name is William [but] where he is she knoweth not'.[7] Far too many question marks. Underwood's next stop was the 'gaole'. Spinster Eleanor Moore was asked 'how longe it was synce she came to [Exeter]' in 1620. Ten years, she replied, but she could only 'geve an accompt' of four of those years and she was promptly and unceremoniously kicked out of the city.[8]

Any magistrate worth his salt questioned things. Never judge a book by its cover was a good adage for these times. I am a Bristol merchant, Godfrey Crosswick told Exeter governors in 1620, who wanted to know who he was and what he was doing in their city. They knew something about Bristol and tried to catch Crosswick out, asking him 'to deliver his knowledge whether he knoweth the parishe church of St Thomas [in] Bristol'. 'He said [that] he doth', the record reads. 'Beinge demaunded who is the minister theire', Crosswick answered, 'Mr Lovering', adding that he had 'been minister for one yeare'. Asked 'if he knew John Powell minister [of] St Thomas', Crosswick said 'he did [but he] died about twelve moneth since'. This seemed to satisfy the governors and he was let go. Joanne Griffin was grilled in Exeter a week later. 'How long synce she was first married and to whome', she was asked; 'about tenne yeares since', she answered, to Allen Griffin 'at a place in Wales called Langdoggin'. The marriage lasted eight

4 LBHC 9, fo. 92; 8, fos. 234v, 335.
5 DHC DC/DOB/8/1, fo. 177.
6 BRO R/AC/1/1/3, fo. 182.
7 BRO R/AC/1/1/3, fo. 127.
8 DRO ECA C1/61, fo. 397.

years, she said, and we lived in Bristol, London, the Low Countries, 'and then he died'. And then I married Thomas Davy 'in Bristol at St. Thomas Church' last November, Griffin said. 'What day did you marry'? she was asked; 'Tewssday or Wensday', she said. 'Who was at that marriage and what tyme of the daye' was it'? 'About one of the clocke', Griffin said, 'Mayne [and] John Sanderford' were witnesses. Governors continued to press her, 'demaund[ing] where she dined that day'. At 'Meanes, porter of the room gate', Griffin answered; they were joined by her sister and 'had for dynner a peece of rost beefe and legg of mutton'. We then moved between Gloucestershire and Bristol until three weeks ago, she continued in her 'what I am' narrative, and arrived in Exeter via 'Stoake', Honiton, Glastonbury, Bridgewater, 'and other places which she knows not'.[9]

There was resistance. 'Idle and suspected' labourer Richard Jennings was picked up in Stoke (Hampshire) in 1647 and 'being demaunded from whence he came and what occasion of busines he refused to give accompt of his being there'. He told the tithingman 'that he scorned to be examined'. An Exeter constable told a court in 1623 'that he overheard [John Bishop] say to his wife whatsoever thou dost or art examined saie nothing' to them. Don't tell them who you are.[10] Swift population growth and more movement meant that fluidity and 'mysprecyson' were the reality of living in England. A guide for local officers cautioned that 'the poore' had 'wavering and straying mindes' and 'wandering and unstaied bodies, which will sooner be disposed to vagrancie than [useful] activitie'. Another chiding voice called this the 'vagabond extravigant life' in 1632.[11]

Many lived like Alice Smith, who was questioned in Exeter in 1560. She said that 'she came out of Wales' by boat two Christmases ago 'and landed at Ylfercombe', where she stayed until Easter before going fourteen miles to Barnstaple to live with Joanne Poor, 'spynning by the week' for three weeks. Next was the short skip to Bishops Nympton until the 'begynnynge of the harvest', after which she walked to 'Lansfrey ii myles from [Barnstaple and] taryed untyl vii dayes before Crystmas'. Smith then made a 52-mile trek to Padstow on the Camel Estuary for Christmas. Boscastle, twenty-five miles up the coast, was her next port of call. Short stints then followed in Barnstaple (25 miles), Hatherleigh (30 miles), Cowley (10 miles), 'Brodwynch' (Bradninch? 5 miles), and, a week later, after ten moves in under two years, she finally found herself in Exeter.[12] 'Idle vagrant wandring rogue' Matthew Bampfield claimed to be Barnstaple born and bred when he was found in the town and marched to magistrates. He said that he left his home town to cross the sea to Ireland 'to see the country' and now he needed local memories to work for him. After six years working in husbandry in Ireland, he returned with

[9] DRO ECA C1/61, fos. 131, 132–3. See also DHC DC/DOB/8/1, fos. 14v–15, 212, 223, 229–30; DRO ECA C1/61, fo. 505.

[10] HA Q1/2, fo. 249; DRO ECA C1/62, fo. 143v.

[11] *An Ease for Overseers of the Poore* (1601), 27; TNA SP 16/21/67.

[12] DRO ECA B/1/4, fo. 16.

eighteen-pence in his pocket to wander the West Country 'from place to place [not staying] in any place more then one day and a night unlesse [it was Sunday when] he tarried two dayes'. He made it 'home' to Barnstaple one afternoon in 1677. Asked 'how he had maintained himselfe', he told the mayor that 'he did pipe for his living' and had 'pipe[d] at two or three places' in the town since 'coming hither' picking up 'three halfe pence'. The next question was, is he known?[13]

Bampfield and Smith moved at will, it seems, living contrary to the stable lives valued by magistrates. Their stories might seem humdrum, but their cumulative outcomes were noticed and led to responses that are covered in this book. 'Wavering', 'wandering', and 'vagabond extravigant' lives in their many thousands contributed hugely to the prevalence of doubt in society and culture and the constant struggle to provide certainty. Life was all too often vague. Not knowing was a revolving ruckus for magistrates. Their uncompromising response to hazy lives like Cooper's is all of a piece with the larger imprecisions that afflicted early modern living. When would plague or fire strike next? Was something what it seemed? Bedfordshire 'gentleman' Richard Drake called the world 'a theator of fiction and disguise'.[14] The twists and turns of many play plots hinged on the moment when someone stepped forward from underneath a disguise. People are constantly confused with someone else in Shakespeare. Cross-dressers fuddle matters: Portia (*The Merchant of Venice*), Julia (*The Two Gentleman of Verona*), Rosalind (*As You Like It*), Viola (*Twelfth Night*), Imogen (*Cymbeline*), and, most famously outside Shakespeare, the gutsy swashbuckling 'man-about-town' Moll Cutpurse in Middleton and Dekker's *The Roaring Girl* (1611); 'a brave disguise', the play lets the audience know in its opening words (Epistle: 15–16).[15] Edgar disguises himself as a Bedlam beggar in tatty clothes In *King Lear*, Kent pretends to be a peasant. Identity puzzles tied people in knots. The twins in *The Comedy of Errors* are taken for each other. The Duke in *Measure for Measure* disguises himself as a friar to shadow Angelo who is pretending to be pious. Still disguised, he writes to a jailer using his real name to get another man to switch places with Claudio, who is due to be hanged the next day. Feste, who masquerades as a priest in *Twelfth Night*, meets someone who he thinks is Cesario, who is Viola's twin (Sebastian), and gets into a sword fight with Malvolio, who thinks he is the man he was supposed to duel with! Audiences laughed along, yet parallels with life offstage were unsettling. The point was always to see 'what our seemers be'. 'Seeming, seeming! I will proclaim thee', Isabella warns 'hypo-crite' Angelo. She asks the duke 'to

[13] NDRO B1/46/499.

[14] Drake is quoted in N. Millstone, 'Seeing like a statesman in early Stuart England', *P&P*, 223 (2014), 114.

[15] See also P. Hyland, *Disguise on the Early Modern English Stage* (Farnham, 2011); M. Holly, 'King Lear: the disguised and deceived', *Shakespeare Quarterly*, 24 (1973); F. Karim-Cooper, 'Disguise and identity in the plays of Middleton', in S. Gossett, ed., *Thomas Middleton in Context* (Cambridge, 2011); S. Orgel, *Impersonations: the Performance of Gender in Shakespeare's England* (Cambridge, 1996); G. Ungerer, 'Mary Frith, alias Moll Cutpurse, in life and literature', *Shakespeare Studies*, 28 (2000).

make the truth appear where it seem hid' (*Measure for Measure*, I, iii, 59–60; II, iv, 163–4; V, i, 73–4). 'Disguise I see thou art a wickedness', Viola says in *Twelfth Night* (II, ii, 27).

Writing about 'spiritual armour', Thomas Walls demanded: 'Now, if a man should put on his face, to wit, a vizard, a false face, as he hath on his head false hair when he teacheth the people, what man or woman would endure to hear him?'[16] Camouflage made things worse. Thief Simon Webb donned 'false haire' that fell apart like his defence in court. Cutpurse Owen Cannon slipped out of prison 'in a false perriwig and beard'. While still seething after being sacked, Thomas Haversly broke into his ex-master's house in a 'false beard'.[17] Certain crimes were linked to disguise like hunting 'with painted faces or other disguising'. 'Egipcians' rambled through England in masks in menacing bands, governors said. Thomas Forster provided a 'model' indictment for this group: 'A.B. and C.D. were in the company or fellowship of T.C. and E.F. vagabonds commonly calling themselves Egyptians and counterfeiting and changing themselves by their apparell, language, and behaviour like such vagabonds commonly calling themselves egyptians.' Author B.E. called 'gypsies a counterfeit brood' of 'rogues and wenches' who lived 'promiscuously…disguising themselves with blacking their faces and bodies' wearing 'an antick dress', who made a living under 'colour of fortune telling, palmestry, [and] physiognomy'. Richard and Roger Bates were both 'convicted and condemned' at the Old Bailey in 1669 'for wandrinng up and downe the country as vagabonds in thee company of other lewd persons calling themselves egyptians pretending to tell fortunes'.[18]

Stepping into someone else's shoes was a witty ruse in theatres but not always elsewhere, as Talboys Dymoke found to his cost in 1601 when putting on a 'stage play', 'the death of the lord of kyme', that mocked the Earl of Lincoln, who was locked in a land dispute with his father. The earl called it 'a very infamous and libellous stage plaie'; Talboys called it a Sunday 'summer lord game' on 'a greene before Sir Edward Dynnock's house'. Talboys took the lead role and 'personated'/'counterfeited' the earl in his 'apparell, speech and gesture and name' in jests with Vice, the Fool, and the Devil. The play ended with a hearty roll call of

[16] T. Wall, *Spiritual Armour to Defend the Head from the Superfluity of Naughtiness Being a Loving and Christian Tender* (1688), 44.

[17] BMM BHCC 4, fo. 123v; LMA MJ/SBR/5, fo. 254; BHCC 7, fo. 135v, 136; 6, fo. 311. See also LMA MJ/SBR/2, fo. 275. Cf. *The Boke for a Justice of Peace* (1544), fo. 23v.

[18] R. Chamberlain, *The Complete Justice Being a Compendious and Exact Collection Out of All Such Statutes and Authors as May Any Way Concern the Office of a Justice of Peace* (1681), 195; W. Sheppard, *A New Survey of the Justice of Peace His Office* (1659), 23; T. Forster, *The Lay-man's Lawyer: Or, the Second Part of the Practice of Law* (1654), 12; B.E., *A New Dictionary of the Canting Crew in its Several Tribes of Gypsies, Beggers, Thieves, Cheats &c* (1699), preface unpag., s.v. gypsies; F. Pulton *An Abstract of All the Penal Statutes…Collected by Fardinando Pulton of Lincolnes Inne, Gentleman* (1577); TNA SP 44/28/folio 26. The Bateses were pardoned by privy councillors to be transported 'into some of our foraine plantations' as they 'were not accused for any thievery or robberye'. See also D. Cressy, *Gypsies: An English History* (Oxford, 2018), chaps 2–5.

the names of the 'known lewd and licentious women' in London, Lincoln, and Boston, with the cast chanting 'ora pro nobis' after each name. Bailiff John Craddock, 'apparalled like a preacher', climbed into 'a pulpitt tied to the maypole [after the play ended] utter[ing] prophane and scurrilous matter in manner of a sermon with a most blasphemous' prayer. A 'dirdge' was sung and a 'slaunderous ryme concerninge the earle' was 'fyxed' to the maypole with 'the earles coate of arms over yt'. The three living defendants—Talboys died before the case reached Star Chamber—were each fined £300, locked up in the Fleet prison, pilloried in Westminster Hall, and whipped under the pillory 'at Lyncolne Assises'. Sir Edward Dymoke was locked up and fined '1000li for beinge a spectator and pryvie to it'.[19]

The Counterfeit Constable (1674) was a short spoof about 'a jolly gang of the town who lived like birds of prey' and thought that there was 'no better way to accomplish their designs than to masque themselves in the mantle of authority'. One of the gang had a 'gown, cap, staff and all the formalities of a constable'. His partners in deceit played watchmen in 'suitable garb'. The gang knocked on doors with a 'pretend warrant' claiming to be searching for a clipper on the run. They took away money, saying it 'was clipped', and the charlatan constable 'pretendedly' gave a name and address for victims to get it back. The gang also took plate when claiming to be searching for stolen plate.[20] Like the 'counterfeit constable', thieves in records stole things 'by colour and pretence' of warrants for recusants, for example, 'searchinge for fleshe' in Lent, or tracking down cutpurses. There were other reasons to pose as officers. A 'counterfeit' man walking home late after curfew in 1632 pretended to be a watchman 'with a holbert' over his shoulders 'seeming to conduct the other [his friend] to his dwelling colorably'. 'Under color and p[re]tence that they were the citties bellmen', John Stringer and his son walked through London for a month before Christmas in 1637 going to the 'houses of the hablest men' to get the year's end 'offering' that was the bellmans' 'right'.[21] 'Deceit-full' con-artists also 'falsely [took] upon them to be messengers of her majesties' in 1596. A royal proclamation told how 'wicked' imposters put on 'scutcheons of armes as the messengers doe' and go 'up and downe the countrey' to 'defraud gentlemen' with bogus warrants to appear before privy councillors, taking fees from them. 'Better to colour their lewd dealing', they offered 'to compound' with the grateful 'deceived' who handed over money with a sigh of

[19] HL EL 2733; C. L. Barber, *Shakespeare's Festive Comedy: A Study of Dramatic Form and Its Relation to Social Custom* (Princeton, NJ, 2012), 39–56.

[20] *The Counterfeit Constable, Or, The Wicked Watch* (1674), 4–6.

[21] LBHC 7, fo. 303. See also LMA Rep. 52, fo. 43; MJ/SBR/1, fo. 592; MJ/SBR/2, fo. 146; MJ/SBR/7, fo. 22; MJ/SBR/5, fo. 379. J. Hurl-Eamon, 'The Westminster imposters: impersonating law enforcement in early eighteenth-century London', *Eighteenth-Century Studies*, 38 (2005); T. B. Hug, *Impostures in Early Modern England: Misrepresentations and Perceptions of Fraudulent Identities* (Manchester, 2009).

relief.[22] 'Craftie' 'vagabond' Thomas Yonge was pilloried for three hours on three market days in London in 1546 for 'counterfeyting [to be a] purveyor for the kings majestie dysceaving' people on authority of a commission in a box he had with him. Clerkenwell's John Leed was brought to court in 1612 'for arrestinge' somone 'pretending to be a messanger and afterwardes discharginge him for money'. Others were caught 'deceaving' or 'cheating' 'under colour' of being informers.[23]

Deceit was defined in one dictionary as 'a subtle, wily shift, or trick, whereunto may be drawn all manner of craft, subtilty, guile, fraud, slight, cunning, collusion, and practice used to deceave'. To 'cheat' was to 'deceive or cozen'; 'dissimulation' meant 'dissembling, hiding, or cloaking'; 'delude', 'to mocke and deceive'.[24] There was rhyme and reason to this exposition of deception on the page, onstage, and in courts. Early moderns believed that meanings were established by exploring their contraries. Opposites pulled together in tension, and the points of friction were highly instructive.[25] Night spoke about day. Knowledge of 'disease' came from a 'pisse prophet' quack with 'piss-pot science'. People could buy ballads for a penny or two and sing of a 'double-dealing husband', 'cozening quacksalvers', or a 'false dissembling, cogging, cunning, cozening young man' who duped maids into sex with false promises of marriage.[26] The 'cant' lingo of criminal underworlds was conceived in opposition to everyday words. 'Cant' terms first: execution day/washing day, mellow/most drunk, gunpowder/old woman, King's Head Inn/prison, wise man of Gotham/fool, poyson'd/big with child, mother/bawd.[27]

Literatures and vocabularies were dedicated to deceptions and fabrications. None more so than 'rogue literature', some of which tried to convince people that there was a fifth column of vagrants doing its best to smash the social order. This 'rowsey ragged rabblement of rakehells', a mirror opposite of so-called conventional society, was organized into finely graded ranks, rules, and roles with 'lewd lousy language'. These picaresque parodies hinged for much of their power on inverting precision. There is deceit all through their pages: cheats, counterfeiters,

[22] *By the Queene. A Proclamation Against Sundry Abuses Practised by Diuers Lewd and Audacious Persons Falsely Naming Themselues Messengers of Her Maiesties Chamber* (1596).

[23] LMA Rep. 11, fo.364v; MJ/SBR/1, fo. 55.

[24] T. Blount, *Nomo-Llexikon,a Law Dictionary* (1691), s.v. deceit, colouring; H. Cockeram, *The English Dictionarie: Or, An Interpreter of Hard English Words* (1623), s.v. delude, defraud, cheat; R. Cawdrey, *A Table Alphabeticall Conteyning and Teaching the True Writing and Understanding of Hard Usuall English Wordes* (1604), s.v. dissimulation; Cf. Thomas Harman, 'A Caveat or Warning for Common Cursetors', first published in 1567 in A. F. Kinney, ed., *Rogues, Vagabonds, and Sturdy Beggars: A New Gallery of Tudor and Early Stuart Rogue Literature* (Amherst, MA, 1990), 128–9.

[25] S. Clark, *Thinking with Demons: The Idea of Witchcraft in Early Modern Europe* (Oxford, 1997), chaps 3–5.

[26] T. Brian, *The Pisse-Prophet, or, Certain Pisse-Pot Lectures. Wherein are Newly Discovered the Old Fallacies, Deceit, and Jugling of the Piss-Pot Science, Used by All Those (Whether Quacks, and Empiricks, or Other Methodical Physicians) Who Pretend Knowledge of Diseases by the Urine* (1679).

[27] Polarities are taken from B.E., *New Dictionary of the Canting Crew*.

coney-catchers, card sharps, and many more. The 'top man [or] chief rogue of the gang [and] compleatest cheat' was the 'dimber-damber'.[28] The founding father of this genre, Thomas Harman, chose his words precisely: 'pretence', 'deluding', 'feign', 'a little show', 'wily wander', and 'appear to all as it were', all turn up in a few pages. He weaves webs of 'deceit': 'deeply dissembling', 'deep dissimulating and detestable dealing', 'deep deceitful practices', and 'the truth cannot appear'.[29] Harman, on the other hand, wrote in 'plain terms', 'according to my plain order', he said. 'I have set forth this work simply and truly'; things are 'laid open', 'truly set forth', and 'manifest'. Rather than 'untrue aspercions', second-hand tittle-tattle, or 'cogging pamphlets and fond baletmakers' (the rivals of 'truth'), or rumours 'blowne abroad' ('misinformacons', London's aldermen called them), Harman worked with 'true report', 'true experience', and 'good proof'. He called one source 'well witness'. 'I was credibly informed by such as could tell well', he wrote, and only use 'matter which I knew well to be true by report of others'.[30] Harman lists the 'true names' of 141 upright men, forty-four rogues, and thirty-one palliards for an appearance of authenticity: Harry Smith ('he driveleth where he speaketh'), John Stradling ('with the shaking head' and five aliases), William Cooper ('hare-lip'), Thomas Gray ('his toes be gone'), Thomas Smith ('scally skin'). Harman was at hand to translate this double-dealing world into something legible. 'Thus I conclude my bold beggars' book', he wrote, 'that all estates most plainly may see / As in a glass well polished to look / Their double demeanour in each degree'.[31]

London's streets were paved with deceit not gold. 'He that walks the streets [and] observes the fatigues used by beggars to make themselves objects of charity must conclude that they take more pains than an honest man doth at his drones', John Cary quipped dryly. Children are educated from cradles to be expert in this 'art', he said, and pick up 'tricks' to manipulate 'anything which may move

[28] P. Burke, 'Perceiving a counter-culture', in his *The Historical Anthropology of Early Modern Italy: Essays on Perception and Communication* (Cambridge, 1987); A. L. Beier, 'On the boundaries of new and old historicisms: Thomas Harman and the literature of roguery', *English Literary Renaissance*, 33 (2003); A. L. Beier, 'Anti-language or jargon? Canting in the English underworld in the sixteenth and seventeenth centuries', in P. Burke and R. Porter, eds., *Languages and Jargons: Contributions to a Social History of Language* (Cambridge, 1995); P. Griffiths, 'Overlapping circles: imagining criminal communities in early modern London', in A. Shepard and P. Withington, eds., *Communities in Early Modern England* (Manchester, 2000); A. Bayman, *Thomas Dekker and the Culture of Pamphleteering in Early Modern London* (Farnham, 2014), chap. 4; M. Eliav-Feldon, *Renaissance Imposters and Proofs of Identity* (Basingstoke, 2012), chap. 4; L. Liapi, *Roguery in Print: Crime and Culture in Early Modern London* (Woodbridge, 2019). Quoting Harman, *Caveat or Warning for Common Cursetors*, 109, 148; and B.E., *New Dictionary of the Canting Crew*.

[29] These last few phrases are from Harman, *Caveat or Warning for Common Cursetors*, 110, 112, 118, 134. Cf. P. Fumerton, *Unsettled: The Culture of Mobility and the Working Poor in Early Modern England* (Chicago, IL, 2006), chap. 2.

[30] Harman, *Caveat or Warning for Common Cursetors*, 112, 111, 113, 120, 143, 137; CSPV 1621–3, 691; M. Aray, *The Discoverie and Confutation of a Tragical Fiction Devised and Played by Edward Squyer Yeoman Soldiar Hanged at Tyburne the 23. of November 1598* (1599), 14v; LMA Reps. 16, fo. 265v; 20, fo. 133v; 21, fo. 317; 40, fos. 49, 69.

[31] Harman, *Caveat or Warning for Common Cursetors*, 153.

compassion' like a 'pretended' leg. They 'fill the streets', he groaned.[32] Beggars dangled empty sleeves or trouser legs that once housed limbs or twisted limbs into odd shapes. One supple beggar conned people into thinking that 'his heels grew to his buttockes'. Others claimed to be lame to 'color begging'.[33] 'Counterfeit criples' crawled along streets. 'Perfect whole' George Croft 'counterfeited fallyng sycknes' in 1559. Career beggar William Worrall was 'well whipped' in 1561 for 'faining' to be 'borne dumb' so 'people should have more pitie on him'. Humphrey Griffen 'stuttereth [a witness said] to melt hearts'.[34] Others tried to get pity and pennies with sighs and cries. 'Idyl' William Hodges made 'mocke falsehood and dysymulacon' on stalls, 'crying out piteously as though he had byn verye sycke'. 'Verie lustie' Bartholomew Symons's trick was to 'lie under a stall and counterfeite as yf he were givinge up the gost'.[35] There was too aggressive begging, but styles for the most part sought sympathy. 'Comon beggar' Margaret Darby 'made herselfe a great belly with clothes' in 1627 to fake pregnancy. Others went 'naked to deceyve people [for] money'. John Haines, who was caught 'naked begging' in Billingsgate Market, had fresh clothes each day but sold them 'of purpose thinking thereby to be pityed'.[36] Some beggars made up stories of suffering and loss. 'Losse by fire' was common. Others were more inventive. 'Marvelously dissemblyng' Sybil Sterre alias Okeley from Stepney was taken to task in 1560 for 'falsely and colorably crav[ing] money of a gret nombre' by 'counterfett suggestions' that her husband was 'borned for religion at Canterbury in Quene Marys tyme', leaving her with seven children with no roof over their heads. 'Comon begger' Elizabeth Barker got 'much money' in 1622 by posing as a homeless, hard-up minister's wife, while governors knew to expect a stream of bogus 'maymed soldyers' once wars ended.[37]

A vow to 'precysion' and its concomitants like honesty and morality must be read in concerns about deceit crimes like cozening, perjury, forgery, or any 'deceavinge'. Samuel Rid put it in a nutshell in 1612: 'beware of cheating'. The author of *Grevous Groans for the Poore* (1621) warned that the 'idle poor' 'practice wrangling, defrauding, robbing, begging, filching, stealing, juggling, conni-catching, cosening, false dicing' and other 'like shifting'. 'Loathsome swine' he

[32] J. Cary, *An Essay on the State of England in Relation to its Trade, its Poor, and its Taxes for Carrying on the Present War Against France* (1695), 152.

[33] R. Bush, *The Poor Man's Friend, or Narrative of What Progresse Many Worthy Citizens of London Have Made in that Godly Work of Providing for the Poor* (1649), 10; BMM LBHC 4, fo. 295; LBHC 1, fo. 211v; 5, fo. 158v; 6, fo. 434v; 9, fo. 645; LMA Rep. 12, fos. 78, 171.

[34] LBHC 1, fos. 26, 183; 2, fo. 35v; LMA Reps. 16, fo. 153; 11, fo. 394v.

[35] LBHC 5, fo. 432v; LMA Reps. 20, fo. 152v; 13, fo. 16v; LBHC 1, fo. 80v; 2, fos. 72, 113; 6, fo. 34v.

[36] LBHC 7, fo. 49v; 3, fo. 359; 7, fo. 97. See also LBHC 1, fos. 35v, 41v; 6, fo. 405v; 7, fo. 254; LMA MSS 5090/2, fo. 291; 4071/2, fos. 199, 229; 5018/1, fo. 22v; 4180/2, fo. 81v.

[37] LBHC 6, fo. 377v; 1, fo. 66; 6, fo.269v. See also BMM LBHC 4, fo. 338v; TNA SP12/261/70; LMA Rep. 21, fo. 53v; MJ/SBR/4, fo. 598; LBHC 7, fo. 309; 9, fo. 620.

called them.[38] Humphrey Mill drew attention to the 'cheating crew' in 1640. William Sheppard discussed the 'trade of cozening' in 1659.[39] Middlesex justices believed that 'greate numbers' of 'cheats' hung around theatres in 'confederacies' in 1604. A 'bill' taken from a cozener's pocket at London Bridewell in 1578 listed the names of sixteen 'cozeners' and remains a 'bill' of federation and knowledge to this day.[40] 'Trade', 'crew', and 'confederacies' all suggest collectivities in these cheating worlds. Cheats were brought to courts in scores. Middlesex swindler Clara New was taken to task in 1640 for 'cheating people pretendinge' to tell fortunes and 'discover stolen goods'. Edward Coke wrote to the king in summer 1616 to tell him that 'I have found out in london thirteen impostors or wysards pretending to tell fortunes to procure love, to alter affections, to bringe againe stollen goods and such like deceits'.[41] Londoner Thomas Beadley was caught red-handed swapping 'a good ring' for 'a countefett ringe' in a goldsmith's shop in 1605; his pockets were stuffed with 'counter-fet' stones. Aptly named John Gold switched copper and gold stones with a quick flick of the wrist.[42] London was the capital city of deceit. Con artists had card tricks and loaded dice up their sleeves. Thomas Buckmaster and Edward Bickerton made a 'living by cheating with false cardes'. Cheats could get rich pickings in one swoop: twenty-one pieces of silver (called 'rex dollars') in a game of 'most at two throws'; £10 playing 'one and thirty'; £8 from a game of 'tecke tacke'. One 'cheat' had a real red-letter day fleecing '79li 17s 6d' from 'a duchman'. Another made money 'with false tallies by a trick called the carrying of the colt'.[43] One case is straight from the country bumpkin/city slicker storybook! 'Simple countreyman' cattle-driver Hugh Pare was taken for a ride by 'cheaters' in a Gracious Street pub who got him 'half drunk' and toasted him with 'jolly carouses and healths' before getting out 'false dice'—'commonly called bars or flats' or 'high fullins'—and milking £200 from him.[44]

There were plenty of provincial cheats also. A smith conned thirty shillings from a turner with 'false dyce' and 'three or iiii pownds' from others at the King's Orchard pub in Southampton in 1582, where a 'true and certayne report' said there was 'great playe at dyce'. 'Whisperinge' three years later reported that 'all

[38] S. Rid, *The Art of Jugling or Legerdemaine VVherein is Deciphered, All the Conueyances of Legerdemaine and Jugling…Cautions to Beware of Cheating at Cardes and Dice* (1612); *Greevous Groans for the Poore* (1621), 7–8.

[39] H. Mill, *A Night's Search Discovering the Nature and Condition of All Sorts of Nightwalkers with Their Associates* (1640), 251, 232; Sheppard, *New Survey of the Justice of Peace His Office*, 20.

[40] LMA MJ/SBR/7, fo. 82; MJ/SBR/1. fo. 585; LBHC 3, fo. 320.

[41] LMA MJ/SBR/1, fo. 417; TNA SP 14/86/49.

[42] BMM LBHC 4, fos. 309, 426. See also LBHC 5, fo. 70v; LMA WJ/SR/NS/36/161; CQSF 105/10, 106/24; P. Griffiths, *Lost Londons: Change, Crime, and Control in the Capital City, 1550–1660* (Cambridge, 2008), 40, 158, 161; *The Diary of Henry Machyn Citizen and Merchant Taylor of London From A.D. 1550 to A.D. 1563*, ed. J. G. Nichols, Camden Society, 42 (1848), 103.

[43] LMA WJ/SR/NS/41/207, 46/189; MJ/SBR/1, fos. 418, 487; MJ/SBR/6, fo. 441; MJ/SBR/7, fo. 139. See also LMA Rep. 13(2), fos. 199, 573v; WJ/SR/NS/41/170, 43/103, 47/68; MJ/SR/506/5, 515/71, 525/80; MJ/SBR/2, fos. 70, 126, 331, 518.

[44] TNA STAC8 241/15.

sorts of people most comonly [the] poorest and ydlest' spent hours there playing 'unlawfull kyttles' and 'dice'.[45] Reading officers got 'informacon' in 1626 'of 2 or 3 cheators or conycatchers' seen 'lately' at markets and fairs who had cards and 'counterfeit rings' in their pockets and sacks.[46] Just like today, gambling debts ended lives. Cambridge alderman Samuel Newton tells the sad story of 'Richard Herring the sone of alderman Herring', who 'did drowne [in 1668] as it is thought betweene 6 and 7 in the morning before it was light betweene Garrett hostle bridge and Trinity Coll. Tenniscourt'. 'He had bin at play at dice the night before [at] John Dods at the Red Heart in Petti cury', Newton noted, 'and lost as was thought there with a London gamester and cheater above 100li'. This 'was thought the only reason he offered vyolence to himself', Newton closed; 'the money was said to be tax money received by him for Captain Story'.[47]

This stain of shame is also evident when someone who had been called a 'cheat' or worse took action against her/his slanderer so that no mud would stick. Westmorland 'gent' Nathaniel Nicholson stood in the dock in 1655 after trying to 'shame and disgrace' yeoman Christopher Stephens 'in ye hearinge' of a crowd shouting 'thou art a perjured fellow'. Jonathan Oldfield from Halifax filed a church court suit against William Rigby for calling him 'a rogue, rascall and thiefe...cheating rascall...cheating thiefe' and 'a clipper and coyner' in 1682.[48] 'What do you call [my father] hoax?', John Cox's son asked Poole shipmaster John Lambert in the mayor's house in 1584. 'I do', Lambert snapped back, 'and cozyner too, make of yt what thou can'. 'In law there is vantage to be taken of those words', the son said, 'will you stand to yt'. 'I that I will', the shipmaster answered, 'and I will prove he hath ben a cosyner'.[49] Constables and other officers were also insulted in the same vein. An Exeter constable was called 'dissembling knave, skabb, dissembling skabb [and] blood sooking skabb'. Philip Romaine called the Dorchester 'constableshipp' a 'cheating and cossening office' in the 'open market'.[50] Allegations of deceit also tarred and feathered religious opponents. Edward Payne called Quakerism 'a great delusion'. The birth of a son to the Catholic royal couple in 1688 was dubbed the most horrible 'cheat, fraud, and imposition put upon mankind since molten calfs [were] adored for gods'.[51] Catholics tried to deceive with 'dastardlie dissimulation'; 'popish priests' 'cunninglie disguise[d] themselves'

[45] SA 6/1, fos. 17, 18. [46] BRO R/AC1/1/2, fo. 199.

[47] J. E. Foster, ed., *The Diary of Samuel Newton Alderman of Cambridge (1662–1717)* (Cambridge, 1890), 37. See also HL SSTM box 1, folder 18, fo. 15; NRO T/C1/2, fo. 82; ESBHRO QI/EW7, fo. 128; HRO Q1/1, fo. 77; GA GBR/G/G3/SO/1, fo. 40.

[48] KAC WQ/I/1, fo. 3v; BIA CP/H/4998.

[49] DHC DC/PL/B/11/2/1, fos. 7v–8. See also BIA CP/H/2970; LMA MJ/SBR/3, fo. 15; MJ/SBR/6, fo. 168; DRO ECA C1/2, fo. 142v; DHC DC/DOB/8/1, fo. 245v; KAC WQ/I/1, fo. 21v.

[50] DRO ECA C1/61, fo. 369; DHC DC/DOB/8/1, fo. 251v.

[51] E. Payne, *Antichrist in Spirit Unmasked: or Quakerism a Great Delusion* (1692); *The Whole Examination of the Birth of the Pretended Prince of Wales and the True Mother of that Notorious Counterfeit and Impostor Fully Discovered and Proved, before the Lords and Commons of England, For the Publick Satisfaction of the Whole Kingdom* (1689), 1.

under 'pretext and cullour of religion [to] cozen', 'cheat', and 'baffall poore simple people'.[52] 'Imposters', Zachary Crofton called the 'vexatious crew [of] anabaptisical spirits' who opposed him when he took up his post in their parish in the heady mid-1650s. 'Little Laud' they called him.[53]

Heated invective was aimed at perjury, a crime that was said to be 'of very deepe dye' because sworn oaths were an 'end of all doubt' and '*ambiguities*'. 'The times are notoriously pester'd, disturb'd, and endanger'd by the variety and frequency of perjury', John Allen wrote in 1682.[54] Perjury snapped a few strings at once and lying under oath was made ten times worse by a promise to tell the truth, so help me God. It was 'an impious and impudent affront to God' that broke two commandments (numbers 3 and 9) in a single stroke.[55] Perjury was 'near kin' to sacrilege, tarnishing national integrity ('a very great blemish to the English air'), trade, and the 'conversation' that society was 'grounded upon'. England would descend into 'Mr Hobb's state of nature' if perjury reigned.[56] It is little surprise that there were calls for death penalties for this 'odious and infamous' sin rather than the 'minute' slap of a wrist in a pillory for 'an hour or two' with the 'empty shouts and laughter of the mobile and rabble' with 'perhaps' a 'little pelting with rotten eggs and turnips'.[57] A 'slight disgrace' for someone who did not value his reputation, Hugh Hare said wryly at Surrey Sessions in 1692. 'Petty larcenies have a more infamous brand set upon them', he added, with no 'just proportion' between crime and punishment in 'cases of wilful forgery and perjury'.[58] But perjurers did get short shrift. 'One of [Yarmouth's] xxiiii', Thomas Sowles, was fined £20 in 1571 for 'perjureing himself intendinge to falsify the verdit of ye admiraltye enquest'. John Blossom, 'otherwaye Jacket,' was 'discomened' in the same town in 1551 for perjury in 'the comon house'.[59] Others got someone else to give 'false' or watered-down 'evidence'. John Prick was sent to prison in London in 1631 'for

[52] T. Sanderson, *Of Romanizing Recusants, and Dissembling Catholicks. A Counter-maund of a Counterfeit Embassage* (1611), 1–4; J. de Chassanion, *The Merchandises of Popish Priests Laying Open to the World, How Cunningly They Cheate and Abuse Poore People, With Theyr False, Deceitfull, and Counterfeit Wares* (1604), Dedication to Sir Thomas Bennet, B1r–1v, B2v, C2v, C3r.

[53] Z. Crofton, *Perjury the Proof of Forgery: Or Mr. Crofton's Civilitie Justified by Cadman's Falsitie* (1657), A2–A5r.

[54] J. Allen, *Of Perjury, A Sermon Preached at the Assizes Held at Chester April the 4th 1682* (1682), 1.

[55] *The Third Commandment: An Essay Tending to Prove that Perjury Deserves Not Only the Pillory but a Much Severer Punishment* (1685), 3, 4, 12–14; Allen, *Of Perjury*, 10, 12, 15.

[56] *An Account of the Proceeding to Judgement Against Thomas Saxton... upon a Conviction of Willful Perjury* (1685), unpag.; *Brief Reflections Upon the Inconveniences Attending Wilful Malitious Forgery and Perjury With Some Reasons Why Such Crimes Ought to be Made Felony* (1685), 1; [H. Hare,] *A Charge Given at the General Quarter Sessions of the Peace for be the County of Surrey Holden at Dorking on Tuesday the 5th Day of April 1692* (1692), 10; *An Humble Address Offer'd to the Consideration of the Lords and Commons Touching a Law Concerning Perjury* (1695), 12, 2, 10; C. White, *Of Oathese, Their Object, Forme, and Bond: The Punishment of Prejuries and the Impieties of Papal Dispensation* (1627), 16.

[57] *Brief Reflections Upon the Inconveniences Attending Wilful Malitious Forgery and Perjury*, 2–3; *Third Commandment*, 10.

[58] [Hare,] *Charge Given at the General Quarter Sessions of the Peace for the County of Surrey*, 9–11.

[59] NRO Y/C/19/3, fo. 11v; Y/C/19/1, fo. 27v.

giving slacke and faint evidence against [professional pickpocket] Henry Waller [who he] charged to have pickt his pocket'. Richard Gamye ended up behind bars in 1611 'for faltering in evidence'.[60] Arch-liars like the Popish Plot architect Titus Oates were often used as counter-examples to urge people to take the straight and narrow road to a life well lived. Perjurer Oates was voted the worst Briton of the seventeenth century and third worst in the last thousand years by *BBC History Magazine* in 2006.

Perjury and forgery were Siamese twins. 'Two pernicious and inseparable companions', one author called them. Norfolk 'grasier' 'gentleman' Richard Dawson called forgery a 'cockatrice-egge of corruption and injustice' when writing about his 'long groaned' trials and tribulations at the 'hellish' hands of 'cheats' who took him on a 'malicious' dance. His hope was that records and 'honest dealing will prove the best policy'.[61] Unlike perjury, forgery did become a capital crime, but not until 1728. The financial revolution and recoinage in the 1690s had a large hand in this.[62] More generally, greater reliance on information and records amplified forgery's injury. 'Abstract[ing]' penal statutes in 1577, Fardinando Pulton 'of Lincolnes Inne' wrote that

> anyone [who] upon his owne heade and imagination or by false conspiracy and fraud... wittingly, subtllye and falsely forge or make [any] false deede, charter, writing, court rolle or the will of any person [should be fined or stand on the pillory and have] both his eares cutt off and his nostrelles slitt, cut, and seared with a whole iron [to] remayne a perpetuall marke of his falsehood.[63]

Royal proclamations aimed at forgers and counterfeiters targeted coins, passports, jewels, books, licences, warrants, miracles, and repentance. Trade guilds fretted about 'counterfeit' goods. Goldsmiths in London were deeply concerned about the rise in 'deceitful working of gold and silver' that they linked to the 'infinite increase' and 'indirect practizes' of 'foreiners' who set up workshops in 'secret' corners. A parliamentary bill to address this did not make it onto the statute book in 1624.[64] W.B. called these 'practizes' the antithesis of 'real and plain demonstration' or anything 'clear and visible'. They were almost inevitable in growing towns where 'legions' put 'faultie' or 'deceitfull' cloth to sale that was often too light or

[60] LMA MJ/SBR/5, fos. 241, 416; MJ/SBR/1, fo. 377; MJ/SBR/6, fo. 312. See also LMA MJ/SBR/2, fos. 127, 346; CA QJB/2/7, fos. 9v, 68v; ESBHRO QI/EW2, fo. 71; QI/EW7, fo. 76v; LA MBC/204; WSHC A1/150/11, fo. 391.

[61] R. Dawson, *The Humble Addresse and Remonstrance of Richard Dawson Gentleman Now Prisoner in the Fleet* (1661), 6, 7, 10, 14, 17, 19, 23, 27, 29, 31.

[62] R. McGowen, 'From pillory to gallows: the punishment of forgery in the age of the financial revolution', *P&P*, 165 (1999).

[63] Pulton, *An Abstract of All the Penal Statutes*, 138.

[64] GCL Company minute books O, fos. 433, 438; P1, fos. 36, 115; P2, fos. 215, 267–7v; HOL Journals, III, fo. 305.

poor quality.[65] The large growth in 'official' documentation also put forgery on a higher illicit footing. Local 'paper states' created more paper: tickets, testimonials, certificates, passports, licences, and more besides. Papers were needed to move, work, or to show 'what I am'. Paper proof was needed to validate service, tenure, title, marriage, residence, and maintenance. There was much more to forge now. London printers pumped out 1,200 passports at one time in 1600 and 1,960 more a little later. Bridport, where Richard Cooper had to show 'what I am', issued passes for 'poore seemen', 'cripells', 'maymed' soldiers, and other 'sicke' travellers who included a grief-stricken 'gentleman' whose 'father and friends were murdered'.[66] Gloucester constables needed 'a tickett in writing' to get a shilling for each vagrant they kicked out of their town in 1652.[67] The Poor Law, we know, made great demands on record-keeping. One Westminster parish handed out 'pewter ticketts' to their poor in 1674 so that they could 'receive almes of victuals'. Some 'poore people' were allowed 'to beg with ticketts' by the same parish one year later. St Benet Fink parish in London had 'a stampe or mould to cast ticketts for pentioners'.[68] Typically, Richard Dunning, in his guide for overseers, told parish officers and officials that anyone of working age asking for a hand-out must have a 'certificate' from their last employer with 'a good account of diligence'.[69] As Richard Cooper found to his cost, authorities required paper proof of identity and character. 'Shereman' 'strainger' James Rowland was told to 'provide and shewe a testimoniall' at Reading in 1635 'or to be gone at his perill'. John and Jane Went, who lived in cheap lodgings in Westminster, were told to get out of the parish in 1613 as she 'could not bring any certificate of her good behaviour from the parish where she last dwelt'. The court had instead a damaging 'certificate' that reported 'that she was a woman of ill life and lewd behavior [and had been] carted out of Clerkenwell where she last dwelt'.[70] Westminster residents Elizabeth Little and her daughter, who were suspected to be 'of evill life and baudry among the best [of] this citty', were told three times by burgesses to get a 'certificate' from St Dunstan-in-the-West 'where they formerly dwelt'. Running out of patience,

[65] W.B., *A Touch-stone For Gold and Silver Wares, Or, A Manual for Goldsmiths and All Other Persons, Whether Buyers, Sellers, or Wearers of Any Manner of Goldsmiths Work* (1677), A3v, 18, 22, 28; Pulton, *Abstract of All the Penal Statutes*, 188; Sheppard, *New Survey of the Justice of Peace His Office*, 28. See also T. Nichols, *Arcula Gemmea: Or, A Cabinet of Jewels. Discovering the Nature, Vertue, Value of Pretious Stones, With Infallible Rules to Escape the Deceit of Such as Are Adulterate and Counterfeit* (1653).

[66] LMA Reps. 26(1), fo. 96; 26(2), fo. 428v; 25, fo. 110v; DHC DC/BTB/M17/1658; DC/BTB/M2/1621; DC/BTB/M4/1663–64; DC/BTB/M4/1686.

[67] GA GBR/B/3/2, fo. 691.

[68] WAC E2416, fos. 10, 12; LMA MSS 2895/2, 1660/1; 1303/1, 1630. See also BRO R/AC1/1/3, fo. 407; DHC DC/LR/B7/D2/1, 23/1/1668; LMA MSS 4071/2, fo. 26v; 4956/3, fo. 45.

[69] R. Dunning, *A Plaine and Easie Method Shewing How the Office of Overseer of the Poor May be Managed* (1686), 9.

[70] BRO R/AC1/1/3, fo. 355; WAC WCB/1, fos. 267–8.

they sent an 'assistant' to the deputy in Fleet Street to 'inquire of their behaviour', who said 'that he could report no good of them'.[71]

England's forgers responded with gusto to these floods of paper. 'Cheators' were put on trial for 'counterfeiting' acquittances, petitions, apprenticeship indentures, warrants, bonds, hue and cries, and letters to get 'money and goods' or hand-outs. Overseer Charles Finfold and 'gent' Thomas Merry from Michinhampton (Gloucestershire) faked 'orders of court' to let some friends keep alehouses.[72] Industries of deceit pumped out 'false' documents. 'Counterfeit' letters crossed the land 'under the hand and seale' in East Sussex cases of the governor of faraway Berwick-upon-Tweed and the 'mayor of the cinque ports'.[73] 'Black market' production lines produced 'false' papers to help the floating poor beg, move, or find a bed for the night. Some London scriveners made money on the side by 'counterfeiting' licences in workshops that we know of in Foster Lane, Long Lane, King Street, and Turnmill Street. One of them made a fake licence out of an expired one that he got from a Northumberland man. He told him to go to a gardener's house who could 'help him to one that would make a copy and amend the date if near expired'.

'Scoller of Oxforde' John Tankerd took 'Irishe boye' Bartholomew Webb to a scrivener's house 'at clastonwell' to get 'counterfeite and false letters of testimoniall to begg'. A Shoreditch forger pocketed 2s. 6d. for making 'a false licence to begg'. Others picked up six-pence or so, and seals could cost a little more—fourteen-pence in one case.[74] It was not hard to get hold of an out-of-date licence, scratch out its contents, and fill in other dates and names. London-bound drifters had 'false' papers made in Wiltshire, Shropshire, Somerset, Essex, Norfolk, and other places.[75] A 'petye chapman' who travelled 100 miles from Audley (Staffordshire) to Hereford in 1601 was questioned about his passport 'subscribed with the hand of Thomas Beeche vicar of Awdley'. He came clean and admitted that the parish clerk charged him three-pence to 'write' and 'seal [it] with two seals' without 'knowledge' of any of the 'signatories'.[76] Acting on a 'hugh and crye' in 1590, Lowestoft constables rounded up vagrant John Houldcroft, 'who said he was 'a scholer'. Seeing him standing before them, 'it appeared plainely' to justices thinking 'in remembrance' that 'vacabonds' caught lately 'with false and counterfeted

[71] WAC WCB/2, fo. 18. See also DHC DC/DOB/8/1, fos. 49, 139v, 181, 233v, 241, 258v; WAC WCB/1, fos. 8–9.

[72] WSHC Q/SaIb/1, fo. 8v. See also ESBRHO QI/EW7, fo. 145v; HA Q1/1, fo. 44; CA QJB/2/7, fos. 18v, 146v; NRO Norwich Sessions Book 1639–54, fo. 11v; GA Q/SO/1/1, fo. 24; NDRO B1/46/514; LMA Reps. 10, fo. 263; 15, fos. 32, 285v; 17, fo. 57v; 21, fo. 371.

[73] ESBHRO QI/EW6, fo. 146v; QI/EW7, fos. 64v, 68. See also SHA 3356/2442, fo. 10v.

[74] LMA MS 12806/2, fo. 150v; BMM LBHC 4, fo. 355; LBHC 2, fo. 35v; 3, fo. 418v; 1, fos. 185v–6; 3, fo. 82; LMA Rep. 17, fo. 10. See also LMA Reps 9, fo. 11; 12, fos. 105, 236, 450v; 16, fos. 138–8v, 462; 17, fos. 111, 182v, 338; 19, fos. 92v, 248.

[75] LMA Reps. 14, fo. 367v; 12, fo. 450v; 21, fo. 447; MJ/SBR/2, fo. 431; MJ/SBR/5, fo. 327; LBHC 1, fos. 79, 189; 2, fo. 83; 3, fos. 9v, 174, 236v, 436; ESBHRO QI/EW7, fos. 44, 120; HA Q3/3, fo. 73.

[76] HEA BG11/17/1/4, fo. 7.

pasports' had said that they were made by 'a scholler having harre and apparall all together lyke' Houldcroft, that he was 'a maker of counterfett pasports'. Their suspicions were confirmed when 'they found about him great numbers of the armes of nobles and gentlemeane of his owne drawing'.[77]

This was a fight without end. Imprecision in its many-sided forms was an unwelcome guest who never left the room. Its eradication was a pipe dream or, more importantly, a never-ending aspiration. The pursuit of precision, as hopeless at it might seem, was not seen like this at the time. It was in effect a permanent condition or strategy that defined governance. We see this in pursing precision in weights and measures, bookkeeping, timekeeping, record-keeping, price-fixing, and rate-fixing. *The Rates of the Custom House Reduced Into a Much Better Order* (1582) reminded readers that 'many things in the former impressions stood confusedly and so out of order that a man often times should have much to doo to finde some things therein contained'.[78] But information had now been put in alphabetical sequence. Ubiquitous, too, were guidelines for measuring life's practicalities such as land, building, trading, height, and distance. John Barker said that he wrote *Measurer's Guide or the Whole Art of Measuring* (1692) for 'carpenters, joyners, plasterers, painters, paviers, glaziers, bricklayers, tylers &c'.[79] *The Carpenters Rule* by Richard More first saw the light of day in 1602. John Bill's *Accompts Cast Up* (1632) usefully helped people to measure 'timber, boord, waynscot, glasse, and land'.[80] 'Sometime professor of astronomy in Gresham Colledge' Samuel Foster also aimed his *Art of Measuring* (1677) at carpenters. William Leybourn produced *The Art of Numbering* in 1667 and *The Art of Dialling* and *The Art of Measuring* two years later.[81]

Precision was quite literally hanging in the balance when it came to weights and measures. This 'half pecke is too little', Thetford officials complained.[82] This was heard again and again in any market anywhere. 'This great evil', William Sheppard called 'deceipts of men in their trades by weights, [and] measures'.[83] A trading reputation was at stake. God looked down with a hawkish eye. 'How odious in the sight of God these deceiptful practizes are', Faversham governors said

[77] NRO Aylsham MS, 175.

[78] *The Rates of the Custom House Reduced into a Much Better Order for the Redier Finding of Any Thing Therin Contained Then at Any Time Heretofore Hath Been* (1582), unpag., front of book. This was a handbook with over 100 pages of indexed rates and measures arranged alphabetically.

[79] J. Barker, *Measurer's Guide or the Whole Art of Measuring Made Short, Plain, and Easie* (1692).

[80] R. More, *The Carpenters Rule or a Booke Shewing Many Plain Ways Truly to Measure Ordinarie Timber and Other Extraordinarie Solids* (1602); J. Bill, *Accompts Cast Up With an Addition of Measuring Timber, Boord, Waynscot, Glasse, and Land* (1632).

[81] S. Foster, *The Art of Measuring Containing the Description of the Carpenters New Rule* (1677); W. Leybourn, *The Art of Numbering* (1667); W. Leybourn, *The Art of Measuring Containing the Description and Explanation of the Carpenters New Rule* (1669); W. Leybourn, *The Art of Dialling Performed Geometrically by Scale and Compasses* (1669).

[82] NRO T/C1/5, fo. 47.

[83] W. Sheppard, *Of the Office of the Clerk of the Market, of Weights and Measures, and the Laws Provision for Man and Beast, for Bread, Wine, Beer, Meal, &c* (1665), A3r.

in 1639. They quoted Proverbs (11:1)—'false balances are an abhominacon unto the lord but a perfect weight pleaseth him'—and Deuteronomy 25:15–16—'Thou shalt have a right and a just weight a perfect and a just measure shalt thou have'. Sheppard also quoted from Deuteronomy in his *Office of the Clerk of the Market* (1665), as well as Leviticus and Micah.[84] The same eight pictures of making and baking bread are at the top of the page in *The Assize of Bread* (1600) with the same messages above them, including 'God blesseth true labour with plentie and favor' and 'Be just with thy weights God plague false sleights'. 'What are unjust weights but a false conscience', Lawrence Wormock asked in 1682.[85] More than 'conscience' was at stake. There were the metaphorical resonances of the scales of justice that ought never to be ordered by 'false balance [and a] bagg of unjust weights'. Sir Philip Warwick lived in hope that the country would find the 'true weights and measures between soveraignty and liberty'. Herbert Thorndike pictured 'the present state of religion [in] just weights and measures'.[86] An off-balance weight gave wrong impressions in an increasingly commercial society. The 'commerce and interchangeable traffique betwene man and man' that was vital for the 'orderly governments of states and people' was, in Powel's words, contingent on 'true observation of the weight and measure between man and man'. The preoccupation with the balance of trade drew sharper attention to working with numbers and weights and measures in markets or anywhere else for that matter.[87]

Every English marketplace should have used the same sets of weights and measures. Thomas Blount put it bluntly: all weights and measures should be 'one' in all parts of the land.[88] The true 'standerd' was kept in Whitehall in the Exchequer. 'There ought to be one weight, one measure, and one yard according to the Exchequer standard in every part of the realm', P.B. told parish and ward officials. 'Weights and measures [must] be marked according to the standerde', Anthony Fitzherbert guided justices in 1544, and anything sold must be 'marked legal with the standerde'.[89] Larger towns took bearings in the Exchequer. There were forty-two in all including York, Appleby, Lewes, Uppingham, Lostwithiel, Ilchester, and Dorchester. Smaller ones travelled to their 'big brothers' for the right measure. Barnstaple governors 'agreed' in 1588 that weights must 'accord to

[84] CKS FA/JM/27/1.

[85] *The Assize of Bread* (1600), B2v/B3r; L. Wormock, *Billa Vera, or, The Arraignment of Ignoramus* (1682), 15.

[86] Sir P. Warwick, *A Discourse of Government as Examined by Reason, Scripture, and Law of the Land, or True Weights and Measures Between Soveraignty and Liberty Written in the Year 1678* (1694); H. Thorndike, *Just Weights and Measures That is the Present State of Religion Weighed in the Balance and Measured by the Standard of the Sanctuary* (1662); Wormock, *Billa Vera*, 15.

[87] *Assize of Bread*, B2r–B2v; P. Slack, 'Government and information in seventeenth-century England', *P&P*, 184 (2004), 51–5.

[88] Blount, *Nomo-lexikon*, s.v. 'weights'.

[89] P.B., *A Help to Magistrates and Ministers of Justice, Also, A Guide to Parish and Ward Officers* (1700), 18; A. Fitzherbert, *The Newe Boke of Justices of Peace* (1544), 122v; Sheppard, *Of the Office of the Clerk of the Market*, 89–92.

the proclamacon and shalbe sent for to London out of hand'. A 'pursevant who brought the proclamacon for weights' to Gloucester in 1587 picked up 2s. 6d. Hungerford spent six-pence to buy 'a statute book to way the bread' in 1673.[90] Directives were precise across a range of trades. This also applied to barrels and sacks or anything else that something was sold in. 'And by this rule', John Every warned, coopers must 'make their casks for all vendible assize': 'a hogshead to contain 63 gallons, a tierce 84, a pipe 126, a tun 252, a barrel for beer 36, for ale 32'. 'Casks made for packing up fish' had specific sizes: a 'herring barrell to hold 32 gallons, a salmon butt 84, an eel barrel 42, a soap barrel 32'. This was 'instituted [for] the prevention of frauds that they might have their due substance'.[91] 'Every city and town [must] have common weights and measures sealed', George Meriton wrote, two centuries after landmark legislation (12 H7.c.5).[92] Records show them forking out money to get hold of necessary 'instruments': 6s. 5d. in Reading 'for gould wayts and skales' in 1618; five-pence 'for makinge of measures' in Kendal in 1613; and 13s. 4d. for making 'beames and scalls' in Manchester.[93] Exeter took 'order for makeinge of the stampes and prynts for imprintinge of everie weight to be stamped' along with 'good beames and scales' in 1588. The clerk was told to 'kepe a booke of all thinges'.[94] Maidstone's chamberlain was told to 'provide a beam, weights, and measures' that was kept in cloisters next to the 'school house [for] comon use of such as will weigh or measure'. Nearby Tenterden stored 'six brasse weights' and 'seaven small brasse weights [weighing] 57li' in 'the presse in the court hall'.[95] Accounts also log payments for 'mendinge'. It cost Windsor 5s. 6d. to mend 'the brasen standard' and buy new seals in 1637. A London blacksmith was paid thirty shillings in 1585 for fixing three beams to weigh meal in Newgate Market and five more for Leadenhall Market.[96]

But it was not plain sailing. 'Measures commonly used within the realme were uncertain and varying one from another', privy councillors noted in 1603, despite statutes and 'good ordinances' to stop 'varietie and deceits'. Towns were told to bring weights and measures to the Exchequer, and 'divers' were found 'defective, differing and disagreeing from the true and antient standard'. This was a national

[90] NDRO B1/3792; GA GBR/F/4/3, fo. 250; BRO H/FAC/1, fo. 41.

[91] J. Every, *Speculum Mercativum, or The Young Merchants Glass Wherein are Exact Rules of All Weights, Coins, Measures, Exchanges, and Other Matters Necessary Used in Commerce* (1674), 20.

[92] G. Meriton, *A Guide for Constables, Churchwardens, Overseers of the Poor, Surveyors of the Highways, Treasurers of the County Stock, Masters of the House of Correction, Bayliffs of Mannours, Toll-takers in Fairs* (1674), 110–12.

[93] BRO R/FA/3/4; KAC WS/MB/1/5, cited by date; J. E. Earwaker, ed., *The Constables' Accounts of the Manor of Manchester From the Year 1612 to the Year 1647 and From the Year 1743 to the Year 1776*, 3 vols (Manchester 1891–1902), II, 110.

[94] DRO ECA B/14, fo. 578.

[95] CKS Md/Acm1/2, fo. 158; TE/S2, fos. 133, 139. See also GA GBR/F/4/5, fo. 146; DHC DC/DOB/24/2; ERO D/B5/GB1, fo. 112.

[96] BRO WI/FA1/1, fo. 100; B. E. Masters, ed., *Chamber Accounts of the Sixteenth Century*, London Record Society, 20 (1984), 75. See also DHC DC/BTB/M2/1635; CKS FA/AC4, fo. 41.

'slander'. New 'true' brass 'standerds and measures' were cut and 'printed with the first letter of the name' so that everything everywhere was 'agreeable'. Proclamation of this was read in markets 'and fastened in a table in the market [to be] seene and read by any that will'.[97] Little was different in 1619, however. 'False and deceitfull' weights and measures were still a national curse, 'especiallie' in 'northern and western parts'. Blame was put on market clerks for not stamping out 'falsities, deceipts and abuses'. Any trade supplying anything for 'sustenance of mans body [and] provision of horses [and] cattell' was told to rid itself of 'deceipts [for the] establishing of the true religion and service of almighty God'. This order was read in churches 'betweene the beginning and ending of common prayer' and put 'in a table to be seene and read at all times'. Ministers were also told to read it on Annunciation Day and Michaelmas for the next five years.[98]

Powel saw the need for his *Assize of Bread* in the 'unskilfulnes and want of knowledge' in officials that made it hard for them to 'perfectly discerne and knowe' true rates and weights.[99] He hoped to put this right, but it was a big hill to climb. Lyme Regis 'corporacon' landed in trouble in 1665 'for not weighing ye bakers bread according to ye statuts'. This had been 'formerly presented and not amended' but little changed. Doubling fines to forty shillings seemed to make no difference.[100] 'A great fawlt is [in the] scales we carry with us [for] tryall of weights and measures', Southampton governors admitted in 1601. They still lacked 'good scales' to weigh bread 'and other things' four years later.[101] 'Inquire of deceits and other offences in trade and traffique', William Sheppard told 'leets for inquiry', with a special eye for 'bakers and brewers [who] keep not the assise' and 'tradesman selling by false weights and measures'.[102] Aletasters in Ashby-de-la-Zouch were told to make 'search and inquirie in all alehouses or victualling houses' at least once every twenty days for 'perfect intelligence of the true assize of ale and beer'. Faversham's market clerk was told to make 'examinacon and tryall' of 'abuses in buyinge and sellinge': summon up 'love you owe to playne and simple uprightnes', governors urged, and 'hatred you owe to fraude and deceipte'. Lists of people with things to weigh (with 'in God is all my trust' written over them) were organized by streets: Nicholas Addy had his hands full with 'a galan pot 2 potle potes, 12 quart pots' and pint and beer pots.[103] 'Artificers' brought products to be weighed to jury foremen, market clerks, 'coroners of ye markett' (Ashby-de-la-Zouch), 'searchers of weights' (Kendal), and 'furers of weights and measures' (Barnstaple).[104] Tewkesbury's bailiffs 'examine[d] the assise of bread, beere, and

[97] *By the King. A Proclamation for Reformation of Great Abuses in Measures, Published by the Kings Commandement* (1603).

[98] *By the King. A Proclamation for Reformation of the Great Abuses in Weights and Measures* (1619).

[99] Powel, *Assize of Bread*, A3r/A3v.

[100] DHC DC/LR/B1/9, fos. 439, 448, 461, 476, 493, 507, 520.

[101] SA 6/1, fos. 25, 29.

[102] Sheppard, *Of the Office of the Clerk of the Market*, 76–88, 117–23.

[103] HL HAM box 2, folder 6, fo. 12v; CKS FA/JM/27/1; FA/JM/26.

[104] NDRO B1/3792, fo.121; B1/3321; KAC WSMB/K/1/5, 1615/16; HA W/A61, fo. 100; BRO R/AC1/1/1, fo. 631.

ale', 'viewe[d] marketts' weekly, and made sure that meat and fish were 'holsome' and 'reasonably' priced. Scales were put under the 'pentise' in Barnstaple, Reading 'woolhall', and on Weymouth streets where sergeants were told to weigh anything anyone 'refused' to put on the scales.[105]

Penalties were stiff but potential damage to character seemed a risk worth taking. Northampton's grand jury 'complayned' that offences were 'very frequent' in 1669. Preston weeded out 'deceivers' and 'cheats' like William Cottam, whose 'lead stone weight wanted 2 ouncs', and John Langton, whose weights 'will not equally balance unles 4 ouncs bee layd on'.[106] Henry Knap was fined 6s. 8d. in Lyme Regis in 1683 when it was found that 'three of his brasse [were] defective': 'one of 8 pounds wanted one ownce', one 'of 4 pounds wanted one ownce and upwards', and a third 'of 2 pounds wanted three quarters of an ownce'. They were 'broken to peeces'.[107] 'False and defective weights' were smashed in Chester, Clitheroe, Lewes, Ludlow, Lyme Regis, Hereford, and other towns in all parts of the land.[108] Lists of offenders stretched all the way down pages in courtbooks. Bakers and brewers breaking 'true' assizes form the longest lists. A list of fines 'for breaking the assize of ale and beere' in Loughborough is sixty-nine names long; another had ten names fewer.[109] Henry Trott from Lyme Regis, who was brought to court in 1653 'for makinge unlawfull measures for beere', told jurors that they were 'simple in presentinge him'. Tom Averill and his wife were put in the stocks in Maidstone in 1600 for making 'ill' and light 'bread myxt with barley' that was meant for prisoners in the town gaol.[110]

Another one of life's staples—fuel—provided more opportunities to swindle buyers. Hawks gathered, knowing that nobody could do without food or fuel. Weymouth governors knew 'by daily experience' that 'many inconveniences and uncertainties are found by measure of coles by heaps in buckets' that were 'sometimes more and sometimes lesse according to the care and regardfulness [of] buyers and sellers'.[111] More than a few colliers tried to con people with 'false defective sackes'. A collier from Ringwood in Dorset who journeyed thirty miles to Dorchester 'with a cart lode of coles' in 1632 was arrested after his 'bagge [was] measured' and his coals 'were found to little [and the bag] deceitfully filled'.[112] Three London servants who were caught 'deceavinge the people [with] sacks of coles sold for

[105] GA TBR/A/1/2, fo.8; M. Weinstock, ed., *Weymouth and Melcombe Regis Minute Book 1625 to 1660*, Dorset Record Society, 1 (Dorchester, 1964), 15.

[106] NA NQS/1, fo. 18; LA CNP 3/2/1, fos. 79, 112, 37.

[107] DHC DC/LR/A3/1, fo. 5.

[108] CA Z/AB/1, fo. 234; LA MBC/173; MBC/232; ESBHRO QI/EW6, fo. 42v; QI/EW7, fo. 74; SHA 3356/2442, fos. 1v, 8; DHC DC/LR/A3/1, fo. 5; HEA BG/11/8/2, 1619, 1627, 1634.

[109] HL HAM box 26, folders 22, 25. See also CA QJB/2/5, fo. 217v; HA Q4/1, fo. 134; ESBHRO QI/EW8, fo. 18; GA Q/Sahib/1, fo. 9v; SHA; SA 6/1, fo. 22; NDRO B1/3973, fo. 465; LMA Rep. 9, fo. 11.

[110] DHC DC/LR/B1/9; CKS Md/Acm1/1a, fo. 70v.

[111] Weinstock, *Weymouth and Melcombe Regis Minute Book*, 59.

[112] DHC DC/DOB/8/1, fo. 151v.

q[ua]rters not beinge half full' were made to 'ryde aboute the markett places and opyn stretes [with] a sack of ther coles hangynge aboute ther neckes'.[113] Other market traders landed in trouble for selling 'deceiptful' meat 'by false blades', cloth, cheese, sheepskins, hay, billets, and wood 'lackynge one inche of length'.[114]

'Seduced', it was said, 'by the subtyll craft of the dyvell', 'covetous' London woodmonger John Sheff was led to the pillory in 1561 after he was caught 'sundrye tymes' 'untruely' stamping new 'marks' on 'billets' that he had already put to sale. London merchant tailor Henry Paradise tried to fob off 'durte and drosse for good and merchuantable woade'. Gardener Robert Dowte was brought to court for selling 'in the name of good cabbage seeds the seeds of coleworts'.[115] An Essex butcher who was put in the pillory for bringing 'an hole calfe kylled and ready dressed and a pigge dead and ready scalded' to London to sell was paraded through the streets with 'one quarter of the calf hanging at his brest, another quarter at his back and bering the head [with] the pigge fastened to a pole in his handes'.[116]

Study 'weight [and] measure', William Petty urged 'rich and poor [and] young and old'. Tame deceit with 'knowledge by plain demonstration'.[117] In such a climate of anxiety about ambiguity and deception many magisterial orders boiled down to two words: be precise. Magistrates never stopped this pursuit of precision and not just in the examination of suspects or getting weights and measures to balance. Their list of demands was long: dense building regulations, microscopic rules for clothing, records needed to be 'perfect', accounts needed to balance, and much else. Precision meant 'knowledge'. Truth or meaning were never self-evident but required corroboration. Truth and precision were related traits but meant something different. Precision is where something is felt to be exact after measuring or calculating that is often represented in numbers. Things are transparent and intelligible. Truth, on the other hand, is better thought of as accepting that something agrees with what are in effect preconceived ideas about the nature of reality and factual precision. Resulting 'facts' are verified and indisputable. They are added to the stock of knowledge. People longed, in Shapiro's words, for probability and certainty.[118] We see this inside vestry rooms, laboratories, courts, guildhalls, and in shops like the one that John Seller ran on a Wapping wharf that was a regular port of call for sailors and anyone looking for a map or 'instrument' for measuring or calculating.

[113] LMA Rep. 13(1), fo. 19v.

[114] GA GBR/G/G3/SO/1, fo. 9; BRO R/AC1/1/5, fo. 45; ESBHRO QI/EW8, fo. 14v; NRO NMCC 12, fo. 472; DRO ECA B/1/4, fo. 268.

[115] LMA Reps. 13(1), fo. 127v; 18, fo. 99.

[116] LMA Rep. 19, fo. 372.

[117] Petty is quoted in T. McCormick, *William Petty and the Ambitions of Political Arithmetic* (Oxford, 2009); 181. See also Every, *Speculum Mercativum*, 5.

[118] B. J. Shapiro, *Probability and Certainty in Seventeenth-Century England: A Study of the Relationships Between Natural Science, Religion, History, Law, and Literature* (Princeton, NJ, 1983).

II

John Seller (1632–97) drew punishments, but the main aim in his large body of work was precision. He would never do anything quite like his *Booke of the Punishments of the Common Laws of England* (1678) again,[119] but he always *aspired* in work covering geography, mathematics, and cartography to be precise through calculation and measurement.[120] England is 29,000,568 acres in size, he noted. 'The north part of America is 1152400000 acres. Africa added up to 15418833000 acres. Little Norway amounted to 28492000. The whole sum of the habitable part of the world is six millars, six hundred and twenty-three million and seventy thousand acres'. Note, he wrote, 'that a millar is one thousand millions'. Seller liked to be precise. Wales had '1016 parish churches, 56 market towns, 40 castles, 230 rivers, 99 bridges, 32 parks, 13 forests, and 1 chase'.[121] He was not always accurate. 'There may be [a] million of people' living in London and Westminster in 1691, he said, 'observed by a scrutinous enquiry in most of the particulars' of the bills of mortality. He was wide of the mark but it is his effort to be exact that matters most in work that tried to 'compute' spending on 'provisions' in the London area over 'a year, week, day, hour, and minute'.[122]

Data was a national issue for Seller. He was worried that England had fallen behind 'the hollander [in] things of publick concernment for the general benefit of navigation'. A 'great treasure' slipped over the Channel, denting the pride of 'our noble spirited countreymen'. England floundered from a 'want of publick information' drawn from the 'experiences' of 'able men of our nation'. Precise knowledge needed to circulate constantly 'for the promotion of a public good' and national 'honour'.[123] Seller's work straddles the final third of the seventeenth century when 'political arithmetic' taught the value of precision in government. He published *The English Pilot* in 1671, the same year that the king made him royal hydrographer, apparently forgiving him for trying to kill him a decade earlier.[124] *The Pilot* is in effect a Mediterranean tour, making the area familiar in the

[119] See Chapter 3, below.

[120] For more on Seller see P. E. Steinberg, 'Calculating similitude and difference: John Seller and the "placing" of English subjects in a global community of nations', *Social and Cultural Geography*, 7 (2006); C. Verner, 'John Seller and the chart trade in seventeenth century England', in N. J. W. Thrower, ed., *The Compleat Plattmaker: Essays on Chart, Map, and Globe Making in England in the Seventeenth and Eighteenth Centuries* (Berkeley, CA, 1978).

[121] J. Seller, *A New Systeme of Geography* (1690), 21, 28.

[122] J. Seller, *A Moderate Computation of the Expences in Provisions, Spent in the Cities of London and Westminster, and the Places Within the Weekly Bills of Mortality, for a Year, Month, Week, Day, Hour and Minute* (1691).

[123] J. Seller, *Practical Navigation* (1669), 310–11.

[124] Baptist Seller was put on trial in 1662 for high treason and found guilty for his part in a plot to kill Charles II, which may have just been repeating rumours about the botched conspiracy. He was put in prison—his 'fellows' were all executed—but was lucky enough to be pardoned. A warrant from London's mayor and sheriffs dated 19 May 1663 extended Seller's monitored release from prison for another month so long as he provided necessary securities: TNA SP 14/15, fo. 23.

details of coasts, capes, rivers, rocks, and sands gleaned from 'judicious navigators'. 'Gentlemen' on ships 'communicated their observations and experience' so that the book would be 'exact' and up to date.[125] Another one of his books 'shewe[d the] courses and distances from one place to another' from 'the south foreland to Flamborough Head' with more information on 'the setting' of tides and currents and 'ebbing and flowing of the sea'. It gave directions for bringing a ship into any harbour along this long stretch of coast, all 'gathered from the experience and practice [of] able and expert navigators of our English nation'.[126]

Seller wanted his books to be workaday manuals to measure distance or to find a place anywhere in the world in 'exact charts' by getting his readers to calculate time and space.[127] Tables let readers thumb across columns to find the 'exact' distance of a particular place from London 'in computed and measured miles'. There was help along the way. Jacob van Langeren reminded readers heading out on a journey that 'It is a usuall manner in many parts where ways bee doubtfull for a traveller to find a standing post with a hand to direct men the ready way'. 'I have endeavoured [to] conceive some rule of ease', John Norden noted, 'being myself a traviler, to finde as neere as possible I could, the certaine distance of townes'. 'They might by this rule', he added, 'be reduced to certainty without error'.[128] Some travel guides provided tables divided by county so readers could move vertically and horizontally over the page to link places and the miles between them. Van Langeren went to great lengths to be precise in a short guide made up of tables for the most part. 'To know the distance between any two cities or townes', he taught, 'seeke place desired in the upper catalogue of townes and direct your eye from either place betweene the lines both from above and the side and where the lines meet in square you shall finde the number of miles'. 'To know whether [to] travell east, west, north, or south, from the place where you are to the place whither you intend to goe', he continued:

> Look in the small mapp of England placed before the great table of shire townes and draw a streight line from the next shire town lying in yor way to the shire

[125] J. Seller, *The English Pilot* (1671), preface. See also J. Seller, *The Coasting Pilot Describing the Sea Coasts, Chanells, Sounding Sands, Shoals, Rocks, and Dangers, the Bayes, Roads, Harbors, Rivers and Ports, with the Buoyes, Beacons, and Sea Marks Upon ye Coasts of England, Holland, Flanders, & France* (1673).

[126] J. Seller, *A Description of the Sands, Shoals, Buoyes, Beacons, Roads, Channels, and Sea Marks on the Coast of England From the Southforeland to Flamborough Head* (1671?).

[127] On the 'active reader' see D. E. Harkness, *The Jewel House: Elizabethan London and the Scientific Revolution* (New Haven and London, 2007), chap. 5; A. John, *The Nature of the Book: Print and Knowledge in the Making* (Chicago, IL, 1998), chap. 6; S. Shapin and S. Schaffer, *Leviathan and the Air-Pump: Hobbes, Boyle, and the Experimental Life* (Princeton, NJ, 1985), 60–72; B. Hackel, *Reading Material in Early Modern England* (Cambridge, 2005); A. Smyth, *Autobiography in Early Modern England* (Cambridge, 2010), esp. chap. 1.

[128] J. van Langeren, *A Direction for the English Traviller By Which He Shal be Inabled to Coast About All England and Wales* (1636), to the gentle reader; unpag. front of book; J. Norden, *England an Intended Guyde for English Travailers* (1625), preface.

towne which is next the place where you desyre to goe and you shall imediately see whether your journie be east, west, north or south.

The example he gave was a journey from London to York: 'Drawe a line or carrie yor eye straight from London to Yorke and you shall finde the way lyeth through Middlesex, Hartfordshire, Huntingdonshire, Northamptonshire, Lincolnshire, Nottinghamshire, and Yorkeshire.'[129]

Much of Seller's work was problem-solving. 'The following useful problems may be resolved', he said in one work: 'the hour of the night by any known star', 'the declination of any known star', 'the suns place in the ecliptick', 'the time of the suns rising and setting any day in the year'. The onus was on readers to do the spadework. Another work taught the tools to find out 'the age of the moon', 'the length of the dayes and nights in the lat[itude] of 52 degrees forever', and 'the hour of the day in all places of the world by the equinoctial compass'.[130] Ambitiously, Seller 'proposed' 'an actual survey' of England in 1679—'having consulted all mapps already extant and finding so great a deficiency therein'—'wherein shall be truly laid down the scituation of all the cities, market towns, parish churches [and] villages', with 'principal roads truly delineated' and an 'exact rule' for 'the ready finding out of any place' in quick time. His maps would be 'more compleate and perfect' and 'ornamental' and 'useful' than anything published before.[131] Like other plans Seller had in in his head, this one remained there. People picked holes in his work, calling it lacklustre or copied. Seller had a rough ride at times. But he was forever practical in his day job selling navigational tools in his shop, The Mariners Compass, handily placed on a Wapping wharf in the middle of London's maritime community. He sold all sorts of compasses, quadrants, scales, 'and other instruments for finding the sun's altitude', charts 'for all parts of the world', globes, maps, blank charts to fill in once a voyage was under way, glasses, dials, rulers, and shelves of books. Whether writing, teaching (he taught classes in arithmetic, geography, algebra, navigation, and gunnery), or selling, Seller lived in a world of numbers, degrees, and measurement, always *hoping* to trade and teach precision.

My next study in precision, Henry Manship (*c.*1550–1625), spent his life in Yarmouth, 137 miles from London. There is affection and confidence in his history of his home town that never saw the light of day in his lifetime. Manship hit heady heights as borough court attorney, soaring higher in 1579 to become town

[129] Van Langeren, *A Direction for the English Traviller*. See A. McRae, *Literature and Domestic Travel in Early Modern England* (Cambridge, 2009), chap. 2.

[130] J. Seller, *A Coelestiall Planisphere* (1678?); Seller, *Practical Navigation*, 31, 32, 33, 193; J. Seller, *Atlas Caelestiss, Containing the Systems and Theoryes of the Planets, the Constellations of the Starrs, and Other Phenomina's of the Heavens* (1677?).

[131] J. Seller, *Proposals for the Carrying on an Actual Survey of All the Counties in the Kingdom of England and Principality of Wales* (1679?), preface.

clerk. But he left this lofty position six years later in foggy circumstances. An offer of a plum position as customs official was withdrawn when it emerged that he had dodged custom duties. Manship hung around doing work for the town before falling heavily in 1604 when he lost his freeman status after calling Yarmouth's MPs—'Mr Damett and Mr Wheeler'—'dunces' and meek 'sheep'. He had a habit of bouncing back and was riding to London on town 'business' soon after. In one of several ironies that light up his life, Manship became solicitor to Yarmouth's MPs. But another fall from grace lurked around the corner when he was caught borrowing money in the town's name without authority to do so.[132]

The seeds of Manship's *History of Great Yarmouth* (finished in 1619) date back to 1612 when, still in favour, he headed a town committee that was tasked to bring order to the town's archives—'the hutch'. Word of his history might have made him the perfect pick for the job.[133] But its inspiration goes back further and it was personal. Manship had a long running enmity with former town clerk and MP 'dunce' Damet, who finished a slim history of the town around 1580 that in Manship's mind was sloppy, incomplete, and an insult to Yarmouth. Manship might also have wanted to show that he was a better archivist than Damet, who in office had failed to put the 'hutch' back in order.[134] So now, in 1612, Manship turned to the 'hutch'. He would outdo Damet and give the town the 'perfect' history that it deserved. The veracity of his text, he wrote, 'doth appear' or 'plainly appeareth' from the records in the 'hutch' or 'as in the court rolls of Yarmouth appeareth'. His history will be written from the records he was asked to put back in order.[135]

> I have for many years with a firm settled study, with my whole heart desired, with all sincerity to antiquity, in this my painful delight or delightsome painfulness, to write the truth so near as I am able, and by probable conjecture seriously collected out of such chronicles, charts, records, old pamphlets and writings as have come to my view and which in any wise might enlighten my understanding in the truth thereof.[136]

[132] For much more on Manship see R. Tittler, *Townspeople and Nation: English Urban Experiences 1540–1640* (Stanford, CA, 2001), chap. 5; A. Wood, 'Tales from the "Yarmouth Hutch": civic identities and hidden histories in an urban archive', *P&P*, supplement 11, *The Social History of the Archive: Record-Keeping in Early Modern Europe* (2016).

[133] See P. Rutledge, 'Archival management at Great Yarmouth since 1540', *Journal of the Society of Archivists*, 3 (1965); Wood, 'Tales from the "Yarmouth Hutch"'.

[134] NRO YD41/104: 'The Foundation and Antiquitye of Great Yarmouth'. See also P. Rutledge, 'Thomas Damet and the historiography of Great Yarmouth', *Norfolk Archaeology*, 33 (1965).

[135] H. Manship, *The History of Great Yarmouth*, completed in manuscript in 1619, ed. C. J. Palmer, Kessinger Legacy Reprints (1854), 171, 100. For Manship's history in broader culture see D. Woolf, *The Social Circulation of the Past: English Historical Culture, 1500–1730* (Oxford, 2003), 281, 284–5, and chap. 8; Tittler, *Townspeople and Nation*, chap. 5.

[136] Manship, *History of Great Yarmouth*, 18–19.

Manship spent days in the 'hutch' 'perus[ing] and copy[ing]' records, but key 'charters, evidences and writinges' had been in the hands 'of sundry persons' for a 'long tyme' and could not be found, forcing the town at 'great cost' to 'take exemplifications' from crown archives 'and other places'. Also vexing, 'charters, rolls, and evidences [kept] in the vestry [and] guildhall' were kept 'dispersedly' and 'very disorderly', making it hard to track down a 'greate number of years' in records. Manship's committee plugged away for two months, noting what each record was about and where it could be found. The fruits of its labour was a 'book' for the town's Assembly that spelt out precise arrangements for the 'hutch'. This included a comprehensive and detailed filing system to help officers and officials find records quickly.[137]

The town gave Manship £50 for his history, but for reasons unknown it was not published for another 230 years.[138] Loose-tongued Manship was back in trouble a year later in 'open sessions' for 'publishing a pamphlet extolling himself and defaming the towne falsely'. Found guilty, he was 'heartily sorry' and returned to Yarmouth's roll call of dishonour.[139] He was dead five years later and had not been in financial good health either. Manship was hardly a pillar of the community, but he wrote its history with love and care. 'O my most sweet beloved native town', he gushed. 'What pains I have herein taken', he wrote, came from 'the desire I have truly to advance the renown of my native township'. His Yarmouth was protestant, proud, civic-minded, and governed according to law. 'I [have] undertaken this work', Manship said, so that 'the posterity to come, especially such as be chosen into the body of the assembly', 'might dip his bucket and draw water of knowledge' of all the 'worthy things' done by the town down the centuries.[140]

He was a busy local William Camden digging in archives. 'My painful delight or delightsome painfulness', Manship wrote, is 'to write the truth, so near as I am able, and by probable conjecture have seriously collected out of such chronicles, charts, records, old pamphlets and writings [anything] which in anywise might enlighten my understandings in the truth'.[141] He reminded readers that his words were backed by records he knew well from his six years as town clerk when archives were needed to clinch points of law, not least in jurisdictional squabbles with the Court of Admiralty, the Barons of the Cinque Ports, and nearby

[137] Ibid., ii–iii.

[138] Charles John Palmer—editor of Manship's history in 1854—noted that the original copy was put in the town's 'hutch' but had long since disappeared.

[139] Manship, *History of Great Yarmouth*, 54, lv.

[140] Ibid., quoting 102, 19, 107, 190, 184. On Manship's sense of the civic see P. Withington, *The Politics of Commonwealth: Citizens and Freemen in Early Modern England* (Cambridge, 2005), 59, 67, 77, 115.

[141] Manship, *History of Great Yarmouth*, 19. In this respect Manship's is 'a 'true relations' text analysed by Dolan that seeks 'veracity' and 'reproduce[s] documents' in 'a kind of archive to substantiate truth': F. E. Dolan, *True Relations: Reading, Literature, and Evidence in Seventeenth-Century England* (Philadelphia, PA, 2013), 3–4.

Lowestoft. 'Let me declare unto you', he wrote, 'what I do find in a record taken out of the Tower in the roll termed *Michaelis* anno 2d Richard touching the force and validity of Yarmouth as such time as great opposition were by Lowestofians made against it'. 'I will not trouble you nor myselfe with the recital of the whole record', he added, 'but with so much as doth concerne the confirmation and approbation of the strength of Yarmouth'.[142] Manship knew Yarmouth's records better than anyone after chairing the 1612 'hutch' committee. His history has characteristics evident in local government record-keeping. He took trips to copy or track down records, quoted from records supplying folio pages, and his margins are peppered with notes with information on where he found something: 'Henry III patent letters', 'ancient parchment book', 'ancient document in the town hutch', 'act of assembly', 'regulations respecting the town common', town charters, 'the men of yarmouth produce their old [Exchequer] records'.

The archive was the last word for Manship. Just like us, he would sit taking notes, jotting down folio pages, and putting things together at home. The range of records he worked with looks like a solidly researched PhD thesis: Yarmouth court rolls, indentures, vestry records, parliamentary legislation, crown proclamations, synodic records, Star Chamber orders and decrees, letters patent, and Yarmouth Assembly books. He was still annoyed by his 1604 expulsion. It affected his *History* as, writing about Yarmouth's 'peerless haven' in 1613, he admits 'I can say but little' as I was 'estranged from town business [and] most willingly submit my imperfections to better judgments'. Manship asked readers to correct mistakes and town leaders to plug gaps in his 'knowledge'. The smell of sour grapes is pungent here. 'The difficulties he had to contend with', Manship said in a margin, 'included the want of sight of many town writings' that 'might have further enlightened my understanding' (he had been sifting through records in the 'hutch' the year before). Great Yarmouth got a new charter in 1608 and scores of laws had been passed since then—'whereof I am ignorant', Manship said, misleadingly.[143]

This is how Manship tackles the question 'Is Yarmouth a renowned town with a lustrous past?' He begins with what he 'found written in commendation' in 'old parchment fragments [in] the vestry'. But, he said, 'I would not ground myself nor persuade you to believe a Yermouth record only'. 'Mr Camden in his last and largest edition' heaped praise on the town: 'folio 477'. 'In the worship of God, the neatness of house, comeliness of apparel, and plenty of diet', Camden wrote, Yarmouth is not 'surpassed by any city of England'. Its people are 'very courteous in bounty and hospitality' and the 'great' annual Herring Fair drew 'a huge multitude' from 'England, France, Holland, and Zealand' ('fol. 478'). 'There is one thing

[142] Manship, *History of Great Yarmouth*, 139. On legal spats and records see R. Tittler, *Architecture and Power: The Town Hall and the English Urban Community c.1500–1640* (Oxford, 1991), 76, 88–9, 128; R. Tittler, *The Reformation and the Towns in England: Politics and Political Culture, c.1540–1640* (Oxford, 1998), esp. 211–19.

[143] Manship, *History of Great Yarmouth*, 75, 190.

[most] worthy of comendation', Camden closed (saving the best till last), 'there hath not dwelled [here] any ecclesiastical person which of any fleshly crime hath been at any time, as our records saith, positively detected'. Manship also 'rode fourteen miles' to 'read' Speed's 'great *Theatre*' that had just been published, to copy 'what there was written concerning Yermouth in Chap. 18, fol. 35' for the 'better confirmation [of] my assertion'. Speed confirmed that the townspeople were 'courteous', and that the town had a 'fair church and pier' and 'the worthiest herring fishery [in] Europe'. Speed was called 'an authentic witness'.[144] Manship turned to a striking range of authors for someone with just a few years in Yarmouth's free school under his belt, including Aristotle, Horace, Ovid, Sophocles, Plutarch, 'a Cornish poet' (on pilchards), the Bishop of Ely, the current king, Cicero, Plato, Constantine, Virgil, Socrates, Livy, Leland, and Holinshed. 'I shall not satisfy all doubts', he said, about the 'original…propagation of the Gospel of Jesus Christ within this island'. 'Yet', he said, I have been 'careful' to 'find out the most authentick writers [on] this subject', mainly 'Mr William Camden in his Britannica fol. 67'.[145]

But Manship's academic home was the archive. 'The first original of most towns is so obscure', he noted, 'by reason of their antiquities [that] are seen afar off which cannot be well discovered by the eye'. Who knew 'the very instant of time when the first stone was laid for the building of Yarmouth'? But Manship went far back in records to be 'manifest'. The town was 'well peopled' in the eleventh century, he revealed, after combing through 'the general survey in the days of Edward the Confessor' that counted 'seventy burgesses'. This was confirmed by the 'Domms-day book or the Notia of England remaining in his majestys excheq[ue]r' and 'an old exemplification' in 'saxon character' in 'the town chest or hutch in the vestry'. He calculated Yarmouth's population to be in the region of 300–400 back then. Now, 'at this present' (1619), he wrote, there are 'not so few as twelve hundred householders' who call Yarmouth their home.[146]

Manship also beavered away in the 'hutch' to clear up what for him was a pressing matter: the exact site of the old hospital. He got his answer from reading 'an old parchment book', deeds (it 'plainly appeareth' and is made 'more than manifest'), and a 'roll of the eighteenth year of Henry VI' that was stored in the 'hutch'. A 'tripartite indenture' and an 'ancient roll in the vestry' told the tale of long-running tiffs with Caister over 'the extent' of each town's 'liberties'. Three-centuries-old 'rolls' told Manship about past housing regulations and transporting

[144] Ibid., 6, 119. [145] Ibid., 29.

[146] Ibid., 20–2, 24. In support of the early burgess/householder estimates Manship also drew attention to the 'writer of a parchment book which I have also perused, containing the originality or antiquity of Yarmouth, who in folios EXTO of the same, affirmeth that in Edward the Confessors time the same began to grow in to sight at low water and that in the days of King Harold and William the Conqueror the same grew to be dry and not overflown' and fishermen started to catch herring: ibid., 22.

wool. He compared an Assembly order passed in his lifetime (1571) banning building houses with board to curb fire hazards to 'many good presentments' for breaking building codes that dated back to the fourteenth century. The old king-provost's home was not called the 'Conge', Manship said reproachfully; it was called the 'kings conge'. He was quick to point out the mistakes of others. He took great exception to a 'return' of Norfolk 'hundreds, towns and lordships' filed in 'Exchequer' in 'the ninth year of Edward the second' and 'a book remayning in the office of his majesties remembrauncer intituled *Copla de Nominbus Villarum & Dmo*' that placed Yarmouth in West Flegg Hundred. It is in East Flegg, he said, as 'ancient records' and Speed's 'late mapp' show. And Yarmouth was not 'an ancient member of the five [cinque] ports'—we don't want to become one, he said stuffily—for 'better confirmation', he added, go back to 'page 8 of this book' and read a 'writ of the ninth of Edward the second'.[147]

Lastly, Kett's Rebellion (1549), the largest shock wave to shoot through sixteenth-century Norfolk: more pages are given to it than anything else.[148] Manship's descriptions of the 'rebels' could have come from Harman's pages. They were a 'cursed crew', a 'rascally rout of rebels', and a 'rabblement of rude rascals'. Like locusts, these 'arch-traitors' or 'viperous villains' surged through Norfolk to 'delude' 'honest' people with false information in classic precision/imprecision binary polarities. 'These villainous traitors' were polar opposites to hard-working Yarmouth men who put down their tools to take up arms to defend their town. They had a 'pretended cause' (anti-enclosure) and issued 'pretended warrants' to cloak their 'develish dealing'.[149] Having 'plainly discern[ed] their jugglings to delude the common people', Manship 'proceed[s] to display them in their true colours'. Still fighting long-dead Kett with his pen, he turned to documents, quoting at length. 'The order and manner' of it all would unravel neatly; 'for willingly I will not insert any thing untruly', Manship reassured his readers. 'The large chronicle of John Stowe' was a good guide to 'the business', but Manship steered readers towards the 'more particular' and 'full information of Alexander Nevill', where 'thou mayst understand to thy full contentment' the 'whole proceedings' of that singular summer.[150] Manship quoted from Kett's 'commission for fetching of victuals' ('Nevill fol. 1,030'), thinking 'good to give thee a true copy' (he had one in his possession), and letters written by privy councillors, the king, and Robert Kett. He told the story from the first fence or hedge that was pulled down at Wymondham to the killing of the Ketts. 'Thus', he told his 'good reader', I have

[147] Ibid., 8, 13, 42, 109, 171–3, 63, 58, 179–80, 100, 64, 57. Manship urges readers to go to other pages in his own book in other places: for instance, ibid., 77, 99, 103.

[148] For Manship's narratives of the 1381 and 1549 rebellions see *History of Great Yarmouth*, 143–58. His account of Kett's Rebellion is analysed in Andy Wood, *The 1549 Rebellions and the Making of Early Modern England* (Cambridge, 2007), 232–5.

[149] Quotes from Manship, *History of Great Yarmouth*, 143, 144, 145, 146, 148, 150, 158.

[150] Ibid., 148, 151, 146.

'delivered unto thee the whole discourse of those bloody businesses so far as I have or could get any certain knowledge'.[151]

Manship and Seller followed words and practices pervasive in the pursuit of precision: truth, exact, survey, manifest, observation, searching, measured, computed, recorded, information, knowledge, authentic, and so on. Neither was exceptional. Far from it. They represented methods that had lasting impacts in local government. In the same vein manorial lords with less in their pockets in inflationary times tried to squeeze money from their estates by turning to surveyors who stalked fields measuring, calculating, and redrawing as lords tried to redefine their relationships to tenants through surveys. John Norden advised 'every lord of a mannor [to] cause his lands' to be 'truly surveyed' at least once a decade to be certain. This became a regular reckoning rhythm. 'What would be more ridiculous', surveyor John Lowe asked, 'than for me to go about to praise an art that all mankind know they cannot live peacably without'.[152] Surveying was a governing art deeply rooted in culture, society, and soil. People peered into dark corners above and below land to survey buildings, lead deposits, rivers, forests, preachers, teachers, sewers, money lenders, Quakers, and much else. Survey was the generic term for chorographical works describing counties and cities that multiplied around 1600, and accounts of other lands: Venice, Virginia, Turkey, Spain, Sweden, the East and West Indies, and, lavishly, 'the whole world'.[153] Towns like Colchester in 1598 spent time and money to survey 'landes, howses, and wast grounds'. Winchester's mayor ordered a 'view' of land and tenements and ribbon developments in 1603.[154] 'Begin at what part of the town you please', David Jenkins wrote in his surveying guidelines, 'go through setting down every parcel of land, messuage or tenement distinctly, abutting and bounding it' and the 'tenure and title of the owner or inheritor'. 'If you begin at the mannor house then begin your survey book: A.B. Esq Lord of the mannor of H'. Not many acres were left unmeasured for long.[155]

Precision was the absence of doubt. In his *Surveiors Dialogue* (1610), John Norden spoke of the absolute necessity for 'a due true and exact view and survey' not 'abused' nor 'wronged' or 'grieved' by 'false informations'. 'It is often seene that one manor lyeth within another', he noted; 'it is necessary therefore that their

[151] Ibid., 157.

[152] J. Norden, *The Surveiors Dialogue* (1610), 30; J. Lowe, *Geodaesia or The Art of Surveying and Measuring of Land* (1688), preface, 1. See also D. Jenkins, *Pacis Consultum... Describing the Court Leet* (1657), 64; A. W. Richeson, *English Land Measuring to 1800: Instruments and Practices* (Cambridge, MA, 1966); A. McRae, *God Speed the Plough: The Representation of Rural England, 1500–1660* (1996), 169–97.

[153] J. Broadway, *'No Historie so Meete': Gentry Culture and the Development of Local History in Elizabethan and Early Stuart England* (Manchester, 2006).

[154] ERO D/B5/Gb1, fo. 160v; HA W/B1/3, fo. 136. See also HL STTM box 3, folder 37; box 12, folder 33; CKS FA/AC3, fo. 153v; Md/Acm/1a, fo. 71; Md/Acm1/2, fo. 59v.

[155] Jenkins, *Pacis Consultum*, 64.

distinctions should be carefully observed and recorded'. 'Bring [to] certainty', he urged, what 'is or may [be] doubtfull'.[156] Ralph Agas wanted surveys to be 'sound and inviolate' with no 'blemish' and 'exact' 'angles, measures [and] numbers'. 'Avoid confusion', he urged. But he was uneasy about the 'difference' of 'instruments used on our practice' that might result in 'uncertaintie and errour'. 'The people generally beginne to doubt whether there be any certainety and perfection in the operation of such instruments', he mused.[157] John Love's surveyor worked with mental maps of the land. He was told to 'walk or ride over the mannor once or twice [to get] as it were a map in your head by which means you may the better know where to begin'.[158]

Seller and Manship came of thinking age in cultures of surveying stressing experience, empiricism, and observation to create 'facts': demonstrated occurrences that were precise. This touched overlapping disciplines such as mathematics, law, natural science, or geography.[159] The time from Elizabeth's coronation to the Glorious Revolution was historic in these intellectual hives. Empirical 'truth' or 'proof' were 'defining' features of these times when the nature of credibility/plausibility caused stormy debates.[160] We see this in common law meanings of legal facts that relied on expert and eyewitness testimony; Francis Bacon's natural and experimental science with grounding in legal protocols and witnessing;[161] tighter standards of evidence (not least in witchcraft cases);[162] fiery debates about the claims and status of science and magic (triggered by storms about the reality

[156] Norden, *Surveiors Dialogue*, epistle to the reader, 2v, 95 (irregular pag.).

[157] R. Agas, *A Preparative to Platting of Landes and Tenements for Surueigh Shewing the Diuersitie of Sundrie Instruments Applyed Thereunto* (1596), 3, 14.

[158] Lowe, *Geodaesia*, 142.

[159] B. J. Shapiro, *A Culture of Fact: England, 1550–1720* (Ithaca, NY, 2000); M. Poovey, *A History of the Modern Fact* (Chicago, IL, 1998).

[160] Dolan, *True Relations*, 5; Shapiro, *Probability and Certainty*.

[161] Shapiro, *Culture of Fact*, chaps 1 and 5–6; Harkness, *Jewel House*, chap. 5; E. H. Ash, *Power, Knowledge, and Expertise in Elizabethan England* (Baltimore, MD, 2004), chap. 5; M. Feingold, *The Mathematicians' Apprenticeship: Science, Universities, and Society in England, 1560–1640* (Cambridge, 1984); C. Webster, *The Great Instauration: Science, Medicine, and Reform 1626–1660* (New York, 1975); H. Wheeler, 'The invention of modern empiricism: juridical foundations of Francis Bacon's philosophy of science', *Law Library Journal*, 76 (1983); M. Ben-Chaim, 'The value of facts in Boyle's experimental philosophy', *History of Science*, 38 (2000); John, *Nature of the Book*, chap. 7; S. Shapin, *A Social History of Truth: Civility and Science in Seventeenth-Century England* (Chicago, IL, 1994); L. Stewart, *The Rise of Public Science: Rhetoric, Technology, and Natural Philosophy in Newtonian Britain, 1660–1750* (Cambridge, 1992).

[162] R. W. Serjeantson, 'Testimony and proof in early modern England', *Studies in History and Philosophy of Science*, 30 (1999); B. J. Shapiro, 'Religion and the law: evidence, proof and "matter of fact", 1660–1700', in N. Landau, ed., *Law, Crime, and English Society, 1660–1830* (Cambridge, 2002); M. Gaskill, 'Witchcraft and evidence in early modern England', *P&P*, 198 (2008); P. Rushton, 'Texts of authority: witchcraft accusations and the demonstration of truth in early modern England', in S. Clark, ed., *Languages of Witchcraft: Narrative, Ideology, and Meaning in Early Modern Culture* (Basingstoke, 2001); C. R. Unsworth, 'Witchcraft beliefs and criminal procedure in early modern England', in T. G. Watkin, ed., *Legal Record and Historical Reality* (1989).

of witchcraft);[163] political arithmetic with key attributes like observation, classification, and calculation;[164] and close attention to detail in architecture, for example, travel writing, or coroners' autopsies.[165]

Scholars often limit discussion to landmark texts/works such as Robert Record, *The Ground of Arts* (1543), John Norden, *The Surveiors Dialogue* (1610), Francis Bacon, *Novum Organum Scientiarum* (1620), Robert Boyle, *The Scepitcal Chemist* (1661), John Graunt, *Natural and Political Observations* (1662), William Petty, *Political Arithmetic* (1676?; published 1690). We can connect these giants and construct compelling narratives of developing factual precision. Thoughts turn (understandably) to book-lined studies, laboratories, libraries, and legal diagnosis. Yet we can miss much when we do this. These agendas are different to mine. It is a question of whether we are talking about science and epistemological knowledge or governing villages and towns. This chapter brings debates about precision to the everyday with archives so treasured by Manship and forms of print aimed at relatively humble people. Empirical precision mattered in vestry rooms, for instance, where governors thought long and hard about facts and figures in their own ways for their own ends. Office-holder(s) became versed in the practices and principles of precision not by reading high-sounding texts but through 'experience' and 'observation'. They plugged away day after day, seeking in their words to be 'true' and 'exact'. They mulled over issues of precision, proof, and truth in workaday settings and offices. The collection, categorization, and application of information was everyday practice in local government. We tend to privilege intellectual projects like 'political arithmetic', but local officers had been doing this long before Graunt put pen to paper (he was one of them!). They did their best, in Manship's words, to be 'as neere as possible'.

We turn next to 'the middle people, betweene cottagers and gentlemen' who dominated local office. They had, in William Harrison's word, 'preheminance' in their communities. They were the 'most substantial inhabitants' (Thomas Forster) or 'cheefest of ye parish' (Oswestry), whose 'course of life', Edmund Wingate of Gray's Inn believed, 'may render them liable to 'hold office'. 'This maketh the State

[163] K. Thomas, *Religion and the Decline of Magic: Studies in Popular Beliefs in Sixteenth- and Seventeenth-Century England* (1971), chap. 18; Clark, *Thinking With Demons*, Part II; M. Hunter, 'New light on the "Drummer of Tedworth": conflicting narratives of witchcraft in Restoration England', *Historical Research*, 78 (2005); T. H. Jobe, 'The Devil in Restoration science: the Glanvill-Webster witchcraft debate', *Isis*, 72 (1981).

[164] P. Kreager, 'New light on Graunt', *Population Studies*, 42 (1988); McCormick, *William Petty*; T. McCormick, *Human Empire: Mobility and Demographic Thought in the British-Atlantic World, 1500–1800* (Cambridge, 2022), chap, 4; Slack, 'Government and information'.

[165] M. Lockwood, *The Conquest of Death: Violence and the Birth of the Modern English State* (New Haven and London, 2017); R. Porter, 'The rise of physical examination', in W. F. Bynum and R. Porter, eds., *Medicine and the Five Senses* (Cambridge, 1993); J. Rudolph, 'Gender and the development of forensic science: a case study', *EHR*, 123 (2008); M. C. Fuller, *Voyages in Print: English Travel to America, 1576–1624* (Cambridge, 1995); McRae, *Literature and Domestic Travel*, chaps 5–6; Shapiro, *Culture of Fact*, chap. 3; V. Hart, *Inigo Jones: The Architect of Kings* (New Haven and London, 2011); C. Anderson, *Inigo Jones and the Classicist Tradition* (Cambridge, 2007).

constant and firm', Walter Raleigh eulogized, 'when both the extreams ['of nobility and gentry and the base rascal, and begarly sort'] are tied together by a middle sort, as it were with a band'.[166]

III

I am thinking of men like Matthew Warren from the 'entirely agricultural village' of Terling in Essex who did the spadework when a longish set of 'articles of enquirey' from justices landed on the vestry table in 1630. 'A man of many parts', tailor, grocer, and one-time alehouse-keeper, Warren was 'well equipped' for this task and relished taking responsibility for it:

> Moreover, he could do it himself as he was literate. His lengthy reply to the justices' articles of enquirey with its careful penmanship, wayward phonetic spelling, and proud signature stands as a monument to his endeavour, the pain it cost him, and to his sense of achievement.[167]

Men like Warren were backbones of local administrative communities. 'Next unto the nobilitie, knights, and esquires', Sir Thomas Smith noted, they 'have the greatest charge and doings in the common wealth, or rather are more travailed to serve in it than all the reast'. Increasingly able to read, write, and count, 'middling' men worked each day in shops, workplaces, counting houses, and around tables fine-tuning skills that were essential for office-holding.[168] This is absolutely key for precision and the chapter to come on information gathering and record-keeping. The extent to which skills honed at home and work were real assets for local government has been insufficiently acknowledged. Trading, retail, and manufacturing sectors grew along with the places they served. Farmers pursued

[166] T. Forster, *The Lay-mans Lawyer: Or, the Second Part of the Practice of Law* (1654), 123; W. Day, ed., *Oswestry Parish Church: The Churchwardens' Accounts for 1579–1613* (Oswestry, 1970), 33; E. Wingate, *The Exact Constable with His Origin and Power in All Cases Belonging to His Office* (1677), A4r; Sir W. Raleigh, *Maxims of State* (1650), 16. The first quotation from George Tooke—speaking in 1635—is quoted in S. Hindle, *The State and Social Change in Early Modern England, c.1550–1640* (Basingstoke, 2000), 207. Harrison is quoted in K. Wrightson, '"Sorts of people" in Tudor and Stuart England', in J. Barry and C. Brooks, eds., *The Middling Sort of People: Culture, Society, and Politics in England, 1550–1800* (Basingstoke, 1994), 39.

[167] K. Wrightson and D. Levine, *Poverty and Piety in an English Village: Terling 1525–1740* (Oxford, 1995), 142, and quoting 23.

[168] Sir T. Smith, *De Republica Anglorum: The Maner of Governement or Policie of the Realme of England* (1584), 29–30, 32. See H. French, *The Middle Sort of People in Provincial England 1600–1750* (Oxford, 2007); K. Wrightson, *Earthly Necessities: Economic Lives in Early Modern Britain* (New Haven and London, 2000), chap. 1; K. Thomas, 'The meaning of literacy in early modern England', in G. Baumann, ed., *The Written Word: Literacy in Transition* (Oxford, 1986); K. Thomas, 'Numeracy in early modern England', *TRHS*, 5th series, 37 (1987); D. Cressy, 'Literacy in context: meaning and measurement in early modern England', in J. Brewer and R. Porter, eds., *Consumption and the World of Goods* (Abingdon, 1993); Harkness, *Jewel-House*, chap. 3.

'improvement'. They developed knowledge and techniques from an active exchange of ideas and 'husbandry' books.[169]

Officers should have been drawn from the ranks of 'subsidie men' or the more 'substantial house-keepers'. The 'ablest inhabitants' are most fit for office, Bedfordshire justice Edmund Wingate advised. Constables, John Layer said in his book on 'dutie' (1641), 'are to be chosen of the abler sort [and never from] 'the meaner sort'.[170] The author of *Ease for Overseers* (1601) advised that 'The statute appointeth overseers of the poore to be subsedie men' or 'substantiall men'. 'A substantiall person [he continued] is he which hath competencie of wealth, of wisdome, [and] care of a good conscience'. 'If he be poore', on the other hand, 'he will not be respected' and people will ask 'shall thou raigne over us'. 'Over-awed', they would surely 'balk their duties'. There would be little to stop them from taking bribes or turning a blind eye to wrongdoing.[171] The defining qualities of a model officer were mirror images of the essential attributes of the middle station of life. 'It is requisite to have these three properties', John Layer urged in his guide for constables: 'honesty, knowledge [to understand what to do], and ability'. A constable needs 'these things', Edward Leigh noted: 'honesty, science, and ability'. Wingate's 'three necessary qualifications' were 'honesty', 'ability', and 'knowledge'.[172]

We have a little library of work that challenges ideas that office-holder(s) were unpaid amateurs who half-heartedly took their turn in office for a mere year when the pick fell on them. Many men from solid 'middling' stock wanted to do a good job in office. A fair proportion served several stretches in various offices down the years.[173] There were inevitably black sheep in their ranks. But many, if not most, had a commitment to do a good job if only because, as property-owners and ratepayers, they had most to lose if the parish peace or purse were put at risk.

[169] P. Slack, *The Invention of Improvement: Information and Material Progress in Seventeenth-Century England* (Oxford, 2015); M. Overton, *Agricultural Revolution in England: The Transformation of the Agrarian Economy 1500–1850* (Cambridge, 1996), chap. 4; C. Clay. 'Landlords and estate management', in J. Thirsk, ed., *Agrarian History of England and Wales, VII, 1640–1750: Agricultural Change* (Cambridge, 1985); M. Overton, J. Whittle, D. Dean, and A. Hann, eds., *Production and Consumption in English Households, 1600–1750* (Abingdon, 2004); J. Thirsk, 'Plough and pen: agricultural writers in the seventeenth century', in T. Aston, P. Coss, C. Dyer, and J. Thirsk, eds., *Social Relations and Ideas: Essays in Honour of R. H. Hilton* (Cambridge, 1983).

[170] Wingate, *Exact Constable*,14, 127; J. Layer, *The Office and Dutie of Constables, Church-wardens and Other the Overseers of the Poore* (1641), 4.

[171] *Ease for Overseers*, 9–10. See also P.B., *A Help to Magistrates and Ministers of Justice, Also, A Guide to Parish and Ward-Officers* (1700), 108; Forster, *Lay-mans Lawyer*, 123.

[172] Layer, *Office and Dutie of Constables*, 3; E. Leigh, *A Phililogicall Commentary or an Illustration of the Most Obvious and Useful Words in the Law* (2nd edition, 1658), 48; Wingate, *Exact Constable*, 13.

[173] J. Kent, *The English Village Constable, 1580–1642: A Social and Administrative Study* (Oxford, 1986); J. Kent, 'The rural 'middling sort' in early modern England circa 1640–1740: some economic, political, and socio-cultural characteristics', *Rural History*, 10 (1999); Wrightson and Levine, *Poverty and Piety in an English Village*, chap. 4; French, *Middle Sort of People*; Hindle, *State and Social Change*, chap. 8; and my *Lost Londons*, chaps 8–11.

'Middling' Berkshire farmer Robert Loder made notes in his accounts (1611–13) of 'payments to the pore' and 'towards the house of correction'. He also made a note about 'some rogues and thieves' who helped themselves to his barley and two sheep.[174] But we should appreciate the sense of obligation felt by numerous 'middling' men for whom a successful stint in office was a source of respectability and a mark of who they were.[175] It is entirely possible that many saw office not as a chore but as an obligation and expectation of their standing. Holding office would not have been a one-time duty for most. Most parishes were too small for that; the pool of 'substantiall' and 'ablest' men might not have been that big, even in some London parishes. Valerie Pearl believes that one-in-ten householders held office at any one time in seventeenth-century London. If she is right, then office-holding was cyclical.[176] The *cursus honorem* of urban corporate life in guilds, councils, and local office was as important for performance in office as it was for the life course of participating citizens. But small villages, in the words of Godfrey Goodman writing in 1616, also operated on the same expectations and accomplishments:

> for here in the country with us, if a mans stock of a few beasts be his own, and that he lives out of debt and paies his rent fuly and quarterly, we hold him a very rich and sufficient man; one that is able to do the king and countrey good service; we make him a constable, a sidesman, a head-borough, and at length a church-warden; thus we raise him by degrees, we prolong his ambitious hopes... Here is the great governor amongst us and we wonder that all others do not respect him accordingly.[177]

'Prolong!' Office-holding unfolds here through adulthood. There was a well-established local office ladder. 'Ye jury' of Ashby-de-la-Zouch 'agreed' that anyone who had 'executed ye office of a constable shall [from now on serve] onely in the offices of churchwarden, overseer for ye poore, feilde ceenes, and coroners of the markett'.[178] 'Middling men' in this East Midlands market town or Goodman's villages took decisions that affect what we see in this book. Talk about the concerns of office was not limited to guildhalls or vestry rooms. It is hardly realistic given the 'associational' pull of the middle walks of life to think that office-holder(s) did not mix in their free time. Who else would they meet up with in this increasingly

[174] G. E. Fussell, ed., *Robert Loder's Farm Accounts 1610–1620*, Camden Record Society, 3rd series, 53 (1936), 13, 85, 36.

[175] H. French, '"Ingenious and learned gentlemen": social perceptions and self-fashioning among parish elites in Essex, 1680–1740', *SH*, 25 (2000); H. French, 'Social status, localism, and the "middle sort of people" in England 1620–1720', *P&P*, 166 (2000).

[176] V. Pearl, 'Change and stability in seventeenth-century London', *London Journal*, 5 (1979).

[177] Godfrey Goodman, *The Fall of Man, Or the Corruption of Nature Proved by the Light of Natural Reason* (Cambridge, 1616), 139–40.

[178] HL HAM box 2, folder 1, fo. 10v.

polarized society?[179] Many became life-long friends and colleagues. They shared fears that hinged on the well-being of their part of the world. Autobiographies and diaries let us into a radius of friends and contacts from similar backgrounds. We see Raleigh's 'middle sort' in a huddle around vestry or parlour tables, swapping thoughts in church porches, or walking somewhere deep in talk—conversations now lost in the main, but they happened and make nonsense of any idea that a year-long stint is how we must measure the accumulated experience of local office-holding. In- and out-of-office talk might soon turn to a local drunk, dwindling collections, troubling 'newecomers', or a roof or road that needed fixing. And in or out of office, someone with more 'experience' might have been at hand to offer assistance and advice. Southampton magistrates asked 'others best experienced in those businesses' to 'direct' officers appointed for 'reforming of abuses about the keyes' in 1602, or, as they asked again in the next year, 'others of experience in such causes'.[180]

The cumulative tools/lessons of work and office were mutually reinforcing. A careful shopkeeper kept up-to-date accounts, organized records, and knew where to buy ink and paper. Starting in the second half of the sixteenth century, there developed what at the time was called 'practical arithmetic' that was pitched towards 'middling' men. Edmund Wingate willed officers to read 'arithmetique'.[181] Advances in local information were powered by commercial prowess and this popularization and necessity of mathematics. We have used the term 'shop arithmetic' for everyday calculating to run businesses. John Graunt's *Natural and Political Observations* (1662) was written and calculated from bills of mortality by someone deeply immersed in 'practical arithmetic' from his many years in a draper's shop.

It begins with numbers!

> I have been so ravished with the study of numbers [William Ingram enthused in 1624] that if any man will ask me, what is the chiefest good next to God, that in this life I take delight in? I must answer, Number; if, what is the second? Number; if, what the third? Number.

'There is no knowledge either rationall, morall, physicall, or metaphysicall', Ingram continued in expansive confidence, that does not have 'cognation or

[179] P. Clark, *British Clubs and Societies 1500–1800: The Origins of an Associational World* (Oxford, 2000).

[180] SA 6/1, fos. 26–7.

[181] Wingate, *Exact Constable*, 14, 127. See also Harkness, *Jewel House*; and L. Stewart, 'Philosophers in the counting-house: commerce, coffee-houses and experiment in early modern London', in P. O'Brien, ed., *Urban Achievement in Early Modern Europe: Golden Ages in Antwerp, Amsterdam, and London* (Cambridge, 2001).

participation with numbers'.[182] Thomas Hylles turned to amateurish rhyme to eulogize 'numbers':

> Though numbers use doth playne appeare,
> In towne and country every where,
> At home, abroade, both farre and neere,
> At sea, at shore, on earth, on ayre.
> In every arte and trade of life,
> In peace, in warre, in merchandise,
> In all contracts...[183]

Numbers were 'everywhere'. 'There is no science in the whole world', John Harpur told his readers, 'that doth increase the knowledge or inrich the mind of man then arithmetick': 'Take [it] away' and how does a shepherd 'differ' from sheep or 'the horse-keeper from the asse?'[184] England's first popular mathematician, Robert Record (1512?–58), related numbers and quantification to government and society. 'Arithmeticke is so many wayes needful unto the first planting of a commonewealth [he wrote, and] for [its] preservation' (a line leads from Record to 'political arithmetic'). 'Oh in how miserable case is that realme where the ministers and interpreters of the law are destitute of all good sciences which be the keyes of the lawes', Record remarked, 'how can they [make] good lawes'? Government would be impaired without (in Ingram's words) 'arithmeticall, geometricall, and harmonical computation'.[185]

Government, but work also. 'It behoveth every good discrete marchaunt to have knowledge and cunning in reading and writing', Hugh Oldcastle wrote in his bookkeeping guide. He must 'bee prompt and ready in his accompt and reckoning', he added, and 'have the cunning and arte of arethmetike'.[186] 'Practical' arithmeticians wrote plainly. Record wanted his pioneering *Ground of Arts* (1543) to be a 'good...meane unto knowledge' for the 'simple [and] ignorant'. Thomas Hylles believed that 'there is no one arte more generally necessarie for all

[182] W. Ingram, *The Secrets of Numbers According to Theologicall, Arithmeticall, Geometri-call, and Harmonicall Computation* (1624), A4r, 1.

[183] T. Hylles, *The Arte of Vulgar Arithmeticke* (1600), Ciiiir.

[184] J. Harpur, *The Jewell of Arithmetick: or, The Explanation of a New Invented Arithmeticall Table* (1617), A3r–v.

[185] R. Record, *The Ground of Arts. Teaching the Perfect Worke and Practise of Arithmeticke...Augmented by Mr John Dee* (1640 edition), A4v–5, A5v; R. Record, *The Whetstone of Witte Whiche is the Seconde Parte of Arithmetike* (1557), Bii.

[186] H. Oldcastle, *A Briefe Instruction and Maner How to Keepe Bookes of Accomptes After the Order of Debtor and Creditor* (1588), unpag., chap. 1. See also Harkness, *Jewel House*, chap. 3; L. B. Cormack, 'The commerce of utility: teaching mathematical geography in early modern England', *Science and Education*, 15 (2006), 311–14; M. Feingold, 'Gresham College and London practitioners: the nature of the English mathematical community', in F. Ames-Lewis, ed., *Sir Thomas Gresham and Gresham College: Studies in the Intellectual History of London in the Sixteenth and Seventeenth Centuries* (Aldershot, 1999).

degrees'.[187] 'Plaine' and 'useful' arithmetic was welcomed in farms, shops, and workrooms. Merchant adventurer John Carpenter hoped that his 1632 account-keeping guide would be 'most usefull for merchants' and anyone who kept 'shops of retaile'.[188] 'I have compiled this book chiefly for advantage of traders', John Hill noted at the start of his *Exact Dealer* (1688), which included 'a store-house of instructions' for 'the trading part of the nation'.[189] 'My design', Arthur Leadbetter wrote in his *Arithmeticall Rules* (1691), 'is to treat only of heads of arithmetick as are necessary and proper for publick commerce'. 'Its end is practical', he added, 'and therefore named practical arithmetick'. John Ayres called his work a 'manual of practical arithmetic...chiefly for the benefit and use of tradesmen'. Edward Cocker put it bluntly in 1678: 'practical arithmetick is the soul of merchandize'.[190]

Many readers who found 'practical arithmetic' 'extraordinar[ily] useful' for 'worldly affairs' would have been office-holder(s). Guidelines for traders replicated advice to officers on what to do with records: pagination, naming books (and writing it on its 'backside or cover'), keeping registers 'for sure keeping and ordering' of letters, making inventories to keep 'in good order', 'kalendering' ('by it you may know in what page of the book the...account stands'), and putting data in columns broken down by date and numbered (so 'there can be no mistake'). This was a busy life of counting, calculating, and categorizing. It relied on accurate transcription, transferring, record-keeping, and on what was called 'reckoning'. The 'middling' walk of life depended on these skills and mental agility for a smidgen of commercial success. We should keep in mind that repetition of this 'practical arithmetick' and keeping accounts (whether single- or double-entry, which had its own guiding texts) created financial records but also a way of doing things with skills that were instinctively transferrable to any task at hand. The habitual reckoning and recording required for order and structure in accounts were brought to social relations, organization, litigation, and local office, where balancing accounts was the crowning achievement of the administrative year. Many churchwardens, constables, or overseers were well versed in keeping accounts and records ('books') from the cut and thrust of making a living and keeping creditors at bay. 'The exact keeping of books', John Hill said, 'is one of the hindges upon which trade turns and commerce is held'. 'A merchant cannot

[187] Record, *Ground of Arts*, B1r; Hylles, *Arte of Vulgar Arithmeticke*, Biir.

[188] J. Carpenter, *A Most Excellent Instruction for the Exact and Perfect Keeping Merchants Bookes of Accounts* (1632), A2v.

[189] J. Hill, *The Exact Dealer Being an Useful Companion for all Traders* (1688), A3r, 129, 4–5.

[190] A. Leadbetter, *Arithmetical Rules, Digested and Contracted for the Help and Benefit of Memory Very Necessary and Useful, as Well for Gentlemen and Tradesmen, as for Youth and Apprentices, in Mercantile Affairs* (1691), A2v, 2; J. Ayres, *Arithmetick a Treatise Fitted for the Use and Benefit of Such Trades-men as Are Ignorant in That Art* (1693), A3r; E. Cocker, *Cockers Arithmetick Being a Plain and Familiar Method Suitable to the Meanest Capacity*...(1678), A2v.

display his reckoning too clearly', Hugh Oldcastle remarked in 1582.[191] John Carpenter advised that the 'books necessary [for] keeping merchants accounts are these': 'a cash or chest booke', 'a booke of charges of marchandizes', 'a copie book for letters', a 'receipt booke', a 'notebooke' (or 'remembrance'), 'a booke of factories or invoices', 'a memoriall or waste booke', 'a journall or daily booke', 'a lidger with kalender or alphabet', and 'a booke of household expences'.[192] 'To keepe a booke well', Nicholas Petri advised in 1596,

> it is necessary that you write in a journal or daies booke all whatsoever you doe touching your affaires, and therein expresse how and in what manner you bargain, either for buying, selling, receiving, paying, bartering, or delivering wares whatsoever, specifying the day and yeare, when it was done, with whome, what goods, what price, howe much, what colour, waight, measure, howe many ells, yards, or peeces, what marke, what number, and for what time the wares are sold, or bought, also by whom they are bought, sold, received, or sent away, with what number and markes as you shall perceave large in the journal.

This done, data about 'debtors, creditors, and wares' was 'transport[ed]' to 'the leager or booke of debts'. Make sure to start each entry on a new line, Petri directed—'part them one from another'—putting details of 'debitors' on the left-hand side of the page and 'creditors' on the right, with dates and folio pages noted in the 'journal' where particulars were first written down.[193]

The next step was how information was best presented. Indexes helped to find something. 'The alphabet or kalender for the lidger serveth to write the names and sirnames of the parties you deale withall', John Carpenter wrote, and 'after writing of names in the kalendar you are to adde the number of the folio of the lidger where such accounts are entered'.[194] 'To render [your book] yet more plain', John Hill told tradesmen,

> I shall say something more particularly of the alphabet [which] is no more than a book of twenty-four leaves left at the beginning of the ledger and on them are placed the 24 letters, one letter to a leaf; and if you look for any account take the sirname and observe under what letter it is [so] that the names [are put] alphabetically in order under the letters, set folio 1 to the first, folio 2 to the second and in like manner proceed. This being done, when you have any occasion to

[191] Hill, *Exact Dealer*, 56; Oldcastle, *A Briefe Instruction and Maner How to Keepe Bookes of Accomptes*, chap. 4, unpag.

[192] Carpenter, *Most Excellent Instruction for the Exact and Perfect Keeping Merchants Bookes of Accounts*, 2, 5.

[193] N. Petri, *The Pathway to Knowledge* (1596), unpag.

[194] Carpenter, *Most Excellent Instruction for the Exact and Perfect Keeping Merchants Bookes of Accounts*, 17.

proceed in the search of a name, it is but looking under the letter that begins the sirname, and it will direct you to it [and] the account belonging to it.[195]

'Perfect ordering' in Richard Dafforne's words, meant numbering at 'the top and bottom of the page'. A book needs to be 'numbered on each leafs side', he wrote, 'the beginning side with 1, the second with 2, and so through all the book'.[196] 'The booke being opened', John Carpenter said, 'set the figure 1 on the left side of the first page [and] number the rest of the leaves' to the end of the book. 'Leaves' must be 'numbred', Hugh Oldcastle insisted.[197]

People should have been busy in the margins also. 'Make briefe notes of the materiall points' of each letter in the 'marget' of a 'copy-booke' of letters, Carpenter told his readers. Don't waste any space. If you make an 'error' in your ledger make 'a marke' like a cross in the 'margent' to 'signifie' it.[198] Remember to enter 'the day, month and mark of the commodity' in the 'margine', Dafforne urged, or, quite beautifully, in 'the whitenesse' of your 'wastebook'. Avoid 'needless sides', he said; write in the 'white'.[199] All of this made it easier to work between records. When shifting something from your ledger to your journal, Petri suggested, always 'marke the folio or leaves' of the ledger entry in 'the margen of your journal'.[200]

Working with and between 'books' (most farmers, traders, and merchants would not have had the full panoply of Carpenter's recommended 'books') would have involved much rechecking and recounting to make sure that transfers were accurate and numbers and pages tallied. We might not give any thought to the self-taught bookkeeper who put them down on paper when we run down the lines of local government accounts. Life outside office was often technical grounding for years of service. Both, it was hoped, would bring order and peace and God's approval. Some individual accounts were dedicated to God or asked for his blessing and/or invoked scripture, just as guides or tables for weights and measures had words of scripture written above them to remind officers and officials that being 'true', 'exact', and 'precyse' was holy work. Balancing weights and accounts was a godly act. 'Mysprecyson' harmed hearts, lives, communities, and God, who was always looking down to see what was going on. 'Precyson', like local government, was a holy matter. Keeping good sets of accounts also imposed

[195] Hill, *Exact Dealer*, 59–60.

[196] R. Dafforne, *The Merchants Mirrour, Or, Directions for the Perfect Ordering and Keeping of His Accounts* (1684), 52.

[197] Carpenter, *Most Excellent Instruction for the Exact and Perfect Keeping Merchants Bookes of Accounts*, 17; Oldcastle, *A Briefe Instruction and Maner How to Keepe Bookes of Accomptes*, unpag., chap. 7.

[198] Carpenter, *Most Excellent Instruction for the Exact and Perfect Keeping Merchants Bookes of Accounts*, 17–18.

[199] Dafforne, *Merchants Mirrour*, 6–7, 52.

[200] Petri, *Pathway to Knowledge*, unpag. Cf. Pepys's diary, assembled, it has been argued, from his other records including accounts, letters, and 'my book of tales'. See M. S. Dawson, 'Histories and texts: refiguring the diary of Samuel Pepys', *HJ*, 41 (2000), 414.

order or at least the appearance of order on lives. The bric-a-brac of work and domestic life could seem coherent, organized, and even fairly dull and predictable. And it spoke well of the person and his accomplished management skills if the two sides of the accounts were in harmony. He was virtuous, pious, and as honest as the day was long. This person strode purposefully and confidently through the middle walk of life. And perhaps best of all, he drew himself in his own accounts as someone with good 'credit' and standing in the world around him. His accounts showed that he was solvent, and that alone bespoke good character and trust in both government and business. On the other side of the same coin, accounts were doctored for appearances' sake and to hide sleaze or incompetence in office. In either case accounts were far more than columns of bald figures in books. They were self-representations. And good accounting in all meanings of that word was a ticket to acceptance and in all likelihood success in the 'middling' worlds of association, work, and office.

'Numberinge', 'computacon', 'kalendering', 'transport[ing]', 'orderinge', and storing were administrative skills taught in texts for 'worldly affairs' that could have equally served as preparatives for local office (which, in effect, they did). Plain and precision were bywords. Like officers and officials, traders and farmers turned to records for verification because they had authority. 'I judge by my note', Robert Loder notes in his own accounts:

> The profits of my orchardes: Imprimis I judge my aples were worth and all charges payd vil Item my cherries were in the whole summer 2MCxv li. besides those which we did eat & lxj li which I knew of by my note, besides all other given and spent by the gatherers which cherries aforesaid were sould for xvjl xxjd.

This is farmer Loder in 1619: 'having cast or viewed over my notes hereto-fore made touching my houskeping I judge we spent about ixl a peice for and because that wheat and mault was cheaper than heretofore'. And this is him one year later: 'Money payd for spurlinge dounge... I judge it cost me (the landes being xx as I may see by my notes made last yeare (therof) with the landes dounged with the pegion dounge and maultdust ye summe of xjs vjd)'. In another place Loder writes: 'I refer my selfe to reade thereof on my note therof made in anno 1617', when tallying profits from wheat and barley in 1619. Records were as much a part of his working life as his horse. 'As in my notes [I] may see and reade', he writes. We see Loder go to his archive for confirmation of something that 'plainly appeareth by the notes' or 'by my notes'—'I having cast over my notes for ye yeares'.[201] In effect, we see him reading, not Livy like Gabriel Harvey, but himself,

[201] Fussell, *Robert Loder's Farm Accounts*, 133, 172, 183, 174. See also ibid., 160, 172, 183, 174. And see ibid., 33, 75, 87, 100, 106, 108, 116, 117, 181, 122. For more on Loder see J. Freear, 'Robert Loder, Jacobean management accountant', in R. H. Parker and B. S. Yarney, eds., *Accounting History: Some British Contributions* (Oxford, 1994).

'to give rise [as Anthony Grafton and Lisa Jardine say] to something else'; a follow-up action to get something done.[202]

John Hill told tradesmen to keep records close at hand 'so that they may be easily found upon any occasion'.[203] 'Middling' men like farmer Loder took these words on board. Loder felt comfortable sorting through his 'notes'. 'I delivered to my wife out of my pourse [in] provicion for my householde', he noted in 1614 ('besides money she receaved for her owne commodities'): 'apparell for myselfe, my wife and daughter' (£7 8s.), 'guiftes at home and abroad (but not to the pore) with a sugar lofe given by my Lady Dunch' (59s. 7d.), 'a safe' (13s.), pewter (9d.), pie plates (£1 4s.), 'a dripping pan' house' (8s. 6d.), harvest gloves (2s. 4d.), 'gave a midwife' (20s.), fixing a lantern (8d.), 'heardes wages' (8s. 2d.), oysters (12d.), 'carrying letters' (4d.), a knife (12d.), and quince trees (9d.). 'Total in this category', Loder wrote under a list that was one of many, 'xxxviiili xiis vid'.[204] He was always pricing and valuing and moving around in his accounts to find something: shepherd's wages, pigeons (£4 9s. 10d.), grain lost through rain, tools, killing mice, orchard profits (in 1612 £12 16s. 8d.; 1618 £29 6s., 'lorde to be prayesed for such an abundance'), 'corne which my men steale (more than I allow of in a yeare)' worth around £3 in 1613. Loder was never just reading. He was actively calculating, shifting stuff, thinking of other records in his archive, making judgments. 'I judge', he wrote in 1614, that I spent 'xxxiiiil xixs viid' on meat this year ('as my notes which I had therof appeared'). Loder added up to compare different parts of his farming operation. 'The summe of the cleare profites (given unto me unworthy therof by the most merciful God)' is 'cxlvil xvis xid', he noted in 1611. He wondered whether wheat or barley had been a higher earner. Profit from 'my wheat landes' 'xxxil viis iid', he wrote ('as I may see in my notes'), 'and barley Liii pounds eight shillings'. 'Not twice so much profitt as my wheat landes', he mused, thinking of the future.[205]

Two seventeenth-century journals/accounts let us dig deeper into 'middling' information cultures through keeping accounts, journals, and other records. One is from two years in the life of Yorkshire farmer Adam Eyre (1647–9); the other is the dozen years when Exeter trader John Hayne kept accounts, ending in 1643.[206]

[202] A. Grafton and L. Jardine, '"Studied for action": How Gabriel Harvey read his Livy', *P&P*, 129 (1990), 30.

[203] Hill, *Exact Dealer*, 52.

[204] Fussell, *Robert Loder's Farm Accounts*, 88–9.

[205] Ibid., 8, 17, 38, 56, 87, 158, 185–6, 19.

[206] A. Eyre, 'A Diurnall or Catalogue of All My Accions and Expences from the 1st of January 1647', in C. Jackson, ed., *Yorkshire Diaries and Autobiographies in the Seventeenth and Eighteenth Centuries*, Vol. I, Surtees Society Publications, 65 (Durham, 1886); DRO Z19/36/14. For domestic archives and account-keeping see Smyth, *Autobiography in Early Modern England*, chap. 2; J. Scott-Warren, *Shakespeare's First Reader: The Paper Trails of Richard Stonley* (Philadelphia, PA, 2019), chap. 2; N. Glaisyer, *The Culture of Commerce in England, 1660–1720* (Martlesham, 2006); N. Glaisyer, 'Calculating credibility: print culture, trust, and economic figures in early eighteenth-century England', *ECHR*, 60 (2007); B. Waddell, 'Writing history from below: chronicling and record-keeping in early modern England', *HWJ*, 85 (2018); D. E. Harkness, 'Accounting for science: how a merchant kept his books in Elizabethan London', in M. C. Jacob, ed., *The Self-Perception of Early Modern*

We can follow the pair into their homes and around their communities and further afield. They were the target audience for 'practical arithmetic' crossing from home life into information systems with regularity that defined them both.

Eyre lived in Hazlehead village on the outskirts of Barnsley in south-west Yorkshire.[207] Sheffield was a little under fourteen miles to the south. York was a longish 50-mile ride, while Derby, where Eyre had business to do at the Spring Assizes in 1647, was also fifty miles away. His journal is just two years long and on its last day he is getting ready to head to London two weeks before the king lost his head (was he there to see it?). He had a 'writ from Chancery to summon mee to be a witnesse [for] Lady Foljamb'.[208] Eyre had been a New Model Army captain (a wartime journal is lost). His *Diurnall* shows him to be a pillar of the community. We see him giving neighbours a helping hand to draw up mortgages, leases, releases, inventories, and wills. He signed and sealed bonds and indentures, brokered master/servant tiffs (dropping a note to a wayward maid's brother advising 'take care that shee might not goe to the house of correction'[209]), crafted petitions for quarter sessions (perhaps with his copy of Dalton's *Complete Justice* open at his side), helped to get rid of tenants who refused to move, settled neighbourly squabbles, combed through letters of attorney, and broke down the legalese thicket of a King's Bench writ into familiar English. His study was the largest lending library in the area. Eyre was proud of his many books, putting up shelves to make sure that they were kept in good condition, and he was happy to let someone borrow them for their benefit. He 'lent to Raph Wordsworth of Waterhall Dalton's "Justice of Peace"' in June 1647 (the next day he wrote 'a note of the statute for shopkeepers bookes' for Robert Ward from Woodseats and 'lent' him 'my statute booke' a week or so later). 'Francis Haigh came hither' a few weeks later on a fast day, Eyre notes, 'and brought my book home and borrowed another'. On 17 May 1647 Eyre 'lent' six books to Reginald Appleyard, who appears as a regular friend in the journal, and later 'lent him a booke of Lillye's called England's Propheticall Merlin and The Starry Messanger both in one volume' after he came to dinner in what was a typical 'middling' evening in Hazlehead.[210]

Eyre's world was filled with paper. He would have got nowhere in private or public life without records. He was bureaucratic and bookish. It is rare for a day to go by without him handling a record. He kept records of household costs, like Loder making notes of buying and selling: 'I bought 3 pair of hose which cost 12s,

Capitalists (Basingstoke, 2008); R. Grassby, *The Business Community in Seventeenth-Century England* (Cambridge, 1995), esp. chap. 6. Women played key roles in this domestic archival culture. See J. Whittle and E. Griffiths, *Consumption and Gender in the Early Seventeenth-Century Household: The World of Alice Le Strange* (Oxford, 2012); J. Spicksley, ed., *The Business and Household Accounts of Joyce Jeffreys, Spinster of Hereford, 1638–1648*, Records of Economic and Social History, NS, 41 (Oxford, 2012).

[207] On Eyre's larger life see A. Hopper, 'Social mobility during the English Revolution: the case of Adam Eyre', *SH*, 38 (2013).

[208] Eyre, *Diurnall*, 116. [209] Ibid., 71. [210] Ibid., 43, 35, 51.

1 pair of gloves 3s, inke and dyurnall 11d, an issue plate 4s 3d, other things for my wife 1s 2d, a ring for keys 3d, a booke at Wakefield 1s. 8d' (13 May 1647).[211] Eyre commonly totted up the miles he covered each day and money spent. He was an inveterate counter with a lighter side that led him away to football, bowls, bathing in rivers, fishing, gambling, and drink. Eyre's journal was also a confessional outpouring for this religious man who liked 'the things of the world' too much. He wrote this down after riding to Mortmoley to meet up with friends at an 'ale': 'This day I abused myself with too much drink, God have mercy on me and forgive mee', not forgetting to add the details of the day's distance and expenditure: 'this days travels were sixteen myles and disburst 8s' (15 February 1648). His reading took him to places where he could not go. He bought a map of the world for two shillings in 1647 and began to read Walter Raleigh's *History of the World* two months later, on the same night that he whipped his maid Jane for the second time in two days for 'foolishnesse' and 'loathfullnesse'. Eyre made a fifteen-day-long trip to London in September 1647, 'and my travel in all these 15 days were in all 836 myles', he duly noted in 'a little parchment covered booke' in which he wrote down the 'particulers' of the trip (including a note that 'my wife procured a touch from the king for the evil, the 13th day'). Our loss is great because 'this little parchment covered booke' was the same one in which he wrote down 'my journal during the tyme I was in the army'.[212] Eyre's contact radius stretched across the country. He kept copies of letters he sent and rode to Sheffield or sixteen miles to Wakefield to meet the London post. Eyre followed the twists and turns of tense interwar years. He got up bright and early on 31 May 1647 to ride ten miles to Woodsome to talk with royalist Sir John Kay, who 'shewed me the king's answeare to ye parliamts propositions' and told Eyre that 'there had bene some stirre of late in London'. 'The news of this time', he noted in the middle of the next month, 'is yt the king is gone to Newmarkett to meete Sr Thomas Fairfax'.[213]

Skills evident in the *Diurnall*, whether reading or working with records, were handy in office: cross-referencing, indexing, calculating, using margins. Eyre stayed at home all day on 26 February 1647 'and began a table to a booke called the State of Europe'. He sat at his desk three months later bringing his accounts up to date, 'which is specified at large [he writes] in the 35 page of this book'. Sitting at home one morning two weeks later Eyre 'red a part of ye American Cobler and writt in the margent as far as I went'. He would later scroll down the margin to pick up where he left off in much the same way as officers would go to the 'white' to find something.[214] It is not clear if Eyre filled office in the years covered by his *Diurnall*, but he was in constant contact with authorities and administrators in

[211] Ibid., 34.
[212] Ibid., 104, 62, 67, 98. Eyre also kept a record of an earlier trip to London in April 1647 in 'a litle booke which I writt in my journey to London, which contaynes the particulers therof', which, like his other metropolitan account, is lost: ibid., 24.
[213] Ibid., 40, 44. [214] Ibid., 43, 48, 110, 45, 113, 14, 36, 42.

Hazlehead and towns and villages in surrounding areas. He travelled a few miles to Penistone to audit churchwardens' accounts in 1648. Constables gave him 'warrants and acquittances' one year earlier and he left word with a sequestrator in Sheffield to find an order he left with him. He travelled sixty miles back and forth to court in Castleton in the same year to file documents. We see him deep in talk with the steward and foreman of the jury in a note in the *Diurnall*. Walking to church, he saw potholes and cracks in the road and when he got back home he 'writ a note' asking the minister to bring it to the attention of his congregation. He was the voice of his village at 'a meeting about the poor' in Penistone a few months later. He also took care of copies of the 'towne assessment' and bills 'for the townes accompt'. Wakefield was on Eyre's map a couple of times when he rode there to sort out leases in the manor court, taking copies of records (he got his hair cut for the first time in three years on his last trip). He made the short trip to Barnsley Sessions the day after hearing that he was indicted by one Mitchell 'for words' in 1648, 'to enquire for a coppy of the indictment'. But he got there too late: 'I was very angry and caryed myself unsivilly. God forgive mee!' Eyre rode twenty miles to Oxley a week later to get copies of the indictment (sleeping at Thomas Barker's house that night; 'an honest roundhead I think'). Eyre with 'a black boxe with some writings in it' in his hands was a familiar sight.[215]

The year 1647 was a busy paper year for Eyre. Two matters took up a lot of his time: back pay from his stint in the New Model Army (after drafting accounts and papers for a review committee he was still out of pocket when Charles I lost his head), and getting rid of Penistone's minister Christopher Dickinson, who was, charges said, 'a man of scandalous life and conversation' with royalist leanings. The parish wanted him gone but he refused to take a £40 pay-off to end things without warrants. Eyre had a big hand in bringing the case to the Committee for Plundered Ministers. He drew up articles of Dickinson's faults including allegations that he slipped into his post 'under pretence' in 'tymes of trouble'; preached daily for three years copying like a parrot the words of others; and drank in pubs all day long including a 'day of solemn thanksgiving' when he went on a three-day-long binge in Barnsley and a fast day when he was too drunk to get out of bed. Eyre was put in charge of getting seventy-five signatures against him. He rode to London in spring 1647 to meet with the national Committee for Plundered Ministers, returning with orders that charges must be examined in full. He made the trip to York twice in May 'after a great deale of waiting on the committee', and at long last got the order his parish had waited for. 'Scandalous' Dickinson had two weeks to appear before the Committee for Plundered Ministers to answer all charges against him. It would not be long before there would be a new minister in Penistone parish who probably knew well before he

[215] Ibid., 106, 6, 15, 67, 43–4, 51–2, 91–2, 93, 61, 30–1, 34, 41.

first climbed into the pulpit that it was a wise move to get Adam Eyre on his side.[216]

John Hayne (1610–43) lived 260 miles from Eyre, in Exeter in Devon. His father (d.1639) was a well-to-do merchant who never made it to the top of the civic tree as mayor but was elected sheriff four years before his death. He also had a single stint as the town's MP. His son lived by trade, and his accounts show a mind familiar with the 'practical arithmetic' of Robert Record and those who came after him. Hayne married in the same year that his father served as sheriff—'spent since my marriage . . . 22 April last in divers expences as appears particularly in folio 13'. He was high on the office ladder at the time of his early death, with a year as collector in 1638 and churchwarden in 1641. Accounts duly balanced in his churchwarden year, Hayne handed '2 keyes of ye chest of writings' to the new wardens. He had information about him at home, work, or office, duly logging public rates and fees in his accounts, moving from his public persona as busy merchant and local government officer to the private Hayne who wanted to make money and move up in the world of trading and accounting.[217]

Hayne had books in his accounting scheme that were split into sections as merchants' manuals suggested. He had a cash book, 'creditor' ('R More xlli wch I set here for want of space to ballance this acct and is borne to a new acc[oun]t in creditor fol. 43'); a day book ('for terceuella [£4 11s.] exprest at large in my day booke in folio 16'); debitor ('My mother in lawe discharged . . . for this sume being lateley deceased wherefore I carrie it to her executors account in debitor folio 89'); letter book ('paide Mr Maddock and Mr Sprage wardens of St Lawrens [2s.] for my 1/2 part of our new seate in ye ile, for a yeare ended ye Easter, as in my letter booke'); and a ledger: 'An acct of profit made of bakers standinge before my dore in St Petroxe from ye 16th of July 1640 till ye 4th of July 1641: when ye whoale is to be posted into my leager to ye acct of profitt and losse received for the first quarter 11/4d'.[218]

Hayne's financial records are accounts of actions. They may seem set in paper for us sitting in Devon Record Office. But for Hayne sitting in his study on the eve of an ugly war reading and transcribing as he put his temporary jottings into formal accounts for his future was a multistep process. In his easy-to-read hand we follow Hayne gliding through his records to find an earlier entry relevant to one he is now writing: 'Henley owes me for a quarter of a 100 of currants and a bagge [as] appears 3 leaves back' (1634); 'I spent [£40 18s.] the first quarter of this yeare as in folio 45 . . . more spent ye 2nd quarter as in folio 46 [£25 2s. 2d.] . . . more

[216] Ibid., 82, 18–20, 22, 24–5, 32, 34–5, 48, 54.

[217] DRO Z19/36/14, fos. 22v, 70v–71v, 72v–73. 62, 123v, 127v, 130v. There is a printed edition with helpful notes on Hayne and his life: T. N. Brushfield, 'The financial diary of a citizen of Exeter', 1631–43', *Reports and Transactions of the Devonshire Association for the Advancement of Science, Literature, and Art*, 33 (Exeter, 1901).

[218] DRO Z19/36/14, fos. 27, 28v, 17, 63v, 61, 34v, 45, 40, 40v, 10v, 96v, 32v, 55. 101v.

spent ye 3d quarter as in folio 48 [£28 5s. 7d.]...spent this last quarter as above [£26 19s. 11d.]' (1638).[219] Hayne builds narratives of deals or debts in numbers and letters through linked entries. I think of him sitting at his desk turning pages with two or three books open at one time:

> Paide Mr Painter [a minister] and Mr Harris [his mother-in law's executors] for their 1/2 of my fathers bookes, as they were praised: viz 5li for one cheste with bookes in ye hall, as 40s for bookes in study, as in ye account of house expences in folio 90. [1639][220]

We follow Hayne moving an item from one book to another or turning to a record to trace a case with all the authority of a capable churchwarden. As well as accounting books, he refers to bills, notes, and letters. We see him surrounded by records in neat retrievable sequence moving across his archive to put his affairs in order. 'This acc[oun]t [he writes] is henceforth to be discontinewed in this booke [and] entered into my leager'. He notes on another day: 'in cr[edit] 106' that 'a former acc[oun]t for ye balance thereof removed'. On another he 'carried to acc[ount] of expences in folio 58'. The painful details of a falling out with James Marshal—a man he shared a pew with—are set down in a page of accounts. Marshal owed him £100 which Hayne had set aside to balance one of his accounts. But he did not pay up and Hayne ruefully records that 'because this is part of mine own private stock [he was going to transfer the debt] to its proper place in my private leager in his account there in debitor folio 4' (meaning that the money would remain a loss). A similar situation left him out of pocket a couple of months later. Christopher Hethbridge was the defaulting debtor this time. At the foot of a list of payments under the title 'Mr Hoppin is creditor' Hayne writes: 'all these parcells are more directly mentioned in his shopp book fo. 238'.[221]

And, finally, John Hayne liked to use margins and other finding aids to help him navigate through his paper train, a merchant at home who would become an effective churchwarden—on the financial side of things at any rate—in a few years time. A price quote for a yard of canvas was 'put downe in ye small alphabet'. His margins look like local government records where writing sums up entries at the side of the page and a finger points at something that needed highlighting. A finger in one of his left-hand margins (a number of merchant manuals suggested using left-hand margins) reminded him that he had 'set not downe my house-rent any more among my expences (as I did formerly) because I now handle it apart in an account of rents in my leager on folio 19'. Another margin finger told him that he had moved payments to James Yeo and William Rowland 'to ye parrishs acc[ount] in page 146'.[222]

[219] Ibid., fos. 8v, 51. [220] Ibid., fo. 83v.
[221] Ibid., fos. 104v, 110v, 52, 45, 32v, 58, 80, 133.
[222] Ibid., fos. 61, 54, 112v.

These were two men who lived many miles apart at more or less the same time, whose lives epitomize the 'middling' male preoccupation with information at work and in office. Men like them were key figures in local information systems. I am not suggesting that every one of England's 'middling' men could compute like Eyre or Hayne (or that they needed to) or that they immersed themselves in 'practical arithmetic'. But enough of them did to make work and office an ongoing exchange. One door shut and another one opened, but the skill sets remained the same. Hayne tried to be 'exact' sitting at home doing accounts and in his year as churchwarden when his accounts successfully balanced. Some sort of celebration often followed to commemorate twelve months of information gathering and counting—and a coordinated financial year that was met with a sigh of relief. The next year counted on this. Windsor brought the financial year to a cheery close with an 'accomptes daye dinner'; the bill for one dinner reached £1 18s. 8d.[223] Accounts audited, Chester's elite sat down to enjoy 'musadell', cakes, and ginger; while the attendees at a 'cofferers supper' in the same town quaffed 'ii quarts of wyne' and '4 quarts of sacke' at The Bull.[224] Accounts done and dusted in 1621, Bridport officials headed off to The Bull to spend six shillings on 'wyne' and 'sacke'. St Martin-in-the-Fields parish (Westminster) forked out fifteen shillings for food and drink at The Greyhound in 1602 after 'the overseers of the poore gave up their accompt' (the new Poor Law might have given more cause to celebrate a job well done).[225] Yarmouth spent a whopping 33s. 4d. 'for the charges of fyre, beare, and other things about the takinge of the townes accomptes' in 1584 (Henry Manship was town clerk in that year).[226]

Why not celebrate precision? It was, after all, the end of another long and hard administrative year. But accounts did not always balance after twelve months of logging stuff and looking from one column to another, sometimes nervously. 'The accompt of Stephen Harryson' was 'corrected' [in Rye in 1598 as] there was some mysprecysion therein'. Another churchwarden in East Sussex was questioned for not handing in a 'true accompt' in 1655.[227] One bad year of accounting could lead to 'greate inconveniences'. Chester Assembly unhappily heard of the 'want' of 'a perfect boucke' of audited accounts' in 1567 that 'left 'many things' not 'perfectly knowne'.[228] 'Want of accompts hath occassioned manifold inconveniences [and] dislike and suspition of unfaithefull dealing', Tewkesbury governors complained in 1618, telling the chamberlain to 'present' a 'perfect accompt [of] money received and paid'.[229] Preston burgesses were troubled in 1641 after 'late bailiff' Luke Hodgkinson ('gentleman') failed to file 'perfecte' accounts to the 'greate losse

223 BRO W1/FA1/1, fos. 53, 56, 60v; WI/FA1/2, fos. 21v, 87v.

224 CA TAR/2/30.

225 DHC DC/BTB/M2/1621; WAC SMF 1602.

226 NRO Y/C27/1, fo. 43v. See also KAC WSMB/A/2/2, 1613; Day, *Oswestry Parish Church*, 86, 133; *Diary of Samuel Newton*, 10–11; Drew, *Lambeth Churchwardens' Accounts*, 43, 161, 201.

227 ESBHRO RYE 1/6, fo. 233; Q1/EW2, fo. 15.

228 CA Z/AB/1, fo. 119.

229 GA TBR/A/1/2, fo. 22.

and damage' of the town and its 'liberties, and priviledgs'. The offence was so great that Hodgkinson was stripped of his freeman status. He would be 'a straunger and forrenor' from now on.[230]

Accounts needed to be 'fully perfected' and 'doubts' cleared up for local pride and authority. Hayne's precision can be read in local records when officers and officials were told to do their duties 'exactly' and asked to 'surveye', 'serche', and 'viewe and see'. Make things 'certyn', Cambridge officers were told when they were getting ready to 'survey' paupers and inmates.[231] On 'Friday the iiii day of October 1616 we did assemble ourselves att Barstead', Kent justice Sir Edward Filmer put down in his notebook, and 'did take an exact survey of all the alehouses' in 'our lymitt'.[232] London's governors asked for an 'exact account' of lazy night watchmen and 'exact search and survey' of 'straungers' in 1639. Hereford's governors wanted 'an exact account' of how the poor 'stock' had been spent in 1682, as well as 'the names and surnames of all inmates'.[233] Magistrates wanted 'trougth': 'a true and perfect accompte' of alehouses (Cheshire); a true and perfect noate' of negligent officers (London); a 'true and perfect accompt in writing of all accons' of scavengers and a 'true and perfect list' of 'strangers servants and journey-men' (Winchester); a 'true presentment [of] the names' of anyone not going to church (Exeter); and 'a perfect note' of recusants (Manchester).[234] 'Yow shall doe the best you can to make trew and perfectt recordes', Poole's town clerk swore on oath, and 'judgements justlie and trewlie enter accordinge to [their] trewe meaninge'. Chester's officers went from street to street in 1571 to make a 'trewe and certayne note' of who deserved hand-outs.[235]

Local governments wanted 'certeynte' not 'doubt' that made policy all the more difficult to put together. 'Certeynte' spawned policies and that could only come from the various 'computacons' and 'particularizing' that are the subject of the last chapter. After hearing that privy councillors had been fed 'foule [and] false informations' that put their town in a 'doubtful' light in 1631, Yarmouth's governors instructed their London representatives to get 'more certayne knowledge what they be'. Confusion or 'cloudie darknesse' harmed governance.[236] Two examples of administrative shambles from Kent show this. Justices were dismayed in 1627 to find that 'recordinge of those that have been burned in the hand at sessions of

[230] LA CNP 3/1/1, fos. 35–6.

[231] CUL VC-CT-vi-15, fos. 80, 118–22.

[232] CKS U120/09, fo. 18.

[233] LMA Jour. 38, fo. 217; Rep. 53, fo. 133v; HEA BG11/17/1/5, fo. 67. See also CA Z/AB/2, fo. 148v; DRO ECA B/1/3, fo. 309.

[234] CA 2QJB/1/3, fo. 277v; LMA Jour. 26, fo. 37v; HA W/B2/4, fo. 53; DRO ECA B/1/3, fo. 19; E. Axon, ed., *Manchester Sessions: Notes of Proceedings Before Oswald Mosley (1616–1630), Nicholas Mosley (1661–1672), and Sir Oswald Mosley (1734–1739)... Volume 1, 1616–1623*, Lancashire and Cheshire Record Society, 42 (1901), 49.

[235] DHC DC/PL/B/1//1/1, fos. 40–41; CA Z/AB1, fo. 126v. See also BRO R/AC1/1/3, fo. 143; HEA Q/SM/4QS 7/1, fo. 162v; NRO Y/C/19/4, fo. 150; HA Q1/1, fo. 44.

[236] NRO Y/C/19/6, fo. 195v.

the peace [is] so dispersed and confused as that it is hard to be founde out and almost impossible to have in a readines in records'. Felons were hidden in this paper mess. 'Many have theire bookes allowed them above once contrarye to the lawe', red-faced justices said, 'to the greate incouragement of malefactors'. A clerk was told to buy 'a parchment boke [to] duely and truly record the names, additions, and dwellinge' of anyone who 'shalbe burnt in the hand' from now on. 'The booke [was] the record to trye when any such shall crave his booke againe, whether he hath beene formerlie burnte in the hand or noe'. The clerk was told to bring it along to 'every sessions of the peace' and to buy a new book when it was 'filled upp'.[237] 'Divers inhabuitants' of Tenterden complained that they were 'very unequally rated and taxed towards reliefe and maintenance of the poore' in 1657. 'The 'tax is made soe confused [they said] by mixing of lands, goods, chattels and personal estates' that they 'cannott well ground their complaints' to get anything sorted out. Governors tried to clarify issues by consulting 'several [county] orders' and getting the 'opinions of severall judges of assize touchinge the makinge of rates and assessments for the poor'. The resulting directive instructed officers to 'conforme unto and in all things observe' a 1651 order about poor rates that was 'the most indifferent, equall, and legal way of assessment'.[238]

Process should not have been clouded by doubt. Winchester was struggling to cope with waves of 'strangers' in 1622, with 'no certaine ordinance [to] expell strangers' who took jobs from 'freemen and inhabitants'. 'For cleering of all doubts and questions [for] future benefitt', magistrates ruled that 'it shall not be lawfull for any stranger or foriner' to set up shop or work in 'anie manner of trade, misterie or occupacon' unless they had been made 'free' of the city by 'a general assembly'.[239] The same city had been plagued by 'doubt' forty years earlier. Governors fretted in 1581 that the 'auncient usages and customes of this citie are nowe partlie growne out of memorie by reason whereof some doughtes are likelie to arise about the same'. They decided that the best way to 'reduce' these 'usages' to 'certeyntye [so that they] maye bee better knowne and dowlie observed' was to meet with hand-picked 'auncient men of this citie of most knowledge and experience [to] vewe of the olde rolles' and draw up in 'writinge' a new and 'certyne' roll of 'lawfull and mete' 'customes and usages'.[240] Regulations, customs, and memories needed to be 'certyne'. Maidstone's governors were mindful of 'ordynances and constitutcons' in force in 1604 that were put in some confusion after the granting of a new charter. They gave orders 'for cleering of all doubt and questions that may be made of the force of them synce the renewing of our charter'. 'Every decree, ordynance or constitutcon' in the 'booke of burghmote' was to be 'newly

[237] E. Melling, ed., *Kentish Sources: VI Crime and Punishment* (Maidstone, 1969), 185–6.
[238] CKS TE/S2, fos. 144–5. See also NDRO B1/1601; B1/1602.
[239] HA W/B1/4, fo. 25v.
[240] HA W/B1/3, fo. 27v.

made', and word of this was taken to all 'places' across the town so nobody was left in any doubt any longer.[241]

IV

The aspiration was that doubt in the case of Maidstone's 'ordynances and constitutcons' or anxious Richard Cooper sitting brooding in Bridport would be clarified. Something or someone recently unknown was now known. 'Mysprecysion' lingered like a nagging cold, but quests for accuracy in local government were for 'middling' officers the grass-roots equivalents of factual precision in learned circles. The parish was their laboratory; its archives were their library. 'Trougth' or 'certantye' were aims that were embedded in governance; in 'What I am' and 'What they be' or 'Who are you?'

Pursuing precision defined the art of local government. This was the thinking behind 'turning inside'. Each one of the remaining four chapters is written with the contemporary principles and practices of precision firmly in mind. The next two chapters are set outside in 'public'. The last two are set inside in 'private' or indoors where punishment was thought to be less risky than a marketplace flogging in front of unpredictable publics; and England's first nationwide system of incarceration inside bridewells developed over the same decades as more sophisticated information systems made local government more effective. 'Precyson' is the common denominator in all that follows. The outside comes first, as movement through time was from what contemporaries termed 'manifestaccon' or public representations of authority to growing recognition of the very real advantages of the inside, institutions, and information for government.

'Manifestaccon' is the subject of the next chapter. Buckingham is the first port of call. This town had just lost one of its most vital 'manifestaccons' of authority: the assizes, with their legal and social pomp and circumstance. Would the status of the town ever be the same again? Would Buckingham be able to think of itself ever again with the pride of yesteryear when the mayor and aldermen rode out in ceremonial 'skarlett' to greet the assize judges at the edge of their town? 'Manifestaccon' mattered that much.

241 CKS Md/Acm1/2, fos. 1v, 95–5v.

2
'Manifestaccon'

> Pictures and images are first the laymans book.
>
> R. Dingley, *Divine Opticks or, a Treatise of the Eye, Discovering the Vices and Virtues Thereof; As Also How that Organ May Be Tuned* (1655), 26.

Buckingham's 'bayliffes and burgesses' were over the moon in 1674. They had got the assizes back from nearby Aylesbury at long last. The wait had been as long as the wound was deep. The town had wallowed in 'decay', having lost the eminence, rituals, and social high points of those choice few days when Buckingham was a stage.

In their moment of triumph civic leaders wrote with warm thanks to the county nobility who had backed them in this long-drawn-out duel. Remember, they wrote, 'how we were honored' when 'Charles the First of blessed memory' camped in our town 'in the heat of the late unhappy and rebellious times'. Unlike Aylesbury, their town had been loyal to 'the royal party'. 'How deep we suffered upon that account from the late usurpers', 'bayliffes and burgesses' mused. We lost 'privileges and benefits of publique meetings' and, to rub salt into the wound, the prized assizes were 'transferred' to Aylesbury, an agonizing fourteen miles away in a straight line. The king came back in 1660, but the town did not get the assizes back. 'Much inricht', Aylesbury 'found meanes and frends to continue this usurpacon'. But now this 'ancient shire towne' could bask in 'its former precedency and lustre'. Thinking that the assizes had come home for good, magistrates asked for a 'generous contribution'—for this was a begging letter also—to build 'a convenient shire hall for yor and the countryes reception' in this 'seat of justice'. This grand hall would stand for all time 'as a monument of yor good will [they said] and of our loyaltye as that of Aylesbury is of the contrary'. They could not resist one last dig at the old enemy.[1]

Buckingham's leaders sprang into action again in 1692 when the town shuddered once more at the thought of losing the assizes. Two Norfolk circuit judges 'refused' to hold assizes there. What followed is hazy but the outcome is not, as '69 principall inhabitants' of this 'loyal towne' wrote to the queen, thanking her 'from the bottom of our hearts' for her 'signal favour to this ancient sheere towne

[1] HL SSTM box 6, folder 13. See J. S. Cockburn, *A History of English Assizes, 1558–1714* (Cambridge, 1972), esp. chaps 3 and 8–9.

Information, Institutions, and Local Government in England, 1550–1700: Turning Inside. Paul Griffiths, Oxford University Press. © Paul Griffiths 2023. DOI: 10.1093/oso/9780192896261.003.0003

in restoring to them the summer Assizes'. Buckingham's summit spectacle continued in the rarified air of the Glorious Revolution. Happy now, the town's great and good basked in the cultural polish of the assizes. They sat down with judges to enjoy an assize banquet with a jaw-dropping menu. 'For the judges men's table': four roast geese, four ducks, four chickens, four turkeys, two capons, and twelve baked chickens. And 'for ye shreeves table': twenty-four roasted ducks, six geese, ten 'boyleing ducks', two dozen turkeys, hens, eleven capons, eight 'carpes', and sixty baked chickens. The '69' added warm thanks to the Crown for this 'blessed' escape from 'popery and slavery', adding that their town had always been 'steadfastly' loyal to the Crown and Church, with just 'one family of protestant dissenters' and not a single 'Jacobite amongst us'. Unlike next-door wavering Aylesbury, we can almost hear them say.[2]

This chapter covers 'manifestaccon' or the visual representation of authority in 'publique' for people to see and assimilate. The first section explains what 'manifestaccon' meant to early moderns. It was a statement of 'civill government' and the 'publique good' seen, for example, in 'skarlett dayes' when towns went on parade, eye-catching civic clothing, as well as maces and staffs. 'Manifestaccon' was also seen in material environments: in market squares, buildings, streets, walls, gates, and 'edfices' like crosses, standards, and conduits. It was intended to display honour, but 'manifestaccon' was also double-edged and vulnerable because its ultimate success depended on the reactions of what Henry Manship called 'the eye-beholder'.[3] Its essence was civic and it can sometimes seem that the projected 'public' was made up of corporate bodies of citizens. But the 'meaner sort' and 'multitude' were also objects of civic messaging, if only because it was thought that they were more likely to compromise ideals of orderly living through slums, rowdy gatherings, crime, 'unsemely' sights, and their insanitary ways.

Pursuing 'manifestaccon' was a continuous task that inevitably made magistrates think long and hard about its effectiveness. But we first turn to contemporary meanings and characteristics of 'manifestaccon'.

I

Buckingham was on show with a new coat of paint from the moment that local luminaries robed in scarlet went to meet the assize judges outside the town. Salisbury's elite put on 'scarlett to accompanye the judges' in 1633.[4] An assize town had to look its best on ritual days that ended with England's most graphic

[2] HL STTM box 7, folder 9; box 6, folder 46.

[3] H. Manship, *The History of Great Yarmouth*, ed. C. J. Palmer, Kessinger Legacy Reprints (1854), 65.

[4] WSHC G23/1/3, fo. 377v. See BRO R/FA/3/1/17; CKS Md/Acm1/3, fos. 197v–8.

public statement at hanging trees. Norwich made payments to 'cleane castell dytches and throw downe the mucke against the assizes' in 1605. It cost six-pence to 'mend' the 'pavement' in Kendal market 'whear the judges hall was set' in 1617 and 1622.[5] Halls were 'sweetened' for assizes and sessions. Gloucester spent 2s. 7d. in 1638 for 'perfume and herbes used at the tolsey and bothal at quarter sessions'. Norwich paid Mr Drake two shillings 'for makinge the guildhall handsome with flowers att sessions' in 1642 and for 'herbes and flowers to dresse up the seates att the newhall the last assize' in 1647. The same city bought an extra broom for the 'assises and sessions' in 1618 and spent eighteen-pence for 'herbes used at the crosse at the assizes' four years later.[6] 'Manifestaccon' also required that scruffy vagrants be kept far from judges' eyes. The home poor were another blot on the landscape. 'A man' in Gloucester got four shillings in 1638 'to keepe the poore from the high sheriffe his house and other places at Lent assizes'. Watches were set 'night and daie' in Leicester 'duringe the tyme of the assises' in 1594.[7] Watchmen guarded Norwich's 'new hall at [the] assizes'. 'Distracted' Christopher Coppin was put in the bridewell as a precautionary measure in 1670, as he was thought 'like to give disturbance in publique next week during the assizes'.[8] But things did not always go according to plan. A Preston plasterer was caught 'waiting among other beggars and old people and children at ye judges return from ye assizes craveing relief' in 1673. 'Divers innholders, hostlers, and other persons' were taken to task in Maidstone in 1674 for letting their servants ride horses 'violently' along high streets 'at the time of assizes, generall sessions of the peace [and] other greate and publique meetings and assemblies'.[9]

The 'greate and publique' had a large hand in defining a town and 'precedency and lustre' as it was called in Buckingham. 'Manifestaccon' was communicated through vocabularies that included 'ornament', 'civil', 'honour', 'stately', 'comely', 'decencie', 'helthful', 'faire', 'clean', and 'sweet'. These vocabularies were used all through James Brome's travels in his 'exact' descriptions of towns and cities. Salisbury was well blessed with 'stately' houses, 'fragrant' gardens, a 'beautiful' guildhall, and 'sweet and cleanly' 'channels'. There was 'nothing wanting to please and gratifie either the eye or palate', Brome closed. Chester had 'fair and uniform houses'. Stafford was 'beautified' by its 'large and uniform marketplace'. Worcester's streets were 'clean and well paved'. Boston had 'beautiful houses [on] both sides of the river'. Taunton was 'beautified' by 'fair houses', while Winchester 'attain'd a great eminency' for 'its publick and private edifices'.[10] These were matters of 'civill

[5] NRO Norwich Chamberlains' Accounts 1603/25, fo. 55; KAC WSMB/K/1/5, 1616/17, 1621/2.

[6] GA GBR/F/4/5, fo. 75; NRO Norwich Chamberlains' Accounts 1625–48, fos. 386v, 488; 1603–25, fos. 303v, 379.

[7] GA GBR/F/4/5, fos. 73v, 48v; LERO BRII/1/3, fo. 91.

[8] NRO Norwich Chamberlains' Accounts 1625/48, fos. 367, 488; NMCC 24, fo. 147v.

[9] LA CNP3/2/1, fo. 403; CKS Md/Acm1/3, fo. 193v.

[10] J. Brome, *Travels Over England, Scotland, and Wales Giving a True and Exact Description of the Chiefest Cities, Towns, and Corporations* (1700), 44, 221–2, 144, 96, 48–9, 223, 14–15.

government' and the 'publique good'. Southampton magistrates complained in 1601 that 'the fishe market is so beastlie and fowle underfoote as there cannott bee a greater annoyance in a towne of civill government'. Winchester governors had harsh words for people who 'preferring theire owne private ease more than ye publique good' did not pay rates in 1652, leaving streets 'very noysome with putrified durt, dung, and filth very undecent and unbeseeminge for good government'.[11] 'Filth and durt' lay in heaps along streets in Civil War Oxford, 'to the scandall of the government'. A well-ordered town was a 'comely' town; random rubbish in piles was a 'scandal'.[12] This was all the more 'unbeseeminge' because people read external things for meanings and significances. 'Pictures and images', Robert Dingley said, were 'the laymans booke' that made things 'manifest'. Edmund Bolton called outward appearances a 'window on the soul' and praised 'outward conformity' in all things.[13] The walker in public observing and seeing should have comprehended a stream of signals. 'Inwardly', Inigo Jones scribbled in a sketch-book, 'the imaginancy was set on fire [in] publicke places'.[14] It could be a building, a procession, or clothes that lit the imagination, or a facial expression or gesture. Full of pride, Thomas Churchyard waxed lyrical on how the 'inward affections of people were playnely expressed by their outward appearance' when the queen was in Norwich in 1578. A dark cloud of 'dolor' hung over the city after the queen left.[15] 'Manifestaccon' said things. This is what William Prynne had in mind when speaking about 'the outward culture' of 'heads and bodies'. William Gouge warned young people that they 'must be so fashioned and ordered as may declare them to be servants and under their masters'.[16]

'These things are visible', Ronald Freart said, thinking of buildings.[17] There was a preoccupation with seeing in both books and records. 'Continuall seeing', Matthew Newcomen called it in a sermon to the House of Commons.[18] The 'eye-beholder', Henry Manship wrote in his history of his home town, Yarmouth, 'can better witness the truth [of] magnificency and sumptuous building than either my pen can enforce to believe by reading or my tongue by uttering of speech can

[11] SA 6/1, fo. 29; HA W/B1/5, fos. 51–3.

[12] OHC C/FC/1/A1/03, fo. 128; LA CNP 3/2/1, fo. 17.

[13] R. Dingley, *Divine Opticks or, a Treatise of the Eye, Discovering the Vices and Virtues Thereof; As Also How that Organ May Be Tuned* (1655), 26; E. Bolton, *The Cities Advocate* (first published in 1629), facsimile copy, The English Experience, 715 (Amsterdam and Norwood, NJ, 1975), 40.

[14] Jones is quoted in T. Mowl and B. Earnshaw, *Architecture Without Kings: The Rise of Puritan Classicism Under Cromwell* (Manchester, 1995), 82.

[15] T. Churchyard, *A Discourse of the Queenes Majesties Entertainment in Suffolk and Norfolk With a Description of Many Things Then Presently Seene* (1578), B1v.

[16] W. Prynne, *The Unlovelinesse of Love-Lockes. Or a Summarie Discourse, Proving the Wearing and Nourishing of a Locke or Love-Locke to be Altogether Unseemely and Unlawfull Unto Christians* (1628), A3r–A3; W. Gouge, *Of Domesticall Duties* (1622), 456, 622.

[17] R. Freart, *A Parallel of the Antient Architecture with the Modern*, trans. J. Evelyn, 2nd edition (1707), epistle dedicatory, 2r.

[18] M. Newcomen, *The All-Seeing Unseen Eye of God Discovered in a Sermon Preached Before the Honourable House of Commons at St. Margaret's Westminster, December 30, 1646* (1647), 13.

deliver'. 'The eye', he added, 'will make a deeper impression into thy mind than the best orator with his pen'.[19] Robert Jenison told Newcastle's great and good that governors must have 'eyes in their head wisely to observe, see and forsee danger'. They 'should not be like Polyphemus, who had but one eye and that a bad one', Samuel Gary told audiences at both Thetford and Norwich Assizes in 1619, but be 'monoculate' like 'Argus, oculatus a fronte and a tergo: eyes before and behind' and 'eagle-eyed'.[20] Charles I had 'a perticuler eye' on London's 'starr' thoroughfare Cheapside that was now an eyesore, and he also 'cast [his] eye' over a shabby-looking St Paul's Cathedral that should have been 'the cheif ornament of the cittie'. Governors spoke of 'viewing', 'espying', and 'observing'. Officers were told to train a 'vigilant' eye on London. 'Divers grave and worthy citizens' griped about unseemly dress worn by young Londoners in 1610 that was 'evident to the view of all men'.[21] Sight (Oasis) was a character in Thomas Heywood's civic pageant *Londini Speculum* (1637). Thomas Dekker advised Londoners that 'good and perfect eye-sight' would root out trouble, and they took him at his word judging by the number of times crimes came to light through keyholes, walls, and holes. 'Eye witnessing' became more important for clinching legal cases.[22]

A counter-vocabulary of 'manifestaccon' that is equally evident in the sources suggests that things did not always work out well. The generic risk in reading meaning in externals or 'outward' show is that anything can be processed in multiple ways. Magistrates struggled to impose an artificial stability and unity of response when they inscribed meanings on vibrant townscapes. But this element of manipulation and control was quite simply unrealistic. There were more ways than one to read representations, and governors found this out to their cost too many times for comfort. Vocabularies of 'anti-manifestaccon' seem steeped in the grit and grind of urban living: 'stinckinge', 'filthye', 'unseemlye', 'uncivily', 'unsaverie', 'unwholesome', 'noisome', 'ruinous', 'decay', 'disworship', 'daungerous', and 'deformedlye'. These are words about outcomes, not ideas, aims, or aspirations. A lane in Kendal was known locally as 'Stinking Lane'. Common Council said that London's streets reeked all year long but were more 'noisome' in hotter summer.[23] Quite typically, Southampton governors said that their town was 'very filthye [in 1574] and full of noysome savors' that drifted from 'donge hills and hepes of

[19] Manship, *History of Great Yarmouth*, 65.

[20] R. Jenison, *The Cities Safetie: Or a Fruitfull Treatise (and Usefull for These Dangerous Times) on Psalm 127* (1630), 7; S. Garey, *Lentaculum Ludicum: Or a Breake-fast for the Bench Prepared, Presented, and Preached in Two Sacred Services or Sermons the Morning Sacrifice Before the Two Assizes at Thetford, at Norwich, 1619* (1623), 4–5.

[21] TNA SP 16/195/32. See also LMA Jours. 20, fo. 323; 39, fo. 122v; Reps. 14, fo. 332v; 17, fo. 39v; 29, fos. 277–8; Letterbooks R, fo. 22v; V, fo. 69v; SRPJ (51), 111; (155), 247; APC 1613–14, 268; 1615–16, 483–4; 1625–6, 251–2.

[22] Dekker is quoted in J. Twyning, *London Dispossessed: Literature and Social Space in the Early Modern City* (Basingstoke, 1998), 73. See also F. E. Dolan, *True Relations: Reading, Literature, and Evidence in Seventeenth-Century England* (Philadelphia, PA, 2013).

[23] KAC WSSMB/K/2/5, fo. 71; LMA Jour. 31, fo. 273.

robidge'.[24] 'Manifestaccon' needed officials and officers to play their parts by the book and conformity and acceptance among the multifarious 'multitude'. There was an inherent potential for 'manifestaccon' to be destabilized by non-compliance or individual inadequacies or eccentricities. William Goodwin stepped down as Mayor of Winchester in 1560 after what must have seemed a long twelve months. His brother governors claimed that Goodwin was guilty of 'enormyties…tendinge [to] the disworshipp of the cytie', including riding 'oftentymes' to Southampton and other places in 'the shreve' in public sight without 'a serjeant waightinge uppon him'. He also once, in what can only be called reverse 'manifestaccon', 'drew his dagar openly [on a sergeant in civic dress] in the chequer betweene the gates' when he was on parade with other civic notables.[25]

In parallel narratives to 'eminency' a city/town struggles to cope with sharp spikes in vagrancy and poverty that hit budgets hard. This had deep consequences for regulation and 'manifestaccon'. It is striking how vocabularies of 'manifestaccon' include words that resonate with the dark sides of urban growth, like 'stinckinge', 'fowle', 'filthye', or 'unwholesome' that stir sensory perceptions. In this respect, sight, smell, and sound could all confound 'manifestaccon'. 'Wee present the women which are dressers of the shambles', Preston magistrates said in 1661, 'for that they throwe guts and garbage into the streetes' making 'a noysome smell' and 'most unseemlye sight in the streete'.[26] A 'comely' town should have been 'clean', 'helthful', and 'fragrant'. Health and the appearance of authority converged in concerns for civic well-being in Norwich in 1559 in an 'Acte for Pavyng of Stretes' that began with a timely reminder: 'tyme oute of mynde there hathe bene a comely and decent order' in paving that had been 'a greate ease and helthefull comodyte [and] a goodly bewtefying' of the city.[27] Shearman William Hall landed in trouble in the same city in 1653 for having a 'swyne style or hogg corte [that gave off] a horrible and abhominable stinke [to] the greate impayerenge of the healthes of good people'.[28]

'Bodily health' was in 'greate' danger in Bideford in 1673, magistrates insisted, putting much of the blame on ugly blemishes like 'stinkinge dungehills or other filth' standing 'in heapes' on streets and hogs running 'up and downe the towne [that] greatly conduces to breed diseases in the bodyes of men, women, and children'.[29] It fell to the vice-chancellor of the university to give a pep talk to the newly elected 'paving leet' in Cambridge in 1671: 'You are strictly and duely' to act at all times for 'the decency and cleanlynes of the streets', he told them, 'as well

[24] SA 6/1, fos. 10, 11.
[25] HA W/B1/1, fos. 124v–5. See also LA CNP 3/1/1, fo. 71; 3/2/1, fo. 159; ERO D/B5/SB2/9, fo. 29v; WSHC G23/1/3, fo. 358; SHA BB/C/1/1/1, fo. 37; DRO ECA B/1/3, fo. 63; GA GBR/B/3/3, fo. 332.
[26] LA CNP 3/2/1, fo. 157.
[27] NRO Norwich Assembly Folio Minute Book 3, fo. 157.
[28] NRO Norwich Sessions File 63/2.
[29] NDRO 1064Q/SO1, fos. 84v–85v.

pleasurable as tending to health'.[30] 'Unseemleye' 'infection' and 'sykenes' could bring matters to a head. 'This towne as yet God be praysed [is not] troubled with plague, pestilence, and other contagious diseases', Yarmouth magistrates said in 1630, and with 'Gods good providence and blessing [they added, we can keep] streets, lanes, gutters, gates [and] walls cleane and sweete' to keep plague at bay.[31] Remembering that 'sundry' people had 'dyed' of plague 'of late', Norwich's Assembly reminded officers in 1579 of a by-law passed a decade or so before to make sure that streets were 'clener kepte and the sykenes by the swetenes of the ayer the soner ease'. Preston's council fretted that 'want of clensinge and washinge' streets [might] procure some pestilentiall disease'.[32]

The 'debit side' of 'manifestaccon' was always on the minds of busy magistrates or 'eye-beholders'. The stark realities of urban governance were infection, sickness, environmental shabbiness, 'publique' shame, and tarnished 'reputacon'. These concerns defined government and were as much a part of urban living as the pomp of a choreographed parade in smart 'scarlet' or what Brome called 'stately buildings'. We could see 'manifestaccon' as a thin veneer for 'the better observance of decencie and good order' in the words of Faversham's magistrates when telling 'citizens' to come to civic events 'in their best apparrell in most comely and descent sorte' in 1614.[33] But peel off the layers one by one and the harsher sides of urban living are soon seen. This was 'manifestaccon' as *an ongoing attempt* to represent towns that was punctuated by red-letter days like that day in Salisbury in 1614 when governors in 'scarlett' gathered to greet the judges. This is a way to think through the strong surge in building and renovating town halls after 1550, for example, or greater expenditure on London's mayoral pageants around 1600.[34] It made a great deal of sense to pay more attention to 'manifestaccon' and 'reputacon' when a town felt itself to be threatened by greater pressures. It was a continual see-saw, with 'reputacon' at one end and escalating troubles at the other. But where did the balance lie at any one point in time? We should not think of 'manifestaccon' as something that either failed or succeeded but as a *continuous process*. Streets, for example, always needed cleaning. This act in miniature embodied 'manifestaccon'. It was always in the making and it was an aspiration rather than an accomplishment. Governors usually got bogged down in cycles of frustration. 'This is very comendable to the government and healthfull', Gloucester's governors commented in 1641, when ordering 'housekeepers' to sweep away filth from the bit of the street outside their doors. But their wishes fell on deaf ears as piles of

[30] J. E. Foster, ed., *The Diary of Samuel Newton Alderman of Cambridge (1662–1717)* (Cambridge, 1890), 61.

[31] NRO Y/C/19/6, fo. 158v.

[32] NRO Norwich Assembly Folio Minute Book, 3, fo. 276; LA CNP 3/2/1, fo. 215.

[33] CKS FA/AC3, fo. 94v.

[34] R. Tittler, *Architecture and Power: The Town Hall and the English Urban Community c. 1500–1640* (Oxford, 1991), chaps 5–6; R. Mackenney, *Tradesmen and Traders: The World of the Guilds in Venice and Europe, c. 1250–c. 1650* (London and Sydney, 1987), 155–65, 172.

'dust and dirt' still soiled the same streets for a long while after.[35] Magistrates, or, in John Dorney's words, 'observators of the manners of the people',[36] continually pursued 'manifestaccon'. It was a thankless task at times but it reveals high expectations of what a town thought it should be and how it ought to appear to the eye. It was an aspiration that was worth striving for because there were times when magistrates could speak proudly of 'honour' and 'lustre'. But its integral 'publique' nature raised fundamental questions and reservations about the effectiveness of representing authority out in the 'open'.

This chapter is about pursuing 'manifestaccon'. There were some notable spectacles: a dazzling royal visit or newly finished town hall standing elegantly on the edge of a market square. But time after time we see the reverse sides of order and 'manifestaccon' in records: 'vagrant' 'porckes or swyne' running amok; someone mouthing off in the stocks; someone else making a mess around the town cross; a slaughterhouse pumping out toxic fumes from inside the walls. Town governors committed themselves to 'manifestaccon' despite its double-edged nature that they knew at first-hand. They put the biggest slice of civic resources behind it. But one of the most important lessons of 'manifestaccon' was to question the effectiveness of each one of its parts and what it meant to represent authority in public. But there was nothing quite like the civic glitter of a successful 'skarlett daye' when a town/city was on display in all its finery and pomp. A day like this might atone for the monotony of governing from one day to the next, if only for a little while. The next section begins with one such day in Cambridge in 1671, when town and gown basked in the glow of a royal visit for a few days at any rate before committing an unforgettable day to civic record and memory.

II

4 October 1671, 'a very cleare sunshiney day', Mayor Samuel Newton of Cambridge put in his diary so that he would never forget anything, for this would be a day to remember. The day when 'his majestie King Charles the 2nd came to Cambridge for the 1st time', and Newton was lucky enough to be mayor in that year. 'The Corperacion met [the king on] Christs Colledge peece', he tells us in his diary, with the mayor and aldermen on horseback dressed in smart 'scarlet' with 'the rest of the gownemen on foot'. Newton knelt down on a mat next to the king's coach to welcome him, holding Cambridge's 'stately' mace in his hand. The king 'strecht out his hand and toucht' the mace in a highly symbolic gesture. Recorder Pepys added his greeting, while the mayor, still on his knees, shuffled forwards to

35 GA TBR/A/1/2, fo. 11.

36 J. Dorney, *Certain Speeches Made Upon the Day of the Yearly Election of Officers in the City of Gloucester* (1653), 76.

give his monarch a gift to seal the bond between him and the city: '100 twenty shilling peeces of brod gold in a crimson coullered velvet or good plush purse with gold fringe and gold strings'. The king climbed out of the coach as Cambridge's elite lined up to kiss his hand. 'Then all the common counsell and gownmen went 2 and 2 [in] order:'

> juniors first then the aldermen on horseback in scarlett 2 and 2 in rank the juniors first, then the kettledrum on horseback [followed by royal trumpeters], then I as mayor on horseback with the town mace in my hand betweene two of his majesties mace bearers with their 2 maces each of which was much bigger than our biggest town mace, then followed his majesties coach [with] his majesties lifeguard [and] the towne souldiers [bringing up the rear].

The procession filed through Cambridge, stopping often with crowds lining the streets. The 'corperacion' escorted the king 'as far as the regent walke' where with pomp and circumstance they handed him over to the university. Their part done, Newton and his brother aldermen walked to the guildhall in high spirits to tuck in to 'a very plentiful dinner', where they were joined by 'most of the knights and gentlemen of the county'. 'The conduit run claret wine when his majestie passed', Newton wrote, ending his account of what had been a memorable day, and he 'was well pleased with it'.[37]

Norwich's elite met the queen two miles outside the city 'in due and comely order' in 1584. 'Master maior and foure and twentye aldermen and maister recorder' put on 'scarlet gownes' along with justices who had served in the highest office. Next in line were those who had 'bin sherifs and were no aldermen in violet gowns'.[38] Colours signified. (See Plates 1–7.) The queen visited Colchester six years earlier, where she was greeted by 'bayliffs and aldermen' riding 'comely geldings' and wearing 'scarlett gownes and black velvett'.[39] These sparkling ritual days were called 'skarlett dayes' in Yarmouth:[40] days when the town dressed in its best at high points in the ritual year. These were days to commemorate its history and honour. 'Skarlett dayes' lit up the year. 'The daies to bee observed for wearing scarlett shall be these onely', Gloucester council ruled in 1644: election day, 'the day kept in memory of our saviours nativity called Christmas day', 'the day kept for memory of the kings inaugaracion', Easter, Whit Sunday, Trinity Sunday, and

[37] Foster, *Diary of Samuel Newton*, 64–6. See also R.W., *A True Relation of His Majesties Coming to the Town of Shrewsbury on the 20 of This Instant September and His Passage From Thence the 23 Day to the City of Chester With the Manner of His Entertainment There* (1642). On urban space and its use see F. Williamson, *Social Relations and Urban Space: Norwich, 1600–1700* (Woodbridge, 2014).

[38] G.B., *The Joyfull Receyuing of the Queenes Most Excellent Maiestie into Hir Highnesse Citie of Norvvich the Things Done in the Time of Hir Abode There: and the Dolor of the Citie at Hir Departure* (1578), A3r–v.

[39] ERO D/B5/Gb, fo. 13.

[40] NRO Y/C/19/5, fo. 106; Y/C/19/3, fo. 82.

'the fifth of September in memory of the citties deliverance'.[41] Winchester's mayor and aldermen were told to wear 'scarlett gownes to the cathedrall' on 'Christmas day, Twelfe day, Easter day, Ascension day, Whit Sunday, the 29th of May Trinity Sunday, All Saints day, coronacon day, and the two burgmote courts'.[42] Yarmouth told 'all those that have bene bayliffs [to] were skarlett gownes with typpets and velvett dubletts [on] these festival daies' in 1574: 'michelmas day', 'twelthe daye', 'easter day', 'whitson daye', 'Christmas daye', 'assencyon daye', 'trynitye Sunday', and the 'sonday next after Halowes day'.[43] Oxford records refer to the 'scarlett cloaks of the citty'. The 'mayor, aldermen, associats' and all former bailiffs wore 'scarlett gownes' at 'soleme meetings and feasts' there in 1578. They put on 'scarlett to hear a sermon to congratulate our princes safe returne' without the Spanish princess in 1623, when a collective intake of breath put the country on edge.[44] Justices wore 'scarlett gownes' on Chester's election day in 1594, with lower-status 'aldermen being not justices' dressed in 'murrey gownes'.[45] But not all 'skarlett dayes' went smoothly. Colchester's mayor and 'aldermen in generall' were fined in 1654 for not wearing scarlet last Michaelmas Day and other festival days. Three Gloucester common councillors were taken to task in 1568 'for not wearing skarlett' on Ascension Day and Trinity Sunday.[46] Gifts were at the heart of ceremonial visits as a Reading 'serjeant' found to his cost in 1646 when he lost his position 'for his ill manner of presentinge the Lo[rd] Fairfax [with a] guift from the company' (he must have leaned towards him).[47]

We have excellent work on the forms and functions of processions that ritualized status.[48] Parades filed through urban arteries portraying the stratified hierarchies of civic bodies. (See Plates 7–8.) William Lithgow called these performed hierarchies 'wondrous commendable'.[49] 'Ryde in order', Oxford's 'worthies' were told when the king came to visit. Town leaders were arranged in carbon copies of 'precedencye' on ritual days: 'eight assistaunts and theire wives shalbe placed in goinge and sittinge ymediatlie after aldermen and their wives in seniroitie and the bailifes for the yere ymediatlie after them and the reste after them in seniroitie'.[50] Chester's civic elite marched in order of 'precedencye'. Banbury governors

[41] GA GBR/B/3/2, fo. 319v. [42] HA W/A6/1, fo. 10. [43] NRO Y/C/19/3, fo. 82.

[44] OHC C/FC/1/A1/O2, fos. 230, 273v.

[45] CA Z/AB/1, fo. 242v. See also Foster, *Diary of Samuel Newton*, 29–30.

[46] ERO DB5/SR/43/8; GA GBR/B/3/1, fo. 30v.

[47] BRO R/AC1/1/4, fo. 301. On the symbolism and status of gifts and giving see F. Heal, *The Power of Gifts: Gift Exchange in Early Modern England* (Oxford, 2015); and I. K. Ben-Amos, *The Culture of Giving: Informal Support and Gift-Exchange in Early Modern England* (Cambridge, 2008).

[48] For example, M. James, 'Ritual drama and the social body in late medieval England', *P&P*, 98 (1983); C. Phythian-Adams, 'Ceremony and the citizen: the communal year at Coventry, 1450–1500', in P. Clark and P. Slack, eds., *Crisis and Order in English Towns, 1500–1700: Essays in Urban History* (Toronto, 1972); P. Borsay, '"All the town's a stage": urban ritual and ceremony, 1660–1800', in P. Clark, ed., *The Transformation of English Provincial Towns, 1600–1800* (1984).

[49] W. Lithgow, *The Present Surveigh of London and England's State* (1643), B1–B2.

[50] OHC C/FC/1/A1/01, fos. 110v, 34v; C/FC/1/A1/02, fos. 102, 230.

escorted newly elected bailiffs from their houses to church 'according to their seniority and degree in office'.[51] This 'seniority' extended to trade guilds who marched in set order on ritual days. This classification was modified from time to time. A new 'order' for 'orderinge' Exeter's midsummer watch was needed in 1561 with the emergence of 'two new companyes'. The civic pecking order required updating. 'It is thus ordered', magistrates said, 'that the companyes shall follow in order as followeth': the lowly butchers first, followed by smiths, cutlers, glovers, skinners, bakers, shoemakers, weavers, tailors, and merchants.[52] These were touchy issues. Walter Merrick was chatting 'at a bonefire' about 'the marching of the severall companyes' in Hereford in 1666 when Edward Parry said that 'he yt graunted ye order for the company of bakers to marche before the companye of weavers should never grant anye suche order agayne'. 'Mr maior' did this, Merrick told him. 'He did not care for a maior', Parry snapped. Weavers, he said, 'would venture their lives' to change this ruling.[53]

Nothing should have been improvised, certainly not the processional order or clothing, that was, a London by-law said, a 'special and laudable marke' of status.[54] Magistrates, William Dugdale said in 1666, must be distinguished from others by dressing in 'grave and venerable garments'. 'As his apparell doth show him to be', he continued, 'so he shall be esteemed'.[55] In a nutshell, you are what you wear. Winchester magistrates ordered citizens to dress in 'decent gownes...according to their degrees [in 1656] which hath beene a very greate ornament [and] putt a distinction between citizens'.[56] It was a custom in some places for the wives of high-ranking officials to wear their husbands' colours when joining them on display. Winchester mayors gave their wives 'a scarlet gowne' when they donned 'scarlet' themselves. I am 'lx yeres or thereabouts', Southampton alderman Beckenham said in 1576, and 'hath biyn a dweller and trader' here 'by the space of xiv yeres' and 'borne' all offices including mayor. 'By reason therefore', he ended, 'he and his wife hath worne the same'.[57] Gowns could be pricey. Samuel Newton was delighted to be chosen an alderman in Cambridge, but he had to dig deep into his pockets. He cut corners, however, and rather than buy a new gown he let 'my 24 mans gowne serve for my aldermans gowne' with some custom tailoring. He 'paid Mr Legg' £1 5s. 6d. 'for 17 yards of lace...for silke 3s 6d, for facing sleeves 1s, and for altering and setting on the tufts 10s'. 'I paid alsoe to Mrs Scott for 1lb and a halfe and 3 ounces of Naples throse silke at 1li 7s per li', Newton

[51] CA Z/AB/1, fo. 131v; J. S. W. Gibson and E. R. C. Brinkworth, eds., *Banbury Corporation Records Tudor and Stuart*, Banbury Historical Society, 15 (1977), 48. See also GA GBR/B/3/3, fo. 425; GBR/A/1/2, fo. 7. The painstaking attention to ritual 'precedence', 'degree', and symbolism is very evident in the intricate plans for the funeral of London mayor John Warner in November 1648: TNA SP 16/516/114.

[52] DRO ECA B/1/4, fo. 117.

[53] HEA BG11/17/1/4, fo. 50.

[54] LMA Jour. 22, fo. 164.

[55] W. Dugdale, *Origines, Juridiaries, or Historical Memorials of the English Laws, Courts of Justice, Forms of Tryall, Punishment in Cases of Criminal Law*...(1666), 98, 196.

[56] HA W/B1/5, fo. 100v.

[57] HA W/B1/3, fos. 18, 23, 27, 30v; SA 6/1, fo. 12.

added. 'So', he summed up, 'the whole charge of altering my gowne stood me in 4li 9s'.[58] This was not small change, but Newton had no choice. Winchester's aldermen needed to have three gowns in 1656: 'a scarlett gowne and two cittizens gownes'. When the time came for him to step down as alderman in the same town in 1673, Richard Nash was told 'to lay downe his gowne' on the ground in a symbolic moment.[59] Thomas Adams's brother aldermen in Windsor were angry with him in 1670, as it had been nine long months since his election and he had still not 'provided himselfe of an aldermans gown'. Without it he cast himself apart from his 'brethren'. Adams could not join them on parade and if he did he would have stood out like a sore thumb. He was given a few days to get a gown or pay a £10 fine.[60]

A line of aldermen in gowns symbolized decorum, unity, and the right order of things. People could see that authority was in good hands. Gowns represented 'corporacon' and 'reputacon'. Thetford's finest put on 'decent apparrell' when the queen stopped off on the way from London to Norwich in 1578, 'to th'ende that the corporacon maye be better liked of her majestie'.[61] Tewkesbury justices were asked to go to church in 'a gowne of the parklet fashion faced with black [for the good] reputation of the towne' in 1639. Bridport's 'capitall burgesses' dressed in 'decent and comely gownes' when they walked to the hall and church on court days, 'for the better reputacon of the borough'.[62] 'It would much redound to the honour of the town', Maidstone's elite said in 1663, if 'jurats' in 'theire gownes' escorted the mayor to church every Sunday. Faversham's governors put on 'decent and comely' clothing for 'the better observance of descencie and good order' on Sundays, court days, election days, 'feast tymes', and when doing rounds of the town on perambulation.[63] 'Chester's clerk made a lengthy list of who 'went to view the libertyes' with the mayor when the 'bonds or limitts of the city [were] ridden' in 1621: eight aldermen, the recorder, two sheriffs, eight 'sheriff peeres', fifteen of ye '40', nine 'gents' (they included two 'sonnes to the maior'), two 'leavelookers', a swordbearer, a mace-bearer, eight 'officers', 'William Webbe the writer hereof', and sixty-three others including a sheriff's son.[64] There were also certain expectations of what governors should wear in public when they were not tending to 'the affaires of the towne'. Winchester's aldermen were told not to 'come into the highe streete [or] markett' in 1566 without 'a gowne or cloke', but they could 'walke before their dores in their shoppes' without a 'gowne or cloke'. Anyone who had served as bailiff or 'anie office above that degree' was told that

[58] Foster, *Diary of Samuel Newton*, 29. [59] HA W/B1/5, fo. 100v.
[60] BRO WI/AC/1, fo. 27v; HA WI/AC1/1, fo. 30. [61] NRO TC1/1, fo. 10v.
[62] GA TBR/A/1/2, fo. 38; DHC DC/BTB/H5.
[63] CKS Md/Acm/1/3, fos. 130–0v; FA/AC3, fo. 94. See also DHC DC/LR/D1/3a, fo. 163; DC/PL/B/1/1/1, fo. 50v; BRO H/FAC/1, fo. 1v; WI/AC1/1, fo. 198.
[64] CA Z/AB/1, fos. 360–1. See also ESBHRO Win/55, fo. 98; LA MCB/639; HA W/K5/8, fo. 346; NRO T/C1/6, fo. 21; SHA BB/C/1/1/1, fo. 27v.

they could not walk along the streets in 'anie hose or stockings of white, greene, yellowe, redd, blewe, wegget, or oringe color' in 1584.[65]

Civic dress was a prickly matter. It was a bad day for magistrates in 'auncient and famous' Winchester in 1656 when they heard that many 'cittizens' had 'noe gownes att all' and 'others' had gowns 'not suitable' to their standing. The city was 'out of joint', they said.[66] The sting was ten times worse because it was public. 'Greate neglecte of attendance on the mayor' by 'jurats' at Faversham's main fairs was something that could not be tolerated in 'well governed citties and townes'. It was 'derogatorie from the credite of this towne', the 'jurats' were told in a stern lecture, 'and a greate discountenancinge and disgrace of the maior [who] ought to be better attended and respected at suche publique concourse of people'. 'Jurats' were told to always join the mayor at fairs 'decentlie apparrelled in gownes' from now on.[67] It was the 'publique concourse of people' that caused the 'corporacon' to lose face. This was 'manifestaccon' turned upside down. Poole magistrates referred back to a fifty-two-year-old order in 1658 directing aldermen and burgesses to 'attend the mayor' on election day in 'comelie and decent attyre'. This had been duly done 'till of late yeares [when] by reason of the late troubles it hath bene neglected [it was said] to the greate dishonor of the town and magestry'.[68] Northampton's 'reverend assemblie' complained in 1612 that 'meetings' of 'assemblies courts and sessions' had been 'shamed' by 'undecencie in apparrell to the disgrace of this corporacon'. The offence was public as these ill-dressed 'members' walked through the town to get to courts.[69] Civic leaders kept a sharp eye on dress as it was a weighty 'matter for the towne'. A ladder of fines punished and deterred. They stretched from a low-sounding shilling in Faversham to a hefty two pounds in Norwich.[70] South Molton told 'corporators' in 1685 that they would be fined ten shillings if they did not 'appear at ye guildhall on ye 9th day [in October] at ye swearing of ye new maior in a decent gowne'.[71] There was nobody there when the mayor arrived at Thetford's hall in 1581 to 'talke places and degrees'. He suspected that his 'brethren' were at 'mr greenes bowling alley [and they] were twice commanded' to join him. They finally arrived 'without ther gownes'.[72] The stain was troublingly 'publique' if someone mocked civic dress in front of others, especially in market squares. Simon Leach overheard William Elliott call Edward Serell 'base rogue' when he was dressed 'in the lyverie of mr recorder' in Exeter's 'open markett' in 1620: 'He shoulde have as muche grace by wearinge his owne wifes petticoate aboute his necke [Elliott continued, reaching for slurs] as he shoulde by wearing mr recorders livery'. 'Opprobrious' Humphrey

[65] HA WB1/1, fo. 148; W/B1/3, fo. 46v. [66] HA WB1/5, fo. 100v.
[67] CKS FA/AC3, fos. 110–10v. [68] DHC DC/PL/B/1/1/1, fos. 50v, 131.
[69] NA 3/1, fo. 345v. See also NRO T/C1/2, fo. 136; BRO R/AZ3/9/73; DHC DC/LR/B1/9, fo. 476.
[70] CKS FA/AC3, fo. 96; NRO Norwich Sessions Books 1654–70, 4/1667 sessions, 1/1668 sessions.
[71] NDRO 1190A/Q2, 17/8/1685. [72] NRO T/C1/1, fo. 73v.

Parker recklessly said that Reading 'was governed by a company of geese in furre gownes in the hearinge of divers witnesses' in 1631.[73] Gestures could also transmit something offensive. Hammersmith labourer Richard Leaver was brought to court in 1637 'for sayeinge that if mr moyle had committed him to the stocks he would have brushed [his] coate'.[74]

Other storms also turned 'manifestaccon' on its head. Preston council cancelled the 'auncient' Easter feast in 1612 because the 'concourse and assemblie of people [grew] verie turbulent and unrullie' and seemed 'very likelie' to shipwreck 'peaceable government'. A Cheshire sheriff was hauled over the coals in 1597 for giving Matthew Wood a box on the ear when he did not 'move aside' as 'sheriffs were passing' him on ritual duty.[75] Policing, as we have seen, was strengthened for royal visits, quarter sessions, and assizes. Extra guards were needed in Gloucester in 1558 when 'frayes [were] made in the street' in the 'sessyons tyme'.[76]

Unsurprisingly, there are more reports of disruption from London than anywhere else. It was standard practice to tighten policing and clean streets for ritual events. Hearing that the king 'intendeth to dyne tomorrowe' at Alderman Cockayne's house in Broad Street in 1616, Common Council passed a 'speedye order' to clean streets 'of all manner of filth and rubbish for the honour of [the] cittie and more delightfull passage [of] the king'. Watches were set at 'thend of every lane and streete' until the king was gone. Governors were aware that 'the most parte of householders' will be 'abroad to behold that royall sight' and 'feared [that] roberyes and other lewde and bad accons may be attempted' by thieves lurking around empty houses. Watch and ward were set from dawn to dusk when the king made his way through the city to Paul's Cross for the sermon in 1620, to 'suppresse any abuse or disorder [by] meanes of [the] concourse of people'. A treble watch kept order in 1641 when Charles I paraded through London after the unpopular Bishops' War. The mayor told householders to warn children and servants not to throw squibs when the royal couple made their way through the city in 1634 'to sup at my house'.[77] These were preventive steps but trouble did break out at royal and civic events. Magistrates constantly worried about vagrants, beggars, thieves, and other 'lewd', 'idle', 'suspicious', and 'suspected persons' when setting watches. They were posted from sunrise to sunset on the mayor's feast day to keep tabs on vagrants. A 'substantiall double watch' was set in 1624 'in or neere such places' where 'pageants or shewes' were staged 'to represse and keepe backe idle and wandring persons'.[78] 'You know there is a lord mayors day', Sir William Smith said in his charge at Middlesex Sessions in 1682,

[73] DRO ECA C1/61, fo. 405; BRO R/AC1/1/3, fo. 177. [74] LMA MJ/SBR/6, fo. 264.

[75] LA CNP 3/1/1, fo. 9; CA ZML/5/152. [76] GA GBR/F/4/3, fo. 72v.

[77] LMA Jours. 30, fo. 70; 27, fo. 76; 31, fo. 164v; 39, fo. 246v; 36, fo. 217. See also LMA Jours. 26, fos. 88, 176v–7; 31, fo. 161; 36, fo. 208v; 28, fo. 164.

[78] LMA Jours. 27, fo. 422; 33, fo. 6v.

> and that consists of a shew in the streets and a feast at Guild-hall; the shew in the streets is the pageants, they draw the vulgar, the mobile together, which gives them opportunity to make a noise and throw about squibs; and when they have spent some time in that and gazing upon the pageants they go home very well satisfied.[79]

Watches were typically set at gates and landing places on the riverside on this chief ceremonial day. Tight restrictions were also put on the movement of 'cartes, carrs, carriages [and] porters'.[80] Showers of squibs and fireworks frequently upset the 'honour' of the lord mayor's big day. City censures from 1634 talk of fireworks 'spitt[ing] downe upon the heads or coaches [of] passengers'. Common Council slammed 'disordered persons [who] nothinge regardinge good government nor peacable and quiett order' or 'the hurte and endangering of others' spent the day 'sportinge themselves [at] windowes and gutters casting squibbes, crackers [and] fireworkes' on people below. 'Manye' were 'endaungered, others hurte', and 'ye pageant [was] in danger of burninge'.[81] 'Many disorders [and] tumults... ordinarily happen', magistrates said in 1610. Clothworker Benjamin Norton appeared before aldermen in 1629 charged with 'throwing of squibbs into the streete uppon the lord maiors day'.[82] Norwich banned fireworks on the mayor's 'feast' and the day before in 1612 'in regard of that lamentable mishapp that befell at the last guild by reason of fyreworkes'. Bellmen walked up and down streets in the same city in 1697 telling people not to 'throwe any squibbs' on the mayor's day.[83]

Officers had key roles trying to keep things clean and orderly, taking part in processions, or standing at landmarks like conduits or crosses. Clitheroe's sergeant was told to 'goe before the bayliffs [to] the church everie saboth', 'festivall daye', 'courte daye and solemne meetinge' in his cloak, with a 'halbert upon his necke'.[84] Reading forked out £18 for cloth for '3 gownes and clokes for ye serjeants, a coate [for a] bellman and wine and cake at ye sessions' in 1646, and also bought 'lace silke and other wares for ye serjeants gownes and clokes' for the assizes in the same year.[85] Civic clothing signified town and office. When 'chosen to be beedell' in Thetford in 1624, John Thorne was given a 'coate and staffe to declare him to be an officer'.[86] London Bridewell's beadles wore 'blewe coates' when going 'abroade', as did other hospital and parish beadles. Warders did

[79] [W. Smith,] *The Charge Given by Sir William Smith, Bart, at the Quarter-Sessions of the Peace Held for the County of Middlesex at Westminster on Monday the 24th of April, 1682* (1682), 4.

[80] LMA Jour. 36, fo. 295.

[81] LMA Jours. 36, fo. 295; 32, fo. 86v.

[82] LMA Jour. 28, fo. 263; Rep. 44, fo. 2. See also LMA Jours. 27, fos. 421v–22; 31, fo. 354; 36, fo. 175v; 38, fo. 319; 39, fo. 364v; and B. Klein, '"Between the bellies and the bums of the multitude": civic pageantry and the problem of audience in late Stuart London', *London Journal*, 17 (1992).

[83] NRO Norwich Assembly Minute Book 5, fo. 417; NMCC 26, fo. 37.

[84] LA MBC/173.

[85] BRO R/FA/3/1/17.

[86] NRO T/C1/4, fo. 7.

rounds in blue, although one parish plumped for bright yellow.[87] Beadles wore distinctive 'blewe' coats in Ipswich and Westminster, purple in Salisbury—'at his majesties cominge to this cittie' (1635)—blue or grey in Liverpool, and a blend of blue and red in Manchester.[88] 'Beadles apparel' in Gloucester in 1635 included 'fine blue cloth', lining for hose, a hat, buttons, two pairs of shoes, doublet, and 'stokens'. The same city spent between £4 and £6 each year after 1650 to buy 'biddles cloathes'; a hat cost six shillings.[89] Norwich's marshals and 'master of bridewell' wore 'blewe cloath coates' in 1664 'after the antient fashion', with the 'city armes as a cognizance on one of the sleeves'.[90] 'Manifestaccon' did not come cheap. Cloth and lace 'for sargents cloaks' cost Windsor £6 3s. in 1656 and it did not end there, as another 9s. 6d. was needed to 'make' them 'with silke and canvas'.[91] The price tag for trimming alone was £2 5s. in Reading in 1645. Gloucester spent ten shillings for a cloak for a 'night bell' man in 1658 (on top of £5 for a beadle's coat) and three times this amount for a cloak for 'the day bell man' (the latter walked along streets in daylight and the former trawled through empty dark streets). The city's six 'publique musicans' were given 'yearly for their liveryes out of the chamber fower pounds' in 1632.[92]

Other officers in civic cloaks, hats, or gowns included clerks, criers, waits, 'sweepers of the markett crosse', swordbearers, and porters. They represented civic honour but they were also in the firing line, evident in the many cases on record when they were bruised by 'abuse' that sometimes focused on their dress. 'Yf she is ever ponished', Londoner Agnes Williams shouted at the beadles who were questioning her on the street: 'she would cut their cloaks from off their backes'. 'Outragious' Anne Phillips ripped 'the watchmans bands and clothes' after he caught her staggering along a London street after a drinking binge. Much is made of torn clothes or bands.[93] Like paupers, officers pinned badges to their coats as a crest of their office. Badges communicated civic symbolism and stigmatization. Thomas Firmin wanted to badge London paupers in 1678: 'For by this badge which is made up of blew and yellow bayes, pinned on their sleeve or

[87] LBHC 6, fo. 297v; 9, fos. 360, 872; LMA MS 4457/2, fo. 213. See also LMA MSS 12,806/2, fo. 38v; 3146/1, fo. 86; 4457/2, fo. 116v; Jour. 28, fo. 278; SBHA Governors' Journals 1, fo. 86; 2, fo. 58v.

[88] SAI C/3/4/1/22, fo. 3v; C/3/4/1/35, fo. 8; WAC F2003, fos. 192–3; WSHC G23/1/3, fo. 391v; M. Power, ed., *Liverpool Town Books, 1649–1671*, The Records Society of Lancashire and Cheshire, 136 (Dorchester, 1999), 93; J. P. Earwaker, ed., *The Constables' Accounts of the Manor of Manchester From the Year 1612 to the Year 1647 and From the Year 1743 to the Year 1776*, 3 vols (Manchester, 1891–1902), I, 83, 271.

[89] GA GBR//F/4/5, fos. 48, 154, 479; GBR F/4/6, fo. 66; GBR/F/4/7, fos. 99, 710.

[90] NRO Norwich St. George's Guild Minute Book 1602–1729, fo. 134.

[91] BRO WI/FA1/2, fo. 99.

[92] BRO R/FA/3/15; GA GBR/B/3/3, fo. 93; GBR/B/3/2, fo. 3. See also WSHC G22/1/205/2, fo. 92v; DHC DC/LR/G/2, fos. 276, 395; BRO R/FA/3/17; N/JQ/1/1, fo. 21; HA WI/FA1/2, fo. 38; KAC WSMB/K/1/5, 1616–17.

[93] LBHC 5, fos. 346v, 304v, 405v; 1, fo. 154; 2, fo. 68v; 6, fos. 116v, 204v; LMA Rep. 25, fo. 227; MJ/SBR/515/36; CQSF 115/1.

breast', he wrote, 'they are known [to be] fit' for hand-outs.[94] Badges were to be worn 'openlye' in 'open and visible manner' in the words of 1697 legislation. London aldermen told parishes to make sure that their 'deserving' poor 'weare badges openly on their upper most garments to be openlye seene whereby they maye be discerned and knowne from others' with no right to charity. Lawful street porters needed 'distinguishing' in 1617, and so Common Council instructed them to put on 'a badge of tinne openly to be seene [for] better manifestation' of their right to work.[95] Oxford's four 'beadles of the beggers' wore 'badges of tynne with a red x' in 1563. The 'six citty musitions' each got a 'handsom livery cloake and a bossed badge of sylver' in 1675.[96] Ipswich's 'seriants' wore 'lyveryes and a cognizance of sylver' in 1578, while Gloucester paid for '5 silver badges for officers' in 1677.[97] There are also payments for cleaning and 'mendyng' badges in civic accounts and coating the 'byddles badge' with silver in 1581 in Leicester.[98]

Maces, staffs, and staves also caught the eye. Maces were the costliest piece of civic regalia. Gloucester spent £85 5s. for a sword and mace in 1651 and another £20 'for the patent for the city armes with new creasts and suporters'. The city calculated that total charges for swords and maces added up to a hefty £107 5s. 10d.[99] William Rason wrote to fellow Reading officials from London in 1652 to let them know that 'the charges of makinge a new mace' will total '26li or 27li besides ye price of the old mace'. Two officials rode to London not long after to get a 'best rate' for selling the old mace and 'best termes' for making a new one that topped the scales at '80oz or thereabouts'.[100] Windsor's mace was a heavy '66 ounces and 3 quarters' but the town still wanted it 'altered with another thirty-three ounces of silver plate'.[101] Maces featured prominently in the king's visit to Cambridge in 1671. Mayor Newton sat proudly 'on horseback with the town mace in my hand betweene two of his majesties mace bearers with their 2 maces [both] much bigger than our biggest town mace' (naturally).[102] 'Paynted' and 'decorated', maces were the focal point of processions. The sergeant-at-mace headed processions with a mace held high. (See Plate 9.) Bridgnorth's sergeants were told in 1633 that for 'order and decencye' in ceremony they should 'decently in their gownes carry their maces on their shoulders' into the church, walking ahead of bailiffs. A sergeant dressed in 'a long gown' led the parade of Banbury's elite after they picked a

[94] T. Firmin, *Some Proposals for the Imploying of the Poor* (1678), 14–16.

[95] LMA Reps. 27, fos. 10–10v; 25, fo. 49; Jour. 34, fo. 70. See also S. Hindle, 'Dependency, shame, and belonging: badging the deserving poor, c.1550–1750', *Cultural and Social History*, 1 (2004).

[96] OHC C/FC/1/A1/01, fo. 9; C/FC/1/A1/04, fo. 145.

[97] SAI C/4/3/1/1/2, fo. 10; GA GBR/F/4/7, fo. 97.

[98] LERO BRIII2/48. See also CA TAB/1, fo. 83v; KAC WSMB/K/1/5, 1582–3, 1597–8; WSHC G22/1/205/2, fos. 92v, 116; CKS Md/Acm1/2, fo. 120; NRO Norwich Chamberlains' Accounts 1625–48, fo. 105; NA 3/1, fo. 224.

[99] GA GBR/F/4/5, fo. 456.

[100] BRO R/AC1/5, fos. 108, 111.

[101] BRO WI/AC1/1, fos. 10–10v.

[102] Foster, *Diary of Samuel Newton*, 64–6.

new bailiff, with 'one end of the mace in his hand and the other upon his right shoulder'.[103] Maces sometimes symbolized the handing over of authority from one mayor to the next. Cambridge governors listened to a sermon on Michaelmas Day and marched back to the hall afterwards to hear the mayor 'declare that he had finished his year'. Sergeants then 'laid downe' their maces on the table while the new mayor made his maiden speech, after which the sergeants were 'sworne' and given back their maces for the new mayoral year.[104] Stamford's governing body walked to St Mary's Church after aldermen were 'sworne' to hear a sermon, and when it was over they escorted the new alderman back to his house 'with the two maces, one of gold the other of silver, borne before him'.[105] Christchurch attorney John Hilderly was well aware of the symbolic freight of the mace. There were dissenting voices when he was elected mayor for the second time in 1637. Opponents insisted that he could not take up the office again. But with supporters in tow Hilderly stormed into the town's court and 'got the mace from the ould portreeve and put him out' of office in a decisive swipe that aped mace exchange.[106]

To damage a mace in word or action was to strike at the very meaning of authority. Even now our hearts might go out to one of Windsor's sergeants who 'much bruised' the mace by dropping it in 1647.[107] This was an accident, but there were times when maces were deliberately degraded. A Chester malster told marketgoers in 1653 that 'the sword and mace carried before the mayor should be layed in the channell for all that mr mayor and his brethren could doe'.[108] Parodies were not welcome either. One of Winchester's sergeants told magistrates that 'about an hour after his majesty passed through' the city, 'he saw Anthony Newman junior carry in procession on his shoulder a large cabbage with the root onto it'. He watched Newman walk in and out of the 'Red Lyon alehouse' and up and down streets in exaggerated poses, 'with an intent to ridicule ye maior and aldermen who carried their mace before his majesty'.[109]

These urban matters were not for the eyes and ears of civic elites only. 'Informacon' reached the king in 1621 that Boston's mayor, 'by himselfe or [with] others', 'had cutt of the crosse from his ma[jes]ties armes uppon the mace belonginge to the towne and caused yt to be caryed before him so defaced'. Ministers leaped into action to try to get to the bottom of things. They picked experienced hands to rush north to see what they could find out. Get 'inform[ation of] the factt', they were told, 'by whome' was it done; 'uppon what pretence'; and did the mayor know anything about it at all?[110]

103 SHA BB/F/1/1/3, fo. 573; Gibson and Brinkworth, *Banbury Corporation Records*, 48.

104 Foster, *Diary of Samuel Newton*, 32–3.

105 R. Butcher, *The Survey and Antiquitue of the Towne of Stamford* (1646), 20–1.

106 DHC DC/CC/A/2/1; DC/CC/A//2/2. There was a counter-petition in Hilderly's case, however, 'with all [the] consents' of 'moste parte of the burgesses and inhabitants' that would seem to pour doubt on this story.

107 BRO WI/A/1/2, fo. 8. 108 CA ZML/3/361. 109 HA W/K5/8, fo. 40.

110 All references to this case are from are from TNA SP 14/121/52; 14/121/52i.

'Examainacons' completed, 'wee finde', the two investigators (Leonard Bawtree, 'seijant at lawe', and Anthony Irby, 'one of ye masters of Chauncery') noted in the first week of April 1621, that there were 'twoe sortes of maces' in the town: one with 'only his ma[jes]ties armes ingraven' that was 'ordinarilye caryed by the sergeants', and another 'greater with the ball and crosse on the toppe of the mace onelye caryed before the maior to the church on sundayes and thursdayes and solemne tymes'. The mace was 'cutt' in the third week of Thomas Middlecott's second term as mayor. His predecessor, William Jenkinson, explained that he 'caused the maces to be made in Michaelmas term 1619 with the crosses as they nowe are' ('which before that time were not in that forme', Thomas Shaw, 'gent' of the town, told a third questioner, royal solicitor-general Robert Heath, in a second round of questioning that began a few weeks later). The new maces were not welcomed by everyone. Jenkinson said that he 'used' them once but, riddled with gout, spent the next couple of months in bed. When he felt well enough to resume his duties, he told Heath, 'some objected against him that he made them for his owne vayn glory' and they were not seen in public again until Middlecott stepped into his shoes.

'Uppon the first of Februarye beeing Thursdaye', royal ministers heard, the maces were taken back to Middlecott's house 'whole and safe' after church. They were put as usual 'in the hall windowe next the streete' until Friday dinner was over ('manifestaccon' from inside), and whoever cut 'the toppes of the crosses' did so in the dark of that night or light of the next day. Middlecott's maid Anne Howett told Bawtree and Irby that 'she thinketh that she was the first which perceaved it' on Friday. But 'finding the maces too alike, thought that ther had been nothing done' and put them in 'cases made for them' in a room upstairs, where they 'rested tyll the Sundaye morninge followinge' (another maid, Ann Bramford, said more or less the same thing). Mayor Middlecott was waiting with his wife to go to church on Sunday morning as the maces were brought downstairs. The sergeant 'espyed' the 'falt' straight away and showed the cut maces to Middlecott and his wife, who were both 'much moved and angrye'. There was no time to think. The sermon bell was ringing. Sergeant Peter Dixon (who 'doth usually carrye ye mace before ye maior when he goeth abroad') told the investigators that he led the procession to the church, maces in hand, 'as they there weare defaced' doing the same the 'next thursdaye and the next sunday after'. Middlecott later explained that his plan had been to 'examine' the matter after dinner and to get the maces 'mended' as soon as the town's goldsmith got back from 'Lynn mart'.

Tongues wagged and there was a lot of head-scratching. Heath said that one of the town's elite, David Lewis, was the 'first [to] complaine of the misdemeanors'. Lewis then walks into the centre of the story, where he stays. Thomas Brown, 'gent', deposed that Lewis, 'being or pretending himself to be a servant to the kings ma[jesty]', camped in his father's house in 'boston fenn ende' talking endlessly about the butchered maces (at this point the clerk tried to cross out 'that he could tell who had bene the means of', but his ink was too thin), saying 'that he would complaine to his ma[jes]ty' first and nobody else. Lewis did indeed head south 'with a purpose to make such complaint'. He later told Bawtree and Irby that Boston's rulers sent a letter to him in London 'persuadinge' him 'to desist from [his] complaint'. William Hill told the investigators that Lewis told him 'something that he warned him not to reveal'; that when 'serieant bawtree did examine diverse [to] any matrriall point [he] would answere before ye examinate and say thou knowest nothing of this businesse and if any examinate did answeare anything which he tooke to be materiall he would say hould thy peace foole'. Unsurprisingly, Bawtree 'found fault with him'. Lewis also claimed that the mayor was present 'during all the tyme of the examinacon of the examinates and did conferr with [all] or most of them imediately before they went to be examined and after'. Bawtree said that Lewis 'tould him he knew who cutt of the crosses of ye mace' but would not give a name 'til he had tould it to his ma[jes]tie'.

It pained Boston's governors that Lewis was now in London and about to tell anyone who would listen to him in Whitehall that the monarchy had been disfigured in Boston, 120 miles away. They got together to send him a letter 'to procure him to desist in his loyall service'. William Bennet, who lobbied for Boston port in London, said that he was down south on the day of the 'cutting', but as soon as he got home the town clerk asked him 'to ioyne in a letter to david lewys not to prosecute his intended complainte touching the cutting of the crosse'. This letter, Bennett said, 'was framed on the behalfe of mr cotton vicar of boston', and the 'mayor churchwardens, and justices'. The town clerk told the investigators that he too was in London when the maces were 'defaced' and that, knowing that his father-in-law was next in line to be mayor, was 'desirous to make peace'. 'Of his owne mynd withowte the privitye of any other man', he added, he tried to stop the letter leaving the town without luck and rode back to London a day or two ahead of the 'messanger' who had the inflammatory letter in his satchel.

It was a classic whodunnit. Lewis said he knew who cut the maces, but the other dozen or so examinants claimed to be in the dark. Thomas Shaw, 'gent', was 'verily persuaded that if ther were a commission directed to sitt and examine witnesses in the countrye touching this misdemeanor it would be easely found who were the actors thereof'. Blacksmith and 'clerke and sexton', John Jenkinson, told the crown's detectives, 'yt he hathe heard himself suspected to have done yt'. But there were bigger fish to fry in the Church. Arch-Puritan John Cotton, who would become the most prominent Puritan to cross the ocean when he went from Boston to Boston a dozen years later, had been the vicar since 1612 when he was twenty-seven years old. It would not be long before controversy shook the town. Unable to conform for one minute more, Cotton turned his back on the Church of England to preach and teach Puritanism. Many in the town were unhappy at this turn of events. Cotton was suspended and then reinstated with the help of some of the aldermen, who also helped him to cope with a stringent Arminian bishop thirty miles away in Lincoln.[111] Fingers pointed at Cotton as news of the crosses drifted through the town. He did not like images and was an eagle-eyed critic of all things 'popish'. One of the churchwardens, 'gentleman' Atherton Hough, told Bawtree that 'he did breake off the hand and arme of the picture of a pope [a short time ago] standing one a pillar... very highe aboute the middest or more of the steeple', knowing that 'some of the towne had taken note of suche pictures as were on the outside of the churche'. Surely the crosses on the maces would have caught Cotton's eye? In fact the town clerk gave evidence that Cotton 'condemened the doeinge of the said fact' and that he heard him tell others that they might as well 'refuse the kings coyne because crosses were on it as forbidd theis crosses'. I am 'persuaded [the clerk insisted, that Cotton] never did consent to the cutting of that crosse'. Nor did mayor Middlecott according to some. But the impression left by documents is that he did have a hand in cutting off the crosses, although sergeant William Smith heard the mayor 'sayeng yt was a plott to doe hime a displeasure'. Asked why he still went on parade with 'defaced' maces, Middlecott answered, 'because he would have the opinion of the house [Boston's corporation] before he sett it on againe' (words implying that there were split opinions about Jenkinson's new maces). 'Vayn glory', angry voices barked, was why the last mayor spent a small fortune on them ('which before that time were not in that forme'). He could not even be seen in public with them. Jenkinson himself informed Bawtree and Irby that 'he knoweth well that Mr Middlecott was much offended' by his innovations and 'caused them to be amended againe' as soon as the goldsmith got home from Lynn. Sergeant Dixon told the Crown's investigators that the maces were 'newe made' now.

Solicitor-general Heath thought that Middlecott was guilty; privy councillors wanted to know if he did it 'by himselfe'. Heath interviewed the mayor and eleven others: 'out of them all I can collecte nothinge whiche can fixe upp middlecoate', he ended in evident resignation. It was all 'presumption'. But the maces were in his house, Heath almost pleads. 'Yett doubtlesse I beleeve it was done purpesely', he said in his last recorded words on the 'defaced' mace, 'whosoever was the actor of it'. But he was a hundred per cent certain that he knew who it was.

Staffs and staves—or 'signes' in one account and 'watchinge staffe' in Colchester—were tokens of office and also weapons. Hospital beadles in London carried 'tip-staves' on their 'rounds' so that they would 'be known for officers'.[112]

[111] Cotton was such a popular preacher that the number of his weekly lectures/sermons was increased, and that is why the mayor went on parade to the church more than once each week: see F. J. Bremer, 'Cotton, John (1585–1652)', ODNB.

[112] LMA Letterbook S, fo. 138; Jour. 28, fo. 278.

They were longish pieces of metal or wood with some sort of insignia at the top or running down the side. Staffs and staves were given to constables, beadles, marshals, 'criers', and watchmen to carry as they walked along streets. Windsor paid 7s. 10d. for 'foure new staves' for the constable, tithingmen, and 'cryer' in 1637. A turner picked up 2s. 6d. in 1656 'for the constable staff', and the town also spent 1s. 6d. for 'ye ferrel and spike' to strengthen it.[113] 'Xiii staves' cost Gloucester 7s. 4d. in 1652. Liverpool's beadle was given a 'suitable staff' in 1665 and was told to 'daily attend his office to hinder or take up vagabonds and idle, lusty [and] sturdy beggars'.[114] Staffs and staves also needed painting, 'oilinge', 'guildinge', and 'colleringe'. Manchester spent a shilling to 'paint' the beadles staff in 1647 and 'laye' it in oil. It cost Chester £1 in 1685 'for paintinge and guildinge 3 constables staves' and £1 13s. 4d. to paint five staves eight years later.[115] Gloucester forked out fourteen shillings to make and paint 'constables staffes' in 1638; £2 5s. 6d. 'for painting xiii constables staves' in 1652; and £4 in 1687 'for paintinge constables staffes'.[116] 'Colloringe' suggests the sort of attention that was paid to cloaks and gowns. William Edge picked up eighteen-pence 'for collering the beadles staff' in Manchester in 1662. Gloucester spent £1 8s. in 1660 to 'colour' and 'guild' seven staves.[117] Norwich accounts list fees 'for coloringe iii beadles staves', 'colleringe beadles staves and badges and ii newe cognizances', and 'paynting' badges and staves at other times.[118] Some officers had halberds to give them a fighting chance if ever they were attacked. Constables, marshalmen, and nightwatchmen commonly carried halberds on patrol in London, where aldermen authorized payment of fifty shillings for 'eight halbereds' in 1626. Kendal's accounts for 1610–20 contain payments of twelve-pence and six-pence (twice) for 'dressinge the sergents holbertes'.[119]

Officers were 'known' by staffs and staves. They confirmed who they were. Walking along King Street in Westminster in 1634, Anne Graynger popped into linen draper William Hawkin's shop to buy 'halfe a dussen of hand-karchers'. She asked if she could take a dozen more with her 'to shew them to one that shee was to buy them for' and left twelve shillings in 'gadge' as security. Graynger went back a little later to return the 'hand-karchers' and get her money back. But Hawkins 'was not willing to deliver [her] money'. Words followed, he changed his

[113] BRO WI/FA1/1, fos. 3v, 99v.

[114] GA GBR/F/4/5, fo. 487; Power, *Liverpool Town Books, 1649–1671*, 176. See also KAC WSMB/K/1/5, 1582–3; CKS Md/Acm1/2, fo. 29; NRO YCA Y/HTG/15, fo. 196; NMCC 20, fo. 487v; ERO D/B5/SB2/7, fo. 121v.

[115] Earwaker, *Constables' Accounts of the Manor of Manchester*, II, 134; CA TAB/1, fos. 14v, 56, 56v, 48v–9.

[116] GA GBR/F/4/5, fos. 73v, 488v; GBR/F/4/7, fo. 434.

[117] Earwaker, *Constables' Accounts of the Manor of Manchester*, II, 147; GA GBR/F/4/6, fo. 368.

[118] NRO Norwich Chamberlains' Accounts 1589–1602, fos. 243, 261, 278v, 297v; 1603–25, fo. 128.

[119] LMA Rep. 40, fo. 346v; KAC WSMB/K/1/5, 1610–11, 1616–17, 1619–20. See also LMA Jour. 28, fo. 278; LBHC 6, fo. 111; LMA MS 4180/1, fo. 175.

mind, and gave her the twelve shillings. But as she left the shop, his wife shouted 'durty slutt' and 'base queane'. Grayngcr hurried away but Hawkins shadowed her as far as the gatehouse, where he 'layd violent hands on' her and tried to grab 'the packe under her arme'. Clinging to it with all she had, Grayngcr started screaming 'theeves and murther'. People soon gathered and Hawkins told them that he was a constable arresting a thief. Thinking quickly on her feet, Grayngcr told the crowd that 'she would not obey [him] untill he would shew his aucthority and demaunded [that he show her] his staff'. She knew that he would not be able to and grabbed her chance: he is 'noe constable', she told the crowd. Some of them began asking Hawkins 'what he would have' of her. People pressed in around him and Hawkins realized that he was in a tight spot. The lack of a staff caught him out, exposing his cock and bull story. All he could mutter as he slinked away was, I 'would knowe her name and dwelling place'.[120]

People expected to see staffs and staves. Ipswich beadle John Kirk was warned in 1609 that he would lose a week's wages 'yf he shall not walke aboute the towne daylie with his beadles staffe in his hande'. He was still in post five years later. Eleven Shropshire towns were fined in 1684 for not having staves.[121] In London, and elsewhere, constables were told to hang staffs outside their doors in a 'signe to demonstrate their office', so that 'every man having occasion to use a constable may readily finde their houses'. But all too often, Common Council complained in 1617, thieves slip away before 'yt can be found where a constable dwelleth'. A ten shilling fine hung over the heads of officers without a staff outside their house. Magistrates were still reminding constables four decades later to 'fix' staves 'at their doores for more ready finding and resort unto them'.[122] Staffs were also turned against officers. Vagrant couple William and Joanne Goddyn broke a beadle's scull 'with his owne staffe' in Holborn in 1611, 'wounding [him] soe dangerously that he is in danger of death'. 'Gownestave' and 'knaves with long staves' were among the insults tossed around on streets.[123] Dorchester watchman Hugh Rogers told a court that John Crinmell 'laid violent hands on him' on Shrove Tuesday 'and went to wrest his bill out of his hands', breaking it in the struggle. Ludlow's bailiff asked Morgan Herbert to help a constable who was trying to arrest butcher Edward Griffiths in 1652 who grabbed his 'blewe staffe' from out of his hands, yelling threats and oaths ('tenn at least').[124]

The morning of a civic parade must have been exciting, but there would also have been tension in the air. People knew what they had to do. Everyone was dressed 'decently', but there was still an element of risk as the sergeant with the

[120] LMA WJ/SR/NS/39/6. [121] SAI C/4/3/1/1/4, fo. 19v; SHA 3365/2430, fo. 19.

[122] LMA Jours. 30, fo. 129v; 31, fo. 68; 34, fo. 9v; Reps. 30, fo. 245; 64, fo. 2; MS 4457/2, fos. 81v, 98.

[123] LMA MJ/SBR/1, fo. 460; DHC DC/DOB/8/1, fo. 113; SHA LB/11/4/78, fos. 13–13v; P. Griffiths, *Lost Londons: Crime, Control, and Change in the Capital City, 1550–1660* (Cambridge, 2008), 343.

[124] DHC DC/DOB/8/1, fo. 113; SHA LB/11/4/78, fos. 13–13v.

gleaming mace in his hand stepped forward to start the march in front of the 'publique concourse of people'. There were always question marks. This is also evident when we read physical fabric or what Brome called Norwich's 'stately structures'.[125] The next section begins with the outer shell of most towns: walls.

III

Steeples were often the first thing travellers saw as a town appeared in the distance. But walls took over as they edged nearer. Newcastle, William Gray said in 1649, 'excels' in four things: a 'long and faire key' lining the Tyne; the bridge with eight 'stately arches' that straddled the river; the steeple crowning St Nicholas Church; and the towers, turrets, walls, and gates.[126] Walls mattered for three reasons, Henry Manship noted: 'comeliness', 'safety', and 'terror of the enemy'. He was proud of the 23-foot-high walls that stretched around his home town Yarmouth. (See Plates 10–11.) He might have forgotten that when he was town clerk in 1583—writing this down—the walls needed 'viewing' due to unauthorized doors 'made' in them. Yarmouth passed two orders for 'ramparing' walls four years later and a third to 'viewe' their 'weake places'. People were taxed to the tune of £63 5s. 2d. soon after for 'fortifieinge and rampeenge the walls' after 'reporte' of a planned Spanish invasion.[127] Walls were supposed to keep things out, not give access through jerry-built doors or holes. They marked space and authority and fortified community for the town within. A regular item in the payment side of accounts was money for walls. Norwich set aside £20 'to be yerly bestowed on the cittie walls' in 1582; Gloucester spent £28 8s. 9d. for 'reparacons done' at the gates and walls in 1592; Yarmouth forked out half this amount twenty-five years later for its tatty walls; while Winchester's walls needed 'clensynge' in 1564.[128]

The state of the walls is a regular refrain in records. One committee after another was set up in London to 'viewe' particular stretches of the walls to deal with 'decay' and 'encroachments' or 'doors and passages through ye citties walls'. Bricklayers were asked to 'stop up' these 'passages' and 'doors'. Aldermen were especially nervous about 'ye passagess, inletts, and wayes through ye cittye walls' in the first year of the Civil War. They wanted the names of anyone 'who made them' and an opinion on whether or not they 'may bee wholly stopped'. 'The citties bricke wall' near Bridewell was 'greatlie ruinated and decayed', people living there said in 1620, and to add insult to injury strangers made away with bricks

[125] Brome, *Travels Over England, Scotland, and Wales*, 136.
[126] W. Gray, *Chorographia, or A Survey of Newcastle upon Tine* (1649), 27.
[127] Manship, *History of Great Yarmouth*, 67, 73; NRO Y/C/19/4, fos. 63v, 128, 139v, 143v.
[128] NRO Norwich Assembly Folio Minute Book 3, fo. 311v; GA GBR/F/4/3, fo. 314; NRO Y/C27/1, fo. 335; HA W/B2/1, fo. 58.

'early and late in the daytime'.[129] Norwich Assembly sat gloomily hearing that 'the walles of the cittie betwixt the gates of Magdalan and Pokethorpp [had] fallen into a sodden and present decaye'. Walls that were meant to be sturdy symbols were on this day in 1555 'very like to falle downe'. The same Assembly heard sixty years later that the walls and towers had 'fallen into great decay'.[130] Things were not any better in Southampton, where governors heard in 1573 that the walls were in 'great [danger of] perrishinge' from 'rayne water' pouring in winter from crumbling houses perched on them. Governors were unhappy to hear in the next year and the one after that 'divers' parts were 'full of noysome savors' from 'donge hills and hepes of robidge'; the area 'behind the walls from the east gate to gods house gate' round to the west quay and 'bedells gate' was the most affected. Walls were still 'in decay and needfull to be looked unto [in] most places' in the town in 1581 and 'more decayed' in 'many places' two decades later.[131]

Walls caused some sleepless nights as they touched many elemental questions of 'reputacon' and security. Gates were an entrance and statement of civic 'esteem'. John Dorney surely beamed with delight when telling Gloucester's officers and officials in 1653 that the south gate 'fallen by the batteries of the late siege' was now 'rebuilt for strength and ornament'.[132] G.B. writes of the moment in 1578 when the queen 'drewe neare' to St Stephen's Gate in Norwich, 'which with the walles there were gallantly and strongly repayred'. 'The gate itself [was] beautified', he enthused; 'the queenes armes were most richely and beautifully set forth in the chiefe front' with her 'badge directly under' them next to the arms of the city.[133] Yarmouth's 'handsome' gates were 'arched over with brick'; Henry Manship describes people 'passing pleasantly [through them in] such comely sort that is a great pleasure [to] behold'.[134] London's seven gates towered over people, announcing the city with crests and other tokens. They were slammed shut after sunset and, as in plague time, the sleeping town was sealed off from the outside world. Gloucester's 'bargates and wickets' were 'locked up each night by nyne of the clock untill sunnrissing'. Lanterns burned all night long at gates from Allhallows to Candlemas in 1626.[135] 'Comon lanthornes' burned in prominent spots like gates, guildhalls, and crosses. It was 'a good act' to hang a second 'watch bell' on Southampton's Bargate in 1579, governors said, as it was hard to hear the other bell 'when the wind is northerrlie'.[136] Ward and watch were posted at gates day

[129] LMA Reps. 27, fo. 148; 28, fo. 250v; 33, fos. 277v, 286; 44, fo. 89v; 54, fos. 180, 283; Jour. 39, fo. 361v; Rep. 34, fo. 530v.

[130] NRO Norwich Assembly Folio Minute Books, fo, 3, 21v; 5, fo. 10.

[131] SA 6/1, fos. 9, 10, 11, 16, 28, 32.

[132] Dorney, *Certain Speeches Made Upon the Day of the Yearly Election of Officers in the City of Gloucester*, 10.

[133] G.B., *The Joyfull Receyuing of the Queenes Most Excellent Maiestie into Hir Highnesse Citie of Norvvich*, 18.

[134] Manship, *History of Great Yarmouth*, 73–4.

[135] GA GBR/B/3/2, fo. 220; GBR/F/4/5, fo. 76.

[136] SA 6/1, fo. 14. See also CA TAB/1, fo.91v; NRO YCA Y/HTG15, fo. 160.

and night for security and 'manifestaccon'. Watches were stationed at gates on the king's 'first repaire' to London in 1603 and when he went to Paul's Cross for the sermon in 1620.[137] Gloucester's gates were painted for pageants. More generally, night watches kept tabs on people coming and going. William Whitcombe earned £3 'for opening and shutting' Gloucester's gates in 1649.[138]

Governors looked to gates in times of trouble. Each one of Gloucester's gates was strengthened with 'iron chaynes' in 1642 'for preventing of the danger of sudden assaulte of horse' and again in 1655 'when the insurrection was at Salisbury'.[139] A part of 'reputacon' was security, so it was a public blight if a gate was out of repair. Ludlow's chamberlain was 'presented' more than once for 'not repayring walles, gates, [and] gildhall'. One of Hereford's gates hung 'very dangerously' in 1664.[140] 'The decayes [of] walls and gates' embarrassed Gloucester in 1659, while Norwich's chamberlain took care of 'amending breaches in St. Augustynes gates' in 1586 and after.[141] Like walls, gates were meant to be sturdy. A porter guarding Gloucester's west gate admitted being 'pryvie to the takinge downe of the gutters of leade' from it and selling them in Tewkesbury.[142] It was an endless task to keep gates looking ornate and secure at no small cost. Gloucester spent four, five, and six pounds at a time on its gates.[143] Gates also needed to be kept clean. Chester spent 6s. 8d. 'for keapynge newgate cleane' in 1594. It cost Gloucester eleven-pence for 'makinge cleane and paintinge the west gate' in 1569. 'All of the gates' in Yarmouth were 'clensed of mucke and fylthe' in 1608.[144] A constant chug of traffic led to chipped stones, boggy paths, and filth splattered walls and gates, all made worse by seeming indifference. 'Theare is a great heape of robidge, dust and other fylth cast in the upper ende of the towne dytch next to the easte gate', Southampton's governors complained in 1576, pointing fingers at the 'inhabitants thereaboutes'. A carpenter's wife made a 'noysome and filthie place [for] a pryvie uppon the walls ag[ains]t [the] posterne gate' in 1587.[145] Most jarring of all perhaps were reports in 1616 of the 'comon use and custome of all sorts of people goeinge in and out of the towne under the barrgate makinge water against both sides of the gate neere unto boothes'. This was Southampton's Bargate, the grand entrance to the town, that still stands elegantly today. (See Plate 12.) But now, governors observed, the gate's entrance 'especiallye in the somer [is] verie unsavoury and stinckinge'. They issued orders to build 'twoo smale gutters the

[137] For these and other examples, see LMA Jours. 26, fo. 127v; 27, fo. 176v; 31, fo. 164v; 32, fo. 273; 35, fo. 182; 38, fos. 172v, 241v; 39, fo. 50v.

[138] GA GBR/B/3/2, fo. 506.; GBR/F/4/3, fo. 16.

[139] GA GBR/F/4/6, fo. 86; GBR/B/3/2, fo. 221. See also NRO Norwich Chamberlains' Accounts 1589–1602, fo. 190; LMA Rep. 56, fo. 9; HA W/B2/3, fo. 3.

[140] SHA LB/11/4/82/18; LB/11/4/83/42; HEA BG/11/4/6.

[141] GA GBR/B/3/3, fo. 52; NRO Norwich Chamberlains' Accounts 1580–9, fo. 205; 1589/1602, fo. 190.

[142] GA GBR/B/3/1, fos. 111–11v.

[143] GA GBR/F/4, fo. 14; GBR/F/4/5, fos. 71v, 274v.

[144] CA TAR/1/22; GA GBR/F/4/3, fo. 133; NRO Y/C/19/5, fo. 64.

[145] SA 6/1, fo. 12.

one on the one side and the other on the other side with a curruant into the towne ditche'. 'No doubt', they said, 'people would rather ease themselves there then as nowe they doe'.[146]

Gates and walls were meant to be 'handsome', but the most 'stately edifice' of all should have been the hall. Around 200 town halls were built or rebuilt in the century after 1540. They were civic parliament buildings expected to radiate authority for what the leading historian of this civic architecture calls 'power' and identity.[147] (See Plates 13–16.) This was a deliberate effort to boost civic pride in tough times of heavy population growth, and it affects all that we see in 'manifestaccon'. The hall often perched on the edge of market squares was the embodiment of the civic. Lyme Regis spent five shillings 'for cleansing and fittinge the townes arms' at the hall in 1663 and £1 10s. to 'mend' the 'townes armes' three years later.[148] Gloucester paid £3 9s. 8d. in 1654 'for worke done in paintinge the cityes armes at the boothall and other things'. Shrewsbury bought 'a crest for its boot hall' in 1566.[149] Henry Manship crowed about Yarmouth's hall. It was 'a fair building' nestled next to the church '76 feet' in length and '22 feet' in breadth and 'substantially repaired and amended' in 1554. The walls were 'new buttressed and supported' and 'a very fair' roof was shipped from Mettingham College after it was 'suppressed [and] placed upon the hall and covered with lead very beautifully'.[150] Faversham's largest project in 1636 was likely to have been 'the beautifyinge of the court hall'.[151] It was a time of building but also repairing. Thumbing through columns of accounts, we see many reports of 'decay'. Preston's 'now bayliff' was told to 'sufficientlie repaire the townes hall' in 1654 and to 'sufficiently repaire the towne hall being in decay in severall places' in 1671.[152] Shrewsbury spent 33s. 16d. on 'reparacons upon the cownsell house' in 1566 and another 34s. 6d. a few months later. Lyme Regis's own 'corporacon' was taken to task in 1685 'for not repairing a dangerous wall att the towne hall'.[153] Buckingham council noted that 'these particulars following are wanting to compleat ye towne hall' in 1688: 'wainscott to be mended and sett up firme', 'playstering to be stopped', 'barrs to be made and hung at the entrance to the gaol dock and both ends of the court', and 'a stepp or block for witnesses to stand upon at the south end of ye court'.[154]

It cost just four-pence to 'cleane' the 'gutter over the counsell howse' in Lyme Regis in 1595 and another four-pence 'for the making clean of the towne hall at the lawe daye', but the value to the town was far greater than this.[155] Broken windows and 'defaced monuments' were a blot on halls elsewhere. Appearance

[146] Ibid., fo. 19. [147] Tittler, *Architecture and Power*, 162–8.
[148] DHC DC/LR/G/2/2, 1662–3, 1665–6. [149] GA GBR/F/4/6, fo. 26; SHA 3365/497.
[150] Manship, *History of Great Yarmouth*, 52. [151] CKS FA/AC4, fo. 23.
[152] LA CNP 3/2/1, fos. 17, 341. [153] SHA 3365/497; DHC DC/LR/A/7/1, 1685.
[154] HL SSTM box 6, folder 38. See also DHC DC/CC/5/2/10, fo. 13; GA GBR/F/4/3, fos. 84, 124.
[155] DHC DC/LR/G/2/2, 1595–6.

mattered in and around the hall. Windsor spent nineteen shillings in 1639 for painting its hall and gave Thomas Biggs two shillings to take away 'rubbish from behind the town hall' in 1668. Reading spent four-pence to get rid of 'dung from the guyeldehall' in 1593 and a shilling to take away 'soyle' in the next year.[156] John Page was twice in trouble in Clitheroe in the mid-1650s for 'layinge' dung 'in the streete over agaiunst the motte hall'. The offence to Clitheroe's 'reputacon' is measured by the threatened fine for his second offence: forty shillings.[157] Someone stepping into a guildhall would expect to see an elegant interior. There was an awkward huddle of governors in gowns outside Preston's hall in 1661, however, as the bailiff refused to hand over the key to the door, leaving the mayor, aldermen, and common councillors outside when they had 'speciall occasion to meete in the mott hall for the good and welfare of this incorproracon'.[158] Our hall was 'ordained for the judiciall hearinge [of] criminal offences [and] solempne meetings and concourse of this howse', Chester magistrates said in 1616, but now it had become 'a stage for plaiers [to] acte their obscene and unlawfull plaies of tragedies [to] the discreditt of the governance of this citie'.[159]

Halls were often spruced up with sweet-smelling things pleasing to the eye and nose in contrast to the 'verie insavoury and stinckinge' smells and sights outside. 'Hearbes', 'halver', 'bysomes', 'rosemary, lawrel and joy' were meant to 'perfume', 'sweeten', and decorate courtrooms and chambers for trials and 'debatinge'. Straw and 'rushes' were put under tables 'to tread on'. Halls were also decked out with flowers and herbs for festivals. Gloucester's beadle was given seven-pence 'to buy holly and ivy at Christmas' in 1639. London's yeoman of the chamber was paid £11 18s. in 1586 for a string of purchases including flowers, herbs, rushes, straw, coal, perfumes, candles, cushions, and other 'sweet' things, and for cleaning the Guildhall.[160] The hall, it was hoped, would be a sealed 'sweet' box. Windsor's accounts for 1644–5 include £1 4s. for locks, bolts, and 'other' work at the town hall. Lyme Regis spent eight-pence on 'dressinge the hall' on election day in 1592.[161] Norwich bought an extra broom for the 'assises and sessions' in 1618. It was Robert Cocket's job to get 'herbes to strowe the chamber and genep to swete the chamber' there in 1595, and he also had 'rewarde' a little later for 'dress[ing] up the councell chamber with flowers'.[162] 'Goodwife' Cocket was paid 'for byrch

[156] BRO WI/FA1/2, fos. 23v, 144; R/FA2/77–78.

[157] LA MBC/201–2. See also GA GBR/B/3/1, fo. 444v; SHA LB/11/4/82/18; LB/11/4/83/42; CRO TAR/1/18; NRO NMCC 8, fo. 539; NDRO B1/185; LA CNP 3/2/1, fo. 132.

[158] LA CNP 3/2/1, fo. 159.

[159] CA Z/AB/1, fo. 333v. See also SHA BB/F/1/1/3, fo. 54; BRO R/AC1/1/5, fo. 199.

[160] GA GBR/F/4/5, fo. 102v; B. E. Masters, ed., *Chamber Accounts of the Sixteenth Century*, London Record Society, 20 (1984), 126. See also GA GBR/F/4/5, fos. 14v, 74v, 112; GBR F/4/6, fos. 28, 474; NRO Norwich Chamberlain's Accounts, 1603–25, fos. 11v, 284, 359v, 417v; 1625–48, fos. 14, 66v, 204v, 205v, 224v, 323, 407v.

[161] BRO WI/FA1/2, fo. 67; DHC DC/LR/G/2/2, 1593–4.

[162] NRO Norwich Chamberlain's Accounts 1589–1602, fos. 187, 199.

and hearbes to dresse and strowe the councel chamber on Maye Daie and the feast daie' four years later. One Mr Drake was paid two shillings 'for makinge the guildhall handsome with flowers att sess[ions]' in 1642 and for 'herbes and flowers to dresse up the seates att the newhall the last assize' five years later.[163] Halls were routinely 'sweetened' for assizes and quarter sessions. Gloucester spent 2s. 7d. 'for perfume and herbes used at the tolsey and bothal at quarter sessions' in 1638. It cost Shrewsbury two-pence for 'candles for the court' in 1578.[164]

Authority (and its representation) should have been clean, 'swete', and 'dressed up' unlike shabby vagrants or slums. Halls should have been impressive. Gloucester drew up proposals for 'the new tolsty chamber' in 1651: glazing with 'good glasse', 'a faire table', new 'wainscot dore', and a pair of stairs. New panelling was also planned later.[165] Panelling and wainscotting needed to be pleasing to the eye because portraits of civic worthies hung on hall walls in increasing numbers in the century after 1550 in another calculated measure to commemorate civic 'fame' and pride. Michael Williams got three-pence 'for setting up some rack hookes about the tolsey chamber to hang up the tables and pictures' in Gloucester's hall in 1647. 'Twelve pictures of benefactors' were hung up 'in the tolsey' in 1678. Oxford's governors gave orders in 1631 for 'a new picture of Sr Thomas White a worthie benefactor to this cittie [to be] drawne [and] hanged up in the upper hall'. The king was also on the walls. Mr Baldwin was paid £28 in Gloucester in 1662 'for making the kings picture'. The same city also spent £4 10s. 5d. in 1635 on 'the studdy at the tollsey'.[166]

It was a cutting irony that 'the howse of offyce' in Southampton 'towne haule' was 'in decaye' in 1575 (Kendal spent six-pence 'for a pisse boll for ye court loft' in 1582).[167] The hall should have been spick and span inside and out. That said, however, the amount of money and time that was spent to maintain halls speaks to the sacred status of civic 'reputacon' and the great expectations driving 'manifestaccon' in the home of government. Many hospitals too were elegant 'works of art' and the buildings where merchants gathered were usually among the finest in any town representing civic ethics and commerce in a tight embrace. 'Statlier' houses lined main streets and there would have been much to see in a short walk from most guildhalls. In fact, walking and walks developed in some places into

[163] Ibid., fo. 274; Norwich Chamberlain's Accounts 1603–25, fo. 303v; 1625–48, fos. 386v, 488.
[164] GA GBR/F/4/5, fo. 75; SHA 3365/511.
[165] GA GBR/B/3/2, fo. 216.
[166] GA GBR/F/4/5, fo. 375v; GBR/F/4/7, fo. 155; GBR/4/6, fo. 446; GBR/4/3, fo. 16; OA C/FC/1/A1/03, fo. 22. Leading works on civic portraiture include R. Tittler, *The Face of the City: Civic Portraiture and Civic Identity in Early Modern England* (Manchester, 2007); R. Tittler, *Portraits, Painters, and Publics in Provincial England 1540–1640* (Oxford, 2012), esp. chap. 7; R. Tittler, 'Portraiture, precedence, and politics amongst the London liveries,1540–1640', *UH*, 35 (2008); T. Cooper, *Citizen Portrait: Portrait Painting and the Urban Elite of Tudor and Jacobean England and Wales* (London and Newhaven, 2012); I. W. Archer, 'The arts and acts of memorialization in early modern London', in J. F. Merritt, ed., *Imagining Early Modern London: Perceptions and Portrayals of the City from Stow to Strype* (Cambridge, 2001).
[167] SA 6/1, fo. 11; KAC WSMB/K/1/5, 1582–3.

high-end leisure and health pursuits in aesthetically appealing settings. Landscaped walks away from cluttered parts were planned for citizens as a welcome alternative to 'anti-manifestaccon': stench, poor hygiene, blemishes, roving animals, heavy traffic, etc. They were conceived for the 'pleasure and recreaccon [of] cittyzens' to breathe cleaner air and enjoy the view. This would be something separate and socially privileged, but urban areas always complicated proscription and exclusivity. Green havens were rarely inaccessible. The king lectured Reading corporation in 1634 on hearing that 'the beautie and pleasure' of 'Brownes Hill [that] was wont to be a place of recreation to walke in and faire and open for ayre' was now 'utterly lost' due to the nearby 'buchers rowe' and 'standing shambles' that blocked the walk. 'Rubbishe' piled up on Reading's walks at other times. The 'mayor and aldermen' of Lyme Regis were presented in 1670 'for not planching the towne walke'.[168]

Most famous of all before Peter Borsay's late seventeenth-century 'urban renaissance' was Moorfields, just outside London's north-west walls. Moorfields had long been a venue for archery and exercise: Alessandro Magno watched 'men and women gather to meet and play' on Sundays at Moorfields in 1562; men shot guns and arrows after the service was over; bowling was also popular.[169] The aldermen were unhappy about the high cost of 'levelling walling and rayling' the fields (and paying for two keepers or guards), but the area was transformed after the king's 1605 blast against the state of the capital city.[170] Richard Johnson published *The Pleasant Walkes of Moore-fields* in 1607 (walking was London's 'chiefest' pleasure). Royal ministers wrote warmly to City governors a decade after the king's stark words 'approving' and 'commending' all 'edifices, structures and workes which tend to publique use and ornamente', amongst other things 'the paving of Smithfield, the planting of Morefield, the bringing of the new streame unto the west partes', 'Britanes Burse [and] the reedifying of Algate and Hicks Hall'.[171] Moorfields was 'most beautiful', healthy, and 'a continual comfort to behold' that reflected the 'noble' minds of London's citizens.[172] The walks are 'sweet and delightful', Richard Johnson gushed in 1607,

[168] LMA Jour. 29, fos. 13v, 351–1v; BRO R/Z5/1; R/FA/3/5; DHC DC/LR/B1/9, fo. 521.

[169] P. Borsay, *The English Urban Renaissance: Culture and Society in the Provincial Town 1660–1770* (Oxford, 1989); C. Barron, C. Coleman, and C. Gobb, eds., 'The London Journal of Alessandro Magno 1562', *London Journal* (1983), 141.

[170] LMA Rep. 29, fos. 13v–14.

[171] R. Johnson, *The Pleasant Walkes of Moore-fields* (1607), A3; SRPC (136) 280–7; LMA Jour. fos. 351–1v.

[172] Johnson, *Pleasant Walkes of Moore-fields*, A3r, B1r; E. Howes, *Annales, Or, A Generall Chronicle of England Begun by John Stow: Continued and Augmented With Matters Forraigne and Domestique, Ancient and Moderne, Unto the End of the Present Year, 1631* (1631), 1024; J. Howell, *Londinopolis: An Historical Discourse or Perlustration of the City of London, the Imperial Chamber and the Chief Emporium of Great Britain* (1657), 301; N. E. McClure, ed., *The Letters of John Chamberlain*, 2 vols., American Philosophical Society (Philadelphia, PA, 1939), I, 235; L. Williams, '"To recreate and refresh their dulled spirites in the sweet and wholesome ayre": green space and the growth of the city',

the air is 'sweet' to stroll in, and trees 'yeelde' much 'delight' to my eyes. Pepys went there 'for a little ayre'.[173] 'Citizens' stretched their legs and took the air along the railed-in walks. The crowds were so large around 1610 that 'the great walkes' were 'found too little'. But we also hear that they were plagued by fruit-sellers, beggars, vagrants, and nightwalkers. City magistrates complained in 1609 of 'wronges, hurts, and impediments to the walke', including 'people easing their bodies' and rudely dumping 'soyle and fylth'. Even the grass was 'growe[ing] amock'.[174] Warders were supposed to guard the walks 'continually' and a pair of stocks was handily put in the 'sweete' fields. But like so much else in this matter of 'manifestaccon' and order, the outcomes were to say the least mixed. Homeless migrants slept in the fields; women with little choice gave birth in them. The keepers were given 2s. 6d. by a parish in 1623 'for bringing word of divers women in laboure', whom they spotted walking across the fields.[175] Moorfields was if anything composite. Thieves swiped 'rayle posts' and 'iron from the rayles'; others pulled railings down. Women continued to hang washing to dry on walls and railings, although keepers told them to stop this in 1609 and many times after. One pimp's 'chefe brokinge' was to 'go to fields among those women that are dryinge clothes' to 'trye them by gevinge them a quart of wyne or som other thinge whether they be for hym'.[176]

The end results were often patchy. It sometimes seemed that the odds were stacked against 'manifestaccon' as towns grew and citizens—the civic/social intestines of 'manifestaccon'—were well on the way to becoming a minority in their own stomping grounds. Improvements were always on the minds of governors, such as the bold achievements in London much admired by privy councillors in 1615. But not all plush buildings were welcomed with open arms. An apothecary's wife living along St John's Street stood in the dock at Middlesex Sessions in 1613 'for giving revylinge speeches [to] Sir Baptist Heckes [who was sitting on the bench] touching the building of the sessions house' named after him (Hicks Hall, one of the 'edifices' highly praised by Crown ministers in 1615).[177] The 'eyebeholder', Henry Manship, on the other hand, was proud of 'the seemly beauty of private houses [and] stately magnificence of public building' in Yarmouth: the 'beauty' of houses 'hastens my pen thither-wards'. 'The uniformity' of buildings, he said, 'concerns' a town's 'magnificence, decency, comeliness [and] beauty' and was the polar opposite of 'deformity of structure' that exuded only 'dishonour,

in Merritt, *Imagining Early Modern London*, 191–2; N. G. Brett-James, *The Growth of Stuart London* (1935), 455–7.

[173] Johnson, *Pleasant Walkes of Moore-fields*, A3v, A2; R. Latham and W. Matthews, eds., *The Diary of Samuel Pepys*, 11 vols (1970–83), IX, 14-3-1668.

[174] LMA Jours. 27, fo.31; 29, fos. 351–1v, 13v–14; Rep. 47, fo. 46. See also LBHC 5, fo. 259; BMM LBHC 4, fo. 29v.

[175] LMA MS 4457/2, fo. 222v.

[176] LBHC 6, fos. 314, 408; 9, fos. 76, 128; 8, fo. 94v; LMA Rep. 29, fo.14; LBHC 3, fo. 110.

[177] LMA MJ/SBR/1, fo. 621.

indecency [and] uncomeliness'.[178] Others hoped to see the same thing. Architectural writer Ronald Freart believed that 'the true and essential beauty of architecture [was seen in] the union and concourse [of] individual parts [in] visible harmony'.[179] Even after seeing 140 buildings in an untidy row on a Yarmouth street, Manship noted that there is 'not any more division in comeliness to be by the eye discovered amongst them than unpleasantness to the ear in music [of] many discords [that] make a perfect concord'.[180] Freart could not have written this and it was not the attitude in London when Manship was writing his home-town history. The City, Crown, and Goldsmith's guild were angry that 'the gouldsmythes row in cheapsyde [once] a great ornament to the citty' was 'broken' and 'defaced'. 'Yt is a thing every man's eye meets with as he passeth up and down' Cheapside, royal ministers observed. There was a time long ago, it now seemed, when only goldsmiths lived along this 'star' row, but it was now home to a hotchpotch of 'mean trades' and 'deformitie [in] the heart of the city'. 'In things of this nature', privy councillors lectured City leaders, 'you ought to account the honour and adorning of the city to be an esentiall part of good government'. They wanted London's 'principall streete [to] be the better beautified and adorned'.[181]

Two conduits—one called 'great'—stood at Cheapside's west and east edges. Water also flowed from a standard that stood next to an eye-catching cross with gilt markings and religious iconography that would lead to Puritans pulling it down in 1643. (See Plate 17.) People went to conduits for water but they were also a civic 'ornament' for 'the publique good'. Exeter's first historian, John Vowell (alias Hooker), was proud of the 'fountains called conduits unto which through canals or pipes lead waters are conveyed from springs rising out of certain places and fields without this cittie'. 'These fountains [four in all] one beeing of great antiquitie and of late reediffyed', he added, 'standeth in the middle of the cittie at the meeting of foure principall streets' (in a similar topography to the drawing of the Bristol cross in *The Maire of Bristowe Is Kalendar*; see Plate 18). Not even the 'rebels' managed to cut off the water supply in the 'commotion' year (1549).[182] Like the capital city, Exeter, Shrewsbury, and Gloucester bragged about their 'greate conduite'. It cost Shrewsbury sixty shillings to build a conduit 'on the hey strat' in 1578. John Ogilby began directions for the trip from Exeter to Truro by

[178] Manship, *History of Great Yarmouth*, 105, 62–3.

[179] Freart, *Parallel of the Antient Architecture With the Modern*, 3.

[180] Manship, *History of Great Yarmouth*, 66.

[181] APC 1621–23, 515; 1629–30, 181. See P. Griffiths, 'Politics made visible: order, residence, and uniformity in Cheapside, 1600–45', in Griffiths and M. S. R. Jenner, eds., *Londinopolis: Essays in the Cultural and Social History of Early Modern London* (Manchester, 2000); J. Newman, 'Inigo Jones and the politics of architecture', in K. Sharpe and P. Lake, eds., *Culture and Politics in Early Stuart England* (Basingstoke, 1994).

[182] [J. Hooker,] *The Discription of the Cittie of Excester, Collected and Gathered by John Vowell Alias Hooker, Gentleman and Chamberlain of the Same Cittie* (1575), 42v–3.

telling travellers to go 'from the great conduit [to] the west-gate.'[183] Conduits appear in civic maps: there was a 'Conduitt Close' in Reading and 'Conduitt Lane' in Bideford.[184] 'Publique' punishments were staged by these 'ornaments' and governors gathered around them on days dedicated to conduits and other eye-catching occasions. London spent £26 8s. 1d. in 1567 'for a dinner at the conduit heads' for the mayor and aldermen 'with the lady mayoress and other ladies and gentlemen [and] wardens of the twelve chief companies.'[185]

Towns took 'viewes' of conduits and they were 'amended' from time to time 'as [was] nedeful'. One in Chester was 'greatlie decayed' in 1583 and quickly 'amended [to make it] more abundant with water in riseinge of the head of the spring to bringe the course of water so ner the high crosse as may be.'[186] Southampton's 'condytte heads' were in 'decaye' in 1580 'and very needeful to be amended' because 'beastes for want of rayles rubbe away the brickes'. 'The conduit head' in the town centre was 'altogeather uncovered' in 1603 with 'bricks broken downe.'[187] Gloucester forked out over £40 on the upkeep of conduits in 1588–92, with additional costs to keep them in working order down through the years, including £4 12s. 4d. in 1564 to fix pipes leading to the walls; £27 18s. 8d. to 'mend' the pipes and leads stretching from the walls to the high cross; and £16 18s. 6d. in 1646 in 'charges about the conduites' and 'mendinge the conduite house at ye hill'.[188] There were payments as elsewhere for 'new cesternes' and 'fynishinge' heads (costing £30 at one time in Shrewsbury). Money was also spent on painting, 'dressinge', 'coloring', 'oilinge', and cleaning conduits, and paving around them for better show and 'credit'. It cost Shrewsbury 14s. 9d. 'for oyll and colors for the condyt' in 1578.[189]

Locks were necessary to stop water being taken from conduits after dark, even more so when some were dry or quarter-full due to broken pipes, cocks not being turned off, or people running pipes for 'private necessitie' to their homes. Some conduits were found without a drop of water in them, wounding the 'creditt of good government'. It was the press of people around Rye's conduit that broke pipes and 'wastlocks' in 1587 so water could not 'runne contynuallye.'[190] The keepers of London's conduits each got 6s. 8d. for the year in 1585, while founder William Palmer picked up 26s. 8d. for 'overseeing' them. Gloucester plumber

[183] SHA 3365, fo. 516; J. Ogilby, *The Travellers Guide or A Most Exact Description of the Roads of England* (1699), 128.

[184] BRO R/FA/3/1; R/AC1/1/4, fo. 262; NDRO 1064Q/SO1, fo. 85v.

[185] Masters, *Chamber Accounts*, 126. [186] CA Z/AB/1, fo. 190. [187] SA 6/1, fos. 15, 27.

[188] GA GBR/F/4/3, fos. 29, 48v, 84, 100, 108v, 139v, 170, 257v–8, 263v–4, 272, 287v, 313v; GBR/F/4/5, fos. 195v, 211v, 342.

[189] SHA 3365, fos. 509, 511, 513, 516. See also CA Z/AB/1, fo. 78v; SAI C/3/4/1/36, fo. 3v; CKS Md/Acm1/1a, fos. 48v–9; SHA BB/F/1/1/3, fo. 562.

[190] ESBHRO RYE 6/1, fo. 184v See also CKS Md/Acm1/2, fos. 176–6v; Md/ACm1/3, fo. 71; GA GBR/B/3/1, fos. 31, 444v; DRO ECA B/1/3, fo. 195; TNA SP 16/214/90, 16/443/41; KAC WSSMB/K/2/5, fo. 22; SAI C/2/2/2/1, fo. 169v.

Thomas Barnes was paid £3 quarterly in 1653 'to locke upp all the conduites' by nine at night in summer and eight in winter and to 'unlocke' them at sunrise. Plumber Widow Barnes was paid £10 in 1675 'for keeping the citty conduits [and] pipes in order'.[191] This was not just a matter of water levels. These pieces of civic 'manifestaccon' were publicly 'defiled' at times. London apprentice John Sampson was whipped for insulting a conduit in 1583! He was 'stripped [from] hys girdle upward [and given] twelve strypes with a rodd at the poste of reformacion' next to Fleet Street conduit for his 'undutyfull speaches of the conduit'.[192] More commonly, people were taken to task for washing clothes or even mops in conduits. 'Many' of Southampton's 'meaner sort' were caught washing their clothes 'at the conduite' in 1604. Magistrates pointed out what was obvious to them, that it was 'verie unsemely in a towne of good government to have washinge of clothes [on] the streats or at anie of the conduits in the hart of the towne'.[193] London's Recorder, William Fleetwood, was on his way to the Guildhall one day in 1592 when his attention was caught by an elderly couple standing on the 'skafold' at 'the lower ende of the cheape syde' who 'entered into the cundeth [at night] and washed theymselffs'.[194] Horses drinking 'in the sistern of the conduit next the gaole' in Maidstone had been a problem for at least fifty years in 1637. John Armstrong landed in trouble in 1659 for letting 'kinne pisse [and] other putrifyeinge water of a base smell' run from the 'backside' of his house in Appleby into the conduit.[195] London aldermen could not put into words on record the 'very fowle' and 'beastlye' acts 'comytted [in the] greate conduyte in Cheape' by Sara Guye and others in 1592 that were 'not fytt to be spoken of for modestyes sake', while Isabel Horne was taken to London Bridewell by a constable in 1618 'for brawling and hurtinge a poore wench att Fleete conduite very dangerouslie'.[196]

It was the prominent location and decoration of conduits that made them valuable and vulnerable. Conduits and crosses were sometimes neighbours in double demonstrations of civic honour. Bridgnorth's conduit was called 'the crosse conduit'. Other towns have left word of 'the conduitt at the high crosse'.[197] The crowning crest was the civic cross in the market or high street. (See Plates 18–22.) 'We begin our computation from the high-cross in Bristol', John Ogilby said, as he guided people out of the city, that like the 'standard in Cornhill is the conjunction of 4 eminent streets' (Plate 18). Gloucester spent £50 on 'beautifying of the crosse' in 1634 and 'inclosing it with iron as Bristoll and other cittyes are'. Ogilby, who mapped and narrated England, thought that its 'statliest crosse' was the one in

[191] Masters, *Chamber Accounts*, 18; GA GBR/B/3/2, fo. 715; GBR/F/4/7, fo. 33. See also GA GBR/F/4/7, fos. 8, 709; CA TAR/1/12; SHA 3365, fos. 511, 523; NA 3/1, fo. 331v; LBHC 6, fo. 74v.

[192] LMA Rep. 21, fo. 4. [193] SA 6/1, fos. 27, 29. [194] BL Lansdowne MS 71/16.

[195] CKS Md/Acm1/2, fos. 162, 60v, 176–6v; KAC WSMB/A/2/1/2, 2-8-1659.

[196] LMA Rep. 22, fos. 387–7v; LBHC 6, fo. 97. See also DRO ECA B/1/3, fo. 195; GA GBR/B/10, unpag.

[197] SHA BBC/1/1/1, fos. 14v, 48. See also CA Z/AB/1, fo. 201v; GA GBR F/4/3, fo. 29.

Coventry market: it was '66 foot high' and 'adorn'd with the statues of several kings' and had been recently 'beautifyed' (Plate 22).[198] Leicester planned to build a 'crosse' in the high street in 1576. James Brome called the same cross 'an exquisite piece of workmanship'.[199] The cross played a large part on 'skarlett dayes'. Banbury's aldermen met the mayor at his house in the morning on 'Ascension [day], Corpus Christi Day, and every fair Day' in 'their best and decent apparell'. They then made 'the perambulation from his house through the faire and market in decent order' to hear 'proclamation made at the market cross'.[200] Winchester's elite met the mayor 'at the high crosse'—'the moste publique and discreate place'—before keynote sermons in 1594. A by-law passed in the same city in 1656 for 'maintaining ye honor and esteeme of this city to th'end [its] citizens may be an ornament' told merchants to greet the mayor 'in their gownes at the high crosse', to 'accompany' him to 'the greate church' on the 'lords day [and] days of humiliation and thanksgiving'. The procession filed back to the cross after the service was over to 'take leave' (they were told to do the same 'when he greets assize judges').[201]

Many crosses had symbols and script linking towns to a glorious past. It cost £3 to 'paint' and 'guild' 'the late king's picture at the cross in Gloucester in 1660. 'Charges' for taking care of the city's cross each year ranged from thirty to three or four pounds or four-pence for a brush to 'cleane the crosse' in 1637.[202] A shoddy cross drained civic 'fame'. We see regular payments to pave, paint, sweep, 'sop', and clean crosses. It cost 1s. 6d. to 'mend' cage doors and to set 'the vayne of the crosse upright' in Windsor in 1639. William Marshal got a few shillings for 'keepinge the crosse cleane and decent' in his Essex town in 1629.[203] This was an essential job. George Wood was fined 3s. 4d. in Clitheroe in 1656 'for breaking the streete neare the cross and not making it sufficient'; Bailiff Wood was fined double this later in the same year for the same offence.[204] Liverpool's 'leave lookers' were told to 'kepe clayne steyres and gryeces off the highe crosse [and] all abowte the stockes [and anywhere] payres, aples, plombes and other frute [were] sold abowt the highe crosse'.[205] Prominent locations made crosses gathering places for governors on parade but for less welcome elements also. 'A world of knaves and cheaters passes [by Cheapside Cross] each day', Henry Peacham wrote in 1641, 'herbwomen on one side and costermongers and tripe-wives on the other'. A 'herbwyfe' selling at

198 Ogilby, *Travellers Guide*, 23, 44; GA GBR/B/3/2, fos. 39, 44.
199 LERO BRII/1/2, fo. 278; Brome, *Travels Over England, Scotland, and Wales*, 77.
200 Gibson and Brinkworth, *Banbury Corporation Records*, 25.
201 HA W/B1/3, fo. 101v; W/B1/5, fos. 108–8v.
202 GA GBR/B/3/2, fo. 39; GBR/F/4/6, fo. 368; GBR/F/4/5, fos. 117v–18, 348v, 42v, 162.
203 BRO WI/FA1/2, fo. 23; F. G. Emmison, ed., *Early Essex Town Meetings: Braintree, 1619–1636; Finchingfield, 1626–1634* (London and Chichester, 1970), 65.
204 LA MBC/200, 201.
205 J. M. Twemlow, ed., *Liverpool Town Books, Proceedings of Assemblies, Common Councils, Portmoot Courts etc. 1550–1862*, 2 vols (Liverpool, 1918–35), II, 7–8.

Cheapside Cross in 1605 was locked in the stocks for tossing 'beane, shales, and other things' at the emperor's ambassador and his train as they filed through the city. A group of chimney sweeps were sent to Bridewell for throwing stones at the same cross in 1634.[206] Robert Arnold appeared at Leicestershire Sessions in 1682 for 'breaking ye stocks and towne crosse' in Bottesford.[207]

'The hart of the towne', the market square, was also the 'hart' of 'manifestaccon'. Many conduits were a stone's throw away from crosses, guildhalls were never far from markets, and principal streets fanned out from them. It was a tall order to maintain expectations. There always seemed to be some sort of trouble waiting in the wings. Just as rich and poor could live cheek by jowl,[208] beauty and ugliness sometimes sat side by side. Building was neglected at times. Thomas Harnam was picked to be 'overseer of the workes' in Gloucester in 1617 with a £5 annual salary after it emerged that his predecessor had presided over 'great neglect in building or making of howses, edifices, structures, waies, causewaies, conduits and water courses'.[209] As people turned off chief streets, they headed into the darker courts and alleys, shabby quarters that were linked in guildhalls with stench, infection, and crime. It was not just scruffy buildings that came under scrutiny but their occupants and uses. A slaughterhouse might not sit too far away from a town hall. It was hoped that the 'stinke' and 'unsemely' sight of slaughterhouses would be consigned somewhere over the walls—yet another struggle over 'manifestaccon' that we can follow in records. Noxious trades made a dreadful sight and stink for what Mark Jenner memorably calls 'the nose of the inhaler'.[210] But like bad neighbours slaughterhouses sat in contested spaces inside walls. Southampton named and shamed butchers in 1603 who 'keepe there slaughter howses within the towne walles', something, governors said, that can no 'longer [be] tollerated beinge a matter excessively against the lawes of this realme in walled townes'.[211] Legislation dating from the reign of Henry VII banned butchers from 'kill[ing] flesh in [their] scalding house or within the walls of London', and it was added that 'this act'—4 H.7.3—'extendeth and shalbee observed in every city, boroughe, and towne walled within England [apart from] Barwicke and Carliel'.[212] It was fitting that Pig Lane in Chester was 'without the bars'. It cost 6s. 8d. to 'keepe swyne within the

[206] H. Peacham, *A Discourse Between the Crosse in Cheap and Charring Crosse* (1641), 1; LMA Rep. 27, fo. 55; LBHC 8, fo. 6.

[207] LERO QS 7/1, fo. 86v.

[208] J. Boulton, 'The poor among the rich: a long-term view of pauperism in London's west end', in Griffiths and Jenner, *Londinopolis*.

[209] GA GBR/B/3/1, fo. 444v.

[210] M. S. R. Jenner, 'Civilization and deodorization? Smell in early modern English culture', in P. Burke, B. Harrison, and P. Slack, eds., *Civil Histories* (Oxford, 2000), quoting 129.

[211] SA 6/1, fo. 27.

[212] *A View of the Penal Laws Concerning Trade and Traffick* (1697), 25; F. Pulton, *An Abstract of All the Penal Statutes Which Be General, in Force and Use Wherein is Conteyned the Effect of All Those Statutes Which Do Threaten to the Offenders Thereof the Losse of Life, Member, Landes, Goods, or Other Punishment or Forfaiture Whatsoeuer*... (1577), 50.

citty walls' in 1629, and a book was kept of hog owners and number of hogs. Ipswich 'surveyed' butchers by ward in 1557 to map their geography.[213] Like other toxic trades, butchers were marginalized at times in law and culture. They were not allowed to sit on the grand jury in Shrewsbury in 1693.[214] Their low status made them an object of insults. Cheapside goldsmith John Foster called 'yeomen of the guarde' the 'kings oxen or butchers' and 'the kings open slaughtermen and bucherly slaves' in 1614.[215]

'Manifestaccon' and the townscape was not just about seeing; it was also about smelling. 'All the butchers in this towne except Thomas Hoskins kyll ther oxen, shepe and other cattell within the walls', Southampton council noted in 1577, and 'annoy' people 'with the infection of the bloud and other noysome savors'. Six slaughterhouse workers—'hogers'—from the same town were told to stop 'beating' calves and 'pricking' veal inside the walls in 1565, but they took no notice, 'whereby wynde entreth and so the fleshe swelleth with boblles as is new blowen which is unwholesome for mans body'.[216] Many butchers fell on the wrong side of the law for offences that we might call insanitary today. Norvician William Lodge was one of them. He was taken to court for 'killing and dressing twenty bullocks and cowes' inside 'the citty and walles' in 1655. Chester's butchers were told to 'kepe ther shops cleane, purged, scoured and washed' in 1565 and not to kill 'beste or cattell' in them, while their fellows in Hereford were not allowed to 'slee' beasts in streets 'nor shed [their] bloud in the highe way nor leye no hedes of beasts in the streets'.[217] Preston also had to deal with similar 'greate and noisome abuse' in 1562 caused by 'butchers throweinge blood ropps and other garbage in the streetes [to] the scandall of the government of this burroughe'. As well as being an eyesore, this 'filth' was a magnet for 'swine and dogges'.[218]

Butchery was not the only noxious trade inside walls. Fish-sellers also turned noses and caused damage. Robert Crosse from Southampton was taken to task in 1577 for 'comonly [throwing] noisome and filthye stinckinge fyshe water owt at his back gardyne dore [that ran] downe the castle hill by the butts [eroding] a greate parte' of the hillside. Fishmongers 'water[ing]' fish in the high street in the same town in 1575 'very muche annoy' this chief street, governors noted not for the first time, aware that these 'very unwholesome smells [were] very daungerous

213 CRO Z/AB/2, fos. 165v, 20v, 7v; N. Bacon, *The Annalls of Ipswiche. The Lawes, Customes, and Government of the Same* (1654), ed. W. H. Richardson (Ipswich, 1884–5), 247. See also WSHC G23/1/3, fo. 284; HA W/B1/5, fos. 51–3; L. J. Skelton, 'Environmental Regulation in Edinburgh and York, c.1560–c.1700' (PhD thesis, University of Durham, 2012), 70–4.

214 SHA 3356/2430, fo. 48.

215 LMA MJ/SBR/2, fo. 139. See also K. Stuart, *Defiled Trades and Social Outcasts: Honour and Ritual Pollution in Early Modern Germany* (Cambridge, 1999).

216 SA 6/1, fos. 13, 5.

217 NRO Norwich Sessions File 95/1; CA Z/AB/1, fo. 108; HEA BG11/18.

218 LA CNP 3/2/1, fos. 17, 59. See also HA B/1/5, fos. 51–3; HEA BG11/17/1/4, fo. 58; CA Z/AB/1, fos. 175–5v; SHA 3356/2442, fos. 2v, 12, 16; SA 6/1, fo. 27.

to breed sycknes this hott somer'.[219] Poor Sotonians buying and selling 'salte fishe' in Holyrood market in the town were roundly reprimanded in 1615 for the 'verie unsavourye odor and smells' that drifted across the surrounding area, 'specially in the somer season'. Southampton's brewhouses were another 'nuisance'. Some of them hugged the walls, and people living 'above the barr' in 1579 complained about 'filthie and unsaverie odors' oozing from the brewhouse next door that hung over them like a foul cloud.[220] Such 'unsemeleye' sights and 'savors' often fill good runs of town or village records. Forty-two Prestonians were taken to task in 1673 for not getting rid of their 'middings'. Anne Ingram was in trouble in the same town for 'continually lay[ing] donng' at her door and 'ye church gate barr' to the 'shame of the government of this burrough'.[221] A dozen people were presented to the Leet court for littering Clitheroe's streets with dunghills in 1657 (a bailiff among them). Future justice Solomon Andrew was one of three men told to remove 'mixons' in 1654.[222]

People pissing in public but not in 'common pissing places' was another corruption of public authority not to be tolerated in a well-governed town. Southampton magistrates complained that their town 'is moste filthilye annoyed by the beastly use of people easinge of themselves' in the streets in 1602. Officers were told to walk 'throughe the towne' to warn people that anyone caught urinating in the 'open' would be locked in the stocks or whipped. 'A poore man' was chosen in each ward 'to fynd oute' offenders. The lane 'leading through Staple Garden into Bridge Streete' in nearby Winchester was said to be 'very noyfull' in 1577. The main offence was stench from 'filthy thinges' and people 'doinge ther needes of easement which is to be done in pryvies or other meete places'.[223] Towns built 'pissing places' or 'public privies' 'for ease of the people and better cleansinge of the towne'. They were placed around markets and anywhere else where people gathered. Reading spent six-pence 'for mendinge the pissinge place' in 1633. It cost a shilling to set up 'a post at the pissing place' in Windsor market in 1639.[224] 'All the wast ground neare [Gloucester's] south gate [was] appointed for the use of the burgesses and inhabitants [for] makinge of water and dryinge of clothes' in 1648. 'The comon privy house at the kay' in Ipswich in 1591 was '12 foote longe and 6 foote broad'.[225] Provision was one thing, upkeep was sometimes another. The 'pryvey at the west keye' was 'very necessary', Southampton governors said in 1573, but it was 'greatly in decaye'. The West Quay privy fell into the sea in 1587 and that left 'the comon sort of people' with little choice but to 'annoye the streate

219 SA 6/1, fos. 13, 11.
220 Ibid., fos. 32, 14.
221 LA CNP 3/2/1, fos. 41, 69, 118, 140, 149, 157.
222 LA MBC/202. See also CKS Md/JLP/1656; NRO Y/C/19/4, fo. 254; SHA 3356/2442, fo. 1; LA MBC/235; CNP 3/2/1, fos. 118, 281, 326, 415; DHC DC/LR/B1/9, fo. 135.
223 SA 6/1, fo. 28; HA Q/B1/3, fo. 10v.
224 SA 6/1, fo. 28; BRO R/FA/3/12; WI/FA1/2, fo. 22v.
225 GA GBR/B/3/2, fo. 461; Bacon, *Annalls of Ipswich*, 364. See also KAC WSMB/K/1/5, 1582–3.

and other places very filthie and noysome to passe by'. The West Quay continued to be a problem spot. 'Notwith-standinge' many warnings, magistrates said in 1589, 'theare ys [still] not a pryvye built at the west keye'.[226]

Repeated refrains of 'wronges, hurts, and impediments' can be read as exasperation but also in terms of standards and aspirations for making things better. It was hoped that built environments would be clean and reflective of effective government. The question here is not whether buildings, streets, or markets were 'stately' and 'clean' 400 years ago, but to think what 'manifestaccon' and sanitation and its regulation meant for early moderns.[227] Age-old stereotypes of rubbish-cluttered streets or steaming dunghills still linger today. Records speak for themselves. They are full of 'gutts', 'sullagdge', 'rubbidge', 'garbage', and 'filthe'. All of this was deeply concerning for 'manifestaccon', and 'contagion' like the 'infectious' 'dede swine [and] horses' that were 'cast' near Oxford's walls and gates or the dead horses left 'neare the highe waies' in Hereford that were 'hurtefull to this comenweale'.[228] We can pile up stories of 'uncleyne things' to weave narratives of dirt and stench, forgetting perhaps that reports of roads 'overlayed' with 'great heapes of donge' (Tewkesbury) or 'many noisome heapes of donge, rubbudge, and other soils' lining streets (Southampton) preface demands for their regulation and eradication.[229]

A good proportion of these insanitary offences came to light after one or more neighbours turned to the courts. They were no longer able to put up with the 'noisome and unseemelye' sights and smells from next door. Many of these cases were the final resort after months of trying to sort things out with words. There were expectations defended by magistrates and shared by some residents of what was acceptable 'reputacon', sanitation, and 'comeliness'. People who soiled streets did so at the risk of condemnation and prosecution by their governors and neighbours, whose quality of life was in danger. This was not an 'us' (governors) and 'them' (governed) state of affairs, although there is evidence of indifference. Neighbours stepped in if someone offended collective standards, tipping off magistrates about people like Norwich cordwainer Thomas Cockwell, who emptied the 'filth' out of his 'howse of office' into his yard in 1653 which ran into 'the comon' street with an 'abhominable stinke' that 'infect[ed the] wholesome

[226] SA 6/1, fos. 9, 19, 20.

[227] Pioneering work includes A. Corbin, *The Foul and the Fragrant: Odour and the Social Imagination* (1996); G. Vigarello, *Concepts of Cleanliness: Changing Attitudes in France since the Middle Ages*, trans. J. Birrel (Cambridge, 1988); M. S. R. Jenner, 'Early Modern English Conceptions of "Cleanliness" and "Dirt" as Reflected in the Environmental Regulation of London c.1530–c.1700' (DPhil thesis, University of Oxford, 1991).

[228] KAC WSMB/A/2/1/2, 2/8/1659; HL EL MS 1956; HEA BG11/4/6, 10/1661, fo. 1. See also GA TBR/A/1/2, fo. 12; HEA BG11/4/6, fo. 4v; KAC WSSMB/K/2/5, fo. 31v; LMA Jours. 23, fo. 403v; 36, fo. 20v; LA CNP 3/2/1, fos. 21, 319.

[229] SA 6/1, fos. 13, 14, 16; GA TBR/A/1/2, fo. 13. Emily Cockayne, in *Hubbub: Filth, Noise, and Stench in England 1660–1770* (New Haven and London, 2007), tends to focus on 'the worst parts' of town life and does more to sustain stereotypes of early modern 'filth' than challenge or modify them.

ayer ther'. The stomach-churning 'ayre' of filthy privies led to appeals to neighbourliness, warnings if they fell on deaf ears, and feisty exchanges if nothing was done.[230] Exeter merchant John Baker had 'conference' with his neighbour, 'troublesome' Michael Gibbins, about 'reformation of his house of office' that bordered on his garden. He pleaded with him to 'reforme' it as his wife had been sick and was slipping from bad to worse due to the 'noysome smells' that floated through their house. 'Rogueronegate' and banckeroute knave', Gibbins sneered, 'he would redresse [it] att his pleasure'. Baker's neighbours gave support, saying that the 'stinke' and 'stenche' from Gibbin's yard had made their lives miserable. He was a 'gamester on the sabbath', they added, linking sanitation with morality in ways familiar to magistrates.[231] These tiffs stayed 'off the record' until nothing else could be done other than to turn to courts in cases that show the grimmer sides of living cheek by jowl. Widow Dent was taken to court in Southampton in 1616 for having 'a slaughterhowse' in her 'backeside' where she 'commonlie' killed pigs, sheep, and calves. She also put 'a great tubb' she used as 'a place of ease' for her household under her next-door neighbour Nathaniel Miles's kitchen wall that 'yeldeth filthie smells [especially] in the somer season'. The stink was so 'odious' that Miles's family and others living around them could not 'continew in theire howses' any longer. 'Odour', Southampton's bench commented, was always worse in hotter summer 'for infecting of the ayre'.[232]

Leona Jayne Skelton calls the 'misconception' that early moderns were indifferent to public hygiene 'the chamber pot in the window' theory.[233] Anyone in Southampton who was caught emptying a pot out of doors or windows in 1602 was fined 3s. 4d. or put in the stocks with 'a pott or tubb before them'. The fine was double this in Hereford in 1622.[234] 'Idle', 'turbulent', 'malicious and envious' Margaret Woodliffe from the same town was taken to court forty years later after she 'did very uncivily cast and throwe... stinkinge pisse out of a chamber pot' in Richard Dubbes's face. We know that Woodliffe was one of a cast of thousands who poured pisspots out of windows with little thought for anyone below or, in the words of Southampton magistrates in 1602, for 'the great indaungeringe of the infection of the ayre whereby great sicknesse may growe'.[235] But this is not grounds for generalizations about attitudes towards sanitation, for example. Many more people were offended by these 'odious' acts. Prosecutions in records are as much a measure of care for personal and community hygiene as any lack of

[230] NRO Norwich Sessions File 62/3; SA 6/1, fo. 18. See K. Wrightson, 'The decline of neighbourliness revisited', in N. Jones and D. Woolf, eds., *Local Identities in Late Medieval and Early Modern England* (Houndmills, 2007).

[231] DRO ECA C1/61, fos. 17, 19.

[232] SA 6/1, fos. 33, 16. See also DHC DC/LR/B1/9, fos. 110, 123, 135; LA CNP 3/2/1, fos. 118, 281, 326, 379, 415.

[233] Skelton, 'Environmental Regulation in Edinburgh and York', 1, 4.

[234] SA 6/1, fo. 26; HEA BG/11/17/1/4, fo. 31; BG/11/17/1/5, fo. 41. See also LA CNP 3/2/1, fo. 29.

[235] SA 6/1, fo. 26.

concern. Environmental regulation in early modern England hinged on the consent and active participation of people to a degree that would be resented today. But most people agreed on the need to maintain levels of sanitation that made life as risk-free as possible. Governors and governed, in other words, had vested interests in regulating sanitation. Effective street cleaning and 'waste disposal' required people to pitch in and work hand in hand with government-appointed scavengers to keep things 'clean'. No matter what the state of affairs in streets and lanes, few towns—or villages for that matter—lacked organized schemes to clean them.[236]

We perhaps ought to see the accumulation of 'dirt' and the operation of such schemes as defining features and tensions of early modern living. The 'decent and sweete keping' of streets was a key element of 'manifestaccon' or, in a word from Gloucester, 'government'.[237] John Evelyn was impressed by Amsterdam's 'straite, even and uniformed streets'. 'Nothing can be more pleasing', he wrote in his diary.[238] Buildings and streets were imagined together in ideas of 'beautification'. A draft parliamentary bill for 'ordering and setting the manner of buildings' in London coupled 'uniformitye in buylding' with 'beautify[ing]' streets.[239] Street-cleaning regulations can seem like comprehensive programmes for urban improvement. 'An acte for keeping clean of the streets' from Gloucester in 1645 included clauses covering 'dirte, dunge [and] other filthy matter' in high streets and 'backesides'; filth jamming channels; pigs running wild; butchers 'cast[ing] blood, dung, or garbidge' into gutters or feeding hogs with 'blood or garbidge'; dumping 'carrion' in ditches or 'water places'; and rules for taking water from 'conduits' for 'necessary use' only.[240]

The central figure was the 'comon scavenger' chosen in Winchester in 1600 for 'clenlynes, decency, and sweetnes of the ayre and avoydinge of infections which happenth by fylthie savours'. His job description was to 'clense' and 'carrye awaye' 'durte, duste, and other things' to a 'convenient place'. Householders were told to stack 'durte' and 'duste' for him to spoon into his cart.[241] George Meriton instructed scavengers to bring 'carts, dungpits or other fitting carriages' into streets each day ('except Sundays and Holy-days'), and to ring a 'clapper' or 'make a loud noise [to] give notice of their coming' so people could bring 'dust,

[236] GA TBR/A/1/2, fo. 13. See Jenner, 'Early Modern English Conceptions of "Cleanliness" and "Dirt"', chap. 3; L. J. Skelton, *Sanitation in Urban Britain, 1560–1700* (Abingdon, 2015), chap. 3; W. J. King, 'How high is too high? Disposing of dung in seventeenth-century Prescot', *Sixteenth Century Journal*, 23 (1992).

[237] GA GBR/3/2, fos. 201–2; TBR/A/1/2, fo. 13.

[238] *The Diary of John Evelyn*, ed. E.S. Beer, 6 vols (Oxford, 1955), II, 46.

[239] TNA SP 14/107/43.

[240] GA GBR/B/3/2, fos. 340–1. See also NRO Norwich Assembly Folio Minute Book 3, fos. 171v–2v, 218–18v; CKS Md/Acm1/2, fos. 175v–6; CA Z/AB/1, fo. 64v; Z/AB/2, fo. 125v; SAI C/4/3/1/1/3, fo. 120v; HEA BG/11/18; GA TBR/A/1/2, fo. 13.

[241] HA W/B1/3, fo. 132.

ashes &c' for them to collect for the 'sweete kepinge of streats'.[242] There were designated dumping grounds for 'durte' like 'the newe enlardged ballastkeye' in Yarmouth or Southampton's 'salt marsh' where it was 'cast' in 'holes [to] levell the ground'. A 'pole' was 'hung up' at each site to bury dung in Exeter in 1564 so that 'it may be knowne to everybodye... where to carrye ther dunge'.[243] Scavengers got helping hands from brother officers including beadles, 'carryers', 'cryers', carters, 'coroners of the market' in Ashby-de-la-Zouch, and 'overseer of the presentments' in Yarmouth, where 'foure able men' were picked 'to carrye away mucke and durte' to keep streets, gates, and walls 'cleane and sweete' in a plague year (1630) when 'generall complainte' was made for 'reformacon' of the streets.[244]

A big burden fell on the shoulders of householders. Southampton's 'cryer' trekked 'through ye towne' in 1569 'to proclayme [that] none doo soyle in ye streats [or] gutters'. Weymouth's 'hall bell' tolled on Saturdays to tell people to 'cleane' the streets and 'gutters before their houses [by] raking them with coler-akes and washinge with water'.[245] Infection was always on magistrates' minds. Preston council fretted that the 'want of clensing and washinge' on streets 'may procure some pestilentiall disease' in 1664. Thetford corporation asked house-holders to get rid of 'filthy mucke' outside their houses to keep 'streets and channels' clean for 'better keeping of the towne free from sicknes'.[246] The representation of a town through its streets was quite literally in householders' hands. There was a risk in this that was recognized in a 1673 Bideford by-law to improve street cleaning. Townspeople were given a week to 'sweep' their piece of the street and thirty 'fitt vessels without any head' were put in the 'leaste offensive' places to store the 'sweepinges of the streetes'. The clerk wrote 'copyes' of this order for the 'cryer' to 'publish [at] convenient places' and 'fix' in open places where people 'may better take notice' and have no excuse to 'pretend ignorance'. But governors were not confident that things would work out well. 'Forseeing' that some people 'will be apt to slight' their order, they offered rewards for information of people 'throw[ing] downe or [tumbl[ing] awaye' any 'vessell' or leaving 'filth' in streets.[247] Reports from other places suggest that they had cause for concern. The same people were presented one year after another 'for not keeping [Hereford's] stretes cleane'. Cleaning streets is 'comendable' for 'government' and 'healthfull',

[242] G. Meriton, *A Guide for Constables, Churchwardens, Overseers of the Poor, Surveyors of the Highways, Treasurers of the County Stock, Masters of House of Correction... &c* (1674), 232. See also DHC DC/PL/B/1/1/1, fo. 55; GA GBR/B/3/1, fo. 185; CKS FA/AC3, fo. 146v; NRO Y/C/19/3, fo. 50v.

[243] NRO Y/C/19/6, fo. 93v; SA 6/1, fo. 12; DRO ECA B/1/4, fo. 254. See also HA W/B1/3, fo. 10v; GA GBR/3/2, fo. 290; Bacon, *Annalls of Ipswich*, 228, 276.

[244] HL HAM box 2, folder 1, fo. 13; NRO Y/C/19/5, fo. 2; CKS FA/AC3, fo. 159v; SA 6/1, fo. 12; NRO Y/C/19/6, fos. 158v, 177. See also SA 6/1, fo. 29; HA W/B1/5, fo. 107; GA GBR/B/3/2, fos. 201–2; NRO Y/C/19/3, fo. 146v.

[245] SA 6/1, fo. 12; M. Weinstock, ed., *Weymouth and Melcombe Regis Minute Book, 1625 to 1660*, Dorset Record Society, 1 (Dorchester, 1964), 57.

[246] LA CNP 3/2/1, fo. 215; NRO T/C1/9, fo.7. See also DRO ECA B/1/3, fo. 292; CA ZAB/2, fo. 156v; LERO BR11/1/2, fo. 362; OHC C/FC/1/A1/03, fo. 128; NRO Y/C/19/3, fo, 202.

[247] NDRO 1064Q/SO1, fos. 84v–85v.

Gloucester's governors said in 1641, yet it is 'very much neglected'. For 'reformacon', 'four persons' in each ward were told to 'survey' streets each Monday and 'house-keepers' were ordered to sweep and stack 'dust and dirt' on Saturday afternoons so that it could be taken away to the 'comon myskin'.[248] Fines ranged widely from a steep ten shillings in Chester and 3s. 4d. in Tewkesbury ('especially after market') to six-pence for Dorchester residents who did not 'sufficiently swepe and cleanse' from their door to the middle of the gutter or 'kennell'.[249]

It's hard to know what proportion of people shirked cleaning duties. Complaining can seem incessant at times, but if we move from blanket condemnations the impression is one of particular trouble areas and repeat offenders. Neglect was frequently brought to light, but it is possible to read complaints as prompts to get things done. Nor did the scavengers whose job it was to clean streets always gets a good press. Gerard Malynes spoke favourably in 1603 of the 'good order observed in other countries for keeping cities and townes cleane without having so many scavengers in every parish as we do'. This blanket condemnation was too sweeping but Malynes knew London well, where complaints about scavengers were more numerous after 1600. 'Oftentymes warned and no redresse', governors in Southampton said in 1581 when 'filth and robbidge' coated the town's streets.[250] Faversham also had a tricky history with its scavengers. 'An acte for a scavenger' is in the margin of a wardmote book in 1615 next to an order noting that there was an 'abundance of durt, dunge, and sullage' on streets as there was nobody to take it to a 'convenient place'. A scavenger was chosen and locals were asked 'not to bring out dust into the streete' until the Friday after his weekly rounds. But this act was 'utterlie repealed' soon after as it did not 'worke so much [as] was expected'. The scavenger did not stick to his timetable, and 'filth and rubbish' clogged streets 'the most parte of the weeke'. A scavenger was selected 'for the markett place' in 1617 and 'jurat' Besbeech was given the task of shifting 'dunge, durt, and sullage' from the streets surrounding the market a decade later. Another scavenger lost his post in 1631. 'A newe order for a scavinger' was passed in the next year. This was a hit-or-miss record, but Faversham continued to try to organize cleaning its streets and market.[251] It was an uphill struggle there and elsewhere. The London record is a chorus of complaints about 'durte and soile' and snow and ice that made streets dirty and slippery.[252] Not many places awarded themselves high marks in this regard. Our town, Preston council said in 1655, has been 'comended for the sweete and cleane keepinge' of streets but now

[248] HEA BG11/4/6, 1661, fo. 2; 10/1662, fo. 14; 4/1663, fo. 4; 10/1664, fos. 15, 15v; 4/1665, fo. 1; 4/1666, fo. 2; 4/1667, fo. 2; GA GBR/3/2, fos. 201–2, 290.

[249] CA Z/AB/2, fo. 66v; GA TBR/A/1/2, fo. 11; DHC DC/DCB/1/1, fo. 25. See also DHC DC/PL/CB/3/5; BRO N/JQ 1/1, fo. 281; NRO T/C1/1, fo. 41; HA W/B1/3, fos. 10v–11.

[250] G. Malynes, *England's View, in the Unmasking of Two Paradoxes* (1603), 101; Jenner, 'Early Modern English Conceptions of "Cleanliness" and "Dirt"', table 3.1; SA 6/1, fo. 16.

[251] CKS FA/AC3, fos. 96v, 110v, 96v, 97v, 110v, 121v, 159v, 163v, 178v, 180v–1v.

[252] LMA Jours. 29, fo. 329v; 34, fo. 297; 36, fo. 20v.

'divers [sweep] their dunge into there channell' to the great 'disapragement of the governmente of this towne'. Scavenger Richard Osbaldtone was fined 3s. 4d. in 1664 for throwing 'fish goots and garbage in the footeway in Mr Sindells bancke goeing downe to ye washing steads'. But Preston could look back longingly to what seemed 'cleaner' times.[253]

There was not a great deal that scavengers could do about 'porckes or swyne goeing vagrant in the streets' in London or the smallest village. Maidstone was 'pestered with infecons and daungerous savours' in 1593 due to 'the 'common' 'runninge of hogges and swyne' through streets. 'Sundry former constitucons' have had little effect, governors said eleven years later.[254] 'Vagrant' hogs caused trouble in Shrewsbury (twenty-nine at one time), Lyme Regis, Ipswich, Hereford, Barnstaple, Ludlow, Preston, Hereford, Oxford (where they roamed 'in every open place'), Faversham (where in 1616 'the nusance encreasethe daylie more and more'), and other places. There are columns of offenders in some courtbooks.[255] Pigs were formidable foes. Windsor's 'cryer' walked through the town in 1668 to give 'notice to keepe hoggs out of the streets'. 'Dayly experience' led magistrates in Maidstone to tell the crier to make 'proclamacon [in] the most usuall places upon the two next markett dayes' to keep hogs from the high street and other named streets in 1645. 'Swyneheards' were chosen to 'impounde hogs running aboute the streets' and lock them in 'pynfolds' until their owners paid a fine.[256] Stray ducks, cats, and 'cowebeats' bothered streets in many towns and cities, though not in the same numbers as dogs. Six named men from Southampton and unnamed others were brought to court in 1587 for 'letting their mastyfe doggs and bitches' run 'dayly abroade in the streats withowt musseling'. The loose dogs charged at 'horsemen endaungering them with overthrowing ther horses and tearyng upp every mans dogg that passe by them', making people 'go together by the eares'.[257] Twenty Prestonians including the mayor were fined five shillings in 1665 for owning 'unruly dogs' that bred 'muche mischeefe'. Seven people from the same town ended up in trouble in 1671 for keeping 'great doggs yt doe byte some persons and are a terror to many'. A Clitheroe bailiff was fined two years in a row for the same offence.[258]

[253] LA CNP 3/2/1, fos. 38, 215.

[254] CKS Md/ACm1/1a, fos. 61–1v.

[255] SHA 3365-511; LB/11/4/82/12; DHC DC/LR/B1/9, fo. 430; Bacon, *Annalls of Ipswich*, 229, 248; HEA BG11/4/6, 4/1661, fo. 8; 4/1667, fo. 1v; NDRO B1/46/374; LA CNP 3/2/1, fos. 15, 215, 321; CKS FA/AC3, fos. 117–17v.

[256] BRO WI/FA/2, fo. 142v; CKS Md/Acm1/3, fo. 10v. For swineherds and pounds see, for example, DHC DC/PL/B/1/1/1, fo. 158; NRO Y/C/19/6, fo. 178; GA GBR/3/2, fo. 719; HEA BG11/18, unpag.; CKS Md/ACm1/2, fo. 71.

[257] SA 6/1, fo. 19. There is a different account of dogs as workers and helpers in C. Rawcliffe, 'Town tykes and butchers' hounds: urban dogs at work in the later Medieval Ages', *Medieval Prosography*, 33 (2018); and for animals more generally, and horses especially, see T. Almeroth-Williams, *City of Beasts: How Animals Shaped Georgian London* (Manchester, 2019).

[258] LA CNP 3/2/1, fos. 374, 241; MBC/201; MBC/202. See also SA 6/1, fos. 14, 25; GA TBR/A/1/2, fo. 12; BRO R/AC1/1/3, fo. 368; HA W/B1/3, fo. 132v; CA QJB/2/5, fo. 112v; Z/AB/1 fo. 109; HA W/K5/8, fo. 1; W/D3/1, fo. 177v.

We know about killing dogs and cats to stop plague in its tracks. John Jerome 'was appointed to kill the dogs [in Reading] which runne upp and downe the towne' in 1646 as a fresh crop of plague cases sharpened anxieties. A Gloucester beadle was given three-pence to buy a 'horse shoe to kyll doggs in tyme of infection' in 1638.[259] Faversham governors made it 'lawfull' to 'kill and destroy such dogs or catts as shall be found in the streets' in 1665, offering a two-pence reward for each carcass. The town appointed a 'warder' to kill dogs.[260] It was also 'lawfull' to kill or whip stray animals at any time in some places. It was 'lawfull' in Winchester to kill any unmuzzled 'bull dogg' or 'mastiffe' that was found rambling streets in 1701 'to the greate terror' of passers-by. William Astley was paid six-pence quarterly 'for whippinge ye doggs' for at least a decade in Ashby-de-la-Zouch (1626–36).[261] Yarmouth's crier walked through the streets in 1595 to proclaim that it was now 'lawfull' to kill any 'vagrant' animal on the spot for a shilling, as the town was 'greatlie annoyed with hoggs, swine, piggs, geese, and ducks [in] every parte'.[262]

The daily tread of animals and people and clutter of traffic wore down roads. There were complaints of holes and other damage and many payments in accounts 'for mendinge streets'. 'The often comminge and passinge' of wagons and carts through Minster Street in Reading that led down to the marketplace and wharfs caused 'great damages and inconveniences' in 1649 by 'reson of the narrowness of the waie' to the market. Magistrates opted to 'chain up' the lane, leaving room for only 'horses and men'.[263] Owners of 'carts and tombrills' loaded down with 'commodities' were told to follow only 'back streetes or lanes' in 1576 in Ipswich and to avoid all 'paved streetes' (this by-law was reissued in 1608 and 1621). Anyone 'comeinge' to the town in 1610 'with [a] cart or tombrell' was told to 'leade the forehorse' with a strap and to 'dryve [on] one side of the channell in the streete with the other whele [on the other] syde' to limit damage to streets and accidents.[264] Drivers and drovers were targeted when wagons and carts blocked streets, damaged houses, broke paving, and injured pedestrians (or worse). 'Postes and rayles and stones' were set up along the sides of streets in Faversham in 1611 'to keepe carriages and wagons from houses' by forcing them to pass 'neere the middle of streets'. But 'great harmes' continued and nine years later carts and wagons were banned from any street unless 'the forehoorse [was] ledd allwaies by a sufficient person'.[265] Wayward piloting by London carmen left streets 'wholly

259 BRO R/AC1/1/4, fo. 302; GA GBR/F/4/5, fo. 73.

260 CKS FA/AC4, fo. 151; FA/AZ/50. See also M. S. R. Jenner, 'The great dog massacre', in W. G. Naphy and P. Roberts, eds., *Fear in Early Modern Society* (Manchester, 1997).

261 HA W/D3/1, fo. 117v; HL HAM misc. box 12, 8/10/1626, 25/12/1631, 8/12/1633, 27/12/1634, 26/6/1636.

262 NRO Y/C/19/4, fo. 264.

263 BRO R/AC1/1/5, fo. 41.

264 Bacon, *Annalls of Ipswich*, 311, 433, 477; SAI C/2/2/2/1, fo. 272v. See also DHC DC/LR/B1/9, fo. 494; DC/LR/G/2/2, 11–1684/85.

265 CKS FA/AC3, fos. 78, 155v.

taken upp' and people ducking and weaving for safety. St Bride's parish petitioned aldermen in 1629 to stop 'the continual passage of horses, carts and carriages through Bride Lane [that] greatly annoyed and indaungered [people and left] pavements much torne and pulled upp'. Carts were banned from 'any rowe, streat or other places within the walls' in Yarmouth in 1614 after 'much hurte hath beene donne to youth and children and the elder sort'.[266] Streets sometimes remained out of repair for a frustratingly long time. The entire Lyme Regis 'corporacon' was 'presented' an awkward number of times in the years after the Restoration 'for not repayringe' streets. This 'neglect' was harmful for what Southampton governors called 'civil government'.[267] Things could always be better. Preston bailiffs were tasked in 1653 to repair streets and pavements 'soe farre forth' than 'their predecesors have been accustomed to repaire the same'.[268]

Like streets, people were expected to take care of pavements in front of their doors, but their perceived casual attitude led to calls in London to hire contractors in the second half of the seventeenth century. 'It is a matter of wonder to all travellers' to see London's 'vast riches' and 'beautiful structures', a parliamentary lobbyist said in making the case for paving legislation around 1700. 'And yet', he carried on, streets 'lie deformedly paved and unwholesomely dirty'. If this was 'remedied', he continued, it would improve the 'healthfulness and beauty of the city'. 'Professional' paviors should take over paving, he ended; only then would streets be 'kept neat'.[269] An 'Acte for Pavyng Stretes' in Norwich in 1569 mentioned older golden days when 'good howseholders' took their responsibility to 'mayntayn' pavements seriously, but now 'paving [was in] decaye and broken to the greate discomodyte and annoyance [of] neybors [and] disworshipp [of] majestrats'.[270] Steps were taken to improve things but complaints reverberated for the next 150 years. Residents were often at fault—seventy at one time in Maidstone in 1656—but local governments bore the burden by forking out large sums at times on 'workemanshipp about paveing'. Windsor corporation spent £39 2s. to pave the 'markett howse' in 1638, 'beinge 1342 feete at viid a foote'. Gloucester dug deep to spend £30 16s. on paving in 1645 and £39 12s. 4d. fifteen years later. It cost modest-sized Faversham £3 17s. 1d. 'for pavyng of the towne' in 1571.[271]

[266] LMA Rep. 43, fo. 266; Jour. 30, fo. 358; NRO Y/C/19/5, fo. 141. See also LMA Jours. 36, fos. 197v, 277v; 41, fos. 103, 103v–4.

[267] DHC DC/PL/CB/3/8; DC/LR/B1/9, fos. 340, 449, 477, 494, 520; SA 6/1, fo. 12.

[268] LA CNP 3/2/1, fos. 23, 35.

[269] *Considerations Humbly Offered to…Knights, Citizens and Burgesses in Parliaments Assembled Shewing the Necessity and Benefitt of Act of Parliament to Incorporate a Certain Select Number of Persons for the More Beautiful and Useful Paving and Cleansing the Streets in the Cities of London and Westminster* (1700?).

[270] NRO Norwich Assembly Folio Minute Book 3, fo. 157.

[271] CKS Md/JLP1/1656; BRO WI/FA1/2, fos. 11v–12v; GA GBR/F/4/5, fos. 310, 433, 454v–5; CKS FA/FAC1-2, document 15. See also CA Z/AB/1, fo. 240v; DRO ECA B/1/3, fo. 383; HA W/B1/3, fo. 63.

A 'channel' or 'kennel' ran down the middle of streets with slopes that tilted down from pavements so 'filth' could move to 'comon' sewers. Blockage was just one potential issue. Stench drifting from choked 'kennels' was another, as well as the people who tipped waste into them. Preston took action against people in 1653 who 'comonlie sweepe myre from before their doors [into] the chanell'. People were caught sweeping 'dunge into ther channell to the disparagment of the governmente of this towne' two years later.[272] 'Many complaints' flooded in a decade later from the 'inhabitants of ye lower ende of Friergate' in Preston that people living at the top of the slope 'doe commonly sweepe myre from before their dores [into] ye channell [and] leave it on heapes' that trickled down to the homes below. After 'the next great fall of rain', they added, the streets in 'the lower part [of the town would quickly be] overflone' with water and muck.[273] There are similar reports from other parts of the country. A 'generall annoyance' that was brought to the attention of magistrates in Maidstone in 1650 was caused by people sweeping 'straw, dirt, and sullage into the gutters or kennells of streets whereby [it was said] the cleer passage of raine water and other waste water is hindered and corrupted'.[274] A dozen people were taken to task in Poole in 1680 'for laying ashes [to] the great damage of the channell and stopping the watercourse', which, they were sternly reminded, is 'the onely watercourse for clensing the streets there'. 'Filthy' gutters were an eyesore that made people in Southampton and elsewhere cover their noses as dirty and stinking 'waters' trickled through waste on the way to sewers.[275]

Again, my aim here is not to call Southampton or anywhere else for that matter dirty or insanitary. That is not a judgment that we can make with our altered understandings, technologies, and ready-made solutions on shop shelves. Physical and cultural sanitation is a relative matter in time and place. Ideas of 'manifestaccon' and its discontents are what bring me to these materials. Pursuing 'manifestaccon' was in effect government/governance from one day to the next, and there were never any guarantees. Material and ecological events made sure of that, amongst other things. We have one more place left to visit and that is the market square. People poured into this large space to shop and bump into friends for a chat. There was a lot going on; more than anywhere else.

IV

The market was the heart and hub of a town; the most 'publique' place to be seen where several things were always going on at once. It was the site for celebration,

[272] LA CNP 3/2/1, fos. 38, 15, 24. [273] Ibid., fo. 251. [274] CKS Md/Acm1/2, fo. 175v.

[275] DHC DC/PL/CB/3/4; J. W. Horrocks, ed., *The Assembly Book of Southampton*, 4 vols, Southampton Record Society, 9 (Southampton, 1917–25), I, 84.

commemoration, punishment, or proclamation. Bonfires burned and bells rang for good news. A Norwich vintner got £6 16s. in 1623 'for a hoggshead of wyne laid at the market crosse and drunke by the captaines [and] their companyes makeing shewe of joy and triumph for the safe return of Prince Charles from Spayne'.[276] Bonfires blazed in Gloucester for proclamations of monarchs, coronations, St George's Day, news that the king had got over a bout of sickness, and 'good news [of] Monmouth being taken'. Bells 'rang for joy' in Norwich after Monmouth was crushed at Sedgemoor and 'a loade of woode' was picked up 'for a bonfyre in ye market place at ye usual place'.[277] Wrongdoers were whipped in and around markets and 'odious' things put to the flames like the 'thirty scandalous ballets' that Alexander Lawes was singing and selling in Norwich in edgy 1642.[278] 'Popish relicts' were put to the flames in New Malton in 1656 and 'popish pictures' in Norwich market in 1644. Markets were fitting spots to burn 'naughty and corrupt hops', 'corrupt meat', 'corrupt herring and fishe', and other rotting food.[279] Market squares were places to put on a show. Lazarus Colleretto arrived in Norwich in 1639 with 'leave' from 'his majesties owne hande to shewe a monster'. Humphrey Bromly got 'libertie' 'to shew [a] strange child with two heads [for] two dayes' in 1616 but was 'forbidden to sound any drumme to drawe company [except for] hangynge up of a picture of [the] child'.[280] There were many more such shows in the final third of the seventeenth century. Dutchman Henry Fisher made 'shew of a litle dwarfe of 37 yeares of age with musicke' for a fortnight in 1688. Folk lined up to see 'a child with six fingers on each hand and six toes on each foot' ('for 14 daies'), 'a monstrous man with two bodys from the Indies', 'a monstrous man taken amongst the hills of Carthinia [who] feeds on roots of trees', 'dauncing beares with trumpets and musique', 'a wonderful monster in the likenes of a lyons whelpe', and 'exotic' fish, elephants, camels, tigers, jackals, and porcupines.[281] 'Artificiall figures called poppets' also drew crowds (with 'waterworkes' sometimes). Matthew Fawes thrilled people with 'figures in waxworke and three livinge turks'. The more scientific-minded enjoyed looking at 'a philosophicall lampe'. If there was a preference for something lighter, touring shows came to town including 'a show called fair rosamond and hocus pocus' and 'a play acted by figures called Englands Glory or The Protestants Welfare with musicke and fower servants'.[282]

[276] NRO Norwich Chamberlains' Accounts 1603–25, fo. 399v.

[277] GA GBR F/4/6, fo. 479; F/4/7, fos. 97, 352, 354, 355; NRO NMCC 25, fo. 186.

[278] NRO NMCC 20, fo. 368.

[279] J. C. Atkinson, ed., *North Riding Quarter Sessions Records*, 9 vols, North Riding Record Society 1–9 (1884–92), V, 220–1; NRO NMCC 20, fo. 415. See also HL EL 2178; NA NQS2, fo. 43; WSHC G22/1/205/2, fo. 19v.

[280] NRO NMCC 20, fo. 266v; 15, fo. 71v.

[281] NRO NMCC 23, fos. 216v, 217v; 24, fos. 80v, 139v, 161, 237, 338v, 360v, 371; 25, fos. 5v, 11, 35v, 164v, 209v, 213, 232, 260, 300v, 315; 26, fos. 21, 39, 62v.

[282] NRO NMCC 24, fos. 116v, 161, 161v, 162, 193v, 301v; 25, fos. 210v, 227, 286, 290, 294v; 26, fos. 5v, 38, 38v, 68v, 73v.

We can imagine applause, laughter, shrieks, and gasps, although all 'shewes' were supposed to be 'civil'. 'Showmen' were told to 'keepe good howers and orders' and behave 'well' or 'civilly'. There was also a trend (like shifting whipping indoors) towards moving shows away from the market to alehouses like the King's Head, Red Lion, Blue Bell, and the Angel 'in the market' where 'hairy Mrs Francis Owen [got] leave to shew herselfe' for one week. Joseph Farel had a week there in 1689 'to show himselfe being 8 foot high with musick'.[283] A 'mountebank' was told to move his stage to the backside' of the Blue Bell in 1693 as he was not 'fitting' for 'public' show. 'Mountebanks' set up stages 'to sell medicinal druggs and performe chirugicall cures' and 'manuall operations' so long as they behaved 'civily' without disrupting trade or 'the use of the pump'. James Kindman had licence to set up 'a stage in ye market' to sell 'medicinall compositions' for two weeks over Christmas 1686, but we read two pages later in the same courtbook that he was banned from 'the markett or any other public place'. Some ballad singers were also given 'leave' to sing and sell ballads, but only if they 'behaved themselves civilly' (at the pump in one case).[284]

A 'civil' market was a requirement for a well-run town. Government proclamations were read 'openly' in halls, churches, or landmarks like Lyme Regis's Cobb.[285] But markets were more likely venues. Proclamations were read aloud in 'the full of the markett' or when a market was 'at the highest'. I will do it 'with the greatest exaltation of my voice that I coulde and with my harts joy and comfort', Southampton's clerk promised when James I was 'proclaymed' in 'the open markett'.[286] James II was 'proclaimed' in '8 places' in Cambridge: '1st at the great market crosse, and on the same marketplace betweene the conduit and rose taverne'. A proclamation voicing horror at 'the great profanation of the lord's day in 1691' was read 'in market time' across the North Riding and pinned up 'in the most open and fit place for view and reading'.[287] Proclamations were 'cryed' at the symbolic stone of crosses. News of an upcoming parliamentary election was read 'publiquelie at the cross' in Windsor in Restoration year, 'beinge the auntient place of publication'.[288] Wedding banns were also 'published' at crosses. Ellen Younge and Lawrence Jackson were able 'to proceed to marriage' in 1656 after their banns were 'published three times at the markett cross of Stoaxley'. 'A lying

[283] NRO NMCC 25, fos. 192, 193, 206v, 229v, 237v, 257, 299v, 330v; 26, fo. 20v.

[284] NRO NMCC 25, fos. 42, 210, 212, 227, 244, 264, 272v, 300, 339v.

[285] DHC DC/LR/D/1/1, fo. 2. See also NRO Y/C/19/5, fo. 136v; HA W/B1/3, fo. 125v; SA 6/1, fo. 29; CKS H/FAC/1, fo. 5; BRO N/JQ/1/1, fo. 243.

[286] Horrocks, *Assembly Books of Southampton*, I, 32. See also BRO R/AC1/1/7, fo. 82; WSHC G22/1/107. fo. 101.

[287] Foster, *Diary of Samuel Newton*, 88; Atkinson, *North Riding Quarter Sessions Records*, VII, 124. See also ESBHRO RYE 1/5, fo. 50v; CKS TE/JQC/1, fo. 6; NRO T/C1/1, fo. 2v; C. Kyle, 'Monarch and marketplace: proclamations as news in early modern England', *Huntington Library Quarterly*, 78 (2015).

[288] BRO WI/AC1/1, fo. 10.

and scandalous pamphlet entituled a true account from Chichester [of] the death of Habin the informer' was 'publiquely burned at the high crosse' there in 1682.[289] Proclamations were nailed on posts 'in the most publique places' where 'they can be seen'. An order banning tying boats to Whitby bridge was 'proclaimed' in the market and 'fixed' on the bridge 'so that all persons may take notice'. Windsor spent ten-pence 'for deal boards and nails for proclamacons' in 1657. Edward Cheetham got ten shillings 'for proclayming 32 proclamacons from the king' in Manchester in 1629.[290]

People with scores to settle appropriated the symbolism of crosses to 'proclaim' adversaries. Anne Dawson told Doncaster magistrates in 1687 that Grace Best sent her children to her house to 'challenge' a 'goose', with her husband walking behind them calling her thief and shouting that he would 'proclaim her a thief at the market cross'.[291] 'Sir Phil Honywood would never be governor of Portsmouth', barber John Thorne told Walter Hartford in 1663. He was 'cashiered in Charles I's time for being a coward', he continued, fled to Barbados to scratch a living as 'a poor planter', and back in England wormed his way into the 'favour' of a lady at court and Sir Charles Berkeley, who helped him become deputy governor of the port. 'The king was sorry that he had knighted him thinking he was another brother', Thorne said, and he is now known as 'the mistaken knight'. Hartford asked 'how he dare such words'; Thorne said he would 'justify them at the market cross'.[292] Proclamation posts were pulled down in Tombland next to Norwich Cathedral. Robert Griffin was 'well' whipped in 1598 'for cursinge' anyone in London who put 'the acte of parliamente for punishinge of rogues' in place and for bad-mouthing a deputy for 'settinge up a post by the conduite in Cheape' to hang up the 'rogues' act.[293] Others took issues into their own hands and pulled proclamations off posts. A 'vagabond' was locked up in London in 1560 for 'pullinge downe the maiours proclamacons'. Some London grocers met the day after a 1617 royal proclamation was made public allowing apothecaries to leave the Grocers' Guild and set up on their own. They vowed to rip up papers on walls or posts or any other 'public place' that authorized this split. Colchester barber William Lawrence glanced 'into the streete' on a 'bright mone lyghte' night in 1624 and saw a man 'take of from posts against the Red Rose twoe proclamacons that had been nailed upp that daye'. Stepping outside 'to see whoe it was [as he]

[289] S. C. Ratcliff and H. C. Johnson, eds., *Warwick County Records*, 9 vols (Warwick, 1935–64), IV, 189–90; Atkinson, *North Riding Quarter Sessions Records*, V, 205; ESBHRO QO/EW8, fo. 102; SAI HD36/A/319.

[290] Atkinson, *North Riding Quarter Sessions Records*, VI, 63; BRO WI/FA1/2, fo. 104; Earwaker, *Constables Accounts*, I, 233. See also DHC DC/CC/4/6; LMA Rep. 61, fo. 4v; NA NQS/4, fo. 35; BRO WI/FA/2, fo. 103; CKS Md/Acm1/2, fo. 62; HEA Q/SM/2, fo. 75v; Masters, *Chamber Accounts*, 89–90.

[291] *A Calendar to the Records of the Borough of Doncaster*, 4 vols (Doncaster, 1899–1902), III, 113.

[292] A. J. Willis and M. J. Hoad, eds., *Portsmouth Record Series: Borough Sessions Papers 1653–1688* (Chichester, 1971), 28.

[293] NRO Norwich Chamberlains' Accounts 1589–1602, fo. 7v; BMM BHCC 4, fo. 24v.

crost by the cage', Lawrence told justices later that he had 'a long lether apron on'. He shadowed the mystery figure with 'his cloake cast over his face soe far as old Peter Beaks house downe North Hill': I 'suspecte it to be Jacob Beake [Lawrence said] rather for his lether apron'.[294]

Others altered the meanings of political posts with their own words and images. A salter's apprentice got in trouble in London in 1612 for 'contemptuously' drawing 'a picture of a gallous and a man hanging' on a proclamation pinned up 'publickely on a post at Queenhithe' for 'the good of the citie'. A bookseller was paraded for a humiliating hour in Cheapside in 1607 for selling four-year-old proclamations and pinning up a fake one 'towching the earle of Tihrone whereby manie people were abused', and 'false reports' spread like wildfire.[295] Knowing that posts grabbed attention, people nailed libels to them. London coal dealer Walter Archibald told the Star Chamber that a Newcastle trader plotted to wreck 'his good name and credit' with a 'most vile and false libel' that he nailed to a post near Billingsgate Market, 'where most merchants for coals daily repair', so that it was 'better viewed and noted of all men'.[296] London Common Council was disturbed in 1640 to hear that libels had been fixed to posts and 'scattered' along streets. William Bray was punished in 1619 'for writinge certayne papers and fixing them on the piller of the Exchange and other places'.[297] While John Cutler had some explaining to do after he 'gathered up a writing [by Hereford market house in 1608] containing a libel which was throwne downe by a welshe man'. He 'showed yt to noe man until this tyme', he told magistrates, adding that 'the welsh man told him [that] it fell from the post of the market howse as he passed by'.[298]

It was a hard task to keep marketplaces 'comely' and 'sweet'. They needed constant attention, with shoppers clogging narrow walkways and stalls packed with food. There are stories of left-over rotting food and putrid puddles as trading days drew to an end. Householders living 'within the compasse' of the 'fyshe markett' in Exeter in 1569 were told to 'cleanse' streets on market days before 4 p.m. People living in 'ye high streete' by Ashby-de-la-Zouch market were told to 'sweep streets every weeke' and 'carry' filth to 'ye hill top'.[299] Market regulations sometimes stretched over two or more pages, covering everything from the location of stalls to the times to ring bells to start and finish buying and selling. ('The ringer of the market bell at the standard in Cheap' in London picked up 8s. 8d. for a year's ringing in 1585.)[300] Market officers tried to make sure that shoppers and traders toed

[294] LBHC 1, fo. 75v; TNA STAC8 26/1; ERO D/B5/SB2/7, fo. 96.

[295] LMA Reps. 30, fo. 317; 28, fo. 105v.

[296] TNA STAC8 41/12. See also TNA SP 12/15/39, 12/60/49, 16/72/45; LMA Reps. 15, fo. 129; 20, fo. 137; 21, fo. 407v; 22, fos. 97, 259v; 23, fos. 191v, 418; 28, fo. 105v; 34, fo. 195v; Jour. 40, fo. 69; LBHC 2, fo. 104v.

[297] LMA Jours. 39, fo. 84v; 40, fo. 69; Reps. 30, fo. 317; 20, fo. 137; 22, fos. 97, 259v; 24, fo. 195v.

[298] HEA BG/11/17/1/4, fo. 11. See also NRO NMCC 25, fo. 187v.

[299] DRO ECA B/1/3, fo. 292; HL HAM box 2, folder 1, fo. 7v.

[300] Masters, *Chamber Accounts*, 18.

the line. Clitheroe appointed 'market lookers'. Kendal forked out sixteen-pence in 1596 'for lokinge to good order in meale marketts'. Marlborough paid 'a poore man' eight-pence in 1627 'for warding on markett day'.[301] Good order and sanitation are coupled in ideas important for representation. Reading market's 'clenser' got two shillings 'wekely' in 1608. Chester's '2 beedles' were paid £1 5s. quarterly in 1696 'for cleansing the market place'. Manchester's 'sciensses' (cleaners) were told to 'cleane ye marketplace once a weeke especiallye aboute ye crosse, stocks, and cadge'.[302] 'One pynte [of] every quarter of corne' that was brought to Maidstone market 'by any forrenor' was put 'towards the [cost of cleaning] the corne crosse and markett place' in 1585. It was the job of the scavenger to clean 'aboute the butter cross and whole market place' in Preston in 1639.[303] Markets took up a sizeable portion of annual expenditure. Windsor's financial accounts show the town paying a great deal of attention to its market house in 1638–40, with payments for amongst other things 'workemannshipp about paveing the markett howse beinge 1342 feete at viid a foote' in 1638 (£39 2s. 10d.); fetching rubbish (2s.); iron work (£3 17s. 9d.); painting rails, doors, and posts (£1 6s.); keys, locks, and hinges (£1 1d.); more paving (£1 17s. 4d.); and ten shillings for sweeping around the market house and opening and shutting its door for one year.[304]

Money could not solve everything. That was the nature of the task at hand. It was always ongoing, seen in Reading by the persistent complaint about 'soile arising weekly in and about the market place'. Reading magistrates 'sent for' scavenger Philip Smith in 1652 to 'reprehend' him 'for permitting the market place to lye soe foule'. He 'promised to amend the same' but was 'reproved' one year later for 'not keeping cleane the market place': he again pledged 'for the future to amend what is remisse'.[305] Preston Corporation was not pleased to hear that George Werden was 'verie negligent in his dutie' in 1653, leaving the market 'uncleansed' for the 'most parte of the weeke'. A Northallerton grocer was taken to task in 1676 'for making a heap of manure and dirt in the market', one of many who appear in records for dirtying markets with 'rubbidge' and 'filthe and dounge'.[306]

301 LA MBC/163; KAC WSMB/K/1/5, 1595/6; WSHC G22/1/205/2, fo. 65v. See also BRO WI/A1/2, fo. 149; NDRO B1/3792, fo. 80; DHC DC/LR/2/2; CKS FA/AC4, fos. 163–3v; SAI C/3/4/1/21, fo. 5.

302 BRO R/FA/3/2; CA TAB/1/84; J. E. Earwaker, ed., *The Court Leet Records of the Manor of Manchester, From the Year 1552 to the Year 1686, and From the Year 1731 to the Year 1846*, 12 vols (Manchester, 1884–90), II, 163.

303 CKS Md/Acm1/1a, fo. 56; LA CNP 3/1/1, fo. 29. See also CA TAB/1, fo. 99; BRO R/FA2/80; R/AC1/1/5, fo. 88; DHC DC/LR/G/2/2, 1587–8.

304 BRO WI/FA/1/2, fos. 11v, 12, 12v, 21v. See also Bacon, *Annalls of Ipswiche*, 60.

305 J. M. Guilding, ed., *Reading Records: Diary of the Corporation*, 4 vols (Oxford, 1886), II, 166, 268; IV, 133, 499; BRO R/AC1/1/5, fos. 137, 180.

306 LA CNP 3/2/1, fo. 13; Atkinson, *North Riding Quarter Sessions Records*, VI, 251. See also CKS Md/ACm1/1a, fo. 37v; LA MBC/211, 211a, 213.

Loose animals were another concern. Untethered horses caused problems in Manchester, along with hogs running around stalls. A 'jebbit' built in the market to punish soldiers 'in the tyme of war' was pulled down in 1651 because it blocked traffic and trading. Reading governors and marketgoers were fed up with daily 'annoyaunces' caused by 'swyne goeinge in the streetes and market places' in 1633.[307] 'Swyne, great and small' were banned from going anywhere near markets. 'Informacons have come before us', Preston governors said in 1665, from 'persons of good rank and quality [and] of our owne knowledge', about 'swine pulling mens sackes in peeces' on market days. 'All owners of swine' were asked to 'keepe them up on market day'.[308] Other obstacles in and around the market included stones, guns, and a 'bulke' that was 'nere the crosse' in Norwich.[309] Reading constables rushed to the scene on hearing in 1631 about 'cudgell playeinge in the markett place' and that players were trampling on wheat that was even more precious in that lean year. Witnesses said that one of them lunged at an officer 'with the hiltes of cudgills', calling him a 'coxcom'.[310] A Devizes man was taken 'before mr mayor and his brothers' in 1580 for 'wordes' that he spoke 'openly [in] ye market to Walter', telling him that the mayor was 'the fyrste breker of orders hyme sellfe'. Reports from other markets show officers doing their best to deal with people squabbling, trading punches, 'gameing or playeinge with dice', 'troublinge market folke', 'mysusing' officers, 'throwing stones, chucking chickens', and much more besides.[311]

Markets were garnished with symbolism, but crosses representing civic 'fame' were focal points that were by no means immune from reverse 'manifestaccon'. Governors noted that the 'covering' on Maidstone's fish cross had 'run much to ruine' in 1685 and passed an order 'that it bee forthwith covered with lead'. The cross in one Hertfordshire town was 'so much out of repayre [in 1670] that the market people [could not] sit under it as formerly without danger of their lives'. People were fined for hanging clothes on Leicester's cross in 1584.[312] There were complaints from all parts of the country about spilt beans, peas, malt, and other 'victuals' 'fowlinge' marketplaces and crosses, including one from Preston not long after the 'butter cross' had been 'handsomely rebuilt'.[313] Any offence

[307] Earwaker, *Court Leet Records of the Manor of Manchester*, I, 177, 260; II, 78, 89, 92, 93; IV, 64; BRO R/AC1/3, fo. 251; Guilding, *Reading Records*, III, 180.

[308] LA CNP 3/2/1, fo. 248.

[309] HEA BG11/4/6, 1663, fo. 12v; KAC WSSMB/K/2/5, fos. 6, 39, 40v, 54v, 79, 82v, 89, 104v, 105, 106v; NRO Norwich Assembly Folio Minute Book 5, fo. 94.

[310] Guilding, *Reading Records*, II, 75.

[311] B. H. Cunnington, ed., *Some Annals of the Borough of Devizes*, 2 vols (Devizes, 1925–6), 76. See also NRO NMCC 20, fo. 282; BRO R/AC1/2, fo. 95; OHC C/FC/1/A1/01, fo. 356; DHC DOB/8/1, fo. 142v; Williamson, *Social Relations and Urban Space*, chaps 4–5; Griffiths, *Lost Londons*, 127–8.

[312] CKS Md/ACm1/3, fo. 265; W. J. Le Hardy, ed., *Hertford County Records: Notes and Extracts from the Sessions Rolls, 1581–1850*, 2 vols (Hertford, 1905), I, 221; LERO BRII/1/2, fo. 382.

[313] LA CNP 3/1/3, fo. 51. See also CKS Md/ACm1/1, fos. 25v, 73; NRO T/C1/2, fo. 221; NA 3/1, fo. 347; SAI C/3/41/35; WSHC G22/1/205/2, fos. 14v, 18v.

committed around a town cross was sharpened by its symbolic freight. London vagrants Anne White and Anne Webb were whipped in Bridewell in the first week of 1631 after they were caught 'abuseinge the place where the lord maior setts att the crosse by theire nastynes'. Norwich's waits were 'suspended from their imployments' in 1683 'for playeinge at the crosse in ye markett [without] Mr Mayors lycence or privity'. John Parnell from the same city was 'whipped at the poast' in 1646 for walking from Ber Street 'into the market place aboute the crosse in the open day time naked'. Robert Greene landed in trouble after he 'mysused Lawrence Hodgson openly at the [same] crosse [in 1564] callyng hym knave' and other 'opprobrious words'.[314]

The last thing any magistrate wanted was 'a hott markett'. Matthew Lynsey told Norwich aldermen that he heard George Fowler 'say in the hearing [of] others [in the market in 1634] that he had taken farthinge tokens for his worke' and did not have enough to buy food. If officers 'woulde not take him', he threatened, he would go back to the market with 'halfe a score more [and] make some stirre'. Questioned later, he admitted saying to shoppers around him 'that yf farthings would not goe in the markett yt woulde be a hott markett'.[315] Abuse given out 'manifestly' in markets was taken extremely seriously because of the sensitive location and potential for large audiences. We know that riots rocked markets when grain was in short supply and people wanted a 'reasonable price' in words from Barnstaple. Lyme Regis market was not the only one to be swamped by an 'inordinate number of badgers, malsters, millers and other ingrossers of corne' who hoarded grain to drive up prices 'before the full of the markett'.[316] Markets were natural places to let off steam when cupboards were bare. Norwich worsted-weaver John Cobb was locked in the cage in 1551 for 'speking of sedycous wordes in the open markett att the crosse', telling 'many persons' that 'the poore can bye no corne there for the ryche chorles take it from them'.[317] Dorchester widow Anne Samways ended up in court in 1630 after she 'call[ed] to a man to sell her some wheat'. When he told her that it had been sold, she 'replyed [with marketgoers listening] that yf they were served aright they should be served as they were in France to cut holes in their baggs for that they sold all to the millers'. Markets were obvious places for the poor to voice their basic entitlement to subsistence.[318]

Markets were one of the few legitimate places for crowds to gather, but with risks. Crowds drew beggars, street sellers, cheats, and thieves on the lookout for

[314] LBHC 7, fo. 210; NRO NMCC 25, fo. 134v; 20, fo. 484v; 8, fo. 193. See also Earwaker, *Court Leet Records of the Manor of Manchester*, IV 257; V, 81, 115; VI, 25, 74; LA MBC/201.

[315] NRO Norwich Sessions Book 1630–8, fo. 44v; NMCC 15, fo. 71v.

[316] NDRO B1/3792, fo. 166; DHC DC/LR/B7/A4/2.

[317] NRO NMCC 6, fo. 98.

[318] DHC DC/DOB/8/1, fo. 46. See also NDRO B1/3792, fos. 188, 274; CKS Md/Acm1/3, fo. 8v; BRO R/JQ/1/1, fos. 18, 133; NRO NMCC 9, fo. 95; OHC C/FC/1/A1/01, fo. 356; J. Walter, *Crowds and Popular Politics in Early Modern England* (Manchester, 2006); A. Randall, *Riotous Assemblies: Popular Protest in Hanoverian England* (Oxford, 2006), chaps 4–5.

opportunities. Word sometimes spread that 'there was a pickepockett around' in a market. Londoner Christopher Lusher was called a 'dayly pickpocket in markets' and earmarked for a ship for Virginia. Katherine Waller was 'noted' to be a 'market pickepockett'. Thomas Gently gave London Bridewell Court the names of seventeen 'pickepurses' in 1560 that he had seen 'many tymes in many fayres and markets'. Countless thieves snatched things from stalls and made a run for it with wheat, meat, meal, gloves, handkerchiefs, cheese, books, and much else. Samuel Pepys looked on sniffily as a 'silly jade' grabbed a piece of mutton from a stall in Leadenhall Market.[319]

People haggling over prices or bumping into friends were sitting ducks for sharp-witted cutpurses. Colchester joiner George Hemming plunged into a 'throng of morrys dancers' to cut purses in the market in 1592.[320] We have good snapshots of cutpurses trying to get a shot at pockets in the same market. John Davis caught Francis Reynolds's eye as he 'drew neare' to one Everett 'as if he would put his hand' in his pocket as he got out his purse to pay for wheat in 1639. Everett turned away in the nick of time, but Reynolds told others and 'bade them take notice of [Davis] and observe what he did'. They agreed that he 'looks like a pickepurse' and someone bet six-pence that he would try for 'Kemptons purse' next as he was 'looking earnestlie' at him as he 'changed' cash. Davis 'drewe neare' to Kempton who was 'bissie in shottinge out his corne' and 'turned up the lappe [of his coat] and slilie put his hand' in his pocket, pulling out 'a lynnen bagge'. He got as far as 'two or three steppes' before people pounced and handed him over to officers.[321] Colchester husbandman John Tooley told justices in 1641 that he was shopping in the 'cornemarkett' and 'as hee walked there hee was followed up and downe' by 16-year-old Kettering 'spinster' Jane Kelley. 'She came so neere', he said, 'that she tread upon his heeles and hee asked her what she meant to tread upon him and shoved her from him'. Without saying a word she 'still followed him as close as she could' before finally leaving Tooley alone. But 'hee having formerlie lost his purse did thinke of his purse and put his hand into his pocket and felt for his purse' but it was 'gone' with 21s. 5d. in it. He looked for Kelley but she had slipped away.[322] Other stories from Colchester and elsewhere tell how thieves 'went into the crowd' jostling and 'jogginge' shoppers, scooping pennies and pounds. Edye Holding had a red-letter day (she thought) in 1629 when she eased 'a purse out of a man's pocket in the corne markett' in Colchester, netting 'two eleven shilling peeces of gold'. She told justices that 'shee hath used picking of purses' for four years 'ever since her owne father dyed'.[323]

[319] ERO D/B5/SB2/9, fo. 246; LBHC 1, fo. 91; 8, fos. 60, 175v, 227v; *Diary of Samuel Pepys*, IX, 285. See also NRO NMCC 13, fo. 436; DHC DOB/8/1, fos. 189, 276v, 343; Guilding, *Reading Records*, III, 98; LBHC 6, fos. 60, 375; 7, fo. 308; 8, fo. 410; LMA CQSF 109/17.

[320] ERO D/B5/SB2/5, fos. 150v–1.

[321] ERO D/B5/SB2/7, fos. 148v–9.

[322] Ibid., fos. 263, 264.

[323] ERO D/B5/SB2/6, fo. 36. See also ERO D/B5/SB2/5, fo. 223v; D/B5/SB2/7, fos. 162v, 262v; NRO NMCC 9, fo. 410; BRO R/AC1/1/2, fos. 9, 105; LMA WJ/SR/NS/34/125.

V

Edye Holding's alternative idea of markets as likely spots to dip into pockets was the opposite of how magistrates or 'observators' saw them. For them they were urbane spaces in 'the hart of the towne' for 'civill government', and the 'publique good'. This was the intrinsic tension with 'manifestaccon' in a world of 'continuall seeing'. There was always a chance that someone might do wrong or something go wrong in a 'publique concourse of people' or hearing of a 'popular auditorie'. This inherent tension is seen in counter-vocabularies of 'manifestaccon': 'sweet', 'clean', 'helthy', 'stately', 'orderly', 'civil', 'filthy', 'fowle', 'unsemlye', 'uncivil', 'disworship', 'noisome'.

There has been plenty of negativity in this chapter, but all of this has been to a purpose: not to evaluate whether a town was clean or if its various rituals worked, but the impacts of these things and much else on the forms and functions of 'manifestaccon'. It is entirely legitimate therefore to draw attention to the consequences of 'filthy thinges' or ragged walls for representing authority for what in London was called 'the honour and creditt of the citty'.[324] The other side to dark clouds were high expectations of standards of sanitation and representation. 'Manifestaccon' mattered for 'civil government' and conversely for 'the disworshipp [of] majestrats'. It was a continuous process and its abiding uncertainty (or aspirational tendencies) helped to define the nature of local government. It cannot be said to have been either a failure or success, but little was ever resolved to the full satisfaction of magistrates. 'Manifestaccon' was pursued and remained in the making. Governors worked hard to 'beautify' their piece of England and address sanitation and public health. They gave 'ornaments' a fresh lick of paint, patched up holes in walls, and took one anti-'manifestaccon' act after another to court (these cases can be read as a guide to flaws, as well as intentions and expectations). They kept on going, doing what they had to do to try to make 'manifestaccon' work.

'Manifestaccon' was a technology as well as an idea. it was the sum of its working parts. These parts needed replacing, cleaning, even oiling. They broke down and some were thrown away. Rust was beginning to set in. Most of these working parts are not with us today, and if they are, we will find them in museums (or somewhere else educational or archival) or they no longer have the partisan political significances of 400 years or so ago. The origins and first stages of these long-term transformations are in the sixteenth and seventeenth centuries.

The punishment of petty crime in front of a 'publique concourse' in a market square or elsewhere was one of the most compelling pieces of 'manifestaccon'. These sharp public shocks were ubiquitous. Each one of England's towns and

[324] LMA Jours. 31, fo. 273; 34, fos. 297, 311.

villages should have had a whipping post and a pair of stocks. These punishments were one of life's routines, but their effectiveness came under close critical scrutiny. This questioning had consequences for 'manifestaccon' broadly speaking and for 'the turn inside' in particular. A sharp quizzical eye was trained on the nuts and bolts of public punishment and 'outward conformity' more generally. The next chapter turns to the forms and functions of punishing petty crime out in the 'open', where a whipper waits to whip another vagrant on a lively market day.

3
Punishment

All punishments are documents to teach us.

Z. Bogan, *A View of the Threats and Punishments Recorded in the Scriptures Alphabetically Composed* (1653), 520

'Whipper' was not a high-end career path, but it was steady work and put food on the table. For someone not born with a silver spoon in his mouth the job had ties to government made visible in coats decorated with eye-catching marks of authority. Barnaby Langdon was Norwich's whipper in the rocky 1590s. We see his footsteps in accounts where he is listed as a payment. He was often paid in batches: 'xv vagabonds' (1593: 2s. 6d.), 'correcting xviii' (1595: 3s. 2d.), 'xii correccons and makinge of a pytt to burye fylth taken out of the comen gayle' (1599: 2s. 9d.), 'xxii correccons' (1600: 3s. 8d.), 'xxtie correccons' (1600: 3s. 4d.). Barnaby also pocketed fees for hiring carts for public whippings.[1]

Domestic strife hit Barnaby's life in 1601. His wife, Marie, was 'whipped at the post' for letting Thomas Welch slip into her house after being 'often' told to stay away from him: 'xx yerkes' next time, she was told. Welch, who 'often' flouted warnings, was locked up for seven weeks after being caught 'lewdlie' in her 'company'. He was warned that he would 'be whipt at a carts tayle iiii severall markett dayes one after another till the blood flow' if he met her again. The next time Welch appears in records he was 'whiped againe at the post with 2 whippes' for 'lewdly keeping the companye of Barnabye's wyfe'. Two men took turns to give him 'xxtie yerkes' each. Barnaby was one and he surely got satisfaction from whipping his wife's lover and getting paid for it.[2]

Barnaby was called a 'gatherer' when getting eighteen-pence for whipping 'ix persons' in 1593. He topped up his salary with other work that brought together punishment and public hygiene. He dug lots of pits: 'a pyt to lye in filthe from Guildehall', 'a pitt withowte the gates to burye excrements', 'a pitt to burye prisoners excrements', 'a pitt for corrupt victualls'. Barnaby had a red-letter day when he got twenty-six shillings for 'carryinge muck from Jackes Pytt'. He got twenty-pence at other times for 'six loads' and three shillings for 'xii loads of muck' that he

[1] NRO Norwich Clavors Book 1, fos. 100, 101v, 102, 103v, 105v, 109, 109v, 135, 136v, 140v.
[2] NRO NMCC 13, fos. 568, 596, 673.

Information, Institutions, and Local Government in England, 1550–1700: Turning Inside. Paul Griffiths, Oxford University Press. © Paul Griffiths 2023. DOI: 10.1093/oso/9780192896261.003.0004

buried in a deep place.[3] He also cleaned civic spaces 'about the Guildhall' (once making ten shillings) and shared 3s. 4d. with 'Gedgboll' in 1605 'for fyringe nyxsons cockey and carrynge away myer'. Barnaby 'carryed' rowdy women 'oute of the cittie' (4d.) and two others 'infected with the pockes' to 'the gates beinge sore diseased' in 1601.[4]

Barnaby did better than a day labourer. Like him, other whippers got lump sums: thirty-four shillings and £1 14s. 6d. on two occasions in Gloucester; 9s. 10d. in Marlborough for whipping '27 idle persons'. We don't see Barnaby whipping anyone tied to a cart, but in Gloucester in 1567 Thomas Wheeler got 2s. 8d. for 'hawling vacabounds about sun-drye tymes', and Thomas Cosent got 5s. 4d. 'for hallying vacabonds about the towne iii tymes'. Fees tended to rise from two-pence around 1600 to four- or six-pence later on.[5] Whips did not cost much. 'Birche and cords' cost a mere penny in Gloucester in 1560 'to whippe a poore fellowe that commited buggerye'. Annual bills for birch never exceeded four shillings in Norwich around 1600 when Barnaby was whipper.[6]

Barnaby Langdon was a foot soldier in civic dress for at least a dozen years. Whipping never stands apart in these few crumbs of his life. He touched dirt each day in substance and bodies with ethical properties. Public punishment was arranged around workaday practices, and this chapter's first section will look at how it was tightly grounded in walking, talking, and seeing. These punishments were embedded in quotidian routines. I cover petty crime only and this is partly polemical, as the prevalence of punishing felony in ideas of historical developments of punishment has led to interpretations that can be questioned and supplemented. We must give more time to petty crime for balance that will give us rather different impressions of punishment over the last five centuries. Misdemeanours mattered, as crime was viewed on sliding scales where the first fault led inevitably to felony unless something was done early in life to put someone on the straight and narrow path. The main aim was to reform minds before it was too late. Critically, the rate of punishing petty crime far exceeded that for capital crime. In incidence alone, punishing felony was the tip of a very large iceberg. The second section covers 'publique' punishments, including whipping, the stocks, pillories, and ducking stools. Each one is broken down by offence, number, and gender. The scope of discretion is measured in number ('duscksyings' or

[3] Ibid., fos. 101, 102, 103, 103v, 105, 134v; Norwich Chamberlain's Accounts 1603–25, fos. 303, 360, 380.

[4] NRO Norwich River and Street Accounts 1598/9, 1599/1600, 1600/1, 1604/5; Clavors Book 1, fos. 102, 138v.

[5] GA GBR/F/4/3, fos. 78, 122v, 123, 274v; GBR/F/4/5, fo, 479; GBR/F/4/6, fo. 120; BRO R/AC/1/2, fo. 205; WSHC G22/1/205/2, fo. 48. Lyme Regis is a good example of this trend. See DHC DC/LR/G/2/2. See also CKS TE/S2, fos. 46, 52, 80, 84, 138; GA GBR/F/4/3, fos. 72v, 274; GBR/F/4/6, fos. 199, 312, 350, 403, 439, 472; WSHC G22/1/205/2, fos. 36, 40v, 48, 49v, 59, 67.

[6] GA GBR/F/4/3, fos. 83, 127v; NRO Norwich Clavors Book 1, fos. 65v, 79, 89v, 95v. See also LERO BRIII/2/47; WSHC G22/1/205/2, fo. 44v.

'strypes'), time (hours in stocks or pillories), length (along streets and across markets), and softer handling due to health, for instance, or age, standing, or family situation. The third section shows that ideas and practices of 'private' punishment were pervasive long before *c.*1680–*c.*1820, which is often said to constitute a decisive turning point. The last section examines why, starting in the second half of the sixteenth century, the advantages of punishing inside began to be seen in a more favourable light than the alternative of punishing before 'a publique concourse'. But we now need to go back to markets and streets to realize the extent to which punishing petty crime in the cold light of day was ubiquitous, familiar, and consequential.

I

It would be a rare day if someone did not pass by a whipping post or stocks. Commerce, ethics, and authority overlapped in marketplaces. It is important to realize how punishments were rooted in workaday routines. They were points on mental maps that helped people to get from one place to another. They walked along 'Whipstreete' in Ipswich, and 'Bridewell Staires' and 'Gallowes Lane' in Gloucester. 'Gallows Hill' loomed over Dorchester. 'Pillory Nooke' was a small lane in Stamford. Henry Newcome passed by 'Hanging Ditch' near Manchester.[7] People in Gloucester peered into 'Hangmans Pitt'. Preston had 'coockstoole pit', Manchester 'cuckingestool poole', and Clerkenwell 'duckinge pond' (people could not walk dogs there).[8] Rogationtide processions also pinpointed penal sites: a 'comon' near Colchester where a gallows stood, 'gallows heath' in Thetford, and 'a place where sometyme stood a paire of gallowes' in Chester 'now called gallowes poole'.[9]

Punishment was fixed in geographies and daily talk. Insults crackled with images of punishment and shame that could bring someone down a peg or two. I was not 'whipt out of Canterbury', a brewer shouted in a Colchester street in 1667, as George Russell followed him throwing stones. 'My mother is an honester women than thine', a Hertfordshire man with a chip on his shoulder told a

[7] SAI C/3/4/1/22, fo. 4v; C/3/4/1/39, fo. 3; GA GBR B/3/2, fo. 419; GBR B/3/3, fo. 745; DHC D/DOR/T/42; R. Butcher, *The Survey and Antiquitue of the Towne of Stamford* (1646), 6–7; *The Diary of the Rev. Henry Newcome, From September 30, 1661, to September 29, 1663*, ed. T. Heywood, Chetham Society Publications, 19 (Manchester, 1849), 161.

[8] GA Q/Saib/1, fos. 40v, 55; LA CNP 3/2/1, fo. 352; J.E. Earwaker, ed., *The Court Leet Records of the Manor of Manchester, From the Year 1552 to the Year 1686, and From the Year 1731 to the Year 1846*, 12 vols (Manchester, 1884–90), II, 10, 16, 18; LMA MJ/SBR/1, fos. 306, 420; MJ/SBR/4, fo. 502; MJ/SBR/6, fo. 300. See also HEA BG11/4/6, 10/1661, fo. 1; WSHC G/22/1/205/2, fo. 33.

[9] ERO D/B5/SB2/4, fo. 7v; NRO T/C1/6, fo. 21; CA Z/AB/1 fo. 360. See also KAC WSSMB/K/2/5, fo. 37v; LA CNP 3/2/1, fo. 323; YCA F7, fo. 351; BRO R/AC/1/2, fo. 297; CKS Md/Acm1/2, fo. 162; NDRO 1064Q/SO1, fo. 85; OHC QS/C/A1/01, fo. 149.

constable in 1614, 'for she never was drawen to the cuking stooll [like] thine'. 'Cart ass whore', a mud-slinger snapped; 'pillory knave', another one quipped.[10] Many injured people took insults to court to clear their name. A Hereford tailor made 'mocks, flowts and divers signes of [scorning] cartesies' to a minister's wife in 1601, calling her 'chit hobbie horse and gillflirt'—this 'by his owne interpretacon' means 'harlot', a clerk noted—and told a servant who tried to help her that 'he would whippe him [and] make him eat his rodde'.[11] 'Thow art a haglett', Richard Black told a curate in 1589, 'a good mr woodcocke worthie to be whipped owt of churche with a dog whippe'.[12] These cutting borrowings show how people versed in penal imagery used it to score points. 'Beastlie' Roger Serrell 'pissed' into Christian Stoverton's Exeter shop in 1620 as she was 'sitting [with] company'. 'Remember the carte', he told her after she 'reproved' him. 'I woulde yt had beene in thy mouth', he hit back, when her maid chided him.[13] An Exeter servant told his mistress that 'his master was a cockholl and better women [than her] hadd binne whipped at the cartes tayle' and bid her 'kisse his asse', hoping, he said, 'to see his [masters] eyes fall out of his heade'.[14] Loudmouths also turned the tables on officials and officers using penal 'engines' that were their responsibility. The mayor stole his coat, Joseph Hall said in Norwich's Mayor's Court in 1616, and he 'thretened [to] whipp [Mr Mayor] unles he payed vis viiid' (a usual fine). Served with a warrant in 1632, a Norwich locksmith told officers that 'he would not sett in the stocks unles mr craske [the justice who signed it] sett with him'.[15] This goading touched raw nerves. Dorset wife beater John Taylor who also threatened to burn down his mother-in-law's house in 1619, warned that he would make 'crowd-strings' of the constables' guts if they dared put him in the stocks.[16] Put me in the pillory, a thief taunted Lavington (Wiltshire) magistrates in 1560. I might lose my ears, he said mockingly, but I will cover the wounds 'with a nyght cappe'. A Colchester feltmaker called an alderman-justice a 'just asse, turd, old foole, old rogue' in 1654, telling him 'that he was as good a man as he [and] bid him sett him in the stocks'.[17]

[10] ERO D/B5/SB2/9, fo. 182v; W. Le Hardy, ed., *Hertford County Records: Notes and Extracts from the Sessions Rolls 1581 to 1698*, 9 vols (1905–39), I, 42. See also BIA CPH/4029; Deposition Book 1676–78, fos. 207–8; DRO ECA C1/61, fo. 37; NRO Norwich Sessions Book 1581–91, fo. 93v; NMCC 8, fo. 365; LMA DLC/214, fos. 32, 103; DHC DC/DOB/8/1, fos. 50, 98v; P. Griffiths, 'Punishing words: insults and injuries, 1525–1700', in A. McShane and G. Walker, eds., *The Extraordinary and the Everyday in Early Modern England: Essays in Celebration of the Work of Bernard Capp* (Basingstoke, 2010).

[11] HEA BG11/17/1/4, fo. 2.

[12] LERO 1D41/91/1, fo. 38v.

[13] DRO ECA C1/61, fos. 520–1.

[14] DRO ECA C1/62, fo. 21v. See also BRO R/AC1/1/3, fo. 162; DHC DC/DOB/8/1, fos. 190v, 247; LMA DLC 214, fo. 103.

[15] NRO NMCC 15, fo. 72; Norwich Sessions Book 1630–8, fo. 22v.

[16] *The Casebook of Francis Ashley JP, Recorder of Dorchester, 1614–35*, ed. J. H. Bettey, Dorset Record Society, 7 (1981) 60.

[17] B. H. Cunnington, ed., *Some Annals of the Borough of Devizes*, 2 vols (Devizes, 1925–6), I, 33–4; ERO D/B5/SB2/9, fo. 92.

People were familiar with the sights and sounds of punishing petty crime, and it is little surprise to see penal prints adding force to their jokes and insults. They also parodied punishments for their own ends. Governors frowned upon any such imitation like the 'ryotous meetinge called vulgarly a rydiunge' in Norwich in 1670 when a group aped penalties handed down by courts.[18] 'There are many that wear horns and ride daily upon collstaves', James Howell noted, 'but this proceeds not so often from the fault of the female as the silliness of the husband who knows not how to manage a wife'.[19] Lincolnshire gentleman John Morris claimed that a rowdy group put him on a horse, 'byndeing both his leggs', and tied a 'halter' to the horse, leading him through heckling crowds for two miles in 'disgraceful manner'.[20] A Worcestershire crowd strapped the curate of Hartlebury to a 'cowle staffe' in 1614 'and carried him up and downe the towne', laughing and mocking him with fiddles playing, horns blowing, and 'making a great disorderly noise'.[21] 'The law calls this a libel', Edmund Wingate noted: 'scandalous words' and 'hanging up' 'pictures or reproachfull signs' of a 'gallowes, pillory, hornes, or cooking-stool' in or near the house of the 'reproached'.[22] 'Punke!' an Exeter fisherman shouted at Edward Dight's wife in 1620 as he 'made hornes unto her with his fingers'. 'Troblesome' Thomas Harrens was brought to court in Norwich in 1585 after 'casting hornes' and a volley of 'rude and railing words' into his neighbours' houses. No one wanted to wake up one day and find 'a huge paier of goathornes' or 'a great payre of hornes' hanging on their doors.[23]

Just as troubling were times when people took it upon themselves to punish someone with no right to do so. Standing in Richard Swift's house on a Sunday morning in Norwich in 1566, Katherine Derrick heard a 14-year-old 'wench' who was guiding 'blyndewoman' Ann to church call her a 'fyne whore'. She pulled her into the house the following Sunday and Swift's wife held her down over a stool while Derrick 'bete' her with 'a byrching rod' for half an hour. A London pewterer got in trouble in 1551 for whipping his apprentice up and down streets 'upon hys owne authoritye'.[24] These vivid parodies of authority were doubly disturbing because they mimicked legal definitions of right and wrong. They were sharp reminders of how hard it was to keep tight control over legitimizing punishments. Margaret Flatman said that a Norfolk 'company' dragged her 'starke naked' into a

[18] NRO NMCC 24, fo. 135v. See M. Ingram, 'Juridical folklore in England illustrated by rough music', in C. Brooks and M. Lobban, eds., *Communities and Courts in Britain, 1150–1900* (1997); D. Underdown, '"But the shows of their street": civic pageantry and charivari in a Somerset town, 1607', *JBS*, 50 (2011).

[19] J. Howell, *Familiar Letters or Epistolae Ho-Elianae*, 3 vols (1903), II, 70.

[20] TNA STAC8 210/11.

[21] J. Willis-Bund, ed., *Worcester County Records; The Quarter Sessions Rolls* (Worcester, 1899), 195–6. See also HEA Q/SM/2, fo. 10; LERO QS/7/2, fo. 135v.

[22] E. Wingate, *Justice Revived being the Whole Office of a Countrey Justice of the Peace* (1661), 163.

[23] DRO ECA C1/61, fo. 343; NRO NMCC 11, fo. 517. See also BRO R/AC/1/1/3, fo. 280; LMA MJ/SBR/1, fo. 368; TNA STAC8 140/29; 152/7; 253/18; DRO ECA C1/61, fos. 23, 120, 151.

[24] NRO NMCC 8, fo. 379; LMA Rep. 12, fo. 508v.

cart, dressed her in a 'mans jerken', and in 'publique mockery and scorne' carted her 'bareheaded' for a mile in 'viewe of a hundred people at the least'. A carpenter's wife claimed that she was ducked in the 'comon cuck stoole [in Leeds to] her publick and open shame and disgrace' by 'base enemies' who 'made greate jollity'.[25] These stories both come from problematic Star Chamber testimony, but in both cases penal imagery was used for effect. Thomas Wells, who lived near Calne (Wiltshire), told a court how a 'company' dragged his wife down the stairs one night in 1618 and 'threw' her into a 'wett hole' outside. They then stamped on her to bury her head in dirt before beating her 'black and blewe' and dumping her in the 'cucking stolle [to] washe hir'.[26] Agnes Keat told Dorchester magistrates in 1631 that a carpenter made her fear for her life by 'threatening to wash her where soever he met her' (Widow Benesfield called her an 'old jade' one year later, adding that 'thou will bee in Bridewell before mee').[27] 'Wee will washe her and make her faire', a group of men said to each other as they watched Darby's daughter ride past them one day in 1607 on her way back home to Bromsgrove.[28]

Penal cultures were embedded in everyday life. Misdemeanours were *ordinary*. They epitomized the difficulties of getting by. Almost anyone might imagine committing one. Anyone could turn a corner walking home late and stumble into the watch. Not many were immune from character labels like lewd, idle, or vagrant. Many hard-up people could imagine snatching food from a stall when there was nothing left at home. This was life's quotidian routine: making ends meet, moving to find a job, sex, or having fun. Enlightenment Europe's leading legal thinker, Cesare de Beccaria, saw this precisely:

> Since men are not induced on the spur of the moment to commit the graver crimes, public punishment of a great misdeed will be regarded by the majority as something very remote and of impossible occurrence, but public punishment of lesser crimes, which are closer to men's hearts, will make an impression which, while deterring them from these, deters them even further from graver crimes.[29]

'Lesser crimes' were 'closer' to hearts. Punishing petty crime week in, week out in 'publique' left impressions. Offenders were not unlike their audience. They shared streets, jobs, and concerns. They could have lived next door. Yet interpretations of the historical development of punishment rarely take this 'ordinariness' into

[25] TNA STAC8 146/15; 266/29. See also TNA STAC8 123/16.

[26] B. H. Cunnington, ed., *Records of the County of Wiltshire* (Devizes, 1932), 65–6.

[27] DHC DC/DOB/8/1, fos. 100, 122.

[28] Willis-Bund, *Worcester County Records*, 106–7. See also LMA MJ/SBR/1, fo. 55; DHC DC/DOB/8/1, fo. 337v; NRO NMCC 14, fos. 57v, 263v; TNA STAC8 34/16; 130/18.

[29] C. de Beccaria, *On Crimes and Punishments*, first published in 1764, ed. H. Paolucci (New York, 1963), 57.

account. They focus on a tiny fraction of 'publique' punishments: punishing felony. It is impossible to be exact, but it is possible that they were less than 1 per cent of all public penalties.[30] The hanging tree intoxicates with stories of human loss in questions of who we once were. Like giants, felonies dwarf anything around them. What appeal is there in a tatty beggar or hard-up thief compared to a flashy highwayman or a witch who spoke to Satan? Yet if felonies hog the limelight, there was a cottage industry in writing on petty crime: cheap literatures on wily bawds and peacock whores, and cutpurse and vagrant ganglands with Moll Cutpurse as *de facto* queen who had a long life and longer shelf life. She was known across the country. A Southampton servant was brought to court in 1626 'for presting women for the warres in the name of Moll Cutpurse [and] putting them in greate feare'.[31] Felony cases are just one route through penal pasts giving us histories of punishing felony but *not* histories of punishment. We get different senses of how punishment developed if we follow petty crime through time: custodial sentences date back to Tudor times and earlier; reforming offenders was an aim of sixteenth-century penal systems; 'private' punishment/whipping greatly outnumbered 'public' or 'open' punishment/whipping before 1700.[32] As mentioned, punishment was seen on a continuum. The first slip-up established an insistent pattern unless something was done to stop it. Stepping stones to the gallows began with the first offence in youth. The first punishment firmly imposed might nip a life of crime in the bud. 'We see by experience', Charles Richardson mused in 1616, 'that many times a little itch turneth into a filthie leprisie'. Do not forgive 'small faults', he warned, but 'labour by smaller and lighter punishments to prevent greater'.[33] 'Punnishinge [a] little fault prevents a greater', the Earl of Huntington told Leicestershire's grand jury in 1639; 'many a rogue that escapes unpunished, if he were whipped and stocked it would keepe him from hanging'.[34] M.R. was willing to wager 'an hundred to one' that if someone 'depart[s a bridewell] and mend[s] not' they will drop into the 'hangmans budget'.[35]

Like tumbling cards, one crime followed on the heels of another in the trials and tribulations of youth. 'Idleness', Richard Haines wrote when championing workhouses, 'is the seed-plot of the hang-mans harvest'. Randolph Yearwood

[30] Bob Shoemaker believes that 10 per cent of crimes prosecuted at Middlesex Sessions in 1660–1720 were felonies. See his *Prosecution and Punishment: Petty Crime and the Law in London and Rural Middlesex c.1660–1725* (Cambridge, 1991), 6.

[31] SA SC9/2/1, fo. 115v.

[32] C. Winter, 'Prisons and Punishments in Late Medieval London' (PhD thesis, University of London, 2012). See P. Griffiths, 'Introduction: punishing the English', in S. Devereaux and P. Griffiths, eds., *Penal Practice and Culture, 1500–1900: Punishing the English* (Basingstoke, 2004).

[33] C. Richardson, *A Sermon Concerning the Punishment of Malefactors* (1616), 13–14, 18.

[34] HL HAM box 26, folder 6, 3.

[35] M.R., *Micrologia. Characters, or Essayes, of Persons, Trades, and Places, Offered to the City and Country* (1629), D7r.

offered 'a word to the youth and apprentices' of London in 1659 after a murderer was put to death at Tyburn:

> Take heed of lesser sins. Little sins will make way for greater sins; if you sip of sin, you'll be drunk of it at last. How modest is sin at first but when 'tis gratified it grows impudent. [This] poor man lately executed [was] of your rank, first he began to game, then to steal, then whore, and then to murder.[36]

These tumbling cards were not just a literary trope or abiding principle of criminal justice. People took these lessons on board to threaten or warn others. A Dorset clothier warned his lazy maid 'that yf shee tooke such [bad] courses they would bring her to the gallowes'. Norwich's mayor gave 'exortacon' to a young man who was caught having sex in a garden in 1562: 'better hold upon Gods Grace & live in ye feare of God or ells he shuld come to ye rope'.[37] 'You see the issue of your sloth', Touchstone tells his former apprentice turned thief Quicksilver in *Eastward Hoe* (1605), who is shortly to hang: 'Of sloth cometh pleasure, of pleasure cometh riot, of riot comes whoring, of whoring comes spending, of spending comes want, of want comes theft, of theft comes hanging'.[38] The 'last dying words' of doomed felons were aimed at young people. In these cradle-to-gallows narratives youth is a 'choosing time' when people could mend if a right path was taken.[39] The young had chances to change, unlike older folk who were stuck neck deep in the quicksand of a wicked world. 'Strike while the iron is hot' and 'best to bend while tis a twig' were guiding adages for these times. Kent justice William Lambarde urged overseers to put people in service 'while they be young and tractable'.[40] There was no time to lose. 'Start while it is called today', John Shower warned the 'younger sort'. 'Bee new men now', the author of *The Prentises's Practice* (1613) urged: 'this day, this hour, this night'. Thomas Powell wasted no time: 'upon this monosyllable now depends eternity'. 'Now they will bend', Robert Shelford said, 'now they will be pliable, now they will worke'.[41]

[36] R. Haines, *Provision for the Poor, or Reasons for the Erecting of a Working-Hospital in Every County* (1678), 6; R. Yearwood, *The Penitent Murderer* (1659), 89.

[37] DHC DC/DOB/8/1, fo. 31; NRO NMCC Interrogatories and Depositions Book, 1561–7, fos. 26–6v.

[38] G. Chapman, B. Jonson, and J. Marston, *Eastward Hoe*, first published in 1605, Tudor Facsimile Texts (New York, 1970), A3, G3.

[39] J. A. Sharpe, '"Last dying speeches": religion, ideology, and public execution in seventeenth-century England', *P&P*, 107 (1985); P. Griffiths, *Youth and Authority: Formative Experiences in England, 1560–1640* (Oxford, 1996), 54–61.

[40] W. Lambarde, *The Duties of Constables, Borsholders, Tythingmen and Such other Law and Lay Ministers of the Peace*, first published in 1584 (1602), 129; F.R., *A Collection of English Proverbs* (Cambridge, 1670), 61.

[41] J. Shower, *Seasonable Advice to Youth* (1692), epistle dedicatory, A2, 35, 37; W.P., *The Prentise's Practice in Godlinesse and His True Freedome* (1613), 28v; T. Powell, *The Beauty, Vigour, and Strength of Youth Bespoke for God* (1676), 56, 61; R. Shelford, *Lectures or Readings Upon the 8 Verse of the 22 Chapter of Proverbs, Concerning the Vertuous Education of Youth* (1606), 126. See also T. Fuller, *Words*

This was a crossroads where ideas of youth and crime came together. Reformation and punishment were twins in this age of life. Punishment also sent warnings 'to terrifie' anyone contemplating crime. 'Example' was secular scripture. Preston rulers wanted 'ordinary hedgebreakers' to be 'publique examples to ye terrifying of all others'. Charles Richardson believed that 'publicke' punishments were 'very profitable for examples and amendment of others [as] feare [extends] to all men'. 'When a man seeth a malefactor brought to deserved punishment', he added, 'he is admonished to take heede of such courses'.[42] But it is unthinkable that courts did not see punishment as a golden chance to reform character. 'Reformation', of course, was the highest priority of Church and State. These are 'times of reformation', Randolph Yearwood said in 1659.[43] Reforming troublemakers was without doubt integral to punishment. 'If punishment is 'properly inflicted', Charles Richardson wrote, the 'party delinquent' would be 'reformed and brought to live in better order'. William Lambarde coupled deterrence and reformation. Punishment is 'for the amendment of the offender', he said, and 'for examples sake that others thereby bee kept from offending'.[44] Minds (and souls) mattered! Thomas Browning revealingly called his prison notebooks *Prison Thoughts*.[45] This is equally evident in cases that were brought to the courts. 'The end of their presentments [is] chiefly reformation', Leicestershire justices said about two drunks in 1671.

Susan Wallys from Somerset was 'severely whipped' in 1621 'to put her in mind how she doth offend in the like hereafter'.[46] Esther Cohen argues that whip-sting shot sensations to minds, urging self-reflection. Thomas Forster called whipping a 'penance' in 1654. The whipping post next to the standard on London's ceremonial pulse Cheapside was called 'the post of reformation'.[47] Whipping, something so crushingly dishonourable that many in elevated circles thought that it should be kept for the 'multitude' only, was meant to humble and reform.[48] Like early modern magistrates, John Dunton coupled bridewells and public whipping

to Give the Young Man Knowledge and Discretion (1653), 88; R. Abbot, *A Christian Family Builded by God* (1653), 25; M. Griffith, *Bethel, or a Forme for Families* (1634), 159; W. Vaughan, *The Golden-Grove* (1600), 3rd part, V8.

[42] LA CNP 3/2/1, fo. 251; Richardson, *Sermon Concerning the Punishment of Malefactors*, 7–8. See also D. Jenkins, *Pacis Consultum... Describing the Court Leet* (1657), 119.

[43] Yearwood, *Penitent Murderer*, 89.

[44] Richardson, *Sermon Concerning the Punishment of Malefactors*, 7; W. Lambarde, *Eirenarcha, Or the Office of the Justice of the Peace*, first published in 1581, facsimile copy, The English Experience, 273 (Amsterdam and New York, 1970), 67.

[45] T. Browning, *Prison Thoughts* (1682).

[46] LERO 28/133; E. H. Bates, ed., *Quarter Sessions Records for the County of Somerset*, 4 vols, Somerset Record Society (1907–19), I, 297.

[47] E. Cohen, 'The animated pain of the body', *AHR*, 105 (2000); T. Forster, *The Lay-man's Lawyer: Or, the Second Part of the Practice of Law* (1654), 23; LMA Rep. 13(2), fos. 293–293v, 401, 486v.

[48] K. J. Kesselring, 'Law, status, and the lash: judicial whipping in early modern England', *JBS*, 60 (2021). See also S. Covington, 'Cutting, branding, whipping, burning: the performance of judicial wounding in early modern England', in J. R. Allard and M. R. Martin, eds., *Staging Pain, 1580–1800: Violence and Trauma in British Theatre* (Farnham, 2009).

in the same sentence that emphasized reformation and shame. He called the whipping post 'an intellectual house of correction (a sort of spiritual Bridewell)'. 'Tye him to the whipping post', Dunton wrote, 'which whipping post [may] explain to him from the argument of his own feeling, how vile and abominable his offence is'. I will 'seek out such rods as will best lash and reform their morals', he added. 'Rods of shame', he called them.[49]

It was hoped that people would change for the better, and again there is telling evidence for this in court cases. London drunk Francis Taylor vowed he would 'become a new man'. A Westminster beadle was stripped of 'his staffe and office' for lodging women after his wife's death until 'it appeared [he was] a new man'. A Norwich tailor who had been drinking and singing in his house all night in 1559 had his fine cut after saying that 'he will become a good and civil man'.[50] Others seeking a second chance promised to become 'a dutifull and obedient citizen'; 'conforme' to 'better manners for the tyme to come'; and 'promise[d] for ye future to live orderlie'. Florence Beales, who taunted Norwich officers in 1672, was let go after a 'promise to reforme her life'.[51] Mind acts like reformation were longed-for outcomes. People 'begged', 'craved', or 'desired' pity. 'Submission' was to be 'gentle' or 'humble'. 'Reverend preacher of God's word' Stephen Egerton was asked to 'convert [two] famous harlots'—Mary Newborough and Ellen Bedford—at London Bridewell in 1603. 'In outward shewe [he said, Mary] seemed [by tears] to have the more repentinge and meltinge hart'.[52] Offenders were 'heartily' sorry for what they had done. A Cumbrian who made a false forgery charge in 1661 said with remorse that 'being conscious to myselfe of the greate wronge I did him do heartely, frely, and willingly acknowledge and confesse' my wrong.[53] Submissions were sometimes staged in set-piece theatre. York merchant Edward Gyllyot sat in church on a fast day in 1642 and in 'a loud voyce' called the minister 'a jew'. 'Thou art a jewe' he said again. 'Noe more and noe more', he shouted as the sermon continued. Moved that he 'shewed himselfe very penitent and sorrowfull', justices told him to keep his word and go to the same church on the next fast day to 'publiquely' show sorrow.[54]

There was much at stake. Punishing 'lesser' faults affected how lives unfolded. Tumbling cards were points in lives. People could lose work, face, and friends. 'Public' penalties had force as they were embedded in 'ordinariness' along

[49] J. Dunton, *Dunton's Whipping-Post, Or a Satyr Upon Every Body* (1706).

[50] P. Griffiths, *Lost Londons: Change, Crime, and Control in the Capital City, 1550–1660* (Cambridge, 2008), 277–8; WAC F2001, fos. 155–6; NRO NMCC 7, fo. 305.

[51] NRO NMCC 24, fo. 206v; 25, fo. 167; LMA Rep. 33, fo. 172v; SHA LB/11/4/83/39. See also DHC DC/DOB/8/1, fos. 238, 252; DC/LR/A3/1, fo. 7; BRO R/AC1/1/3, fo. 302.

[52] BMM LBHC 4, fo. 346.

[53] KAC WQ/1/2, fo. 16v. See also NRO NMCC 9, fo. 692; 20, fo. 414; 26, fo. 46v; SHA BB/C/2/2/3, fo. 6; DHC DC/LR/D/1/1, fos. 45–6.

[54] YCA F7, fo. 158. See also LMA MJ/SBR/2, fo. 232; MJ/SBR/6, fo. 48; Reps. 14, fo. 2; 22, fo. 27; DHC DC/PL/CB/1/1, fo. 49; KAC WSMB/A/2/1/2, 15/4/1668.

'whipstreete' and in what Sicinius Velutus calls 'the people's eyes' in *Coriolanus* (IV,vi, 3088). Months after getting dumped in the stocks in 1611 with 'intollerable' people around him, Edward Edyton—'a gentleman of very good respecte'—claimed that word of it had 'growne soe vulgar and generall and comon' that it was a 'public adage and proverb'. The deeper injury for Wiltshire vicar Richard Hine was not that Ethelred Alande called him 'a black devil and a black crowe', but that he always tried to 'villifye him in public'.[55] Shame lingered like a brand on a hand. This sense of self was why well-to-do men gave money 'to the poor' rather than be punished in public and face people they knew in mortifying moments. Norvician William Tesmond begged 'that his faulte might not be openly knowne for feare yt shoulde be an occasyon he shold be put owte of servyce' when on trial for 'evell rule' in 1562. An under-bailiff at St Paul's Cathedral lost his job when it emerged that he was 'of very evil name', having 'stood on the pillory' not long ago.[56] Ten men from Atherton who were asked to make a report on John Astley's 'conversation, credit, and reputation' ended on the damning note that he had been 'whipped and stocked' for helping himself to malt.[57] Everyday penalties for everyday crimes. But this ordinariness was not at all disparaging. It was in fact extremely powerful and this is evident in how punishments in public were so often staged to trace the rhythms of daily living.

II

It was no surprise to see seven men sitting in the stocks at noon in Norwich market in 1566 in 'the cheife of the markett'.[58] People knew full well that this was the time of day and place for these staged penalties that were in fact meant for them. Light-fingered Isaac Hill was 'stripped from the waste upwards' in the same city 133 years later and 'whipped from one end of the market to the other', stopping at the highly symbolic cross where six more 'stripes' cut his back. Saturday lunchtime shoppers watched as Thomas Carpenter was led through Northampton market for an hour in 1673 'with a paper on his breast written in capitall letters convicted of assault and attempt to ravishe Ann Andrew'. He stood still for fifteen minutes 'in ye 4 most eminent places [in the market] where most concourse of people is for people to read his fact'.[59]

[55] TNA STAC8 130/18; Cunnington, *Records of the County of Wiltshire*, 111.
[56] NRO NMCC Interrogatories and Depositions Book 1561–7; LMA MJ/SBR/7, fo. 182.
[57] HL STTM box 19, folder 1. See also HEA BG11/27/1/5, fo. 72; LMA MJ/SBR/4, fo. 209.
[58] NRO NMCC 8, fo. 411.
[59] NRO Norwich Sessions Book 1691–1702, 4/1699 sessions; NA NQS/1, fo. 37. See D. Postles, 'Penance and the marketplace: a Reformation dialogue with the Medieval Church (c.1250–c.1600)', *Journal of Ecclesiastical History*, 54 (2003).

Public penalties were 'commonplace'. People made plans to watch them. Robert Wrey met with four others on one Saturday afternoon in Dorchester in 1631 'to see the fellow stand in the pillory'. Inveterate correspondent John Chamberlain thought it newsworthy that Sara Swarton 'was expected by great multitudes' when she was due to be put on the pillory at Westminster in 1619. But Swarton talked her way out of it at the last minute and was taken back to prison after telling the authorities that she had made up charges of incest and poisoning against Lady Exeter.[60] These dramas brought essentials to mind and view: blood, pain, water, fear. The noise of the lash, jeers, cheers, clattering wheels, and tinkling was part of 'official' soundscapes like bells and the crier's booming voice. Punishment was aimed at eyes and ears that were windows to minds. Millicent Pierson, who was prosecuted for having sex with her brother-in-law in 1638, was whipped in Leicester market 'whereof she may bee best *seene and hard* of ye people'.[61] Sound and vision were essential elements in the effectiveness of punishing petty crime out in the 'open'. Governors spent money 'colleringe' stocks, pillories, whipping posts, and ducking stools. Whippers wore distinctive clothing.[62] Lyme Regis spent 3s. 6d. 'for iii yardes of canvas to make a coate [for a whipper] to whipp rogues' in 1596. A blue and red 'gowne' was made for Mercer, who whipped rogues in Gloucester in 1575, along with a cap with 'a ribband and sarcent'.[63] Some whippers were disguised as a precaution. Norfolk's market towns and parishes were told to buy a 'canvise shirte' for their whipper and 'a beaver to cover [his] face'. St Martin-in-the-Fields (Westminster) vestry told overseers to buy a 'disguise' for the whippers in 1661: 'a coate, vizard and cap of hayre'. Wiltshire parishes were ordered to pick 'an able man with a hood and disguised garments and whippes' to punish vagrants in 1598.[64]

'Yt is very necessarye to have a peyre of stocks above ye bar [gate]', Southampton governors said in 1569, as 'many vacabonds for ye want thereof goithe unpunished'.[65] Punishment 'engines', as they were sometimes called, were put in 'open' or 'common' spaces, some side by side, ready to be used. They also acted as visual deterrents when not in use (which was nearly all the time). Faversham's pillory stood next to the stocks 'with a frame and a paire of manacles' in 1623. A pillory nestled against Maidstone 'gaole' in 1658. Stocks stood 'under the pillorye' in Leicester and inside a cage in Marlborough in double cautions.[66] A ducking

[60] DHC DC/DOB/8/1, fo. 87v; TNA SP 14/105/43.

[61] LERO 1D41/14/1, fo. 48.

[62] For example, WSHC G22/1/205/2, fos. 126v, 153v, 165; NRO Norwich Chamberlain's Accounts 1625–48, fo. 302v; GA GBR/F/4/5, fo. 348v; J. M. Guilding, ed., *Reading Records: Diary of the Corporation*, 4 vols (Oxford, 1886), II, 247; J. P. Earwaker, ed., *The Constables' Accounts of the Manor of Manchester From the Year 1612 to the Year 1647 and From the Year 1743 to the Year 1776*, 3 vols (Manchester 1891–1902) I. 152.

[63] DHC DC/LR/G/2/2, unpag. 1595/6; GA GBR/F/4/3, fo. 184.

[64] NRO Aylsham MS 17/26; WAC F2003, fo. 253; WSHC G22/1/107, fo. 101.

[65] SA 6/1, fo. 7.

[66] CKS FA/AC3, fo. 138v; Md/Acm1/3, fo. 96v; LERO BRIII/2/46; WSHC G22/1/205/2, fo. 65.

stool was 'chained to the pillory' in Reading market. While plans were made in Norwich in 1550 for a three-in-one contraption: a cage was 'made' in the west part of the 'newe repared' pillory with 'a newe per of stoks' 'sette' on the pillory.[67] Much thought was given to settings. A whipping post loomed large 'in the cliff' above Lewes. A pillory on top of a hill in Ipswich and a cage on London's Tower Hill were impossible to miss.[68] Ducking stools sat next to rivers, pools, pits, and docks: 'the watering pool at the lower end of Mr Cross's field' in Liverpool, 'Jacks Pitt' and 'Fybridge' on the banks of the Wensum in Norwich, a 'horsepoole in marketside lane' in Manchester, Reading's 'sawepitt', and Bridewell wharf on the Thames to punish 'wenches, yonge girles, fishwives [and] hearbewyves'.[69]

The market square was a focal point, with streets delivering people from all directions. There was a whipping post in Oxford's 'corne markett', a 'malefactors post' in Norwich market, and a 'rogues post' in Manchester market.[70] Stocks were put in Kendal's 'fish shambles as neare [to] the gibbet as conveniently can be', Gloucester market by a pillory, Shrewsbury's 'corne markett', and Leicester's 'Saturdaye market'.[71] A pillory and cage stood side-by-side in 'the north ende' of Oxford's 'corne markett place' and in York and Rye markets.[72] A cage was put at the east end of London's Newgate Market next to 'The Signe of the Bell' where a 'lamp hangeth'. A 9-foot-long and 4-foot-wide cage was put at the 'west end of the meale markett house' in Bishopsgate, London, in 1636.[73] These 'engines' were also placed next to civic buildings and monuments. There was a cage next to Norwich Guildhall, and stocks next to the 'hyghe crosse' in Liverpool, Ormskirk, Barnstaple, and Gloucester, where they were also placed by the 'little wicket', 'aylegate', 'mynster gate', and the south gate, where a 'newe payre…weying x pounds' were put in 1560.[74] Stocks stood next to Leicester 'town hall', the south, north, and east gates, and (with a whipping post) the 'Senvye' and 'hyghe crosse'. A cage at 'the end of [Maidstone's] great bridge' was decorated with insignia. An order was

67 Guilding, *Reading Records*, IV, 460; NRO NMCC 6, fo.83. See also LMA Rep. 19, fo. 197.

68 ESBHRO QO/EW8, fo. 83v; SAI C/3/4/1/17; LMA Rep. 16, fo. 479v.

69 M. Power, ed., *Liverpool Town Books, 1649–1671*, Records Society of Lancashire and Cheshire, 136 (Dorchester, 1999), 101; NRO Norwich Chamberlain's Accounts 1580–9, fo. 317; NMCC 9, fo. 263; Earwaker, *Court Leet Records of the Manor of Manchester*, II, 12; IV, 25; BRO R/AC/1/3, fo. 272; LMA Rep. 11, fos. 364v–5. See also LMA Reps. 27, fo.72; 29, fos. 103–3v; 34, fo. 10; MJ/SBR/1, fos. 306, 336, 378; MJ/SBR/4, fo. 502.

70 OHC C/FC/1/A1/03, fo. 155; NRO NMCC 12, fo. 312; Earwaker, *Constables' Accounts of the Manor of Manchester*, I, 14.

71 KAC WSSMB/K/2/5, fo. 88; GA GBR/F/4/3, fo. 183v; GBR/G/G3/S)/1, fo. 108; SHA 3365/522; LERO BRIII/2/34; BRIII/2/32. See also SAI B/105/2/4, fo. 82v; LMA MJ/SBR/1, fo. 135.

72 OHC C/FC/1/A1/2, fo. 277; YCA F7, fos. 377, 381; ESBHRO RYE 1/5, fo. 236.

73 LMA Reps. 23, fo. 505; 49, fos. 80v–1.

74 NRO NMCC 11, fo. 135;.J. A. Twemlow, ed., *Liverpool Town Books, Proceedings of Assemblies, Common Councils, Portmoot Courts etc. 1550–1862*, 2 vols (Liverpool, 1918–35), II, 96; F. R. Sharpe, ed., 'The Order Book of Ormskirk, 1613–1721', in F. R. Sharpe, ed., *A Lancashire Miscellany*, Lancashire and Cheshire Record Society, 109 (1965), 33; NDRO B1/3792, fos. 65, 118; GA GBR/F/4/3, fos. 79v, 83v, 183v, 184, 207v; GBR/F/4/5, fo. 15; GBR/F/4/6, fo. 77.

passed in 1654 to 'handsomelie cover' it.[75] Punishments were timed for maximum effect at 'the height of the markett', the 'chief time of the market', or 'full' or 'open faire'.[76] They were tailored to suit local needs. Cicely Lane was whipped 'in the most public place' in Burnham (Somerset) in 1622. A Gloucester couple who were caught living 'incontinent[ly]' were 'openly carted [in] full market' in 1631.[77] A Glastonbury woman was 'whipped about the markett house' in 1638 'when the market is at the biggest'. While Lodowick Bowyer, who was a member of an underground Catholic letter ring, was put in the pillory 'in full market' in Reading in 1633 with 'an abundance of people' milling round.[78] Saturday and Wednesday were the days of choice, and most open-air 'correccons' took place between '12 and 2', '11 and one', 'or 12 and 1'.[79] Key civic landmarks like crosses, standards, and conduits were naturally included in this penal semaphore. Londoner Roger Popley was 'tied to the post besyds the standard in Chepe' and whipped in 1559 for 'shamefull betyng' of his mother. A waterbearer who 'most lewdlye, falsely, and vylely rayled openly' at London's mayor in 1553 'was whipped naked abote all the conditts'.[80] John Errington was whipped from 'the high cross to the lowe crosse' in Appleby market, while thief Richard Clarke was flogged 'round the crosse' in Norwich market in 1689, getting '25 lashes' in all.[81]

John Seller finished his *Booke of the Punishments of the Common Laws of England* in 1678. It is eleven pages of drawings. A half-naked thief looks back in pain in one, as a whipper cuts his back at a 'carts tayle' ('for petty larceny and other offences') (Figure 3.1). Some people are jeering. Gloucester spent 2s. 4d. in 1563 on 'papers made for offenders and for hiring carts and horses' to whip them through the city; eight-pence in 1559 when 'egyptians' were 'brought aboute the citie and scourged'; eight-pence 'for wryting the supscription for punyshinge the egyptans' in 1578; and two-pence in 1568 for 'cordes to binde' vagrants whipped across the market.[82] Thousands criss-crossed markets, sometimes standing still at specified spots. Norwich thief Robert Beecham stopped 'under the signe of every

[75] LERO BRIII/2/33, fos. 34, 36 41, 45, 48; CKS Md/Acm1/3, fo. 70v.

[76] For example, SHA 3356/2430, fos. 37v, 40v, 103v, 131; Bates, *Quarter Sessions Records for the County of Somerset*, IV, 217; KAC WQ/O/4, fo. 147v; DRO ECA B/1/4, fo. 260; LERO QS6/1/2, fo. 47v; NA NQS/3, fo. 79v; NQS/1, fo. 61v.

[77] Bates, *Quarter Sessions Records for the County of Somerset*, I, 312; GA GBR/G/G3/SO/1, fo. 159.

[78] Bates, *Quarter Sessions Records for the County of Somerset*, II, 301; BRO R/AC1/1/3, fo. 279. See also CA ZML/1/5. A document dated 13 November 1633 notes the varying opinions of members of the Star Chamber on how Bowyer should be punished, ranging from 'whipping but stigmatised' to '3000 fine: stand pillory here in the pallace with a pap[er], stand in cheapside likewise: at Reading likewise with his eares nailed: [ending] if he be putt from the felony to returne to perpetuall imprisonm[en]t in som house of correccon': TNA SP 16/250/59.

[79] For example, OHC QS/C/A1/O1, fo. 128; NA NQS/2, fo. 92; HEA Q/SM/2, fo. 20v; ESBHRO RYE 1/6, fo. 284; HA Q3/3, fo. 97; NRO T/C1/2, fo. 166.

[80] LMA Reps. 14, fo. 169v; 13(1), fo. 75.

[81] KAC WQ/M/1, fo. 2; NRO Norwich Sessions Book 1671–91, unpag. See also SAI B/105/2/6, fo. 177; KAC WQ/O/5, fo. 205; NA NSQ/1, fos. 43, 49v; DRO ECA B/1/4, fo. 251.

[82] GA GBR/F/4/3, fos. 100, 199, 78, 127v, 100.

Figure 3.1 'The Manner of Whipping at the Cart's Tail'.
Source: John Seller, *A Booke of the Punishments of the Common Laws of England* (1678), Guildhall Library, London, AN 18.3.25.

house he passes [to] have three stripes' when he was whipped around the market.[83] Exeter cutpurse Thomas Logan, who had 'too wyfes', was given 'syxe strypes' each time the cart rolled to a stop 'in the myddle of the fysh markett', 'the myddle of the butter markett', 'the meale markett', 'the whet markett', 'the malte market', 'beare corner', St Peters Church, 'the east gate', the lytle conduit at St Martyns Lane', 'and the guyldhall' (sixty-six 'strypes' in all). His older 'wyfe' got 'fyve strypes' when the cart stopped; the younger wife got three.[84]

Carts rolling along streets with offenders 'barefaced in publique view' were near relics by 1700. Fifty-five women and nine men were carted in London, Gloucester, Norwich, Exeter, and Rye records. Carting was coupled with sex: 'as they passe the people scoffing say / Ho-la ye pampered ladies of Asia'.[85] Men, however, committed a wider range of offences. A London nightman stood 'upright in a tub' in a cart for dumping dung in a sewer in 1591; 'a comon barretor' was drawn through markets in 1555 with 'basons and panes ryngynge before hym'.[86] Women were carted for sex-related offences: 'harlot', 'lewde liffe'

[83] NRO Norwich Sessions Book 1691–1702, 5/1698 sessions.
[84] DRO ECA B/1/4, fo. 250. See also SHA 3356/2430; DRO ECA B/1/4, fos. 141, 239; SAI B/105/2/6, fos. 22v, 30v; NA NQS/1, fo. 37; NRO NMCC 13, fo. 649; LMA Rep. 11, fo. 153v.
[85] M.R., *Micrologia*, D7r. See also M. Ingram, *Carnal Knowledge: Regulating Sex in England, 1470–1600* (Cambridge, 2017), 338, 343.
[86] LMA Reps. 13,(2), fo. 323v; 22, fo. 262v.

'incontynent lyfe', 'fylthie and naughtie lyffe', and 'whoredome'. Widow Leman was caught red-handed in a Norwich barn in 1561 in 'the abhomynable acte of whoredom' and carted through the Saturday market and 'over Costamny brydge and Fybrigg wth a bason tynclkyd before hyr and so onto the cokingstoole and ducked in the water'.[87] Thirty-nine couples in the same records were punished differently: a woman was carted; a man was whipped at its 'arse'. A Gloucester bigamist was 'tyyed to the tayle of the cart [and] well whipped through all the streets' in 1618. Jane Bonham, his lover and mother of their child, sat in the cart. More commonly, couples stood in carts for 'evill rule', 'lechery', 'whoredome', 'adultery', and 'bawdrye'.[88]

Civic maps of display set routes when governors went on parade. Punishments often followed the same route, sticking to the 'principall thoroughfares', 'comen marketts', and 'notable stretes'. 'Lewde' Christian Wallis, who stripped children and stole their clothes in 1587, was 'tyed to a cartes tayle' and whipped across London from Bridewell to Ludgate, stopping for 'open proclamacon [of] offence' at 'Ludgate, Paules Churchyarde, the lyttle counduicte [and 'crosse'] in Cheape, the greate conduyte, the Stocks, the Exchaunge, Leadenhall, Allgate and Whytechapell Barres'.[89] A couple who 'very unreasonablye beat' their 12-year-old maid were whipped from Newgate Prison to their house in 1582, with the 'childe borne before them [so] the people may see howe unreasonablye she hath bynn dealt'. They stood outside their house and were then taken through Newgate Market, Cheapside cross and conduit, the Royal Exchange, and Leadenhall Market, with 'proclamacons published' at each stop.[90] Symbolic touches magnified the spectacle and shame. A London woman was 'garnysshed with images of yong infants' after she abandoned her child. A 'lyttle pillorie devised for the punishment of suche offenders [was] openly borne' before a baker who sold bread at the wrong weight and price. A carpenter's wife and a second carpenter who sold two pigs in Lent in 1551 were led through London with 'one quarter of the hog hangynge on his brest and [another] at his bake', the 'hed on the top of a longe pole', 'one of the pygges hangyng upon their brests and the petytoes of the pygges in garlands upon their hedds in example [and] terror'.[91]

Large towns also drew maps of display over their length and breadth. York's penal circuits ran 'from Owsebridge [to] Walmegatebarr' and along 'the shambles to Micklegate Barr'. Shrewsbury's troublemakers were taken from 'the castlegate

87 NRO NMCC 7, fo.521. Cf. ESBHRO RYE 1/6, fo. 284; NRO NMCC 9, fo. 72; LMA Reps. 12, fo. 492; 18, fo. 35; DRO ECA B/1/4, fos. 172, 243, 343; LERO BRIII2/42.

88 GA GBR/G/G3/Sib/1, fo. 66. Cf. NRO NMCC 9, fo. 729; ESBHRO RYE 1/5, fo. 65v.

89 LMA Rep. 21, fo. 427v. See S. Minson, 'Political Culture and Urban Space in Early Tudor England' (DPhil thesis, University of Oxford, 2013), chap. 5; S. Minson, 'Public punishment and urban space in early Tudor London', *London Topographical Record*, 30 (2010).

90 LMA Rep. 20, fo. 315.

91 LMA Reps. 15, fos 22v, 221v–2; 14, fos. 103v, 12v; 13(2) fo. 410v; 12, fo. 460. See also LMA Reps. 11, fo. 329; 12, fos. 55–5v; 13(1), fo. 144v; 15, fo, 465v; 18, fo. 456; 27, fo. 396.

prison to the salt markett up the high street to the Wild Hop and back to the welsh bridge'; 'from castle gate downe to hye markett house to the stone bridge'; and 'from the prison to and round the markett house to ye stone bridge'. Exeter steered its whipped along 'Rock Lane and Southgate streate' up to the guildhall.[92] Processions in 'lesser' towns might have had more impact in their smaller boxes. Lewes whipped wrongdoers from the bridge or sessions house to the market house or west gate. In other Sussex towns routes ran 'from the bridge to the Running Horses' (Midhurst); from 'the north gate to the south gate' (Chichester); and from 'the church to the gaole' or Arundel bridge to Mary Gate (Horsham).[93] Doncaster whipped its black sheep from the 'guildhall up Baxtergate to the Butcher's Cross and to the Hall Cross' or from 'the Wheat Cross through the buchers shambles to the Friars Bridge'. Wellingborough's parade of shame ran 'from ye Hind Inne to ye White Hart and back againe'. Vagrants and others were whipped 'from the bell corner to the marcat place' in Thetford.[94]

Wrongdoers were also lashed outside at a post: 2,248 men and 1,011 women (31 per cent) in records consulted. They were whipped 'for publique example' or 'terror, staye, and example'. Public whipping was familiar, and people were whipped for something trivial for the most part. They were not seasoned thieves with a string of crimes as long as their arms. If living locally, they probably stole something cheap or had one drink too many. In another Seller drawing, a beadle whips a vagrant at a whipping post ('for vagrants and sturdy beggars'), with a constable close by with a staff (Figure 3.2). A woman has a basket of food on her head representing 'ordinariness'. Mundane maybe, but pain and shame still stung. Symbolism could add extra meaning. Going threshing in Doncaster in 1686, Edward Watson spotted turkeys 'in the parsonage garth' and told John Wand, 'I will kill one of those turkeys'. 'Do', Ward urged. He 'knocked down' two with a stick, unaware that someone was watching. The pair were whipped outside their homes.[95] The parents of a 'base child' were whipped along Gaston High Street (Somerset) with 'fiddles playing before them to make known their lewdness'. A Norwich 'ladd' who poisoned his master was 'whipped with rodds by too lads'.[96]

A drunk sits glumly in a set of stocks ('for drunkerds and other unruly persons') in Seller's first sketch (Figure 3.3). Children are laughing; a pedlar walks by

[92] YCA F7, fos. 366, 427, 366; SHA 3356/2430, fos. 143, 131, 133; DRO ECA C1/61, fo. 237. See also CA QJB/1/6, fo. 122; GA GBR/G/G3/SO/1, fos. 45, 79v.

[93] ESBHRO QO/EW2, fos. 58, 95v; QO/EW7, fos. 26, 64v; QO/EW8, fo. 83v; QO/EW/10, unpag.; QO/RW9, unpag.; QO/EW3, fo. 77; QO/EW8, fo. 145v.

[94] *A Calendar to the Records of the Borough of Doncaster*, 4 vols (Doncaster, 1899–1902), IV, 111; NA NQS/4, fo. 6v; NRO T/QS/1, fos. 19v, 25. See also ESBHRO RYE 1/5, fo. 65v.

[95] *Calendar to the Records of the Borough of Doncaster*, III, 111.

[96] Bates, *Quarter Sessions Records for the County of Somerset*, I, 211; NRO NMCC 8, fo. 430. Cf. LMA Rep. 15, fos. 432v–3; M. Ingram, 'Shame and pain: themes and variations in Tudor punishments', and my 'Bodies and souls in Norwich: punishing petty crime, 1540–1700', both in Devereaux and Griffiths, *Penal Practice and Culture, 1500–1900*.

Figure 3.2 'The Punishment of the Whipping Post'.
Source: Seller, *A Booke of the Punishments of the Common Laws of England.*

with a sack on his back. A new set of stocks cost from 4s. 10d. to 22s. 4d. They were used to 'secure' folk 'till their heat be over' or until they were taken to magistrates.[97] Riding through Leigh one morning in 1665, Roger Lowe 'found Raph Jenkins in the stocks', where he had been all night with 'a fire upon the cross by him'.[98] But they are best known for links to heavy drinking. A ballad warned that 'If you sweare and be drunk / the stockes will have you'.[99] Six hours is the time stated on statute to punish what the Earl of Huntington, addressing a grand jury in 1639, called a 'sin' 'frequently committed', 'especially in market towns'. Dorchester drunk William Croome was 'stocked' for six hours in 1635 'when he is fresh'; John Spurrier was caught 'dronk 2 times' in three weeks and locked in the stocks for twelve hours.[100] But offences punished were larger in range, from putting up maypoles and hedge-breaking to travelling by boat on Sundays. A total of 426 people were locked in stocks in the records I have seen: 335 were male (79 per cent), although Dorchester, where ninety-eight men and six women were put in stocks in the 1630s, tilts the figure (it would be 68 per cent without that town).

[97] G. Meriton, *A Guide for Constables, Churchwardens, Overseers of the Poor, Surveyors of the Highways, Treasurers of the County Stock, [and] Masters of the House of Correction* (1674), 13, 18, 44–5, 75, 113–14. For costs see NRO Y/C/19/4, fo. 261; HA Q1/3, fos. 38, 78, 147, 383; DRO ECA C1/61, fos. 244, 253; DHC DB/DOB/8/1, fo. 25.

[98] *The Diary of Roger Lowe of Ashton-in-Makerfield, Lancashire, 1663–74*, ed. W. L. Sachse (New Haven, 1938), 92.

[99] *A Statute for Swearers and Drunkards or Forsake Now Your Follies* (1624).

[100] HL HAM box 26, folder 6, fo. 3; DHC DC/DOB/8/1, fos. 274, 24. See also DRO ECA C1/61, fo. 257; LMA MJ/SBR/6, fo. 204; DHC DC/DOB/8/1, fos. 25, 313v; CKS TE/JQC/1, fo. 8.

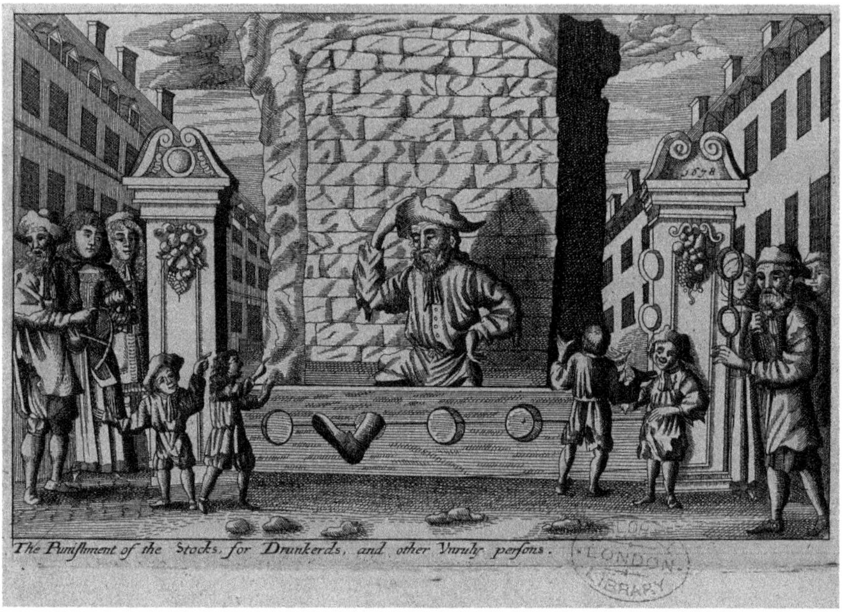

Figure 3.3 'The Punishment of the Stocks'.
Source: Seller, *A Booke of the Punishments of the Common Laws of England*.

Men sat in stocks for spells that ranged from one hour to a whole day. A Thetford man spent all day in the stocks in 1583 for playing cards when he should have been in church; John Rolfe was put in the stocks in Westminster all night after grabbing a beggar from a constable (his wife was let go at sunset).[101] One-hour stints were handed out for 'evil' words, vagrancy, and helping someone break out of stocks; two-hour stretches for bad-mouthing constables, leaving church early, lodging inmates, and to a libeller who 'fixed' a 'paper' on a maypole; three hours for clowning around in court, 'slaunderous speeches', 'playing trap for money' on Sunday, forging passes, refusing to give officers a helping hand, and bickering with masters; four hours was felt to be right for not paying poor rates, trading punches, and for a sexton who hid a plague corpse in his church; six-hour stints for drinking too long, brawling, housing 'masterless' men, and for taunting officers.[102] Men tended to sit for longer spells. Most women were given one or two hours for crimes that included scolding, beating children, vagrancy, and lodging women 'with childe', and a Norwich single woman who tried to 'poyson herselffe with rattenbone'. A number of women got six-hour stretches for being drunk.

[101] NRO T/C1/2, fo. 103; WAC WCB/1, fo. 262.

[102] See, for example, GA GBR/G/G3/SO/1, fos. 16, 47v; NRO NMCC 7, fo. 290; 25, fo. 183; LMA MJ/SBR/1, fo. 135; WAC WCB/1, fo. 210; DHC DC/DOB/8/1, fos. 23, 169v, 277v, 319; OHC C/FC/1/A1/O1, fo. 356v.

A few scolds were also put in the stocks for six hours. Jane Browne and her husband from Whitechapel spent six hours in the stocks for 'emptieinge great quantitye of nightworke into the comon sewer' in 1613.[103] As with whipping, symbolic splashes sharpened embarrassment. Thieves in Norwich sat in the stocks with hay, saye, yarn, bread, hens, linen, or geese straddling their shoulders or hanging from their necks. 'Vacabonde' Robert Archer who tried to trick people with 'counterfett ringes' in 1568 was 'whipped at a cartes tayle and after set in the stocks wth a paper and the ryngs hangyng thereon that the people myght knowe of hym and souche as he ys'.[104]

No marketplace would have been complete without pillories that were associated with 'deceiptfull' selling. A dictionary described pillories as 'engin[es] of punishment or rather shame by which petty malefactors are made gazing stocks to the people [with their] necks locked into a hole, as it were, peeping through a door'.[105] Manchester's pillory cost 34s. 1d. to make in 1625, including 12s. 6d. to cut down a tree and chop it up. Other towns spent 24s. 2d., twenty-two shillings, sixteen shillings, and 13s. 4d. for a pillory. Pillories were 'taken' up and down at a cost of four-pence in Norwich (1580–1620).[106] A perjurer stands in a pillory ('for perjury, cheating, and other misdemeanors') in Seller's sixth drawing (Figure 3.4). Guards ring the pillory to stop trouble, but a crowd mills around and someone throws something. A total of 222 people were put in pillories in records I have seen (159 from London alone): 169 men and 53 women (24 per cent). Exeter 'pilloried' a large number of women, each one for theft. Men stood in shame for theft, bribes, libel, seditious words, rumour-mongering, kidnapping, coaching begging, plotting murder, 'discovering the queens secrets', and most often for 'deceit' crimes like counterfeiting, forgery, and selling 'light' food or fuel. Women spent two or three hours in pillories for ill-treating children, 'harlotry', theft, witchcraft, light coal sacks and other 'deceit' crimes. One woman wished that London would burn to the ground. 'Harlots' had their hair 'clipped of above theire eares' in symbolic shaming that had a long past. 'Comen and abhomynable harlott' Elizabeth White, 'otherwyse called Flounsing Besse', had her hair 'rounded as short as her eares' on the pillory next to the 'standered in Chepe' in 1548. Twenty-one-year-old Magdalyn Dawyn, who crossed London 'contrary to all honestye of

[103] NRO NMCC 8, fo. 281; 13, fo. 454; LMA MJ/SBR/1, fo. 645. Other offences included selling stolen goods, tippling, faking pregnancy, and illegitimacy.

[104] NRO NMCC 9, fo. 519. See also NRO NMCC 12, fos. 71, 179, 472; 13, fos. 76, 173; 15, fo. 162; 8, fos. 461, 650; 10, fo. 222. And for other towns and cities see GA GBR/G/G3/SO/1, fo. 47; WAC WCB/1, fos. 3, 9, 12; WCB/2, fo. 45; ERO D/B5/SB2/9, fo. 176; LMA MJ/SBR/1, fo. 391.

[105] Phillips, *New World of Words*, s.v. 'Pillory'. See Wingate, *Justice Revived*, 184; R. Chamberlain, *The Complete Justice Being a Compendious and Exact Collection Out of All Such Statutes and Authors as May Any Way Concern the Office of a Justice of Peace* (1681), 191, 276–7, 280–1.

[106] Earwaker, *Constables' Accounts of the Manor of Manchester*, I, 150–1. See also WSHC G22/1/205/2, fo. 13; NRO Norwich Chamberlain's Accounts, 1580–9, fos. 110v, 267v, 308v; 1589–1602, fos. 140v, 170; 1603–25, fo. 321v; T/C1/1, fo. 78v; GA GBR/F/4/3, fo. 99v; SAI C/3/4/1/25, fo. 9.

Figure 3.4 'The Punishment of the Pillory'.
Source: Seller, *A Booke of the Punishments of the Common Laws of England.*

womanhood apparelyd in mannes clothinge' in 1575, was put in the pillory 'in mans apparell' with her hair hanging 'women like' over her shoulders.[107]

Seller drew whipping, stocking, and pillorying, but not ducking. There is no clear reason for this. Ducking was still being used, although less so, and it was the only gender-specific penalty at this time. Only women were 'duckt', 'kuckt', 'cooked', 'pumped', or 'plownsed' in a 'cockeinge stoole', 'cock queane stool', 'duck-stoole', or 'gomstoole'.[108] 'Cucking-stool or cokestool', in Blount's *Law-Dictionary* (1691), was 'an engine [for] punishment of scolds and unquiet women by ducking in water'.[109] A *c.*1630 ballad told how 'This little Devil / With her unquiet tongue / In a wheele-barrowe brought…into the cucking stoole'.[110] Ducking stools were for 'idle, lewd and disorderly scolding women' (Deptford), 'harlots [and] skowlds' (Southampton), and 'unreasonable women' (Salford).[111] Our 'cucking stoole in

[107] LMA Reps. 13(2), fo. 179; 11, fo. 451; 12, fos. 128v–9. See also LMA Reps. 18, fo. 372; 19, fo. 93v; Letterbook V, fo. 271.

[108] WAC WCB/1, fos. 76–7; DHC DC/DOB/8/1, fo. 79; LMA MJ/SBR/4, fo. 417; MJ/SBR/2, fo. 174; SA SC9/2/1, fo. 2. For stools see BRO R/FA/3/11; WSHC G22/1/205/2, fo. 59v; GA GBR/F/4/3, fos. 145v; 273; SAI C/3/4/1/15; LMA MJ/SBR/4, fo. 502; HEA BG11/4/6, 4/1659, fo. 7.

[109] T. Blount, *Nomo-lexikon, A Law-Dictionary* (1691), s.v. 'cuckingstool'.

[110] *The Cucking of a Scould to the Tune of The Merchant of [?]* (*c.*1630).

[111] E. Melling, ed., *Kentish Sources VI: Crime and Punishment* (Maidstone, 1969), 193; SA 6/1, fos. 13, 14, 25, 27, 28; J. G. de T. Mandley, ed., *The Portmote or Court Leet Records of the Borough or Town and Royal Manor of Salford, 1597–1669*, 2 vols, Chetham Society Publications, NS, 46 (Manchester, 1902), I, 61.

the tyme of the late warres [was] destroyed', Southwell constables told Nottinghamshire justices in 1654, 'the want thereof [they added has] 'encoureged many lewd and turbulent women to continue in their unquiett and unpeaceable behavior'. The 'great lacke' of a ducking stool in Southampton in 1579 left the town without anything to 'terrour' 'harlotts [and] skowlds'.[112] 'Wicked' Jane Sampford from Exeter was 'cuckt' for 'roaring' in 1619, shouting that John Jewell was a sheep thief whose wife was a 'whore', holding up fingers to 'maketh hornes' crying 'bitch a hundred tymes'. She also called Katherine Wilcox 'carted whore' and John Taylor 'cuckoldy Taylor'. Heavy-drinking Alice Thomas, who was also from Exeter, was 'cuckt' in the same year for calling a doctor's servant 'whore-monger and murderer', Thomasine Oliver 'scabbed whore', and Wilmott Prud a 'tinckered [tinckled?] whore' with 'wormes crawl[ing] from her', whose husband was 'a murderer and theefe'.[113]

Winchester forked out £1 5s. 5d for a ducking stool weighing thirteen pounds in 1685 (rope 'to let down' the chair cost 5s. 9d. one year later). An Ipswich sawyer picked up a few shillings 'for sawinge of 45 foote for the coocking stoole' in 1615. A new ducking stool cost £2 8s. 4d. in Reading (1631), 18s. 5d. in Marlborough (1611), and 9s. 8d. in Gloucester (1656).[114] Some stools needed taking to water at a cost of six-pence in Colchester (1579), a shilling in Marlborough (1625), and fifteen-pence in Gloucester (1571).[115] Three 'dusckyngs' was the standard dose, although 'abhomynable' Agnes Richards was 'duckyd in the water iii tymes at the leaste' in Norwich in 1633.[116] Stools were taken straight to scolds in symbolic moments. Augustine Loggins got 3s. 4d. in Gloucester in 1656 'for haulinge ye ducking stoole into everye streete to affrite the scolds'. Southampton put a 'cucking stoole' on wheels in 1604 'to bee carried from dore to dore as the scold shall inhabitt so that they may receave punishment'.[117] Some scolds 'rode' on stools. Elizabeth Marten, who called Elizabeth Webb 'whore' on Devizes streets in 1583, was made 'to ryde in the cucking stole from the Guyldhall' to her home, where it was left at the door.[118] 'Evell' John Willows is the only man I have seen who was humbled in a ducking stool after getting Agnes Knagges 'with chylde' in Norwich in 1549. He was 'sette on the cockestoole with a ray hoode uppon his hedd' and 'caryed abote the market' in a flush of blushes.[119] In variants, scolds were tied to 'a

[112] NOTTA C/QSM/1/13, fo. 12; SA 6/1, fo. 14. See also GA GBR/G/G3/SO/1, fos. 91v, 93; DRO ECA B/1/4, fo. 88; DHC DC/DOB/8/1, fo. 160v.

[113] DRO ECA C1/61, fos. 196, 197, 199.

[114] HA W/K5/8, fo. 40.

[115] WSHC G22/1/205/2, fo. 13; GA GBR/F/4/3, fos. 99v, 145v.

[116] NRO NMCC 8, fo. 108. See also ESBHRO RYE 1/6, fo. 144v; NRO NMCC 10, fo. 735; 13, fo. 129; DHC DC/DOB/8/1, fo. 180v.

[117] GA GBR/F/4/6, fo. 203; SA 6/1, fo. 28.

[118] B. H. Cunnington, ed., *Some Annals of the Borough of Devizes*, 2 vols (Devizes, 1925–6), II, 2. See also OHC C/FC/1/A1/O1, fo. 213; NRO NMCC 6, fo. 11; DRO ECA B/1/4, fos. 127, 135, 170; ECA C1/61, fos. 341, 661.

[119] NRO NMCC 5, fo. 541.

boats tayle' and 'towed' or 'rowed' along rivers. Three Exeter scolds were 'towed at the sturnne of a bote through the whole [River] Ex' in 1562.[120] Westminster scold Maudlin Tichon was tied to 'a boats tayle' wearing 'mortars' in 1611 ('according to the ancient custome of the citty') and 'drawn through the water to the other side of the Thames'. 'Comon disturber of her neighbours' Alice Webb, who 'abused constables' and a burgess in 1614, wore 'the mortars around her neck to her house… fast stapled with iron'.[121] I have seen fees for 'a bridle for scoulds' and 'reines' to lead them along streets. A few scolds were warned to be quiet 'or have the bridle' [one 'through the towne']. But only one scold (from Salford), who chided a constable 'uncivell[y]' in 1655, had 'the bridle upon her [for] one whole hour'.[122]

Like felony cases, discretion guided decision-making. 'Some servants deserve to be beaten with more stripes', one author advised; 'weigh ye disposition of delinquents, some are more flexible than others'. Hand out 'diversitie of punishments according to the desert of the offender', Charles Richardson advised in 1616.[123] There were sliding scales. Offenders were 'grievously', 'soundly', or 'severely whiped'. A Norwich 'procurer' was 'specially ponyshed'. Frances Webb, on the other hand, was 'privately and gently whipped'. Three Northampton thieves were 'moderately corrected'.[124] We never find out what 'severely' or 'gently' mean. The fewest 'stripes' was six and the sharpest sentence was sixty-six 'strypes' that cut cutpurse and bigamist Thomas Logan's back in Exeter; 'incontynent' Joanne Kent had 'xl lashes' there in 1564.[125] A Hampshire thief was given 'six good stripes'; Devon beggar Anne Noble got 'a dozen whips' in 1623'; Lawrence Poynton winced through 'xxiiii lashes' in Thetford's 'open marcate' in 1633; light-fingered John Billings endured '30 lashes' at Norwich's cross.[126]

People were treated differently. Richard Gates and John Findall from Northampton were whipped 'about' the market in 1675, but Findall was given 'more severe punishment'.[127] Northampton had a 'great'/'long' or 'little'/'short round' through the market. Two thieves were whipped on the 'long round', but

[120] DRO ECA B/1/4, fo. 187.

[121] WAC WCB/1, fo. 81; WCB/2, fo. 18. Alice Howte, who was 'taken' in London late at night with a 'suspected person in her howse' in 1554, was 'drawen throughe the ponde in Smythfelde': LMA Rep. 13(2), fo. 179.

[122] Mandley, *Portmote or Court Leet Records of the Borough or Town and Royal Manor of Salford*, II, 145. See also Earwaker, *Constables' Accounts of the Manor of Manchester*, II, 59; Earwaker, *Court Leet Records of the Manor of Manchester*, III, 283; LA CNP 3/2/1, fos. 42, 43, 122; SHA 3356/2430, fo. 46v.

[123] HL EL 1163; Richardson, *Sermon Concerning the Punishment of Malefactors*, 20.

[124] NRO NMCC 9, fo. 110; NA NQS/3, fo. 28; NQS/4, fos. 24v, 25. For severe: ESBHRO QO/EW/8, fo. 83v; LERO QS6/1/2, fo. 6v; SAI B/105/2/6, fo. 90; and gentle: LERO QS6/1/2, fo. 47v; NA NQS/3, fos. 26, 84; HA Q1/1, fo. 115. See P. King, *Crime, Law, and Discretion in England, 1740–1820* (Oxford, 2000), chaps 7–9.

[125] DRO ECA N/1/4, fo. 245.

[126] HA W/D3/3; NRO T/C1/9, fo. 4; DRO ECA C1/2, fo. 144; NRO Norwich Sessions book 1691–1702, 10/1699 sessions.

[127] NA NQS/1, fo. 69.

their partner in crime was whipped 'privately'.[128] Women were more likely to go the shorter distance; 98 of 107 men went the 'long round' (92 per cent).[129] William Findon was ordered to be 'whipt the long round' in 1694 but a change-of-mind 'afterwards' sent him on the 'short round' instead.[130] 'Long' or 'short' are crossed out in records as courts had second thoughts. Crossings-out make decision-making visible. Rye's clerk drew a line through 'whipped' after Margaret Dore was found guilty of 'whoredom' in 1599 and put 'carted about the towne' instead. 'Next market' was blacked out next to the name of a thief in 1690; 'to be whipt privately' took its place. A dark smudge blots out 'at the post', shifting the whipping of a dice-addicted Norwich apprentice to 'the great chamber' in 1588.[131]

Courts could soften or sharpen punishment according to a string of variables like character, status, age, or gender. The pleas of family could matter. William Brame and Margaret Bond from Norwich were set free in 1576 after 'promising to marye and live honestly as man and wife ought to doe'.[132] Like 'pleading the belly' in felony cases, pregnancy tailored decisions. Two 'comen harlots' were ordered to be 'doppyd in the Theamys' in 1551 but a third 'with child' was 'spared'. Dorothy Baskerville from Gloucester was whipped for stealing pewter bowls in 1618 'as she be not with child'.[133] It could help husbands if their wife was pregnant. A Southampton 'cryar' who opened a gate in the middle of the night to steal wood had his whipping 'deferred' as his wife 'lyeth in childbed'.[134] Health was another consideration. Mary Homes was to be whipped in Northampton 'if in health'. A scold was 'ordered to be plownsed when the weather is warmer'; an 'unfitt' woman was spared the stocks in Dorchester. A London widow who was put in the pillory for 'sedycous words' in 1559 was allowed to 'sytt in an old chayre parte of the tyme' owing to her 'age and weaknes of bodye'.[135]

Courts toned down the letter of the law when it felt right to do so. This had a large hand in framing the scope of public whipping. Already in the last quarter of the sixteenth century people found guilty of 'felony' were getting whipped in Norwich. Greater numbers were whipped on suspicion of committing a felony: fifty-seven in a single sessions book in the city covering 1571–81 (forty men and seventeen women). Numbers were larger still at London Bridewell. Justices sent growing numbers of 'suspected' and 'acquitted' felons to be whipped there after 1600. Whipping tended to focus on petty larceny. 'Pious perjury'—devaluing stolen goods to under a shilling—had a role in this. The whippings of forty-nine

[128] NA NQS/4, fo. 22. [129] Figures are from NA NQS/1–4. [130] NA NQS/3, fo. 45v.

[131] ESBHRO RYE1/6, fo. 284; HEA Q/SM/2, fo. 71v; NRO NMCC 12, fo. 165. See also HEA Q/SM/2, fo. 35; LERO QS5/1/1, fo. 62; NRO T/QS/1, fos. 2v, 42; NMCC 10, fo. 749; 13, fo. 180.

[132] NRO NMCC 10, fo. 43. [133] LMA Reps. 12, fo. 495v; 14, fo. 195.

[134] J. W. Horrocks, ed., *The Assembly Book of Southampton*, 4 vols, Southampton Record Society (Southampton, 1917–25), III, 58–9.

[135] NA NQS/4, fo. 64; GA GBR/G/G3/SO/1, fo. 70v; DHC DC/DOB/8/1, fo. 117. See also NRO NMCC 8, fo. 692; 9, fo. 631; DHC DC/DOB/8/1, fo. 322; SAI B/105/2/8, fo. 25v; DRO ECA C1/61, fo. 79; BRO N/JQ/1/1, fo. 24.

small-time thieves are noted in a Norwich Sessions book covering 1602–18. Many petty thieves were whipped more than once: John Child three times (1630–48); Bridget Nobbs four times (1645–53); Cicely Fuller was also whipped four times, once with Nobbs (1648–51). John Quantrell was whipped four times and branded at least three times until the day arrived in 1674, as the tumbling cards said it would, when a judge told him that he would ride 'to the place of execution there to be hanged by the necke' until your 'body be dead'.[136]

We should keep this theft focus in mind as we turn next to patterns of punishment over the sixteenth and seventeenth centuries. To cut a long story short: the number of 'publique' whippings fell as whipping inside soared; people continued to be put in pillories at a steady rate; ducking stools and stocks were well on the way to becoming antique museum pieces by the start of the eighteenth century, though they could still have a valuable role as warning signs.

III

Historians of criminal justice over the 'long eighteenth century' pay too little attention to events before 1675. They want to emphasize how far the period 1680–1820 constituted a key turning point. The first chapter of Faramerz Dabhoiwala's book on England's 'first sexual revolution', for example, covers 'The Decline and Fall of Public Punishment' and argues unconvincingly that whipping rates fell after 1700 (not earlier), since it is then, he believes, that attitudes towards sex softened. Robert Shoemaker similarly has little to say about anything before 1660 in arguing that the first significant falls in public whipping in London occurred after 1700. His first run of statistics begins in 1723. He also points out that 'the distinction [between "public" and "private" whipping] first emerges in the Old Bailey Proceedings around 1757'.[137]

But it is clear that the frequency of public whipping fell before 1700 and that the extent of 'private' whipping grew at the same time. There was in fact an

[136] NRO Norwich Sessions Books 1571–81, fo. 176; 1581–91, fo. 115v (for felons). For multiple whippings see NRO Norwich Sessions Books 1629–36, fo. 35v; 1637–64, fo. 33; 1639–54, fos. 74v, 81v, 101; 1654–70, 1/1661 sessions. For Quantrell see NRO Norwich Sessions books 1639–54, fos. 110, 130; 1637–64, 4/1659 sessions, 1/1661 sessions; 1654–70, 9/1661 sessions, 4/1663 sessions, 12/1663 sessions; 1671–91, 4/1674 sessions. See Kesselring, 'Law, status, and the lash', 516.

[137] F. Dabhoiwala, *The Origins of Sex: A History of the First Sexual Revolution* (2012), chap. 1; R. Shoemaker, 'Streets of Shame? The crowd and public punishments in London, 1700–1820', in Devereaux and Griffiths, *Penal Practice and Culture*, 254, n. 23; R. Shoemaker, *The London Mob: Violence and Disorder in Eighteenth-Century England* (2004), chap. 4. Peter King charts a fall in public whipping in Essex (statistics start in 1760): *Crime, Justice, and Discretion*, 272–3. John Beattie notes a fall in Surrey and Sussex: *Crime and the Courts in England, 1660–1800* (Oxford. 1986), 614; and a sharp fall at the Old Bailey after the 1718 Transportation Act: J. Beattie, *Policing and Punishment in London 1660–1750: Urban Crime and the Limits of Terror* (Oxford, 2001), 446. And further north: G. Morgan and P. Rushton, *Rogues, Thieves, and the Rule of Law; The Problem of Law Enforcement in North-East England, 1718–1800* (1998), 72–5.

expectation that punishment would take place indoors. Household heads were told to punish rowdy dependents at home and it was a natural step for courts to rule that youngsters could be whipped 'at home at ther owne howsys'.[138] A Westminster maid who said 'that the most part of English women were whores' in 1612 was punished at home by her mistress after 'she confessed in open court'. The master of a Dorchester lad who sat in church with his hat on laughing when a 'sidesman' asked him to take it off was 'willed' to 'correct him' in his house. Two brothers landed in court in 1632 for 'quarelling' in church after one of them would not let the other sit down. Their father was asked to take them home and 'whippe them well'.[139] Punishing inside was routine in trade guilds, schools, and hospitals. 'Divers idle boyes' who poked fun at Reading's Free School master as he walked home in 1642 were either whipped in the school or 'by their fathers in their owne houses'. The London Fishmongers had three options when punishing apprentice James Johnson after he outraged a liveryman's wife with 'very vile and lewde speeches' in 1617: 'openly in the house [company hall], at Bridewell, or by the apprentice's master in his owne howse'. They plumped for the third course.[140]

Shoemaker's 'first example of the phrase "private whipping"' in London area sessions records is in 1733. This is a late date for the metropolis and the country. 'Private' whipping is noted down on record in the first quarter of the seventeenth century; 'private' punishment crops up earlier. 'Private' differentiated penalties, but more often clerks jotted down indoor sites. There had been a turn to punishing inside since the first bridewell took its first batch of prisoners in 1555. Many thousands were whipped in bridewells all over England over the next 150 years. 'Private' punishment was a routine feature of decision-making in early modern courts. Magistrates sometimes shifted penalties from outside to inside. Thief John Blussever, who swiped a sheet off a Gloucester hedge in 1625, was ordered to be 'whipped against the whipping post' and put in stocks for an hour: 'whipped in bridewell this day', the clerk wrote under the entry.[141] Wrongdoers were also 'privately whipped in ye gaole', though it's puzzling to see Herefordshire thief Edward Davie being whipped 'in gaole' in 1687 with a line drawn through 'privately'. A sheriff took a pair of Wiltshire wood thieves 'to prison without delay' in 1653 to be 'whipt on the naked shoulders untill they bleede'.[142]

[138] NRO NMCC 11, fo. 318v.

[139] WAC WCB/1, fo. 161; DHC DC/DOB/8/1, fos. 261v, 111. See also DHC DC/DOB/8/1, fos. 57, 75, 81v, 84v, 90, 110v, 164v, 174v, 175; NRO NMCC 9, fo. 165; 11, fo. 318v; 12, fo. 491; 15, fo. 230v. For domestic punishment see Griffiths, *Youth and Authority*, chap. 6; M. T. White, 'Ordering the Mob: London's Public Punishments, c. 1783–1868', (PhD thesis, University of Hertfordshire, 2009), 227–32 251–2.

[140] Guilding, *Reading Records*, IV, 36–7; GL MS 5770/1, fos. 494–5. In London, there was 'ye crosse or place of correccion' at St Bartholomew's Hospital and a 'cross for correction' at Christ's Orphanage: SBHA Governors' Journals 2, fo. 39v; 3, fo. 45v; LMA MS 12806/2, fo. 247v.

[141] GA GBR/G/G3/SO/1, fo. 115.

[142] HEA Q/SM/2, fo. 35; WSHC A1/150/10, Easter/1653 sessions. See also CA QJB/1/4, fo. 25; HA Q3/3, fo. 225; LERO QS/5/1/1, fo. 19v; OHC QSM I/1II, fo. 73; NA NQS/3, fos. 171v, 189; NQS/4, fos. 6v, 25.

Far more people were whipped inside bridewells than outside walls. Whipping was the 'usual correction' at Norwich Bridewell.[143] Offenders were often whipped when they entered and left a bridewell. Six or twelve 'stripes' were the norm in Norwich. The head of 'house' in Tenterden got six-pence 'for everie rogue, vagabond, sturdye begger, and idle and disorderly person' he whipped in the 1640s. Reading constables claimed thirty-eight shillings for whipping rogues in the bridewell in 1626, although governors gave them half of this.[144] There was a growing resort to punishing 'privately' or 'privily' in the case of two vagrant women in Westminster in 1612.[145] Anyone not giving a helping hand to constables to take vagrants to London Bridewell in 1581 was punished 'privately'. 'Counsel gever' Agnes Walker, who gave tips to a woman who left her child on a street in 1574, was 'punished secretly'.[146] This calculated use of 'private' by courts can only mean that punishing inside was an accepted part of deliberation. Wiltshire petty thief Joanne Mason was 'privately whipped [until] her backe doe bleede' in 1610.[147] Westminster Court of Burgesses, whose records survive for six years (1610–16), punished a good number of offenders 'privately'. A 'vagrant strumpett' was 'stripp'd naked from the wast upward [and] privately whipp'd in the courthouse' in 1612 for giving birth to a 'base' child. A waterman's daughter who called 'diverse' women 'whores' was 'privately whipped' in 1615.[148] After they were caught having sex in 1614, Mary Lilly was whipped 'at a cart's tail' along the Strand to Temple Bar and David Seogall was 'privately whipped', 'for it appeared that [he] was drawn thereunto by [her] allurement [and] she was a comon strumpet'.[149]

England's two largest cities—London and Norwich—show significant levels of indoor whipping.[150] Thousands were whipped inside London Bridewell not in the cold light of day; the whipping-room was handily placed next to the courtroom. A noteworthy number of offenders were whipped in the 'chamber', 'great chamber', or 'assembly chamber' in Norwich, and this gathered a head of steam after 1600. But they were whipped inside before 1600. Ninety-six thieves, vagrants, and

[143] NRO NMCC 25, fo. 181. For typical cases: HA Q3/3, fo. 113; HEA Q/SM/4, fo. 211v; SAI B/105/2/6, fo. 181; DRO ECA C1/61, fo. 339; ESBHRO QO/EW3, fo. 67v.

[144] NRO NMCC 14, fos. 39, 405; 15, fo. 169v; 20, fo. 396v; CKS TE/S2, fos. 46, 80, 84, 98, 138; BRO R/AC1/2, fos. 205, 206.

[145] WAC WCB/1, fo. 198.

[146] LMA MS 12806/2, fo. 117v; SBHA Governors' Journal 2, fo. 194v; SAI B/105/2/3, fo. 68v; B/105/2/4, fo. 23; LMA WJ/SR/NS/36/162; WAC WCB/1, fo. 164.

[147] Cunnington, *Records of the County of Wiltshire*, 29.

[148] WAC WCB/1, fo. 30; WCB/2, fo. 112.

[149] WAC WCB/1, fo, 164. See also WAC WCB/1, fos. 99, 156, 238, 273; WCB/2, fos. 10, 34, 30, 99; NA NQS/1, fo. 104; NQS/3, fos. 171v, 189; NQS/4, fos. 6v, 25.

[150] I traced Norwich's whipping patterns in 'Bodies and souls in Norwich', esp. 90–1. A total of 3,179 people were whipped in Mayor's Court records up to 1700: just 139 after 1660. Nobody was whipped in the 1690s; 627 people were whipped in sessions books in 1570–1700; numbers fell around 1650 but rose after 1690. The last person put in stocks by the Mayor's Court was in 1687; the last scold was ducked in 1670. Just six people were put in the stocks and pillory by justices and nobody was ducked.

others were flogged in the 'assembly chamber' in 1576–95.[151] Other towns followed suit. Judith Brading ('approved to be a whore' by confession), who mixed with 'notable bawd' Goody Bande, was 'whipped closelye' in Southampton's town hall in 1615 (Bande was 'sowndlye whipped at a carts tayle throughout the towne').[152] Warminster apprentice William Matthew, who 'thrust' a knife into Walter Rudman's thigh in 1603, was 'whipped in the towne Hall [to] the end yt might be an example of warninge to him and other lewd mynded boyes'. A runaway apprentice was 'whipt' inside Dorchester's 'hall' in 1636.[153]

Turning inside was the dynamic element in punishing petty crime. Punishment inside was quicker and easier to control. A hand-picked audience was sometimes invited. 'Myching and fylching' Robert Davy was 'whipped' in Norwich 'new hall' 'in the face of other servants' in 1571. Three Exeter boys whose 'wanton lyffe' got them in trouble in 1561 'were whypped naked in the gulydhall in the presence of bayliffs [and] skolers of the highe scoole'.[154] It was standard practice in trade guilds to whip disruptive apprentices in company halls before brother apprentices. London apprentice Robert Coles, who stole cloth from his master in 1573 and 'confederated with his fellow to cutt broad clothes and carseys brought to his masters house to tacke thinkinge to make his master banckroupte [was] ponished' in the hall 'before sundrie householders and apprentices'.[155] Some fishmongers' apprentices were taken to task for 'great abuses' in the stocks market in 1610. Wardens ordered a 'mynister' to be 'ready' and 'masked' as the apprentices were 'stripped to the girdle' before 'as many boyes and apprentizes of the company [as] could be gotten hither to see there punishment for examples sake'. The audience was 'streightly charged' not 'to speak word to anyone [of] the matter, nor [to] cast in the teeth of them that is punished', who were 'exhorted to take a new course of liff'.[156] There were no 'public' blushes. Indoors was a softer alternative to the public glare of the post or what in Exeter was called 'the open shame of the cart'.[157] A Norwich apprentice who was caught playing dice in 1588 was whipped in the 'great chamber'—'at the poast' is crossed out—and warned that he would be 'whipped at the poast' if he was ever found to be 'disobedyent' again.[158] Indoor settings were pleasingly or disconcertingly mild for some. A Chippenham thief told county justices in 1618 that 'he had [had] no open punishment but was whipped in the Comon Hall at Marleborough'. Justices 'demanded how yt came to pass that he was not openlye whipped; 'he sayeth he knoweth not'.[159] John Dixon was 'tyed at a carts taile' at London Guildhall in 1610 for his 'intollerable abuses'

[151] NRO NMCC 10–12. [152] Horrocks, *Assembly Book of Southampton*, I, 176.

[153] Cunnington, *Records of the County of Wiltshire*, 8–9; DHC DC/DOB/8/1, fo. 57. See also DRO ECA B/1/4, fos. 169, 297, 375; DHC DC/DOB/8/1, fos. 223, 322.

[154] NRO NMCC 9, fo. 148; DRO ECA B/1/4, fo. 120. See also LMA Rep, 13, fo. 127; GL MSS 5770/1, fo. 140–1; 11,588/1, fo. 168v; WSHC G22/1/205/2, fos. 72v, 74v.

[155] CH Company Minute Book 1558–81, fo. 177. [156] GL MS 5770/1, fos. 594–5.

[157] DRO ECA B/1/4, fo. 152. [158] NRO NMCC 12, fo. 165.

[159] Cunnington, *Records of the County of Wiltshire*, 62.

to his master and whipped along 'publique streets' to his home. I 'never expected such publique punishment', his master told aldermen; 'he is the son of a gentlewoman of worship'. Dixon was duly whipped in 'private' at Bridewell instead.[160]

Existing work on 'private' and 'public' penalties tends to play down coexistences. Reading constables asked this question in 1633: 'in what stocks swearers and drunkerdes and alehouse haunters shalbe put into whether private or publicke?' A clothworker who fathered a 'base' child in 1577 was told that he would 'either be whipped in London Bridewell privately' or holding the child on a pillory.[161] Penalties we think of as public were integral to punishing inside. The bridewells at Clerkenwell and Oxford both had arsenals called 'instruments of punishment'.[162] 'In Bridewell', an inventory drawn up in Gloucester in 1635 listed a 'payer of stocks' and 'whipping stock'; a 'pillory with iron pinns' was added later. Norwich Bridewell had 'two whipinge postes', a 'paire of stockes', and 'chaire for unruly persons'.[163] Bridewells had stocks in Salisbury, Devizes, Durham, Dorset, Oxford, and Reading; a cage and stocks in London; pillories in Dorset and Oxford; and a 'correctione poste' at Ipswich (the prison had '2 payer of stocks' in 1580).[164] Stocks were called imprisonment. Richard Chamberlain believed that 'the escaping of a person out of the stocks [is] a breach of prison'. Richard Bradley, who was fined 3s. 4d. for hitting a Prescot constable in 1552, was back in trouble soon after for 'breaking' the king's gaol or 'stockys'.[165]

Standing on streets, cages were in some senses liminal, neither public nor private. Seller drew 'the cage for vagrant beggars and other unruly persons' in his second sketch (Figure 3.5). It was called the 'vagrant cage' in East Sussex and the 'cadge for punyshment of roges and other offenders' in Oxford.[166] The cage that stood next to 'the meale markett house' in Bishopsgate (London) was 'nine foote in length east and west and four foot or thereabouts in breadth'. Shrewsbury had a cage that was ten feet long and two feet wide. St Martin-in-the-Fields spent £25 for a cage at Charing Cross with 'the bedells chamber over' it in 1602.[167] Vagrants

160 LMA Rep. 29, fo. 184v. See also NRO NMCC 11, fos. 145, 216, 251; Le Hardy, *Hertford County Records*, I, 298–9.

161 Guilding, *Reading Records*, III, 200; LMA MS 12806/2, fos. 174–6.

162 LMA MJ/SBR/2, fo. 274; H. E. Salter, ed., *Oxford Council Acts, 1626–1665*, Oxford Historical Society, 95 (Oxford, 1933), 33–4.

163 GA GBR/F/4/5, fo. 33; NRO Norwich Bridewell Treasurers Accounts 1, 1622; 2, fo. 17.

164 Cunnington, *Records of the County of Wiltshire*, 58; B. H. Cunnington, ed., *Some Annals of the Borough of Devizes*, 2 vols (Devizes, 1925–6), II, 118; C. M. Fraser, ed., *Durham Quarter Sessions Rolls 1471–1625*, Surtees Society, 199 (Newcastle-upon-Tyne, 1991), 268; Hearing and Bridges, *Dorset Quarter Sessions Order Book*, 279, 299; Blades, *Oxford Quarter Sessions Order Book*, 28, 54, 66; BRO R/FA/3/5; R/FA/3/17; B. E. Masters, ed., *Chamber Accounts of the Sixteenth Century*, London Record Society, 20 (1984), 74, 76; SAI C/3/4/1/13.

165 Chamberlain, *Complete Justice*, 385, 305; F. A. Bailey, ed., *A Selection from the Prescot Court Leet and Other Records, 1447–1600*, The Record Society of Lancashire and Cheshire, 89 (Chester. 1937), 118.

166 ESBHRO QO/EW1, fo. 37v; OHC C/FC/1/A1/02, fo. 336v.

167 LMA Rep. 49, fos. 80v–1; SHA 3365/545. London records show that cages were for vagrants, beggars, rogues, and 'lewd' people: LMA Reps. 12, fo. 287; 16, fos. 519v; 23, fo. 505, 514; 51, fo. 79.

Figure 3.5 'The Punishment of the Cage'.
Source: Seller, *A Booke of the Punishments of the Common Laws of England.*

were not the only troublemakers to suffer a stint in a cage. A number of scolds were put in the cage in Norwich for up to three hours in the 1660s. Norwich worsted-weaver John Cobb was put in the cage in 1551 'with a paper on his hede' for 'speking sedycous wordes in the open markett att the crosse'. London hosier Hugh Eton, who in 'fonde fassyon and dysguysed' was taken 'irreverently walkyng up and downe before the moste blessed sacrament disturbing prests at masse' in St Brides Church in 1544, was put in a cage in his 'dysguysed garments' with a 'paper' that was 'taken from his hed' and 'fyxed on the outsyde' of the cage.[168] Whippings also took place next to cages. Christopher Wheatly was 'whipped at ye cage by the guildhall' in Norwich in 1583. 'Singleman' Robert Croft and Cicely Rochester were sentenced to be whipped in the same city 'in the great chamber with rodds' one year later, but he 'did before ponishment leape out the wyndow' and for this aggravated offence he was taken outside to be 'whipped openly at ye cage'.[169]

The choice to punish someone in 'publique' or 'private' remained on the table all the way through the seventeenth century. Magistrates in Preston compiled a 'remembrance of such persons as were punyshed' in the town in 1604–5.

[168] NRO NMCC 6, fo. 98; LMA Letterbook K, fo. 102. See also NRO NMCC 23, fos. 248v, 126v, 152v, 226, 245v, 273; 24, fo. 20v.
[169] NRO NMCC 11, fos. 243, 135.

This 'remembrance' shows a creative readiness to carefully consider whether to punish people in private or public (or both). Offenders were locked up in prison or whipped behind closed doors for the most part. But some of them were punished outside in 'the open', like Hereford shoemakers 'Dist Bowper' and 'Dick Wicked Will' who were carted through the busy marketplace. Ralph Birley and saddler Edward Glaze were 'punnished in prison' and later 'proclamed' at 'the crose' in the heart of Preston.[170] Separate ideas of punishing someone inside and outside were clear at this time, but they were also deliberately coupled to powerful effect. Northampton thief Thomas Bennett was whipped both 'privately' and 'publickley' in 1672. Vagrant Isaac Phillips was 'whipt in the house of correccon' at Lewes in 1686 and at the market post afterwards. Joanne Kent, who was carted for 'incontinent life' in Exeter in 1564, was also given 'xl lasshes' 'inside' in the hall.[171] In other cases, 'public' and 'private' were merged when someone was locked up in a prison or bridewell and also whipped 'in the open markett'. Lawrence Poynton was put in Thetford Bridewell in 1633 and 'whipped [with] xxiiii lashes' a few days later in the middle of the 'open marcatte'.[172] Others were sentenced to a spell in prison or a bridewell cell and locked in stocks with people looking on afterwards. A Mile End drover was sent to the bridewell in Colchester in 1669 for 'imbeazelling a hole bays woofe', where he remained until the following Saturday, when he was locked in the stocks 'before the bayhall door' for three long hours 'with a skayne [wrapped] about his neck and paper on his hatt'.[173] It has been argued that privacy was becoming more attainable and even desirable at this time.[174] Whether that had any effect or not, ideas and practices of 'private' punishment were becoming more pervasive. 'Private' penalties still worked hand in hand with age-old public displays, but there was no doubt which way the wind was blowing. The next question is why?

IV

Unlike hanging, there was no single decisive legislative stroke to get rid of carting, ducking, or locking someone in stocks. The last use of the ducking stool that we know of was in 1809; the last time someone sat in the stocks was in 1872. But neither stools nor stocks were used much after 1700. They might have remained on view as a reminder to toe the line but little else. Pillories continued to make

170 LA CNP 2/1/9, end of book.

171 NA NQS/2, fo. 26; ESBHRO QO/EW9; DRO ECA B/1/4, fo. 245. See also NRO NMCC 11, fos. 196, 503, 667; 12, fos. 124, 290, 495; T/QS/1, fo. 19v; DRO ECA B/1/4, fo. 245; DHC DC/DOB/8/1, fo. 167v; SAI B/105/2/6, fos. 96, 154v.

172 NRO T/C1/9, fo. 4.

173 ERO D/B5/SB2/9, fo. 176. See also SAI B/105/2/2, fo. 54; CKS TE/JQC/1, fo. 5; NA NQS/1, fo. 86; GA GBR/G/G3/SO/1, fo. 115.

174 Cf. L. Cowen Orlin, *Locating Privacy in Tudor London* (Oxford, 2007).

'gazing stocks' of mostly cheats and sodomites over the eighteenth century before being finally abolished in 1837. Public whipping was on a downward spin over the eighteenth century but went through a late 'Indian summer' in London in the final fifth of the century.[175] Public whipping rates were low but steady in Essex until they plunged after 1790 (there was a sudden surprising spike in 'private' whipping that ended in the closing stages of the century).[176] Peter King describes 'a renaissance of public whipping' in Cornwall that peaked at the end of the 1790s, although a sharp slump set in after that.[177] Whipping women in public was ended by statute in 1820. It was not formally abolished for men until 1862, although whippings were few and far between by the 1830s. 'Private' whipping inside prisons was not brought to an end until 1948. My question is not about whipping's 'Indian summer' or parliamentary legislation but about the downward trend in 'public' punishment before 1700 and parallel growth in 'private' options. I have not come across one order in any of my sources that states bluntly that we ought to whip fewer people outside and more inside, stop ducking altogether, chop up the stocks for good, or no longer cart anybody through a town. It did not happen like that. Nor have I read in a pamphlet or treatise an argument to phase out the public punishment of petty crime, though I have read strongly worded cases for bridewells and workhouses. This does not mean that they are not somewhere to be found. But the roots of the long-term fall of publicly punishing petty crime are not in the lofty realms of learned treatises but in what was called 'experience' at the time. There were no sustained debates about reforms as there soon would be about public hanging. Key decisions were more likely to have been taken locally for practical reasons that were motivated by 'experience'. This was a development in England's localities that cumulatively became something 'national' in scope and scale.

The twists and turns in the downward trend of public whipping are another reminder that there was no neat displacement in punishing inside or outside. We have instead a string of overlapping thoughts and actions over a long span of time that were grounded in local 'experience'. Not one was enough to impact the nature of punishment on its own, but together they were sufficient to do so. They included, in no particular order: (1) the acceptance that putting petty offenders behind bars made a good deal of sense; (2) the concern that any public display of authority carried with it an inherent risk factor; (3) general concerns about any audience; (4) neglect by officials and officers that could compromise

[175] Shoemaker, 'Streets of shame', 239–40; G. T. Smith, 'Civilized people don't want to see that sort of thing: the decline of public physical punishment in London, 1760–1840', in C. Strange, ed., *Qualities of Mercy: Justice, Punishment, and Discretion* (Vancouver, BC, 1996); White, 'Ordering the Mob, 227–32 and chap. 6 *passim*.

[176] King, *Crime, Justice, and Discretion in England*, 272–3.

[177] P. King, *Crime and Law in England, 1750–1840: Remaking Justice from the Margins* (Cambridge, 2006), 274–5. For the situation in the north-east see Morgan and Rushton, *Rogues, Thieves, and the Rule of Law*, 134.

'manifestaccon'; (5) scruples about the number of times people appropriated forms and words of punishment for their own ends; (6) the many times that someone took it upon themselves to punish somebody with no right to do so; and (7) the need to keep tight control over any sort of 'manifestaccon' of authority.

Not everything went according to plan. Things turned comical in Exeter in 1560 when a brewer's wife, who was turned out of doors by her husband for 'wantonly' with no 'shamefastness or womanhoode of womankynde' mixing with the Earl of Bedford's servants, was being carted 'throughe the whoal markett' and 'the carte broke downe in the meale market'.[178] This was impossible to legislate for but awkward nonetheless. It was a knock to pride if something went wrong and appearances did not meet expectations. Manchester magistrates were unhappy to see rubbish 'layd betwixt the stockes and the crose to the damage of the towne' in 1685. John Mason was taken to court in Liverpool in 1655 'for letting dung lie at the pillory'.[179] This should not have happened in what Knutsford governors called 'a verie proper markett towne' when expressing fears about punishment.[180] 'Publique' punishment in other words was subject to the same sensitivities and broader critiques of representations of authority and ethics of which it was an essential element. The contagion of 'unseemely' sights or neglect of penal 'engines' mattered a great deal in 'a verie proper markett towne'. The full panoply of posts, pillories, stocks, and stools in fine fettle was a statement. It is a puzzle why Preston did not have a ducking stool or fully functioning pillory for six years (1662–7) and Lyme Regis for one year longer (1652–58).[181] Clitheroe had recurring issues with pillories, ducking stools, and stocks all through the second half of the seventeenth century.[182] Ludgershall, Ludlow, Hereford, East Havant, and Kendal had similar stories to tell.[183] Pride was dented, not to mention the deep cost to peace of mind. It was claimed that absent punishment 'engines' allowed 'roges and vagrant people' to roam at will (Hampshire and Staffordshire); gave 'malefactors and unrulie persons' all the time in the world to do bad (Liverpool); and allowed 'thieves and nightwalkers' to do whatever they wanted (Middlesex).[184] Governors usually put the blame on careless officers, but they should have shouldered some of it too.

[178] DRO ECA B/1/4, fo. 69.

[179] Earwaker, *Court Leet Records of the Manor of Manchester*, VI, 230; Power, *Liverpool Townbooks*, 68.

[180] HL EL MS 678. See also DHC DC/LR/B1/9, fo. 156.

[181] LA CNP 3/2/1, fos. 169, 247, 265, 274; DHC DC/LR/B1/9, fos. 95, 110, 123, 135, 144.

[182] LA MBC/200; MBC/201; MBC/202; MBC/209; MBC/215; MBC/216; MBC/232; MBC/234.

[183] Cunnington, *Records of the County of Wiltshire*, 202; SHA LB/11/4/82/18; LB/11/4/83/42; HEA BG/11/4/6, 4/1659, 6/1659, 10/1663, 10/1664, 4/1666, 4/1670; ESBHRO QI/E3, fo. 41v; KAC WS/SMB/2/5, fo. 33.

[184] HA Q1/3, fo. 40; S. A. H. Burne, ed., *Staffordshire Quarter Sessions Rolls. Vol II, 1590–1593* (Kendal, 1932), 296; Twemlow, *Liverpool Town Books*, I, 271; LMA MJ/SP/1680/May Sessions.

Norwich servant Prudence Murrell was crossing Fye Bridge on a 'sabbothe daye morninge' in 1660 when she saw John Buckingham 'and two fellowes' pick up the ducking stool and throw it into the river. It might have been horseplay for Buckingham, but this was a mockery of 'manifestaccon' in the ghastly image of a ducking stool half in and half out of water.[185] Smashing or removing penal 'engines' challenged representations of authority. Robert Arnold was caught red-handed 'breaking ye stocks [and] towne crosse' in Bottesford (Leicestershire) in 1682. A 'disordered' group in Thornbury (Gloucestershire) broke authority into smithereens when they 'cutt, rend, and toare in peeces' the 'cocking stoole' and set the 'peeces' on fire.[186] Eleven men ruined the sleep of Widow Hewget's neighbours in Lyonshall (Herefordshire) in 1680, 'drinkeing, curseing, sweareinge, wrangleinge, quarreleigne [and] fighting', before heading off to James Browne's house, where they stayed until the sun rose. Going outside in the early dawn, they 'broke the stocks and spoyled ye whipping post and broke down a bridge'.[187] The ashes of the Thornbury stool would become 'experience'. So, too, tales of wrong-doers in other parts of the country who set the stocks on fire on May Day night, dumped another set in a churchyard, cut down pillories, or pulled up whipping posts. 'Manifestaccon' was tarnished by a 'principall watchman' in Southampton in 1609, who was put in the stocks for not giving 'anie enformation' about a group who 'removed' the 'pannel stocks standing by hollyrood churche [and] tyed [them] to the bull ringe' in the upper high street that was used for 'baiting'.[188]

We can add punishing petty crime to the list of risky 'manifestaccon' and question its effectiveness. This is a question with many answers, as outcomes depended on local 'experience'. Most offenders appear once on record and then disappear. Some did learn their lesson. A Holborn wife reported in 1608 that her neighbour Dorothy Charlson, who was 'carted about the strets' three years ago, had 'synce that tyme kept company with women of the best sorte' and was now 'accompted an honest woman'. Elizabeth Pearce, who was also carted through the city, now mixed with 'the best sort of women of citizens wives and tradesmens wives'.[189] These success stories are from depositions, but records more generally are less likely to speak of someone changing for the better. We are far more likely to read about recidivists than Pearce or Charlson. We can follow Joan Garroll in London records for thirteen years (1628–41) or Jane Sellars in Norwich for eight years until she ran out of tumbling cards in Christmas 1631.[190] The number of recidivists

185 NRO NMCC 23, fo. 119.

186 LERO QS 7/1, fo. 86v; TNA STAC8 128/1.

187 HEA Q/SM/4, fos. 117v–18.

188 Horrocks, *Assembly Book of Southampton*, II, 41. See also LMA Rep. 12, fo. 523; LBHC 4, fo. 56; TNA SP 12/252/94; SHA 3365/2242, fo. 17v; Cunnington, *Annals of the Borough of Devizes*, II, 8; Atkinson, *North Riding Quarter Sessions Records*, II, 98.

189 LMA DLC 218, fos. 75–7.

190 For Garroll see my *Lost Londons*, 154–5; and for Sellars see my 'Masterless young people in Norwich, 1560–1645', in P. Griffiths, A. Fox, and S. Hindle, eds., *The Experience of Authority in Early Modern England* (Basingstoke, 1996), 146–7.

or 'bad examples' predictably dwarfs the count of 'good' outcomes. 'Much evil and hurt will follow', Charles Richardson warned, when recidivists mix freely with others; 'the offender [and] others are animated [and] more emboldened to sinne'. 'Godlinesse and honestie' cannot 'flourish [he added] where wicked persons are uncontrouled'.[191] A Norfolk justice was unhappy to hear that a labourer's wife 'convicted before me' for running an unlicensed alehouse 'brags' that 'she will draw beer again in despite of the townsmen'. 'The presedent beinge so evill', Southampton governors said in 1601, hearing that a shipmaster whose 'harlot [had] receaved open punishment in most places [now] shamelessly walked upp and down the streats' in front of many people with her on his arm.[192]

Recidivism here is 'public' and painful for courts that saw this flaunting as taunting. We can imagine salty alehouse talk as recidivists rubbed shoulders with others. Staffordshire justices heard that one Woodall 'receaved ['Goodwin's yonger brother'] as a good guest' in 1595, even though he 'hathe ben sundrie tymes indyted arrayned, pylloried, sett in the stockes and whypped'. Neighbours frustrations are also evident. We hoped that 'publycke punishment myght wrought some shame and repentaunce', Richard Nicholl's neighbours told the same bench, but 'wee fynd farr other wyse': he still steals 'dayly' and 'encrease[s]' his 'ill behaviour with tonge and handes'.[193] Repeat offending was harmful to authority. London aldermen were at a loss about what to do with eight 'comen harlots' in 1552: 'Neither doppynge in the theamys nor eny other ponyshment' will 'stey or reforme them'. The same court agreed in 1549 that 'no care or indifferent correccon or punishment will stey, reforme, or wthdrawe ["ii auncyent and comen harlotts of their bodies", Elizabeth Bell and Alice Hassott] from their detestable and devylysshe vice and synfull lyffe'.[194] Repeat offenders, in effect, were living and breathing bad 'examples'. Crime gave the wrong sort of encouragement to people who might not know any better. People could turn 'good or bad', Samuel Garey cautioned at Norwich and Thetford Assizes in 1619, depending on the 'example' that was set. 'If you follow examples follow the best and not the worst', Thomas Hall warned his readers. 'It is the corruption of mans nature', Charles Richardson regretted in 1616, 'to be led by the example of others'.[195] Cumbria magistrates put into words their fears that 'evell example' might infect anybody 'ther present' at 'publique' gatherings. Hearing in 1577 that 'slowfull

[191] Richardson, *Sermon Concerning the Punishment of Malefactors*, 3–4, 5, 7.

[192] *The Notebook of Robert Doughty, 1662–1665*, ed. J. Rosenheim, Norfolk Record Society, 54 (Norwich, 1989), 35; SA 6/1, fo. 25.

[193] Burne, *Staffordshire Quarter Sessions Rolls*, IV, 101–2, 393–4.

[194] LMA Rep. 12, fos. 435, 128v–9. See also LERO QS6/1/2, fo. 33; LMA Rep. 21, fo. 447; DRO ECA B/1/4, fos. 135, 267; NRO NMCC 1, fo. 658; 10, fos. 350, 754; 25, fo. 307; HA Q1/3, fo. 48; WAC WCB/2, fos. 127–8; ESBHRO RYE 1/6, fo. 1v.

[195] Garey, *Lentaculum Ludicum*, 23; T. Hall, *Comarum Askomia: The Loathsome-nesse of Long Haire* (1654); 68; Richardson, *Sermon Concerning the Punishment of Malefactors*, 42.

people' arriving late at church in Thetford would be fined, John Hyllary 'openly reported in the hearinge of diverse persons' that he for one would not pay it 'to the discreditt of the mayor and recorder and annymatinge of the inferior people'.[196] Gloucester records, like others elsewhere, show fears that crimes were an 'evell example [to] others', in cases as varied as heavy drinking, keeping pigs on highways, sabbath-breaking, and running 'a comon house of play [with] shefel-board and skettles'.[197]

The worst situation was when black sheep set bad 'examples' for a long time. One such was alehouse-keeper and 'hedborowe' George Pannell from Rugeley on the edge of Cannock Chase. Twenty-seven neighbours signed 'Articles of information' filed against this 'common drunkarde', 'scolder', 'barretor, quarreller [and] player at cardes [and] tables' at Staffordshire Sessions in 1592. A string of charges included letting servants and apprentices drink and gamble 'daylie and nightlye' at his house; 'quarrellinge and brawlinge' with the vicar; breaking into a widow's orchard; beating up his 'naturall father and divers of his own brethren'; and, with 'his brethren', 'disquyetting' neighbours at home and causing such 'uprorers' on 'journeyes in other straunge countreys that whole townshippes have rysen agaynste them'. Pannell was also a sore loser. He 'commanded' Robert Orchard (as 'hedeborowe') to hand him his dagger after 'fallinge out in playe' with him and losing money. Orchard did as asked and Pannell hit him on the head with it. The town steward told a constable to lock him in the stocks, but Pannell stood his ground, 'us[ing] moste opprobrious and undecente wordes against them all'. The constable 'either coulde not or woulde not sette him in the stockes to the evill example of others'. To add insult to injury, Pannell bragged later 'that before he had gone to the stockes there shoulde have ben soche a daye as never was in Rugeley...two or three should have ben slayne'.[198] And now the twenty-seven hoped that their complaint would end this bad 'example'. Fingers crossed.

Like unauthorized punishment or the appropriation of penal dialogue/imagery, recidivism was one element in a wider collective attrition that cast doubt on punishing petty crime in public. It must have been grating when people did not do what they were told to do. Two North Riding men 'contemptuouslie refused' when a constable asked them to whip a vagrant in 1608. He asked two other men, who 'in neglect of justice did strike their rodes against the postes in the street instead of the rogue to give coulour as though they had cruelly beaten him'. Justices heard that there was 'no shew of any stroak on his back or shoulders'.[199]

[196] KAC WSMB/A/2/1/1, fo. 7v; NRO T/C1/1, fo. 4.

[197] GA GBR/G/G3Sib/1, fos. 483, 519, 548; GBR/G/G3Sib/2, fos. 38v, 39; See also SA 6/1, fo. 11; KAC WQ/1/1, fo. 12; LA QDO/2/28, fo. 10; CNP 3/2/1, fo. 86; CA QJB/1/6, fo. 87v; OHC C/FC/1/A1/O4, fo. 91; WAC WB/1, fo. 262.

[198] Burne, *Staffordshire Quarter Sessions Rolls*, II, 289–90.

[199] Atkinson, *North Riding Quarter Sessions Records*, I, 133.

Wiltshire justices were unhappy in 1603 that William Matthew from Warminster (who we saw stabbing someone) had not been whipped weeks after his offence. A constable, 'being of kynne to the boye', said 'that it is done'; but another said that he 'knowes not of yt nor any body els'. A Manchester constable landed in trouble in 1648 because he had not 'cuckt' 'comon scould' Mary Kempe.[200] Punishment needed to run smoothly for the appearance of authority. But reversals continued to accumulate. A Norwich beadle was stocked for 'favouryng' Hugh Jones after 'beyng comaunded specyally to whipp [him] well'. Whipper William Woods from the same city was taken to task after he 'whipped wagstaffe on his cloathes'.[201] A 'tymorous' officer who would not whip fiery hedge-breaker Margaret Franklin after she 'drewe her knife' in 1623, was told 'to tye her to the maypole' and whip her. But he stopped whipping her 'after a fewe light blowes' on her shoulders, governors heard, 'with out shewe of strooke'. Urged once more to flog her, he brushed her skin 'in a very moderate manner without any rygor att all'.[202]

Audiences saw these awkward moments and gossiped about them afterwards. One irony of 'manifestaccon' (and public punishment) was that it depended on an audience for full force when governors did not like people to gather most of the time. 'So dangerous at all tymes are unlawfull and unnecesarrie assemblies', Faversham governors warned in words that would have struck chords anywhere:

> that moste men observe and use it as a good and orderly course and methode whensoever an assemblie by commandment is caused, before they be any wayes ymployed, to signefye and make knowne unto them as well the authoritie whereby as the occasion wherefore they are so called together.

The 'one', they said, is 'to embolden them to willinglie undertake'; the 'other [to] encourage them carefullye and dilligentlye to prosequete those things [that are] required at theire hands'.[203] Crowds, in other words, needed proper schooling. Market 'assemblies' were a little unpredictable as they comprised who was there at a given time. Impulsiveness was challenging. An unwelcome crowd all too often caused consternation: demonstrating, playing rough sports, or gathering to hear someone speak. 'It is found by dayly and frequent experience', Maidstone's magistrates said in 1656, that 'heady and turbulent persons'

[200] Cunnington, *Records of the County of Wiltshire*, 8–9; Earwaker, *Court Leet Records of the Manor of Manchester*, IV, fo. 25. See also ESBHRO QI/EW2, fo. 56v; RYE 2/1, fo. 5v; BRO N/JQ 1/1, fo. 310; CA QJB/1/6, fos. 183–3v; SHA LB/11/4/82/18; DHC DC/DOB/8/1, fo. 73.

[201] NRO NMCC 11, fo. 415; Norwich Sessions Book 1639–54, fo. 161v.

[202] TNA STAC8 289/1. See also TNA STAC8 33/10.

[203] CKS FA/JM/27/1.

> intrude [into] publique meetings [in] a confused and tumultuous manner [attracting] greate assemblies [in] open streets and market places [and] other places of concourse [to] publiquely [preach] giddy fancies [in] raylinges and revilengs [in alarming] open contradictings, contests, debates, wranglings, and quarellings.[204]

Quaker preachers who made the long trip from the Lake District to Norwich in 1654 to 'declare the truth' ('as he calls it', the clerk noted snootily), set up impromptu pulpits 'in the publique markett place' and drew 'a great company of rude and idle people [to] the disturbance of the peace'. Norwich was also troubled in 1629 by 'many' seemingly spontaneous 'meetings and concourses' on consecutive Sundays, where people 'under pretence of cudgell play and hearinge of musick' formed 'troops and multitudes' at the cross.[205] Spontaneous gatherings lacking 'official' backing made governors uneasy about losing control in public settings. Crowds could gather on the spur of the moment if they heard shouting or something else turned their heads. 'Yow honest women', Londoner Mistress Griffen shouted 'openly in the market [in 1591] with such an open mouth that a great multitude of people assembled...why did you let that whore and thief stande amonge yow [when her place is] beneath the carts arse'.[206] An Exeter constable 'took' Giles Geale 'by the shoulder' on a dark street in 1620 and willed him to 'goe home to his wife'. He glanced over his shoulder a little later and saw Geale following him calling him 'drunckerd' and 'base knave' at the top of his voice, 'by which meanes [it was said] the whole streete was full of people'.[207] The nature of an audience could change suddenly. A full Sunday church was the last place where governors wanted someone to set a bad 'example'. 'I was reading the chapter', Earls Colne vicar Ralph Josselin noted in his diary in 1656, when all of a sudden Sam Burton and James Byat who 'were sitting in the maids seate...made a disturbance'. A justice sitting in the front pew 'commanded the constable to take them forth to the cage', he continued, but one of their mothers 'tooke her son and said her husband paid scott and lott in the towne and her son should sitt any where'.[208] 'Come downe, come downe', Abraham Moates shouted with a 'loud voice' in a Gloucester church in 1652, when the minister was preaching in the pulpit; 'believe

[204] CKS MD/ACM1/3, fos. 84–84v.

[205] NRO Norwich Sessions File 63/25; Norwich Assembly Book 5, fo. 253. See also NRO Norwich Sessions Files 64/1; 64/30.

[206] LMA DLC 214, fo. 102.

[207] DRO ECA C1/61, fo. 435. See also DHC DOB/8/1, fo. 251v; LMA MJ/SBR/5, fos. 179, 465; Rep. 13(2), fo. 336; NRO T/C1/1, fo. 16; Norwich Sessions File 63/25; GA GBR/G/G3Sib/1, fo. 553; NDRO B1/3973, fo. 437; 1064q/SO1, fo. 155.

[208] *The Diary of Ralph Josselin*, ed. A. Macfarlane, British Academy Records of Social and Economic History, NS, III (Oxford, 1976), 377.

him not', Moates roared, 'he is a deluder of the people'.[209] This is the risk of what Reverend Oliver Heywood called 'a huge publick' when jotting down the details of 'a strange tumult' in Halifax Church in 1678 as curate Gill was reading an excommunication order against 'stout' smith John Butterworth. As he began reading, Butterworth, who was in the trained band, drew his sword and stormed into the 'mid-alley' and 'bad him if he durst' to read he would pay for it. Gill 'desisted not daring to read it' and asked 'officers to doe their office'. 'Put him in the stocks', some worshippers urged. I 'durst not', a constable said lamely. 'A huge publick there was', Heywood noted in his last words on a Sunday that went horribly wrong.[210]

Any thoughts magistrates had about the crowds at public punishments should be seen in larger considerations of audiences more generally. There was always a potential for something to go wrong at hustings or processions, for example, or in churches or theatres. Oxford governors were keen to track down the ringleaders—and 'make them exemplary to others'—of 'a very great disturbance of the publique electing of officers' in 1670 when there was 'hissing att mr mayor and the magistrates'. Norwich freemen were banned from going to plays in 1589 'as experyence hath taught', an order of the Assembly said, that they caused 'quarrels and brawls'.[211] Like gallows crowds, market crowds were supposed to watch and learn. The ceremonies were less elaborate but expectations that the central characters would show sorrow and that audiences would behave well and pay attention were the same. There were no last speeches at the post or pillory but people still grabbed the opportunity to speak their mind. A London wax chandler who stood on the pillory on Cheapside after he was caught in a bowling alley in 1552 'shamefully, dyspytefully and slaunderouslye raylie[d] openly before moche people allegynge that [the magistrates] had wrongfullye adudged hym to that penaunce'. Mabel Grunyon, who stood on the same pillory one year later for trying to poison her husband, 'moste falselye denye[d] her wycked dede alledgynge [that] she was wrongfullye ponyshed with owte enye good or just cause'.[212] 'It was his glory to be in the cage', John Bagley shouted at Manchester constables after a late-night drinking spree in 1631, and he then turned on the constables, calling them 'knaves and rogues'.[213] Richard Akin wrote from Gravesend to a friend in 1667,

[209] GA GBR/G/G3/Sib/2, fo. 24.

[210] *Reverend Oliver Heywood, B.A., 1630–1702; His Autobiography, Diaries, Anecdote and Event Books*, ed. J. Horsfall Turner, 4 vols (Brighouse, Bingley, 1881–5), 253–4.

[211] NRO Norwich Assembly Book 5, fo. 53v; OHC C/FC/1/A1/04, fo. 91. See also LBHC 6, fo. 389; 7, fo. 75v; TNA SP 12/260/16; LMA MJ/SBR/1, fo. 559; MJ/SBR/4, fo. 396; Jour. 27, fo. 263; NRO Norwich Assembly Book 6, fo. 45; A. B. Dawson and P. Yachnin, *The Culture of Playgoing in Shakespeare's England* (Cambridge, 2001); I. Munro, *The Figure of the Crowd in Early Modern London: The City and its Double* (Basingstoke, 2005), esp. 41–4, 118–22; C. Whitney, '"Usually in the werking daies": playgoing, journeymen, apprentices, and servants in guild records, 1582–92', *Shakespeare Quarterly*, 50 (1999).

[212] LMA Reps. 12, fo. 519v; 13(1), fo. 9.

[213] Earwaker, *Court Leet Records of the Manor of Manchester*, III, 82.

telling him that 'this day the person convicted of forgery did stand in the pillory and is likewise to stand there the next markett day'. 'The fellow [who is never named] att the first was very stoubberne', he wrote, 'and did not stand quietly till the mayor caused a person to put hand cuffes uppon him which person could not of himselfe till fower or five seamen went upp on the pillory and fourced him to itt'. The man on the pillory was a 'very bould and audacious rogue', Akin continued, 'and did not vallue the disgrace att anything'. Quite the reverse, he 'tooke a pride in sayinge that he had many ticketts in that nature and was only sorry that he was apprehended for such a small one'. Akin ended by telling his friend that the nameless man on the pillory went on 'to tell many other storyes in pride of his rougues accons'.[214]

There were never gaurantees at the end of the day. Many in the crowd probably felt the same indignation that made magistrates order public punishments in the first place. This is what Provost in *Measure for Measure* calls an 'unpitied whipping' (IV, ii, 197). Others may have felt nothing and walked past without even a slight glance. There might have been some fun and games like the scenes in the foreground of Hogarth's Tyburn engraving. Action was sometimes taken ahead of time in case something went wrong. When William Phillips alias Taylor was ordered by Somerset justices to 'make public confession [for] publishing vile, unseemly, scandalous & untrue speeches' about Mary Gill in 1616, they told him that he would be bound over to appear in court if he 'shall refuse to do so or shall do not sincerely but after a scoffing manner'.[215] Guards were sometimes posted to make sure that nothing went wrong. 'Hunt and Milnes' were paid eight-pence 'for watching Robert Hulme all night in ye stockes' in Manchester in 1623. Edmund Buckley was given two-pence in 1624 'for tending Robert Costerdine whoe was putt in the ould stockes for beeinge druncke'.[216] 'Gardes' ringed the Smithfield pillory in London on an 'open markett daie' in 1581 when 'lewde and seditious persons' were punished after 'reskewing' someone who was being escorted to prison. '200 halberds' lined London's streets in 1621 when an apprentice was whipped for taking part in a 'great tumult' against the Spanish ambassador.[217] Guards were also stationed around pillories in 'the Pallace-yard Westminster, Temple-Bar, and the Royal Exchange' when a perjurer was pilloried 'in three publick places' in 1679 'to prevent the multitude from throwing things, as their usual manner is'.[218]

[214] TNA SP 29/199/100.

[215] Bates, *Quarter Sessions Records for the County of Somerset*, I, 180.

[216] Earwaker, *Constables' Accounts of the Manor of Manchester*, I, 96, 133.

[217] *William Whiteway of Dorchester, His Diary 1618 to 1635*, Dorset Record Society, 12 (1991), 35; LMA Remembrancer Book 1, fo. 102v.

[218] *The Proceedings Against Mr. J. Reading who Being Found Guilty of High Misdemeanours, was Fined to the King in One Thousand Pounds, to Suffer One Years Imprisonment, and to Stand Three Several Days in the Pillory, at Three Several Places* (1679), 6–7. See also ERO D/B5/SB2/5, fo. 84; D/B5/Aa/25; LMA MS 9680, fos. 14, 16, 21, 27; LERO ID41/12/59, fo. 33.

It was at times like these that thoughts turned to the potential risks of 'publique' representation. Even more so when the central characters were political figures with plenty of support whose appearance on a pillory was an opportunity to proselytize on both sides and to observe at close quarters in person and print 'manifestaccon' in high echelons. It is entirely possible that the only seventeenth-century execution that got more column inches than the ruthless pillorying of John Bastwick, Henry Burton, and William Prynne at Westminster Palace Yard at the end of June 1637 was the killing of the king a dozen years later. The focus so far has understandably been on the politics and religion of this grisly event.[219] But I want to treat Bastwick, Burton, and Prynne on the pillory as a failure of 'manifestaccon'. Things fell apart and what is more this failure was broadcast widely in print and talk. The writing seemed to be on the wall from the first moment. 'When I came to the sight of the pillary my spirit was mightily cheered', Burton wrote six years later, 'and all the while I stood in the pillary I thought my selfe to be in Heaven and in a state of glory and triumph'.[220] One observer wrote later to the Earl of Northumberland that 'the light common people strowed herbes and flowers' in front of Bastwick as he walked from the Gatehouse Prison to the pillory. Bastwick and Prynne stood on one 'scaffold'; Burton stood alone. 'All three talkt to the people', the same observer said, Bastwick 'was pleasant and witty all the tyme' saying that 'this was his coller daye in the kings pallace'. Prynne 'protested his innocency to the people'; 'Mr Burton said it was the happiest pulpett hee had ever preacht in'. The hangman started to cut off their ears two hours later, beginning with Burton. 'Very many people…wept and grieved' for him as if it was them who were losing their ears. Bastwick in a loud voice told the hangman 'to cutt off his eares quickly and very close that hee might not come there noe more'. Prynne, however, was in dire straits. When branding his cheeks with a sizzling hot iron the hangman 'burnt one cheek with a letter the wrong waye' and a surgeon 'clapt on a plaster to take out the fire' when the letter was put the right way up. The hangman then botched his next job, 'hew[ing] off Prinns eares very scurvily'. 'The humours of the people were various', the Earl of Northumberland was told; 'some wept, some laught and some were verie reserved'.[221] But the public wound for the authorities did not end there. John Maynard, deputy warden of the Fleet Prison, was examined by the attorney general a few months later. He had been part of the guard that escorted Prynne to Caernarfon Castle after he lost his ears, passing through St Albans, Coventry, and Chester on the way west to Wales. Maynard continued the narrative of public embarrassment in the post-pillory procession with Prynne as victim/martyr who was greeted by the prayers and blessings of well-wishers 'in the streetes and highwayes'. Another deputy warden

[219] Most recently, M. A. Kishlansky, 'Martyr's tales', *JBS*, 53 (2014); M. A. Kishlansky, 'A whipper whipped: the sedition of William Prynne', *HJ*, 56 (2013).

[220] H. Burton, *A Narration of the Life of Mr. Henry Burton* (1643), 13–14.

[221] TNA SP 16/363/42.

of the Fleet, James Joyner, who just took Prynne on the 7-mile leg to Barnet, was also questioned in late September. He told Attorney General Bankes that a 'great store of people' lined the 'streetes [and] high wayes' shouting 'God blesse you and God bee with you' as Prynne passed by (Prynne was supposed to talk to no one).[222]

The voices of 'common people' evident in sprinkled herbs and flowers (the opposite of cruelty) and street-side prayers, constant chattering, jokey Bastwick, counter-protests of innocence, the hangman's 'scurvy' butchery, the 'various' 'humours of the people': all this sabotaged 'manifestaccon' and would do so for the rest of the century. There were other high-profile breakdowns in 'manifestaccon'. John Lilburne famously talked all the time on the pillory until he was gagged. He had his local counterparts. 'Here he lets me prate like one i' the stocks', Volumnia says about her son Coriolanus (V, iii, 369–70). Husbandman William Martin turned punishment on its head when he was put in the stocks for 'swere[ing] blasphemously' in Dorchester in 1632: he sat swearing 'oaths by the name of God vi and 4 by the blood of God'. Norwich officials watched as Mrs Emery shouted 'unfyttyng wordes' when she was carted around the market in 1588 for 'sufferinge whoredome and bawdrye' in her house, saying 'that as she hath doon she wyll do'. A Southampton weaver was taken to task in 1616 'for resisting the cryer' when he was 'whipping a prisoner'.[223]

Quizzical talk sometimes started in the run-up to actual punishment. On hearing that some young men were due to be whipped for stealing flowers from Mrs Carter's garden in Dorchester in 1632, John White's wife said 'in the walke and hearinge of many people that if the boyes were whipt it should be a deere whippinge to Mris Carter'. Word also circulated that constable Edward Bagley said that 'if those two boyes were whipt they had wronge'. He was bound to his good behaviour.[224] Some people cried revenge after they had been punished, which is why some whippers wore masks and hoods. Samuel Phillips, who worked in Northwich's salt-works, struck Catherine Basnett in the 'publick market' and 'struck' the constable who asked him why he had hit her. He was locked in the stocks for 'neare three quarters of an hour' and when he was free he swore 'twenty oaths' and threatened that he would kill the constable and his family. Norfolk justice Robert Doughty signed a warrant 'against' constable George Brooke in 1663 'for abusing the watchmen of Aldborough who set him in the stocks'.[225]

222 TNA SP 16/368/14.

223 DHC DC/DOB/8/1, fo. 136v; NRO NMCC 7, fos. 211–2; SA SC9/2/1, fo. 24v.

224 DHC DC/DOB/8/1, fo. 141. See also BRO R/AC1/1/3, fo. 204; Guilding, *Reading Records*, II, 130–1.

225 H. E. Bennett and J. C. Dewhurst, eds., *Quarter Session Records With Other Records of the Justices of the Peace for the County Palatine of Chester, 1559–1760*, Record Society of Lancashire and Cheshire, 94 (Chester. 1940), 201–2; *Notebook of Robert Doughty*, 25.

It was not at all unusual to hear troublemakers mocking their own punishment. 'Moore an aturney', who was put in the Cheapside pillory in 1624 'for speaking very lewdly & scandalously of Quene Elizabeth and Henry the eight…', laughed all the while, even though both of his ears were cut off.[226] The danger was that others similarly inclined might join in. People watching might say something out of order that changed the performance of a scripted event. Norwich labourer Thomas Holme, who was in the audience when William White's ears were cut off on the pillory 'for speaking sedicous wordes' in 1550, said out loud 'that if Whites ears shulde be cut of by his hedde he thoughte he shulde dye' (the clerk noted that it 'appered by his words he shulde be againste suche ponysshment').[227] Ralph Thrower from the same city called Mayor Bacon 'vyllayne, cherle, slave, and bocher' at 'the signe of the gryffen' in 1557, 'revyling him' for 'the ponnyshmente' of a Yarmouth woman, adding with some Dutch courage that 'if he came abroade out of the towne he shold never goo further'.[228] Two men from Rye told town officials in 1593 'yt they did here olde Bull saye [that his son who had been whipped for 'lewde demeanor' in 1593] was as honest a man as the best and yt he cared not for the governors and yt yf he were as his son he wolde putt his cappe where the paper stood under his tayle'.[229] Yeoman Thomas Samford was sitting talking with 'a group of men' after John Lone had been 'punnyshed in the cart for whoredom in Colchester' in 1575. Lone had become the talk of the town and one of the group said that he had been 'rigorursly handled in that punishmentt farr other wyse than hadd bene sene in that towne before'. Samford told his friend that Lone's 'punishment might happen to cost the towne a hundred marks'.[230] A sailmaker from the same town told justices in 1650 that 'this daie he and Mary the wife of John Pirkis [were] speakeinge about the whippinge of John Alexander (whoe was whipped for the cutting and stealing of Mr Thomas Talcotts wood)' when she said that he 'had as much honour by that whipping as Christ had by his sufferinge upon the crosse'. 'Shee had as good a call to doe those things which she hath done', Pirkis told magistrates later, 'as Abraham had for the offering his sonne Issac' (rumours were rife in the town that she had left her husband some time ago to 'goe awaie' with Alexander).[231] John Whitcombe's mother stood weeping at his side when he sat in the stocks in Barton in Somerset in 1656. Seeing her, a minister with a book in his hand said, according to witnesses, 'troble not yourself as this is the best days work that ever he did, for by the statute no justice can punish him after twenty days and [it] will allow him five pounds for every hour in the stocks'. They also told the court that the minister 'brought [Whitcombe] beer'

226 TNA SP 14/159/70.
227 NRO NMCC 6, fo. 82.
228 NRO NMCC Interrogatories and Depositions Book 1554–61, 13/4/1557.
229 ESBHRO RYE 1/5, fo. 302v.
230 ERO D/B5/SB2/2, fo.99v.
231 ERO D/B5/SB2/9, fo. 37.

while he sat in the stocks and that he said in his (next Sunday) sermon that Paul 'was whipt and stockt and did not grieve at it [and] neither should we'.[232]

We might not be surprised if a relative or friend broke the rules, but a minister was a different case. Disruption more usually took the form of ill-timed comedy, heckling, or taunting, including a piece of gleeful *schadenfreude* in Norwich marketplace in 1610 when a fight broke out when Dutchman John de Pute was spotted 'rejoyc[ing' as he watched some English apprentices being whipped for threatening his fellow countrymen.[233] A pair of widows told a court in Thetford in 1582 that Abraham Bass's wife shouted 'that ther were a hundred hores in ye towne besydes Bodmans wyfe' when the latter was 'punyshed [in the market for] playing ye harlot'. John Little, who went to watch Cecily Bootty getting whipped in Norwich market in 1567, ended up in trouble himself after he 'swore and sayed wold they wold whyp hym but I shall once come owt and then I will be even with my cozen the mayer and the proudest of them'.[234] When 'straunger' John Bullhead was 'sett in the stocks' in Barnstaple in 1580 'for refusinge to paie [fines] for 5 oathes', John Davie started to shout 'in rayleing and reproachfull manner att the heighe crosse [in] the hearinge of very manye taxin[g] mr maior [who was standing nearby] for injustice sayeing that hee had done basely to sett [him] in the stocks [and] done more than he could justify'. Davie's location next to the 'heighe crosse' with the mayor standing a few steps away magnified his offence, with 'very manye' hearing his loud denunciation.[235]

Davie, Little, and the rest gave contrary signals in the public eye to the practices and principles of 'manifestaccon'. This story continues in Carmarthen, where in 1610 Katherine Griffith, who had not lived with her husband 'for a long tyme', was put on trial for giving birth to 'diverse bastards' and her 'incontinent livinge, scouldinge, and defaminge of her honest neighbours'. She was found guilty and told that she would be 'cucked in a cuckingstoole'. According to testimony, Griffith turned to one of the aldermen who was a friend to take steps to 'spare' her shame. He came up with a plan to get the ducking called off by hiring a few roughnecks to create a diversion by pushing the mayor 'in his gowne into the river' that was 4 fathoms deep. Griffith was sitting in the 'cuckingstoole' a few days later, perhaps smiling to herself, while a few yards away the mayor was thrashing about in the water and an open-mouthed crowd had a juicy story to tell for a long time to come. The alderman claimed it was an accident, but most people took that with a pinch of salt.[236]

A Norwich ducking also ended badly. Bennet Goodwyn was caught 'comitting the abhomynable acte of whoardome' by constables in a garden shed in Norwich in 1562. She was taken to the Mayor's Court in the morning, where it was ordered

[232] Bates, *Quarter Sessions Records for the County of Somerset*, II, 342.
[233] NRO NMCC 14, fo. 290v.
[234] NRO T/C1/2, fo. 84; NMCC 8, fo. 542.
[235] NDRO B1/3792, fo. 437.
[236] TNA STAC8 208/1.

that she would 'ryde in a carte wth a pap[er] on her hed and tycnkelyd wth a bason [on the next Saturday and at] one of the clocke to be had to the cokingstol and duckyd in the water'. Goodwyn was sitting strapped in the stool on the banks of the Wensum when, tailor Richard Harleston and 'calendarer' Robert Tryll told magistrates a couple of days later, 'servingman' Robert Lloyd who was standing behind the ducking stool gave 'a twytche at the paper that was pynned on her hed' and managed to 'losen' one of its 'corners'. Harleston stepped in straight away and 'pynned it to her hat agayne'. But 'afterwarde', as an alderman's wife 'was talking and perswading with Bennet that she sholde amende her evyll lyfe and confesse her faulte to the people', Lloyd reached in for a second time and, in Tryll's words, 'twiched off the paper [and] rolled yt up in his hande and caste it in to the ryver abowte ii or iii yards from the backsyde'. Tryll 'ran' to get a sheriff, who rushed to the riverside to restore order and reclaim the 'publique' stage. Lloyd's 'twytche' in effect denied Goodwyn's offence at the same time as an alderman's wife was urging her to leave her 'evell lyfe' behind for good. We don't know if Goodwyn was ducked once the dust had settled. She probably was. But talk in the alehouses that Saturday night would have turned to the crumpled piece of 'paper' in the river.[237]

Also worth talking about were the times when troublemakers broke out of cages. Manchester spent 1s. 2d. to fix a 'caige dore broken by a prisoner' in 1613. A London cutler's apprentice who broke open a cage to let out a 'dysordered person' was punished with 'tenne stripes' in 1590,[238] while 'a lewd person' who was suspected of stealing clothes off a hedge and put in a cage next to Exeter's east gate in 1622 was freed by locksmith Philip Parkhouse, who 'brought a keye this morning [and] opened the cage dore'. The 'prisoner' was still on the run a few days later. Parkhouse said that he did not open the cage but gave the key to a woman whose name he could not remember who opened the cage, not him.[239] It was also a 'publique' slap in the face for authority when someone broke out of the stocks. A Worcestershire labourer was locked in the stocks in 1619 for drinking too long in William Wilks's alehouse, who 'brought him a drink and let him out'. When he was 'reproved' by a constable, Wilks fired off 'beastly' words and offered the officer a provocative 'cup of ale'.[240] Dorchester carpenter George Brine could have built the stocks from which he let several people go in 1631, including miller Robert Waddam: 'the fellow was no more dronk than' me, he told the mayor. This was the same carpenter who called Agnes Keat, a witch telling her he would 'wash her'. He was also put in the stocks for 'sweareing 3 oathes blasphemously' in 1632, and was

[237] NRO NMCC Interrogatories and Depositions Book 1561–7, fos. 8, 24–4v, 25, 38, 39; NMCC 8, fos. 8, 24.

[238] Earwaker, *Constables' Accounts of the Manor of Manchester*, I, 12; LMA Rep. 22, fo. 60v.

[239] DRO ECA C1/62, fos. 76–6v. See also LMA Rep. 14, fo. 200; MJ/SBR/6, fo. 607; DLC/218, fo. 179; TNA STAC8 206/18.

[240] Willis-Bund, *Worcester County Records*, 307–8.

once in trouble for 'misdemeanors against John Oldish in the markett'. Philip Nichols 'lookyd out at his window' and saw Brine 'let Dare out of the stocks'. He rushed outside and asked him why he set Dare free; Brine answered that he helped a 'blind boy' who asked him to 'loose his shoe' as his foot was 'brused' and 'pluckt out his feet of ye stocks'.[241] In other cases the stocks (and authority) were smashed to pieces. Cheshire drunk William Jones, who could not pay a fine, was put in the stocks for three hours in 1654. Thomas Jones (a relative?) came up to him after an hour or so and 'swore several oaths that if he were not let out he would fetch an axe and break the stocks'. Running out of patience, he got his axe from home and smashed the stocks, saying 'the divell take him that lockt it'.[242]

I want to end this section with a story from Wolverhampton that, although it is on the short side, conveys 'anti-manifestaccon' in a series of stinging strikes. Two constables (Richard Aukers and Thomas Collye) filed articles at Staffordshire Sessions in 1591 against 'brawler', 'quaraller', and 'comon drunkarde' John Greene. They had taken a 'stranger' in his house ('he keepethe comon ale sellinge') for stealing a cloak off a hedge. Peeved, Greene turned up at Aukers's house later on the same day, 'callinge [him] villen and false knave', and yelling 'openly yt weare a gode deade he weare hanged'. Aukers 'willed' him not to speak 'suche unseemely speaches' but Greene did not calm down and so the constable with help 'putt him in the stockes'. It was not long before Greene 'with force brake open the stockes [and] cutt them in peeces'. He was soon back at Aukers's door, 'bragginge howe he was out of the stockes [and] calling for a freshe payre' as someone had chopped up the old pair. Greene 'threatened to set fyre' to Aukers's house a little later and kill him 'with his dagger'. His public vendetta was not over yet, however. To 'the grette astonishment of the congregation', he sauntered into church on Easter Day with a feather in his hat and 'in derision [made] a very low obeysaunce' to Aukers, and then walked out of the church 'lookinge over his shoulder'. Once he was outside, Greene put on a 'blewe coate' in imitation of the constable and 'in derision of his office. He waited for the congregation to make their way out of the church and then resumed his spoof, strutting around the churchyard poking fun at the constable in the most public way on the holiest day of the year.[243]

John Greene's feisty anti-theatre fused many elements of counter-'manifestaccon': gesture ('very low obeysaunce'), mockery ('lookinge over his shoulder'/calling for 'freshe' stocks), appropriating penal imagery (hanging), counter-display/anti-authority expression (cutting the stocks 'in peeces'), signs

[241] DHC DC/DOB/8/1, fos. 78, 80v–1, 80v, 83v–4, 100, 144. See also NRO NMCC 10, fo. 524; 25, fo. 183; CA QJB/1/3, fo. 164v; DHC DC/DOB/8/1, fo. 78; LMA MJ/SBR/1, fos. 202, 632; MJ/SBR/7, fo. 48; Atkinson, *North Riding Quarter Sessions Records*, I, 113–14; Bailey, *Selection from the Prescot Court Leet*, 118; Willis-Bund, *Worcester County Records*, 66, 433–4.

[242] Bennett and Dewhurst, *Quarter Session Records with Other Records of the Justices of the Peace for the County Palatine of Chester, 1559–1760*, 163, 201–2.

[243] Burne, *Staffordshire Quarter Sessions Rolls*, II, 110–12.

(feather in hat), and parody (blue coat). He must have been the talk of the village for a long time to come, although Aukers did have his day in court where justices ordered that Greene should pay for a new pair of stocks and also be 'bound to his good behaviour'.

V

But in all likelihood the damage had already been done. A binding-over did nothing to stop people talking or to wipe out memories. Greene's satirical Sunday was on the way to becoming a folk tale. Perhaps this Staffordshire story travelled across the county and made its way into neighbouring areas as people moved around (a progress that was more like an oil slick for governors). Word of mouth worked like this at other times. There would not have been many parts of England that did not have similar stories to tell. Lambasting and lampooning penal performances, 'engines', and officials/officers are part of the rich streak of anti-authority subversion, sabotage, and satire outside England's established order. These actions were aimed at the powers that be, but they were also profound acts of anti-'manifestaccon'.

They are also likely to be the tip of an iceberg. We know about them because someone heard someone else 'speakeing words of disliking of the punishment' or saw someone doing something wrong and felt strongly enough to report it and go along to court to support the prosecution. They were in the right place at the right time from the point of view of magistrates or somebody was apprehended red-handed by constables. In any event, the people in the records were caught, and we have no idea how many others got away with saying or doing something that was against the law. Like hangings, the majority of whippings, duckings, and stockings were completed without major hitches, marred at worst by overly boisterous spectators. But there were more than enough 'twytches', 'breakinge', 'prateing', and bad 'examples' to give governors food for thought. It has long been argued that disruption was a factor in the abolition of public execution, and there is little reason to think any differently about the decline of the public punishment of petty crime.[244] This risk that something might not work out right had greater force when there were larger scruples about more general 'manifestaccon'. Neglect, vandalism, as well as appropriation through 'unlawful' punishment or insults, emphasized the need to keep control of representations in local settings. All of

[244] On gallows disruption see T. Laqueur, 'Crowds, carnival, and the state in English executions, 1604–1868', in A. L. Beier, D. Cannadine, and J. Rosenheim, eds., *The First Modern Society* (Cambridge, 1989); V. A. C. Gatrell, *The Hanging Tree: Execution and the English People, 1770–1868* (Oxford, 1994), chap. 2.

Plate 1 'Alderman John More of Queenhithe Ward'

Source: From *A Caveatt for the* City *of London* (1598), Folger Library, Washington DC, MS v.a.318, fo. 19v

Plate 2 'The Mayor and Swordbearer'

Source: From *A Caveatt for the Citty of London* (1598), Folger Library, Washington DC, MS v.a.318, fo. 8

Plate 3 Lucas de Heere, 'Mayor and Aldermen'

Source: British Library, ADD MS 28330

Plate 4 'Sir Thomas Bell the Elder, Mayor of Gloucester'
Source: @Gloucester Museum Service, unknown artist (n.d.)

Plate 5 'John Falkner, Mayor of Gloucester'
Source: @Gloucester Museum Service, unknown artist (n.d.)

Plate 6 'John and Joan Cooke, Mayor and Mayoress of Gloucester'
Source: @Gloucester Museum Service, unknown artist (n.d.)

Plate 7 'The Lord Mayor in Procession'
Source: From Michael van Meer, 'Album Amicorum', University of Edinburgh Library, special collections department, MS la. iii.283, fo. 101r

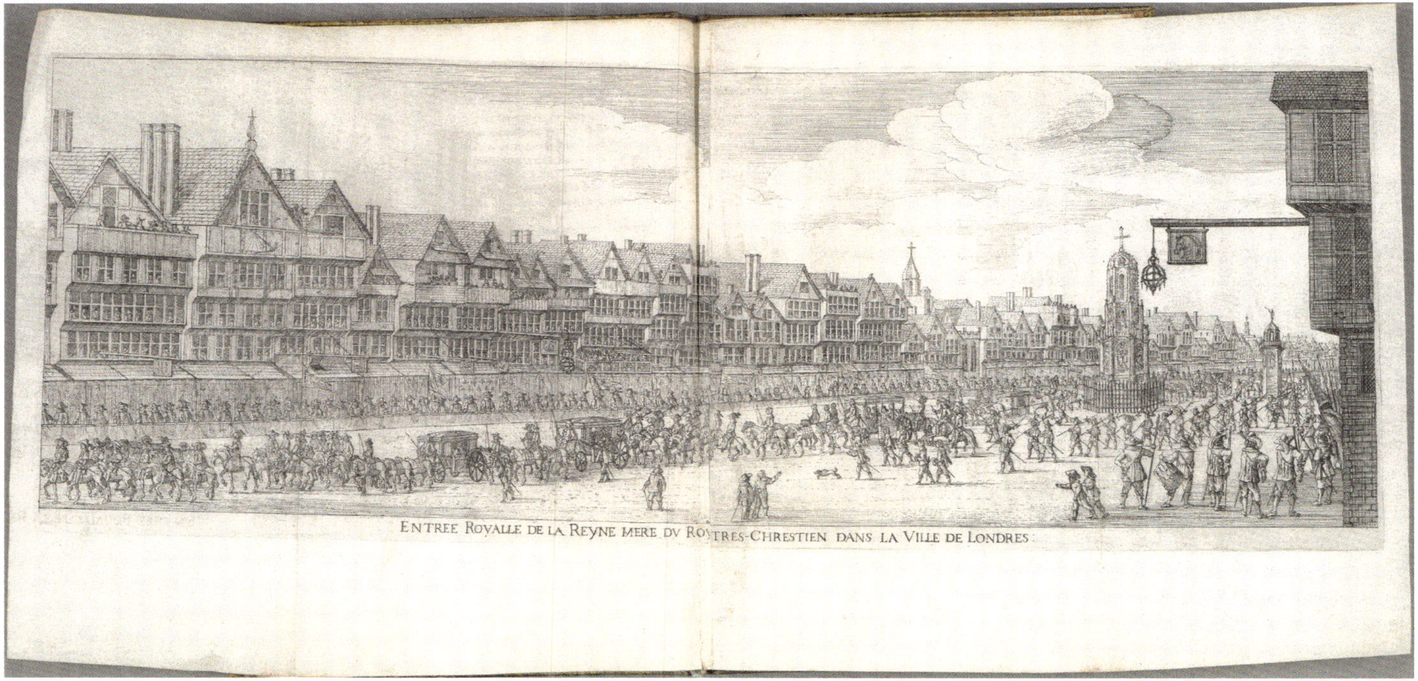

Plate 8 Jean Puget de La Serre (*c.*1594–1665), *Histoire de L'entree de la Reyne Mere Dv Roy Tres-Chrestien, Dans la Grande-Bretaigne, A Londre* (George Thomason and Octauian Pullen, 1639), engraving

Source: Yale Center for British Art, Paul Mellon Collection

Plate 9 Stratford-upon-Avon mace, late fifteenth century with mid-sixteenth-century decoration

Source: Shakespeare Birthplace Trust, SBT 1868-3/1043.1

Plate 10 Great Yarmouth medieval town walls

Source: Wikipedia Commons; Tim Heaton, Geograph Britain and Ireland, CC-BY-SA-2.0

Plate 11 Great Yarmouth medieval town walls
Source: Wikipedia Commons; Tanya Dedyuukhina, Own work, CC-BY-3.0

Plate 12 Southampton Bargate
Source: Wikipedia Commons; Editor5807, Own work, CC-BY-SA-4.0

Plate 13 Thaxted Moot Hall
Source: Wikipedia Commons; T Christopher, Own work, CC BY-SA 3.0

Plate 14 Lavenham Guildhall
Source: Wikipedia Commons; cc-by-sa/2.0 - @Marathin—geograph.org.uk/p/4134571

Plate 15 Evesham Booth Hall
Source: David Hunter/Alamy Stock Photo

Plate 16 Aldeburgh Moot Hall
Source: Wikimedia Commons; Michael Garlick, Own work, CC BY-SA 2.0

Plate 17 Cheapside Conduit and Cross

Source: From *A Caveatt for the Citty of London* (1598), Folger Library MS v.a.318, fo. 15

Plate 18 'Bristol Cross'

Source: From Robert Ricart, *The Maire of Bristowe Kalendar* (1478–9), Bristol Archives, CC 2/7

Plate 19 Malmesbury Market Cross
Source: Wikipedia Commons; Arpingstone, Own work

Plate 20 Chichester Cross

Source: Wikipedia Commons; Simon Burchell, Own work, CC-BY-SA-4.0

Plate 21 Devizes Cross

Source: Wikipedia Commons; Rodw, Own work, CC-BY-SA-4.0

Plate 22 Coventry Cross
Source: Wikipedia Commons, Jim Linwood, Uploaded by Oxyman, CC-BY-2.0

Plate 23 Parish chest, Corby Glen, Lincolnshire

Source: Wikipedia Commons, Acabashi, Own Work, CC-BY-SA-3.0

Plate 24 Parish chest, Beckley, Sussex

Source: Wikipedia Commons; Julian P. Guffogg, Geograph Britain and Ireland, https://www.geograph.org.uk/photo/2661374, CC-BY-SA-2.0

Plate 25 Parish chest, Shotteswell, St Laurence
Source: Wikipedia Commons, Motacilla, Own work, CC-BY-SA-4.0

this amounted to 'experience' that was by definition local. It also spread doubts about 'huge publicks' and staging punishment in front of the 'poorer sorte' or 'inferior people'.[245]

What we do know is that many more people were punished inside walls than outside in 'publicke' in the 150 years after 1550. The little quantification we have on this score from Norwich clearly points in this direction. We also know that 'private', 'privy', or 'secrete' punishment existed in idea and practice from as early as the final quarter of the sixteenth century. While whipping has had the lion's share of coverage so far—there was far more of it—it's clear to me that ducking stools and stocks as punishments were being used less often the deeper we travel into the seventeenth century, with this caveat: the fall in punishing petty crime in public is a mosaic of local stories with local cadences, although there is no doubt about the overall drift of things. And this is backed up by the simultaneous proliferation of bridewells, to punish the petty crimes of the poor for the most part with time in a cell, but much more often whipping with a quick release. Bridewells are the central characters in the next chapter.

Just one of John Seller's eleven drawings is set inside. His third sketch takes us inside a house of correction where five gloomy looking prisoners are 'beating hemp for rogues, whores, and vagrant persons' (Figure 3.6). There is no audience.

Figure 3.6 'The House of Correction'.
Source: Seller, *A Booke of the Punishments of the Common Laws of England.*

[245] NRO Norwich Assembly Folio Book 5, fo. 19.

It looks dank and dreary inside these walls; tedium on a page. Not much would have changed inside from one day to the next. This is where we need to go now. The chapter sequence in this book structurally represents turning inside. Chapters 2–3 have been set outside in the main; the remaining two turn inside. The first of them covers institutions. It starts with a guided tour of a house of correction in the south-west of the country.

4
Institutions

> Few are sent 'to the house of correction or working house but they come out better'.
>
> E. Coke, *The Second Part of the Institutes of the Lawes of England* (1644), 729.

There was dark 'benchinge' running along three walls in the hall. A large seat in front of the chimney was impossible to miss. A 'cubbord' holding 'drawinge boxes and an open presse' sat 'under the hall'. A door 'with lock and keye' took people to 'the foote of the staires'. An 'enterclose divide[d] the hall from the entrie' that had two doors 'with lock and key'. Bright light streamed in from 'a great wyndowe with sixe lights towardes the streete'. A kitchen had two ovens.

We are inside a bridewell. This one is in South Molton, a dozen miles inland from Barnstaple on Devon's north coast. A parlour stood next to a hall where 'a bedsted hede' was 'joyned to the seillinge [ceiling]'. The door was locked if no one was in the room. Eight stairs led to an upper floor with three 'chambers over the hall, parlor, and entrie'. One had a 'newe windowe of 4 lights'. 'The chamber over the hall' and a room 'over the entrie and prison' both had 'olde' windows. Outside, 'a newe gate with 4 hookes and twists and iron staple' was in between 'the gate house and house on the west' that had 'a doore with hooks and twists, a staire with 9 stepps' and a 'window of 4 lights'. 'The chamber over the gatehouse' also had 'a windowe of 4 lights' and a 'stoppe for the correccon of rogues with irons'.

We hardly ever get inside a bridewell. The year is 1644 and Humphrey Buckingham had just been made 'master' of the 'house'. 'It seemed good [to open this] house', magistrates said, 'consideringe the greate number' of jobless drifting here and the 'daylie' growth of home poor. It was the best 'remedy'. Buckingham got a five-year term and £50 to buy wool, flax, and yarn to put 'poore people on worke'. Long-winded 'house' rules were finalized: (1) Buckingham would take care of all 'repairs'; (2) provide things 'necessarie' for the 'safe keepinge [of] rogues and idle persons' and 'mills and cardes' for work; (3) keep 'a booke to recorde the names of rogues and idle' people and their committal dates; (4) inmates would get for 'sustenance' what they earned from 'labour'; (5) wages inside would be the same as outside for 'like worke'; (6) Buckingham was to provide lodgings and food at town rates; (7) healthy inmates were 'corrected by moderate whippinge everie seconde daye'—Sunday 'excepted'—men 'one mornynge' and women the next; (8) men and women could not mix at 'diet, laboure, and lodginge [so]

Information, Institutions, and Local Government in England, 1550–1700: Turning Inside. Paul Griffiths, Oxford University Press. © Paul Griffiths 2023. DOI: 10.1093/oso/9780192896261.003.0005

lewdness and suspicion thereof may be avoyded'; (9) Buckingham had to update justices on the 'house' at each sessions; (10) prayers were to be said 'everie daie' 'reverentlie and orderlie'; (11) the 'master' took care of the sick; (12) any child without work on the streets was to be sent to the 'house'; (13) anyone who 'marred' their work or refused to work would get 'reasonable correccon'; (14) no more than four children would be in the 'house' at any one time; and (15) the master would lose his job if he did not do it properly.[1]

This was how things should have been inside this particular bridewell. Local peculiarities aside (for example, the nature of economies), these South Molton 'house' rules were fairly typical. This chapter covers the sequence of events and thoughts behind the idea, development, and effectiveness of England's bridewells in town and country (comparisons with prisons and other institutions are made all the way through). It begins with the institutional comprehensiveness that was developing in most towns and cities. This started with households (and service/apprenticeship) and fanned out through linked pipelines to connect domestic settings to bridewells, workhouses, almshouses, hospitals, prisons, orphanages, and lazar-houses. Institutions were coming to play more prominent parts in solutions to the trials and tribulations of urban living: grim conditions, health, disease, wrongdoing, need, keeping families together, and negotiating life-cycle change. Although often swamped, they were to become indispensable in testing times when the number of people living in urban areas doubled.

This chapter sketches the sequence of events in Parliament and early innovations in towns and cities that culminated in legislation in 1610 that set up England's first ever nationwide system of incarceration in bridewells. The emergence of bridewells was often patchy, a series of stops and starts, but the compulsion in the 1610 House of Correction legislation changed things. The next issue is numbers of bridewells in towns and counties, their size, and nitty-gritty matters such as costs, building, upkeep, and remodelling. Prisoners and their offences are quantified and categorized, and the lengths of sentence are measured and broken down by crime. Recorded bridewell populations make it clear that this 'revolutionary' project was intended to take care of the marginal and troublesome poor, petty crime, and family breakdowns. The fourth section moves to life inside bridewells. The status, terms, and conditions of keepers and other officers form one aspect of this; another is the conditions in which the prisoners were kept—food and board, health, hygiene, and medical care. It was hoped that bridewells would lead the way in keeping some deep social troubles in check. The question of their effectiveness lingers and while this chapter gives due coverage to 'mysgovernment', one of its main aims is to reconsider the terms through which we evaluate bridewells. But we turn first to the scope and scale of institutionalization and the words in which it was expressed that bring to mind the interconnectedness

[1] NDRO 3058add7/44/1–2.

between different types of institutions and the domestic language that coupled them with the first link in the chain: the household.

I

Governors imagined institutions in networks that criss-crossed towns. The Duke in *Measure for Measure* talks about 'our city's institutions' (I, i, 10). The whole was greater than the sum of its parts. England's second city, Norwich, exemplifies this interconnectedness. It was a city of prisons, hospitals, almshouses, lazar-houses, and an early bridewell. 'Bridewell' first turns up in Mayor's Court records in 1571 when Joan Gedding was locked up after she was carted for 'mysrule'. 'The Boke for Brydewell' is written in a margin in the Assembly Book in the same year. It is also called 'a booke drawne for the order of the poore' on the same page, as if this institution was synonymous with the grand plan for poverty and order that was put together after the famous 1570 census.[2] Norwich had several prisons at any one time. There was an 'aldermans prison' and 'free pryson' in 1551, a 'guildhall prison' in 1580, a 'gaolehouse', 'the citie prysone' or 'comon gayle' in the east wing of the Guildhall in 1588, a prison in 'the howse called the Lambe' in 1600 that was 'one of the new prisons', a 'comon gaole in the markett place' in 1609, and the 'womans prysone at the guildehall'.[3] Payments for a 'hows' in Bridewell's Yard, 'where in the madd people bee putt', are logged in 1586: a 'lunetyke' minister was kept there for a handful of years. The city also had a number of hospitals. The 'Great Hospital' near the cathedral was home for seventy-eight 'poore people' in 1622. Numbers hovered between eighty-five and ninety-five, peaking at a hundred in 1682. It looks like a retirement home: the ages of 'poore people' at first entry ranged from sixty-one to eighty-one.[4] In his 1617 will, the founding father of the Childrens' Hospital, first called 'the hospitall for orphans', Alderman Anguish, said that its main aim was the 'good bringing up' of children loitering in 'streets' who caught 'grievous diseases', leaving them unfit for work 'ever after'. 'Tene boyes and two gyrles' were the first intake in rooms 'on the east part' of his house. Just 'nyne children' were there in 1633 but that number soared to 'xvi boyes' in 1642 and settled at a steady dozen from around 1660. Anguish's will put age at entry at 'five, six, or seven', although one child was thirteen. Children stayed until they were 'fitting

[2] P. Griffiths, 'Inhabitants', in C. Rawcliffe and R. Wilson, eds., *Norwich Since 1550* (2004); NRO Norwich Assembly Folio Book 3, fo. 186v.

[3] NRO Norwich Bridewell Treasurers Account Book 1, 1586; Norwich Clavors Book 1550–1601, fos. 104, 105, 108; NMCC 6, fo. 117; 10, fo. 538; 11, fo. 556; 12, fo. 105; 14, fos. 251v, 459; Norwich Chamberlains' Accounts 1580–9, fos. 29v, 236, 251v; 1589–1602, fos. 60v, 159v, 187, 218; 1625–48, fo. 14; Norwich Assembly Book 5, fos. 177, 190v, 193v.

[4] NRO Norwich Great Hospital Account Rolls, 1621/2, 1631/2, 1633/4, 1641/2, 1643/5, 1648/9, 1649/50, 1665/6; NMCC 25, fo. 10; 24, fo. 45; 25, fo. 312; 26, fos. 8, 13, 15v, 19, 26, 28, 33, 61, 65, 74v, 78.

for service [at] fourteen or fifteen'.[5] Aldermen were tasked to 'find a roome' suitable for 'a girles hospitall' in 1652. 'The house in the dark entry at the newhall' was chosen, although two decades later the city hoped 'to build or hire a convenient house for the girles hospitall'. The 'girles' ranged in age from nine to fifteen.[6] Once leper refuges, lazar-houses ringing the city at its gates offered a crumb of comfort to 'sore diseased' and 'very fowle' folk. Women laid low with 'the pockes' or 'frenche disease' were sent to one, along with the 'sicke' poore including Great Hospital inmates and 'diseased soldiers'. The 'guyder of the poore at St Bennetts gates' took in fifty-three 'poore children' in 1600–1 and five 'poore women', sometimes 'after the rate of iis vid the weeke' and 'vid' at other times. They included 'diseased young wench' Jane Bartle, a 'child left in the towne closse borne in the cytty gaylle', and Robert Graye, whose legs were 'almost eaten upp with a canker'.[7]

Norvicians grew up and old in a city where the threat of Bridewell or the warmer prospect of a hospital bed were ever-present possibilities. Institutions straddled the life course, touching many lives at any one time. Hospitals gave room and board and training to children as they set out in life, while almshouses gave shelter to people in the winter of their lives: Salisbury's almshouse gave a last home to 102-year-old Nicholas Harding, who was no longer 'able to subsist'; 'very decrepped' Thomas Johnson; and, very poignantly, an old man who had 'nothing lefte'.[8] Returning to Norwich, institutions worked hand in hand with city government, parishes, and each other. This interconnectedness was buttressed by communication pipelines, government policies, cross-referrals, and pooled resources: hospitals sent rowdy inmates to Bridewell; sick prisoners went in the other direction; 'fowle' patients and prisoners were put in lazar-houses.[9] Ties between the Guildhall, parishes, and institutions tightened after the 1598/1601 Poor Laws, not least if we follow flexible definitions of institutions to include apprenticeship and households. England might have been half-a-million households. A well-governed country began with households that were the backbone of work, discipline, and order: reformation, Daniel Cawdrey said, 'sticks here' (that is, the household).[10] Householders were lynchpins of order and took their turn as office-holder(s) to protect the parish peace and purse. This instinctive thinking about domestic discipline was translated into hospitals and bridewells.

[5] NRO Norwich Assembly Folio Book 5, fos. 113v, 125–5v; Norwich Children's Hospital Book, front of book, 1632/3, 1641/2, 1648/9, 1649/50, 1659/60, 1660/6; NMCC 25, fo. 3; 26, fos. 13, 17v, 19, 32, 58, 59, 80v.

[6] NRO Norwich Assembly Folio Books 6, fos.25, 126v, 129, 138v; 8, fo. 12v; NMCC 26, fos. 5, 21v, 41, 65.

[7] NRO Norwich Clavors Books 1, fos. 9v, 39, 40v, 65v, 80v, 82, 86v, 87v, 109, 134, 136–40v; 3, fo. 3; NMCC 23, fos. 154, 164v, 191v, 196; 24, fos. 298, 328; 25, fos. 92, 213, 224; 26, fo. 32; Norwich Great Hospital Account Rolls 1608–9, 1631–2.

[8] WSHC G23/1/3, fo. 414; G23/1/37. And see NRO Y/C/19/5, fo. 122; T/C2/5, fos. 9, 87; GA GBR/B/3/1, fos. 20, 37v; HA W/H3/15, fo. 24; LERO QS6/1/2, fo. 27v.

[9] See M. Pelling, *The Common Lot: Sickness, Medical Occupations and the Urban Poor in Early Modern England* (Harlow, 1998), 97–8.

[10] D. Cawdrey, *Family Reformation Promoted* (1656), 46.

They were imagined as 'houses' and their inmates were thought of in terms of dependency as 'the poor'. Norwich's Great Hospital was called 'God's howse' or 'howse of the poore people'. The lazar-house at St Augustine Gate was known as 'the house of the poore'. The bridewell was called a 'house', 'hospital', and 'prison', and one of its chief tasks was to settle domestic tiffs and fix fragmented households including breakdowns in service. This domestic spin signified care and teaching. Norwich's mayor was called Bridewell's 'governor or heade master' in 1571. The person in charge of running bridewells was often called the 'master', although its inmates were to 'be kept as presanors'.[11]

This word jumble signifies the multifaceted nature of institutions that were meant to punish, heal, shelter, and reform. 'Hospital' was an umbrella term that could catch each of these functions. Plans were made in Ipswich in 1659 to turn the 'house of blacke fryers' into 'an hospitall for the poore' to be called 'Chrystes Hospitall'. 'Masterlesse servants, idle persons, hedgebreakers, harlotts, and drunkards' were among the 'hospitalls' population, but it also gave room and board to a 'blynde woman', elderly people with nowhere left to turn, and 'poore children' who 'learned to worke'.[12] Yarmouth had a 'pore howse at the hospitall' or 'pore howse comonly called brydewell'.[13] This double or treble function was the *modus operandi* in many 'houses'. The one in Salisbury housed 'poore children' along with the 'baser and lewder sort of people' who needed 'correctinge'.[14] People in Thetford 'workehowse' either had no help at home or broke the law like 'comon hedgebreaker' Edward Meadows, who had 'a clogg allwayes [on his leg] dureing his abiding'.[15] Arch-Puritan Ignatius Jourdain noted that an Exeter man was punished for his 'filthy adultery [with] twenty stripes' in the 'house of correction [that was] commonly called the bridewell'. 'Correction house or Bridewell', William Sheppard called it.[16] 'Bridewes-well or Brudgtswell', M.R. wrote, is a 'free hospital for the remedie of sundry diseases' that drove 'lazy drones from idle-nese, lewde letchers from luxury, vaine unthrifts from prodigalitie, old persons from vild-nesse, youth from wild-nese'.[17] House of correction and workhouse were also twinned. Woodbridge's 'workehouse master' was told to run it 'as a house of correccon' in 1649. Bungay had a 'workehouse and house of correcon' in 1650. A Barnstaple clothier was put in charge of the 'bridewell or worke-house' in 1687,[18] while plans were made in Southampton in 1632 for a 'worke house' and 'house of correccon'

[11] NRO Norwich 'Mayors Booke for the Poore, 1571–79', fo. 2v.
[12] SAI C/4/3/1/1/1, fos. 47, 48v, 54v, 120, 181–2; C/4/3/1/1/5, fos. 14, 196.
[13] NRO Y/C/19/3, fos. 82v, 89; Y/C/19/4, fo. 124v.
[14] WSHC G23/1/3, fo. 289v. [15] NRO T/QS/1, fos. 20v, 38.
[16] TNA STAC8 161/10, Ignatius Jourdain answer; W. Sheppard, *New Survey of the Justice of Peace His Office* (1659).
[17] M.R., *Micrologia. Characters or Essayes, of Persons, Trades and Places Offered to the City and Country* (1629), D7r.
[18] SAI B/105/2/1, fo. 133; B/105/2/1, fo. 140; NDRO 1064Q/SO1, fo. 212.

to shelter the 'impotent and aged pore' and put 'idle, lewd, and vagrant persons' to hard work to make them 'better' people.[19]

People walked past 'houses' and 'hospitals' each day of the week in urban England, and their thoughts must have turned to what it was like inside. Like punishment before 'people's eyes', they became embedded in life. People walked up and down 'bridewell staires' in Gloucester, 'Old Gaole Lane' in Dorchester, and 'Gaole Lane' in Hereford. Institutions appeared in directions to get somewhere: 'Old Scull Streete' in Hereford needed patching up 'from the bridewell up to the gaole lane' in 1661; Faversham's 'comon pounde adioyninge the comon gaole or prison called the white-house' also needed fixing.[20] Bridewells and prisons also added extra edge to street slang and gibes. Mary Badham called Ann Luck 'bridewell whore' as they washed clothes in London in 1602; Mary Sadd called Magaret Eddis 'hospital whore'. 'Bridewell rogue' and 'bird' and 'Newgate bird' were also heard on streets and bandied about in print.[21] 'You old jade, you will be in bridewell before me', a Dorchester widow snapped at Keate's wife in 1632. A Hereford baker who was sitting around a bonfire on a 'publique daye of thanksgiveinge' in 1661 'disgraceful[ly]' said that the 'company of weavers were all a company of theeves being often in the gaole and out of the gaole'.[22] Bridewells were also lampooned and lambasted on streets. and things got touchy when words slammed these symbols of local authority. A woman was 'well whipped' in London in 1559 for 'rayling most unhonestlye and slaunderouslye upon [Bridewell] and [its] governors openly in the hearyng of fyve hundred persons'. A thief who snatched a hat from a man walking along a street 'curse[d] this hospitall and the founder thereof' (King Edward VI).[23] Matters were made worse if it was one of the government's own who bad-mouthed a bridewell. A Norwich bellman lost his job in 1613 after he 'publiquely shouted [that] yf any [were] desirous to have their neckes broke yf they came to bridewell yt should be done'. A rash quip perhaps, but it was a poor choice of words in 'publique'.[24]

We ought to remember how new bridewells were and that they had no precedent. They sprang up in towns and cities in the second half of the sixteenth century and their ties to harsh confinement and hard work made them seem heavy-handed, intrusive, and controversial.[25] England's first bridewell in London has been called 'revolutionary', 'unique', and 'pioneering', and the first of its type to

[19] SA SC9/2/1, fos. 66v, 134v. Cf. DRO ECA B/1/3, fo. 411; WRO QS0040/1/1, fo. 11v; OHC C/FC/1/A1/03, fo. 2v; HEA Q/SM/3, fo. 39; DHC DC/BTB/M2/1630.

[20] GA GBR F/4/5, fo. 376v; HEA BG11/4/6, 10/1661, fo. 1; DHC DC/DOB/8/1, fo. 259v; CKS FA/AC3, fos. 97v, 180v. See also DHC D/DOR/T/40–1.

[21] LMA MS 9057/1, fo. 1; D/L/C/214, fos. 407, 412.

[22] DHC DC/DOB/8/1, fo. 122; HEA BG/11/17/1/5, fo. 49. See also DRO ECA C1/62, fos. 55v, 152; WAC WCB/1, fo. 174; GA GBR/G/G/SO/1, fo. 39; DHC DC/DOB/8/1, fo. 98v; HEA BG11/17/1/4, fo. 76.

[23] LBHC 1, fos. 17v, 87v, 38, 51–1v; 2, fo. 76; 8, fo. 212v.

[24] NRO NMCC 14, fo. 378v.

[25] J. Innes, 'Prisons for the poor: English bridewells 1555–1800', in F. Snyder and D. Hay, eds., *Labour, Law, and Crime: A Historical Perspective* (Oxford, 1987).

twin character-changing work with custodial sentences.[26] It is hard for us to imagine what it was like when a bridewell first opened its doors. People had not known anything like this before. Imprisonment was not new. Troublemakers had been locked up in prisons long before 1500. Work on urban records especially has got rid of the myth that prison sentences were not handed down in medieval England.[27] But bridewells made a real difference after 1550. They had no equivalent before then. Work so far does not suggest that people were put in prison in fifteenth-century England for being idle, vagrant, out of service, or simply suspicious in anywhere approaching significant levels. The scope and scale of the war on marginal living as population growth boomed and Protestantism sought to establish itself are distinctive. A part of that lies in an attachment to bridewells that were submerged in the cut and thrust of workaday living. They were synonymous with the poverty and trouble that was enveloping England in the Tudor population flood. This will be evident as we turn to their origins and first decades.

II

The first nationwide system of incarceration inside bridewells was set up by statute in 1610 (7.Jac.1.c.4). Each town and county had to open at least one bridewell. Plans for the needy, sick, and bad increasingly turned to institutions for solutions. This institutional momentum stretched back to the time when London opened five 'hospitals' in a short seven-year span (1546–53) as streets 'swarmed with beggars and rogues' and aldermen fretted about a 'daylie increase in [the] great number [of home poor] then have bin in tymes past'. The first—Bethlem (1546)—housed lunatics and was followed one year later by St Bartholomew's for the sick. Another 'hospital' for the sick, St Thomas's, and Christ's Hospital for the 'comfortless' and 'parentless' children opened their doors in 1552. The final piece of the jigsaw was Bridewell in 1553, with sweeping powers to 'seke owt [all] ydell ruffians and taverne haunters, vagabonds, beggars', and 'persons of yll name and fame' in London and its north-west fringe.[28] Bishop Ridley called the hospitals a

[26] A. L. Beier, *Masterless Men: the Vagrancy Problem in England, 1560–1640* (1985), 164; A. L. Beier, 'Foucault Redux?: The roles of humanism, Protestantism, and an urban elite in creating the London Bridewell, 1500–1560', *Criminal Justice History*, 17 (2002); P. Slack, 'Hospitals, workhouses, and the relief of the poor in early modern London', in O. P. Grell and A. Cunningham, eds., *Health Care and Poor Relief in Protestant Europe, 1500–1700* (1997), 237; Innes, 'Prisons for the poor', 42, 53; P. Spierenburg, *The Prison Experience: Disciplinary Institutions and Their Inmates in Early Modern Europe* (New Brunswick, NJ, and London, 1991), 23–5; R. Jutte, *Poverty and Deviance in Early Modern Europe* (Cambridge, 1994), 169–70, 172–3, 174.

[27] C. Winter, 'Prisons and Punishments in Late Medieval London' (PhD thesis, University of London, 2012); H. Carrel, 'The ideology of punishment in late medieval English towns', *Social History*, 34 (2009), 312–14; H. Carrel, 'Civic Government and Identity in the Provincial Towns of Late Medieval England, c. 1370–c. 1500' (PhD thesis, University of Cambridge, 2007), 78–85; R. Pugh, *Imprisonment in Medieval England* (Cambridge, 1968).

[28] P. Griffiths, *Lost Londons: Change, Crime, and Control in the Capital City, 1550–1660* (Cambridge, 2008), 12; LMA MSS 6, fo. 6v; 9384; Jour. 16, fos. 370v–1; *The Thirty-Second Report of the Charity Commissioners of England and Wales. Per Acts 38 Geo.3.c.91 and Geo.3.c.8.81*, part IV, 1840 (219), xix; *John Howes MS, 1582*, ed. W. Lemprière (1904), 56–60.

'blessed work of God' in his final farewell to London before his martyr's death in 1555. The 'citizen' in Richard Johnson's *Pleasant Walkes of Moore-fields* (1607) bragged about London's 'immortal commendations' including Christ's and Bridewell. Bishop Gilbert Burnet spoke glowingly about Bridewell in his *History of the Reformation* (1679), calling it one of the 'noblest' acts in Europe since Luther nailed up his ninety-five theses.[29]

England's first bridewell in London was its biggest. It was a former royal palace sitting on the riverside next to the west wall at the point where the Fleet River met the Thames. It was finished in 1523 but Henry VIII never set foot in Bridewell Palace again after divorce talks with Rome broke down there. The terms 'bridewell' and 'house of correction' became synonymous, and I will do the same here. The idea of bridewell as a tough response to crime and joblessness quickly became a blueprint for other cities, counties, and countries. Some got copies of Bridewell's charter and letters patent (the Duke of Portland had a copy of the letters in his Nottinghamshire home).[30] 'Bridewell-like institutions' followed soon after the first one opened its doors in 1553: Oxford (1562), Salisbury (1564), Norwich (around 1565), Ipswich (1569), Gloucester (around 1569), and perhaps another ten towns and cities by the end of the century. Towns took leading initiatives but at least one quarter of England's counties had bridewells by 1600 in most parts of the country—in Cornwall, for instance, Suffolk, Yorkshire, and Gloucestershire (although the North-west looks a little sparse). Norfolk and Devon might have had as many as four or five.[31] It is logical to think of county bridewells as serving predominantly rural regions, although they were located in market towns for the most part. The intention of the 1610 legislation was to put all areas on the same footing. There had been a law before (in 1576) to prompt localities to open a 'correccon house'. The group framing this legislation talked about setting up bridewells all over the country. Privy councillors put their weight behind this disciplinary apparatus, turning to leading civic figures who had first-hand experience. One of them, Norwich alderman John Aldrich, sat on the committee that drew up the 'bill for setting the poor on work and for avoiding of idleness' (that became the 1576 Act), and had a large hand in the ground-breaking scheme that followed the Census of the Poor (it was his wife who stood next to Bennet Goodwyn on the banks of the Wensum as she was about to be ducked in 1562, urging her to change her ways).[32] A clutch of parliamentary legislation restated

[29] 'A Treatise or Letter Written by Dr Ridley Instead of His Last Farewell to All His True and Faithful Friends in God', in *The Acts and Monuments of John Foxe*, ed. S. R. Catley (1841), 559–60; G. Ridley, *The Life of Dr Nicholas Ridley, Sometime Bishop of London Shewing the Plan and Progress of the Reformation* (1763), 377–9; R. Johnson, *The Pleasant Walkes of Moore-fieldes* (1607), B1v; G. Burnet, *The History of the Reformation of the Church of England*, 1679, ed. N. Pocock (Oxford, 1865), 367–8. See Slack, 'Hospitals, workhouses, and the relief of the poor'.

[30] NOTTA DD/4P/68/23, fo. 23. See Spierenburg, *Prison Experience*, 24.

[31] Innes, 'Prisons for the poor', 61.

[32] *Journals of the House of Commons, I: 1547–1629* (1802), 68.

the need for 'houses' including the Poor Law (39.Eliz.c.3) and 'An Act for Erecting of Hospitals or Abiding and Working House for the Poor' (39.Eliz.c.5), under which anyone could 'bequeath in fee-simple' money to 'incorpo-rate [a] hospital, maison de dieu [or] house of correction' as a 'body corporate and politick'. The 1598 Poor Law seems to have been a strong influence that made Sussex, Shropshire, and Westmorland, for instance, open a bridewell. Essex magistrates made plans to open twenty-three in that year.[33]

The compulsion in the 1610 legislation made a big difference. Earlier laws, its framers explained, had 'not wrought so good effect as was expected'. Either bridewells had 'not been built [as] was intended', Edward Coke wrote in his commentary on the Act, or laws had not been 'duely and severely put in execution' ('Execution', he added, 'is the end and life of the law').[34] Parliament set a timetable. Towns and counties had to open bridewells by Michaelmas 1611; a £5 fine was dangled over justices who fell behind this schedule. The law, work, and order triangle was on the minds of MPs in this parliamentary session, who also passed legislation covering crime in the 'north parts', 'manual occupations', apprentices, 'unlawful hunting', and the 'reformation of alehouse-keepers'. The king also waded in, telling assize judges to urge counties to open bridewells. Joanna Innes notes that England had a 'network' of bridewells by 1630: there were 'seventy or more county bridewells alone'. These were 'unusually large numbers' for Europe. Central government added more pressure to get things done in the same year when the Privy Council's Book of Orders put the question to towns and counties: do you have a house of correction?[35]

Civic magistrates took it upon themselves to open bridewells as basic planks in social schemes to put 'problem' paupers on the right track and get work for the poor. But it was rarely smooth sailing. The plan to open a bridewell was a starting point only. Yarmouth is a good case study of a town that saw the benefits of bridewells in their early dawn but ended with a mixed record of stops and starts. The 'south side of the storehowse [was] made ready for poore people' in 1573 ('hospitall for the poore' is written in the margin in the Assembly book). 'New surveiors at bridewell' were named in 1574, although 'surveior of the pore howse at the hospitall' appears in the margin. Their task was to 'take order' if 'the brydewell shalbe contynued or not' ('auditors' and 'persons to take order for brydewell' were picked in 1575).[36] I wish I knew what was behind this question, as it is intriguing this early. In any event, records run dry for a while until 1582, when a committee was tasked to 'oversee the house late used for a bridewell' to report if it could be used again to tackle 'idlenes'. The Assembly ruled in 1587 that the town needed a

[33] Innes, 'Prisons for the poor', 67.
[34] E. Coke, *The Second Part of the Institutes of the Lawes of England* (1642), 728–9.
[35] Innes, 'Prisons for the poor', 62; P. Slack, 'Books of orders: the making of English social policy', 1577–1631', *TRHS*, 30 (1980).
[36] NRO Y/C/19/3, fos. 50, 60, 71, 73v, 82v, 89, 102, 107v, 113.

'hospitall or bridewell' and a committee was set up to advise on the best way to get this done. Funding may not have been sought until 1590, when bailiffs levied a subsidy 'through ye wholle towne' and got Mr Drury to lend £20 for 'a bridewell or house for bringing up of youth'. Yet another committee met soon after 'to conferre' about the 'charge' for a 'bridewell' for 'poore idle persons' who 'greatly encombered' the town. The 1590s was a tough time, and governors struggled to find the 'meanes' to 'bringe to passe so good a pece of work'. Assembly members were themselves slammed for not giving towards 'the building of the hospitall'. The 1598 Poor Law seems to have roused them from their slumber. 'Mr Baylfyy' made a 'motion [for] errecting of a bridewell' in that year. Magistrates 'viewed the hospitall' and its 'garden or orchard' to see if it was 'convenient [for a] house of correction or hospitall for the placing of [the] poore and settinge of idle persons on worke'. An audit book logs a £30 payment for 'prepareinge the hospitall howse [to] be a house of correction accordinge to the forme of the [1598] statute'. Orders for its 'government' were drawn up, overseers were picked, and inmates put to work. Further articles for 'good order and government' in Bridewell were read to the Assembly in 1603. Regular orders were passed before and after the 1610 Act for 'better ordering [or reforming] of brydwell or the howse of correccon'. All for the 'best advantag of the towne'.[37]

Yarmouth magistrates were energized by the 1598 Poor Law, but the 1610 Act urged many towns and counties to wake up. Cheshire justices fell into immediate talk on plans for a bridewell. Middlesex magistrates could finally think about laying the foundation stone for Clerkenwell Bridewell in 1615, although they had been slowed down by jurisdictional concerns about London Bridewell's powers to police the north-west metropolitan area. The county bridewell in Lancashire at Preston opened its doors for the first time in 1620.[38] But there was still uncertainty, false dawns, and money matters along Yarmouth lines. Geography was an issue in Cheshire as it was elsewhere. 'Experience', justices there said in 1631, has 'taught that the due execucon' of laws to tackle vagrancy 'have not wrought that good effect' they had hoped for because the county bridewell in Northwich 'is farr remote from divers partes'. 'Few or none' take offenders there, they said, owing to the high 'charge and trouble' of sending them from places far and wide. The answer, justices decided, with the recent Book of Orders in mind, was to have two county 'houses' from now on: one in Chester Castle and the other in 'Nether Knuttford'. But things did not work out. There was a change of mind and justices plumped for Tarvin instead, where Robert Hitler 'hath already prepared a

[37] NRO Y//C/19/4, fos. 53, 124v, 147v, 187v. 192, 201, 216, 220, 271v, 278, 281v, 282, 283; Y/C27/1, fos. 217, 226v, 244; Y/C/19/5, fos. 23, 37, 37v, 46, 65, 73, 86, 121, 142v, 220, 264, 271v, 274–5; Y/C/19/6, fo. 182. Henry Manship tells us that the 'storehouse'—the site of the 'hospitall for the poore'—and a school were 'used for a house of correction' in 1598: *The History of Great Yarmouth*, completed in manuscript in 1619, ed. C. J. Palmer, Kessinger Legacy Reprints (1854), 43.

[38] Innes, 'Prisons for the poor'.

convenient house'. But they continued to make 'sute' for the castle without any luck as they could not get 'leave' from the king. In the end they opted to have 'onely one house of correccon [in] Northwich [being] seated neerest of all other towns to the middle of this county'.[39] There were similar issues in Richmondshire four decades later. The grand jury filed a complaint about a surge in vagrancy that they 'imputed' to moving the bridewell from Richmond—'where it hath formerly been kept time out of mind'—to a 'place so far remote as Thirske'. The 'greatest part' of vagrants are now no longer punished, they added. The ideal solution was to open two new 'houses' 'within this Riding', in Richmond and another 'where the justices shall think fit'.[40] More than a few county benches decided that two bridewells was the right number for their needs. Hearing that as many as nine bridewells were being mooted for their county in 1624, Hertfordshire's grand jury insisted that nine was far too many and that two would be more than sufficient.[41]

It was not cheap to run bridewells and start-up costs were high and sometimes led to delays. The final bill in Shropshire in 1631 was a whopping £520 4s. 2d. We have wonderful itemized cost sheets for 'purchasing and building' this 'house of correccon': £18 to cut and carry stone from quarries, £28 11s. for 'thirty-two 'thousand of slate', six shillings to dig a vault 'for the house of office', 17s. 8d. for '10 iron cramps to tye the new and old buildings together', 5s. 9d. for 'worke to make a little roome to keepe irons in', £1 17s. 6d. to buy '500 boards to floore the womans house' and, when all the work was done, £1 7s. 4d. for a celebration 'dinner at ye Raven'.[42] The cost for 'workmanship' and materials for the 'correction howse in Tutlefeildes' in Westminster in 1622–3 came to £155 4s. 1d. including £7 7s. 6d. for 'xx blocks to beat hempe on', 6s. 6d. for '44 printed passes', and £1 for 'presidents and orders transcribed out of other houses of correccon' in Middlesex, Surrey, and the 'old bridewell in London'. Middlesex Bridewell was 'finished' in 1615 with the help of large 'somes' from 'honorable and well affected persons' and £500 from London.[43] Assize judges 'moved' Wiltshire justices to make plans for four bridewells costing £1200 in 1630 after the county bridewell in Devizes burnt down.[44]

As with compulsory taxation in the Poor Law, some better-off people took exception to being told that they must contribute to the cost of opening bridewells.[45] Getting rates collected was often a hard slog. Michael Shorditch was

[39] CA QJB/1/5, fos. 286, 294, 306–7.

[40] J. C. Atkinson, ed., *North Riding Quarter Sessions Records*, 9 vols, North Riding Record Society, 1-9 (1884–92), VI, 249, 263–4.

[41] J. C. Cockburn, ed., *Calendar of Assize Records. Hertfordshire Indictments. James I* (HMSO, 1975), 275.

[42] SHA QS/2/1, unpag.

[43] WAC E13, 1622–3; LMA MJ/SBR/2, fo. 120; Rep. 32, fo. 120; Jour. 13, fo. 13v.

[44] WSHC G22/1/269. Roger Langton was given £250 'towardes the erecon of a howse of correccon' in Preston in 1618 'for the whole countie': E. Axon, ed., *Manchester Sessions: Notes of Proceedings Before Oswald Mosley (1616–1630), Nicholas Mosley (1661–1672), and Sir Oswald Mosley (1734–1739)... Volume 1, 1616–1623*, Lancashire and Cheshire Record Society, 42 (1901), 46–7.

[45] P. Slack, *Poverty and Policy in Tudor and Stuart England* (Harlow, 1988), chap. 7.

hauled before Middlesex justices in 1614 'for speakinge divers unfitt and mutynous speeches touchinge a rate [for] the makinge of a house of correccon'. William Newman from Greenford in the same county was charged in 1615 with 'givinge false reporte to the courte touchinge the house of correccon'.[46] Collections dragged on past their due date, falling 'behynde hande'. Middlesex justices moaned that rates had been 'unduelie made in divers parishes' in 1615, that officers were 'remisse in collectinge the somes rated', and that some among the rated were either dead or had moved elsewhere. Northall and Ealing constables were taken to task for 'not collectinge money for the howse of correccon' in the same year.[47] Cheshire also had regular shortfalls in collections. Justices berated officers who 'have not yet paid their money [for] the house of correction' in 1616 and again two decades later when a lack of funds was 'hindering' the 'work'. Lawyers were instructed to speed up action against 'divers' constables, but 'the worke lyes still unfinished', justices said, with considerable impatience.

Slack officers were given one month to get collections in or else face a spell in Chester Castle.[48] The Middlesex bridewell was probably the costliest and running costs continued to be a drain on county and civic budgets. Like Buckingham in South Molton, 'masters' gave regular updates to magistrates. Three justices 'at the least' were instructed to 'oversee the government' of Middlesex Bridewell in 1617. Hampshire justices wanted to see how the 'house standeth' in 1632. Four Oxford magistrates met at the 'house' each Friday in 1631 for its 'better over-sight and ordering'. Justices sent four delegations to 'visitt the house of correccon' in successive weeks in 1627 to make 'reportes [on] disorders [in the] government of the house'.[49] Committees were regularly appointed to 'take care for the ordering of all things concerninge the house'. Many towns and cities like Norwich, Chester, and Faversham appointed overseers and 'surveyours for bridewell' to 'enforme themselves' of what was going on inside.[50]

Running costs tended to be on the lower side, but neglect caused by financial shortfalls or organizational issues could put a big dent in budgets. Somerset justices sat frowning in 1608 on hearing that Taunton's 'house' was 'ruinated'. The old master was owed back pay and his successor told them that the 'howse' needed 'reedifyinge beinge so fare [from] reparatyone by means of [the] governor before myself'. The 'cheffeste rooms have fallen downe to the grownd', he added; 'I have towe onlye rooms that I cane detayne pryssoners' and they are 'verye symple'.

[46] LMA MJ/SBR/2, fos. 125, 199, 245.

[47] DRO ECA B/1/3, fo. 457; LMA MJ/SBR/2, fos. 245, 182.

[48] CA QJB/1/4, fo. 132v; QJB/1/5, fo. 505; QJB/1/6, fos. 14v, 23, 30v. See also HA Q4/1, fo. 98; Q1/2, fo. 216v; ESBHRO QI/EW8, fo. 17v; HL HAM box 49, folder 6; KAC WQ/I/1, fos. 7, 9v; HEA Q/SM/4, fos. 97v, 121v–2.

[49] LMA MJ/SBR/2, fo. 411; MJ/SBR/4, fos. 406, 515; MJ/SBR/5, fo. 355; MJ/SBR/6, fo. 604; MJ/SBR/7, fo. 103; HA Q1/2, fos. 48v–50, 69v; OHC C/FC/1/A1/02, fo. 30.

[50] CKS FA/AC4, fos. 11, 141; CA Z/AB/2, fos. 42v–3; NRO Norwich Assembly Folio Book 4, fo. 24v; Norwich Assembly Book 5, fo. 38v; HEA Q/SM/4, fo. 2.

Justices said that they would view the 'house' and find the money to put things right.[51] 'Ruination' was a matter of security and an awkward public stain. Putting the Cheshire 'house' in 'good repaire' was 'of publique concernment' in 1667. A committee in Gloucester was asked 'to consider how the bridewell may be put in good condicion and repaire [as] it ought to bee' in 1650.[52] Cheshire appears to have had a notably patchy record. The 'house' there was 'much decayed', justices heard in 1621. 'Ymplements and toles [were] lost' and people 'sent thether' could not be punished. A new master changed nothing. The building was 'muche decayed' in the next year, justices said, 'tooles' were still missing, and prisoners did not work or get 'due correccon'. The 'house' got its third 'master' in a little over a year and £49 16s. was set aside for 'necessary repayring of the decayes of the house'.[53] Few bridewells reached a state where inmates could not be punished, but there were complaints of 'oute of repaire' houses. Windows and towers needed to be 'repaired and amended' in Oxford in 1638. Reading scrambled to find £30 to repair the bridewell after it 'was made a court of guard by soldiers' in 1653 who 'ruinate[d] and pull[ed] downe a great parte' of the 'house'.[54] Nor was weather a friend at times. 'A greate storme' hit the Hampshire 'house' in 1704, while wind made 'a breach on the north side of bridewell howse' in Norwich in 1621. Something always needed to be done: fixing gates, 'making stoops and doors', fitting iron doors with locks, or making iron bars for windows.[55]

Not too many bridewells were physically imposing like the first one in London that loomed large over the Thames. South Molton, with half a dozen rooms or so, was more typical. Norwich Bridewell was in a 'great hows convertyed to a brydwell' in 1585. James Thurleby's house, 'stable, curtliage and other premisses [and] tenements' and 'greate orchard' were 'made fitt [for a] house of correccon' in Clerkenwell in 1615, while the 'kitchen or brew house' (of Christ's Hospital?) was set aside for Ipswich Bridewell at the end of the sixteenth century.[56] Oxford's new bridewell in 1631 was in a building by Northgate and the next-door corner house ('or tower following') after 'a verie worthie guift' of £150 from William Tipping 'esq'.[57] Hospitals and almshouses were 'converted' to bridewells in some places. Others took up parts of a guildhall (or 'moote hall' in Colchester in 1608) or castle, or shared space with prisons. Northamptonshire Bridewell was moved to a courtyard in Northampton 'gaol' in 1696, 'with a stable and chambers over the

51 Bates, *Quarter Sessions Records for the County of Somerset*, I, 19–20, 114.

52 CA QJB/3/1, fo. 171; GA GBR/B/3/2, fo. 534.

53 CA QJB/1/5, fos. 64v–5, 86v–7; QJB/3/1, fo. 41; QJB/3/4, fo. 8.

54 OHC C/FC/1/A1/03, fo. 83; BRO R/Z8/4/2.

55 HA Q3/3, fo. 369; NRO Norwich Treasurers' Accounts 1, 1621; 2, fo. 42v. See also ERO D/B5/AB/14; D/B5Aa/12; GA GBR/F/4/5, fo. 84; NDRO B1/721; B1/724; HA Q3/3, fo. 255; CKS Q/SM/A/1, fo. 5v (Maidstone); ESBHRO QO/EW2, fos. 16v, 38v; BRO R/AC1/1/3, fo. 227; R/FA/3/8.

56 NRO Norwich Bridewell Treasurers' Accounts 1585–1646, 1585; LMA MJ/SBR/2, fos, 157–9; SAI C/2/2/2/1, fo. 218.

57 OHC C/FC/1/A1/03, fos. 2v, 4v, 9v, 21.

same...consisting of 4 bayes of building'.[58] Some bridewells were fittingly in a 'house'; 'howses [were] appointed for the howse of correction' in Salisbury in 1602. Faversham's bridewell was

> sictuat behind the middle rowe neere the markett place [with] one roome leading into the back cellar, one other roome lyeinge over [the] cellar [another] roome called the slaughterhouse [and one more] roome or lofte lyeinge over the stable [with] a well and house of office [and] a passage [linked rooms and land around them].[59]

Poole's bridewell consisted of 'two ground roomes at the west end of the old almshouse' in 1694. St Martin-in-the-Fields (Westminster) vestry instructed churchwardens to 'take order to build a shedd fitt for a private house of correction' in 1617.[60] Prisons by way of comparison ranged from large 'gaoles' in cities to parts of the 'tollhouse' in Great Yarmouth, 'mote hall' in Colchester, or 'olde courte hall' in Faversham and Tenterden.[61] Maidstone's 'brambles' prison was in a 'towne house' in the centre of the town, A 1661 'view' of rooms in Oxford's 'Bocardo' prison has left us with a good sense of its size and shape. It shows a 'freemans ward over the gate', an 'inner ward' on the north side, a 'womans ward with a little room wythin yt' on the west side, a 'little warde under the fremens ward where the women beg' from a window, another ward for men to beg, a 'condemned roome under the womens ward', and a 'dungeon' under the 'condemned roome'.[62] Like London and Norwich, many towns had more than one prison. A half-dozen prisons are noted in Gloucester (and not only there): 'ye boothall' or 'bothall', 'the castle', 'aylegate', 'the northgate' (also called the 'comon gaole'), the 'watchgate gaole', the 'maine gaole', and 'wemens prison' that was called the 'womens prison in aylegate' in 1560.[63]

Numbers behind bars in houses of correction ranged from over 100 in London Bridewell to a half-dozen or so in smaller houses elsewhere. 'A note of the number of all such prisoners as have been sent into the howse of [London] bridewell' from the first day of November to Boxing Day 1597 logged fluctuating numbers from one day to the next. There were 129 'preseanors' in this former royal palace on the first day, 121 on the next day, twenty-two more a week later, and 123 on the

[58] ERO D/B5/Cb/6, fo. 129v; D/B5/Gb2, fo. 130v; BRO R/AC1/1/1, fo.598; OHC C/FC/1/A1/01, fo. 213; HEA Q/SM/4, fos. 97v, 121v–2, 222v; Bates, *Quarter Sessions Records for the County of Somerset*, I, 349; NA NQS/3, fo. 73.

[59] WSHC G23/1/3, fo. 169v; CKS FA/TL/6.

[60] DHC DC/PL/CB/1/1, fo. 39v; WAC F2001, fo. 114. Cf. WRO QS0040/1/1, fo. 96.

[61] Manship, *History of Great Yarmouth*, 60; ERO D/Y/2/3/15; D/B5/SB2/3, fos. 110v–11; D/B5/SB2/4, fo. 61v; D/B5/SB2/7, fo. 150v; CKS FA/AC4, fo. 45; TE/S2, fos. 171, 175–6.

[62] CKS Md/Acm1/3, fo. 21; OHC C/FC/1/A1/O3, fo. 92v.

[63] GA GBR/G/G3/SO/2, fo. 32v; GBR/F/4/3, fos. 51, 83, 89, 113v, 118, 258; GBR/F/4/5, fos. 29v, 42, 99v, 107; GBR/F/4/6, fos. 29v, 474; GBR/G/G3/SO/1, fos. 7, 8, 21v; GBR/G3/SO/2, fos. 32v, 47; GBR/B/3/2, fo. 514; GBR/G/G3/Sib/1, fo. 62v; GBR/B/1/10, unpag.

day after that. The number slipped below 100 in the middle of November, falling to a low of seventy-one on 22 November. It did not rise above 100 until three weeks later, when the number of inmates rocketed from seventy-eight to 186 on a single day (14 December), though it dropped by sixty-six by the end of the next day. Eighty-three men and women spent Christmas Day inside Bridewell. These numbers were added up in the margins; the final tally was 5,468 'men, women, and children', along with nine recusants and twenty-five Spaniards who 'remaine[d] in the house of bridewell' on the last day.[64] These ever-changing numbers dwarfed those in smaller 'houses'. There were three men and three women in the Cheshire bridewell when it was inspected by justices in May 1617. Exeter 'workehowse' was home to five men and two women on one day in 1686: 'idle and disorderly' Lydia Maddice, who was not in service, and 'idle wandring' Elizabeth Edleigh, who did not go back home to Plymouth after being whipped.[65] There were eight 'presaners' in the Herefordshire 'correccon house' in April 1693; five two years later; and two men and five women six years later, including 'incorrigible, lewd, idle [and] disorderly' Mary Male.[66] Ten men and six women filled Dorset Bridewell in April 1631, including a number who needed to find masters and Mary Bryant who was waiting to go back to Hampshire to her master who was the father of her child.[67] Prisons, needless to say, also had wide variations in numbers inside. A January 1639 'calendar' lists a dozen prisoners in Colchester prison: eight men and four women, including three alleged murderers. Nine men were inside Suffolk Prison on 30 April 1652, including six pirates and Thomas Hall, who had been acquitted of witchcraft. The 'calendar of prisoners' in Exeter Castle 'gaole' in January 1656 lists twenty-seven inmates: twenty men and seven women. Another from sixteen months later lists fifty-eight prisoners, including men charged with 'wife murder', libelling a privy councillor, stealing horses, and 'affrontinge' tax collectors (thirteen men were waiting to be 'transported by conscent'); and women charged with infanticide and theft (two of them were waiting to be transported).[68]

So there were a fair number of people inside bridewells and prisons, and we can add the inmates of hospitals, almshouses, and workhouses to get a fuller picture of institutional experiences. Numbers in the large London hospitals peaked at 180 at St Bartholomew's in 1588; a cap of 200 was set at St Thomas's in 1624. The number of children admitted to Christ's Hospital in its first dozen years was estimated to be 1,916 in 1564 (it soared in later years).[69] Numbers were smaller elsewhere. Twenty 'poore blew coate boys' filled Gloucester's 'blue coate hospital'

64 TNA SP 12/84/22.

65 CA QJB/1/4, fo. 161; DRO QS/32/3b.

66 HEA Q/SM/3, fos. 53, 114v–15; Q/SM/4, fo. 57.

67 T. Hearing and S. Bridges, eds., *Dorset Quarter Sessions Order Book 1635–1638: A Calendar*, Dorset Record Society, 14 (Dorchester, 2006), 173.

68 ERO DB5/SR/38/29; SAI B/105/2/3; DRO QS/32/1; QS/32/2.

69 Griffiths, *Lost Londons*, 261–2.

in 1668 that was run 'according to the lawdable usage of Christ Church Hospitall in London'. The number of 'hospital children' in Westminster's Greencoat Hospital was 'sometimes xx a moneth sometimes more and sometimes lesse' in 1627, and 'sometimes in number xxviii and sometimes lesse' in the next year.[70] Looking back in his autobiography, John Shaw tells us that when he took up the post of master in Hull's Charterhouse in 1651—'God's Howse', he called it—it was £100 in debt, with 'about twelve poor people' housed inside (its foundation charter called for twenty-six). Shaw turned things around. The debt was paid off inside seven years, while the 'number of poor encreased to forty'. 'If I had continued four or five years master there more', he bragged, that number would have reached 100.[71]

Institutions touched lives but to what effect? We know that bridewells had teething problems—whether financial shortfalls or incompetence, to name just two—that led to the stop-start experiences in Yarmouth and Cheshire. But we must keep in mind the valuable roles that bridewells performed in local settings. It's not hard to stitch together a narrative of financial and administrative setbacks, but this is insufficient grounds to assess bridewells. Again, we should remember how unique they were in a society with a deep past of resistance to losing liberty and forced levies. We must think of them—like the Poor Law—in terms of what they were able to get done despite the tough obstacles that lay in their way. But bridewells have not fared too well in the court of historians. Steve Hindle believes that 'their record of achievement was poor'. 'It was in the 1630s almost sixty years after the statute', he continues—misleadingly, as statutory compulsion came in 1610—'that they became virtually universal'. This was a decent achievement but, Hindle adds, 'they were badly managed and underfunded'.[72] If money and management are the basis for evaluation, then England has never had an effective bridewell or prison. They have been leading criticisms since England's first prison opened its doors. Hindle's thin conclusions have nothing to do with why early modern governors saw solutions in bridewells. There is nothing about the people who spent time in one of them. Joanna Innes believes that 'bridewells frequently failed to fulfil precisely the roles their sponsors assigned to them'. But she has more expansive understanding of the contexts in which they operated. They were essential elements in 'social and penal projects' and 'instruments' of policy framed by broader social relations.[73] In other words, we should assess bridewells through their roles in supporting the authority and social structures in which they came of age. They were creatures of their economies and societies and tailored towards the

[70] GA GBR/B/3/3, fos. 367, 375, 378; WAC E15/1626; EC/1628.

[71] J. Shaw, 'The life of Master John Shaw', in C. Jackson, ed., *Yorkshire Diaries and Autobiographies in the Seventeenth and Eighteenth Centuries*, Surtees Society, 65 (Durham, 1877), 147–8. For almshouses/workhouses see WSHC G23/1/3, fo. 339v; DHC DC/PL/B/13/1, fo. 17v; NDRO B1/719; KAC WQ/O/1, fo. 29v.

[72] S. Hindle, *The State and Social Change in Early Modern England, c.1550–1640* (Basingstoke, 2000), 164.

[73] Innes, 'Prisons for the poor', 43, 44, 45–6.

organization of work and regulation in local societies including households and anyone who tried to cut the strings of family life.

Bridewells were embedded in their local economies and societies, but maybe more than anything else they were, in Innes's words, 'prisons for the poor'. A nationwide system of incarceration worked hand in hand with the first national Poor Law that taxed 'middling' households to give hand-outs to needy and worthy neighbours. The first bridewells were not imagined alone but working in tandem with poor rates and plans to put paupers to work. Work creation was a new departure. London Bridewell was a 'house of occupations' and a prison for the poor. Work was pivotal in any bridewell. Yarmouth governors said in 1587 that 'the 'great necessitie and godly consideration of the state of the poore people of this towne urgeth the erecting of an hospitall or bridewell'. 'The poore' and 'idle' would both be housed in it.[74] The reason why Southampton made plans to build a 'howse of correcction' in the 'upper ende of the friars where the french churche stood' in 1616 was 'the continuall increase of poore people'. The 'want of imployment and government' was the compelling argument for the Nantwich Bridewell in 1617.[75] The poor were bunched in titles and categories like 'idle' and 'derserving', but the boundaries between them were in 'experience' porous and someone might cross them one day without even knowing it. With bridewells, magistrates patrolled these borders and therefore poor relief, where the needy were warned that they could lose their precious pennies and get locked up if they did something wrong. Bridewells loomed over the lifestyles of the millions at the sprawling bottom of the social pyramid. Vagrants in towns were as likely to be residents as travellers. Vagrancy was the embodiment of what governors deemed to be wrong lifestyle choices: someone moving to get a job or stuck in a rut of joblessness. Anyone who was not seemingly doing anything could be called idle and/or disorderly. A justices' handbook said that bridewells were for 'the correcting and setting of work of rogues, vagabonds, sturdy beggars and other idle and disorderly persons'. Thomas Forster provided a template 'mittimus to the house of correction' in *The Lay-mans Lawyer* (1654): for I.S. 'a sturdy vagrant beggar, dangerous to the inferiour sort of people'.[76] 'This house [is] for punishment of rogues, vagabonds, wandring, [and] idle and disorderly persons', William Sheppard noted in his widely read advice for justices. Something that was made clear, he thought, 'by the express words of 7 Jac.4'.[77] Local magistrates followed suit. A 'correccon howse' was for 'rogues, vagabonds and sturdy beggars and idell persones' (Colchester), 'idle and disordered persons' (Aylesford), 'roagues, vagabonds, and

[74] NRO Y/C/19/4, fo. 124v. [75] SA 6/1, fo. 33; CA QJB/3/3, fos. 44, 109v.

[76] B.P., *A Help to Magistrates and Ministers of Justice, Also, A Guide to Parish and Ward-Officers* (1700), 125; T. Forster, *The Lay-mans Lawyer: Or, the Second Part of the Practice of Law* (1654), 140–1.

[77] Sheppard, *New Survey of the Justice of Peace His Office*, 32. See also R. Chamberlain, *The Complete Justice* (1681), 180–1.

sturdy beggers' (Uxbridge), and 'rogues, vagabonds, sturdie beggers and other ydle and disorderly persons' (Cheshire).[78]

The 1610 Act targeted the 'idle and disorderly'. 'By particular words', Edward Coke noted, the 1598 Poor Law 'did not extend to rogues, vagabonds and sturdy beggars'. It used 'generall words', he explained, that in 1610 are 'explained to be wandring or idle persons [and] idle or disorderly persons' with reference to 'the branch whereby the authority of justices to commit to the house of correction is warranted'. Coke believed that this law gave justices 'a generall and large power' to lock up 'all idle or disorderly persons without exception of any person'.[79] General and flexible ideas of what it meant to be 'disorderly', 'idle', or 'vagrant' had been used for committals to bridewells for half a century before the 1610 Act. In practice, these elastic labels, whose appeal for magistrates was that they were 'general' and 'particular', covered a large range of wrongdoing. When they sent 'vagrant and dangerous persons', the father of an illegitimate child, a husbandman charged with 'misdemeanors', and Edward Drewett, who left his family to a bridewell, East Sussex justices made it clear that they were to 'be dealt with as an idle, lewd, and disorderly person'.[80] The operation of bridewells stretched interpretations of the legislation to its outer limits. Anyone defined as a 'rouge', in B.P.'s words, was 'liable' to be put in a bridewell.[81] They were weapons to curb marginal lifestyles or those the 1601 Poor Law called people who 'use no ordinary daily trade of life to get their living by'. This 'mysprecyson' was a defining feature of bridewell 'presaners', many of whom did not have a home, job, master, or documents. Some did not even have a name. There was little else that Suffolk justices could do in 1657 but to 'continew' a vagrant in the bridewell who would not 'tell the place of his last settlement or xpian name'. A woman in Norwich Bridewell 'would not make known her name'.[82] Bridewells conferred identities by taking in those who did not fit in, like Yorkshire weaver Thomas Jackson who told Reading governors in 1625 that he left home two weeks earlier 'to seeke service' in London. But he 'can[not] answere to any purpose', they said, and he had no 'testimoniall of his travell'. He is 'found to be a wandering person', Dorchester governors said in 1629, after hearing John Cawpin admit that he had 'not had any certaine dwellinge these many yeres but wandred up and downe the countrey' getting some money by 'curing divers ruptures in men and children'.[83]

Bridewells were for marginals and had a large hand in re-establishing social relations in the case of people like Nicholas Cox, who was found 'living

[78] ERO D/B5/Cb/6, fo. 129v; CKS U120/09, fo. 35; LMA MJ/SBR/3, fo. 278; CA QJB/1/4, fo. 108; BRO R/Z/8/1; Axon, *Manchester Sessions*, 9.

[79] Coke, *Second Part of the Institutes*, 730.

[80] ESBHRO QO/EW2, fo. 71; QO/EW3, fos. 25, 31.

[81] B.P., *A Help to Magistrates and Ministers of Justice, Also, A Guide to Parish and Ward-Officers* (1700), 125.

[82] SAI B/105/2/4, fo. 17v; NRO NMCC 23, fo. 130v. See my *Lost Londons*, 189–92.

[83] BRO R/AC1/1/2, fo. 175; DHC DC/DOB/8/1, fo. 11.

maisterlesse' in Dorchester in 1632 or 'lazie living' Ben William or the thousands who could not 'render an account' of how they made a living.[84] People with loose ties to families, work, and service, living 'at their own hand' or 'out of service', spent their days under the large shadows of bridewells. Any 'younge man' who lived 'idely' in Maidstone in 1569 ran the risk of being locked up 'untill he shall reforme'.[85]

III

Bridewells became indispensable. This is not to make light of Yarmouth-like complaints about fits and starts and thin funds. But governors did not question the need for bridewells that were integral to providing for and regulating the poor. They gave a handy option to deal with the 'dangerous' poor, increasing penal choices and giving more power to police the frontiers of poor relief. They loomed large when crunch questions were on the table: what to do with the poor, vagrant waves, or 'fit' people who turned their backs on work? Their longevity speaks to their indispensability. 'No one thing was requisite for government of this countye', Middlesex justices said in 1614, 'as to provyde a house of correccon'.[86] The real concern was what to do without one. Chester governors spoke of 'the great losse' we 'sustain by not having a howse of correccon', ordering that one 'be forthwith built where the former stood'. 'Manie great inconveniences and mischeifes daily [trouble] this countrey', Nottinghamshire justices complained in 1653, for 'want of a house of correccon'. 'For want of a house of correction', Cheshire justices said in 1638, a 'great number of rogues, vagabonds, and sturdy beggars do daily increase [who] live in idlenese stealing and feed upon the labours of such as live honestly'.[87]

A steady stream of offenders were sent to bridewells. Unbroken entries in London Bridewell courtbooks (from 1617 onwards), for example, Southampton sessions book (1609–35), Norwich Mayor's courtbooks (continuous), or the Dorchester Offenders Book (1629–37) get us inside bridewells for long enough to see a regular flow of committals. Most prisoners appear once and disappear; maybe the bridewell made them, in Coke's word, 'better'. People, culture, and the aims of governors are missing when we limit interpretations to money and management. But people were the reason why bridewells were opened in the first

84 DHC DC/DOB/8/1, fos. 156, 358.

85 CKS Md/Acm1/1a, fos. 43, 74v. See also BRO R/AC1/1/3, fo. 218; NRO T/QS/1, fo. 11v; P. Griffiths, 'Masterless young people in Norwich, 1560–1645', in P. Griffiths, A. Fox, and S. Hindle, eds., *The Experience of Authority in Early Modern England* (Basingstoke, 1996); T. Wales, '"Living at their own hands": policing poor people and the young in early modern England', *Agricultural History Review*, 6 (2013).

86 LMA MJ/SBR/2, fo. 117.

87 CA Z/AB/2, fo. 109; QJB/1/6, fos. 70v–2; NOTTA C/QSM1/12, fo. 9.

place. We should put ourselves in their shoes when with little by way of warning bridewells reshaped lives. The experience must have been profound. We cannot take too lightly the shame and fear of bridewells. Oliver Heywood went to visit fellow dissenter Mr Hardcastle in Wakefield Bridewell in 1668: 'I dined with him', his diary reads, 'in his reproach-full prison'. John Lilburne's wife was bundled into a Bridewell cell with 'common sluts and whores whose society is a hell upon earth to one that fears the Lord'. The friends of a 'gentlewoman of good berth' who was locked up in London Bridewell hatched a rescue plan, 'thinking bothe for theire owne reputacon and hers to avoyde the shame and infamie of so open and reproachfull a disgrace'.[88]

'Infamie' and forced confinement fuelled fear of bridewells for many whose liberty was part of who they were. 'Mere fear' of bridewells, Joanna Innes says, made people think twice about breaking the law.[89] Nottinghamshire justices wanted Southwell Bridewell to be a 'house of terror'. Norwich governors said that it was 'the feare and terror of the house of bridewell [that caused the number of] whoremasters, whores, and vacabondes' to drop by nine-tenths after it opened. Somerset justice Edward Hext said that vagrants begged with 'bytter teares' to go to prison rather than bridewell. 'Distressed' Elizabeth Pinfould said that she would rather die 'a happie death' than spend another day in Bridewell in 1632 in a petition to privy councillors who had locked her up for 'troublinge' them with too many petitions.[90] Bridewells were manipulated within the lifestyle, service, and work matrix. People drifting 'out of service' were given time to get a master. Mary Savidge, who had lived 'idely and disorderly' for a 'long time' in Dorchester, in 1632 was told to 'live orderly' in service or go to bridewell. Sarah Harris was told to stop living with her mother 'to goe abroade a chearing' in 1634 and given a month to get into service or go to the bridewell on the twenty-ninth day.[91] Wiltshire justices ruled in 1649 that 'apprentices which shall refuse to be bound' will be 'sent to the howse of coreccon'. Middlesex justices asked Dorothy Mill 'to certifie her behavior and course of life' within a few days in 1626 or go to Bridewell.[92] Anyone without any right or reason to be somewhere was usually given a specific time to leave. Tinker Joseph Marwood who had 'wrought long' in Dorchester was given ten days to leave in 1635 to go back to his home in Melbury. The town's Offenders' Book where he appears reveals threats to pressure vagrants like him or masterless people and others like watchman's wife, Elizabeth Bull,

[88] *Rev. Oliver Heywood, B.A., 1630–1702; His Autobiography, Diaries, and Anecdote Books*, ed. J. Horsfall Turner, 4 vols (Brighouse, Bingley, 1881–85), I, 249–50; LMA Remembrancer Book 1, fo. 153; HOL MP, 21/12/1640.

[89] Innes, 'Prisons for the poor', 105.

[90] Hindle, *State and Social Change*, 164; NRO Norwich 'Mayors Booke for the Poore, 1571–9', fo. 5v; BL Lansdowne MS 81/62; TNA SP 16/229/35.

[91] DHC DC/DOB/8/1, fos. 152, 216. See also ibid., fos. 8v, 90v, 185v, 294, 349v; DRO ECA C1/61, fo. 493; Hearing and Bridges, *Dorset Quarter Sessions Order Book*, 44, 175, 364, 426; Griffiths, 'Masterless young people', 160–1.

[92] WSHC A1/160/1, Hilary 1649 sessions; LMA MJ/SBR/4, fo. 391.

who was told 'to continue at home [in 1634 and] dresse meate as a wife ought to doe' or go to the bridewell 'to work hard'. William Lovelace, who called Rebecca Cornish 'whore' as she drew water at a well in the same town in 1635, was warned to live 'quietly' or go to the bridewell.[93]

This was all that was needed for most people. Success did not actually hinge on committals. But who did end up behind bars? 'Which persons are fit to be sent to the house of correction' was scribbled on the back of a piece of paper in Reading in 1621. The question on governors' minds was what is 'comprehended within the words disorderly persons, although they be not wanderers' (clearly a hangover from the 1610 legislation). Reading justices, it emerged, had 'thus far agreed' that these offences fell within the broad word 'disorderly': 'reputed fathers of basterde children', 'persons usually druncke', 'unlawfull games' on Sundays, someone 'being no subsedy man [hunting] in warrens by night', 'great swearers and blasphemers of the word of God', 'cosenage or deceipt', abusing officers, 'teareing' hedges, making off with wood, robbing orchards, 'settinge doggs or netts to take deere, partridges or phesants', and servants stealing from masters or hitting them. Any of these, justices concluded, are grounds to send someone to the bridewell.[94]

The offences of 1,125 Bridewell inmates are noted in records I have seen from across the country. They cover every 'lesser offence' under the sun including vagrants, jugglers, 'peekers', and 'nightwatchers'. Stiff-necked Nonconformists and Catholics also ended up in bridewells. Lodowick Muggleton and John Reeve were put in London Bridewell for six months in 1653 and warned not to spread their dangerous doctrine in the workshops and cells.[95] 'Presanors' have been grouped under umbrella categories that seem arbitrary but necessarily so. One in five committals were for moral and religious regulation, putting this in first place. (See Table 4.1.) Unlike in London (it was half of recorded cases heard at London Bridewell in 1605–55), vagrancy was not a runaway leading offence in the provinces.[96]

There is more balance elsewhere. Vagrancy/street cases are not far behind moral regulation. Lifestyles are in third position at 14.57 per cent. While theft ranked fourth at 13.33 per cent. Domestic disorders ranked one point lower. Justices used bridewells for people who escaped hanging but deserved punishment. Home Circuit judges ruled in 1616 that anyone who was discharged or acquitted of a felony could be put in a bridewell. The bridewell population included prisoners who successfully read the 'neck verse' and others found not guilty or suspected of felony. Samuel Hartlib believed that anyone 'acquitted for

[93] DHC DC/DOB/8/1, fos. 281v, 23, 23v, 107v, 182v, 265v, 239, 90, 237, 358. See also DRO ECA C1/61, fo. 676; BRO N/JQ/1/1, fo. 257; R/AC1/1/2, fo. 300.

[94] BRO R/Z8/2.

[95] CA QJB/2/5, fo. 206v; DHC DC/DOB/8/1, fos. 229–30; DRO ECA C1/61, fo. 216; BRO R/AC1/1/3, fo. 211; TNA 12/230/57, 29/103,75; LBHC 9, fo. 628.

[96] For London see my *Lost Londons*, appendix.

Table 4.1 Houses of correction: offences[1]

Category of offence	Number and % of committals
Moral regulation/religion[2]	233–20.71%
Vagrancy/street offences[3]	206–18.31%
Misfit lifestyles[4]	164–14.57%
Theft/cozening[5]	150–13.33%
Domestic disorders[6]	142–12.62%
Court referrals[7]	125–11.11%
Public disorders/violence[8]	94–8.35%
Court disorders[9]	11–0.97%

[1] Figures are from county/urban bridewells in Berkshire, Cheshire, Devon, Dorset, Durham, Exeter, Gloucestershire, Hampshire, Herefordshire, Kent, Lancashire, Leicestershire, Middlesex, Norfolk, Northamptonshire, Oxfordshire, Shropshire, Somerset, Suffolk, Sussex, Warwickshire, Westmorland, Wiltshire, and Yorkshire.

[2] Unlicensed pubs, keeping bawdy houses or being taken in one, blasphemy, drunkenness, false paternity charge, fornication, illegitimacy, keeping company, and prostitution.

[3] Begging, counterfeit bedlam, counterfeit licence, settlement offences, rogue, vagrant, and wandering.

[4] Living at own hand, dangerous, disobedient, disorderly, dissolute, distempered, evil life, idle, impudent, incontinent living, incorrigible, lewd, lewd/idle/disorderly, lewdness, licentious, loose, masterless, nightwalking, having no account of life, being out of service, suspicious, whore, and refusing to work or go into service.

[5] Cozening, cutpurses, receiving stolen goods, and theft.

[6] Abandoning children, abusing apprentices, apprentice/children disorders, abusing spouses, and neglecting and deserting families.

[7] Referred from quarter sessions after clergy and branding or acquittals for felony or petty larceny, suspected of felony, and after being sentenced to transportation.

[8] Arson threats, driving cattle on land, stabbing horses, escaping from a bridewell, hunting, juggling, abusing people, ministers, or officers, taken late at night, abuses by officers, scolding, swearing, threatening people, traffic disorders, tumults, being unruly, violence, damaging wares, and being found inside a disorderly alehouse.

[9] Being in contempt of court, courtroom disorders, not having sureties, not paying fines, and abusing magistrates.

petty larceny' should go to a bridewell 'to make them serviceable to the commonwealth by reforming their ungodly life'.[97]

One bridewell population is not in this sample: the 'lunatique', 'madd', and 'distracted'. Some 'lunatiques' from outside London were put in England's only asylum (Bethlem/Bedlam), although the keeper was told in 1624 'that the number [of "lunatiqe persons" should] never exceede above xxv'.[98] 'Poore man' Henry Bedlam from East Sussex, 'being distracted', was 'sent to Bedlam' in 1646 and is now 'recovered', justices noted. 'Distracted' Joan Browne's husband from Hampshire, who was sinking in 'greate wante' after 'a longe tyme' caring for her, asked if she could be 'removed' to 'bedlem in london' in 1622, 'the place appointed for such distempered people'.[99] But the clear majority of Bethlem's 'mad' were

[97] S. Hartlib, *London's Charity Inlardged, Stilling the Orphans Cry* (1650), 10.

[98] LBHC 6, fos. 368, 48v.

[99] ESBHRO QO/EW1, fo. 44v; HA Q1/1, fo. 443.

Londoners in the seventeenth century (three-quarters came from the city and built-up Middlesex in 1640–80).[100]

Nearly all 'lunatiques' were put in the nearest bridewell or cared for at home. People sometimes took matters into their own hands. An entry in Oliver Heywood's diary from 1680 tells us how he heard 'multitudes of people shouting' and, looking outside, he saw a crowd hurrying [a woman] to the house of correction upon a sledge who threatened to burn the town. 'Some said she was mad', others that she was drunk, but all whipped her 'fearfully' as they dragged her to a 'dark entry or dungeon' where 'she lay all night'. She woke up covered 'in blebs and miserably sore'. 'Oh horrid cruelty', Heywood wrote.[101] The families of 'lunatiques' got top-ups to poor relief to 'take [them] into ther care as one of the poore', including a poor soul from Ravenstonedale in Cumbria who was said to be 'in ye highest manner lunatick' in 1686.[102] Danger posed was often the tipping point. 'Distracted' and 'distempered' Susan Barter from Warminster 'walketh up and downe the towne', her neighbours said in 1647, and is 'likely [to] sett the towne one fyer if shee be not prevented'. Somerset justices told six villagers and two brothers of orphan 'lunaticke' Richard Hygdon to 'rule' him at his own house in 1612 or he would be marched to the bridewell.[103] This is where many were sent after they broke windows, broke into houses, or, like John Alden from Hackney, ran about streets all night 'making great noise and uproare'.[104] A 'distracted' Wapping widow 'was for prevencon of danger restrained in the house of correccon' for five months in 1639, where she 'broke downe the walles and spoiled goods'. 'Distracted' Thomas Cottrell's stint in Norwich Bridewell in 1682 was called 'his restraynt' after aldermen, hearing 'his son in tears' say that he 'would fyre his house', 'thought fit to secure him' there.[105] 'Secured' was often the word of choice, although 'distracted' Thomas Vincent from Fontmell in Dorset needed 'to be watched all the time'.[106] Threats of arson were often the last straw. 'Severall' neighbours feared that Martha Carr from Norwich, 'beinge much distrayned in her brayne,' would 'fyre their houses' in 1669. 'Now lunatic' Emme Carter from Frome (Somerset) was locked up in 1613—as 'law requireth for all such

[100] J. Andrews, A. Briggs, R. Porter, P. Tucker, and K. Waddington, *The History of Bethlem* (London and New York, 1997), 323.

[101] Heywood, *Autobiography*, II, 270.

[102] KAC WQ/O/3, fo. 70v. See also P. Rushton, 'Idiocy, the family and the community in early modern north-east England', in D. Wright and A. Digby, eds., *From Idiocy to Mental Deficiency: Historical Perspectives on People with Learning Disabilities* (London and New York, 1996); P. Rushton, 'Lunatics and idiots: mental disability, the community, and the Poor Law in north-east England, 1600–1800', *Medical History*, 32 (1988).

[103] WSHC A1/160/1, Michaelmas/1648 sessions; Easter sessions 1653; Bates, *Quarter Sessions Records for the County of Somerset*, I, 88.

[104] LMA MJ/SBR/7, fo. 20.

[105] LMA MJ/SBR/6, fo. 60; NRO NMC 25, fo. 120.

[106] Hearing and Bridges, *Dorset Quarter Sessions Order Book*, 29. See also WAC E2416, fos. 18, 51; CA QJB/1/6, fos. 251–1v; ESBHRO QO/EW3, fo. 29.

dangerous and disordered persons'—after neighbours became convinced that she would burn the town down.[107]

There were no tailor-made institutional developments for 'lunatiques'. Some were put in bridewells when all else failed but they were a small fraction of the inmate population. There was no indiscriminate herding of the down-and-out into bridewells in what Foucault calls 'the great confinement'. But there is no doubt that bridewells touched the lives of countless paupers. One way we can measure this is by the length of sentences, keeping in mind their novelty. Imagine a life sentence inside a bridewell! After a long history of vagrancy and theft, Margaret Utting from Norwich was 'delivered to the master of brydewell' in 1598 'to dwell and remayne for ever'.[108] She did not spend her last days there, however. Utting was 'whipped for filching' in January 1600 and sent to the lazar-house at 'Mawdelyn Gates [from] whence she came'. She was again 'whipped at the poste' for 'fylchinge' in April and December and her last time in records was in Christmas 1601, when she was 'whipped for receaving a roaguish wench into hir tower' at Magdalene Gates (in Norwich).[109]

We do not know how long most prisoners spent behind bars. All we have is a name and offence, and sometimes just a name. Some were locked up 'till further order'. Edward Flatman was 'acquitted of murder' in Norwich in 1663 and sent to the bridewell 'till further order'. John Child from the same city was also kept until the court thought fit after his 'acquitt[al] for two sheep skins by the grand jury' in 1650. Another Norvician, Martha Wild, was found not guilty of felony and locked up in 1669 'till mr maior and the court of aldermen discharge her'.[110] Other prisoners were told that they could go home after filing sureties or paying fines or 'charges'. Robert Foot was put in Dorchester Bridewell 'for want of sureties' in 629 after bad-mouthing the mayor and 'abusing mr bailiffs saying a turd in [their] teeth'.[111] Norwich cutpurse John Welham was 'acquitted of cutpursinge' in 1654 and locked up until he got the money for sureties (he was back in bridewell nine months later after 'he was acquitted of felony' once more for 'pickinge a pocket').[112] The fates of Mary Bishop and Margaret Goose were in the hands of their husbands. Bishop, who was 'acquitt[ed] of felony' in 1662, was told that she would not leave bridewell 'untill her husband shall desire to have hir out'. Goose was told that she would stay 'till her husband fetch hir out' in 1598. Roles were

[107] NRO NMCC 24, fo. 103v; Bates, *Quarter Sessions Records for the County of Somerset*, I, 99–100; 224. See also HEA Q/SM/4, fo. 45v; B. Capp, 'Arson, fear of arson, and incivility in early modern England', in P. Burke, B. Harrison, and P. Slack, eds., *Civil Histories* (2000).

[108] NRO NMCC 13, fo. 183.

[109] Ibid., fos. 183, 404, 430, 546, 677.

[110] NRO Norwich Sessions Books 1639–54, fo. 132; 1654–70, 4/1663 sessions, 8/1669 sessions. See also HA Q3/3, fo. 113; ESBHRO QO/EW2, fos. 69v, 71; YCA F7, fo. 390; SAI B/105/2/1, fo. 26; NDRO 119OA/Q1, fo. 8.

[111] DHC DC/DOB/8/1, fo. 8.

[112] NRO Norwich Sessions Books 1654–70, 7/1654 sessions, 4/1655 sessions. See also HA Q3/3, fo. 185; LMA MJ/SBR/4, fo. 612; NRO T/QS/1, fo. 19v; Hearing and Bridges, *Dorset Quarter Sessions Order Book*, 111, 173, 220, 261, 308, 395.

reversed for Abraham Raves, who 'forced' his wife out of their Warwickshire home in 1628 and was told that he would remain in his cell until he agreed to 'receave his wife home to him [and] live together as man and wife oughte to doe'.[113] Magistrates used bridewells to support households, marriage, and service. Records from across the country repeatedly show 'preasners' getting released after a domestic relation had been (re-)established. Joseph Barnes was not allowed to leave Dorset Bridewell in 1637 until he married the woman who was pregnant with their child. Thomas Betts was branded after reading the 'neck verse' in Norwich in 1646 and told that he would stay in bridewell 'until his master can fetch him'.[114] Others, like Richard Cooper who began the first chapter, were waiting for a piece of paper that would make something 'certain' to get them out of prison/bridewell. Husband and wife Henry and Mary Mills were stranded in Dorset Bridewell until their residence could be known for 'certain'. Their cellmate James Payne needed to 'certify' his place of birth. An Oxford inmate was told to get a 'certificate' of his marriage before he could go back home.[115]

One day is not a long time! A vagrant was put in Gloucester Bridewell 'until tomorrowe'. Richard Sawister had to get through just 'two daies of hard labour' in Northampton in 1681. Warwickshire widow Jane Wheeler was 'well whipped' in bridewell for the 'space of two dayes' for 'misdemeanors' in 1629.[116] 'Just' is the wrong word, as we should not judge sentences by our standards. These short sharp shocks might have left raw impressions. We should not dismiss a handful of days out of hand or forget that the upper reaches of time spent in bridewell cells would be considered lengthy today. Seven days was long enough to interrupt routine and convince someone not to go back again. Four-in-ten prisoners in a sample of 200 spent a week or less in London Bridewell.[117] People given a week elsewhere included a woman of 'wicked life and conversacon', a South Molton man who threatened to stab two men, a runaway apprentice, and an 'idle girle' (to 'receive correccon', twice).[118] We might think about the stories such people told once they got home. Bridewell's fear and stain was spread by them. There were braggarts for whom time inside was a trophy. Others took it in their stride.

113 NRO Norwich Sessions Book 1654–70, May sessions, 1662; S. C Ratcliff and H. C. Johnson, eds., *Warwick County Records*, 9 vols. (Warwick, 1935–64), I, 56.

114 Hearing and Bridges, *Dorset Quarter Sessions Order Book*, 360; NRO NMCC 13, fo. 198. Some males were told they would stay until they were 'reteyned in service or sent for a souldier': NRO Norwich Sessions Books 1630–8, fo. 97; 1637–64, fo. 19v; 1639–54, fo. 89; NMCC 25, fo. 195; WRO QS0040/1/1, fo. 44; Hearing and Bridges, *Dorset Quarter Sessions Order Book*, 180, 253, 308, 340, 360, 384, 407.

115 Hearing and Bridges, *Dorset Quarter Sessions Order Book*, 173, 196; Blades, *Oxford Quarter Sessions Order Book*, 3.

116 GA GBR/G/G3/SO/1, fo. 110v; NA NQS/2, fo. 21v; WRO QS0040/1/1, fo. 69. See also SAI B/105/2/3, fo. 41; NRO T/QS/1, fo. 2v.

117 Griffiths, *Lost Londons*, 279.

118 NDRO 1190A/Q1, fo. 10v. See also ESBHRO QO/W8, fo. 108; CKS Q/SM/A/1, fo. 17 (Maidstone); LERO QS5/1/1, fo. 3; NRO Norwich Sessions Book 1630–8, fo. 103v; NMCC 14, fos. 450, 459v; OHC QSM 1/11v, fo. 22; QS/C/A1/O1, fos. 92–2v.

But imprisonment was a hard time for many. 'Loose' Thomas Punt who handled stolen goods was put in Norwich Bridewell for nine days. 'Evil' Elizabeth Taylor was locked up for one day longer in 1698.[119] 'Presansers' locked up for a fortnight included Richard Parker from Needham (Suffolk) who was 'acquitt by verdict for a rape', 'lewd' Thomas Goodman from Norwich who was 'suspected of evill practices' ('to be whipt at his goeinge in and cominge out'), vagrants, thieves, 'a clerke convict', and a loudmouth who taunted watchmen.[120] The number of days grows: sixteen for 'dissolute' Francis Coombes who did not follow a 'good course of life' in Tenterden in 1634; three weeks for 'ydle pilfering' Anna Tilly in Canterbury in 1623 ('as [I] thoughte lawfull and fitt in discretion to doe', the committing justice noted, 'being thereunto guided and directed by a late booke called Daltons Justice of Peace'); and twenty-four days for Catherine Scott who was caught 'living at her own hand' in Norwich.[121]

Norfolk justice Robert Doughty issued a warrant to bring Thurgarton labourer 'idle and disorderly' Edmund Bell into custody in 1665. He had 'bene often compayned of unto me [for] misusing his owne wife', Doughty noted, yet 'notwithstanding he hath bene admonished of his duty as an husband hath used her the more hardly'. Ever since, he added, he has 'constantly continued his course of running and cursing her and her two children, grudging the very bread they eat as much as they scarce dare eat any of his'. He is 'threatening to be the death of them'. Last night, Doughty finished, he 'held out of doores [his wife] and hir owne suckling child' and their other children. Bell was put in the bridewell 'to worke' with 'fetters upon him' for a month.[122] Vagrant William Williams and his wife were locked up in Cheshire for a month with 'moderate correction' in 1632. 'Vagrant and dangerous' Thomas Atherington and John Broadwater spent a month in the Lewes 'house' in 1657 doing 'hard labour'. Thomas Manning, who was 'acquited of felony' in Norwich in 1635, was 'sett on worke in Bridewell a moneth'. Also in Norwich, 'clarke convict' Thomas Manning was 'barbored close' in 1638 and given a four week stretch in the bridewell. One-month sentences were handed down for scores of other offences including bad-mouthing masters, pulling down trees, taunting and threatening neighbours, throwing punches, stealing, selling beer with no right to do so, ignoring court rulings, and being seen to be 'idle', 'incorroigible', 'disorderly', or 'lewd'.[123]A mixed bag of thieves, pickpockets,

[119] NRO Norwich Information and Examinations Book 1690–9, 29/9/1698, 8/10/1698. See also NMCC 13, fo. 19; BRO R/AC1/1/2, fo. 169.

[120] SAI B/105/2/2, fo. 40; NRO Norwich Sessions Book 1691–1702, 1/1696.

[121] CKS TE/JQC/1, fo. 5; TNA STAC8, 13/7, bill of complaint, Justice Sedley, answer; NRO NMCC 24, fo. 148. See also NRO Norwich Information and Examinations Book 1690–9, 8/10/1698; WSHC A1/150/11, fos. 600, 601.

[122] NRO Aylsham MS/304. Bell had already appeared before Doughty on a number of occasions for beating his wife and for threatening to kill her and their children: *The Notebook of Robert Doughty, 1662–1665*, ed. J. M. Rosenheim, Norfolk Record Society, 54 (1989), 35, 46, 64.

[123] CRO QJB/1/5, fo. 306; ESRO QO/EW3, fo. 31; NRO Norwich Sessions minute books 1629–36, fo. 132v; 1637–64, fo. 26. See also HEA Q/SM/4, fos. 57v, 73v; ESBHRO QO/EW1, fos. 13, 62; QO/EW3, fos. 39v, 67v; LERO QS5/1/1, fo. 20; NA NQS/2, fo. 70v; NSQ/3, fo. 11; NRO Norwich Sessions

vagrants, nightwalkers, beggars, and drunks were locked up in London Bridewell for around a month. A woman who was sent there for 'lewdnes' walked free after four weeks in 1606 in regard [of her] 'longe imprisonmente and repentance'.[124] 'One whole moneth' is sometimes written down, giving us a sense of the length of time that was thought to be long enough to make a difference. Clerks also scribbled that inmates had spent 'a longe tyme in the house' or 'great while'. Katherine Flood and Elizabeth Constable were allowed to go free in 1606 'in regarde of their longe imprisonmente and repentance'. It was noted that a Gloucester apprentice had 'long lyen' in the bridewell in 1625.[125]

Knowing full well the effects of time, courts handed down sentences that reflected the possibility that certain offences might have been treated more harshly in some places. Activist magistrates had an impact, as we see in Puritan Dorchester and Salisbury.[126] As with the number of lashes or time sitting in the stocks, the length of sentences was influenced by the nature of offenders, offences, and conditions. A 'whole' month was a landmark but many prisoners spent longer inside bridewells. John Stephens spent five weeks in Lavenham Bridewell in 1642 for a 'third time convicted for drawing beere without licence' ('accordinge to lawe'). A Dorset apprentice was locked up for six weeks in 1627 for treating his master badly and told that he would be kept for a year if he ever repeated his offence. 'Lewd' thief Francis Rochester spent fifty-seven days in Norwich Bridewell in 1698.[127] 'Longe ponyshment', London Bridewell's clerk wrote at the end of an entry noting that Cicely Alexander was locked up on 20 December 1559 for eating flesh on 'dayes prohibited' and 'discharged of the same the xxv of february 1559 [1560]'. 'Naughty pack' Jone Cocks, who was 'taken in the strets as a lewd straggler', left prison on the day that Alexander arrived, having been 'brought into this house the xiiii of october 1559'.[128] Others spending similar stretches in bridewells included a married couple from Thetford for 'exorbitant offences [against] the government of this buroughe', a Norwich maid who ran away from her master, and Alice Christian, who 'counterfeited' a justice's signature on a petition to East Sussex Sessions in 1673.[129]

minute books 1629–36, fo. 99; 1639–54, fos. 77, 119; T/QS/1, fos. 2v, 43; NOTTA QSM/13, fo. 50v; OHC QS/C/A1/O1, fo. 127v; QSM 1/1/I, fo. 56; KAC WQ/O/4, fo. 145v; SROI B/105/2/1, fos. 106v, 130v; B/105/2/3, fos. 44, 91v; B/105/2/6, fos. 40, 154v; SHA 3356/2430, fos. 3, 108.

[124] LBHC 5, fo. 30v. See also LBHC 1, fos. 35v, 73v; 5, fos. 101v, 229, 249v; 6, fos. 34, 39v; 8, fos. 215, 249, 329, 377v, 383, 405, 414; 9, fos. 341, 342, 343; BMM BHC 4, fos. 79v, 189v.

[125] LBHC 5, fo. 30v; 1, fos. 63, 42; GA GBR/G/G3/SO/1, fo. 115v. See also LBHC 5, fos. 30v, 98v, 109, 300; 8, fos. 363, 383; NRO NMCC 14, fo. 287v.

[126] D. Underdown, *Fire from Heaven: Life in an English Town in the Seventeenth Century* (1992); P. Slack, 'Poverty and politics in Salisbury, 1597–1666', in P. Clark and Slack, eds., *Crisis and Order in English Towns, 1550–1700: Essays in Urban History* (Toronto, 1972).

[127] SAI B/105/2/1, fo. 51v; Hearing and Bridges, *Dorset Quarter Sessions Order Book*, 43; NRO Norwich Informations and Examinations Book 1690–9, 4/8/1698, 12/8/1698, 17/8/1698, 8/10/1698. See also NRO NMCC 13, fo. 598; 14, fo. 426v; 25, fo. 117v; NA NQS/1, fo. 69; OHC QSM 1/1/1v, fo. 47.

[128] LBHC 1, fos. 63, 42.

[129] NRO T/QS/1, fo. 13; NRO Norwich Informations and Examinations Book 1690–9, 9/8/1698, 8/10/1698; ESBHRO QO/EW7, fos. 13, 26. See also HEA Q/SM/4, fo. 73v; LERO QS5/1/1, fo. 13.

This sense of 'longe' may not seem so today but it helps us to grasp how early moderns thought about incarceration. Richard Plattin spent three months in Thetford Bridewell for 'petti larcenie' in 1633. Fifteen-year-old 'masterless' 'single woman' Phillipa Bartlett was locked up in Dorchester for '3 monethes' in 1676 for 'incontinency'. John Dawkes was 'sett to hard labour with moderate correccon' for the same period in Suffolk in 1658 after causing trouble in church.[130] Others spending three months inside included a poacher, wanderer, shady 'newcomer', and housebreaker.[131] Four- or five-month stays are rarely noted. More people were locked up for the six-month milestone that stretched out like an eternity for some. Prisoners spending half a year inside bridewells included London 'gadder' Bridget Abell (1560), Colchester thief John Sallones (1639), and apprentice Jeremy Black—'not to be let out till the six monthes from this day be expired' (1646).[132] London 'gadder' and 'harlot' Frances Knolls was 'comytted to the labor' of Bridewell on 23 October 1559 and set free on 'the xxi of maye 1560 because she was with child'. While light-fingered Henry Morgan was released from the same place after more than six months ('a great while').[133]

A year is the next milestone. The 1610 legislation that made bridewells mandatory also sentenced 'lewd' women who 'shall have any bastard which may be chargeable to the parish' to bridewell for 'one whole year'. Warwickshire mother of 'three bastards' 'evell' Bridget Walker was locked up for a symbolic 'yeere and a day' in 1627, as she never had 'condigne punishmente' and took 'encouragement to goe on still in that lewde course'.[134] Mothers of 'bastards' were sentenced to twelve months at a steady rate. Mary Needles was put in a bridewell for 'one whole year' in the year of the Infanticide Act (1624): 'she hath had a bastard before', Somerset justices said, and 'seemeth to be more lewd'. Margaret Mott was locked up in Colchester a 'month after her delyvery' for 'one whole yere' in 1619.[135] Illegitimacy is often seen as a male economic offence, and it is revealing to see the 'mother of a bastard childe' locked up because she was 'not able to releeve' her child. Ann Stanley from Northampton was sentenced to a year in 1671 'unles', magistrates said, 'she shall give security to the parish'. Mary Needles paid four-pence weekly 'out of her labour in bridewell' towards the upkeep of her child.[136] Other mothers did not see out the full year. There is evidence that, like Stanley, some left after finding money to take care of their child. Discretion also played a part. Eleanor Rudge was set free after ten months in Gloucester in 1631, as 'she

[130] NRO T/C1/9, fo. 2v; DHC DC/DCB/1/1, fo. 2v; SAI B/105/2/4, fo. 57.

[131] For example, HEA Q/SM/3, fos. 43v–4; Q/SM/4, fos. 73, 93; NA NQS/3, fo. 82; LERO QS5/1/1, fos. 62, 111v; ESBHRO QO/EW9, 12/1/1688.

[132] LBHC 1, fo. 63v; ERO DB5/SR/38/28; NRO NMCC 20, fo. 481.

[133] LBHC 1, fos. 28v, 29v; 8, fos. 362, 383. See also HEA Q/SM/4, fo. 80; SAI B/105/2/4, fo. 117; NA NQS/2, fo. 73; OHC QS/C/A1/02, fo. 145.

[134] WRO QS0040/1/, fo. 36v.

[135] Bates, *Quarter Sessions Records for the County of Somerset*, I, 322; ERO D/B5/SB2/6, fo. 289v.

[136] NA NQS/1, fo. 84. See also KAC WQ/O/1, fo. 26v; HEA Q/SM/2, fo. 97; BRO Q/JQS/1/1, fo. 78; ESBHRO Q1/EW1, fo. 53v; CKS U120/09, fo. 141.

has lately growen into such dangerous fittes [that she] is not likely to live [if] shee bee not inlarged'. Jane Fidge was 'set on worke' for 'one whole yeare [in Kent in 1619] unlesse through penitence and amendmente of liefe we shall thinke fit to respite the same'.[137] This was not quite the letter of the law—there was room for manoeuvre in decision-making. Illegitimacy, of course, was not the only reason why people spent a 'whole' year in bridewells. 'Lewde' Jane Leech was led to London Bridewell by Parliament's purger Pride 'to worke for a yeare' in 1649 (she 'will not be reformed', the court said). Suffolk thief Deborah Symper was 'whipped in the open market' in Bury St Edmunds in 1675 and put in the bridewell 'to remaine for one yeere'. Matthew Redshaw from Worlingham (Suffolk) was locked up for 'one whole yere' in 1641 after a string of 'fowle misdemeanors against his last master'.[138] These were custodial sentences. Other cases show how justices used bridewells for people acquitted of felony or branded after reading the 'neck verse'. Grace Herring was 'burned in the hand for felony' in 1652 and sentenced to 'a yeare'. Edward Bunn and John Giddens were 'acquited of felony' in Norwich in 1638 and put in the bridewell 'to remayne a yeare'.[139] Others spent one year behind bars for leaving a child on a doorstep or for 'incontinencye'. 'Comon nightwalker' Martha Jackson was 'content to stay a yeare' in London Bridewell if 'ever she came in againe'.[140]

Others were locked up for over a year, including 'a poore humble man' in Warwickshire in 1634, 'whose name is unknowen', who had been 'inside' for fourteen months and was 'not able to give an account from whence he came or able by his worke to gayne anything towards his lively hood'. 'Altogether destitute', he had no clothes to cover his 'nakednes'. He got some clothes but not his freedom.[141] Jane Prosser was in Herefordshire's 'correccon house' 'kallendar' in April 1693. She was sent in three months earlier 'for abuseing her parents' and was called 'dangerous and disorderly' in October 1693. Prosser appears in April 1694, October 1694, and January 1695, but not afterwards.[142] Millicent Kempe from the same county was locked up under 'the discipline of the house' in 1631. She had had 'bastard children' before and justices said that she 'liveth so dissolutely that she is like rather to have more than to bee reformed'. She was still there two years later, 'very weake and sickly by reason of her longe imprisonment'. Kempe was finally allowed to go home, but justices were unhappy to hear that her parish had not yet got her 'fitt and convenient apparrell'.[143]

Bridewells and prisons worked very closely together; sometimes in the same sentence or building. The author of *A View of the Penal Laws* (1681) made it clear

[137] GA GBR/G/G3/SO/1, fo. 133v; CKS U120/09, fos. 118–19.
[138] LBHC 9, fo. 376; SAI B/105/2/8, fo. 33; B/105/2/1, fo. 27.
[139] LBHC 9, fo. 436; NRO Norwich Sessions Book 1637–64, fo. 26v.
[140] LBHC 8, 404. See also SAI B/105/2/2, fo. 102v; ERO D/B5/SB4/3, fo. 16; HEA Q/SM/1, fo. 161v; LERO QS5/1/1, fo. 58v; OHC QS/C/A1/01, fo. 135.
[141] WRO QS0040/1/1, fos. 98, 124v.
[142] HEA Q/SM/3, fos. 65, 72v, 82, 90v–1.
[143] Ibid., fos. 43v, 53.

that anyone who decided to 'kill, hunt, or take away red of fallow deer' did so at the risk of spending six months in a bridewell 'or the common gaole for a yeare'.[144] It is revealing that for this author six months in a bridewell is the equivalent of a year in 'gaole'. John Salter and Richard Standen were 'found guylty of an enormious assault and threatning words to fire William Bowells house' in Kent in 1640. Justices sentenced them 'to remaine in gaole for one moneth and then to goe to the house of correccion [for] sixe moneths' and back to 'gaole' afterwards until they paid a £5 fine.[145] Norfolk Justice Robert Doughty said that Thomas Martins had no 'calling' or home 'but the bridewell and gaol' in 1665.[146] Prisons and bridewells were seen as alternatives and this widened the scope for judicial decisions. William Sheppard noted in his justices' handbook (1659) that anyone spouting 'blasphemous opinions'—'that he is a God almighty, infinite &c.'—should be sent 'to prison or house of correction for six months' (only 'bridewell' is in the margin).[147] This idea of alternatives took firm hold in the 1706 legislation that gave courts the option of locking up people who committed minor felonies in bridewells for up to two years—assize judges had been sending 'lesser' offenders to bridewells from the early seventeenth century and perhaps before.

Prisons held people ahead of trial and until execution, but they did far more (some suspects were put in bridewells ahead of their trial).[148] Courts sentenced offenders to custodial sentences; alternatively, they were locked up without a specific length of time and this could drag on for months or even years. The crimes of 1,190 prisoners in 'gaole' or 'prysone' are noted down in records that I have worked with (many more have nothing next to their names). This is what we see after putting these offences in the same brackets as bridewell 'presaners': there are differences but also similarities in prisoner profiles inside bridewells and prisons. Twelve times as many were locked up in bridewells for domestic disorders and this is unsurprising given their heavy hand in keeping households together. Twice as many people were behind prison bars for public disorders/violence. One-third of people in prison were thieves or cozeners; the figure was just over one-in-ten in bridewells. (See Table 4.2.) There was a seven-point difference (favouring bridewells) in vagrancy/street cases, when we might have expected it to be higher. The largest contrast is in the misfit lifestyles bracket that was three-quarters of 1 per cent in prisons and 14.57 per cent in bridewells. The 1610 legislation linking

[144] *A View of the Penal Laws Concerning Trade and Traffic* (1681), 130.

[145] E. Melling, ed., *Kentish Sources VI: Crime and Punishment* (Maidstone, 1969), 97.

[146] *Notebook of Robert Doughty*, 53.

[147] Sheppard, *New Survey of the Justice of Peace His Office*, 19.

[148] For example, ESBHRO QO/EW8, fo. 184v; HA Q3/3, fo. 155; HEA Q/SO/1, fo. 90; SAI B/105/2/6, fo. 154v; NRO T/QS/1, fo. 20v; KAC WQ/O/1, fos. 8v, 28v.

Table 4.2 Prisons: offences[1]

Category of offence	Number and % of committals
Theft/cozening	387–33.33%
Public disorders/violence	212–17.81%
Court referrals	211–17.73%
Moral regulation/religion	167–14.3%
Vagrancy/street offences	131–11.01%
Domestic disorders	13–1.09%
Court disorders	13–1.09%
Misfit lifestyles	9–0.76%

(Forty-seven prisoners were charged with murder: 3.95 per cent.)

[1] Figures are from prisons in Cambridgeshire, Cheshire, Devon, Dorset, Essex, Gloucestershire, Hampshire, Herefordshire, Kent, Lancashire, Middlesex, Norfolk, Northamptonshire, Oxfordshire, Suffolk, Sussex, Wiltshire, and Yorkshire.

bridewells with 'idle' and 'disorderly' lifestyles made the difference here. The proportion of women in bridewells was double that of the female prison population (42.75 per cent/21.43 per cent). The ratio of female vagrants and other street offenders was almost equal (31.30 per cent prison/31.55 per cent bridewell), though numbers were higher in bridewells (206/131). But difference is more par for the course. Over eight-in-ten of 233 bridewell prisoners imprisoned for moral/religious offences were women; the figure for prisons was below four-in-ten. Women were five times more likely to end up in bridewells for public disorder/violence (29.33 per cent). Female thieves on the other hand were one-quarter of the female prison theft population but just 7.7 per cent inside bridewells. The largest disparity was again with marginal lifestyles. Numbers were higher in bridewells (164) than prison/gaol (9). All nine in prison were men; women were six-tenths of the bridewell group.

Norwich has gaol calendars wrapped in sessions files covering twenty years (1646–66) that take us inside cells to see who was there. Olive Blancher was locked up for two decades and probably longer as calendars run dry in 1666. She is in the August 1646 calendar with no hint of what she had done and was still behind bars at Christmas 1666. Olive was in prison as the dust settled on the Civil Wars, when England shook as a king was put to death, through each day of the rocky republic, as bells rang and bonfires blazed when the king came back, and as plague and fire crushed London. Her husband, John, was 'sent' from London to the prison 'by order of the chief justice to remaine in safe custodie' in September 1652 until he could be set free by 'the law and custome of England'. He was called 'John Browne alias Blancher' in 1665. Seven months later, John Browne 'al[ia]s Blancher' was 'convict of felonie', but 'judgement [was] respited' and he was put in 'safe custodie'. John Blancher was back in court two months later, 'convict of felonie upon his inditement for break of prison [and] had judgement to be hanged'. It had been fourteen years since he first walked into Norwich Prison.[149]

The highest number in Norwich Prison at one time was twenty-eight in April 1658; the lowest was five in June 1662. A large variety of crimes appears next to 'the names of the prisoners in the prison', from murder to misdemeanour. John Blancher's companions when he joined his wife in autumn 1652 included William Emerton, who 'dangerously' wounded a sheriff's officer; Elizabeth Reeve, 'delivered of a bastard child in a towne of Lincolneshire which she saith was dead'; and Gilbert Hughes, who was 'suspected to have murdered' her child. Edmund Gosling was jailed for misdemeanours in 1657, sharing prison with the Blanchers and a spinster who, 'seduced' by the devil, used 'divellish arts' called 'inchantments, witchecraftes, charms and sorceries' to harm John Callowe. Another suspected witch had three Lake District Quakers for company at New Year 1654, who had made the long trip to Norwich 'to declare the truth'. The Blanchers were joined by a Jesuit in 1658.[150]

Some 'presansers' were held as process took time to draw to a close. Tobias Bliss and Richard Gater were put in 'gaole' in Fisherton Anger (Wiltshire) in 1651 until justices 'conceeveth [that] they are bayleable' after Jane Cowles said they tried to burn her house down. They were 'honest poore labouringe men' justices heard who 'never intended' the 'burnynge [of her] howse but onely to fire some thatch suspect[ing] her to be a witch.'[151] A fine unbroken set of Dorset gaol calendars (1629–38) shows prisoners being 'cleared out' of 'gaol' each quarter, though some were sentenced to be punished elsewhere. They were locked up for theft for the most part, though other offences included illegitimacy, barratry, and giving shelter to inmates and vagrants from as far afield as Ireland, London, King's Lynn, Chelmsford, Tiverton, and Penzance. Prisoners were let go, sent to the bridewell, branded, whipped, pilloried, or put in stocks. Three men and two women of the total 581 prisoners (130 women, 22.4 per cent) died on the gallows. The largest number of prisoners at any one time was forty-nine in January 1638 (nine women): six were released; three were branded with the letter 'F', four with 'R', and two with 'T'; three were held for sureties and a dozen until they paid fines; thirteen were whipped; and one was kept for the next sessions.[152] Prisoners elsewhere were told that they could leave once they paid fines or fees or pledged sureties. They included Rose Reynolds, who was fined twenty-five shillings in Suffolk in 1655 for being 'several tymes indicted for being out of service', and Norwich 'jailer' John Quash, who was locked up in 1583 until he got sureties for his

[149] NRO Norwich Sessions Files, 52/37, 77/18; Norwich Sessions Book 1654–70, 7/1667 sessions, 9/1667 sessions.

[150] NRO Norwich Sessions Files, 69/62, 62/22, 67/27, 65/39, 67/36, 67/23, 68/62, 63/25.

[151] WSHC A1/160/1, Hilary 1651 sessions.

[152] Hearing and Bridges, *Dorset Quarter Sessions Order Book*, 304–5, 315, 394–5.

'contemptuous' words to the recorder.[153] Others were kept until they 'submitted'. Southampton 'gent' Francis Demery was fined £10 and put in 'prison' in 1620 for 'rayling wordes' to the mayor until he 'acknowledged his offens [in] the audett howse' before the 'mayor, aldermen and th'assistants'.[154] Others were sitting in prison waiting to be transported after a pardon, like Oxford burglar Peter Beer, who was 'reprieved after judgment' in 1687 and 'pleaded pardon of transportacon' six months later.[155] Some prisoners were left in the dark, not knowing when they could get on with their lives. They were locked up 'till further order' or at the court's 'discretion' or 'pleasure', like 'sometime beadle' now fruit 'gatherer' Thomas Jackson, who was put in a Gloucester cell in 1628 for calling Thomas Cox's wife 'rotten nosed geldinge' who had been 'of good life and honest demeanor all her life' and married to 'a very honest subsedy man'.[156]

We often know for how long someone was put in prison and the range is again from one day to a life sentence. Two quarrelling 'strangers' were put in Norwich Prison for just a single day in 1567; Margaret Needham was 'imprisoned for the rest of her natural life' after she was found in the same city in 1583 with a rosary 'consecrated called a hallowed bead' (I have no idea if she spent her last days in a prison cell).[157] Some prisoners spent less than a week behind bars. 'Yf anie person shall misuse the mayor [by] evell language', the people of Thetford were warned in 1574, they will spend 'ii dayes and ii nights' in prison. Robert Wetheridge from Barnstaple was 'stayed two daies' in prison in 1617 for keeping neighbours awake and giving a constable a mouthful of abuse. 'Clerke convict' Ann Barre was put in prison 'tyll Fryday' in Norwich in 1640.[158] A few days in prison could mean more than lost wages. Fittingly named Giles Toogood from Dorset was locked up for three days for tippling with no licence in 1636. Others spending three to five days in prison committed 'fellonie', picked purses, taunted aldermen, preached 'dissent', broke the sabbath, and more besides.[159]

A nagging issue with records of imprisonment is that it is not always clear whether someone was in prison for a particular length of time or with no time specified. What does 'stayed' mean? It could have been time to cool off. Prison was used in various ways. The Dorset calendars show prisoners waiting for a

[153] SAI B/105/2/3, fo. 116v; NRO Norwich Sessions Book 1581–91. fos. 58, 59v. See also SAI B/105/2/3, fos. 109, 122v; B/105/2/4, fos. 16, 180; B/105/2/6, fos. 73, 165v; NRO T/C1/2, fos. 82, 83; DHC DC/DOB/8/1, fo. 185v.

[154] SA SC9/2/1, fo. 58.

[155] OHC Oxfordshire Sessions Rolls E/46, T/34, M/43, EP/57, M/24, E/43. See also SAI B/105/2/4, fo. 82v; B/105/2/6, fo. 165v; OHC C/FC/1/A1/01, fo. 191; C/FC/1/A1/02, fos. 32v, 166.

[156] GA GBR/G/G3/SO/1, fo. 132v. See also ESBHRO RYE 1/5, fo. 7; NRO Norwich Sessions Book 1581–91, fo. 72; OHC C/FC/A1/01, fo. 356v; C/FC/1/A1/02, fo. 50.

[157] NRO Norwich Sessions Book 1581–91, fo. 80; NMCC 8, fo. 498.

[158] NRO TC1/2, fo. 41; NDRO B1/3792, fo. 189; NRO Norwich Sessions Book 1637–64, fo. 62.

[159] Hearing and Bridges, *Dorset Quarter Sessions Order Book*, 332. See also OHC C/FC/1/A1/02, fo. 9; DRO ECA B/1/3, fo. 138; CA QJB/1/3, fo. 164v; YCA F7, fos. 65, 389; SAI B/105/2/3, fos. 48, 96v; NA 3/1, fo. 210v.

decision. But this analysis of time spent behind bars is also drawn from court minutes where magistrates are sending someone to prison or letting them go home. Imprisonment is punishment whether or not the length of time is spelt out on record. It often was. Bridgnorth residents were told in 1573 that they would stay 'one whole weeke' in prison if they spoke 'undecent langwege' to the bailiffs or aldermen.[160] Two 'singlemen' 'taken' begging in Norwich in 1565 were 'imprisoned by the space of vii dayes' after telling people that 'they were marchande men robbyd' by pirates. Leonard Thursby also spent a week in the same 'gaole' after being 'acquitted as an incorrigible rogue' in 1615. Other prisoners who spent a week behind bars included loudmouths who insulted constables, constables who turned a blind eye to vagrants, and vagrants who spoke out of turn.[161] Liverpool's 'scolders and chiders' could either pay a fine or go to prison 'by the space of tenne dayes' in 1587. A fortnight in 'St Johns Howse' in Winchester was the chilly prospect for anyone trading with plague-hit London in 1593.[162] 'Singlewoman' Frances Saunders, whose master said that she had stolen 'an angel', was released from Norwich Prison after two weeks in 1575 so long as her master 'will laye no fellony'. The 'keper' of Exeter Guildhall spent eighteen days locked up in his own prison in 1562 for letting a prisoner go 'out of the pytt'.[163]

Varying stretches in prison reflect several things: a length of time that fitted a crime and sense of offence, particular sentences for particular offences, or the stage of process. A defined piece of time like a week or month feels like a determined sentence. A Somerset feltmaker who travelled to Dorchester to 'seke work' in 1630 was locked up for '21 dayes [for] want of a testimonial'. Rye servant Richard Tate faced a month in prison after he punched 'a precher of Gods worde' in 1591 (he was on a list of people who believed 'dyverse heresies and errors' in the same year).[164] Robert Batch from Thetford who beat up his master in 1620 spent a 'whole month' in prison, as did Nicholas Wade who was 'acquitted of burglary' in Norwich in 1638 and told that he would 'remayne in the gaole for a moneth'.[165] 'Whole' brings us back to understandings of what a long length of time might be. Richard Sweet had a history of 'incontynent lyff' when he appeared before Exeter magistrates in 1562. 'Extreme punnyshmente' was the only option, they said; 'open shame of the cart used in such cases' did not fit the bill. Sweet was told that he 'would 'remayne in a strayght pryson yn the pytt of the guildhall' for forty days and get fed on Wednesdays and Fridays with only bread and water.

[160] SHA BB/C/4/1/1.

[161] NRO NMCC 8, fo. 277; 9, fo. 580. See also NRO Norwich Sessions Books 1602–18, fo. 206v; 1571–83, fo. 3v.

[162] J. A. Twemlow, ed., *Liverpool Town Books, Proceedings of Assemblies, Common Councils, Portmoot Courts etc. 1550–1862*, 2 vols (Liverpool, 1918–35), II, 350; HA W/B2/3, fo. 4; Q1/1, fo. 115.

[163] DRO ECA B/1/3, fo. 83. See also NDRO B1/3792, fo. 189; CA QJB/1/2, fo. 198v; DRO ECA B/1/4, fo. 3; OHC C/FC/1/A1/O1, fo. 356v.

[164] DHC DC/DOB/8/1, fo. 38; ESBHRO RYE 1/5, fos. 214v, 216v.

[165] NRO T/C1/9, fo. 1v; Norwich Sessions Book 1637–54, fo. 33. See also DRO ECA C1/61, fo. 405; WSHC A1/150/11, fo. 223; HA Q/SM/3, fo. 6v.

There were glimmers of discretion even here in these gloomy quarters. The mayor told Sweet that he could decide to 'shorten' his sentence 'at his pleasure' if any signs of 'repentaunce and amendement shall appeare'. 'One Dible' was let out of Colchester prison after six weeks in 1583 after the recorder decided that this was 'condigne punishment for his offense'.[166] Forty days was 'extreme' in Exeter, but three months was the standard sentence for 'fornicacon' in 1650s Suffolk as the republican regime cracked down on immorality.[167] Norvician Nicholas Salter spent three months in prison in 1664 for 'destroyinge a swanns egg'. Thomas Bugg was told to 'remayne in gaole three monethes' in Suffolk in 1662 for 'taking connies'. Other offences that merited three-month sentences included speaking seditiously, barracking ministers, refusing to take an oath, and taking part in an 'unlawful assembly'.[168]

I have few words from prisoners about what they felt about their time behind bars. We do hear their voices in petitions protesting against their treatment and the time they had spent in prison. The 'miserable' and 'poore convicts' in Oxford Castle '[had] suffered longe hardship and tedious imprisonment', they said, in a 'humble peticon' to justices in 1688. Prisoners grumbled about 'tedious confinement' and 'want of reliefe' three years later, 'especially' two of them who had been locked up for over two years.[169] But prisoners are mostly mute. I don't know what Martha Simpson thought about her four months in Norwich Prison for adultery in 1651, but she must have been relieved, as her infidelity was now a felony. Nor do I know what Abraham Whissater/Whisstler felt about his six months in prison in 1646 after he was 'convict[ed] of felony' and 'read the book' in 1640, whipped, locked up, and branded again one year later, and whipped through the Saturday market in 1645. Toughened prisoners like Whissater were more likely to take things in their stride. He was back in prison with Olive Blancher in August 1649 and stayed until autumn 1651, when he disappears with no word why.[170] Wiltshire weaver William Bond might have used his time in prison to make others see the light. Meaning 'wholely to extirpate religion', he was sent to 'the comon gaole [for] six moneths' in 1656 for 'thise athiticall, blasphemous and execrable words':

> That there was no God or power ruleinge above the plannetts and that there was noe Christ but the son that shines upon us and that there was no such Christ as is menconed in the scripture [and] that yf the scripture were to making againe that Tom Lampier [from Melkham] would make as good scripture as the bible

[166] DRO ECA B/1/4, fo. 152; ERO D/Y/2/8/319. See also DRO ECA B/1/3, fo. 176; C1/61, fo. 208; SAI B/105/2/2, fo. 7v; B/105/2/6, fo. 165v.

[167] SAI B/105/2/4, fo. 173.

[168] NRO Norwich Sessions Book 1654–70, 7/1664 sessions. See also HA Q1/2, fo. 216v; NA NQS/2, fo. 75; CA QJB/3/1, fo. 60; DRO QS/32/1; YCA F7, fo. 408; LA 3/1/1, fo. 47v; SAI B/105/2/3, fos. 50, 108, 133.

[169] OHC Oxfordshire Sessions Rolls EP/39, EP/41.

[170] NRO Norwich Sessions Files, 59/37, 60/45, 53/44, 54/135, 59/37, 59/59, 60/57.

> and there was neither heaven or hell but in a mans owne conscience for yt he had a good fortune and did live well in the world that was heaven and yf he lived poore and miserable that was hell and death ytselfe for then he would dye like a cowe.[171]

We have seen both houses of correction and prisons being used to lock up religious 'radicals'. Both Anna Trapnel and James Nayler ended up spending time in London Bridewell. Labourer Christopher Atkinson from Kendal was one of the Quakers who came to Norwich 'to declare the truth' in winter 1654. He was sent to prison in December 1654, when justices heard he 'did moleste and disturbe the visitor of the prisoners [in] the time of his sermon', shouting 'leave off then hypocrite, thou deceive the people'. Atkinson was not released until August 1655, when in 'open court' he repented and apologized for heckling the minister.[172]

The Norwich Sessions calendars have a lot to say about the long-term prison population. Bridget Nobbs, who stole stockings, is in calendars with Blancher and Whissater for twelve months in 1650–1. Nobbs was well known, as she had been whipped four times for petty larceny in 1645, 1646—'till the blood come'—1648, and 1653. She was back in the calendar in the same year for eight months for 'suspicion of felony and burglary'. This would be her final appearance. She was 'convict of felony for stealinge of goods above xs' in December 1653 and sent back to prison 'and from thence to be caryed to the place of execucon and there be hunge by the necke till she be dead'.[173] William Thurgar was in prison when Nobbs left for the last time. He had been there before, in Easter 1652, for stealing money from a shop and was let go after being whipped at the post. Suspected of felony, Thurgar was back behind bars in December 1652 with nine men and seven women including recently arrived John Blancher and three suspected murderers. A Matthew Thurgar was found guilty of felony, branded, and 'delivered' in the same month. William Thurgar, 'felony confessed', appears in the April 1653 calendar; William Thurgar, 'hanged', is in the sessions book for the same month. Luckily for him he was 'reprieved after judgment' four months later. Bridget Nobbs had joined him by then. Thurgar is in calendars for the next three years. His companions included the Lake District Quakers, among them Quaker leader George Whitehead from Westmorland who only wanted 'to declare the will of God (as he calls it)'. Thurgar was finally released in March 1656, thirty-one months after his reprieve, but he did not learn his lesson. In March 1657 William Thurgar and William Youngman were 'convict of several felonys' and sentenced to

[171] WSHC A1/150/11, fo. 356.

[172] NRO Norwich Sessions Books 1637–64, fo. 62; 1639–54, fos. 23v, 70; 1639–54, fo. 89; 1654–70, 8/1655 sessions; See also HA Q1/1, fo. 340; SAI B/105/2/6, fo. 93; DHC DC/PL/CE/2/1; CA QJB/3/1, fo. 260v; ERO D/B5/SB3, fo. 13.

[173] NRO Norwich Sessions Files 59/37, 59/59, 62/29, 63/25, 63/22; Norwich Sessions Books 1639–54, fos. 74v, 135; 1637–64, 3/1646 sessions; 1639–54, fos. 81v, 101, 166.

hang.[174] William Rix walked in through the door in March 1656. He was sentenced to hang in the same month but was also reprieved—but not released, as he is in calendars up until April 1659 when he was a 'closse prisoner'. He is missing in the next one but is back in August 1660 for the last time. Rix could have been in prison for fifty-three months.[175] Mary Gooding/Goodwin was locked up at the same time as Rix and left with him in summer 1660. She and Thomas Gooding were charged with burglary but he broke out of prison in September 1656. She 'pleaded that she is quick with childe and within six weeks of the time of her delivery' and was kept 'until she be delivered and then to be hanged'. Mary was still in prison one year later. There is a seven-month gap in calendars from autumn 1657 to April 1658, when she appears with 'after judgment' written after her name. Had she been released in between times and gone back to her old ways? Gooding was 'reprived' exactly one year later. Her last time in the calendar was, like Rix, in August 1660.[176]

Other 'long-stay' prisoners were in prison from one year to twenty-one months. The calendars, however, survive in broken sequence: thirty-six survive from August 1649 to August 1660; fifteen more take us to December 1666. Like Gooding, there is a chance that someone was freed and locked up again in times of silence. But we know more about why people were locked up and for how long. Bridewells were integral to discretionary justice. Some of this was spelt out in legislation, but also evident is recognition in court of the unpredictability of the human condition and situation. Ideas of custodial sentencing at this time need to be flexible to include specified lengths of time, views of the right amount of time for a particular person or crime, and tinkering with the letter of the law. Prisoners were kept from one court session to the next. Olive Blancher is the most compelling case. She was told that she would 'remayne according to former order' in the month when her husband joined her in autumn 1652. Courts punished offenders after acquittals and reprieves. Like Thurgar and Rix, who spent three years in prison after a reprieve, they thought that freedom waited around the corner, only to find that courts had other ideas. The worst day of Christopher Baxter's life was in winter 1640 when he heard his death sentence; the best was two years later when he was reprieved. But he did not go home until the month after Parliament won the war at Naseby (June 1645).[177] This is in effect prison in place of hanging. Anne Rickner/Cricknell was 'reprieved' in Norwich 'after judgement' in September 1651 but remained until March 1653. She is not in the next calendar

[174] NRO Norwich Sessions Files 61/26, 62/26, 62/29, 62/30, 63/22, 63/25, 64/32, 64/39, 65/35, 65/39, 66/24, 66/36, 66/40; Norwich Sessions Book 1639–54, fos. 152v, 166v; 1637–64, 3/1657 session.

[175] NRO Norwich Sessions Files 66/36, 66/33, 66/40, 67/19, 67/23, 67/36, 68/52, 68/62, 69/16; Norwich Sessions Book 1654/70, 3/1656 sessions.

[176] NRO Norwich Sessions Files 66/33, 66/36, 67/19, 67/23, 67/27, 67/36, 68/52, 68/62, 69/16, 69/62; Norwich Sessions Book 1654–70, 9/1656 sessions (Gooding/Goodwin).

[177] NRO Norwich Sessions Books 1639–54, fos. 20, 23, 29, 37, 49, 61v, 62v, 67, 70v, 75; 1637–64, 9/1642 sessions.

but the one after tells us that she was reprieved with William Thurgar. She stayed in prison for nine months and appears for one last time in September 1655 as 'a condempned person [who] did lately make an escape out of prison'.[178] Like others, she had to go through months of not knowing. Sara Fairfax was convicted of felony in winter 1614 but 'reprieved in gaole'. Her world changed eight months later when, still in prison, she was told that her reprieve would be reviewed at the next sessions, but she was again 'repryved in gaole' and went home (a Sara Fairfax was 'whipped for peti larceny' in April 1617).[179] There are similarities between Fairfax's not untypical rollercoaster ride from judgment to reprieve and a custodial sentence. There is the appearance of making sure that a thief gets punished just as acquitted felons were locked up inside bridewells.

We have met 'presaners' who spent days, weeks, months, or years inside. We know little else about them. Nor have we said much about their time behind bars. Like them, we need to go inside bridewells and prisons to see how they were run and what prisoners might expect from one day to the next.

IV

Exeter governors wanted a 'sufficient and mete' man to fill the post of bridewell master in 1579 and a 'person of better credytt' when looking for 'a new keper for the counter' not long after; 'capable' was the word in Cheshire in 1662; Yarmouth plumped for 'meete' in 1614.[180] The 1610 Act wanted 'fit' men to be 'governor or master'. Wiltshire justices interviewed two men to be master of Devizes Bridewell in 1643: Abraham Hall turned out to be 'fittest in respect [of] ability [and] understanding [of] theire trade and sufficiency of the securitie [and] the better spirited man'.[181] It was a good idea to turn to someone with a pedigree. 'Rauffe moore bedell of this towne [was given] the guidinge and charge' of Ipswich's 'house' in 1599. 'Eldest sergeant' Thomas Belcamber took over the 'counter' in Reading in 1657.[182] Women, too, needed to be 'discrete' and 'mete'. Middlesex justices asked 'gentleman' John Stoyle, the first master of Clerkenwell Bridewell, to pick a 'discrete and honeste woman' to be 'matron and governes over the women'. Henry Savage's widow was 'a fitt woman to be governor or mistr[es]s of the poore wemen' in Exeter Bridewell in 1579 with 'ii rooms [for] her selfe and stuffe'. The widow of the 'late keeper' of Hampshire's bridewell became keeper 'by herself' in 1696 after showing her 'fitness' in a self-penned petition.[183]

178 NRO Norwich Sessions Books 1639–54, fos. 20, 23, 29, 37, 49, 61v, 62v, 67, 70v, 75; 1637–64, 9/1642 sessions.

179 NRO Norwich Sessions Files 59/59, 61/18, 61/24, 61/39, 62/23, 62/26, 63/22, 64/32, 65/35.

180 DRO ECA B/1/3, fos. 414, 429; B/1/4, fo. 538; CA QJB/3/1, fo. 46; NRO Y/C/19/5, fos. 142v, 271v.

181 WSHC A1/160/1.

182 SAI C/2/2/2/1, fo. 218; BRO R/AC1/1/2, fo. 134; R/AC1/1/7, fo. 62.

183 LMA MJ/SBR/2, fos. 242–3; HA Q/1/2, fo. 162; Q3/3, fo. 159.

Keepers could stay in post for a long while. A Dorset keeper was in post for at least a decade. Robert Henfield ran Yarmouth Bridewell for seven years and probably longer.[184] The job was handed down the family line. A Henry Tubb was in charge of Reading Bridewell in 1625 and 1647, getting £18 in 1635 for '12 paires of cards, 12 wheeles, 1 paire of stocke cardes [and] 1 frame'. Thomas Cooper followed George Cooper in Sherborne. Augustine Cooper stepped into the shoes of his father in 1638 in Hampshire. John Page, 'maister' of Middlewich, was sinking in debt in 1662 'through the calamities of the late tymes', and his son Hugh, a person 'very capable', was asked to give him a helping hand. 'Very antient' John was dead a dozen years later when the full £40 salary was paid to Hugh;[185] £40 was a decent annual wage for the 'middling sort'. Salaries varied in time and place. Ben Garfield picked up £100 'yearly' for ruling the roost in Clerkenwell Bridewell in 1618. The keepers of Speenhamland and Reading bridewells got £40. George Cooper in Sherborne 'prayed' justices 'to have a larger allowance' than £20 in 1635 (he got a 50 per cent hike).[186] The Berkeley keeper received £26 in 1673 (a Cirencester keeper was paid the same). Norwich keeper Richard Wright earned £24 in 1631. Keepers in Yarmouth, Southwell, and 'the cliffe nere Lewes' got £20 for the year.[187] Others fared less well: £13 6s. 8d. (Westmorland: 1661), £8 (Colchester: 1617), £6 13s. 4d. (Thetford: 1630), £6 (Appleby: 1690), £2 (Tenterden: 1640, topped up by six-pence 'everie' time the keeper whipped a 'rogue, vagabond, sturdye begger and other idle disorderly person' and five shillings for each hanging), and fifteen shillings (Manchester: 1621).[188] As in Tenterden, top-ups put more money in pockets. Edward Wright, who was keeper of Norwich Bridewell for two decades, at least, got 'a penny out of every shillinge' prisoners earned in 1617.[189]

These salaries were just one source of income for most 'masters' and their range reflected the size of a particular house, whether the job was full- or part-time, or whether the payment was a portion of an annual wage. The job involved a lot of responsibilities. Life's essentials like eating, drinking, sleeping, heating, and hygiene were catered for in rudimentary ways at a price. 'Poore prisoners' could hope to get regular rations of bread, beef, and beer. The rule of thumb was that they ate what they earned 'by their own labour', as Cheshire justices put it. If they

[184] Hearing and Bridges, *Dorset Quarter Sessions Order Book*, 167, 380, 387, 363, 413; NRO Y/C/19/5, fo. 274; Y/C/19/6, fo. 182.

[185] BRO R/AC1/1/2, fo. 91; R/AC1/1/3, fo. 355; R/AC1/1/4, fo. 48; CA QJB/3/1, fo. 46; QJB/3/2, fo. 144; HA Q/SM/1, fo. 48.

[186] LMA MJ/SBR/3, fo. 58; BRO R/Z8/1; R/AC1/1/2, fo. 91; Hearing and Bridges, *Dorset Quarter Sessions Order Book*, 413–14.

[187] GA Q/SaIb/1, fo. 7; Q/SO/1/1, fo. 58; NRO Norwich Sessions Book 1629–36, fo. 43v; Y/C/29/5, fo. 274; NOTTA C/QSM/1/12, fo. 267; ESBHRO QO/EW2, fo. 4v.

[188] KAC WQ/O/3, fo. 98; ERO D/B5/Gb1, fo. 161; CKS TE/S2, fos. 46, 29, 46, 98; T/C1/4, fo. 89; T/C1/5, fo. 247; J. E. Earwaker, ed., *The Constables' Accounts of the Manor of Manchester From the Year 1612 to the Year 1647 and From the Year 1743 to the Year 1776*, 3 vols (Manchester, 1891–1902), III, 74. See also ESBHRO WQ/I2, fo. 12; CKS Q/SM/A/1, fo. 11 (Maidstone); OHC C/FC/1/A1/03, fo. 81; NA NQS/3, fo. 73; NRO Norwich Bridewell Treasurers' Accounts 1, 1585–6; 2, fo. 59v.

[189] NRO Norwich Sessions Book 1602–18, fos. 177v, 196, 247v.

do not work, they said, 'then noe foode allowed but water and very thin drink [and] coarse bred or a few food beanes [and] a piece of bullocks liver or sheeps liver' three days each week (and 'for their lodgeing only strawe'). Men 'earne by theire worke 4d daily', Reading's governors ruled in 1621, women '3d daily', and '2d daily for boys and girls'.[190] Prisoners were given hand-outs now and then and were sometimes allowed to beg from an appointed place. A storehouse inventory from Ipswich in 1592 listed 'one longe cheyne for the barr gate for to tye a prysoner to begg at'; 2s. 8d. was spent in Norwich in 1588 for 'a tymber wyndow wheare the prysoners [in bridewell] looke out', hoping to get something from passers-by.[191] 'The prisoners of alegate' in Gloucester had a ladder in 1550 'to go up to the wyndowe' to beg.[192] Fuel was a priority in cold times. There was extra coal for prisoners in Norwich 'in tyme of could wether' in 1597. The 'master of the bridewell howse' in Thetford spent 26s. 8d. in 1630 to buy 'two able chalders of coale' for the 'comforte of inmates'. Prisoners in Gloucester 'northgate' were given 3s. 2d. worth of 'coales' 'in colde weather' and 3s. 6d. 'in ye great frost' in 1613.[193] 'A paire of bellowes' kept prisoners warm in Norwich in 1625.[194] Hygiene was taken seriously for the most part, evident in payments for 'sweepinge' and 'clensinge' and 'caryeng mucke' away. Other fees covered 'fyringe the howse of office' in Norwich Bridewell in 1617; 'makinge cleane' Gloucester Bridewell in 1643; and washing linen and supplying 'fresh strawe everie moneth' at Clerkenwell Bridewell.[195] Salisbury's steward was told to 'see' the 'howse and people cleanly kepte by howskeepers and laundres'. Marlborough 'blindhouse' had a 'tubb' for prisoners to clean themselves.[196]

Some of this was papering over cracks. Prison, Geoffrey Mynshul said, was 'a grave to bury men alive'. It was 'a little world of woe' and 'map of misery', he continued, and 'stinks more than the lord mayors dogg-house or Paris Garden' in hot summers. Prison was an 'unholsom...pitifull dog-hole' and a health hazard with its own sickness—'gaol fever'—that took many lives.[197] Southampton 'gaole' was reported to be 'very fowlie and filthily kepte' in 1600, with 'noysome stincks very dangerous to breed some infectious diseasse'. The 'vaults of [Maidstone] gaole' were 'very noysome' and needed emptying in 1640, with neighbours complaining bitterly that they were 'much troubled' with 'smoake which

[190] CA QJB/1/5, fos. 127–7v BRO R/Z8/1. See also HA Q/3/3, fos. 122, 176; LMA MJ/SBR/2, fo. 273; GA GBR/G/G3/SO/1, fo. 4.

[191] SAI C/3/4/1/22, fo. 10; NRO Norwich Bridewell Treasurers' Accounts 1, 1588.

[192] GA GBR/F/4/3, fo. 29v.

[193] NRO Norwich Bridewell Treasurers' Accounts 1, 1597; T/C1/4, fos. 105–6; GA GBR/F/4/6, fo. 479.

[194] NRO Norwich Chamblerlains' Accounts 1603–25, fo. 417.

[195] NRO Norwich Bridewell Treasurers' Accounts 1, 1604; Norwich Chamberlains' Accounts 1580–9, fos. 29v, 302v; GA GBR/F/4/5, fos. 41, 222v; LMA MJ/SBR/2, fo. 274.

[196] WSHC G23/1/3, fos. 291–1v; G22/1/205/2, fos. 113v, 131, 135v, 139v, 143v, 166, 174. See also CKS TE/S2, fo. 134; BRO WI/FA1/2, fo. 23.

[197] G. Mynshul, *Characters of Prisons and Prisoners* (1638), 3.

commeth out of the gaole' all winter long.[198] Life began and ended in prison. 'Poore' Susan Gardner breathed her first breath in Ipswich Bridewell in 1639 as her mother was breathing her last. Jane Wiseman was 'begotten with child whilest she was in [Bury St Edmunds] gaole' in 1641 waiting trial for 'felony confessed'. A blind fiddler's wife gave birth in a Manchester dungeon 'not halfe an hower' after being picked up for begging in 1624, 'whilest the passe was makinge' to send her home.[199] Edward Hext wrote to Lord Egerton from Somerset around 1600 to tell him about the 'multytude [in] the gaole' perched 'over a river so cold' that it poisoned people coming into the 'gayle'. He reckoned that 'above cxl' had lost their lives 'by the very infecon of the gayle'. Judges set aside a 'thowsand markes' to build 'a newe gayle and with yt a house of correccon'; 'I have nowe xl men at worke about yt', Hext ended, more upbeat now.[200] Prisoners' deaths in Dorchester 'gaol' were noted down in the 'Offenders' Book': 'condemned man' John Degoma fell sick one morning in 1632 and 'died' that day; Christopher Pepper 'languished of a sicknes' for three months before he left this life in 1635.[201] Inmates were 'decentlie buried' in the Middlesex 'house'. The bridewell dead were buried at a cost of sixteen shillings each in Norwich in 1697. The 'master of [Herefordshire] house of correccon' got twenty shillings in 1677 for 'shrowds, burialls and other things' for six 'felons' who were taken by smallpox. Prisoners also dropped dead from plague.[202]

Like Humphrey Buckingham in South Molton, keepers were supposed to take care of their sick. This often meant paying 'churgions' to treat sick prisoners. A Maidstone 'chiurgeon' filed three 'bills' for 'physick and churugery' for 'prisoners in the gaole and house of correccon' in 1584, with three following later in the same year: £6 8s. 9d., £4 2s. 6d., and £6 12s. 5d.[203] Similar payments turn up in Norwich Bridewell accounts: twelve shillings for 'apothecary' Valentine Pell in 1695; 'Mr Lad the surgeon' got £1 for curing a man's hand in 1637; and 'Mr Hobart the surgion' got fifteen shillings for 'healynge of a woman' in 1605. Other 'hurts' healed included lame hands and legs and a boy with no name whose illness was called 'his hurt'.[204] A 'surgion' was 'appoynted' at London Bridewell in 1580 with the help of St Bartholomew's Hospital. The first of them, William Pickering, got £3 in 1581 'for heling of dyverse poore within brydewell'. There was a quick traffic in 'surgions'. Pickering was soon followed by Henry Terry, who lasted months

198 SA 6/1, fos. 24, 73; Melling, *Kentish Sources*, 213.

199 SAI B/105/2/1, fos. 6v, 63v; ERO D/B5/SB2/9, fos. 173v–4; Earwaker, *Constables' Accounts of the Manor of Manchester*, I, 130. See also CKS Q/SM/A/1, fo. 18v (Maidstone); NRO Norwich Clavors Book 1, fo. 97v.

200 HL EL/2688.

201 DHC DC/DOB/1, fos. 63v, 65, 67, 111v, 121v, 266v.

202 LMA MJ/SBR/2, fo. 274; NRO Norwich Bridewell Treasurers' Accounts 1, 1585/7, 1609, 1612; 2, fo. 63v; HEA BG/11/7, fos. 3, 13, 17, 21, 22, 25; Q/SM/4, fo. 55.

203 CKS Q/SM/A/1, fo. 17v (Canterbury); Q/SM/A/2, fos. 2, 9, 11v, 17v (Maidstone).

204 NRO Norwich Bridewell Treasurers' Accounts 1, 1591, 1599, 1603, 1605, 1609; 2, fos. 24, 61; NMCC 14, fo. 246; 20, fos. 306v, 350v; 25, fos. 11v, 66v, 113.

before Edward Bailey stepped into his shoes to 'faythfullye cure deseased people within brydwell'. A July 1581 memorandum lists 'patients cured [by] henry terry surgion' in the last month, whose 'hurts' included 'lame leggs', 'yoints', and toes; 'swoellne' legs and knees; face, feet, and arm ulcers; 'sore' legs, mouths, hands, throats, and cheeks; foot strains, finger wounds, 'wrenched' hands, 'broken' heads and arms, and an 'ynposton in chyne'.[205] Herefordshire justices issued payments for 'distempered' 'poore prisoner' Frances Davis in 1683, but the outlook was bleak as she struggled 'in a very sad condicon with smallpox'.[206]

There was another sort of recovery that was an aim inside bridewells and prisons, although it is not one that is always associated with punishment at this time. Michel Foucault in *Discipline and Punish* (1975) told us that the idea of reforming offenders to make them think about what they had done and might become developed after 1800 with solitary confinement at the flagship Pentonville Prison (1842). Before then authority focused on physical punishment rather than reforming offenders. Most scholars now moderate this argument, but an unspoken assumption persists that reforming wrongdoers was a low priority in early modern times. In fact, it was quite the reverse! 'Do it vigorously [and] spedily', John Kitchin preached in 1660, 'reform and reform vigorously and speedily'.[207] These thoughts were readily put into practice in legal fields. 'The end of punishment', Nathanael Ellison told Newcastle's elite, 'is to make bad men good and good men better'. 'Correction without instruction makes the master a tyrant', Thomas Browning said in *Prison Thoughts* (1682).[208] If punishment is 'properly inflicted', Charles Richardson said in *Concerning the Punishment of Malefactors* (1616), 'the party delinquent is by this means reformed and brought to live in better order'. Edward Cressy believed that any 'prison ought to be a school of repentance'.[209] Some commentary on the 1610 Act dwelt on reforming offenders. 'I may assign severe punishment and hard labour in the house of correction' according to the statute 7.Jac.1.c.4, Hugh Hare said in his 'charge' at Surrey quarter sessions in 1692, 'for so long time as shall be thought necessary for their chastisement and reformation'.[210] The author of *An Ease for Overseers of the Poore* (1601) urged that the 'willfull and incorrigible must be constrained to worke in the house of correction [so] that by applying labour and punishment of their bodies their forward natures may be bridled [and] their evill mindes may be bettered'. These words appeared almost unaltered in Michael Dalton's *Country Justice*

[205] SBHA SSHHB/HA/1/2, fos. 142v, 147v, 154, 159–9v, 165.

[206] HEA Q/SM/4, fo. 172v.

[207] J. Kitchin, *The Grand Statute: or the Law of Death Unalterable, Opened and Applied in a Sermon Preached May 11 1660* (1660), 18.

[208] N. Ellison, *The Magistrates Obligation to Punish Vice* (1700), 34; T. Browning, *Prison Thoughts* (1682), 31.

[209] C. Richardson, *A Sermon Concerning the Punishment of Malefactors* (1616), 7, 22; E. Cressy, *Spiritual Directions for Hospitals, Houses of Corrections and Prisons* (1675), 14.

[210] H. Hare, *A Charge Given at the General Quarter Sessions of the Peace for the County of Surrey Holden at Dorking on Tuesday the 5th Day of April 1692* (1692), 18.

(1618). Cheshire justices wanted their new county bridewell to 'subdue the people to subjection' in 1631 in the words of E. M. Leonard. Acle Bridewell (Norfolk) was revealingly called the house of 'reformation'.[211]

Local magistrates echoed these words of reformation. Oxford council 'desired for theire reformacon that idle people [who] wander aboute being able of bodye to worke' should be sent to the bridewell in 1655. 'Obstinate persons as shall refuse to be reformed' must be sent to the bridewell, Salisbury magistrates ruled in 1596.[212] Any 'of able bodyes refusing to work', Cheshire justices ordered in 1638, should be put in a bridewell 'to remayne and worke [until] they shalbee reclaymed from lewd and idle life'. The main aim in Kent in 1612 was 'reformation of the idle and disordered' in bridewells, while vagrants were put in Clerkenwell Bridewell in 1617 to be 'reduced to goodness'.[213] Intent matters; we draw interpretations from intentions. Offenders played to this hope of reformation of life. Margaret Rutter left Norwich Bridewell in 1683 to go to her brother 'upon her promise to reforme her evell and lewd life'. Norwich scold Martha Mason promised 'to live orderly'. Another offender said that he would 'become a good and civill man'. Softer treatment was possible if offenders seemed 'penitent' or gave their solid word not to 'offend in the like faulte again'. Mary Soamer was set free from Norwich Bridewell in 1618 on her 'promise of reforemacon'. A London nightwalker was sent home to her husband in 1641 after he 'promised to kepe her at home and reforme her'.[214]

But there were also times when magistrates put their hands up in the air in despair, knowing that someone could not be 'reclaimed'. 'They will not be by any frynds reclaymed', Norwich governors said, casting rueful looks at the Bate brothers. 'Idle [and] dangerous roague' William cannot 'be reformed' of 'his roageishe lyfe', Hampshire justices concluded in 1650, knowing that he had been whipped 'in severall places' and 'branded on the shoulder with the letter R'.[215] Anne Goodier is in London Bridewell records for eleven years starting in 1630: for vagrancy (twelve times), nightwalking (five), walking late at night and mixing with men 'suspiciously' (both twice), and cheating (once). She was also sent across the river to St Thomas's Hospital four times to be healed of the 'fowle diesease'. The last time she appears is a midnight walk in 1641. 'She will not be reformed', Bridewell's governors sighed, and we never see her again.[216]

In a world where medical and spiritual healing went hand in hand it is no surprise that religion was part of daily diets in hospitals for the sick: Mr Batho was

[211] *An Ease for Overseers of the Poore* (1601), 19; M. Dalton. *The Country Justice* (1661 edition), 122; LMA Jour. 20, fo. 502v; E. M. Leonard, *The Early History of English Poor Relief* (1900), 248.

[212] OHC C/FC/1/A1/03, fo. 230v; WSHC G23/1/3, fo. 156v.

[213] CA QJB/1/5, fo. 471; CKS U120/09, fo. 35; LMA MJ/SBR/2, fo. 411.

[214] NRO NMCC 7, fo. 305; 8, fo. 11; 15, fo. 180; 20, fo. 368; 24, fos. 206v, 385; 25, fo. 167; LBHC 8, fo. 356; 5, fo. 361; BMM LBHC 4, fos. 5v, 95v, 193v, 337, 419v, 467v.

[215] NRO NMCC 12, fo. 105; 25, fo. 307; HA Q1/3, fo. 48.

[216] For Goodier see my *Lost Londons*, 155–6.

paid £12 'for servinge and ministeringe the poore folkes in God's howse' in Norwich in 1618/19; Tooley's Hospital in Ipswich picked Mr Paddle 'to catechise and instructe [inmates] in the principles of religion' in 1610.[217] Magistrates hoped that religion and confinement with time to think would bring desired 'reformation'. Middlesex Bridewell was nearing completion in 1615 when justices began a job search for a 'discreete and honest person' to be 'reader of divine service and praiers [in] the howse'. He was to 'reade publique prayers' every day 'at the leaste [and] twice everie sabboth daye'. The successful candidate would see that inmates were 'carefullie instructed and chatechized in the articles of theire faythe [and] points of religion as tend to salvacon of their soules'.[218] Prisoners prayed in the 'morninge or eveninge' each Wednesday and Friday in Christ's Hospital Ipswich and 'morninge and eveninge' on Sundays. 'Mr Owen of St Peter of Hungate' was paid £4 for leading 'divine service and prayer' at Norwich Bridewell each Sunday and 'other times' in 1616 (he got £3 two years later). Minister John Russell, who was locked up in the debtors' prison in Dorchester, became minister of the bridewell there in 1629.[219] London's two 'compters' had preachers, though aldermen were unhappy to hear that the 'word of God is seldome preached' in them in 1632 and made plans to choose 'a good and hable man [to] reade divine service and preach the word of God every Sonday'. Hampshire justices praised John Haselrine's 'good service [for] condemned persons and other prisoners in praying and preaching amongst them in the county gaole to prepare them for a future better life'.[220] It was the 'poore prisoners' in Herefordshire 'county gaole' who begged justices to agree to continue Mr Walker's 'yearely allowance' in 1678 for 'preaching and praying to theire greate comfort in theire confinements'.[221] Another way to work reformation in combination with religious lessons in bridewells was character-changing work. Work inside 'correccon houses' was supposed to heal. The bell 'tolled everye morninge at sixe, everie noone at xi and againe at xii and everie eveninge at vii' at Middlesex Bridewell in 1616 to let prisoners know when work began and ended.[222] The 'occupacons' at London Bridewell included spinning, knitting, weaving, and making buttons, pins, gloves, shoes, hats, and tennis balls. Outside Bridewell, prisoners 'clensed' Smithfield pond; dredged soil and sand from the Thames (getting six-pence if there were two tides

[217] NRO Great Hospital General Account Rolls, 1618/19, 1621/2, 1624/5; SAI C/4/3/1/1/4, fos. 33v, 111v, 228; C/2/2/2/1, fos. 182, 257–7v, 263v. See also NRO Norwich 'Childrens Hospital Booke', 1628–32, 1638–9, 1643–4; GA GBR/B/3/1, fo. 37v; GBR/B/3/3, fos. 47, 127, 630; NA 4/1, fo. 58; NDRO B1/179.

[218] LMA MJ/SBR/2, fos. 242–3.

[219] SAI C/2/2/2/1, fos. 181–2, 207; NRO NMCC 14, fo. 421v; 25, fo. 114v; Hearing and Bridges, *Dorset Quarter Sessions Order Book*, 78. See also NRO Norwich Great Hospital General Accounts 1601/4, 1604/8, 1608/9, 1610/12, 1615/26, 1618/19; Norwich Bridewell Treasurers' Accounts, 1616, 1629.

[220] LMA Rep. 27, fos. 182v, 195; HA Q/3/3, fos. 142, 188. See also LMA Rep. 47, fo. 64; Jour. 41, fos. 128, 169; NRO NMCC 25, fo. 114v; Norwich Chamberlains' Accounts 1603–25, fo, 30; 1625–48, fo. 264.

[221] HEA Q/SM/4, fo. 83.

[222] LMA MJ/SBR/2, fo. 274.

on one day); cleaned 'comon sewers and ditches' (with 'a collar of iron about the necke'); 'skowered' Tower Ditch; and cleaned streets (men and women could not 'mingle').[223] Widow Choke kept the 'weomen young and olde at worke in spinninge and cardinge' in 1634 in Reading Bridewell (she was 'knowne to be a good spinster'). We can read work in Ipswich in payments for mills ('to sett idle and stubborne and unrulie persons on worke' in 1612), wool, hemp, looms, thread, yarn, hammers, spinning wheels, 'reeles', 'beetles', 'quearnes', 'stock-cards', and other 'worke stuffe'.[224]

These were the intentions put down in rules. In 'ideal' bridewells 'mete' masters and matrons would stay in post for a decent stretch of time, running a 'house' with basic hygiene, diet, and medical care, and making sure that their 'poor' had work and religious/moral guidance. Whether or not this was the case, most prisoners did not come back. But there is a record of problems inside bridewells and prisons caused by rogue masters (and their underlings) as well as unruly inmates. We can retrieve aspirations in policies and strategies and typically we read governors complaining about what had not been done or what had gone wrong. A 'conference' was held for 'ordering' Middlesex Bridewell in 1632 to investigate the governor William Parkes. A damning charge sheet was drawn up after 'serious debating' of the 'misgovernment' of the 'house' that included 'disablinge of milles and [the] bakehouse', 'extortious and exactious fees', 'excessive and riotous expence [by] prisoners', 'undue easing of them of labour by suffering prisoners to become keepers', and letting prisoners go home without punishment. Hugh Marvyn stepped into Parkes's crooked shoes not long after.[225] Corruption tarnished other bridewells but not often on the scale that we can find in 'gayles', where keepers leaned much more heavily on squeezing fees from prisoners. Magistrates sometimes questioned what a keeper did with the 'stock' which he had pledged to use for the good of the 'house'. Some of the more stinging complaints were about work that was crucial to the bridewell project. Warwickshire justices had a 'full hearing and longe debating of the matter touchinge the house of correccon' in 1630. The master, one Hemming, was questioned 'along with witnesses'. A grand jury 'surveyed' the 'house', finding it 'altogether unfurnished of materials for ymployment and ye settinge on worke of vagrant [and] idle persons'. Also, money that was thought to be going to the 'house' was 'misymployed'. Hemming duly got his marching orders after 'divers proofes' that he was a man of 'evill behavior'.[226]

There were 'rogue' keepers and others who were quite simply not up to scratch. Somerset justices believed that 'the age and unfitness' of the bridewell 'master' was the reason why Taunton and its surrounding areas were 'pestered with great numbers of wandering and disorderly persons' in 1624. Something needed to be

[223] Griffiths, *Lost Londons*, 253; LBHC 7, fo. 298.

[224] BRO R/Z8/1; R/AC1/1/3, fo. 307; R/FA/3/17; SAI C/4/3/1/1/4, fo. 71. See also HEA Q/SM/2, fo. 3; Q/SM/4, fo. 46; NRO NMCC 14, fo. 417v; 15, fo. 53v; NA NQS/3, sheet inserted inside book.

[225] LMA MJ/SRB/5, fos. 329, 330, 358.

[226] WRO QS0040/1/1, fo. 79.

done, North Riding justices said, on hearing that the master of Thirsk Bridewell was now 'old and infirm'. This they felt spelt danger.[227] Other 'masters' were said to be 'very unfit' or 'of small abilities'. A lengthy investigation concluded that the fire that 'consumed' Devizes Bridewell in 1630 'began through the [master's] negligence' in making a 'kiln [in] that part of the howse which was soe burnt for the dryeinge of mault'. The cost of rebuilding was put at £137 10s.[228] Even political affiliations intervened at times to cast doubt on the integrity of a bridewell keeper. 'Informacion' flooded into Preston Guildhall in 1691 saying that William Tomlinson, 'governor of the howse of correccon', was 'ill affected to their majesties and the government' and 'very unfitt' for his post. He was sacked at the first opportunity. Tomlinson was not the first Preston keeper to alienate magistrates, who asked in 1683 whether Thomas Anderton 'should continue' in post after hearing that he was 'an unfit and falty person in several respects and in particular by his non residence'.[229] John Evans of Great Torrington in North Devon filed a 'humble peticon' to justices. He 'hath ever byn a loyal subject unto his late majesty of famous memory [he said] and alsoe his royall majesty that nowe is kinge charles the second'. Richard Vann, on the other hand, took 'accon against his late majesty' yet is 'intrusted with the bridewell [and] stock of the county' that he uses to 'a great benefit unto himselfe'. His 'humble request' was that 'your worshipps will in due time settle the bridewell [on me and be sure that I will] ever pray for your happines'. There were twenty other signatures at the foot of his petition, which was successful in this political climate when the monarchy was restored after eleven long years. 'We conceave [that] the petitioner [is] as fitt as any other' is written down under Evans's words.[230]

There was an expectation that there would be trouble inside bridewells and prisons. In 1616 orders for 'government of the howse of correccon... att Clerkenwell', justices told officials to do everything necessary for 'ye sure making of all places for safetie so as none can breake out'. Women were 'not to be intermingled with the men or lodged in their lodginges' but live in 'decencie' in seven rooms that were set aside for them. A 'hatch' was added in 1626 to 'restraine souldiers from enteringe weomens wards'.[231] Reading Bridewell had 'distinct roomes for men [and] weomen by themselves to lodge and work' in 1621. 'A particon' was built in a cellar to keepe men asunder from women' in Oxford Bridewell in 1638.[232] Bridewells were equipped with restraints to immobilize anyone who caused trouble. A 1622 list from Norwich included 'two paires of shackles', 'two paires of pothookes', 'two paires of manacles', and 'three blockes with shackles'.

[227] Bates, *Quarter Sessions Records for the County of Somerset*, I, 352; Atkinson, *North Riding Quarter Sessions Records*, VII, 23.

[228] WSHC G22/1/26. See also CRO QJB/1/5, fos. 127–7v; DHC DC/DOB/8/1, fo. 68v; Hearing and Bridges, *Dorset Quarter Sessions Order Book*, 387.

[229] B. W. Quintrell. ed., *Proceedings of the Lancashire Justices of the Peace at the Sheriff's Table During Assizes Week, 1578–1694*, Lancashire and Cheshire Record Society, 121 (1981), 161, 145.

[230] NDRO 2558M/11/8.

[231] LMA MJ/SBR/2, fos. 274, 242–3; MJ/SBR/4, fo. 370.

[232] BRO R/Z8/1; OHC C/FC/1/A1/03, fo. 90. See also NA NQS/4, loose sheet; LMA Rep. 57, fo. 218.

'Handcuffes' were listed in 1660.[233] A 1592 inventory from Ipswich prison listed five pairs of shackles, five 'manackles', a 'neck coller without a chayne', and another collar 'with a chayne'. 'Fetters and revetts' and 'cloggs' were added not long after. 'Pothookes', 'cheans', 'manacles', 'shakells', and 'boults' are listed in other inventories and accounts.[234] Troublemakers were 'shackled', 'manacled', or 'fettered' in London Bridewell. Thomas Venables was 'mannacled and fettered' there after lunging at officers with a bottle. 'Prissner convict and mutinous in Newgate' John Gwyne was 'kept at worke in chaynes and fettered' in 1618.[235] 'Rogues and vagabonds' in Sherborne were shackled 'using fetters [and] gyves' in 1629. Nottinghamshire justices were troubled to hear that there were not enough 'lockes, bolts, gives, [and] beetles' to restrain a recent surge of 'wandring persons' in 1654 (and six months later).[236] There was resistance. 'Yf you laye a blocke on my hele', 'great molestor, trobler and disquyeter' Thomas Ebbots growled in prison in Norwich in 1577, leaving threats hanging in the air. He had been locked up for 'wish[ing that] the cittie [was] better governed'. William Corkell was put in the stocks in the same city in 1600 'for lewdly behaving himselfe [in prison by] offeringe' to set the doors 'a fyer and breaking his yrons'.[237] There was also 'close' confinement. The lord chief justice ordered that John Bingham 'be kepte a close prisoner' in 1606 in London Bridewell 'and noe body to speake with him'. A 'room' was 'made over the gatehouse' in the same 'house' in 1626 to keep 'close prisoners in security'.[238] 'Rude' Frances Wootten was 'putt in [a] turret' in 1641 until she became 'quiet'. Thomas Cockerell was 'put in the hole' in Norwich 'gaol' in 1660 for causing trouble 'amonge [the] prisoners' and was told later that he could go back to the 'free chamber so longe as he behaved himself civilly'.[239]

We think of whips when we think of punishment inside bridewells. Whips and work were meant to 'reform', 'subdue', or 'correct'. East Sussex justices ruled in 1655 that anyone sent 'to remayne for one yeare' would get 'correction' at 'their coming in and going out' and 'every month'; anyone who was there for a shorter time was whipped 'every fortnight' and 'at their coming [and] going out'.[240] 'Every rogue, vagabond, idle wandering and disorderlie person' was whipped on Friday afternoon in Speenhamland Bridewell; the number of lashes was lower for anyone judged to be 'milde, penitent', and 'conformable' (no one could leave until they had been whipped twice).[241] 'Masterles' Judith Stile was given xx 'whipps at her

[233] NRO NMCC 23, fo. 115.

[234] SAI C/3/4/1/22, fo. 10; C/3/4/1/34, fo. 9. See also CA QJB/1/5, fos. 127–7v, 286; LBHC 5, fo. 97; 6, fo. 414; 8, fo. 35v.

[235] LBHC 1, fos. 8v–9; 5, fo. 229v; 6, fo. 58v; 8, fos. 132, 136v, 151.

[236] Hearing and Bridges, *Dorset Quarter Sessions Order Book*, 80; NOTTA C/QSM/1/13, fos. 8v–9, 18. See also NRO NMCC 8, fo. 690; 10, fo. 677; 15, fo. 275; DRO ECA B/1/4, fo. 72. For prison restraints see CKS TE/S2, fo. 314; NA 3/1, fo. 338; LMA Rep. 13(2), fos. 281v, 516; NRO NMCC 7, fo. 461; 8, fo. 249; 9, fos. 28, 265; GA GBR/F/4/5, fos. 33v, 201v; GBR/F/4/6, fo. 383.

[237] NRO NMCC 10, fo. 10; 13, fo. 418.

[238] LBHC 5, fo. 97; 6, fo. 414.

[239] LBHC 8, fo. 35v; NRO NMCC 23, fo. 115.

[240] ESBHRO QO/EW3, fos. 9, 16v.

[241] BRO R/Z8/1.

entrance' to Exeter Bridewell in 1620. Mary Hartley, who was 'indicted for felony' in York in 1653 but 'found guiltie of pettie larceny, [was] severely whipt daily in the house of correction'.[242] Escape was on the minds of more than a few. A 'complaynt' was filed against the Lewes keeper in 1684 after 'several' escapes in under a week. John Tapscott—'as he named himselfe'—was caught in Bideford after breaking out of Exeter prison in 1685 with twelve other prisoners.[243] Prisoners broke walls, windows, bars, and 'boordes' to escape. Inmates in Ludgate Prison in London dug a tunnel. Thief Henry Locke with four others sawed a 'great hole' in the porter's wall in London Bridewell. A Norwich smith, 'having his eyelede hanging downe', escaped from bridewell 'att a windoe' in 1600.[244] Compulsory quarantine orders in the high heat of plague were not enough to stop people slipping out of 'infected' houses. It's hardly a surprise, then, to see offenders trying to break out of prison. No bridewell or prison was escape-proof. Keeper John Ackland told Exeter magistrates that Alice Broadmead, who stole clothes off a hedge in 1622, had not long broken out of his bridewell by 'undermining a wall'. 'She is a verie whore', he added. Ackland told the same magistrates two years earlier the story of how John Sampford 'came into the house of correccon to speak with his wyfe' and 'seeing' that Ackland was not there 'wilfullie' got his wife and took her away shouting that 'he woulde be the deathe of him' that tried to 'take' them. Husband and wife walked to the 'west gate' where they pawned her smock for cash to 'drincke in ale', arguing with others who 'reproved' them. 'He would fyre the howse', Sampford said, if they were locked up. The pair then strutted up and down the high street in full public gaze and she was rearrested soon after and put back in bridewell. The last we hear is Sampford telling Ackland that he would be hanged and putting 'his hand to his throate sayinge yt woulde be but a halter and a knott'. Asked 'where he hath lead his life for these sixe weekes' one year later in the same city, Alexander Skinner, who was suspected of felony, said that he had been 'committed to bridewell by Mr Ignatius Jurdayne but made an escape' on Christmas Eve. 'Ever synce', he said, he had lived 'about the cytie'.[245]

Escape is one part of Susan Hobbs's larger story about a family on the fringes of society that takes a shocking turn towards the end. Hobbs was examined in Reading in 1627 and told magistrates that she 'liveth by travelinge the countrye and sellinge small wares'. She was on her way from Middlesex to Hampshire and stopped off in Reading as she was 'acquainted with a woman' who was locked up

[242] TNA STAC8 161/10, Ignatius Jourdain answer; DRO ECA C1/61, fos. 121, 339; YCA F7, fo, 350. See also NRO NMCC 14, fo. 459; T/QS/1, fo. 49v; YCA F7, fo. 402; CA QJB/1/4, fo. 182v; SAI B/105/2/2, fo. 54; KAC WQ/O/4, fo. 174v. Prisons also had whipping posts, stocks, and pillories. See, for example, NRO T/QS/1, fo. 11v; NA NQS/3, fo. 110; OHC C/FC/1/A1/01, fo. 356v; Hearing and Bridges, *Dorset Quarter Sessions Order Book*, 97, 185, 279, 368.

[243] ESBHRO QO/EW8, fo. 188v; NDRO 1064Q/SO1, table.

[244] Forster, *Lay-mans Lawyer*, 161; Griffiths, *Lost Londons*, 156; NRO NMCC 13, fo. 498; 14, fo. 394; 15, fo. 253v. See also BRO R/FA/3/15; NRO Norwich Bridewell Treasurers' Accounts 1, 1603, 1611; Chamberlains Accounts 1589–1602, fo. 187.

[245] DRO ECA C1/62, fo. 5; C1/61, fos. 486–7, 579–80.

in the 'gaole' (how did she know she was there?) but was 'apprehended as a vagrant' as she made her way through the town. A surprise followed when Hobbes said that she had 'ii daughters in the house of correccon' (had they travelled with her from Middlesex?), adding that 'her sonne Matthewe was hanged abowt the duches of Lenox plate'. It was 2 May. Hobbs was put in Reading Bridewell on May Day (there are smudges over this line that block out words written there later, and I can only make out 'being…wth the…childe') but 'ran awaye out of the house'. She was soon back and 'rayled against the officers and voluntarily saide that [bridewell] was noe place for her [for] she had killed a childe' by knocking him or her on the head, 'and buryed it at Colebrooke townes end about ii yeeres past' (Colebrooke in Devon?). After this bombshell, one of Hobbs's daughters—spinster Grace Allen—admitted helping her mother to kill and bury 3-year-old orphan Elizabeth (whose parents 'dyed at Newgate') in a gravel pit. They dug her up the next day and buried her in a churchyard with help from 'a poore wandering symple fellowe'. A second daughter—Joyce, who was nineteen years old—backed up her sister's story, adding that it had been 'a trouble' to 'carrye it aboute with them [as Elizabeth did not stop] byting and scratchynge'. 'The will of God be done', her mother said. The mother and her eldest daughter were committed to the 'gaole until the next assizes'.[246]

Keepers often had a bad press. They 'most commonly are insinuating knaves and mercenary rascals', lawyer Geoffrey Mynshul said icily in 1638. 'They will doe anything' for money, he mocked, 'cruelty to prisoners is policy'. This is too general, but Mynshul's 'mercanaries' existed in stories of 'excessive' fees, 'abuses and injuries', 'hardship', 'greate calamities', and cases when 'gaolers' either turned a blind eye or gave prisoners a helping hand to escape.[247] Reading 'gaole' was turned into 'a comon alehouse' by its 'gaolers', magistrates there claimed in 1652. 'Maye it please you to be advertized', a mole tipped off Reading magistrates, 'that the keeper of the howse of correccon (Ballard by name) intertayneth poore mens children [and] servants by daye and by nighte suffering them to be typlinge and spending their money until they be druncken'. Goodwife Miller, who was in charge of female inmates in Winchester 'Hospital', lost her job for 'making the hospital a comon alehouse'.[248] Bridewell became London's biggest brothel for six months in 1602. Sinking finances were behind the aldermen's decision to hand over its running to 'private' 'undertakers' led by Thomas Stanley, who promised to put finances back in order. But rumours of 'misgovernment' soon circulated. There did not seem to be many vagrants walking in and out of Bridewell's great

[246] BRO R/AC1/1/2, fos. 250, 255.

[247] Mynshul, *Characters of Prisons and Prisoners*, 50, 57. See also LMA Reps. 45, fo. 22; 49, fos. 306–6v; NA NQS/1, fo. 89v; OHC Oxfordshire Sessions Rolls E/31; M/22; EP/39; NRO NMCC 20, fo. 488. For examples of collusion in escapes see CA QJB/3/1, fo. 238; LMA WJ/SR/NS/36/55; SAI B/105/2/1, fo. 63v; DRO ECA B/1/3, fo. 83.

[248] BRO R/AC1/1/5, fo. 112; R/Z3/13; HA W/B1/7, fo. 189.

gate any more. What aldermen found instead was Stanley as brothel-keeper not Bridewell-manager. There were no vagrants to be seen in the cells. But the women who should have been behind bars were now Bridewell's star attraction. City inspections discovered 'lighte and lewde' women dressed in 'gorgeous apparrell sitting and supp[ing]' with well-heeled gentlemen 'in the fairest roomes', tucking in to 'crabbs, lobsters, artichoque pyes and gallons of wyne' before peeling off in pairs.[249]

One reason why bridewells needed 'fitt' masters was that the threat of disorder always lingered below the surface. A hothead might walk in through the door or a row break out in cramped quarters. But nobody could have anticipated the trouble at the Middlewich 'house' in 1643 when two dozen people broke in and occupied it. They included two widows, a mother and three children, two married couples and their children, and a childless couple. They were accused of 'entering and abuseing the house of correction'. Justices ordered constables in the next year to remove 'lewde persons as have unlawfully entered the [bridewell] and made there abode'. The 'house is much spoyled', they said, putting the blame on officers who left the squatters alone.[250] The edgy atmosphere inside many bridewells could spill over into unrest as when Dutch cutpurses 'made a mutiny' in London Bridewell. Norwich governors were 'enformed' in 1617 'that Gurny Delfe and Clem Blynge prisoners in the house of correction conspired together that [if] the master should offer to laye hold or correct any of them that then they woulde strike [him] with whatsoever they had in their hands'. 'By that meanes', aldermen were told, 'the women and other prisoners in the house began to be in a mutyny'.[251] Alice Sandes said that Dorothy Smith tried to 'force her to hange hirself' in London Bridewell in 1575, telling her 'that yf any... did so the howse sholde be put downe'. She also 'saide that manie whores saide they wolde hang themselves'. Sandes, Smith, and three others were brought to court for being 'unrulie' in the cells 'and swering and thretnynge to hange them selves'. We also have fevered reports of 'insurrecons and mutinyes' from various 'gaols'.[252]

Resistance more commonly took the form of lashing out with fists or words or refusing to toe the line. Gloucester servant Arthur Wheeler 'persevered in obstinancie' after he was locked up in 1633 for behaving 'verie disorderlie towards [his] master', shouting 'that hee would come out of bridewell this daie in spite of his masters teeth'. Prisoners got in trouble for 'abusinge' keepers like John Gape, who made a second court appearance in Dorchester in 1629 for 'playing vives in the gaole and abusing the keeper of the house of correction and his people'.[253]

249 Griffiths, *Lost Londons*, 221; G. Ungerer, 'Prostitution in late Elizabethan London: the case of Mary Newborough', *Medieval and Renaissance Drama in England*, 15 (2003), 182–91.

250 CA QJB/1/6, fos. 112v, 133v.

251 Griffiths, *Lost Londons*, 163; NRO NMCC 15, fo. 149.

252 LBHC 2, fo. 135. See also WSHC A1/160/1, Hilary 1650 sessions; LMA Reps. 51, fo. 325; 60, fo. 37; BRO R/Z8/1; NRO Norwich Bridewell Treasurers' Accounts 1, 1619; NMCC 20, fo. 346.

253 GA GBR/G/G3/SO/1, fo. 16; DHC DC/DOB/8/1, fo. 6v. See also NRO NMCC 13, fo. 53; 14, fo. 251; LBHC 2, fo. 135; Blades, *Oxford Quarter Sessions Order Book*, 1–2.

The work that mattered so much could go horribly wrong. We could most likely pluck examples from any bridewell. A large number of prisoners in London Bridewell 'downed tools' or ruined their work in the mid-1570s. Nearly all were women who were taken to task because they 'will not worke' or be 'ruled by the matrone'. Jane Dale (alias Witton) was whipped and 'sett to labor' in 1575 'for that she will not worke with the matron and stryveth with her and will not be ordered'. Others 'spoyled' or 'marred' work. Sibyl Love and three other women were called 'comon spoylers of their worcke' in the same year. She was whipped again in the next year for not working and was one of four women who with Alice Sandes said that they would hang themselves in Bridewell.[254] Not many months passed by in most bridewells without something going wrong, but bridewells became essential elements in law and order cultures and systems in the century after 1550.

V

Not unsurprisingly, fewer 'new' bridewells were opened in the second half of the seventeenth century. Innes counts one new one in every four years after 1630, though there is also a busier parallel story of refurbishments and repairs. But there were worrying lags too when a county or town found itself without a fully functioning bridewell. There was streamlining, as when Devon closed down bridewells that were too far from Exeter to create a single coordinated focus on the county town.[255] But the value of bridewells for unruly paupers and managing poor relief systems was rarely if ever seriously questioned. Far from being considered failures, there was a spate of new bridewells in the three decades after 1690 in growing urban and industrial regions for the most part. A parallel movement resulted in perhaps three dozen towns opening workhouses that were partner institutions to bridewells in ongoing efforts to discipline the poor. Legal records also show that a good number of people prosecuted by Societies for the Reformation of Manners around 1700 were sent to bridewells.[256] Houses of correction still housed the troublesome poor in the eighteenth century and were seen in a new creative lights as somewhere to lock up felons under groundbreaking legislation in 1706 that was the culmination of a century long call to use hard labour as an alternative to hanging (the number of committals dwindled after the 1718 Transportation Act).[257] Bridewells continued to play a large role in these

[254] LBHC 2, fo. 87; 3, fo. 58v. See also Ibid., fos. 69, 75, 76v, 210, 266; 3, fos. 12, 69, 75v, 79, 84, 187.

[255] Innes, 'Prisons for the poor', 77.

[256] Ibid., 79, 83; T. Hitchcock, 'The English Workhouse: A Study in Institutional Poor Relief in Selected Counties 1696–1750' (DPhil thesis, University of Oxford, 1985); R. B. Shoemaker, *Prosecution and Punishment: Petty Crime and the Law in London and Rural Middlesex, c.1660–1725* (Cambridge, 1991), chap. 9.

[257] J. M. Beattie, *Policing and Punishment in London 1660–1750: Urban Crime and the Limits of Terror* (Oxford, 2001), chap. 7.

felony fields over the next 100 years. Growing numbers were held in them until trial for felony; more convicted felons were put in bridewells in the final third of the eighteenth century. Differences with prisons grew thinner.

So it seems premature to sum up the record of bridewells in earlier periods as 'poor'. There were nagging issues like funding or keeping order, and management was a shambles at times. But as damaging as such things could be, they should not detract from the extent to which bridewells were embedded in social welfare/discipline schemes, legal/penal systems, and local economies and societies. Imagined in terms of domesticity and dependency and charged to restore broken domestic relations, bridewells were synonymous with households. Whether operating around households or the margins of poor relief, bridewells became key tools in governing apparatus. They were crafted to suit the local needs of industrial, agricultural, coastal, or thickly populated urban areas. This flexibility was amplified by the 'generall and large power' to lock up people in bridewells for leading 'unsettled' lives. Bridewells affected the lives of countless thousands on the lowest rungs of social ladders. Their origins, development, and meaning lay in pressing questions of the times: how to cope with the 'imployment and government' of growing numbers of poor. The recognition, acceptance (or rejection), and practice of this is why bridewells mattered.

More people were punished inside rather than outside after 1550. They were put in bridewells or whipped in one or in civic 'halls'. This was one of two major changes in times when local government was turning inside. The other was more expansive and effective information systems. The two changes shared chromosomes including chronologies and trajectories, and they developed in similar conditions and governing mindsets. The 'inside' seemed more manageable and controllable. It was certainly possible to argue that there was more left to chance 'outside'. This was the direction in which thoughts turned. That said, it did not always work out well, as we have seen. Institutions and information systems had their systemic 'problems'. But the real advantage was that people did not see them for themselves, although they might well have heard about them from someone else.

We no longer punish troublemakers in public today and rely on data in almost every aspect of life. This continues to develop at a scintillating pace to an extent that is controlling. None of this looked inevitable in 1700. But with the advantage of hindsight we can see that 'private' punishment, whether whipping or incarceration, was firmly established by then. The second key component in turning inside also developed over the same 150 years: developing information systems. The story of this historic configuration whose consequences still affect us today is brought to a conclusion in the final chapter on information. It starts in Winchester, where civic authorities are about to send officers on another 'search' to count and categorize 'nuisances'.

5
Information

Records give us 'lights'.

M. Johnson, *Ludgate, What It Is, Not What It Was, Or, A Full and Clear Discovery of... That Prison* (1659), 2–3

Winchester was not in good shape around 1600. The cathedral still reassuringly dominated the skyline. Churches were full each Sunday. Fine buildings lined the high street and cathedral green. Winchester felt prosperous but records reveal its darker sides as speedy growth made this town of 'ancient fame' more trouble-prone. Vagrants were not welcome but still came. 'Searches' or 'surveys' turned up 'inmates' and 'newcomers' in cheap lodgings. There seemed to be more theft nowadays. The poor needed more help to put food on the table. Black sheep were found sitting drinking in one of the 'excessive' number of alehouses. So magistrates made plans for another survey, as they often did if troubles were on the rise. Numbers helped. They gave a better sense of the dimensions of disorder. More finely tuned policies could follow. Governors told constables to 'survey' their patch and note any 'problems' in 'returns'. This is what constables found on that day in Winchester: forty-two alehouses, many without licences; sixteen recusants; eleven inmates and 325 'newcomers' who were coupled with disease and disorder; five 'souldiers married' (?); six 'fire places dangerous'; and six people caught 'gaming' on Sunday in church time. Numbers now at hand with date and place duly noted, magistrates had a clearer sense of the scope and scale of issues on their doorstep.[1]

Winchester could not have been effectively ruled without information or 'making known'.[2] Local governments used information for what in Salisbury was called the 'better government of this citie' in 1596 when officers drew up a 'certificatt and information' of 'newecomers', 'base born children', 'straungers', and 'disordered houses'. A committee was formed in the same town in 1613 for 'vewye' of the poor to find out 'in what sorte they may be relyved'.[3] A Norwich committee was tasked to 'take notice of the state and condicion of the poore' in 1649 to find out who should work, get handouts, or go to the bridewell.[4] 'Knowledge' was a key word.

[1] HA W/K5/8, fo. 35.

[2] E. Coles, *An English Dictionary* (1673), and E. Phillips, *The New World of Words. Or a General English Dictionary* (4th edition, 1678), s.v. information.

[3] WSHC G23/1/3, fos. 231, 291v, 153v.

[4] NRO Norwich Assembly Folio Minute Book 6, fo. 88v.

Information, Institutions, and Local Government in England, 1550–1700: Turning Inside. Paul Griffiths, Oxford University Press. © Paul Griffiths 2023. DOI: 10.1093/oso/9780192896261.003.0006

Maidstone's mayor met fortnightly with his 'brethren' in 1629 to take steps 'for more readye suppressinge of disorders and disorderly persons and taking knowledge of them'. 'A boke of freemen freehoulders' was compiled in the same town for 'better knowledge' in 1604. Governors took 'knowledge' of mischief-makers sitting in pubs rather than churches in the same year.[5] 'Information' was used as it is today. Maidstone officers were told to 'walke in the streates' for two hours with staves in 1614 to 'view' alehouses and 'take information' of 'foreyn rogues and other lewde and idle persons'. While Leicestershire justices sought 'informacon' in settlement cases and were disappointed whenever they got in their word 'misinformacon'.[6] 'Informacon' was, of course, critical in court. Southampton's beadles gave 'information' in 1603 that Joan Harvey, who rented a cheap room from Goodwife Mitton, had two husbands. Shrewsbury weaver John Arnkdale 'gave informacon [in 1686 that Widow Anne Sandford] yesterdaye was buried in the parish church of St Chad [and] contrary to the law for burying wollen was buried in linnen'.[7] 'Informacon' was a key word in vocabularies of local surveillance along with 'viewe', 'survey', 'certifie', 'enquire', 'take note', 'observacon', and 'knowledge'. Suffolk alehouse-keepers were warned in 1584 that 'if open knowledge come to the towne of anie roberie', they must give the 'names, apparell and dwelling places' of anyone renting rooms within two days either side of the robbery.[8] Yarmouth wanted 'certayne knowledge' about 'foule, false, rude, and reprochful aspercons' that harmed the town in London. Southampton governors 'referred' to 'bydels rolls' for 'knowledge' of hucksters in 1604.[9] 'Intelligence' had similar meanings. Prescot churchwardens spent a long day 'perfectinge presentments' in 1636 with the help of 'ancient men' with 'better intelligence of recusant's goods and lands'. Ashby-de-la-Zouch aletasters made 'inquirie in all alehouses or victualling houses once every twenty days at the least [for] perfect intelligence of the true assize of ale and beere'.[10] 'Intelligence' was also a tip-off. Norfolk justices got 'intelligence' in 1592 that Garboldisham glover George Turner had been 'loking for backing' among 'ye worst people' to attack a constable from nearby Kenninghall. On 'search' one night in 1620, two Exeter constables got 'intelligence' that a 'straunger' had slipped into Joanne Chapman's house. They soon found her with John Adams in one of her rooms: 'she being unready and he setting by her having noe candle nor any bodie in the roome with them'.[11]

[5] CKS Md/ACm1/2, fos. 2, 124v; Md/ACm1/1a, fo. 82.

[6] CKS Md/Acm1/2, fo. 29; LERO QS6/1/2, fo. 73; QS7/1, fo. 113.

[7] SHA 3356/2430, fo. 23; SA 6/1, fo. 27.

[8] NRO Aylsham MS, 181.

[9] NRO Y/C/19/6, fo. 195v; SA 6/1, fo. 28.

[10] T. Steel, ed., 'Prescot Churchwardens' Accounts, 1635–1663', *Record Society of Lancashire and Cheshire*, 137 (2002), 8; HL HAM box 2, folder 1, fo. 12v.

[11] NRO Aylsham MS 17, fo. 62; DRO ECA C1/61, fo. 431.

'Information' and 'knowledge' were part and parcel of local authority in idea and action.[12] The demonstration of this in times that we refer to as 'the Age of Discovery' is the main aim of this chapter. There was far more to 'survey' in times that were marked by deep demographic and social strain. Improvements in the technologies of information gathering and application were also important for their pervasive deployment. Existing narratives of information for governance are overwhelmingly told in terms of (1) Church and State and (2) the 'political arithmetic' pursued by William Petty and others. Much less explored is a third narrative from the bottom up in local government that relied routinely on surveillance to keep on top of all sorts of issues ranging from the humdrum like rotting wooden walls or hogs or dogs on the loose to emergencies like plague that closed a town down. But what we still need perhaps is a comprehensive grasp of local data use as practice and process. This was given more clout and agency as the records that were produced possessed authority in themselves. They were consulted as a final determination or last word.

This is all covered in the first section of this chapter, which also considers how archives were put together for custom-made local 'knowledge'. Subsequent sections examine information systems in their entirety, from event to entry on record and making to using (for example, census-taking, books, catalogues, lists); the impacts of 'precyson' in calls for 'exact' and 'trew' information; the need to improve the safe storage, security, and 'secresie' of records/information; more effective presentation of information in records for use by officers and officials (for example, indexes, calendars, alphabetization, marginalia); information, records, and policing; and local information networks. But I shall turn first to interpretations and chronologies of local information cultures and systems.

I

Collecting and processing data had long been a tried and trusted method. The Domesday Book, after all, was the most spectacular national headcount before England's first national census in 1801. Medieval manorial record-keeping with lengthy surveys of tenants and holdings was an end in itself, but also provided grounding for later times. Surveying was more vital in all fields of government in what Peter Burke calls the 'paper state'. The need to know England and its people

[12] P. Slack, *The Invention of Improvement: Information and Material Progress in Seventeenth-Century England* (Oxford, 2015); P. Slack, 'Government and information in seventeenth-century England', *P&P*, 184 (2004); P. Griffiths, 'Local arithmetic: information cultures in early modern England', in S. Hindle, A. Shepard, and J. Walter, eds., *Remaking English Society: Social Relations and Change in Early Modern England* (Woodbridge, 2013); P. Griffiths, 'Surveying the people', in K. Wrightson, ed., *A Social History of England, c.1500–c.1750* (Cambridge, 2017).

better grew with a population boom and its after-effects that still rocked towns after national growth settled down around 1630. There was more to survey.[13] As ships set sail for faraway lands and telescopes were trained on the heavens, governors learned more than ever before about their subjects (Francis Bacon applied narratives of overseas discovery to pursuing knowledge). James Brome wrote in his late seventeenth-century travel guide that 'it is very incongruous to pretend to be acquainted with other countries and to be strangers to their own'.[14] Understand your home turf first. The domestic faces of discovery went beyond Whitehall to include travel writing, mapping, surveying, communications, and work on counties and cities ranging from the remote past all the way up to the present.[15]

The early modern period is often seen as a stepping stone to what historians call the 'modern information state' read in terms of military and fiscal apparatus.[16] This has been one of three leading narratives in the development of information systems. The sustained growth in information gathering by sixteenth-century central government was unprecedented. A full list would run on for many pages but picking high points we can start with Henrician muster counts, the mountain of paperwork in fiscal returns to the Great Subsidy (1524–5), Wolsey's corn surveys and enclosure and chantry commissions, the *Valor Ecclesiasticus* that tried to take stock of Church wealth in the wake of the royal supremacy (1535), parish registers (1538), and a string of state-sponsored surveys. The Church was also an inveterate counter. The 1563 Bishop's Census was a high watermark, seeking numbers of families in each diocese. The Bishop of London commented that 'it hathe not byn accustomed in anie ecclesiasticall visitaycon to enquire of the number of householdes in everye parishe and therefore we have no recorde thereof'.[17] The number of communicants was added up in 1603 and it is from around then that the royal government started to collect data on burgeoning

[13] O. Coleman, 'What figures? Some thoughts on the use of information by medieval governments', in D. Coleman and A. H. John, eds., *Trade, Government, and Economy in Pre-Industrial England* (1976); P. Burke, *A Social History of Knowledge From Gutenberg to Diderot* (Oxford, 2000), 117–19. See K. Wrightson, *Earthly Necessities: Economic Lives in Early Modern Britain* (New Haven and London, 2000), chaps 4, 7, and 10; V. Groebner, *Who Are You? Identification, Deceptions, and Surveillance in Early Modern Europe*, trans. M. Kyburz and J. Peck (New York, 2007), chap. 3.

[14] J. Brome, *Travels Over England, Scotland, and Wales Giving a True and Exact Description of the Chiefest Cities, Towns, and Corporations* (1700), 1.

[15] See B. Klein, *Maps and the Writing of Space in Early Modern England and Ireland* (Basingstoke, 2001); A. Alexander, *Geometrical Land-scapes: The Voyages of Discovery and the Transformation of Mathematical Practice* (Stanford, CA, 2002); A. McRae, *Literature and Domestic Travel in Early Modern England* (2009).

[16] See E. Higgs, *The Information State in England: The Central Collection of Information on Citizens Since 1500* (Basingstoke, 2004); D. R. Headrick, *When Information Came of Age: Technologies of Knowledge in the Age of Reason and Revolution, 1700–1850* (Oxford and New York, 2000).

[17] The bishop is quoted in A. Dyer, 'The Bishops' Census of 1563: its significance and accuracy', *Local Population Studies*, 49 (1992), 28. See also A. Dyer and D. M. Palliser, eds., *The Diocesan Population Returns for 1563 and 1603*, British Academy Records of Social and Economic History, NS, 31 (Oxford, 2005); N. Goose, 'The Bishops' Census of 1563: a re-examination of its reliability', *Local Population Studies*, 56 (1996).

trade. The first Council of Trade was set up to gauge 'the true balance of the trade of this kingdom' from 'records and writings as you shall find needful for your better information' (1622). The quest to balance trade generated reams of paper on coal, fisheries, shipping, and draperies.[18] Information collection picked up pace after 1660, touching anyone alive. The Hearth Tax (1662) invaded households in more ways than one. Settlement laws from the same year toughened up residence requirements through surveillance by record. The Compton Census (1676) stretched across the country to classify religious affiliation, while the Marriage Duty Act (1695) called for registers of vital statistics in returns that Gregory King used to see if the population was growing or falling.[19] The British took surveying with them when they crossed the ocean to build new worlds. John Smith counted 1,500 'warlike' warriors around Jamestown. 'A faithful and true record' of vital statistics was begun there in 1611. The colonial Assembly passed registration legislation in 1619. An 'official' census of Virginia counted 4,914 people in 1635. There were at least twenty-three censuses in the Atlantic colonies before 1700.[20]

The other leading narrative in the development of information is the 'political arithmetic' of the final third of the seventeenth century and its antecedents. Francis Bacon imagined 'Solomon's House' in *New Atlantis* (1627): a 'depot' propelled by collection and research. Little came of this in hard practical terms, but ideas circulated and we can trace group discussion in wavering lines from Robert Boyle's 'invisible college' and meetings of physicians, scientists, and philosophers in London from 1645 on, through Samuel Hartlib's circle to the scientific and philosophical 'club' in Interregnum Oxford, and the founding of the Royal Society.[21] Hartlib first talked about an 'Office of Address' in the middle of the seventeenth century to send information across borders. William Petty discussed compressing knowledge into 'one booke or great worke' in a letter to Hartlib from

[18] Slack, *Invention of Improvement*, 51–5, quotation at 52; P. Slack, 'Measuring the national wealth in seventeenth-century England', *ECHR*, 57 (2004).

[19] N Tadmor, 'The settlement of the poor and the rise of the form in England, c.1662–1780', *P&P*, 236 (2017); N. Landau, 'The laws of settlement and the surveillance of immigration in eighteenth-century Kent', *C&C*, 3 (1988); R. Wall, 'English population statistics before 1800', *History of the Family*, 9 (2004); C. Brooks, 'Projecting, political arithmetic and the Act of 1695', *EHR*, 97 (1982); J. Boulton, 'The Marriage Duty Act and parochial registration in London, 1695–1706', and A. Whiteman, 'The Compton Census of 1676', both in K. Shurer and T. Arkell, eds., *Surveying the People: The Interpretation and Use of Document Sources for the Study of Population in the Later Seventeenth Century* (Matlock, 1992); T. Arkell, 'Illuminations and distortions: Gregory King's scheme calculated for the year 1688 and the social structure of later Stuart England', *ECHR*, 59 (2006).

[20] J. H. Cassedy, *Demography in Early America: Beginnings of the Statistical Mind, 1600–1800* (Cambridge, MA, 1969), 12, 15, 18, 19, 20–1, 26–31; Slack, 'Government and information', 47; M. Farrell, *Counting Bodies: Population in Colonial American Writing* (Oxford, 2016).

[21] C. Webster, *The Great Instauration: Science, Medicine and Reform 1626–1660* (New York, 1976), 54–67, 88–99, 154–78; J. Soll, *The Information Master: Jean-Baptiste Colbert's Secret State Intelligence System* (Ann Arbor, MI, 2009), 97–8; S. Mandelbrote, 'William Petty and Anne Greene: medical and political reform in Commonwealth Oxford', in M. Pelling and S. Mandelbrote, eds., *The Practice of Reform in Health, Medicine, and Science, 1500–2000: Essays for Charles Webster* (Aldershot, 2005).

the same time. We are still a decade from John Graunt's *Natural and Political Observations* (1662), 'which effectively founded' historical demography and social statistics. But in privileged intellectual circles (to which Graunt would not belong until his election to the Royal Society after his only book came out) the idea of using data in Colbertian ways to govern states had been gaining ground for a while.[22] Graunt (1620–74) was the son of a London draper and a haberdasher's apprentice who beavered away in local government, ending up as a common councilman. His reasons for writing his book were grounded in London and working with its 'bills of mortality' on the raw materials of human life. Bacon saw population as a potential quantity that could be measured through observation and recording. Graunt followed this when conceiving a book that would reach its fourth edition before its fifth year. Like Bacon, his guiding principle was that population figures were key for government. It is 'necessary', he said, 'to know how many people there be of each sex, state, age, religion, trade, rank, or degree [as by] knowledge whereof trade and government may be more certain and regular'. 'I conclude', he wrote in the final paragraph of *Natural and Political Observations*, 'that a clear knowledge of all these particulars [is] necessary in order to good, certain, and easie government'.[23] William Petty is called the founding father of 'political arithmetic' but one of its more storied definitions came from William Davenant: 'the art of reasoning by figures upon things relating to government'.[24] The impacts on government of empirical methods to generate quantifiable information were not as far-reaching as Petty intended. But this 'science' was coming of age. Working with fiscal sources and vital statistics, Gregory King calculated the national population to be 5.3 million in 1696.[25]

But data had been used by local government long before either Graunt or Petty wrote a single word.[26] There is in fact a third narrative on the timing of

[22] Webster, *Great Instauration*, 67–77; Soll, *Information Master*, 163; T. McCormick, *William Petty and the Ambitions of Political Arithmetic* (Oxford, 2009), 58, 67; Slack, 'Government and information'; Slack, *Invention of Improvement*, 102–6.

[23] J. Graunt, *Natural and Political Observations Mentioned in a Following Index and Made Upon the Bills of Mortality* (1662), 73–4.

[24] C. Davenant, *The Political and Commercial Works*, ed. Sir C. Whitworth, 5 vols (1771), I, 128.

[25] See McCormick, *William Petty*, 132, 283; Slack, 'Government and information', 42, 59; P. Slack, *Perceptions of Population in Early Modern England*, (Stenton Lecture, 2010, University of Reading 2011); Slack, *Invention of Improvement*, 116–28, and chaps 5–6; A. A. Rusnock, *Vital Accounts: Quantifying Health and Population in Eighteenth-Century England and France* (Cambridge, 2002), 5–6, 16–25; J. Innes, 'Power and happiness: empirical social enquiry in Britain from "political arithmetic" to "moral statistics"', in her *Inferior Politics: Social Problems and Social Policies in Eighteenth-Century Britain* (Oxford, 2009).

[26] I disagree with Paul Slack, who believes that 'The lasting contribution made in the sixteenth century to what became political arithmetic did not come in the shape of new methodologies'. He does not consider the organization and use of information by local administration in his narrative, personified in the life and work of London office-holder John Graunt. The key thing for Slack was the emergence 'of new documentary sources, whose accumulation created archives to be plundered and manipulated in the future' ('Counting people in early modern England: registers, registrars, and political arithmetic', *EHR*, 137 (2022), 1120).

government through information and quantification that rarely gets the same attention as 'intellectual' political arithmetic. Government through knowledge developed over longer time frames in towns and villages where Graunt looks like a late arrival. We might remember the last line of his *Natural and Political Observations*: 'but whether the knowledge thereof be necessary to many or fit for others than the sovereign and his chief ministers, I leave it to thy consideration.'[27] Needing information and solutions, local elites 'surveyed', in their word, on a scope and scale that had not been seen before 1550.

In *Human Empire* (2022), Ted McCormick imposes linear chronological stages on the development of demographic thought in England and its colonies. His interests in the period *c.*1550–*c.*1680 are intellectual for the most part: reason of state, natural philosophy, and—the subject of his first book—William Petty and the making of political arithmetic.[28] McCormick recognizes quantification and the application of information by local governments in Elizabethan England, but 'local' lacks deep significance. 'The numbers', he writes, 'remained local: focused on a particular type, with significance in a particular place, for purposes of local administration.' These numbers were 'embedded' in limited 'local' settings with little bearing on rarefied 'political arithmetic'. They had seemingly constrictive attributes, being 'contingent, multivalent, and local'.[29] McCormick looks at one piece of 'local arithmetic', the Norwich Census of the Poor (1570). But this most famous of censuses is treated in isolation, when in fact enumeration and quantification were essential elements for governing towns across the country long before the death of the last Tudor monarch. McCormick's interests are in the emergence of population as knowledge for thinking about the nation in structural analysis. The intellectual streams that led to 'political arithmetic' are his province, not 'municipal initiatives' that are not considered in their own right but in the long run as cogs that 'helped create the conditions for demographic quantification'.[30]

Yet Elizabethan towns have long been seen as pioneers of the use of information and quantification for 'better government' in ground-breaking social discipline/welfare schemes. This was done for practical and pragmatic governance, not to make arguments about population as an intellectual construct or endeavour.

[27] Graunt, *Natural and Political Observations*, 74.

[28] McCormick, *William Petty*.

[29] T. McCormick, *Human Empire: Mobility and Demographic Thought in the British-Atlantic World, 1500–1800* (Cambridge, 2022), chap. 3; 67, 68. McCormick notes that 'the creation of parish-level overseers tasked with counting, classifying, and reporting numbers of the poor implied a more immediate purpose for empirical census-taking' or what he calls the 'instrumental use of quantification' (ibid., 67).

[30] Ibid., 66. McCormick also tones down the long-held view that urban policies and programmes were innovative and influential, writing that they represented 'the enforcement and elaboration of existing law and policy' in the final third of the sixteenth century (ibid., 76). His considerable strengths are not so evident in his social and urban history, and his idea that 'marginal subpopulations came to be treated as national rather than local and permanent rather than historically specific problems for government', or that it was only towards 1600 that vagrants were defined in terms of 'physical capacity' and 'moral incapacity' (ibid., 101, 78).

But it still concerned knowledge of population for law and order and the human good that was guided by what at the time was called 'experience'. What is more, towns were in regular conversation with Whitehall and each other, sharing knowledge about people and process. McCormick gives urban local arithmetic no real significance in his account of the quantitative past. Nor does he give any more thought to its progress and impact after his second stage/chapter ends with the death of the queen in 1603. Yet England's first historical demographer, John Graunt, came of age in a haberdasher's shop in London in the 1630s, with a role in the years ahead in the practical parish arithmetic that became the backbone of local government well before William Petty was born in 1623.

The practices and principles of Elizabethan local administration were in large part shaped by information and quantification. This owed much to the increasingly regular 'intrusions' of central government in local affairs culminating in the Poor Laws towards the end of Elizabeth's reign. Whitehall combed the country for information on social, economic, and financial issues. The State's data machine could only work with local surveying that included Wolsey's corn surveys in the 1520s. Parishes kept registers of vital statistics and dealt with the nuts and bolts of the Poor Laws. Local officials drew up tax listings. Information relations between parish and polity were two-way cogs. Surveying people and things was a matter of course in government, from Whitehall all the way down to the smallest English parish. Local officers might not have read anything written by Jean Bodin, Giovanni Botero, or Francis Bacon (the key pre-Petty texts for McCormick). Their great teacher was 'experience' in and out of office, and they could also turn to their peers for guidance and instruction texts like William Lambarde's *The Duties of Constables, Borsholders, Tythingmen and Such Other Law and Lay Ministers of the Peace* (1584) or the anonymous *An Ease for Overseers of the Poore* (1600). Information streamed into Whitehall, but it was mainly collected for local issues. It was possible to develop local information systems to levels of finesse and use that were truly distinctive. This has not gone unnoticed. We have top-drawer work on particular exercises in local surveillance including rate assessments, landholding registers, and counts of 'newecomers' or settled residents that were, in James Scott's words, 'a project of legibility and simplification'.[31]

Information depended on 'experience' and 'surveying'. To 'survey' was to discover, delineate, calculate, and categorize someone or something that needed to

[31] J. C. Scott, *Seeing Like a State: How Certain Schemes to Improve the Human Condition Have Failed* (New Haven and London, 1998), 9. See, for instance, Schurer and Arkell, *Surveying the People*; P. Slack, ed., *Poverty in Early-Stuart Salisbury*, Wiltshire Record Society, 31 (Devizes, 1975); P. Clark and J. Clark, 'The social economy of the Canterbury suburbs; the evidence of the census of 1564', in A. Detsicas and N. Yates, eds., *Studies in Modern Kentish History* (Maidstone, 1983); N. Goose, 'Household size and structure in early Stuart Cambridge', *SH*, 5 (1980); J. F. Pound, ed., *The Norwich Census of the Poor, 1570*, Norfolk Record Society, 40 (1971).

be more fully understood. Local governors wanted a quantifiable present to help cope with an unsteady future. Thousands of surveys that were cut from the same cloth revealed the particles of England from the bottom up in information 'or making known'. Each one of them was a narrative of a particular place at a particular time conducted locally in response to change. They are for us the raw materials of history.

II

What are archives for us were working records for local magistrates 400 years ago. Records were intended for certain eyes and ears only. Local secrets were supposed to be hidden from the very people they documented. Unlike books, they did not see the light of day or get passed around alehouses. Records were not meant to be read by anyone else unless governors said otherwise or someone leaked something. They were constructions from first to last shaped by governing definitions, deliberations, and decisions. Records are versions of something made by governors for their own reasons. We find a place written in its records. Each new record, whether it is a general courtbook for 'affairs' or something more particular, tells us something more about life there.

We rarely see the creative chain from talk to record, but Maidstone governors have left a snapshot of their deliberations from 1652. They met for an hour 'after dinner' each court day to talk about 'publique matters concerninge the towne' as 'they shall see cause'. Once the mood of the meeting became clear, they spent time 'digestinge and preparing in writinge in the forme of orders'.[32] This was called 'the town's record' in Liverpool.[33] Strategies to govern or crack crime or any other 'sore' consequence of socio-economic change had better chances of success if understood through surveillance. In response to a constable's warrant, St Martin-in-the-Fields (Westminster) officers went around counting in 1603, noting that 'wekely almes' were handed out to seventy people: 'whereof xii have been verie good parishioners and have paid all duties'. 'The number of poore' hovering around the poverty line and 'likely to come to have reliefe' in harsher times was calculated to be 123 'men and widdowes besides their wives and children'.[34] Another parish surveyed, revealed in little local atoms.

Like governors back then, historians use such surveys to draw pictures of families and communities. We map social structures—household size and composition, occupations, profiles of poverty or wealth—and keynote social trends like

[32] CKS Md/Acm1/3, fo. 61.
[33] M. Power, ed., *Liverpool Town Books, 1649–1671*, Records Society of Lancashire and Cheshire, 136 (Dorchester, 1999), 58.
[34] WAC F6039. See also WAC F3348–51.

population growth or the widening rifts of a harshly unequal society. Smart detective work has been based on single surveys or combinations of records. But what we lack perhaps is an overall understanding of early modern surveying as a process. We know its intriguing documentary products but it reflects something greater than the sum of its parts. Communities are imagined in their records. Like labelling crime, censuses and surveys categorized and commented on character and circumstance. Locally assembled reconfigurations of life in records speak of the graphic human consequences of living in changing times in formatted lists, columns, and entries.

Thomas Hariot believed that English settlers were superior to natives on Roanoke Island as they had 'no letters nor other suche meanes as we to keepe records'.[35] Records possessed authority in their own right. They 'signify', Edward Phillips noted, 'an authentical or uncontroulable testimony in writing'. Thomas Blount used the same wording.[36] Edward Chamberlain called records 'memorials or monuments of things done before judges' in his much-read justices' handbook. 'If a record say anything', he continued, 'no man shall be received to aver or speake against it'.[37] Records 'import in them[selves] such incontrollable credit and verity as they admit no averment', Edward Phillips pronounced with confidence. 'Such is the excellency of a record'—'a register of things done'—Edmund Wingate wrote in 1661, that 'there shall be no averment against it to avoyd confusion'. Gerard Malynes called 'public records' 'jewels of inestimable value' in which our 'laws and liberties [and] estates, lives, progenitors, and predecessors do reside and are recorded'.[38] Many record books were resplendently elegant in dignified colours, with crests stamped on covers or title pages. They embodied authority and amity. Preston burgesses reported that everything went smoothly, 'tending to unity, concord, and satisfaccon' after Leet presentments were filed in 1665.[39] Records were worth more than the paper they were written on. The written word became more vital to make a point in law. People were more likely to turn to records for 'evidence' to clinch questions of custom, for instance, where custumals were compelling legal weapons.[40] Records were 'jewells' of 'memories'. 'Record is derived of recorder to remember', Edward Leigh said:

[35] Hariot is quoted in Cassedy, *Demography in Early America*, 5.

[36] E. Phillips, *The New World of Words, Or a General English Dictionary* (4th edition, 1678); T. Blount, *Nomo-Lexikon A Law Dictionary* (1691), s.v. 'record'.

[37] R. Chamberlain, *The Complete Justice Being a Compendious and Exact Collection Out of All Such Statutes and Authors as May Any Ways Concern the Office of a Justice of Peace* (1681), 318.

[38] E. Leigh, *A Phililogicall Commentary or an Illustration of the Most Obvious and Useful Words in the Law* (2nd edition, 1658), 200; E. Wingate, *Justice Revived Being the Whole Office of a Countrey Justice of the Peace* (1661), 212; G. Malynes, *England's View, in the Unmasking of Two Paradoxes* (1603), 17.

[39] LA CNP 3/2/1, fos. 238–9.

[40] A. Fox, *Oral and Literate Cultures in England, 1500–1700* (Oxford, 2000), chap. 5; A. Wood, *The Memory of the People: Custom and Popular Senses of the Past in Early Modern England* (Cambridge, 2013), chap. 5.

> The records [are] lively representations of time and truth and reputed the treasures of the kingdom . . . A record or sufficient matter in writing are good memorials [and] therefore it is said when we will by any record or writing commit the memory of anything to posterity, it is said *tradare memorie*. And this is the reason that regularly a man cannot prescribe or alledge a custom against a statute because that is matter of record.[41]

Writing about 'records of immunities' in 'courts christian' on issues like tithes, Thomas Powell noted that 'These by custome and continuance have attained to such reputacon that notwithstanding the records should bee lost, yet the remembrance or prescription of them holdeth wonted force and validitie'. It seemed 'most strange' to Powell that even when people and courts had 'records to cleare the prescription in question', they 'often use no other argument but the memorie of man which may erre'. But he was 'forward looking' in 'wishing that the severall registers of all dioscesse would collect all such records thereof there might bee a perfect volume digested for succession'.[42]

The pen was becoming mightier than speech. Maidstone magistrates said that 'authenticall' records must have the last word. Two Southampton men were 'convicted by ther [own] records' for taking over another man's house in 1613.[43] A churchyard fence in Abberton in Essex was falling to the ground in 1657 because, it was said, the villagers did not 'repair their parts' as they should have done. The case was sent to justices, who ruled according to an 'ancient booke kept in the parrish [that] doth sette downe every p[ar]ticuler peece of pale and who hath [to] make the same'.[44] Even people trying to insult each other reached for the power of records. A Norwich worsted-weaver told 'singleman' Richard Picking 'in hearinge of others': 'you are a rogue and a recorded rogue and [Benjamin Lane] will prove that you are a recorded rogue . . . I will prove that you are a recorded rogue'. Picking was not just a 'rogue'; he was a 'recorded rogue'.[45] Court cases were won or lost after something 'appeareth by the booke'. 'A matter of record', Thomas Blount explained in 1691, 'is that which [is] proved by some record'. 'Nude matter', he said, 'is a naked allegation of a thing done to be proved only by witnesses and not [by] record or speciality in writings under seal'.[46] A Yarmouth legal spat ended when one side 'appeared' right by 'particulars' in 'bookes beinge viewed'.[47] Thinking about landlord/tenant disputes, an anonymous author argued that manor customs 'should be fairly written and publickly exposed to the tenants view every court

[41] Leigh, *Phillilogical Commentary*, 199–200.
[42] T. Powell, *Directions for Search of Records Remaining in the Chancerie, Tower [and] Exchequer* (1622), 75.
[43] CKS Md/Acm1/2, fo. 162; SA SC9/2/1, fo. 12.
[44] D. H. Allen, ed., *Essex Quarter Sessions Order Book, 1652–1661*, Essex Record Office Publications, 65 (Chelmsford, 1974), 102.
[45] NRO Norwich Sessions File 67/19–20.
[46] Blount, *Nomo-Lexikon*, s.v. 'matter of record'.
[47] NRO Y/C27/1, fo. 177.

day' to end 'perjury, law-suits [and] other mischeifs'.[48] It was a decisive day in Norwich in 1627 when, after two years, 'records of diverse assemblyes' established that basketmaker John Kettle with his 'ambiguous answers' did indeed break with civic amity when refusing to serve as feast-maker in St George's Guild.[49]

A 1673 dictionary defined an archive as 'the place where old records are kept'. Another substituted 'ancient' for 'old'.[50] We cannot think of retrieving long-dead lives without archives, but many are broken. It is sobering to think for a minute about what did not make it this far. We will never know what is lost to what Gerard Malynes called 'careless keeping' and the 'rage and troubles of former times'. The 'records of petty and inferior courts of ancient times' still with us today, he said, 'do not amount to [a] ten thousandeth part of [what is] lost'. Not one 'sheriffs turn or county and hundred courts', he said, had records that stretched back over two decades. They were either 'not entered at all' or 'not well kept'. For each record of 'inferior courts' that 'exceeds one hundred years', Malynes added, there are ten [that] do not reach to half a hundred'. What did we lose in 'Wat Tylers, Jack Cades, or Ketts popular frenzies?' he mused.[51] Concerned by what he saw, Thomas Powell hoped in 1622 'that some course might be taken in time for the repayring of those records' in the Tower and equity courts that 'are worne out with their antiquitie before it be too late'.[52]

Fire and water were deadly enemies of archives, then and now. 'A dangerous and sodaine fire' raced through 'buildings and roomes [of] the office of the clarkes of the high court of Chancerie' in 1622, 'consum[ing] many bills, answers and other pleadings [and] depositions of witnesses and other decrees, divers patent rolles, warrants, and other records'. Steps were taken to get replacement copies if at all possible.[53] 'I find a great difficulty in my undertakings', William Gray admitted when working on his 'survey' of Newcastle in the heat of civil war, 'because the records of this country are but few and confused being so often infected by the Scots and Danes who consumed and fired all before them'.[54] We would know far more about early modern Tenterden if 'disaster' had not struck in 1661 when the 'comon gaole and court hall' were reduced to ashes by a fierce fire that 'consumed... our charters and records' (a clerk wrote 'letter concerninge our late greate losse' in the margin).[55] Some administrators made what for us were terrible

48 *Perjury, the National Sin, or, An Account of the Abuses and Violations of Oaths Among Us of This Nation Humbly Offered to the Consideration of the High Court of Parliament* (1690), 20.

49 NRO Norwich St. George's Guild Minute Book 1602–1729, fos. 57, 63–63v.

50 E. Coles, *An English Dictionary* (1673); Phillips, *New World of Words*, s.v. 'archive'.

51 Malynes, *England's View*, 18–19.

52 Powell, *Directions for Search of Records Remaining in the Chancerie, Tower [and] Exchequer*, 19. See also J. Bidwell, 'The study of paper as evidence, artifact, and commodity', in P. Davidson, ed., *The Book Encompassed: Studies in Twentieth-Century Bibliography* (Cambridge, 1992).

53 *By the King. A Proclamation for Reliefe of the Subject that Might be Otherwise Damnified by the Late Burning of Records in the Sixe Clarkes Office* (1622).

54 W. Gray, *Chorographia, or, A Survey of Newcastle upon Tyne* (1649), A3r.

55 CKS TE/S2, fo. 177.

choices. A 'list of records delivered to the mayor' was drawn up in Barnstaple in 1691. It included 'a bundle of old recognizances', 'a booke of notes of the court of survey', 'bundles' of accounts, 'old writs', various grants and rents, 'some proceedings in the court of record', and 'proceedings in the court of sessions in 1676'. Someone added a note to this entry a century later: 'I have very carefully examined the papers in this bundell and am of opinion [that] they are of no sort of use'. He threw them away in a shrug that closed doors on parts of the past that we will never get back.[56]

It is agonizing when there is a hole in a record and we can do nothing about it. 'The foregoing tenn leaves were lost before I had the booke', Thetford's clerk wrote in evident panic in the same book in 1624. St Mary Aldermanbury (London) vestrymen were shocked to see that 'divers leaves have bin torn or cutt out of the vestry booke and aught is knowne of great concern to this parish'. It 'cannot at present be discovered by whome', they added.[57] St James Garlickhythe vestry ordered that their book be 'provided with alphabetts and nombered throwout to prevent abuse by tearing out of leaves as is to bee seene in the present booke'. Two members of a Herefordshire grand jury found themselves in the dock in 1684 when 'of their owne accord without the privity and consent of their fellow jurors' they 'cutt off and imbezelled a parte of the parchment' from constable's presentments. To protect someone, I imagine.[58] Hearts sink when we open a record and something is missing, or wavy words dance across a page, or a thick black squiggle crosses out something that mattered because it was worth obliterating. It is rarely possible to get underneath the inky blotch. 'Blot not your book or raze' it, I. C. Gent cautioned merchants. Legal handbooks warned that records should be 'well and faithfull kept from rasure, corrupcon [and] imbeselling'.[59] A concerned Robert Cecil wrote to the lord keeper in 1604: 'My good lord the king is very desirous you should send for Mr Attorney about ye extinguishing and defaceing of the records whereof I spoke.'[60]

Records were altered by authority. 'Big' is crossed out and 'great' put in its place in an order from Ashby-de-la-Zouch to get a '... bellyed woman' out of the town in 1628.[61] There are orders to cross out entries for reasons that are long lost. 'Words to be blotted out of the 39th article of the ordinance of ye hospitalls', Gloucester governors noted in 1655. 'These words following interlyned therein that is to say (or of ye overseers of the poor there) shall be blotted out and become

[56] NDRO B1/1748. [57] NRO T/C1/6, fo. 11; LMA MS 3570/2, fo. 160.

[58] LMA MS 4183/1, fo. 59v; HEA Q/SO/1, fo. 39. See also KAC WQ/I/3, fos. 143–50, 161–4; HL EL MS 2134; LMA MSS 1240/1, fo. 108; 4072/1, fos. 240, 332; 4214/1, fos. 20, 37v–8; CA QJB/1/3, fo. 265.

[59] I. C. Gent, *A Most Excellent Instruction for the Exact and Perfect Keeping [of] Merchants Bookes of Accounts* (1632), 18.

[60] HL EL MS 2912. See also Chamberlain, *Complete Justice*, 117, 215, 318–19; Fitzherbert, *Newe Book of the Justices of Peace*, 115v; Wingate, *Justice Revived*, 212–13.

[61] HL HAM misc. box 12.

void.'[62] Words were also crossed out when balancing accounts, making payments, or doing town 'busines', as well as in cases of illegitimacy, 'scornefull words', 'breakinge the assize of ale and beere', setting the poor to work, caps on numbers of sheep, settlement orders, baptisms, burials, or striking a dissenting minister from a 'freeholders book'.[63] Names were crossed out from lists in deliberate strokes. Two names on a note of ratepayers and three more 'from the names of the poore' in St Giles parish in Reading for reasons that we can only try to guess at.[64] We have also lost ten names from a list 'of those that keepe waightes and meysures' in a Hereford ward in 1624; eight Barnstaple tipplers and five butchers who broke the assize; and nineteen names daubed with ink in a lengthy presentment for not taking care of Maidstone's pavements in 1652. Mistakes needed to be crossed out.[65] Three names were cut from a list of men who took the oath of supremacy in Kent in 1684. The clerk wrote 'voyd, mistake' in the margin.[66] A blot sometimes spreads over a whole page. 'Voide' orders were often erased. 'Peruse all orders', Chester governors told a city committee in 1579, and 'sett downe' those 'moste meetest and profitable to the comonweale and howe many growen out of use and voide'.[67] Winchester's mayor and 'the xxiiii' combed through the 'black booke' in 1552 to see what 'acts and ordyances [as] thei thinke good bye their discretions to remayne and be newlye wrytin [in] the newe paper booke bownde wth bords'. Any thought to be no longer 'mete' were 'utterlye abolished forever'.[68] Maidstone governors pointed out in 1626 that some 'acts and orders enacted by the court of burgh-mote' were 'contrarye the one to ye other'. 'Others [were] defective [and] superabundant'. A committee was set up to 'peruse acts, orders, and constitucons' and report on what needed to be 'alter[ed], change[d], supplie[d] and putt out'—their 'doings'—at the next court.[69] National events could also change things in local settings. Thoughts about 'prejudical' orders led to common council acts 'made in the time of the late troubles' in Gloucester being 'expunged' in 1672.[70] Political twists and turns had a hand in events in Preston in 1660 when former bailiff and royalist Henry Chorley, who was taken to task for swindling town accounts in 1654, was absolved after the king came back. Chorley's 'presentment' on record was forever 'expunged [or] obliterated' and ruled to be 'null and void' in the Restoration air.[71]

The clash between king and Parliament caused storms not long after brewer Thomas Stanley was 'elected' for a second stint as Maidstone's mayor in 1641. His election was challenged by John Wall, who filed a 'sute touchinge legalitie'.

[62] GA GBR/B/3/2, fo. 845.
[63] For example, LA MBC/172; MBC/209; MBC/233; BRO R/AC1/1/2, fos. 9, 264; WI/FA1/2, fo. 76v; WI/AC1/1, fo. 8; NDRO B1/1602; CKS FA/AC3, fo. 23v; Md/JLP1/1652 (B); SHA QS1/3, fo. 30.
[64] BRO RP/1/4; R/AP1/1; R/AP/2/1.
[65] HEA BG11/17/1/4, fo. 34; NDRO B1/1855; CKS Md/JLP1/1652 (B).
[66] CKS Q/SM/A/2, fo. 2 (Canterbury).
[67] CRO Z/AB/1, fo. 178.
[68] HA W/B1/1, fo. 99.
[69] CKS Md/Acm1/2, fos. 95–5v.
[70] GA GBR/B/3/3, fo. 503.
[71] LA CNP 3/2/1, fo. 113.

Wall nailed his colours to the parliamentary mast, while Stanley backed the king in all things. Stanley survived this challenge, but Wall was 'put out of his place of common counsel' in summer 1642 and fined £5 for 'contemptuously misdemeaning him selfe towards the new mayor and comon counsell'. Stanley, too, was wounded by war when royalist troops—'our soldiers', he called them—threatened to storm Maidstone, a parliamentary garrison town. He was stripped of his militia captaincy and worse followed when his political enemies hounded him out of government. 'Thomas Stanley did of late usurpe and take upon him the office and place of maior', charges read, 'not beinge in nominacon'. Oddly, he was said to be 'personally in open rebellion againste the kinge and parliamente'. Wall's future suddenly looked brighter at the same moment as Stanley's turned bleaker—the entries in records with details of his humiliating 'expulsion' and fine were 'obliterated...by vertue of an acte of burghmote' in 1643. Wall was back. This was reiterated in the second year of the Republic when 'the order made concerninge his outinge' in the time of 'the usurpinge maior' was called 'unjust' and together with the lines on fines was 'obliterated, vacated and defaced' (the original 'obliteration' did not pass muster?). But we can still read words under the thick page-size X and the black lines drawn through John Wall's 'outinge' entries. Wall became town chamberlain in 1650. Stanley, meanwhile, had a rocky war. His assets, worth £8,110 in 1640, slumped to £2,201 in 1653, slashed by fines, compounding, bad loans, and poor choices of people to run his brewhouse. But things looked sunnier when the king came back in 1660 and he was 'restored to his place and office of a jurat'. 'Severall orders of burghmote' for his (and others) 'outing' were 'defaced and obliterated' and 'made void' with big black Xs. Wall was no longer alive but Stanley was an active jurat and took his justices' oath before dying aged eighty-eight in 1669.[72]

At least local governors made all decisions in this tit-for-tat 'defaceing' and 'obliterating'. Sometimes, however, it was done without their say-so by turncoats, including a 'destructive' Winchester recorder who was not named in the record. He was a celebrity drunk who had a fight with an alderman in an alehouse around midnight in his first month in office in 1652, and who fell into trouble again five years later for calling the mayor 'a 'drunckard and swearer' in front of Winchester's elite. He was drummed out of office for this and also for his 'evell councell' when he managed to convince a former mayor to have 'orders entered in an assembly booke made and agreed upon by ye assembly erased and obliterated'.[73] Chichester

[72] CKS Md/Acm/1/2, fos. 191, 194v, 196v; Md/Acm/1/3, fos. 1, 1v, 2v, 17, 111v, 113, 115, 120v. Other orders removing royalist common councillors were reversed and 'obliterated'. See CKS Md/Acm/1/3, fos. 34, 44v–5. Maidstone royalists were removed from office by Parliament in 1647. I drew heavily on Stanley's *History of Parliament* entry: http://www.historyofparliamentonline.org/volume/1604-1629/member/stanley-thomas-1581-1669 (accessed 3 January 2016). See also HL HAM box 2, folder 1, fos. 34, 39; CKS FA/AC3, fo. 106v; Md/Acm1/3, fos. 19, 40v–3; TE/AC2/6; HA W/B2/1, fos. 2v, 91; GA GBR/B/3/3, fo. 310; NRO Y/C/19/4, fo. 25v.

[73] HA W/B1/5, fos. 119v–20v.

yeoman Joseph Bennett landed in trouble 'for altering and strikeing out certaine figures in the poore booke'. Richard Dudman of North Bersted in West Sussex—a constable, I presume—was taken to task in 1684 'for blotting out his presentments bill after it was sworne and signed' by a justice of the peace. While Daniel Sefton from Arundel appeared before the same court for 'blotting out and defaceing the presentments of the jury at the last court leet'.[74]

How did Winchester's recorder last five years in office? Was it the war and its fallout again? And how did two-time Southampton mayor and long-time justice Andrew Studley imagine that he could get away with his 'wronges, corruptions, and misdemeanors' that were 'contrary' to the town 'constucons' and caused 'great damage'? Studley had 'been putt greatlie in trust manie yeares with the townes affaires especiallie in matters of awdit'. An 'assembly' met at the 'audict howse' to hear articles against him in 1603, and now Studley had to face the music before colleagues of many years standing. The articles were read out one by one: Studley (1) burned an account book in front of a 'late deputy steward'—John Ireland—that 'hath benn longe tyme missinge out of the awditt howse'; (2) 'ripped up sondrie of [Ireland's] bookes of accomptes after they had been brought unto the awditt [and] putt other leaves into them in there places'; (3) wrote 'errnonious parcells puttinge more to accompt of paym[en]t then was dew'; (4) snatched £15 out of the audit house; (5) wrongly 'entered three parcells on the collections side' in 'the fortheth leafe of the lidger booke' to line his own pockets to the tune of 'thirtie poundes three shillings and seaven pence in discharge of sums dew by James Ireland on the debitor side'; (6) owed the town another £43 17s. 6d. 'as in the one and thirtieth leafe of the lidger appeareth'; (7) 'contrarie to trueth with his owne hand writtinge dischardge[d] his accompt of the whole sum' and to cover his tracks wrote a 'false discharge' in the name of dead mayor Peter Stone, moving it to his own account 'as a matter given him'; (8) 'detayne[d Stone's] booke of casualties or accompts' so the town had 'no meanes to recover the debt'; (9) took bribes for leases on town houses; and (10) was the focus of 'manie other complaints [from] sundrie poore victuallers [and others] for takinge victuals [of] them by vertue of his aucthoritie and not payeinge for [them]'. There was no shred of doubt about Studley's guilt. He was trapped by his 'owne hand writinge'. It was 'a matter very odious for a man of his place to deceave the towne in such grosse and palpable manner', made far worse as he 'procured' an 'inferior officer' to work 'deceipts and unhonest practizes'. You 'shall for ever from and after this daye be secluded from the societie of the howse', governors told the man who had once been one of them. Studley was removed 'from the counsell' and stripped 'from his assistauncie' and position as 'awditor'. This former mayor was 'utterlie disgraded of his burgeship' and relegated to the subterranean ranks below 'good' citizens.[75]

[74] ESBHRO QI/EW6, fo. 55; QI/EW7, fos. 152v, 154v.

[75] J. W. Horrocks, ed., *The Assembly Books of Southampton*, 4 vols, Southampton Record Society, 9 (Southampton, 1917–25), I, 26–30.

It is hardly surprising that there were failings in information systems. Their operation was a comprehensive exercise with the potential to be adversely affected by individual inadequacies, ambition, and greed. No system this extensive exists without glitches. Yet the very stories of problems are also evidence of the real efforts amongst administrators to bring about higher levels of expectation in local government and to normalize more efficient record-keeping that were defended in court if necessary. Studley's case is jaw-dropping precisely because it was so exceptional and he was found out in the end after James Ireland turned the tables on him. Southampton magistrates took steps to put things right and make sure that nothing like this could ever happen again. Even seemingly minor cases like tearing off a piece of a 'presentment' were relatively rare.

It can be productive to study a system at work by observing responses to its particular problems. This we should keep in mind as we move now to look at information systems as a whole from their being made to being used. The great bulk of records remained relatively safe and sound, although weather and destruction got some of them in the end. They were locked up in chests that were put behind locked doors until the day that they were no longer administrative materials but research records and were moved to public archives. We turn next to making records, and the clerk in the middle of this, to follow production lines from event to entry on record.

III

Making records was a lonely pursuit. A clerk sits at a desk turning his court shorthand into full sentences, sometimes taking records home to finish the job if allowed. He is the front door to local knowledge. Clerks handled secrets each workday. Surrounded by records, they ought to have been from thoroughbred 'middling' stock. Precision was the watchword of their oath of office. 'Yow shall doe the best you can to make trew and perfectt recordes', Poole's town clerk pledged, and 'judgments justlie and trewelie enter according to true meaning'. If you are 'doubtefull' about anything, he was told, 'take the advice' of the recorder. Records were to be kept 'safelie and surelie in a chest fast locked in the towne howse'. He was warned never to let anyone look at them without high-ranking officials in the room. He would be in serious trouble if he was found 'dymnishinge or alteringe anie article, worde, or sentence' when making copies. All 'entries' were to be stored 'secretlie'. Nor was the clerk to 'disclose' or 'conceale anie matter that [came to his] knowledge touchinge the state of the towne'. 'The secretts of the towne', he was told, 'yow shall secretlie keepe'.[76]

[76] DHC DC/PL/B/1/1/1, fos. 40v–1. Cf. *The Office of the Clerk of Assize Containing the Form and Method of the Proceedings at the Assizes, and General Gaol-Delivery... Together with the Office of the Clerk of the Peace* (1676).

It was a plum job. Many clerks stayed in post for a long time. They made good livings and could top up their salaries with fees for making documents. It was 'thought fitt' by St Martin-in-the-Fields 'vestrimen' to pay the clerk forty shillings each year from 1606. He was told to come to all of meetings for 'writing and entring of suche orders and businesses as should be there comuned and concluded'.[77] Towns had 'tables' of fees with built-in add-ons. Thetford's clerk got four-pence for 'copies of all matters taken out of the courte', a shilling for a victualler's recognizance, and two shillings for 'recording of evidences'. Yarmouth's clerk was paid two-pence 'for every billett' and six-pence for 'judgements' written down in the 'courtbooke'.[78] These men made the records that we hold today. Robert Smith, who worked wonders reforming London's archives, had a red-letter day in 1586 when he got £30 for 'collecting' Common Council Acts 'into one volume' (a stationer got 53s. 4d. for binding it).[79] Benjamin Monger picked up £40 in 1602 for 'making of many writings' at London Bridewell. Arthur Good was paid 363 shillings 'for writing of 363 orders' at Hampshire sessions in 1694. Walton-on-the-Hill's clerk got a shilling 'for wryteing presentments to the head constable to the assyzes' (the minister picked up 2s. 6d. 'for wrytinge of the booke of cristhninges, weddinges and burialls').[80] Westminster clerks got 6s. 8d. for writing the 'twoe laste scavengers accomptes in twoe newe bookes' in 1599 and 52s. 2d. 'for writing books of assessment, indentures of apprenticeshipp, peticons and other writings for the parish' in 1624.[81]

Paper places needed paper to make their records. England's paper industry took large strides forwards in the seventeenth century,[82] although prices were volatile at times. London spent a fair amount of money on paper in the mid-1580s. Leatherseller William Prestwood—he was said to be a stationer in the next year—supplied a pile of paper to City government in 1585:

> one roll of parchment, 2 paper books for my lord mayor, 6 quires of parchment for the account, 6 quires of parchment for the journal of letter Z, 6 quires of parchment for freemen, 2 quires of paper royal, 6 quires of parchment for common council, and for a second book of parchment covered with leather to serve the lord mayors court for entering of reprieves of prisoners to actions

[77] WAC F2001, fo. 45v.

[78] NRO T/C1/6, fos. 30v–1; Y/C/19/5, fo. 165v. See also NRO Y/C27/1, fos. 26v, 80, 190v, 292v; KAC WSSMB/K/2/5, 1703 (end of book).

[79] B. Masters, ed., *Chamber Accounts of the Sixteenth Century*, London Record Society, 20 (1984) 82, 89. See P. Cain, 'Robert Smith and the reform of the archives of the city of London, 1580–1623', *London Journal*, 13 (1987–8).

[80] BMM LBHC 4, fo. 288; HA Q3/3, fo. 113; E. M. E. Ramsay and A. J. Maddock, eds., *The Churchwardens' Accounts of Walton-on-the-Hill, Lancashire, 1627–1667*, Lancashire and Cheshire Record Society, 151 (2005), 24, 55.

[81] WAC E14, 1624–5; SMF, 1599. See also HL HAM misc. box 12, 26/6/1636; box 2, folder 1, fos. 39, 42v; BRO WI/FA1/2, fos. 75v, 159v.

[82] D. C. Coleman, *The British Paper Industry, 1495–1860: A Study in Industrial Growth* (Oxford, 1958).

> commenced in the said court... one roll of parchment, 5 quires of royal paper, 6 quires of parchment for common council, one skin of vellum and one forel of vellum, 4 quires of parchment for the journal of the repertory, and 6 quires of parchment for freemen.

Total costs came to a hefty £12 2s 4d. and would keep rising.[83] Costs varied elsewhere: £4 7s. 'for makinge twoe books for the towne' in Lyme Regis in 1672; fourteen shillings 'for a greate boke for towlseye' in Gloucester in 1580; 3s. 4d. for 'a newe booke to write certen records of the towne' in Shrewsbury in 1578; and three-pence for 'a booke of paper to write strange ministers name in' at Walton near Liverpool in 1665.[84] Growing towns needed more books, ink, and paper. It cost Windsor 3s. 4d. to get ink and paper 'for one whole yeare' in 1657.[85]

William Dugdale spoke tersely about 'the unhappy neglect of the clerks in all ages'.[86] His blanket condemnation is severe. Most clerks did good jobs and became valued members of governing bodies. But not all of them. Chester was hit by another problem in 1626 and the cause this time was one of their own: city clerk Robert Brerewood. Harmful gaps had come to light in city records and Brerewood was thought to be the villain of the piece. His conduct was already causing concern. He was 'intemperate', some said, and 'uncivel' to a number of mayors in a row as well as city justices. And, to add insult to injury, it seemed that he had not been doing his job by the book. Allegations piled up. He had been looking after himself, not his city. Assembly orders had not been put on record ever since he began to moonlight elsewhere. Nor had he written down the names of people who sat on juries as he was bound to do. The clerk also farmed out his office for three years, lining his pockets with rents (even though it was 'annexed to the person'). The investigating team also found 'imperfect orders' in records that had not been 'agreed on by the assembly' and a judgment 'wrongfully' put in the books. On one occasion Brerewood 'entered [an] accon' on record that sent someone to a cell for a long cold night when he had been granted bail. To cap it all, he was ripping out records that he did not want anyone else to see. A 'declaracon and a record' had been 'razed' and 'altered', and a 'judgement' was 'blotted out' to hide something or someone. The details of 'other misdemeanors' more than serious enough to 'hinder' justice and 'dishonor' were not noted down. There was now nothing left of the trust the town had once put in its clerk. Brerewood had no leg left to stand on as one witness after another painted ugly pictures of him.

83 Masters, *Chamber Accounts*, 29–30, 89.

84 DHC DC/LR/G/2/2, 1671–2; GA GBR/F/4/3, fo. 208v; SHA 3365, fo. 511; Ramsay and Maddock, *Churchwardens' Accounts of Walton-on-the-Hill*, 163. See also CA TAR 1/9; SHA 3365, fo. 513; BRO R/D/QR/19/2/1, fo. 17v; KAC WSMB/K/1/5, 1594–5.

85 BRO W/FA1/2, fo. 103v.

86 W. Dugdale, *Origines Juridiales, or, Historical Memorials of the English Laws, Courts of Justice, Forms of Tryall, Punishment in Cases Criminal, Law Writers, Law Books*...(1666), A3v.

Little time was lost. He was sacked on the spot and a search started straight away for a 'fitting clerke'. A note was made in the margin of the assembly book: 'Mr maior to put in one to execute the place and take care of the records and bokes'. Nothing mattered more than that Chester got its records back in 'good order'.[87]

Brerewood's cavalier disregard for Chester and its records was out of the ordinary. More commonly a clerk was quite simply not up to the job. Pocklington's (Leicestershire) parish clerk was 'not sufficient' for the post in 1635 as 'hee can neither write nor reade'. He was also in a spot of bother for a 'fame of adultery'.[88] A Yarmouth clerk lost his post after he was caught 'extorting' fees, while a Norwich clerk wrote libels on the side in 1635.[89] Others fell behind. Maidstone governors warned the recorder's clerk in 1644 to 'carefully and truly' record 'all acts and orders made at courts of burghmote and not yet entered'. Thomas Rix got a pat on the back in Norwich in 1608 for 'registeringe of freemen by their sycencs and trades in a booke which was discontynewed for many yeares'.[90] Names were 'left out' of the assessment books in St Martin-in-the-Fields in 1644, while Oxford governors were dismayed to hear in 1672 that 'there hath beene little or noe true accompt' kept of 'forraigne freemen' who had paid forty shillings to become citizens. The mace-bearer was ordered to 'buy a booke [and] keepe the accompt therein exactly' including 'the day and yeare when it was done'.[91] We know all too well the gaps in records that maddingly break narratives and patterns. 'In my last years progress', Bishop Turner of Ely noted before doing the rounds of his diocese in 1685, I 'found no fault so common and almost general as the careless making up and keeping of parish registers'. 'Great care should be taken of those records', he scolded, as they 'may be brought to evidence in law'. 'You are to make them up exactly', he told his parishes, and 'bring them in so perfected to the *matricula* [i.e. Bishop's Register] and to see them kept hereafter under three locks and keys'.[92] A Westminster parish reminded its officers to 'register the names of all children baptized' and all burials and marriages in 1680: 'such as are behinde and not entered in the time of John Stogdell late clarke [to] be registered in the old register booke' to 'be kept in ye old vestry roome'. Lambeth's 'regester booke' was 'lefte unwritten' for three long years (1592–5). The minister of St Cuthbert's

[87] CA Z/AB/2, fo. 12v. Brerewood was locked in a spat involving his father-in-law (Sir Randle Mainwaring), and it is possible that charges against him were manipulated. Lawyer Brerewood was elected recorder in 1639 and MP in 1640, but local gentry and aldermen said his 'reliability was suspect' and he lost his seat in the Long Parliament election. He backed the king (he was knighted in 1643) but lost his place as recorder in 1646 after the parliamentary siege. See G. C. F. Forster, 'Civic government in Chester, 1642–1660', *Northern History*, 37 (2000), quoting 85, 92.

[88] LERO 1D41/21/1635.

[89] NRO Y/C/19/5, fo. 156; Norwich Sessions Book 1630–8, fo. 66v. See also CKS TE/AC3/3; NRO T/C1/1, fo. 58v; *The Vestry Minute Book of the Parish of Stratford-on-Avon* (1899), 149.

[90] CKS Md/Acm1/3, fo. 4v; NRO Norwich Chamberlains' Accounts 1603–25, fo. 107.

[91] WAC F2002, 1644; OHC C/FC/1/A1/04, fo. 107v.

[92] F. Turner, *Letter to the Clergy of the Diocese of Ely From the Bishop of Ely Before and Preparatory to His Visitation* (Cambridge, 1686), 18.

in York landed in trouble in 1660 after marrying couples 'without recording them in the register'.[93]

But despite these gaps paper records were everywhere. Gloucester had a 'paper office'.[94] Paper was produced in bulk for London in 1585–6: 300 proclamations to stop anyone from 'infected places' coming to the city, 500 constable's oaths, 200 freeman's oaths, 300 books of orders for clothing, 300 Common Council Acts aimed at alleys and inmates, and 300 to get 'foreigners and straungers' to pay taxes (this was a fraction of the paper that piled up in the Guildhall).[95] It was almost certain that a 'booke' would be compiled for any pressing problem. The ones that I have seen cover a myriad of matters including alehouses, almshouses, apprenticeship, bastardy, the bellman's 'doeings', branding, bridewell, cattle, Catholics, corn, 'the 5th of November', foreigners, hospitals, inmates, markets, pews, paupers, prisons, punishment, recusants, sickness, strangers, vagrants, whipping, and town 'affairs'.[96] Books were to govern by and were to be read and read again. 'A booke' was left at 'the round house' in St Martin-in-the-Fields in 1659 'to record the names of all vagrants passed away'. It was 'shewed every three weekes at the vestry' so governors could monitor the situation.[97] A guide for clerks of the peace recommended that they should 'keep a register book [with] true names, sirnames', and addresses of anyone with a licence to buy and sell corn or run an alehouse 'to the end it may appear to the court who be licens'd and by whom and who be not'.[98] Yarmouth governors wanted 'a booke [made] of all the almes howses [to] ye intente [that] the churchwardens maye see ye same howses employed to the uses they were given unto'.[99]

We see paper places in inventories of records that were one way of catching neglect and abuse. 'Mr maior required of the towne clerke a catalogue of all the books, evidences and writings of the towne in his hands', Cambridge alderman

[93] WAC E2416, fo. 85; C. Drew, ed., *Lambeth Churchwardens' Accounts 1504–1645 and Vestry Book 1610*, Surrey Record Society, 3 vols., 60 and 63–4 (1940, 1941, 1943).

[94] GA GBR/F/4/5, fo. 459. [95] Masters, *Chambers Accounts*, 89.

[96] GA GBR/F/4/3, fos. 107v, 266; GBR/F/4/5, fo. 34v; GBR/G/G3/SO/1, fo. 29; TBR/A/1/2, fo. 38; NRO Y//C/19/1, fo. 41v; Y/C/19/3, fo. 21v; Norwich Assembly Minute Book 5, fo. 83v, 143; HA W/B2/1, fo. 83; W/B1/3, fo. 167; W/K1/12, fos. 225–37; BRO R/AC1/1/1, fo. 600; R/AC1/1/3, fos. 17, 351; R/AC1/1/4, fo. 156; WI/FA1/2, fos. 116v, 123v; DRO ECA B/1/3, fo. 411; B/1/4, fo. 456; CKS FA/AC3, fo. 106; Md/Acm1/2, fo. 194v; YCA Y/HTG/15, fo. 156; WSHC G23/1/3, fo. 418v; KAC WQ/O/4, fo. 18v; WAC F2003, fos. 192–3; DHC DC/PL/B/1/1/1, fo. 99; CA Z/AB/1, fo. 4; NA 3/1, fo. 196; SHA 3365, fo. 513; BB/C/7/7/1/1; E. Melling, ed., *Kentish Sources: VI Crime and Punishment* (Maidstone, 1969), 185–6; B. W. Quintrell, ed., *Proceedings of the Lancashire Justices of the Peace at the Sheriffs Table During Assize Week, 1578–1694*, Record Society of Lancashire and Cheshire, 121 (Bristol, 1981), 150; J. P. Earwaker, ed., *The Constables' Accounts of the Manor of Manchester From the Year 1612 to the Year 1647 and From the Year 1743 to the Year 1776*, 3 volumes (Manchester, 1891–1902), I, 30, 214; II, 149; G. Meriton, *A Guide for Constables, Churchwardens, Overseers of the Poor…&c* (1674), 89–90, 95, 282–3; W. Lambarde, *The Duties of Constables, Borsholders, Tythignmen, and Such Other Low and Lay Ministers of the Peace* (1614), 5, 67, 68; R. Dunning, *A Plaine and Easie Method Shewing How the Office of Overseer of the Poor May be Managed* (1686), 9.

[97] WAC F2003, fos. 192–3. [98] *Office of the Clerk of Assize*, 91–2.

[99] NRO Y/C/19/3, fo. 21v.

Samuel Newton noted in 1669, referring to an order 'in a great booke page the 45 or 145'.[100] A committee was set up in Norwich in 1609 to 'set downe in an inventory all the bookes and recordes remayning in the clossett in the Guildhall'. Thetford governors also set up a committee in 1593 'to viewe the evidences of the towne [and] to inventorye the same'. Their peers in Salisbury asked for 'an inventorye [of] all the writings, deeds, and other things in the cheaste [in 1634 to be] inserted in a booke'.[101] A catalogue of papers 'for the towne' drawn up in Bridport in 1610 plunges us into the infrastructure of local administration-by-information. This is some of what we see: vagrant passes, 'hue and cr[ies]', the examination of a vagrant with no name, bridewell committals, Henry Lack's 'writing' to 'show cause of his ponnishment', orders 'for seats in the church', 'entries' for children, leases, releases, rentals, bonds, 'a booke for a voluntary benevolence of the best ablest for the sicke', 'examinacons of Robert Burrows that robbed a woman', 'a note' of ratepayers, 'entries [about the] stock of the poore', and more examinations, certificates, passes, warrants, and letters to and from Dorchester (outgoing letters were always copied), and much else.[102] This large range of issues is very revealing of the synergies between change and administration. All of this from a small Dorset town not far from the county seat but not sitting on a busy corridor. Records were also 'inspected' to check that they were complete and accurate. Oxford parishes were told to bring 'yee poore bookes' to 'the hall' in 1687 'to be inspected by ye justices'. Preston put the workhouse clerk in charge of 'keeping and tak[ing] care of all the note bookes of accompts paper and other writtings' in 1679. He was told to be 'ready and willing [to] shew forth [all] notebooks and accompt of papers' when called upon.[103]

Magistrates were compulsive list-makers, making lengthy inventories 'of all things belonginge' at regular intervals. A list put things in order and sequence, for a time at any rate. Information was first categorized and sorted in descending lines that were easy to take in. The names of owners of London's 700 hackney coaches were put in neat columns in 1681. A 'list' of conventicles in the London area was drawn up two years later, listing forty-one in the city, eleven across the river in Southwark, and twenty-three in Middlesex and Westminster (with the names of preachers and the 'factions they profess' written next to addresses).[104] Two lists from many thousands from all over the land. Some ran over many pages

[100] *The Diary of Samuel Newton Alderman of Cambridge (1662–1717)*, ed. J. E. Foster (Cambridge, 1890), 39.

[101] NRO Norwich Assembly Book 5, fo. 385v; T/C1/2, fo. 28; WSHC G23/1/3, fo. 387; WAC F2062; DRO 2203A-99/PO/2, fos. 61–2; 4767 A-99/PF/1.

[102] DHC DC/BTB/C88, fos. 30–30v. See also GA GBR/G/G3/SO/1, fo. 29.

[103] OHC QS/C/A1/01, fos. 8, 37v, 59v; QS/C/A1/02, fo. 95; LA CNP 3/1/1, fo. 171v.

[104] GA GBR/F/4/3, fo. 232v; *A View of the Penal Laws Concerning Trade and Traffic* (1681), 45; *A List of the Conventicles or Unlawful Meetings Within the City of London and Bills of Mortality* (1683). See also DRO ECA B/1/3, fo. 8; GA GBR/F/4/5, fo. 32; GBR/3/1, fo. 104; NRO T/C1/2, fo. 166; OHC C/FC/1/A1/02, fo. 79.

including 'true', 'exact', or 'perfect' 'lists' and 'catalogues' of Catholics, Scottish soldiers killed or taken prisoner at Dunbar (1650), Newgate prisoners, Rye House Plot conspirators, rebels put to death in 1686, high court judges, Royal Society fellows, and sailors captured by pirates in North Africa. Listing for multiple reasons was normal practice in local government. Some of the longest lists are columns of people who are about to be brought to court: fifty-one 'tiplers' in Barnstaple in 1676; fifty-one butchers from the same town who were caught 'not bringeng ther skynnes hangeng to the fleshe' in 1596.[105] Lists of indicted Cheshire recusants stretched for many pages; sixty-eight Wintonians were on a list of non-ratepayers in 1599; seventy-two recusants in Loughborough were put in a list in 1686; and the names of twenty Prestonians who kept 'great and unruly doggs' were noted in 1665 (the mayor among them).[106]

Numbers governed localities. Local arithmetic was becoming virtually indispensable. We have known about a surge in local 'census' taking at this time for a long while now. 'Survey' was often the word used. But things changed quickly in larger urban areas, making surveys obsolete in no time at all. St Martin-in-the-Fields pointed out in 1659 'that the present rate made for the poor will not serve [as] the numerous multitude of poore' was 'dayly increasing'.[107] The underlying reasoning for updating John Stow's *Survey of London* nearly a century after its first publication was that London was 'so much alter'd since his time as to be quite another thing'. Richard Carew needed a quick second edition of his Cornish *Survey* in 1602, as his 'countrie hath undergone so manie alterations since I first began these scribblings'.[108] Almost anything human, animal, or material was surveyed, people more often from the mid-sixteenth century on as inhabitants or the 'poore'. 'The poore surveyed', Chester governors noted after one more count.[109] Villages also counted when something needed noting, but towns were pioneers in this question of using information to discover populations. A census was commonly taken in troubled times, not least when the cost of taking care of the poor shot up and information was needed to fine-tune regulatory and relief systems. Officers and officials, as in Norwich in 1570, went from door to door to take 'note' of pauper households. We use these counts to establish levels of poverty and vulnerability and who lived where. A census is a source to mine, but it was also surveillance. Seventeenth-century lexicographers Edward Phillips and Elisha Coles

105 NDRO B1/3321; B1/46/374.

106 CA QJB/2/6, fos. 7–20v, 22v–6; HA W/B2/3, fos. 22–3; HL HAM box 27, folder 88; LA MCB/191; CNP 3/2/1, fo. 241.

107 WAC F2003, fo. 215.

108 *The Model of a Design to Reprint Stow's Survey* (1694), 2; R. Carew, *The Survey of Cornwall* (1602), preface to the reader.

109 CA Z/AB/1, fo. 4. See P. Slack, *Poverty and Policy in Tudor and Stuart England* (Harlow, 1988), 73–80; C. R. Chapman, *Pre-1841 Census and Population Listings in the British Isles* (1999); W. B. Stephens, *Sources for English Local History* (Cambridge, 1981), chap. 2; Laslett and Wall, *Household and Family*, 74–85 and chaps 4–5.

both thought of a 'census' as 'a mustering of an army' and 'a cessing of the people'. Francis Bacon believed that 'the population may appear by musters'.[110] Particular vocabularies of census-taking are evident in orders. 'The names and surnames of all inmates' (Hereford), 'take the names' (Rye), 'take notice' (Liverpool), 'a note of the number of the poor' (Oxford), 'set down the names' (Cambridge), 'trewe billes of all inhabitants' (Yarmouth), and 'present' or 'certifie' names (Chester and Maidstone).[111]

Magistrates asked the same question again and again: 'how many?' 'Articles to be inquyered of' are portraits of urban disfigurement. Exeter wanted information in 1561 on 'skowldinge [or] brawlinge women', 'any vagabond, upright men, qwyer byrds, mightye beggars, bawds, whores [or] mysliving people', anyone living 'suspiciouslie', victuallers serving too late at night, any 'hopster' not 'of good name and fame' keeping 'bawdrey [or] nighte watchinge', apprentices not 'seemely apparrelled', forestallers, crooked measures, 'swyne fylthe' or 'dunge hills', 'decayed' houses, and filthy 'jaks house of office'.[112] Questions crossed landscapes seeking information. All done, Yarmouth council said, for 'taking knowledge' for 'the better governmente' of a town and 'better discovery' of troublemakers.[113] The human and physical debris of change fills surveys: idle poor, 'singlewomen' living alone who 'goe to thir owne hands', vagrants, inmates, crumbling walls and buildings, or workers without seven-year apprenticeships under their belts.[114] 'Articles to be inquired of' by Cambridge 'surveyers' in 1600 are a textbook example of a town trying to discover the dimensions of its difficulties. 'Surveyers' were told to 'diligently inquire and faythfully sett downe in writing' the names of anyone who had lived in the town for less than three years with no right to be there; hard-up paupers 'able to gett theire living by labour in whole or in part'; householders who could not get by without hand-outs; better-off people who could 'give' to the poor; innkeepers, alehouse-keepers, and any householders who rented rooms to beggars and inmates; and any cottages that had been built on Cambridge's fringes.[115]

Cambridge was better known after it had been surveyed. People were slotted into columns and categories such as orderly/disorderly, deserving/undeserving, employed/unemployed. This is hardly unexpected when Whitehall and local governors created strategies and vocabularies for surveillance through legislation

[110] Coles, *English Dictionary*, and Phillips, *New World of Words*, s.v. 'census'; *Francis Bacon: Major Works*, ed. B. Vickers (Oxford, 1996), 302.

[111] HEA BG11/17/1/5, fo. 67; ESBHRO RYE/5, fo. 282; Power, *Liverpool Town Books*, 14; R. Blades, ed., *Oxford Quarter Sessions Order Book 1614–1637*, Oxford Historical Society, NS, 29 (Woodbridge, 2009), 41; CUL VC-CT-vi.15, fo. 80; NRO Y/C/19/3, fo. 91v; CA Z/AB/2, fo. 17v; CKS Md/Acm1/3, fo. 102.

[112] CUL VC-CT-vi.15, fos. 71–2. 80; DRO ECA B/1/4, fo. 106.

[113] NRO Y/C/19/5, fos. 20v–1, 83.

[114] CKS Md/Acm1/1a, fo. 62; FA/AC3, fo. 76v; NRO Norwich Assembly Book 5, fos. 244–5; GA TBR/A/1/1, fos. 8–9; GBR/B3/2, fo. 284; HEA BG11/17/1/5, fo. 45; DRO ECA B/1/4, fo. 396; WAC E2413, fo. 82.

[115] CUL VC-CT-vi.15, fo. 80.

and directives. Towns counted but did they always get it right? Constables went to Cambridge's Midsummer Fair in 1626 to take 'note' about the Sign of the George where word was that students boozed all day Sunday. One constable said that there were twenty students 'drinkinge and conversinge and smoking tobacco [with] 4 fidlers playing'; another said that 'there were some xii there' in the alehouse.[116] 'I have heard of twenty or thirty thousand catholics' in St Martin-in-the-Fields, Peter Petit noted in 1689, 'but the account was taken there and as exact a one as could be, and I am assured by some that should know [that the real figure] upon most careful scrutiny was about 600'. 'We hear of vast numbers [of papists] in the north', Petit continued, 'but I believe there are much fewer than we hear'. 'People', he ended snootily, 'multiply the number of papists in common talk at least ten-fold'.[117] Surveying and counting were sometimes neglected. 'A very smale appearance', St Martin-in-the-Fields vestry noted glumly in 1659, when just two officers filed a 'returne of ye inmates'. They also slammed 'the greate neglect' of beadles who filed inmate lists in dribs and drabs a few weeks later.[118] Southampton's beadles were taken to task in 1604 for 'neglecting duties in not presenting weekly the names of newcomers, inmates and undertenants'. We lack lists of all who 'keepe guns and greyhoundes', Westmorland justices complained in 1648.[119] Mistakes, but we should acknowledge the aspiration to be accurate. Lancashire constables were told to bring information 'as nere as they can' of the 'names and nomber' of 'strandge beggers' in 1586.[120] Officers in all parts of the country were told to inquire 'diligently' and 'faythfully' and 'truely certifie' findings in 'a true note', 'perfect book', 'certayne note', 'exact survey', 'trew certificate', 'true accompt', and 'true and perfect callendar' or 'list'.[121]

There were other pressures, such as a need for speed. St Martin-in-the-Fields overseers were told to list the 'names of all poore people [who can] worke with all convenient speed' in 1656. Northampton officers were told to 'searche immediately' for inmates in 1585 and 'certifye' their findings 'immediately'. Rye constables were told to put the names of every householder 'in a fayre booke' 'in 1593 'without delaye'.[122] Other 'serches' appear to have been on the spur of the moment—'this night' or 'this day'—or dictated by emerging situations as in Ipswich in 1593 when

[116] CUL VCT/49, fo. 15.

[117] P. Petit, *A Discourse of the Growth of England in Populousness and Trade Since the Reformation* (1689), 140–1.

[118] WAC F2003, fos.189, 203.

[119] SA 6/1, fo. 28; KAC WQ/0/3, fo. 48; WQ/M/1, fo. 10.

[120] Quintrell, *Proceedings of the Lancashire Justices*, 69.

[121] For example, CUL VC-CT-vi.15, fo. 80; LMA Rep. 54, fos. 271–2; E. H. Bates, ed., *Quarter Sessions Records for the County of Somerset*, 4 vols, Somerset Record Society (1907–19), IV, 281; CRO Z/AB/1, fo. 126v; CKS U120/09, fo. 18; NA 3/1, fo. 227; NRO Y/C/19/4, fo. 150; HRO W/B2/4, fo. 53; DRO ECA B/1/3, fo. 411. On the reliability of surveys, Steve King notes that Bolton's 1699 census is 'unquestionably' 'accurate': 'Locating and characterizing poor households in late seventeenth century Bolton: sources and interpretations', *Local Population Studies*, 68 (2002), 59.

[122] WAC F2003, fo. 97; NA 3/1, fo. 225; ESBHRO RYE/5, fo. 282.

officers 'serched' for anyone arriving from plague-struck London.[123] Time was always of the essence as troubles struck 'dayly'. Attention was on 'this tyme' or 'nowadays'. 'Surveys' were timetabled 'once every weeke at the leaste' (Yarmouth, 1622). Officers there had a week to draw up 'trewe billes of inhabitants' in 1574. Yarmouth pubs were surveyed 'every weeke twysse' in 1599 and in Winchester in 1572, along with 'newe dwellers' and anyone dirtying streets.[124] Chester had monthly surveys around 1600 (on Saturdays, moved later to Fridays). 'Newecomers' were surveyed monthly in Colchester (1597), Chester (1590), Leicester (1574), and St Martin-in-the-Fields (1622).[125] Inmates were counted 'every Munday' in St Margaret's Westminster (1683), each third Wednesday in next-door St Martin-in-the-Fields (1659), quarterly in Northampton (1581), 'every six weekes' in Ashby-de-la-Zouch, and weekly 'duly and carefully' in Yarmouth (1622) and Norwich (1600).[126] Gloucester had 'surveyes at severall tymes' in 1646. Winchester porters were told to 'dailie bringe certificates to mr maior of theire dailie proseedings and events in their wardes' in 1593.[127]

Most things were counted because anything was a potential concern: apprentices, dog owners, men pressed for war (twenty-nine in 1628 in Reading), rickety houses, people letting sheep eat corn 'in this time of scarcitie', fishing boats, people with weights and measures at home (sixteen in one Hereford ward in 1624, with ten other names crossed out), and a page of people with buckets in Chester in 1659.[128] Roger Lowe went around Ashton-in-Makerfield with two others in 1666 'to see what people would give towards the relief of such needie persons as had sustained losse by the great fire in London and to set their names downe'. 'Over the one halfe of Ashton' gave something, Lowe noted.[129] Loyalty was measured in lists of people taking or not taking oaths: 307 Maidstone men signed the Solemn League and Covenant in 1662 (four refused); 208 men signed the Oath of Allegiance in Lyme Regis in 1661; and there were 307 signatures on a loyal address to the new king in Bideford in 1685.[130] A catalogue of offenders/

[123] SAI C/4/3/1/1/3, fo. 34. See also HEA Q/SM/2, fo. 61; WAC F2002, fo. 266; HA W/H3/15, unpag.; CKS Md/Acm1/3, fos. 49v–50.

[124] NRO Y/C/19/5, fo. 83; T/C1/1, fo. 8; Y/C/19/3, fo. 91v; HA W/B2/1, fos. 3, 24v.

[125] CA Z/AB/1, fos. 259v, 261, 263; ERO D/B5/Gb1, fo. 134; LERO BR11/1/2, fo. 246; WAC F2001, fo. 162. See also NRO Y/C/19/5, fos. 20v–1; GA TBR/A/1/2, fo. 9; LERO BR11/1/2, fo. 246; WSHC G23/1/3, fo. 321; CA Z/AB/1, fo. 231v.

[126] WAC E2416, fo. 134; F2003, fo. 192; HL HAM box-2, folder-1, fo. 13v; NA 3/1, fo. 209; NRO Y/C/19/5, fo. 266; Norwich Assembly Book 5, fo. 244.

[127] GA GBR/F/4/5, fo. 349; HA W/B2/3, fo. 3v.

[128] HA W/B2/1, fo. 61v; W/B1/4, fos. 137v–8; W/B1/5, fos. 45–5v; LMA MJ/SBR/1, fos. 25–6, 560–62v; MJ/SBR/2, fos. 121–2, 413–14; Rep. 62, fos. 169–172v; 63, fos. 167–70v; CA QJB/1/5, fos. 2–5, 86–6v, 530; CUL VC-CT.15, fos. 71–2; ESBHRO RYE/5, fos. 260v–1; CKS Md/Acm1/1a, fos. 5v–6.

[129] *The Diary of Roger Lowe of Ashton-in-Makerfield, Lancashire, 1663–74*, ed. W. L. Sachse (New Haven, CT, 1938), 107–8.

[130] CKS Md/Acm1/3, fos. 12v–15v; DHC DC/LR/B1/9, fos. 366–9; NDRO 1064Q/SO1, fos. 192v–4. See also SHA BB/F/1/1/365/71; LA CNP 3/2/1, fos. 23, 87; and J. Walter, *Covenanting Citizens; The Protestation Oath and Popular Culture in the English Revolution* (Oxford, 2017), esp. chaps 4–6.

offences was a logical step towards eventual prosecution. Unsurprisingly, the variety of lists was as broad as the range of offending: 'wenches that goe att their own hands', mothers of 'base' children, 'comon gamesters', wood stealers, hedge-breakers, begging, breaching market regulations, or not cleaning streets.[131] An Exeter constable was 'comaunded by mr maior to go and take the names of suche as were playinge at cudegells about St Johns Rowe' one day in 1619 (his reward was a volley of threats).[132] We also see orders to note names and numbers of anyone caught since the last court or set free from a bridewell. Leicestershire officers were told in 1610 to 'provide an accompt upon oath in writinge under the hand of the minister' of how many 'vagabonds' and 'rogues' they took into custody and 'how many' they ended up punishing. These 'dirreccons ' were 'to be publickly read [in] parochiall churches or at the church dore and to be registered [in] parish books [for] the better informacon and example of those that shall succeed them'.[133]

Plague made people count. 'Eight houses visited', Chester's mayor reported in 1654, 'but all the families remaine out in the cabins which are remote from any passage to the cittie'. 'Not any sicke within the cittie at present to our knowledge', he added with fingers crossed. Since 'the first beginninge onely eleven persons dyed and three of them lately', he reported, evidently pleased at this 'light' toll.[134] 'There are at this present 4 howses infected', privy councillors heard from Reading in the first stirrings of plague in 1625, 'and 2 more being suspected wee have caused to bee shutt upp'.[135] More general tallies were called for as the first deaths were reported. Yarmouth deputies were told to 'deliver unto Mr bayliffes a trew note of all suche persons as doe dye in ther wardes as also what howses be infected' in 1590 and to keep 'notes' of plague deaths 'by themselves'.[136] Thomas Usher was paid well 'for certifieng [the] names of the deceassed wekely' in Norwich in 1579, while two Northampton men got twenty-pence weekly in 1578 for 'certyfying what disease' any parishioner 'dyeth of [as] nere they can'.[137] Bills of mortality are the most well-known course of action to count and explain deaths. In London, parish lists were merged in columns by the Parish Clerks company and sold in droves. We can imagine anxious readers thumbing through

[131] For example, ESBHRO QI/EW2, fos. 25v–6; LA CNP 3/2/1, fos. 216–17, 315; CKS U120/09, fo. 106; Md/Acm1/11a, fo. 74; NRO Y/C/19/4, fo. 230; SA 6/1, fo. 27; SAI C/4/3/1/1/1, fo. 95v; NA 3/1, fo. 422; LERO BRII/1/3, fo. 938.

[132] DRO ECA C1/61, fos. 25–6.

[133] LERO QS6/1/2, fos. 62–2v. For advice in handbooks see Meriton, *Guide for Constables, Churchwardens, Overseers of the Poor...*, 97–8; Lambarde, *Duties of Constables, Borsholders, Tythingmen...*, 28–9; Chamberlain, *Complete Justice*, 181.

[134] CA ZML/3/376.

[135] BRO R/Z3/9. For plague and surveillance in Florence, see J. Henderson, *Florence Under Siege: Surviving Plague in and Early Modern City* (New Haven, CT, and London, 2019), esp. chaps 3–5; N.A. Eckstein, 'Florence on foot: An eye-level mapping of the early modern city in time of plague', *Renaissance Studies*, 30 (2015).

[136] NRO Y/C/19/4, fo. 190v.

[137] NRO Norwich Clavors Book 1, fos. 77v, 78; NA 3/1, fo. 195. Officers fleeing plague-hit towns were sometimes added up. See, for instance, LMA Jours 26, fo. 131v; 33, fo. 130.

columns to map death by number to follow its pitiless drift across London. Humphrey Crouch put this in verse in a work on death in London and Newcastle: 'The day the weekly bills come out / to put the people out of doubt / How many of the plague do dye / We summe them up most carefully'.[138] Graunt believed that people read bills to see 'how the burials increased or decreased', so 'they might take the same as a text'. He thought that 'the rich might judge of the necessity of their removal' by reading the bills, 'and tradesmen might conjecture what doings they were likely to have in their respective dealings'.[139] Ralph Josselin sat in his house a comfortable sixty miles from London thumbing through weekly death tolls to track plague there in 1665: 267 one week, followed by 684, 1,268, 2,785, 3,014, 4,030, 5,568, 7.496, 8.252. 'Plague increased' to 267, he noted on 2 July; 'London sad days increase 1268 buried' (16 July); 'Great increase of plague' (13 August); and, finally, 'abatements' as cooler autumn arrived. He also tracked plague through Colchester and other Essex towns.[140] Alderman Newton, sitting in Cambridge, copied figures from London's bills into his diary, while John Squire used the bills in 1636 to trace a fall in deaths over a seven-week stretch after a fast, sharing his findings in a sermon at St Paul's Cathedral.[141]

This is a veritable hotchpotch of enumeration. But population and poverty were counted more than anything else. Manchester spent four shillings for 'wryting two bookes of the names of all inhabitants' in 1628 (a list from 1648 stretches to twenty pages and another in 1666 to twenty-two). An Oswestry clerk was given four-pence in 1609 'for engrossinge ye names of ye townesmen'. A 'catalogue of all the names of the householders' was drawn up in Chester in 1630 ('a kalendar to be made of their names').[142] Moving south, the names of 'every house-holder' in Rye were put 'in a fayre booke' in 1593. 'Trewe billes of all inhabitants' were prepared in Yarmouth in 1574. A skinner got a few shillings for 'makeinge' a 'booke of all inhabitants names' in one London precinct in 1601.[143] 'In this booke [are] contayned the names of all thinhabitantes yownge and old', a clerk has written with a sense of accomplishment after constables went round Poole to count people on 5 May 1574: 'We find that there is dwellinge in this towne, menn, of wymen, and of chyldren as by the accompt dothe appeare to the some of 1373

[138] H. Crouch, *London's Vacation and the Countries Tearme* (1637), B1r. See also J. C. Robertson, 'Reckoning with London: interpreting the bills of mortality before John Graunt', *UH*, 23 (1996).

[139] Graunt, *Natural and Political Observations*, preface.

[140] *The Diary of Ralph Josselin*, ed. A. Macfarlane, British Academy Records of Social and Economic History, NS, III (Oxford, 1976), 519–21 and 522–33.

[141] *Diary of Samuel Newton*, 14–15; J. Squire, *A Thankes-giving for the Decreasing and Hope of Removing of the Plague* (1637), 25–6. Robert Jenison compared mortality in London in 1603/4 and 1625 in his *The Cities Safetie: or a Fruitfull Treatise (and Useful for These Dangerous Times) on Psalm 127* (1630), 160–1.

[142] Earwaker, *Constables Accounts of the Manor of Manchester*, I, 214, II, 181–201, 202–21, 225–46, 247–59, 261–83; W. Day, ed., *Oswestry Parish Church: the Churchwardens' Accounts for 1579–1613* (Oswestry, 1970), 36, 175; CA Z/AB/2, fo. 24v.

[143] ESBHRO RYE/5, fo. 282; NRO Y/C/19/3, fo. 91v; LMA MS 9680, fo. 10.

persons [of] the which nombre are 165 howse holders [and under tenants]'. The 'booke' also notes 180 'masstrs, maryners, and sea fayringe men' and 180 'merchants, artificers, and others'. The town was quite literally on paper now.[144] We have lists of inhabitants (men only sometimes) and orders to count them from Rye (1681 and other years by ward), Lyme Regis (1658) Hereford (1663 by ward), London (1640 by precinct), Ealing (1599), Maidstone (1656), Thetford (1550 and 1578 by ward), Ludlow (by ward), Winchester, Bridport, and little Wollaston on Nottingham's fringe (1637–8): 'a trewe copie of all householders with the number of families'.[145] Cambridge parish returns in the 1630s/40s list households broken down by 'towne borne' and 'forreyners', with notes on ages, landlords, and 'sojurners'. We get little insights into lives: a locksmith's family with 'a child very poore but yonge and lustye', Widow Sisson with '2 children poor but lusty', and a waterman not long married but his wife now 'impotent'.[146]

Males were also listed for reasons that reflect their roles as taxpayers, voters, landowners, tenants, governors, citizens, officers, and fighters on land and sea.[147] 'The names of those that were made burgesses' in Gloucester were noted each year: fifty-one in 1645, eighty in 1661.[148] Marlborough officials made lists or 'nota' 'of burgesses and freemen'. Barnstaple, Reading, Clitheroe, Poole, and Christchurch did the same.[149] Yarmouth listed 'names of the bailiffs, aldermen, burgesses, and commonaltye' in 1626.[150] It was vital to check that records of freeholders, copyholders, and customary tenants were up to date when more land changed hands and landlords schemed to redefine relationships to tenants. Names of Loughborough freeholders who had died since the last 'court of inquiry' were 'certifyed' to the court to keep things up to date (ninety-one in 1646).[151] Towns also updated lists of ratepayers for taxes or more mundane matters like patching up bridges or roads. A Maidstone 'survey' from 1651 listed people 'that doe pay towards the reliefe of the poore people [and] those who doe not pay' (with a note

[144] DHC DC/PL/B/13/1, fos. 10, 17v, 3.

[145] ESBHRO RYE 15/2, 15/20; DHC DC/LR/B1/9, fos. 71–3; HEA BG11/4/6, fo. 10; CKS Md/JLP1/1656; NRO T/C1/1, fo. 8; HL HAM box 54, folder, 26; HA W/K5/3, 30v; DHC DC/btb/E6; A. Rogers, 'An early seventeenth-century listing: Wollaton, Notts', *Midland History*, 5 (1980); P. Styles, 'A census of a Warwickshire village in 1698', *University of Birmingham Historical Journal*, 3 (1951); K. J. Allison, 'An Elizabethan village "census"', *Bulletin of the Institute of Historical Research*, 36 (1963); for London see my *Lost Londons: Change, Crime, and Control in the Capital City, 1550–1660* (Cambridge, 2008), chap. 11.

[146] CUL CUR 37.3, fos. 109–16.

[147] For Gloucester alone see GA GBR/F/4/5, fos. 306–6v, 404, 452; GBR/F/4/6, fos. 7, 122, 254, 296, 392, 342; GBR/F/4/7, fos. 5, 90, 345, 419, 455, 500, 705.

[148] GA GBR/F/4/5, fos. 306–6v; GBR/F/4/6, fos. 296, 392.

[149] WSHC G22/1/20, fos. 43–4, 92–3, 134–5, 178–9; NDRO B1/3792, fo. 80; BRO R/FA/3/1, 1587–8; LA MBC/225; DHC DC/CC/B/2/2/1; DC/PL/B/7/2/1.

[150] NRO Y/C/19/6, fo. 109. See also NRO T/C1/1, fo. 34; CKS Md/Acm12, fo. 2; HA W/B2/3, fo. 3; Q2/2, fo. 58.

[151] HL HAM box 26, folder 14. See also HEA Q/SM/2, fo. 61; J. Norden, *The Surveyors Dialogue* (1610), 93, irregular pag.

on 'abilities and qualities').[152] Such lists became routine as poverty dug deeper. Ratepayers in a Reading parish appear in alphabetical order from William Ambrose to Mr Webb (forty-four names in all, with two crossed out).[153] If they fell in the age group 16–60, these men also appeared on muster lists. Typically, Rye officers went 'to every house [in 1583] to wryte downe householders names with their sonnes and servants and guests able to serve'.[154] Officers and 'captaynes' knocked on doors to 'wright downe everry serviceable mans name' in Yarmouth in 1590. A Manchester scribe earned 2s. 6d. for writing 892 names on a muster roll. A 'B' against names 'in the margent' in a Marlborough muster role from 1587 meant that this person had 'black billes' (thirty-six in total).[155]

Columns of paupers give us the bare details of the lives of victims of change, though they were rarely recognized as such. They get us inside the doors of the poor. The down-and-out in two Salisbury parishes were listed by address, life-cycle stage, age, 'ability', and hand-outs in 1635. Magistrates picked through measly household budgets to paint pictures of people perched precariously on poverty lines. The value of child labour to drag have-not households from one week to the next is plain to see. Eighteen of the 'surveyed' limped through life crippled or lame. Five could not get out of bed. Seven were blind. One was blind in one eye. Another could barely see anything. Three more had weak eyesight. One could not hear anything. Sixteen were 'sick' or 'feeble'. Three paupers were 'impotent'. Five wives (one pregnant) fended for themselves with no idea where their husbands were. 'Surveyours' found 24-year-old Eleanor Macy in a shabby house with her 70-year-old feeble mother. 'Sometimes distracted' Mellor Jones lived with his 'crook-backed' daughter on twenty-five-pence weekly, while John Butler's wife was left with 2s. 6d. weekly to put food on the table for Crisse, Ann, Thomas, and Nabb after he was put in prison [156]

There are similar-sounding stories in the Norwich Census of the Poor (1570) that is our best bird's-eye view of the English poor. Families are listed as 'myserable' or 'verie poore' in plights that repeat themselves. Work is hard to get; women with children have no 'helpe' (one with eight mouths to feed); household heads 'not in occupieinge'; hard-up widows aged anywhere from 20 to 100; people 'past' work or 'not able to work'; and child breadwinners. We see paupers knee-deep in poverty's quicksand: Widow Jenkinson who would 'spyn when she can get ytt'; Widow Peck who was 'beside hyrselfe [and can] do no worke'; and Widow Maude

[152] CKS Md/Acm1/3, fos. 49v–50.

[153] BRO R/AP1/4. See also ESBHRO RYE 1/6, fo. 43v; DRO ECA B/1/5, fos. 16–18; LA CNP 3/1/1, fo. 42; WSHC G22/1/107, fos. 13, 41, 66.

[154] ESBHRO RYE 1/5, fo. 34.

[155] NRO Y/C/19/4, fo. 187; Earwaker, *Constables' Accounts of the Manor of Manchester*, I, 170; WSHC G22/1/107, fo. 10. See also NRO Norwich muster lists/13a/1–39; NDRO B1/3792, fo. 97; SAI C/4/3/1/1/1, fo. 94v; WSHC G22/1/107, fos. 9–10, 32–4; BRO R/AX/1, fo. 22; SAI HD36/A/306.

[156] P. Slack, ed., *Poverty in Early Stuart Salisbury*, Wiltshire Record Society, 31 (Devizes, 1975), 75–80.

House 'that is a desolate thing and beggeth'. More than a few had not long arrived in Norwich, like 40-year-old lace-weaver 'Alice-lyve-by-love' from Diss. We see suffering in graphic tales of sickness, disability, and pain: lame (34), 'diseased' (14), 'sycke' (32), one hand or leg (5), deaf and/or dumb (8), 'croked' (2), blind (8), and not far off blind (2). A note was made of anyone on the wrong side of the law, including thieves (more women than men) and women 'out of service'. Idle 'drones' and scolds turn up along with 'unruly' folk and 'grasse maydes' with 'base' children. Twenty-nine-year-old Rose Fidemund from the 'west contree' had been in Norwich for four years living with her out-of-work brother and his wife (a working spinner). She was called a 'gressemayde' and 'harlot that spyn webbynge'.[157]

The anonymous author of *An Ease for Overseers* (1601) urged that 'the multitude of the poore must be reduced to number' and provided a 'readie forme for a speedie inspection of the poor'.[158] Officers in one London precinct made a book 'conserninge numberinge of all the powre [that] had relefe of us' in 1603. 'The number of poore people' was written down in 'two bookes' in St Martin-in-the-Fields in 1603: 'one for the vestrie to see and the other for justices'. A Chester parson got six shillings 'for making of a boke of all the names of the pore folke of the cittye' in 1572.[159] This is what St. Martin-in-the-Fields vestry saw in constables' returns in 1603: 448 people getting hand-outs or likely to need one soon; ten landlords housing inmates cheaply (names, addresses, and rents set down); and 'i carman, ii nightmen, iii water bearers, and ii oyster wives (or cryers of fishe)'.[160] 'The names of the poore' were listed in St Giles parish in Reading in 1650: nineteen men, twenty-two widows, and three goodwives (three names crossed out). There were fifty-five poor in another Reading parish: sixteen men and thirty-nine women including thirty-four widows (four names crossed out).[161] 'Certificates' from Ipswich revealed 122 households in 1597: sixty-two headed by married couples; forty-eight by women (thirty-six widows); six by males; five with two women including two pairs of widows and a pair of 'sturdye' sisters; and one house shared by two frail men. The paper bristles with classifications: 'able', 'sound', 'sick', 'ympotent', 'inmate', 'diseased', 'blind', 'lame', 'bedred', 'sturdye'.[162]

The poor were surveyed everywhere. Gloucester's governors 'surveyed the poore' in 1640; St Martin-in-the-Fields drew up alphabetical lists of 'pensioners' and orphans (1654–96); Oxford put together 'a note of the number of poor'

[157] J. F. Pound, *The Norwich Census of the Poor, 1570*, Norfolk Record Society, 60 (Norwich, 1971). See M. Pelling, *The Common Lot: Sickness, Medical Occupations and the Urban Poor in Early Modern England* (1998); and P. Griffiths, 'Inhabitants', in C. Rawcliffe and R. Wilson, eds., *Norwich Since 1550* (2004), 65–6.

[158] *An Ease for Overseers of the Poore* (1601), 17, 4.

[159] LMA MS 9680, fo. 21v; WAC SMF, 1603; CA TAR/1/14.

[160] WAC F6039. [161] BRO R/AP1/3; R/AP2/1.

[162] J. Webb, ed., *Poor Relief in Elizabethan Ipswich*, Suffolk Records Society, 9 (Ipswich, 1966), 119–40.

(1618).[163] Norwich made 'a note fairely written of the names of [the] poore' (1699); 'double chardged' Chester took a 'viewe and certayne note' of the poor (1571); Ipswich constables 'certifye[d] the number' of the poor to magistrates in 1582.[164] There were 'surveys' of the poor in Worcester (1557), Canterbury (1563), Bolton (1674, 1686, 1699), Huddersfield (1622), little Walton-on-the-Hill (1652), Preston (1675), Bristol (1696), Norwich again (1691), and Cawston village twelve miles from Norwich.[165] South Newington had 'a register booke for the poore' (1579); a 'paper booke' listed 'the names of the poor' in Preston in 1697 as 'are to bee registered'; 'a booke' was bought in Salisbury in 1625 to bring three parish 'abstracts for the poore' into one document.[166] 'A booke of the names of such as are most poor and necessitated' was completed in Liverpool in 1656; a note was pinned to it saying that 'the number of the poor are to be computed at 60 odd'—'computed' is a memorable term.[167] Tewkesbury (1639), St Katherine-by-the-Tower (1609–10), Great Yarmouth (1636), and Manchester (1626) all had a 'poore booke'.[168] 'Particularizing', in a wonderful word from Walton village, was on magistrates' minds. The Ipswich census had these headings: 'names and condicions', 'ages', 'woorkes', 'wages', 'child[ren]', 'reliefe', and 'wants'.[169] The poor were broken down into their parts. Winchester set up quarterly 'strict examinacon[s]' of paupers 'fit' to get 'almes' in 1655 in set categories: 'impotent, aged and decrepit, the infant, ye fatherlesse and ye motherlesse, blind and lame', which were entered into a 'booke'. St Martin-in-the-Fields split their 'chargeable' poor into those who were 'able to labour' or 'impotent through age or infirmitye' in 1662.[170]

'Particularizing' allowed governors to focus process on specific groups. Kendal poor's children, for instance, were put down on paper to see who was 'fitt for apprenticeships'. A note was made of Faversham's children in 1627 to find the best way to keep them 'from idlenesse and disorderlie course of life and for theire better meanes of living'.[171] It was crucial to have current knowledge of matters such as these with consequences for the peace and purse. St Martin-in-the-Fields

[163] GA GBR/B/3/2, fo. 170; WAC F3348–51; Blades, *Oxford Quarter Sessions Order Book 1614–1637*, 41.

[164] NRO NMCC 25, fo. 275v; 26, fo. 59v; CA Z/AB/1, fo. 126v; SAI C/4/3/1/1/3, fo. 50.

[165] Slack, *Poverty and Policy*, 73; Clark and Clark, 'Social economy of the Canterbury suburbs'; E. Ralph and M. E. Williams, eds., *The Inhabitants of Bristol in 1696*, Bristol Record Society, 25 (Bristol, 1968); T. Wales, 'Poverty, poor relief, and the life-cycle: some evidence from seventeenth-century Norfolk', in R. Smith, ed., *Land, Kinship and Life-Cycle* (Cambridge, 1984), 369; Ramsay and Maddock, *Churchwardens' Accounts of Walton-on-the-Hill*, 90; LA 3/1/1, fo. 155v.

[166] E.R.C. Brinkworth ed., *South Newington Churchwarden's Accounts 1553–1684*, Banbury Historical Society, 6 (1964), 13; LA CNP 3/1/3, fo. 11v; WSHC G23/1/3, fo. 317.

[167] Power, *Liverpool Town Books*, 92–3.

[168] GA TBR/A/1/2, fo. 38; LMA MS 9680, fos. 21v, 12; NRO Y/C/19/5, fo. 264v; Earwaker, *Constables Accounts of the Manor of Manchester*, I, 171.

[169] Ramsay and Maddock, *Churchwardens' Accounts of Walton-on-the-Hill*, 90; Webb, *Poor Relief in Elizabethan Ipswich*.

[170] HA W/B1/5, fos. 109–10; WAC F2003, fo. 294. Cf. CUL VC-CT-vi.15, fo. 80.

[171] KAC WSSMB/K/2/5, fo. 55; CKS FA/AC3, fo. 156. See also BRO R/AC1/1/3, fo. 301; KAC WSSMB/K/2/5, fo. 100; WAC F2003, fo. 294; HA W/B1/5, fos. 109–10.

vestry clerk was asked to make an 'abstracte [of orphans and "pencioners"] as have dyed or beene placed awaye' over the last year and any 'new put in'. Twenty 'penconers [were] allowed' there in 1657.[172] 'Inquyre what penconers are lately dead', Bury St Edmunds magistrates told officers in 1651; find out 'when they dyed, whoe are livinge and when last paid, and whoe are fitt to have ther pencons discharged or abated and whose pencons are fitt to be augmented and upon what grounds'.[173] Norwich magistrates wanted the names of paupers whose hand-outs 'may be abated by reason of the cheapnes of corne' in 1686.[174]

'Unnecessarie members', as Preston governors called them, were also surveyed. They were inmates who 'crept' into the town in hard times, hoping to strike it lucky.[175] This was the 'unruly 'sort' who, Cambridge magistrates said in 1631, were 'unhoulsomly thronged and thrust together' in clammy little box rooms that were breeding grounds for 'deseases'. Officers counted them in 'a trew certificate'. 'Wee are credibly informed', governors said, 'that there are [543 inmates] harbored' in St Andrews parish, 360 in Trinity parish, 396 in St Giles parish, 179 in St Clement parish, 148 in Little St Mary's parish, and eighty-five in St Benet's parish. The total figure was 1,278, but some parishes had not yet filed certificates.[176] Officers were told to 'certifie' inmates twice weekly in Yarmouth (1599); every third Wednesday in St Martin-in-the-Fields (1659); monthly in Hereford (1662), Liverpool (1666), Faversham (1584), Winchester (1690), Northampton (1629: 'continuallie and successivelie'), and Ipswich (1607); every six weeks in Ashby-de-la-Zouch (1625); and quarterly in Northampton (1581) and Tewkesbury (1608). We have orders to 'survey' inmates from Oxford (1600)—'within one weeke of their comynge'—Southampton (1603), Barnstaple (1690), Maidstone (1659), Reading (1635), and Salisbury (1656) when returns were called 'information'.[177] Beadles in St Margaret's Westminster gave overseers 'a perticuler account of all inmates and lodgers' in 1683. They were told to meet 'from time to time to compare [their] perticuler accounts' before handing them to overseers. It was 'agreed' in next-door St Martin-in-the-Fields in 1659 that three 'gentlemen' of the vestry would fortnightly 'take an acompt' from parish officers of what 'newecomers do come into the parishe'.[178] Towns were like revolving doors, with people coming and going all the time. 'Good, perfite, and suer searches, surveys, and viewes' tried to keep tabs on inmates in bulging London, but they would have been out of date as soon as they were put on paper. A London precinct kept a 'perfect booke of entry' of new arrivals. Portsoken ward had an 'inmate booke'. Other parishes

172 WAC F2002, fos. 47, 266; F2003, fo. 116.
173 SAI B/105/2/1, fo. 171.
174 NRO NMCC 25, fo. 198v. See also NRO NMCC 25, fo. 275v.
175 LA CNP 3/2/1, fo. 111.
176 CUL CUR 37.3, fos. 127–30.
177 NRO Y/C/19/5, fos. 20v–1; LA CNP 3/2/1, fo. 147; WSHC G23/1/3, fo. 153v; CUL VC-CT-vi.15, fos. 118–23; OHC C/FC/1/A1/02, fo. 68v; NA 3/1, fo. 225; SA 6/1, fo. 27; SAI C/4/3/1/1/4, fo. 24; BRO R/AC1/1/3, fo. 371; HA W/B2/4, fo. 53; CKS FA/AC3, fo. 14.
178 WAC F2003, fo. 394.

had 'a booke for the inmates'.[179] Bideford had 'generall overseers to discover inmates', a job that was done by 'houselookers' in Preston. Bideford's 'overseers' netted two dozen 'inmates' at one time in 1677, including a Cornish bricklayer, a 'dorsettshire man', a London tailor and his wife, a 'welshe man whose name [his landlord] would not discover', and a feltmaker from nearby Great Torrington. Phylis Stribling was found in the clerk's house and promised to go to Horwood five miles away 'as soone as her arme is healed'. Spinster Jane Cooke was allowed to 'tarry in towne' as she had 'an estate' fourteen miles away. Seven men and a spinster pledged to get 'discharges' to live by their own means.[180]

Towns were also destinations for 'foreigners' or 'strangers'. England opened its doors to religious refugees fleeing Catholic tyranny who set up home in East Anglian and south-east towns in the main. They, too, became numbers on record. Norwich was a different place after a decade of immigration after 1560. Officials counted 2,519 'strangers' in the year before they added up the poor in 1570. This number soared to 3,925 in 1571 ('names and faculties to be entered in a book'). 'Numbers of persons in the duch congregacon' were said to be 1,200 in 1613. This fell to 999 in 1624 and 678 ten years later ('where of aliens 103 [and] natives 575').[181] 'Strangers' in London also became statistics noted by name, nation, location, and job. An 'Extract of the Whole Number of Strangers' crossed London to gauge the dimensions and complexions of the 'alien' presence in 1593. The final numbers were 3,477 'strangers' born across the Channel and 2,068 London born and bred (1,345 'englishe' served/worked in their households). 'Strangers' were also added up in the sprawling suburbs. There were 320 across the river (135 native-born). A little over 7,000 were counted on London's eastern fringes (2,443 native-born and 4,570 immigrants). The 'Extract' ends with a list of 142 'trades used [by] straingers' arranged in alphabetical order from 'armorers' to 'yarne twisters'.[182] Further counts followed in 1627, 1635, and 1639—'an exact search and survey of all the straungers'. There were parish/ward surveys on top of city-wide counts. Local officers were told in 1610 to take 'speciall care both for the truth and certentie of yor certificate'.[183]

[179] LMA MSS 9680, fo. 927; 1176/1, 1624; 4524/1, fo; 115; 2088/1, 1637–8; 818/1, fo. 99; Griffiths, *Lost Londons*, 410. See also LMA Jours. 19, fo. 164v; 26, fo. 266v; 30, fo. 129; Reps. 16, fo. 40v; 17, fos. 131v, 452v; 18, fo. 130v; 20, fos. 294v, 366v.

[180] NDRO 1064Q/SO1, fos. 126–7.

[181] NRO Norwich Dutch and Walloon Strangers Book, fos. 22, 69v, 31v; Norwich muster list, case 10/H, number 11.

[182] HL EL MS 2514.

[183] LMA Jours. 30, fo. 129; 26, fo. 293v; 28, fo. 155v; 29, fos. 5v, 50v; 30, fo. 381v; 38, fo. 223v; TNA SP 12/160/27, 14/47/28–28i, 16/305/11; L. B. Luu found twenty-four surviving returns from the period 1561–93: '"Taking the bread out of our mouths": xenophobia in early modern London', *Immigrants and Minorities*, 19 (2000), 7. See also I. Scouloudi, ed., *Returns of Strangers in the Metropolis 1593, 1627, 1635, 1639: A Study of an Active Minority*, Huguenot Society of London Publications, 57 (1985); Griffiths, *Lost Londons*, 407–9.

Religion and belief were also 'particularized'. Dissenter Oliver Heywood made a note in his diary of a Sunday in 1665 when constables on the trail of conventicles knocked on his door 'to surprize us'. 'They would shew me no order [he wrote] yet they came furiously in [and] searcht the house.' Luckily for Heywood there were 'but four persons besides my family'; the constables wrote down 'all their names'.[184] This spoiled Sunday was one of countless local dramas as authorities tried to chart the extent of dissent culminating in the countrywide Compton Census in 1676. In London, as elsewhere, lists of conventicles and dissenters were compiled for better grasps of their numbers and geographies.[185] Communicants were also added up at Easter and other times in pursuit of order and orthodoxy. All Saints Northampton drew up 'a true' record of everyone 'of what degree soever [that] shall communicate' in 1585. Walton-on-the-Hill's 'old schoolemaister' got two shillings 'for writeing the names of communicants' in 1630.[186] Sabbath-breakers also ended up in lists. Gloucester common councillors teamed up with constables 'every Lords Day' in 1651 to take the names of 'disorderly persons'.[187] Lyme Regis listed thirty-eight people missing from church on 15 July 1648 (split evenly between men and women). Two men were told 'to take notice' of anyone walking and talking on Sundays around Norwich Cathedral in 'sermon time' in 1644.[188] Recusants also became data. Lambeth 'laid out' fourteen-pence when 'honest men' 'went about to enquire after recusants' in 1590.[189] Master Kaye picked up eight-pence for writing 'certificates [of] converted recusantes' in Walton-on-the-Hill in 1642. Recusant lists in Middlesex Sessions registers include one from 1608 listing fourteen men and eight women and another three years later noting twenty-one men and a dozen women.[190] 'True' registers of 'popish recusants and persons popishly affected' took up a lot of space in some record books. One from Hampshire filled as many as eighteen pages.[191]

Alehouses, the sabbath-day enemy of the Church, attracted near blanket surveillance. Their numbers always seemed 'excessive', causing Northampton's governors to claim in 1624 that 'the horrible and loathsome disease of drunkenness' grows 'daylie'; 'whoredome and idlenes are much crepte' in, they added.[192]

[184] *Rev. Oliver Heywood, B.A., 1630–1702; His Autobiography, Diaries, and Anecdote Books*, ed. J. Horsfall Turner (4 vols.; Brighouse, Bingley, 1881–85), I, 198–9.

[185] For example, TNA SP 29/71/48, 29/88/73, 29/105/37, 29/111/67, 29/121/38.

[186] NA 3/1, fo. 227; Ramsay and Maddock, *Churchwardens' Accounts of Walton-on-the-Hill*, 11, 26, 50. See also J. Boulton, 'The limits of formal religion: the administration of holy communion in late Elizabethan and early Stuart London', *London Journal*, 10 (1984).

[187] GA GBR/B/3/2, fo. 590.

[188] DHC DC/LR/A3/1, fo. 8; NRO Norwich Assembly Folio Minute Book 6, fo. 21.

[189] Drew, *Lambeth Churchwardens' Accounts*, 180, 186, 149.

[190] Ramsay and Maddock, *Churchwardens' Accounts of Walton-on-the-Hill*, 70–1; LMA MJ/SBR/1, fos. 67, 256–7, 367, 439.

[191] HA Q4/1, fos. 118v–22v, 124v–28v. See also TNA SP 12/118/73; KAC WQ/I/1, fo. 54v; DRO ECA B/1/4, fo. 228; OHC County Sessions Roll E42; SHA LB/11/4/83/42; ERO D/Y/2/5/117; ESBHRO QI/EW5, fos. 110–18v; QI/EW6 fos. 83–91.

[192] NA 3/1, fos. 423v–4.

The aim was a 'fitt number' of alehouses, not their eradication. Lewes set up a 'survey' to cut the 'great number' of alehouses to a 'fit number' in 1651. One Sherborne parish had a 'superflous and needles' six alehouses in 1637, when 'twoe or three' were deemed sufficient. 'Wildersley [in] Salop', 'a small village in the syde of a mountayne', had just eight houses, 'wherof there be three alehowses'.[193] Larger Bridgnorth put caps on the number of alehouses in certain streets: 'high street tenn', 'hangry street three', 'lessles street one', 'the castle one', 'underhill three', 'bridge street one', 'whotborne street three', etc.[194] 'How manie [alehouses] stand lycenced in everie village and towne and registered and recognised', Manchester justices asked in 1618. 'Uppon Friday the iiii day of October 1616', a Kent justice reports, 'wee did assemble [at] Barstead and did take an exact survey of all the alehouses': twenty-one licensed in Eyhorne hundred, four 'suppressed'; six alehouses licensed in Maidstone hundred, eight 'suppressed'.[195] There were two dozen approved alehouses in Lyme Regis in 1654 (nineteen male keepers) and the same number twelve months later (twenty male keepers).[196] A 'list' of Barnstaple tipplers noted thirty-eight men and thirteen women in 1676 and another fourteen men and one woman who were 'not bound'. Thirty-seven men and nine women were 'lycensed' to sell beer in Newbury in 1667.[197] 'Alehouses counted', one 'note' says. Maidstone's officers were told to take 'knowledge' of everyone they found hanging around alehouses in 1604.[198] Listing let governors 'compute' and 'particularize' in this case the alehouses around them. These were records to use. Because of this their storage and security caused constant concern.

IV

The English Revolution was just one year old and things once taken for granted no longer seemed certain. The war dropped question marks over records. So Wiltshire justices took steps at their 1643 sessions to keep records safe 'in this time of danger'. The world was turning, but records were a reassurance of the order of things. 'Deputie clerkes of the peace' were tasked to see that 'a stronge cheste' with two locks and keys was speedily made 'for safe keeping' of records. The locked chest was 'placed' in the vestry house next door to Warminster Church, where it was hoped the ravages of war would not intrude. Keys were put

193 ESRO QO/EW2, fo. 20; HA Q1/2, fos. 120v–1; HL EL MS 1764.

194 SHA BB/F/1/1/3, fos. 20, 105.

195 E. Axon, ed., *Manchester Sessions: Notes of Proceedings Before Oswald Mosley (1616–1630), Nicholas Mosley (1661–1672), and Sir Oswald Mosley (1734–1739)... Volume 1, 1616–1623*, Lancashire and Cheshire Record Society, 42 (1901), 51; CKS UI20/09, fo. 1.

196 DHC DC/LR/B1/9, fos. 145, 172.

197 NDRO B1/3321; BRO N/JQ 1/1, fo. 11. See also HEA Q/SM/4, fo. 65v; ESBHRO RYE 1/5, fo. 460; KAC WQ/O/4, fo. 77; NRO T/C1, fo. 5; Y/C/19/5, fos. 20v–1; TNA 16/247/35, 16/250/22.

198 CKS Md/Acm1/1a, fo. 82.

in the hands of the clerks, 'that they may have recourse thereunto as occasion shall require'. They were told to take the last three years of 'bundells' and 'bookes' home to make sure that 'granting forth of proces of this court againste such persons as are or shalbe indicted or presented' would still sail smoothly in war.[199]

A chest was called variously the 'parish chest', 'comon chest', 'stronge cheste', 'great chest', 'black chest', 'towne chest', 'chest of writings', 'chest of records', and proudly in Salisbury the 'yron cheste of this corporacon'.[200] (See Plates 23–5.) Reading had a 'great' and 'little chest' in 1624: 'this daye the great chest was opened and the litle chest unlockt, and the deedes and quitt taken oute [and] perused and many lockt upp in the chest as by note of remembrance thereof in the little chest'.[201] The first in a string of 'necessarie orders' for Heavitree parish in Exeter in 1586 called for a 'strong chest bounded with iron with three lockes' to store 'the parish stock, writyngs, and evidences'. Four 'sidesmen' took charge of the keys and the chest could only be opened when three of them 'at the least' were in the room. Northampton's records were put 'in a presse with iii lokks' in 'the vestry of our Lady chapell' in 1553. Tenterden's 'records and munuments' were 'laide in the press' in 1604 except for 'charters and customalls' that were given to the mayor and any 'books and records which the towne clerke shall daillie use'.[202] Records were also stored in boxes and bags. Barnstaple spent eight-pence in 1585 for 'new boxes to keepe writings in the guildhall'. 'A list of borough documents' from the same town over a century later included 'a blacke box containing feo[ff]ments', 'a box' with '26 old writings', six boxes storing 'writings', and 'a bag' holding almshouse writings.[203] Banbury's chamberlain carried five boxes of 'writings concerning the borough all sealed up' to the mayor in 1662 to be put in 'the common chest secured for the use of the corporation'.[204] Rye and St John's parish (Exeter) both had a 'great boxe'. 'A bagg for the towne books' cost Lyme Regis 4s. 4d. in 1672; a 'bagg to keepe the records' cost Hereford 1s. 8d. in 1662.[205]

Records were often stored in a 'vestry house' or 'vestry roome'. Vaults or cupboards offered further peace of mind. St Dunstan-in-the-West and St Peter Cornhill in London put their records 'in the cubbard in the vestry'. A Westminster parish put assessment books 'in the cupboard'; St Katherine-by-the-Tower

199 WSHC A1/160/1.

200 DRO 2203A-99/PO/2, fos. 61–2; Z19/36/14, fo. 130v; ECA B/1/3, fo. 420; B/1/4, fo. 103; WSHC G23/1/3, fos. 289, 375. See also NA 3/1, fo. 327v; EBHSRO Win/55, fo. 29; BRO WI/AC1/1, fo. 53v; HA W/B2/3, fo. 37v; KAC WSMB/K/1/5, fo. 152v; SHA BB/C/1/1/1, fo. 48v; W. E. Tate, *The Parish Chest: A Study of the Records of Parochial Administration* (3rd edition, Cambridge, 1969), esp. 35–42.

201 BRO R/AC1/1/2, fo. 80.

202 DRO 3004A/PW/2; NA 3/1, fo. 8v; CKS TE/C1, fos. 113v–14.

203 NDRO Bi/3792, fo. 8; B1/1738.

204 J. S. W. Gibson and E. R. C. Brinkworth, eds., *Banbury Corporation Records: Tudor and Stuart*, Banbury Historical Society, 15 (1977), 209.

205 DRO 4767 A-99/PF/1; NA 3/1, fo. 327; DHC DC/LR/G2/2, 1671–2; HEA BG/11/23/14, fo. 15. See also NRO Norwich Chamberlains' Accounts, 1669–70, fo. 12; CKS TE/S2, fo. 113; LERO BRII/1/3, fo. 31; GA GBR/F/4/5, fos. 74, 139.

precinct used the vestry 'cubbard' for 'safe keeping' of 'rolls [and] bookes' in 1655.[206] London's records were put in the Guildhall 'bookhouse' ('a place att hand for storage of them'), but this did not make them impregnable. Aldermen took 'knowledge of the bookes and records of this court belonging to the citty in the threasury and bookehouse' in 1633 and were unhappy to find that they 'lye up and downe in a disorderly manner and oftentymes are missing and not to be had upon occasion of use'. A committee drew up orders for 'keeping of the bookes and records'.[207] Towns kept records close at hand in a 'hall', 'cownsell house', or 'chamber'. Faversham council ordered that 'broader shelves than now' be 'set up' in 'the studdie in the court hall', with 'partitions and dores with locks and keyes' in 1623 'to holde rolls and records'.[208] Marlborough paid 3s. 6d. in 1633 for '3 locks and 2 keys for cubbords in the counsel howse'. Oxford, Norwich, and Gloucester locked records in the 'treasury'. The one in Gloucester had five keys that were kept by the chamberlain, mayor, sheriffs, and coroner. [209] St Martin-in-the-Fields put papers in an 'armory' with three keys in the hands of the churchwardens and minister. Thetford and Yarmouth put their 'wrtyings' in the 'hutch'. Thetford had a 'little hutche' and a 'great comon hutche' with three 'kepers of the keyes'.[210]

But the security of the chest and its contents was never fail-safe. Stratford-upon-Avon churchwardens John Noble and William Wright 'privately' took their 'unjust' accounts from the chest in 1696 after it was found that they had cooked the books. Things went wrong but governors tried to put them right. The Stratford-upon-Avon vestry filed a 'protestacion against [Noble and Wright's] accounts', ordering that they must be filed 'within a weeke'. To avoid any cover-up 'for the future', they ruled that accounts must 'bee entered into this [vestry] booke [or another] register booke' as soon as possible.[211] A yeoman ended up in court in Southampton in 1619 for 'taking away of certen writings'. Someone unknown 'inserted' 'certen things' in 'the vestree booke' and 'quest booke' in St Dunstan-in-the-West (London) in 1600 containing 'very scandalous and reproachful matters of supposed inconteynence malyciouslye…donn and sett downe to disgrace and defame' four parishioners who had spotless 'reputacons'.[212] What should be appreciated is the aspiration and effort to take good care of records. Speaking to officials and officers on election day in Gloucester in 1653, John Dorney called stewards and chamberlains 'treasurers…intrusted [with]

[206] LMA MSS 3016/1, fo. 314; 4165/1, fo. 356; 9680, fo. 119; WAC E2413, fo. 93. See also CKS TE/S2, fo. 374; WAC F2002, fo. 206; NA 3/1, fo. 8v.

[207] LMA Reps. 34, fos. 348v–9, 522; 47, fos. 292v, 303; 20, fos. 31, 133v.

[208] CKS FA/AC3, fo. 138v.

[209] WSHC G22/1/205/2, fo. 74; OHC C/FC1/A1/01, fo. 261; NRO Norwich Assembly Book 5, fo. 259v; GA GBR/B/3/3, fo. 512; GBR/F/4/3, fo. 151v.

[210] WAC F2002, fo. 46; NRO Y/C/19/3, fo. 129; Y/C/19/4, fo. 144; Y/C/19/5, fo. 184v; T/C1/1, fos. 11, 23, 65v.

[211] *Vestry Minute Book of Stratford-on-Avon From 1617 to 1699 A.D.* (1899), 151.

[212] SA SC9/2/1, fo. 34v; LMA MS 3016/1, fo. 38.

charters and evidences [with] a solemn duty' to see that they were 'rightly used and safely kept'.[213]

A town was nothing without its records. Like Wiltshire, Bridgnorth moved 'bonds and writings' to a safe place in 'these dangerous tymes' in 1645.[214] A 'strong and convenient room' was built next to Wells Cathedral in 1619 for 'safe keeping' of records. Herefordshire justices made plans to build 'a house or roome in the castle' for 'preservacon' and 'securing' of 'publick' records in 1678.[215] Plenty of attention was paid to care and repair. It felt 'requisite' for 'proclamations' to be 'carefully fyled in the towne hall [in Maidstone to] remaine without spoyling, tearinge, or looseninge'.[216] Books were 'cleaned'. Norwich Great Hospital spent 2s. 6d. for 'makinge cleane the bookes, boxes and room' in the 'treasury' in 1619. One Bedford got 6s. 6d. 'for dustinge' Chester's records in 1614.[217] There was also concern for environmental conditions. A clerk from Rodmarton (Gloucestershire) left this piece of advice in the parish register for his successors: 'If you will have this book last, bee sure to aire it att the fier or sunne three or four times a yeare [and] it will not be amisse [to] wipe over the leaves with a dry woolen cloth [as] the place is very much subject to dankishness'.[218] A Herefordshire sessions clerk kept 'a constant fire in the castle house' in 1688 for 'airing records [made] wett and damp in this extraordinary wett winter'. Oxford's 'key kepers' were told to 'bring upp all writings as ly belowe in the treasure howse' in 1583 and 'laye them above in chests as the nether howsse is some what moyste and will hurte the writings'.[219] There was a failed attempt to turn the preservation of parish registers into a statutory matter in the 1563 Parliament. A bill 'for an Office of a Register [in each diocese] to keep the Church Books for Wedding, Christening and Burying' was drafted, but it did not get past its first reading, even though it was apparently 'very well liked' by 'all' members of the house. A seven-strong committee that included the first ever 'keeper of the state papers', Thomas Wilson, was asked to 'draw' a similar sounding bill 'for the safe keeping of the Church Books, or Registers of the Christenings, Marriages and Burials' in the 1576 Parliament. They met on the next Sunday afternoon—'at Mr Wilson's Chamber in the Arches'—but this bill too ended up on the parliamentary scrapheap.[220]

[213] J. Dorney, *Certain Speeches Made Upon the Day of the Yearly Election of Office in the City of Gloucester* (1653), 18.

[214] SHA BB/F/1/1/3, fo. 45v.

[215] Bates, *Quarter Sessions Records for the County of Somerset*, I, 247; HEA Q/SO/2, fo. 88v–90.

[216] CKS Md/Acm1/2, fo. 170v.

[217] NRO Norwich Great Hospital Account Rolls, 1618–19; CA TAB/1, fo. 30.

[218] The clerk is quoted in J. C. Cox, *Churchwardens' Accounts from the Fourteenth Century to the Close of the Seventeenth Century* (1913), 16.

[219] HEA Q/S0/2, fo. 225v; OHC C/FC/1/A1/01, fo. 261.

[220] *Journals of the House of Commons, I: 1547–1629* (1802), 68, 104–5. It was Thomas Bowesey, a clerk in the Signet Office, who made the comment on support for the 1563 bill in a letter to Archbishop Parker, with a copy of the bill enclosed, in a probable attempt to get backing for his bid to become the registrar of registers in Canterbury Diocese. See Slack, 'Counting people', 1121–2.

Books were also rebound. London stationer Hugh Singleton was paid 82s. 6d. in 1584–5 for binding 'book Z serving the lord mayors court' and 'making up' a parchment book for 'acts of common council' with a 'calendar'.[221] Norwich's 'old court books and assemblie bookes' were 'decently bound' in 1680. 'Forrel' was bought 'to cover' books in St Martin-in-the-Fields; it cost eighteen-pence to cover 'ye regester booke' 'with calves leather'.[222] Some places left it until the last minute. Oxford's recorder hopped on a horse for London in 1663 to get 'transcribed [in] legible character' two 'auntient bookes of records commonly called the red book and the litle white book' that were 'much obliterate and hardly to be read'.[223]

It ought to be no surprise that concern for records and their care was a parallel development to growing concerns about access to records. Government needed to be tighter and cohesive in challenging times. Tighter meant leaner. Vestries were trimmed in size in many parishes to streamline decision-making. Authority was put in fewer hands. In the words of one directive: 'all vestrys [were to] be dissolved and none but ministers and gentlemen of the best estates, quality, and reputation [were to be] chosen [in future] and a certain number limited'. Whether or not they were in fact 'select' (formally reduced in size), participation in vestries was 'circumscribed' as secrecy was a watchword.[224] Local government was turning inward. This is also seen in limitations on who could read records. Clerks and other officers of London's Mayor's Court had power 'to commit' anyone slipping into the 'bookehouse' without 'license' to prison.[225] Local governors made plans to keep a tight check on people and records going in and out of the archive. Nothing could be taken out of Thetford's 'hutch' 'without the presence and assent of iiii burgesses', the mayor, and six 'comoners'. Bridgnorth's high bailiff, high chamberlain, and coroner, who kept the keys to the chest, were told that there must be three or four burgesses at hand when they had 'cause [to] see or use any of the writeings'.[226]

Records were handled more selectively and stored more securely. The London Goldsmiths' guild ruled that liverymen could read its 'bookes, writeings, or papers' but only as wardens 'thought fit to conduce to the good' of the guild.[227] Maidstone's freemen had 'free accesse' on 'request' to read town charters in 1642, but they could not see records of 'the busynes' of the town. The town's chamberlain

[221] Masters, *Chambers Accounts*, 30, 89.

[222] NRO NMCC 25, fos. 61v, 69; WAC SMF, 1574–6; E5/1574–6.

[223] OHC C/FC/1/A1/03, fo. 311. See also DHC DC/BTB/M2/1578; DRO 4767 A-99/PF/1, fo. 2; BRO R/D/QR/19/2/1, fo. 30v; CA TAR/1/22.

[224] HL EL MS 8571; S. Hindle, *The State and Social Change in Early Modern England, c.1550–1640* (Basingstoke, 2000), 210–18 (quoting 214); J. F. Merritt, 'Contested legitimacy and the ambiguous rise of vestries in early modern London', *HJ*, 54 (2011); P. Griffiths, 'Secrecy and authority in late sixteenth- and seventeenth-century London', *HJ*, 40 (1997).

[225] LMA Letterbook Y, fo. 217v.

[226] NRO T/C1/2, fo. 211; T/C1/4, fo. 37; SHA BB/C/1/1/1, fo. 48v.

[227] GCL Company Minute Book T, fo. 35.

was told in 1567 that the book of laws and 'constituycons' should never be 'redde, seene or consideyid' unless six common councillors 'and mr maiors assistants' were in the room.[228] In nearby Tenterden, on the other hand, an addition to the 'custumal' in 1604 let freemen 'see every record, decree, or other matter [that] shall concerne himselfe freely' at the end of court days, with officers and officials hovering close by.[229]

There was a clear tendency to limit sensitive records to a chosen few. St Brides vestry in London ruled in 1662 'that the great ledger booke of churchwardens accompts be not lett [to] lye publqiuely open in the vestry as formerly' but be 'locked up'.[230] It begins with the keys that opened chests and records. Exeter's 'great coffer' had nine locks; eight of the ruling 'twenty-four' had a key each and the mayor took care of the 'litle key'.[231] A handful of locks was more typical. Tenterden's four keys were in the hands of the mayor, his next in line, the town clerk, and chamberlain. The three keys that opened 'the desk in the councill house' in Lyme Regis were looked after by the 'three eldest capitall burgesses', while the mayor, chamberlain, and 'eldest jurate' were in charge of the keys that opened Maidstone's 'strong cheste'.[232] London vestries put chest keys 'in ye custodie' of ministers, churchwardens, common councillors, aldermen, or the 'ancient men of the parish'. St Mary Aldermanbury vestry 'ordered' in 1568 that 'books and evidences [shall] remayne locked up in a chest in the vestry' that could not be opened by anyone 'except [the] common councell and churchwardens'. The same vestry ruled nineteen years later that 'noe writings [can] be taken out of the chest but by order of the vestry'. Each 'writing' was to be 'registered' on its safe return.[233] Not all of them did get back safely, however. 'He could not presently fynde yt', Mr Spooner said rather sheepishly when Thetford's mayor asked him for 'the key of the towne chest' in 1626.[234] 'One of the keies of the kubbered' in Winchester, where 'auncient recordes and presidencies of the citie' were stored, went missing after Mr Bethell who had 'custodie' of it left the city. Nobody knew where he was.[235]

Equally disquieting were times when someone held onto records that should have been in the chest. Poole needed its records back after Mayor Trew breathed his last in 1682. James Hallibred stepped into Trew's shoes and one of the first things he did was sign an indenture with his widow to hand over 'things' 'belonginge unto the corporation'. It began with maces and the impression is that Trew had all of this paper at home:

[228] CKS Md/ACm1/2, fo. 197v; Md/ACm1/3, fo. 65; Md/Acm1/1a, fo. 38v.

[229] CKS TE/C1, fos. 113v–14.

[230] LMA MS 6554/1, fo. 238.

[231] DRO ECA B/1/3, fo. 25.

[232] CKS TE/C1, fos. 113v–14; TE/S2, fo. 374; DHC DC/LR/D1/3a, fo. 182; CKS Md/Acm1/1a, fo. 66; See also BRO WI/FA1/1, fo. 53; SHA BB/C/1/1/1/1, fo. 48v; SAI C/4/4/1/34, fo. 9; DRO ECA 3004A/PW 2.

[233] LMA MS 3570/2, fo. 82. See also LMA MSS 3016/1, fo. 232; 3570/2, fos. 81, 156; 943/1, fo. 52; 4214/1, fos. 153–4; 4072/1, fo. 224v; 3908/1, fos. 12, 55v.

[234] NRO T/C1/1, fo. 37.

[235] HA W/B1/3, fo. 64.

> the towne booke of records, the two charters in two black boxes, the booke of entrys of statute, the old statute booke att large, the booke of entryes of leases, [a book] of corporation lands with a brasse seale, the admiralty courtbook, five seales, fourteen keyes belonging to the boxes in the towne hall, an iron seale, a stamp for yards and measure, the brasse standard foryads and ells, the brasse box of tray weights…two lead tray weights, two brasse measures, a small booke [of] statutes lately made, the booke of mayors, the charter of Winchelsdey, the booke of assize of bread, the table of fees, the incorporation book, Mr orchards two accts 1674/5 and 1675/6 and Mr Fords accts anno 1673 and 1680, Mr Jn Willis acct 1674, Mr John Carter anno 1667, all audited, and Mr Moses Durells 1679, unaudited, Edward Linorons lease of his shop, a chancery writ for adminsteringe the oathes of allegiance and supremacy, overseers account anno 1679 and 80, severall letters from the councell table…and other books, bonds, leases, accounts, and contracts.[236]

When the post of Gloucester's mayor changed hands in 1613, the old mayor handed over to his successor 'an auncient ledger booke for inrollinge leases', 'a boke of orphans', a 'great booke of the stewardes accomptes', 'two bookes of common councell', a 'booke of survey', 'a paper booke of mr maiors notes for corrections out of the sessions', sessions rolls, 'bundles' of letters from the privy council, 'certen notes concerning the boothall', and a 'great bundle of proclamacons'.[237]

Records fell into wrong hands at times. People hoarded them at home. Not even London's remembrancer could take 'books of the cittie home [to] kalendar'. They could 'not be carryed out of the hall'.[238] But some people did take records home, putting at risk what Essex justices called 'the publique interest'. Like Mayor Trew, former officials were told to bring in 'writinges' that had been in their home for too long. The son of Faversham's 'late steward and town clerke' got £5 for 'voluntarilie' bringing in 'writinges' on lands and tenements in 1605. It was believed that 'want thereof (in all likelihood) would have greatle weakened our estate'.[239] Thomas Merwin from Windsor was told to bring in 'a booke oute of the hall called the maiors booke began in ye yeare of our Lord 1559' in 1658. A former 'common clark' kept Dorset sessions 'records, books, recognizances, presentments and other things' in his house despite warnings. He was told to bring his trunk to the court.[240] Officials were asked to hand back 'charters, evidences, wrytings, and mynym[en]ts', 'bookes of orders', accounts, exchequer decrees, court rolls, 'and other bookes, wrytings, and records belonginge to the towne'. Faversham's governors complained that 'much inconvenience' resulted by 'hidinge and obscuringe' records.[241] Some people did not give books back. Yarmouth had to

[236] DHC DC/PL/B/11/1/1. [237] GA GBR/G/G3/SO/1, fo. 29.
[238] LMA Rep. 17, fo. 177. [239] CKS FA/AC3, fo. 61.
[240] BRO WI/AC1/1, fo. 7v; DHC DC/DCB/1/1, fos. 1–2. [241] CKS FA/AC3, fo. 80v.

deal with this at regular intervals. A former recorder's clerk held on to two decades of court rolls. Mr Gryce and Mr Tompson had records at home when they should have been in the 'hutch'. So, too, did Mr Johnson, who 'brought in' four 'court rolles EL3, EL11, EL17 [and] EL18' at another time, while Mr Gray 'brought in these court rolls' to an Assembly in 1620: '8Eliz, 8Jac [and] 13Jac [to] 17Jac'. But 'there are now still wantyng the court rolle of two yeres 15 and 22Eliz', governors noted after checking the paper pile. 'All men which have in their houses or custody bookes of charters, asemblyes, water bookes and other bookes' were told to bring them back straight away in 1627 'to bee layd up in the vestrye hutch'.[242] These situations dragged on for months or years, marring the ability to make policies and cases. It took Tenterden six years to get 'Mr Alcroft gent late comon clerke' to bring in 'writings concerning settlement of the cottage' of the 'late' Thomas Thorpe 'for use of the poore'. Governors also heard in 1671 that he had an 'indenture' detailing 'uses of the gramer schole'. Aldcroft handed in some seals and records a year later, but not the cottage 'writings'. A disapproving note tells us that he still held onto one indenture and a second was now in the hands of Edward Finch esq. It took seven orders until a clerk could finally write: 'see more hereof below with this marke #'. Edging down the page we see: '# Att a vestry here holden 28 die December 1677 [Aldcroft] fully delivered abovementioned writings' that were 'imediately locked up in ye chest [in] ye vestry house'.[243]

A London story puts the chest at risk in the centre of the stage. St Botolph-without-Aldgate parish was split into two camps of 'substantial men' in 1622, who both claimed to be the legitimate body for 'keeping, ordering, and disposing' records. The row rumbled on and reached the lord keeper's table. The plaintiffs—'the minister, churchwardens and vestrymen'—alleged that the defendants had by hook or by crook got hold of the 'common chest' and 'bondes, evidences, writinges, church bookes, vestry bookes, accompts, and stockes of money'. 'Custodie' of these records belonged to the sitting vestry, they said, but the chest was now shut up in a 'private' house. The plaintiffs argued 'that no vestry ought to be kept in a private mans house nor by any private person'. The chief defendant was Portsoken ward deputy Mr Vinton, who with a group of common councillors took the chest 'into their hands [and] particular custodies'. After 'longe debating', the lord keeper ruled that Vinton and his cronies as 'officers chosen for civill government' of the ward 'cannot nor ought to assume authority' to grab parish 'books and writings'. His 'pretended usage' was 'voyd in law and againste reason, discretion, and common understandinge' and 'contrarie to the laudable customes and usages' of parishes. The defendants were told to carry the chest to the vestry

[242] NRO Y/C/19/4, fos. 1, 83v, 158v; Y/C/19/5, fos. 122, 220v, 238, 306v; Y/C/19/6, fo. 86v. See also HEA Q/SM/4, fo. 187v; DRO ECA B/1/3, fo. 420; NRO T/C1/1, fos. 26v, 82; NMCC 20, fo. 487; CKS TE/S2, fos. 38, 124.

[243] CKS TE/S2, fos. 254, 262, 265, 269, 273, 276, 280, 291. See also LMA MSS 6554/1, fos. 75v, 135v; 4165/1, fos. 356, 377.

house—the 'parliament' of the parish—'to be kept and disposed of by the minister, churchwardens, and vestrymen [as] hath ancientlie bene accustomed'. The parish got its records back but in dribs and drabs. But there was worse to come. When the plaintiffs opened the records they found that 'divers partes [were] torne and defaced so that the truth of accomptes cannot appeare'. The lord keeper ordered commissioners to go through papers with Vinton and common councillors to try to get to the bottom of the 'defacing of books and detaining of any others concerning the parish'. We do not have the last word in this taxing parish/ward duel, but the chest was back in the hands of parish not City officials.[244]

St Botolph breathed a deep sigh of relief. It was lost without records. There were also qualms about copying records. When Thomas Watts 'and his councell' asked to see a Northampton by-law for inmates in 1660, governors got stuck on whether to give them 'a coppy of the by-law' or 'a sight' of it 'in the booke itselfe'. The town's 'maiors clerk' was not allowed to 'make owte any coppye [of] any order sett downe in this [Assembly] booke or any other booke withowte the special lycense of the maior'. The size of the fine hanging over him—forty shillings—quantifies secrecy.[245] Members of London's Apothecaries' guild could not get copies of ordinances without 'consent', but they could read them or have them read aloud by the clerk. Oxford council ruled in 1640 that 'noe acts of comon councel shalbee copied [or] delivered to any person without [the] consent of mr maior [his] brethren and mr bailiffs'.[246] Obstacles were put in the way of anyone outside the elite who wanted to read its records. A distinction was drawn in London between Common Council Acts that were in effect law and Court of Aldermen Repertories that recorded the discussions and decisions of governors. 'Anye freeman [can] have accesse to actes of common councell and have sight or coppie of any of them', aldermen ruled in 1620, so long as a clerk was in the room to 'the end that noe freeman may be ignorant of those lawes they are bound to observe'. 'But as for the acts and orders of this courte', they said, changing tune, 'it neither standeth with justice nor conveniency' for them to be 'communicated to any [except] members' of the court. Repertories could only leave the 'bookhouse' by 'speciall licence'. To avoid doubt, the journals were not to be 'mingled' with repertories.[247]

John Strype ran into snags when he tried to read City records for the 'abundance of additions' he needed to bring John Stow's *Survey* up to date. 'It was not only necessary to gather up and present the many and most important' Common Council Acts, he wrote in his preface, 'but also to have recourse to authentick books and records belonging to the chamber of London'. But getting into the 'bookhouse' was 'very difficult to obtain'. At last, with the help of 'friends of

[244] LMA MS 9236/1. [245] NA 3/2, fo. 15; 3/1, fo. 207v.
[246] LMA MS 8200/1, fos. 402, 375; OHC C/FC/1/A1/02, fo. 103v.
[247] LMA Rep. 34, fos. 521v–2.

quality and good account', he was allowed to 'transcribe' what he thought was 'convenient'. But he was told to 'leave' his notes with a clerk 'to be reviewed and examined lest some things published from them might seem prejudicial some way or other to the city'. After another 'delay', Strype was told that there was nothing in his 'very considerable' notes that could 'prejudice the custom of this honourable city' and he went home to put the finishing touches to his new Stow.[248]

Strype found out what he knew already: secrecy was a rule of thumb in government. London's aldermen would not put into words on paper 'a matter of great secressie and waight which is not thought mete to be named towchinge the citie' in 1572.[249] Speaking to Cambridge's civic body on Grand Common Day in 1669, Alderman Newton—after word from the mayor that 'too much [was being] discovered' of late—reminded 'freemen' to 'take speciall notice of that part of their oathes that enjoynes secrecy for towne affayres'.[250] Leicester's officials swore oaths to always keep the 'secrets and counsell of the bodie politique'. Wokingham's sergeant-at-mace swore never to 'reveale secrets' of the town. Mayor's clerks and town clerks assistants were 'sworne not to reveale any secrets in the bookes of this citie' in London in 1571.[251] Governors were imagined as a body made whole by this secrecy and broader concerns for ethics and the well-being of a village or town. The last of twenty-six 'artycles' passed by the 'chieffe inhabitants' of Swallowfield (Berkshire) three weeks before Christmas in 1596 focused on secrecy: 'what so ever shal by any of us don or sayd in or meetyngs…shalbe kept secret [and] not revealed'. 'None of us', they said, 'shall use any comunycation or means co[n]sernynge our meetyngs or any thynge ther in don or sayd w[hi]ch may tend to [our] discredett or disgrace'. The fine in Northampton for revealing 'secret councell' or 'eny maner of thing secret' in 1557 was twenty shillings for a first offence and double that for a second breach. A third leak led to 'expuls[ion]' from the 'consell'.[252] A hefty £5 fine was dished out in Tewkesbury to anyone who was caught revealing 'any secretts' of common council meetings and in Leicester for 'disclosing anye speeches, secretts, or matters oute of this comon hall'.[253]

Steps were taken to keep rooms as watertight as possible. Guards were stationed at doors to check who went in and out. London's Stationers' guild was rocked by a 'disturbance' in 1651. 'The court dore is not kept shutt', governors complained, 'soe that persons come in suddenly when the court is private whereby business is

[248] J. Strype, *A Survey of the Cities of London and Westminster: Containing the Original, Antiquity, Increase, Modern Estate and Government of Those Cities, Written at First in the Year MDXCVIII by John Stow…Corrected, Improved and Very Much Enlarged: and the Survey and History Brought Down From 1633*, 5 books in 2 vols (1720), i, iii, v. Cf. M. Johnson, *Ludgate, What It Is, Not What It Was, Or, A Full and Clear Discovery of…That Prison* (1659), 16.

[249] LMA Rep. 17, fo. 246. [250] *Diary of Samuel Newton*, 39.

[251] LERO BRII/1/2, fo. 144; BRO WO/AC1/1/1, fo. 1; LMA Reps. 17, fos. 102, 222; 48, fo. 312v.

[252] HL EL MS 6162, fos. 36–6a; NA 3/1, fo. 103.

[253] GA TBR/A/1/2, fo. 36; LERO BRII/1/3, fo. 80. See also ERO D/B5/Gb1, fo. 9v; CKS FA/AC3, fo. 48v; TE/S2, fo. 247; LMA MS 3016/1, fo. 250.

interrupted'. The beadle was told to take 'speciall care' to '[keep] the court private and [see] that noe person be suffered to come in untill the bell be rung by the master or wardens'. The beadle was the cause of trouble three decades later when he was lectured not to 'come into the counsell chamber or court roome while the court is sitting untill he be called in by the ringing of the bell'.[254] William Ravenscroft got forty shillings in 1585 'for keeping the door leading out of the council chamber' in London's Guildhall. St Brides (London) vestry told the staffman in 1646 to 'attend without at the vestrie doore [to] keepe men at distance from hearkinge to any proceedinges for want whereof some inconvenience happened [at] the last vestrie'.[255] Orders spelt out who could be in rooms when governing 'affayres' were on the agenda. Norwich's mayor, aldermen, and justices met 'in the councell chamber' to hear 'causes' in 1568 in 'moste secret manner among themselves commaunding all others out of ye house except ther comon clerke'.[256] London's aldermen drew up directions for 'what persons ought to bee present in court' to talk over 'publique or private affaires' in 1627. 'None excepte vestriemen and the clerke of the vestrie' were allowed to be 'present' when St Brides vestry was 'debatinge of busines'.[257]

The regular repetition of orders concerning secrecy suggests that secrets did indeed slip out. The issue in Oxford in 1637 was that 'the towns office', where the mayor, 'thirteene', and bailiffs met weekly 'to treate of businesse and affaires', was no longer secure. They had not been able to 'consult [in] secret manner as they ought'. Meetings were moved to the more secure 'audit house'. This was restated three years later with further orders to keep 'writinges' safely with a fire burning for 'airinge' of them.[258] 'One of [Winchester's] xxiiii' was 'excpellyed the councell house' in 1624 'for that he revealyed the secrets spoken in the same howse unto straungers'. Secrets were still leaking three decades later. 'Ye private and secrett actings and affaires as well in counsells [and] common assemblies are divulged and made knowne', governors noted in 1656, 'which doth very much occasion the disturbance of ye peace and good government'. The fine for 'making knowne private transaccons touching affaires of the citty [in] counsells or comon assemblies' was increased to ten shillings.[259] Tenterden governors found themselves in a sticky spot in 1668:

> Some of the members of this corporacon have att severall times past published and divulged divers transactions which have passed att severall comon halls [that] have required secresy contrary to the oaths which they tooke when they became freemen [and] very much to the damage [of the] corporacon.

[254] Stationers Company Minute Books C, fo. 266; E, fo. 153v.
[255] Master, *Chamber Accounts*, 35; LMA MS 6544/1, fo. 18v. See also LMA H1/STA1/1, fo. 44; H1/STA1/2, fo. 14v; H1/STA1/3, fo. 167v; H1/STA1/5, fo. 130v.
[256] NRO NMCC 8, fo. 584.
[257] LMA Rep. 42, fo. 2; LMA MS 6544/1, fo. 18v.
[258] OHC C/FC/1/A1/03, fo. 103v.
[259] HA W/B2/1, fo.30v; W/B1/5, fos.105, 156v.

A note in the margin read, 'a decree to enjoine secresie'.[260] Jurat John Hallett from nearby Faversham got in trouble in 1600 for 'infourm[ing] our lorde warden that the towne were agreead to acquaynte [him] with theire proceeding concerninge the release of Christopher Hudson from his refusall of appearance at the court of Saynte James of Dovur'. Governors were fuming after hearing that Hallett also confided that 'they would trye the validitye of theire charters by lawe'. Did he not realize that he 'had disclosed the privityes of the wardemoate', they asked, and 'the townes meaninge and order in proceedeinge therein in sute'? He 'aunswered that if my lorde should ask him any questyons he would tel him' the answers. That was not what his fellows wanted to hear. You 'hathe disclosed the privityes' of the town and 'overthrown proceedings of the corporacon in their sutes and affayres', they told him, and are 'very likely hereafter to offende in like manner'. 'For this and other misdemeanours', Hallett was 'dissfraunchised for ever' and would remain a pariah in Faversham.[261]

This uncompromising language epitomizes the vital need to keep 'publique affaires' secret. Government and regulation were tightening; information was locked up out of reach except for a select few. Secrecy was secular scripture. But records were, as Tenterden rulers said, for 'daillie use'.

V

We see 'bookes' on tables waiting to be used. Once open, we notice that information is often arranged and presented for use. A few words in margins give quick summaries of entries; pointing fingers in 'the white' direct users to something of consequence. Books are paginated and an impressive number are indexed or 'kalendared'. These finding aids signify use. 'Kalendars'—or 'sumarie index[es] of direction'—put things in handy columns to take users to pages. This was so in royal and local archives. Yorkshire entries in the 'Booke of Domesdaie' had a 'kalendar... which if you observe the manner of it [Agard said] it will marvalously ready the searcher'.[262] Malynes thought that Chancery decrees were 'so methodically kept and kalendered [in "books of orders"] as the search hath nothing at all of hardship in it'. They were put in 'the chapel of the rolls where they are most orderly kept and easie to be found'. Another observer noted how Chancery bills were 'orderlie filed in bundelles' with a 'true and perfect register, kalender [and] booke of entrée' to be 'the more redilye founde'.[263]

[260] CKS TE/S2, fo. 247. [261] CKS FA/AC3, fo. 48v.

[262] A. Agard, *The Repertorie of Records Remaining in the 4 Treasuries on the Receipt Side at Westminster* (1631), 132–3.

[263] Malynes, *England's View*, 50–1; HL EL MS 2912. See also CA ZML/3/486; Powell, *Directions for Search of Records Remaining in the Chancerie, Tower [and] Exchequer*, A3r; HL SSTM box 9, folder 4.

An index, Edward Phillips wrote, was 'a token or mark [to] direct the table of a book'. Another lexicographer called indexes a guiding forefinger (like the one we see in margins) or the hands of a clock.[264] 'The index I am sure must be of good use [to] understand the history and affaires of this country', Laurence Echard wrote in his 'exact description of Ireland'. It stretched to forty pages.[265] Many London area records had finding aids. There was a handy index listing orders by page numbers at the back of St Benet Paul's Wharf parish accounts (1605–57). A goldsmith made 'a callendar of names' to steer readers through St Peter Westcheap accounts (1435–1601). Guides to St Katherine Coleman Street's accounts included 'branches' of wills and orders and 'a table of the accomptes' at the front of the book (1609–71).[266] A St Martin-in-the-Fields vestry book was indexed by subject and the names of churchwardens (1651–6). 'A register of writings belonging to the parrish and poor' begins in 1685 but goes all the way back to 1607 to index documents and orders from then on.[267]

Outside London, an Oxford Council Act book was indexed by order, title, and subject, with short synopses of subjects written in the margins (1591–1628). The one after has shorthand in margins and 'a table of all acts conteyned in this booke' as well as a guide to the contents of each page (1629–63).[268] A Tewkesbury Order Book has an 'abstract' with orders summed up in a few words including 'revealing the towns secretts'. Ordinances are indexed in a Yarmouth Assembly Book with a note on subject and page reference (1550–9). A Bideford Sessions Book has a 'table' at the front—continued at the end of the book—with a year-by-year list of offences and offenders.[269]

Peter Burke notes that alphabetization was used more often at this time to put records in better order. St Margaret's (Westminster) vestry book was organized for use with an alphabetical index tied to page numbers with running heads that included 'tickets for poore people', 'poore children', 'records', 'register', and 'workehous'.[270] Richard Issac, Exeter's chamberlain from 1653 to 1683, added a nineteen-page 'index' to an early City Act Book (1560–84) 'of the moste remarkable things contayned in this booke... alphabetically digested under proper and particculer heades' by page number, from 'accomptes' to 'watches'. He did the same

[264] Phillips, *New World of Words*, and Coles, *English Dictionary*, s.v. 'index'. See also P. Halliday, 'Authority in the archives', *Critical Analysis of Law*, 1 (2014).

[265] L. Echard, *An Exact Description of Ireland Chorographically Surveying All its Provinces and Counties* (1691), A2r–A2v, 104–44.

[266] LMA MSS 878/1; 645/1; 1124/1. See also LMA MS 1432/3, back of book.

[267] WAC F2003; F2001, fo. 14v; F2062.

[268] OHC C/FC/1/A1/02; C/FC1/A1/03.

[269] GA TBR/A/1/2, fos. 31, 35; NRO Y/C/19/1; Y/C/19/5; NDRO 1064Q/SO1. See also HA W/A6/1, fo. 140; KAC WSSMB/K/2/5, back of book; WSSMB/K/2/6, front of book; CKS FA/AC3, back of book; Md/Acm1/2–3, separate sheets of paper listing contents; GA GBR/F/4/5, fo. 283v; GBR/B/3/1, front of book; GBR//B/1/10, end of book; WAC F2001, fo. 4v; F2004, front of book.

[270] Burke, *Social History of Knowledge*, 184–7; WAC E2416; E2419.

for the next book.[271] Kent's Process Indictment Books were sorted alphabetically by defendant's name, parish, status, and job. A note was made in the margin of the indictment roll in which he/she appears for cross-reference. The index is in columns, with last names beginning with the same letter listed together in chronological order from tailor Paul Allen (1649) to husbandman Edward Young (1669).[272] There are more A–Z indexes from all parts: Colchester's Book of Examinations and Recognizances (1610–19) and Quarter Sessions book (1677–85), East Sussex prisoner files, a Herefordshire Sessions Order Book (1665–73), a fourteen-page index in a Gloucester Sessions Indictment Book (1638–53), and a forty-four-page index in a Common Council Book from the same city (1632–56).[273] London Bridewell courtbooks open with A–Z lists of offenders some with folio numbers next to names. Three Middlesex Sessions Process Register of Charges Books have indexes that are thirty-nine, twenty-six, and thirty pages long. Seven seventeenth-century Norwich Sessions Search Books list the names of anyone indicted by date in alphabetical sequence. Letters were cut into the side of some books in alternating black and red.[274]

The appearance and organization of pages helped people to navigate through records. Issac Bothomley compiled an 'alphabeticall book' of benefactors for St Martin-in-the-Fields in 1623. The same parish had alphabetical lists of pensioners and orphans in 1654, 1659, 1673, and 1696, with payments next to names.[275] An 'alphabet of the last sessions att Chichester and Lewes' was made for future use in East Sussex in 1661. The names of 502 Bideford men who signed oaths of allegiance were listed from A to Z, ending with Stephen Zeller. A book of seventeen double-sided pages lists indicted recusants in Oxford Diocese from A to Y, with surnames written in alternating shades of pink or red. Recusants were further catalogued by parish or hundred in alphabetical order. A separate list of gentry, knights, and squires (and their wives) was seven pages long.[276] Alphabetical sequencing was also followed for copyholders, freeholders, leases, tenants, ratepayers, and anyone not taking civic oaths. Later London Bills of Mortality listed cause of death by the alphabet.[277] Clerks had an able awareness of spaces and borders. For 'perfecting of [a] surveigh', Agas advised in 1596, 'make a fair parchment book with a large margent' for details of a 'plat' and its date.[278] Margins were rarely empty. Fingers pointed to John Hallet's 'disenfranchisement from his

[271] DRO ECA B/1/3, fos. 474–92; B/1/4, fos. 588–95. [272] CKS Q/SPI/1; Q/SPI/2.

[273] ERO D/B5/SB2/6; D/B5/SB3/1; ESBHRO QI/EW2; QI/EW3; HEA Q/SO/1.

[274] LMA MJ/SB/P001-3; NRO Norwich City Sessions Search Books 1–7.

[275] WAC F2001, fo. 163v; F3348, fo. 51.

[276] ESBHRO QI/EW2, fo. 58v; NDRO 1064Q/S01, fos. 12–13v; HL EL MS 2178.

[277] HL EL MS 2514; CA TAR/2/29; DRO 2945 A-99/PO/2; BRO R/AP/1/4; HL HAM box 25, folder 12; box 26, folder 14; box 27, folder 16; LA CNP 3/2/1, fo. 248. See also T. Cummins and J. Rappaport, 'The reconfiguration of civic and sacred space: architecture, image, and writing in the colonial northern Andes', *Latin American Literary Review*, 26 (1998), 178.

[278] R. Agas, *A Preparative to Platting of Landes and Tenements for Surueigh* (1596), 15, irregular pag.

juratshippe' in a Faversham wardmote book in 1600, and 'chamberlens to account' or 'accons and sutes to be brought' in Maidstone's Burghmote Minute Book in 1630.[279] Fines are noted in margins in Dorchester's Offenders Book (1629–37). Names and a note on subject matter run down the side of London Bridewell Courtbooks. Three Oxford Council Act Books have shorthand summaries of entries in margins (1520–1663).[280] Pointing fingers fill margins in London's repertories and journals. 'By the notacion in the margent of last years booke to this article', a note in Southampton's Leet Book reads in 1603, 'it is said no reason to charge the towne with anie more watche'. 'The precept for the clearke of the markett court as in Mr Mawdleys letter book f. 6' was written in a margin in Poole's Market Book in 1649. While Norwich's clerk wrote a note to himself in 1632 in a Sessions Book margin: 'remember to speake to Mr Alex Anguish about Mr Merricks sonne and for evidences against Ann Hynds'.[281] There are marginal notes all the way through a Gloucester Common Council Minute Book (1632–56) summing up entries about 'the gaole to be amended', for example, 'keepe the streets and lanes cleane', roads, 'setting the poore on worke', 'gentlewomens seates in the colledge', and 'porters allowance for trimming their cloaks'.[282]

This was a book that was designed for use. Officers and officials also worked between records for information and verification. Folio page references in other books show a collection of records as a single working resource. London chamber accounts record £1411 4s. 7d.,

> paid to the use of divers orphans from Michaelmas 1584 unto Michaelmas 1585 as particularly appears by an acount thereof kept by James Pele by two books the one called the ledger folio 44 and the other called the journal [as] also by the repertory kept in the inner chamber of the guildhall.

The city spent £2635 8s. 4d. on orphans over the next twelve months, duly logged in accounts and two books in the hands of John Benson 'called the journal folio 41 and the ledger folio 47'.[283] Moving between books created continuous data chains. Yarmouth's clerk noted in 1616 that an 'ordinance' for 'thimployment and relieffe of the poore' was in 'the booke of ordinances folio 193'. The town 'delivered… Queene Maries charter menconed in fol. 170 and Queene Elizabeths charter menconed in fol 159' to Mr Felton 'to use at London' in 1589.[284] There are references to folio pages in Preston's books (with dates added for good measure) to spotlight court cases, waste, tottering buildings, 'keepe the streets and lanes

[279] CKS FA/AC3, fo. 48v; Md/AC,1/2, fos. 102v, 171v.

[280] DHC DC/DOB/8/1, fos. 257v, 258v; OHC C/FC/1/A1/01–3.

[281] SA 6/1, fo. 27; DHC DC/PL/CLA/179, fo. 8v. See also NDRO 1064Q/SO1, fo. 176; WSHC G22/1/107.

[282] GA GBR/3/2, fos. 55, 63, 68, 69, 79, 91, 102, 111, 112, 113, 147, 151, 152, 162, 172, 201, 252, 255, 292, 295, 312, 355, 363, 702, 719.

[283] Masters, *Chamber Accounts*, 50, 67.

[284] NRO Y/C/19/5, fo. 164; Y/C/19/4, fos. 176, 146.

cleane', 'middings', soil, dung, and putting the poor to work.[285] 'Hutch folio 171' is in the margin of a Yarmouth Assembly Book.[286] People also looked elsewhere in the same book. Faversham governors checked a lease 'in this booke fo. 89' when giving orders to build 'a mill and mill house at the new sluice' in 1613. 'As appears in the next page' is in a Bideford Sessions Book (1659–1709) that also refers readers to 'folio 26' in 'the monethly meetinge booke' for information on another matter.[287]

Clerks looked for people in books. Recidivists left paper trails. Vagrant Thomas Wear was 'taken' in Exeter on 27 November 1563, and a note confirmed that he had been found vagrant on 21 April 1562. Records showed that another Exeter vagrant who was caught in 1563 had been whipped four years before, while 'evell and incontinent' Ellen Hunt, who was caught rambling on 29 July 1564, had been 'taken' thirty-two days earlier in a house.[288] Records were these vagrants' undoing. John Robinson from Derby was found in Manchester on 26 January 1625, and a book showed that he 'had beene whipped and sent out of the towne afore the xxix of December last'.[289] Standard practice in Bideford was to note the date and details of a case in the margins of a Sessions Book (1659–1709): '16th January 1682 William Gorwell bound to the good behaviour for beateinge his servant'; '9 March 1682 informacon of Robert Boscombe of Northam agt Walter Peeke, Symon Burgess and Samuel Griffiths concerninge the stealinge of his duck'. Bideford Sessions clerk was asked to 'see what wandring vagrant rogues' Passion Hodge and her son Daniel Tooslow 'are by theire examinacons taken and filed with the records of the generall sessions the 24 of Oct. last past'.[290] Norwich justices turned to the officer's 'examination' in the 'courtbook xi Apr. 1640' for more on John Bonfield, who 'abused' a constable in June 1640.[291] Telling phrases like 'here before' or 'often here' appear next to names in London Bridewell Courtbooks. They could be more specific. 'Common nightwalker', 'rude' Francis Wotten stood in the dock on 23 June 1641: 'here 2 June' is next to her name. Elizabeth Cooley was caught walking late in June 1638 and a note said that she 'hath bene often here [and] 25 March last passed to Ware'. Katherine Curtis was caught walking after dark in winter 1637; 'here the vi of September last' for being a 'comon nightwalker', the book says.[292] Books also confirmed that 'very giltye'-looking Godfrey Lambright had been in trouble 'five years sens for lewde life' and that 'comon rogue and begger' Edward Griffin had been in Bridewell five years before. A clerk

[285] LA CNP 3/1/3, fos. 30v, 36, 44, 52, 53; 3/2/1, fos. 2v, 26, 35, 71, 230, 308, 321.
[286] NRO Y/C/19/6, fos. 182v, 190.
[287] CKS FA/AC3, fos. 92–3v; NDRO 1064Q/SO1, fos. 7v, 125v. See also GA GBR/B/3/2, fos. 55, 63.
[288] DRO ECA B/1/4, fos. 238, 234, 259.
[289] Earwaker, *Constables Accounts of the Manor of Manchester*, I, 136.
[290] NDRO 1064Q/SO1, fos. 176, 127.
[291] NRO Norwich Sessions Book 1639–54, fo. 10v.
[292] LBHC 8, fos. 338, 176v; 6, fo. 117.

'search[ed]' back through books 'for five yeares last past' in 1608 to find out 'what proceedings were had againste Erasmus Percivall' and to 'extract the same'.[293]

Working between records was routine. St Martin-in-the-Fields vestry ruled in 1601 that churchwardens should 'declare their recypts for all buryalls [in accounts]' that were to be 'compared with the ministers register' to check that they 'agreed'.[294] Norwich justices asked in 1679 'that for the future a noate of all indictments and presentments be at the next sessions presented in open court' to see 'what process' had been taken. Governors had Assembly books at hand when working on 'businesse' in the Mayor's Court. 'Searche', 'viewe', or 'peruse' were verbs of choice.[295] A case was secured by something in the books: 'as 'expressed in the booke of orders', 'as appered by particulars thereof in bookes viewed and seene'. The proper 'order' of civic processions in Poole in 1658 was sorted out as 'appeareth by an order or constitucon made in this towne booke the 19th day of September 1606'.[296] Courts checked data in wills, deeds, leases, rent rolls, leet books, charters, and other 'evidences'. The churchwardens of 'Allhallows' Newcastle were sitting drinking in an alehouse 'after evening prayer' in autumn 1623 when Godfrey Comyn asked if he could move into the 'stall' left empty by a recent death. They said yes but had second thoughts when Comyn reached for his purse, telling him instead that he should pay later, 'for they did not knowe what to take and they would searche the church book and see what was usuallie taken'.[297] In Gloucester alone we see courts 'searching evidens [in the] powncell howse' (wine and cake followed); getting copies of parish registers from other places; paying ten shillings to copy York's charter; reading 'writings' from the 'treasury' to check burgesses' 'comonable places'; choosing 'agents' to read 'charters and writings [to] sollicite' for 'the rights, liberties and privileges of this city'; and setting up a committee in 1664 'to examine the books of the acts of comon councill and the stewards accompts' to 'see what monyes have been disbursed by the mayor and burgesses for the use of the hospitalls' and the amount collected from rents.[298]

Records were checked to settle tricky issues with fiscal consequences such as paternity or settlement. London's Commissary Court asked William Norton—a governor of Christ's Hospital—in 1592 for details of a case from Christ's court a

[293] LBHC 3, fos. 346v, 384; 5, fo. 295;. See also LBHC 1, fo. 90v; 5, fos. 377v, 395v; 8, fos. 260, 352, 371.

[294] WAC F2201, fo. 96.

[295] NRO Norwich Sessions Book 1671–91, 1679 sessions; NMCC 23, fo. 210v; 25, fo. 215v. See also SAI C/4/3/1/1/4, fos. 10, 12; HA W/B2/1, fo. 21; NDRO B1/3792, fo. 110; HEA Q/SM/2, fo. 96v; WSHC G22/1/205/2, fo. 99.

[296] DHC DC/PL/B/1/1/1 fos. 131, 99, 101–1. See also BRO R/AC1/1/3, fo. 349; NRO Norwich Clavors Book 1, fos. 18, 26v; SA 6/1, fo. 31; NRO Y/C27/1, fos. 84, 177.

[297] Durham University Library, Archives and Special Collections DDR/EJ/CCD/1/11, fos. 316v–17 (I must thank Keith Wrightson for this reference).

[298] GA GBR/F/4/3, fos. 202v, 225v, 290; GBR/B/3/2, fos. 360, 491, 554; GBR/3/3, fos. 78, 209, 283, 301. See also HA W/B2/1, fo. 21; ESBHRO RYE/6, fos. 10–10v; NRO Y/C27/1, fo. 237v; CKS FA/AC3, fos. 92–3v; LA CNP 3/2/1, fo. 71.

decade earlier. He checked 'a speciall booke and recorde [for] particuler proceedings and examinacons' in 'a matter' involving Evan Thomas and his maid. Norton found what he was looking for in an entry from 26 May 1582, where Thomas admitted that 'he had the use of [her] body'. He put a 'mark' next to it.[299] A Flint justice, faced with a sick 'poore woman' who had been 'lurkeinge' for six months in 'Hamme' in 1608, was sent an 'examinacon' by request from Chester's mayor to confirm 'that she was borne' in his city and she was soon on her way there.[300] 'See his examanacon in mr maiors booke and hers in this booke', Dorchester magistrates said in 1631 when getting to the bottom of a charge of fathering 'a basterd childe' made by Joan Benvill against a clothworker. They also copied entries from 'mr maiors booke' into the Offenders Book on a regular basis and turned for evidence to 'Mr White's book' (this is Puritan John White). A list of 'offenders with their offences taken out of mr maiors booke' covered one-and-a-half pages in the Offenders Book; folio pages sit next to names. Offenders included ten people missing from church, twenty-seven 'drunkards', and twenty 'tiplers'. Glover John Merrifield had been in trouble for 'dronkennesse' before, 'as in mr Whites booke is recorded'.[301] London Bridewell's clerk made copies from records for parishes that needed material on one of their own. Stepney requested 'true coppies' of 'accusacions' about parishioner Daniel English in 1603. Parishes paid for confessions and 'examinacons' in illegitimacy or child abandonment cases. A parish was sent 'examinacons of the midwife and others about Wheelers childe'. Another got a copy of 'the womens examinacons about St Gregorys child' in 1640.[302] Vital statistics in parish registers cleared up doubts about paternity, provision, burials, or marriage. 'For the solemnization of the marriage itselfe', Thomas Powell advised, 'search the parochiall register'.[303] St Sepulchre parish (Middlesex) paid St Thomas Apostle's clerk for 'a certificate of the marriage of John Preston and Joane his wife (nowe in the hospitall) whose child is left to the parrish'. William Goldsmith got eight-pence from Lyme Regis 'for sercheinge the churche booke of Exeter for Warwoods daughter'. Two men got four shillings from Lambeth parish in 1593 to cross the river 'with Robert Russhe to Whitechappell to] search the regester'.[304] Crowfield (Suffolk) had a 'problem' with Alice Austen, who was 'privately brought' from Loddon in Norfolk and 'left in a hay house' in their town. Parish officers spent four years 'constantly enquiring for the place of her birth'.

[299] LMA D/L/C 214, fos. 160–1. [300] CA ZML/2/219.

[301] DHC DC/DOB/8/1, fos. 81v, 306–6v, 181, 103v, 314v, 348. See also DRO ECA C1/61, fo. 598; BRO R/AC/1/3, fo. 442; NRO Norwich St. George's Guild Minute Book 1602–1729, fos. 74v–5.

[302] LBHC 3, fos. 180v, 240v, 242v–3; 5, fos. 115, 292v, 414v; BMM LBHC 4, fos. 10, 187, 234, 331, 418, 451; WAC E15/1627; LMA MSS 590/1, fo. 149v; 7706, fo. 8v.

[303] Powell, *Directions for Search of Records Remaining in the Chancerie*..., 77.

[304] LMA MS 9080/4, 1654; DHC DC/LR/G/2/2, 1595–6; Drew, *Lambeth Churchwardens' Accounts*, 188. See also CA QJB/1/6, fo. 228v; LERO 1D41/13/11, 49a; GA GBR/F/4/3, fo. 225v; WAC WCB/1, fo. 280.

Finally, in 1647, her grandmother told them that she had been 'borne and nursed' forty miles away in Loddon. Paper confirmation was needed and good news arrived a few days later: 'yt itt doth appeare by the Register booke of lodden that the child was there baptized' seven years ago.[305]

There was a brisk traffic in records. The job description of London's yeoman-of-the-chamber included 'carrying of books and records [for] the necessary business of the city'.[306] Windsor spent 10s. 10d. in 1664 for wine, beer, and tobacco for the mayor and 'company' when 'the new charter was brought home'. All of Maidstone's charters and 'burghmote books' were 'carried' to London by the mayor in 1654 for 'counsell' to examine. They were to be 'carefully preserved' and back in Maidstone inside two weeks.[307] Local governments shipped parcels of records in one trip. 'A note of such things and writings' taken to London in a 320-mile round trip by Exeter's clerk in 1580 included 'a bondell of rolls for the towne', '3 customes of the port in the tyme of Richard the second', 'xviii rolles whereof some are very shorte', 'fower rolles of King Edward the third', 'and a 'bundell of parchment in several rolles concernynge sutes agaynste the earle of Devon which are for the moste part eaten with wormes'.[308] A shipment of 'wrytings' that were sent on the 420-mile round trip from Barnstaple to London on 6 April 1613 was even larger: '31 old receavors accompts in one bundell', '21 in another bundell', forty-five in six more bundles, leases, releases, bonds, records of a squabble 'betweene Sir Jn CH and the towne', '9 peeces of writtings concernyng Castell fayres', '5 antient charters', 'writtyngs sent for London in maie 1613', '3 courtbooks', '1 old parchment booke being a rentall', '19 courte rolles and acommpts', '40 severall deeds and wrytinges', and three town charters.[309]

A legal suit was often the nub of the matter. Paperwork mounted up as litigation rates soared. Tenterden gave 'moneyes' to the town solicitor in 1664 'for suing out of coppies of the two peculiar charters belonging to this corporacon [Henry VI and Elizabeth to help] us to make our defence at the tryall of Robert Gibbon'. All Hallows Lombard Street (London) spent £4 10s. 7d. to read 'records concerninge the naked boye and for charges of law' in 1618.[310] Legal counsel combed through records for prize pieces of evidence. Reading governors sent 'the English coppy of the [charter and] ordinances or bi lawes' to Walter Knight of Staple Inn to put their side of a case in 1547. Mr Felton got to see 'xvi court Rolles' and two charters to help him build a case for Yarmouth in 1574 (he would do so again fifteen years later). Charters went back and forth. Ipswich paid Richard Dawtry 46s. 8d. in 1578 'for copying out of the charter of London'.[311] Local governors took the time and trouble to copy 'orders' and 'constitucons' from other places. Windsor's

[305] SAI B/105/2/1, fo. 98v. [306] Masters, *Chamber Accounts*, 37.

[307] BRO W1/FA1/2, fo. 123v; CKS Md/ACm1/3, fo. 143v. [308] DRO ECA B/1/3, fo. 460.

[309] NDRO B1/46/366. [310] CKS TE/S2, fo. 221; LMA MS 4051/1, fo. 17.

[311] BRO R/Z4/3/3; SAI C/3/4/11; C/2/2/2/1, fo. 227v. See also BRO WI/FA1/2, fo. 109; R/FA2/77; GA GBR/B/3/2, fo. 554; HL EL MS 555e.

John White picked up £2 10s. 'for his jorney to Readinge' in 1640 and for 'writing oute copies of orders or by-laws'. Westminster officials got copies of orders for Newgate and Cheapside market in 1615 and 'presidents and orders' from 'houses of correccon in Middlesex and Surrey and old Bridewell in London' in 1622. Ipswich governors 'agreed' in 1589 that 'artycles exhibited by the duchmen touchinge ther abode' needed to be 'reconsidered' and a delegation was sent to Norwich 'to understand the certentye of the orders of the dutche companye there and to bring a perfect copye'.[312]

Legal matters shaped cross-country pipelines. 'Books', 'examynacons', and 'informacons' were ferried to and from assizes and sessions. John Yonge was put in charge of 'books and records that were taken out of [Yarmouth] vestrye to be carried to the assises when the trial of the cause' between Thomas Dassett and William More was heard in 1598. A 1657 note from Walton-on-the-Hill reads: 'paid [1s.] for writing a coppie of this account for the justice of the peace'.[313] It cost money to read records in London's 'bookhouse'. St Benet Gracechurch parish sent someone to find an order in the repertories for 'buylding' sheds 'by the churchside wher the yerbwifes sell hearbs'. Bridewell kept an up-to-date archive of Court of Aldermen orders, copied by a Guildhall clerk soon after they were passed.[314] Towns and villages also went to London to 'search' through central/equity records for fees ranging from 3s. 4d. to read King's Bench pleadings 'as ancient as from the harmlesse King Henry the sixt' to four-pence 'for sight' of any Chancery record 'you call for by the index or kallender', eight-pence more 'for everie sheet' copied, and two shillings 'for the hand of the Clarke to anything you coppy'. It cost 6s. 8d. 'for search of Domes-day booke' in 1622, plus four-pence for each line copied 'written in the old Saxon letter'.[315] Norwich Great Hospital spent two shillings in 1607 'for a search in Domesdaye Booke'. St Dunstan-in-the-West precinct (London) forked out twenty-three shillings to copy 'records of the Tower' in 1630. A copy of a Chancery decree 'concerninge schoole money' cost Walton-on-the-Hill three shillings in 1657.[316] Windsor spent £2 for 'twoe surveyes towchinge this corporacon out of the exchequer' in 1640 and 6s. 8d. seven years later 'for procuring the will of King Henry the Eight touching his guifte to the poore of Windsor'.[317]

[312] BRO W1/FA1/2, fo. 38; WAC WCB/2, fo. 121; E13/1622–3; SAI C//4/31/1/3, fo. 2. See also SAI C/4/3/1/1/1, fos. 4–5, 8, 52v, 57v; GA GBR/F/4/3, fo. 290.

[313] NRO Y/C/19/5, fo. 10v; Ramsay and Maddock, *Churchwardens' Accounts of Walton-on-the-Hill*, 111.

[314] LMA MS 1568, fo. 160; BMM LBHC 4, fos. 160, 178, 249. See also HA Q1/3, fos. 14–15; DHC DC/LR/G/2/2; SAI C/4/3/1/1/1, fo. 57v; NRO Y/C/19/5, fo. 10v.

[315] Powell, *Directions for Search of Records*, 14–15, 36–7, 53, 62–3, 65–6, 68–9; Agard, *Repertorie of Records*, 11.

[316] NRO Norwich Great Hospital Account Rolls, 1607–8; LMA MS 2968/2, fo. 214v; Ramsay and Maddock, *Churchwardens' Accounts of Walton-on-the-Hill*, 114.

[317] BRO WI/FA1/2, fos. 30, 87. See also CKS FA/AC3, fo. 38v; WSHC G22/1/205/2, fo. 59v; WAC F2002, fo. 132; DHC DC/BTB/M2/1610.

Hue and cries with physical descriptions chased after fleeing suspects 'to every town round about east, west, north and south'. 'Describe him by his apparel', Richard Chamberlain wrote, and 'give notice of the thing stolen as horse &c of the colour and special marks'.[318] Accounts from Manchester list thirteen hue and cries in 1614, sixteen in 1617, and twenty-six in 1627. They included little pen portraits: 'a man lowe in stature with a broune broade beard thin of haire and smale'; 'a yonge manne in a brownishe sute of aperrill and greene stockeinges'; 'a suspitious person blak heared haveinge sad collared clothes'.[319] Chester officials asked constables in Derbyshire 'to rayse hue and cry' for 'wandering soldier' Robert Butterworth in 1610. He was 'a bigg bare faced younge fellow with black haire on his head and som on his upper lipp appareled in russet' who had 'stolen' a 'livery cloake of russet color cloth faced with watchet velvet and silke lace' and 'a guilt rapier sworde with embroidered hangers'.[320] We can follow a hue and cry from Drayton (Norfolk) in 1587 on its way to nearby Hellesdon 'and so forthe to Norwich and Yermouth'. It carried 'informacon' about 'a man of tall personage having a red berd and a broad russett hat with the verge buttened up and blacke freise coate with a longe dagger at his backe and a gould ringe on his finger'. 'A yonge fellowe of meane stature aboute thage of xxliiii yeres' who stole twenty-six shillings was the protagonist in another Norfolk hue and cry five years later. He had on 'a white canvas doblet, a payer of clothe venisicons [of] velvet color, [a] payer of knit stockins of watchet and grene and a blacke felt hatt' and carried 'a pack of old clothes'.[321]

Information was also circulated by letter. Thomas Fuller (alias Daniell) made off with clothing and household goods from a Norwich lodging house in 1568. Hearing that he was heading for London, magistrates posted information about his friends and relatives living there. They also gave details of his clothes (and a 'dagger with a yealowe scabbur') to officers on the road to London, adding that he was 'of personage a very black man with very few heares on his beard [and] of meane stature but of good thickness and anckles somewhat bigg above his shoes'.[322] Leicestershire justices wanted 'a description of the person' in a vagrant 'pass or testimoniall', something that was also spelt out by authors of legal handbooks.[323] I find myself asking how they knew that someone was thirty, forty, or eighty miles away? Exeter's mayor wrote a letter to his opposite number in Lyme Regis (30 miles

[318] Chamberlain, *Complete Justice*, 183. See also J. Layer, *The Office and Dutie of Constables, Churchwardens and Other the Overseers of the Poore* (1641), 27–8.

[319] Earwaker, *Constables Accounts of the Manor of Manchester*, I, 14–17, 34–6, 45–8, 35, 162, 204, 241.

[320] CA ZML/6/33.

[321] NRO Aylsham MS/181. See also DRO ECA C1/62, fo. 145; WSHC G22/1/205/2, fo. 23v; G23/1/38, 27/12/1612; ERO D/B5/Sb2/7, fos. 146v, 148–8v, 247.

[322] NRO NMCC Interrogatories and Depositions Book 1567–72, 24/8/1568.

[323] LERO QS6/1/2, fos. 59v–60; P.B., *Help to Magistrates*, 59v–60. See also DHC DC/DOB/8/1, fo. 120v; ERO D/B5/SB2/6, fos. 32, 137, 173v, 254v; Griffiths, *Lost Londons*, 255–7.

away) in 1670. Thieves were on the run. 'Two young men' (Joseph Williams and Francis Butcher) were 'suspected' of stealing 'neare fortie pounds' from John Browne, who ran an Exeter pub. They sneaked into shadows but were chased by a shower of hue and cries. One made its way to Lyme Regis on the coast. Word reached Exeter's mayor that the pair slipped into Plymouth (45 miles from Exeter; 75 miles from Lyme Regis), where they bumped into someone they knew and, fearing getting turned in, 'went suddenly from thence'. The mayor was in touch with Plymouth officials, who told him that Williams and Butcher had gone back to the town. The pair sent a 'box' from there to Lyme Regis on a 'shipp called the Jone of Luic' skippered by John Alford, who was told to leave it with John Burridge, landlord of the Three Caps. The mayor even knew that the thieves had changed their clothes. Information flows within a seventy-five-mile radius. Exeter's mayor asked his colleagues in Lyme Regis to search Burridge's house and anywhere else their suspicions took them. This 'good worke' shall be 'acknowledged by yor friend and servant' the 'mayor of Exeter'.[324]

Cross-country communications were essential for policing. Oxford justices double-checked Anthony Lamborne's claim that he had murdered a man in Hampshire in 1624. A 'certificate' arrived to say that this was 'his own foolish affirmation'.[325] Cripplegate surgeon Edmund Cage stopped at Dorchester for dinner on his way to Plymouth 'to seeke a place to goe to sea as a surgeon on a merchant voyage' in 1631. He was drinking with a 'company' when constables surprised them and 'apprehended' Cage for 'a misdemeanor of cheating laid to his charge' thirty months ago in London, over 100 miles away. He owned up and was soon on his way back to London. How did those constables know who he was, what he had done, and where he was?[326] Exeter governors found £10 5s. 9d. in 'vagabond' Henry Burton's pockets in 1566, who said 'that he got it by begging'. Finding out that he was from a parish near York, a letter was 'written to Yorks mayor' asking him to 'advertyse [Burton's] person, estate and honesty'.[327] 'God alone have the glory', Essex minister Ralph Josselin said on hearing that thieves who stole goods worth 'nigh 50li' from his son in 1669 had been tracked down to Cambridge, thirty miles away.[328] We see information travelling from Exeter to Wells (47 miles), and from there to Launceston (108 miles), before ending up in Tavistock (14 miles): 169 miles in all![329] Word also went from London to Salisbury (80 miles) and Colchester (65 miles), from Ipswich to Norwich (45 miles), and between other towns across England.[330]

324 DHC DC/LR/B7/D2, 16/3/1670.
325 Blades, *Oxford Quarter Sessions Order Book 1614–1637*, 108, 118.
326 DHC DC/DOB/8/1, fos. 86–6v. 327 DRO ECA B/1/4, fo. 300.
328 *Diary of Ralph Josselin*, 550–1. 329 DRO ECA B/1/4, fo. 239.
330 WSHC G22/1/205/2, fos. 15, 47; ERO D/Y/2/9/75; D/Y/2/9/253; SAI B/105/2/4, fos. 16, 90; B/105/2/6, fo. 134; DHC DC/BTB/M2/1610.

Chester's archive includes letters to and from the mayor that give telling glimpses of contact fields. A Warwickshire justice wrote in 1593 to tell the mayor that he was 'enforme[d]' that horse-thief Coventry fuller John Stanfield, who broke out of Warwick Prison, was ninety miles away in Chester 'gayle'.[331] Wigan's mayor asked that Thomas Almond, who was in prison 'upon suspition of felony' in 1612, be sent forty miles to Wigan. He sent 'the bond or recognizances [to] make it playne' that Arnold 'is the man that hath stolen plate called a beaker from Susan Greene of Wygan'.[332] Chester's mayor also got word from Liverpool's mayor: I have detained the person you asked about in your last letter. From justices in Lancashire: information about a robbery and murder. From Newport's vice-chamberlain: a request to release Henry Leigh from prison 'for suspicion of fellony' so that he could go with his family to Ireland. Master of the Mint Isaac Newton wanted word from the mayor as soon as coiner William Cook arrived from Dublin, so 'that I may order a heabus corpus' to take him to Newgate: 'I can satisfy you that this is my hand', Newton ended.[333]

Local governors were in dialogue with places near and far on issues like crime, poverty, trade, and religion. Appleby, Ashby-de-la-Zouch, Chester, Bridport, Hungerford, Faversham, Shrewsbury, Lyme Regis, Manchester, and Thetford all have documented extensive links with other places. We can follow Yarmouth officials on 'town busines' at Norwich, King's Lynn, Beccles, Ipswich, Thetford, London, and the Privy Council.[334] The little Nottinghamshire village of Upton was in contact with Southwell, Nottingham, Newark, Morton, Rampton, Averham, Stoke, Scrooby, and Norwell on issues such as weights and measures, 'criples', a disputed meadow, the 'protestation', soldiers' wages, poor children, corn, and hay, as well as taking village 'busines' to sessions and assizes.[335] Walton officials near Liverpool made trips to Chester, Wigan, Lancaster, Manchester, Warrington, Ormskirk, Prescot, Huyton, Sefton, Preston, Chorley, Tarbock, Childwall, Crosby, Liverpool, and London on 'parish busines'. They travelled to file 'presentments', buy a Book of Common Prayer, 'deliver' orders to mayors and justices, make payments for 'maimed souldiers', hand over 'names of able men' at one time and people taking or refusing the 'protestacion' at another, get copies of court orders and 'the kinges book' (Book of Sports) and advice about their poor, 'bastard' children, and outsiders setting up home in the parish. The village also sent

[331] CA ZML/1/140. [332] CA ZML/2/254.

[333] CA ZML/1/92; ZML/6/68; ZML/1/94; ZML/6/85; ZML/6/60; ZML/5/547. See also CA ZML/1/147, 159–62, 164–6, 169–71; ZML/2/186, 192, 239, 278; ZML/3/352, 487; ZML/5/78; ZML/5/79–80, 220; ZML/6/62.

[334] NRO Y/C/19/3, fos. 6v, 8v, 10v, 13v, 40v, 67v, 82v, 83v, 93, 105, 214v; Y/C/19/4, fos. 8, 10, 49v, 98v, 131v, 166, 189v, 199v, 210, 217, 218v, 220, 222, 242, 253, 264v, 279, 284; Y/C/19/5, fos. 149, 288v, 328–8v; Y/C/19/6, fos. 13, 45v, 54v, 65, 85, 123v, 138, 142.

[335] M. Bennett, ed., *A Nottinghamshire Village in War and Peace: the Accounts of the Constables of Upton, 1640–66*, Thoroton Society, 39 (Nottingham, 1995), 5, 7, 11, 12, 13, 15 18, 20, 22, 25, 29, 31, 35, 38, 39, 41, 47, 57, 58, 59, 63, 64, 72, 80, 81.

papers and delegations to assizes, quarter sessions, 'my lord bishops corrections', 'commicioners for pious uses', and 'the inquisition'. Officials travelled to London to put their side in legal cases with nearby Kirkby and Liverpool, spending £7 15s. 13d. to send Master Finch there in 1657.[336] Barnstaple had 'affaires' to take care of in nearby South Molton, Torrington, Ilfracombe, Ottery St Mary, Chichester, Honiton, Plymouth, London, and Exeter, including a day in 1582 when 'xvii pyratts' were taken there at a cost of 58s. 5d. with 'cord to bynd them withall'.[337] Larger Gloucester had bigger contact fields for 'city businesse' including Manchester, Chester, Cirencester, Worcester, Tewkesbury, Bristol, Hereford, Taunton, Ludlow, Ireland, the Council of the Marches, privy councillors, the Committee of the Kingdom, the Archbishop of Canterbury, and Parliament's speaker on 'affaires of this citty'. These 'affaires' included corn, conduits, customs, wages, plague, 'suspected' people, and paperwork for courts. Roger Lowe got 2s. 8d. in 1584 'for rydinge to Kingeswoode for the preste that murdered the woman'; Edward Harris picked up 1s. 6d. 104 years later 'to goe to Newnham to make enquiry after the gent that was killed'.[338]

VI

Questions crossed landscapes. Information or 'makinge knowne' was oxygen for local government that could not have run without it. Courts would have rolled to a grinding halt. Lights would have gone out in guildhalls, leaving magistrates in the dark in more ways than one. Information was bright light that could 'take knowledge' of the dark corners of a town, open up nooks and crannies, establish geographies, and reveal the 'undiscovered'. All for the 'better government' of towns, in words from Salisbury. The scope and scale of information collection at local levels was unprecedented after the middle of the sixteenth century. So, too, were the uses to which all this 'knowledge' was put. The extent of quantification changed things. Numbers on paper could display a town like a map. With information and statistics at hand, officers and officials could now 'digest', 'compute', 'number', 'order', and 'particulerize'. They could now try to answer the questions that mattered: 'who are you?', 'what am I?', 'what number?', 'what they be?', 'where have you been?', 'what are you?' There were more of these questions as more

[336] Ramsay and Maddock, *Churchwardens' Accounts of Walton-on-the-Hill*, 4, 5, 7, 10, 14, 15, 18, 19, 21, 24, 25, 29, 31, 33, 39, 47, 53, 64, 68, 72, 74, 78, 82, 84, 87, 89, 95, 100, 110, 116, 120, 131, 132, 133, 138, 142, 143, 149, 153, 157, 167.

[337] NDRO B1/379, fos. 65, 70, 73, 76, 86, 87, 102, 114, 116, 118, 121; B1/3118.

[338] GA GBR/F/4/3, fos. 29, 36v, 54v, 67v, 99v, 101v, 123v, 184, 232v, 243v, 274v, 290, 328, 411v; GBR/F/4/5, fos. 13, 15, 40, 69–9v, 75v, 111, 220, 249v, 282v, 319v, 348v, 375, 411, 437, 487; GBR/F/4/6, fos. 75, 78, 82, 85, 87, 187, 272, 320, 364, 444, 478; GBR/B/3/2, fos. 235, 239, 594, 751; GBR/B/3/3, fos. 220, 260.

jobless people took to the road to look for work to get through the ravages of a population boom in a harshly unequal society.

More questions, more answers, more 'making knowne'. There were empirical dimensions to the great growth in local surveillance. 'Experience' was a good teacher; learning on the ground doing 'observation' time after time to the point of repetition so that information gathering developed a strong interior momentum. 'Precyson' as aspiration was another motivating factor, although we have also come across a fair amount of 'mysprecyson' caused by neglect, sleaze, or incompetence. The quality and commitment of 'one-year' officers has long stirred debate, although there has been more optimism lately. Office-holder(s) were overwhelmingly drawn from the middle walk of life, and it seems to me that a highly significant number of them stepped into office (for the first, second, third, fourth, fifth, or sixth time?) equipped with all the skills necessary for record-keeping, managing information, and handling accounts. The same economic and commercial changes that challenged local information systems to improve also produced an army of 'middling' men with personal and professional reasons to get things done as churchwarden or constable. England's first 'political arithmeticians' were the prime movers in the 'turn inside', making sure that institutions and information became indispensable for local government.

Coda: Turning Inside

> 'We humans hate ambiguity more than almost anything else in the world'.
>
> Jeff Tweedy, *Let's Go (So We Can Get Back)* (2018), 162.

Counting, Dr Johnson told Boswell, 'brings everything to a certainty, which before floated in the mind indefinitely'.[1] This aimless floating infuriates any sort of government. Little is ever settled in these floating worlds. 'Precise' and 'exact' information and counting, however, were intended to put a stop to this drifting. They would create certainty and the reassuring confidence of being in the know and in control, in the minds of magistrates at any rate.

There was a time when it was thought that London's vagrants, needy, and down on their luck could be counted in their entirety and put down in a 'booke'. This was from around the start of London's population surge in the middle of the sixteenth century. It was then, John Howes wrote in his gushing history of the five 'hospitals' opened in 1546–53 (1582), that the 'xxxtie persons' (a City committee of aldermen 'and other grave cyttezens') 'devysed to send precepts to every alderman and to the wardeines of every companye to this effecte',

> that they wth theire officers shoulde make dilligente searche wthin every of their wardes and companyes what nomber of poore fatherlesse children, what nomber of aged, lame, and impotent persons, and what nomber of ydell roges as well woeman as men. As allso what nomber of decayed householders were in every ccompanie and warde wthin the cytue of london and lyb[er]ties of the same. And after this searche so made they all agreed to sette downe in wrighting theire whole nombers in a booke.

'What nomber' was always the end in sight. 'This was a very good course', Dignity tells Dutie (Howes's manuscript is a dialogue), 'and incydent to the matter'.[2] It begins with counting: 'What nomber?' This is pure political (practical) arithmetic on London's busy streets nearly three-quarters of a century before

[1] Quoted in A. A. Rusnock, *Vital Accounts: Quantifying Health and Population in Eighteenth-Century England and France* (Cambridge, 2002), 1.

[2] *John Howes MS, 1582, Being a Brief Note of the Order and Manner of the Proceedings in the First Erection of the Three Royal Hospitals of Christs, Bridewell, and St. Thomas the Apostle*, ed. W. Lemprière (1904), 19–20.

Information, Institutions, and Local Government in England, 1550–1700: Turning Inside. Paul Griffiths, Oxford University Press. © Paul Griffiths 2023. DOI: 10.1093/oso/9780192896261.003.0007

either John Graunt or William Petty drew their first breath. 'What nomber' for thinking, discussing, making policy, and, one day if all went according to plan, for 'present relefe' and new ideas to tackle the tides of vagrants. 'Searche' was 'diligently made throughoute ye cyttie'. Numbers noted down with people in place, the wardens and aldermen 'broughte in theire reportes [of] everye of the sortes of the pore' to the Guildhall to be 'particularized', 'computed', and brought together in 'one whole number'.[3] 'Everye'; they were so sure of themselves! Their certainty was their knowledge, authority, and motivating drive. This was a process that became just about intuitive in local government: 'search', 'reporte', 'examyne', 'particularize', and put it all down in a 'booke' to use again and again.

'The number was greate', Howes wrote in a work that we know was read by governors (he was one of them), 'viz: of fatherles children [300], of sore and sicke persons [200], of poore men overburdened with theire children [350], of aged persons [400], of decayed house-holders [650], of ydell vagabondes [200]'. Howes did his sums: 'the whole number ys as appeareth to be of all sortes which requyred present relefe 2160 (sic)'.[4] Howes's twentieth-century editor—William Lemprière, like Howes a governor of Christ's Hospital—could not resist a dig with his belittling 'sic': it was 2,100 poor souls, not 2,160, he chides. Lemprière tells us that he 'discovered' this 'small volume' in the 'ancient archives of Christs Hospital' in 1888 when he was looking for supporting materials to make a case to the Privy Council, but he does not tell us what it is about. All this reminds us of the fragility of the past and also how it can surprise us. An 'interesting' little book is dug up when someone was looking for something else, and there are some iffy calculations on one of its pages. Nothing can be taken for granted. It is not just that Howes's figures do not add up; they seem to be on the low side. They are also suspiciously neat in their tidy multiples of ten. Exactly 200 'vagabondes' roam through London, adding to the anguish of 650 'decayed householders' who need help because they are in great danger of drowning under the poverty line. Reasons follow for why London is so 'overchardged' and 'greate' numbers beg all over the streets and fields that all boil down to 'neckligente governmente'.[5]

There are 200 missing in Howes's 'whole number', although he was not among those who set up the 'searche' to govern by numbers. Like Dr Johnson, they believed that counting would lead to 'certainty'. Like Jeff Tweedy, they did not like ambiguity. Even if their figures look on the low side, they now had 'knowledge' at their fingertips and they acted on that. The last thing any magistrate worth his salt wanted was ambiguity. We owe a great deal to Terling's Matthew Warren and his fellow toilers in local soil and government who asked 'what they be?' or 'what number?' They were England's first political arithmeticians, if by that term we mean that they used information in practical ways to make local government more effective. They spent their time in office pursuing 'precyson'. They did not

[3] Ibid., 20–1. [4] Ibid., 21. [5] Ibid., 22.

like to see question marks hovering over anyone or anything. Government needed the brighter light of 'making knowne'. To get this necessary intelligibility, local officers and officials 'surveyed', in their own word, doing the best they could with what they had to make the 'undiscovered' known. Not floating any longer, but 'noted' down on record.

Nothing changed in a flash. The only possible watershed moment is the 1610 bridewell legislation, but even that was the consequence of six decades of social thinking and planning in towns and cities (maybe the opening of England's first bridewell in London was the watershed moment?). So much changed in the 150 years after 1550! England was a foreign country in 1700 for anyone alive when Edward VI took his last breath in 1553. An empire grew so large so fast, becoming the biggest in the world in less than a century. The most market-minded and productive agriculture anywhere in the Western world fed its more than five million people with no help from anywhere else. A brand-new political arrangement in the wake of the Glorious Revolution softened the royal prerogative. The Bank of England was open, as was Lloyd's of London, helping shipping that went to far-flung parts of the empire. 'Middling' people spearheaded local 'practical' and 'political arithmetic' that they brought with them to local administration. They forged a new political activism and drove economy, empire, and trade ineluctably forwards. They also developed distinctive cultures of knowledge, consumption, and conviviality. There were around ten times more Londoners at the end of the seventeenth century than two centuries earlier, and two-in-ten people lived in towns, an increase of somewhere in the region of 250 per cent. There were victims, too, capsized new arrivals in towns who clung to meagre livings to get by or the 'losers' in the dirty war in the countryside who lost their precious acre to land-hungry enclosers and were now forced to scratch a living labouring for an uncertain pittance. In sunnier climes, information paved the way ahead in agriculture, finance, trade, and empire. Like 'experts' on ships hugging America's shore to discover and map, 'middling men' collected and categorized back home in England.

This, then, was 'turning inside': principles and practices of local governance in which magistrates put their faith in information systems that in their procedures and range were innovative and developed institutions that were distinctive in their numbers and purposes. We have seen governors trying hard over the seventeenth century to make 'manifestaccon' work, but at the same time spending ever more thought, effort, and resources on developing information systems and institutions from around 1550 on. Information and institutions became necessary to moderate the after-effects of England's population boom and constant surges in the growth of urban populations. They became required methods to deal with some of society's basic and draining 'problems', such as fractured families, crippling poverty, chronic bad health, infection, the 'undiscovered' and vagrant, putting young people on the road to 'respectability', trying to cope with growing numbers of young singlewomen in towns, and giving some poverty-stricken elderly people room and board in their twilight years.

Yet 'turning inside' was only ever possible because of the perceived appeal and advantages of governing with information and institutions. Expectations were extremely high and that ought to be commended. There should have been bridewells in each town and county. People should have been 'better', Edward Coke said after leaving one of these 'houses of reformation'. Bridewells became indispensable for local government, economies, regulation, and policing poor relief, even if that need was frustrated at times by financial shortfalls and flawed inadequate administration. But this was not a 'poor' performance by any measure. We would have to hunt high and low before 1700 for a comprehensive argument that bridewells were a failure and that government would be more effective without them. Quite the reverse. We will find many times in early modern records when concerned magistrates reel off the dark and damaging consequences of not having a fully effective bridewell in their town or county.

Another leading theme in *Information, Institutions, and Local Government in England, 1550–1700* has been the varying relation between the 'public' and the 'private' in authority and government. There is a tendency to treat 'public' and 'private' as things apart and other oppositions, like inside/outside, follow naturally. After all, it is entirely possible to move from something 'public' into something else that is designated 'private' in a matter of seconds. It can feel quite different when we do this. With 'private' we might sense something that is hidden away, secluded, intimate, protected, exclusive, inside. 'Private' can seem ominous and that is often the intention. It can be a warning: 'PRIVATE, KEEP OUT'. I cannot help but think back to the guards at the door in, say, 1624 making sure that nobody got into the room where governors put their heads together to deal with 'towne busynes', 'affayres', and 'secreates'.

Public, on the other hand, seems more open at first glance. A public holiday is ours, we are told. A public celebration is intended for all of us, though not everyone will take part, and some might resent what it represents. Like 'manifestaccon', it stands for something that might be lampooned or lambasted. But in intention at any rate the 'public' is inclusive in the idiom of those in power, with established conventions and rules that were not always followed to the letter. Of the two, 'public' is less rigid in the sense of meetings behind closed doors for the 'public' interest and/or good of a public corporate body. Overlaps like these, whether linguistic or physical, are in fact integral to 'private'/'public' distinctions. We have seen this in penal outcomes when someone was punished both inside and outside in the same sentence, or in the sliding scale of penalties when the implications of punishing behind walls or out of doors were weighed up to match punishment to particular offenders and offences. The same early modern technology or culture can manipulate the 'public' and 'private' even at a time when the balance between them was tipping in changes that might be only faintly realized, if at all.

The incremental nature of change makes it highly unlikely that shifts in penal practices and cultures, for instance, were quick or confined to a particular epoch. It was not—as in Foucault—the abrupt leap from the brutal drawing and quartering of regicide Robert-François Damiens in a Paris plaza in 1757 to a solitary cell with prisoners sunk deep in angst-ridden self-reflection in Pentonville Prison, which first opened its doors in London in 1842. 'Private' and 'public' penalties coexisted for centuries before Damiens. *Information, Institutions, and Local Government in England, 1550–1700* looks at the balance between them, but it has never claimed that they were unavoidably opposed or that any tension between them was inevitably negative. 'Manifestaccon' still mattered after 1700. Black sheep were still punished outside but in lesser numbers, on record at any rate. Parliament passed badging legislation at the end of the seventeenth century. Civic panoramas were still draped with insignia and, like walls, most of which would come clattering down in the next two centuries, they spoke of might and right. But to what effect it is hard to say except that a long-term decline had begun. Public processions still strut along England's main streets today, but no longer with the urgent political intentions of yesteryear through which authority and the regulation of populations, resources, and environments depended to an extent that is simply inconceivable now. Rituals today might still toast pride and history (local/national) with 'recreational' features, but that age-old intense and regulatory identity-authority-politics has all but disappeared from 'official' scripts.[6]

Some ideas in this book modify long-held interpretations, and they include that local government reliance on information was stock practice long before 'political arithmetic' came of age; that towns developed substantial institutional apparatus in the 150 years after 1550; that the roots of 'private' punishment/whipping lie far back in the second half of the sixteenth century; and that custodial sentencing was part and parcel of early modern judicial process. These major developments changed practices, principles, and representations of local authority and government as well as judicial decision-making. Important aspects of local government turned inside, where they have remained ever since for the most part.

* * *

[6] B. Roberts, 'Entertaining the community: the evolution of civic ritual and public celebration, 1860–1953', *Urban History*, 44 (2017); M. Freeman, '"Splendid display, pompous spectacle": historical pageants in twentieth-century Britain', *SH*, 38 (2010); T. Hulme, '"A nation of town criers": civic publicity and historical pageantry in inter-war Britain', *Urban History*, 44 (2017); H. McCarthy, 'The league of nations, public ritual and national identity in Britain, c.1919–56', *HWJ*, 70 (2010). An influential early expression of changes in civic rituals is D. Cannadine, 'The transformation of ritual in modern Britain: the Colchester Oyster Feast', *P&P*, 94 (1982).

'Turning inside' began slowly and awkwardly five centuries or so ago with setbacks and glitches that could outnumber its early successes. Things often changed at a snail's pace. Local government by 'private' and 'public' means coexisted all the way through the sixteenth and seventeenth centuries. Looking back now, with the gift of reflection after the fact, we know that the 'private' and the 'public' in local government were heading in different directions, where they remain to this day with no signs of shifting anywhere else soon. The one inside is all-pervasive for us in our own time when a great deal of local government tends to take place far away from the public gaze. We get to see little today except for bills, messages, and online minutes. Our local governors do little in the public outdoors when it comes to expressing their authority and its defining values.

This 'turning inside' in critical aspects of local government was nowhere near complete by the end of the seventeenth century; a long line of key breakthroughs and turning points lay ahead in the near and distant futures. But it was clearly evident before 'the long eighteenth century', defended, and expressed repeatedly with impacts that changed the practices and principles of governing towns and villages for good. The roots of all of this lie deep in early Elizabethan local 'computing' and 'particularizing' and the day in 1555 when England's first bridewell opened its doors to receive its first batch of prisoners.

Bibliography

Manuscript Sources

Berkshire Record Office: Reading

N/JQ/1/1 Newbury Sessions Book (1666–1739)
R/AC1/1/2 Reading Corporation Minutes (1622–8)
R/AC1/1/3 Reading Corporation Minutes (1628–37)
R/FA/3 Reading Chamberlains Accounts (1606–48)
WI/FA1/2 Windsor Chamberlains Accounts (1637–1735)

Bethem Museum of the Mind: Beckenham

Bridewell Hospital Courtbook 4

Borthwick Institute for Archives: York

V1684-5/CB/1a 'Archbishop Dolben's Primary and Metropolitan Visitation of the Diocese of York'
York Diocese Deposition Book (1676–8)

British Library

Lansdowne manuscripts

Cambridge University Library

CUR 37.3
VC-CT-vi-15
VCT/4

Centre for Kentish Studies: Maidstone

FA/AC3 Faversham Wardmote Book (1579–1633)
Md/Acm1/1a Maidstone Burghmote Minutes (1561–1604)
Md/Acm1/2 Maidstone Burghmote Minutes (1604–44)
Md/Acm1/3 Maidstone Burghmote Minutes (1644–94)
Md/JLP/1 Maidstone Court Leet (1652–6)
TE/C1 Tenterden Custumal
TE/JQC/1 Tenterden Summary Conviction Memoranda Book (1632–69)
TE/S2 Tenterden Corporation Minute Book (1641–1762)
U120/09 Sir Edward Filmer Justicing Notebook (1609–25)

Cheshire Archives and Local Studies: Chester

EDC 6/1 Chester Diocese Penance and Excommunications
QJB/1/3 Cheshire Sessions Recognisance and Order Book (1594–1609)
QJB/1/4 Cheshire Sessions Recognisance and Order Book (1609–18)
QJB/1/5 Cheshire Sessions Recognisance and Order Book (1618–40)
QJB/1/6 Cheshire Sessions Recognisance and Order Book (1640–50)
QJB/3/1 Cheshire Sessions indictment and Presentment Book (1660–9)

TAB/1 Chester Treasurers Accounts and Rentals (1683–97)
Z/AB/1 Chester Assembly Book (1539–1624)
Z/AB/2 Chester Assembly Book (1624–84)
ZML/1 Mayor's Great Letter Book (1541–98)
ZML/2 Mayor's Great Letter Book (1599–1650)
ZML/3 Mayor's Great Letter Book (1651–73)
ZML/4 Mayor's Great Letter Book (1674–1715)

Clothworkers' Hall: London

Clothworkers' Company Minute Book (1558–81)

Devon Record Office: Exeter

ECA B/1/3 Exeter Chamber Act Book (1560–84)
ECA B/1/4 Exeter Chamber Act Book (1581–8)
ECA C1/61 Exeter Sessions Minute Book (1618–21)
ECA C1/62 Exeter Sessions Minute Book (1621–30)
Z19/36/14 John Hayne Account Book
Various miscellaneous and individual documents

Dorset History Centre: Dorchester

DC/DOB/8/1 Dorchester Offenders Book (1629–37)
DC/LR/A3/1 Lyme Regis Misdemeanour Book (1683–1729)
DC/LR/B7/D2/1 Lyme Regis Town Correspondence (1570–1696)
DC/LR/D/1/1 Lyme Regis Orders of Mayor and Council (1594–1671)
DC/LR/G/2/2 Lyme Regis Sundry Mayors Accounts (1573–1685)
DC/PL/CB/1/1 Poole Sessions Book (1678–99)
S235/A/2/1/1 Sherborne School Order and Account Book (1591–1850)

East Sussex and Brighton and Hove Record Office: Brighton

QO/EW1 East Sussex Sessions Order Book (1642–9)
QO/EW2 East Sussex Sessions Order Book (1650–4)
QO/EW3 East Sussex Sessions Order Book (1655–60)
QO/EW7 East Sussex Sessions Indictment Book (1690–1706)
QO/EW8 East Sussex Sessions Order Book (1679–84)
QO/EW9 East Sussex Sessions Order Book (1685–90)
QO/EW10 East Sussex Sessions Order Book (1690–6)
RYE 1/1/5 Rye Hundred and Assembly Book (1582–95)
RYE 1/1/6 Rye Hundred and Assembly Book (1595–9)

Essex Record Office: Chelmsford

D/B5/AB Colchester Chamberlains Bills
D/B5/Gb1 Colchester Assembly Book (1576–99)
D/B5/SB1/4 Colchester Sessions of Peace Justices Book (1630–64)
D/B5/SB2/3 Colchester Book of Examinations and Recognizance (1576–81)
D/B5/SB2/4 Colchester Book of Examinations and Recognizances (1581–9)
D/B5/SB2/7 Colchester Book of Examinations and Recognizance (1619–45)
D/B5/SB2/9 Colchester Book of Examinations and Recognizances (1647–87)
D/B5/SB3/1 Colchester Sessions Book (1677–85)
D/Y Morant Manuscripts

Gloucestershire Archives: Gloucester

GBR B/3/2 Gloucester Common Council Minute Book (1632–56)
GBR/B/3/3 Gloucester Common Council Minute Book (1656–86)
GBR/F/4/3 Gloucester Stewards-Chamberlains Accounts (1550–96)
GBR F/4/5 Gloucester Stewards-Chamberlains Accounts (1635–54)
GBR/F/4/6 Gloucester Stewards-Chamberlains Accounts (1653–63)
GBR/G/G3/Sib/1 Gloucester Sessions indictment book (1638–53)
GBR/G/G3/Sib/2 Gloucester Sessions indictment book (1653–85)
GBR/G/G3/SO/1 Gloucester Sessions Order Book (1608–43)
Q/SaIb/1 Gloucestershire Sessions Indictment Book (1660–8)
TBR/A/1/2 Tewksbury minutes and order book (1608–90)

Goldsmiths' Company Library: London

Goldsmiths' Company Minute Book O-P2

Guildhall Library: London

5770/1 Fishmongers' Company Minute Book, (1592–1610)
5770/2 Fishmongers' Company Minute Book (1610–31)
7090/2 Pewterers' Company Minute Book (1561–89)
7090/3 Pewterers' Company Minute Book (1589–1611)
8200/1 Apothecaries' Company Minute Book (1617–51)
11588/1 Grocers' Company Minute Book (1556–91)

Hampshire Archives and Local Studies: Winchester

Q1/1 Hampshire Sessions Order Book (1607–28)
Q1/3 Hampshire Sessions Order Book (1649–58)
Q3/3 Hampshire Sessions Minute Book (1679–1716)
W/B1/4 Winchester Book of Ordinances (1617–47)
W/K5/8 Winchester *A Retrospect of Civic Manners & Customs 1576–1888*
W/D3/3 Winchester Sessions Minute Book (1714–42)

Herefordshire Archives and Record Centre: Hereford

BG11/4/6 Hereford Tourns (1657–71)
BG11/17/1/4 Hereford Miscellaneous Papers (1600–44)
BG11/17/1/5 Hereford Miscellaneous Papers (1641–1857)
Q/SM/2 Herefordshire Sessions Minute book (1684–91)

Huntington Library: San Marino

Ellesmere Manuscripts
Hastings Manuscripts
Stowe Manuscripts

Kendal Archive Centre

WQ/1/1 Westmorland Sessions Indictment Book—Kendal (1656–67)
WQ/1/2 Westmorland Sessions Indictment Book—Appleby (1661–85)
WQ/1/3 Westmorland Sessions Indictment Book—Kendal (1669–91)
WQ/M/1 Westmorland Sessions Minute and Memorandum Book—Appleby—Kendal (1733–7)
WQ/O/4 Westmorland Sessions Order Book—Appleby (1699–1724)

WQ/O/5 Westmorland Sessions Order Book—Appleby—Kendal (1725–37)
WSMB/A/2/1/1 Appleby Memoranda and Minute Book (1614–61)
WSMB/A/2/1/2 Appleby Memoranda and Minute Book (1662–85)
WSMB/K/1/5 Kendal Chamberlain Account Book
WSMB/K/2/5 Kendal Sessions Oder and Indictment Book (1685–1710)

Lancashire Archives: Preston

CNP 3/1/1 Preston Common Council Orders (1608–1781)
CNP 3/2/1 Preston Proceedings of the Great Court Leet (1653–73)
MBC Clitheroe Court Leet Verdicts (1593–1700)
QDO/2/28 Lancashire Sessions Order Book (1655)

Leicestershire Record Office: Leicester

1D/41/4/28 Leicester Diocese Court Proceedings
1D41/12/59 Leicester Diocese Box (1628–30)
1D41/14/1 Leicester Diocese Archbishop Laud's Metropolitical Visitation Papers (1638)
1D41/91/1 Leicester Diocese Court Act Book Peculiar Jurisdictions of Groby, Evington, Rothley
BRII/1/2 Leicester Hall Book 2 (1553–87)
BRII/1/3 Leicester Hall Book 3 (1587–1707)
BRIII Leicester Chamberlain's Accounts
QS5/1/1 Leicestershire Sessions Minute Book (1696–1726)
QS6/1/2 Leicestershire Sessions Court Order Book (1678–1700)

London Metropolitan Archives

Old Guildhall Library references are provided in the cases of parishes and wards with the current London Metropolitan Archives reference at the end of each entry.

DLC London Diocese Consistory Court Depositions
Journals of Common Council 20–27 COL/CC/01/01/020-028
Letterbooks R-Y COL/AD/01/017-022
MJ/SBR/1 Middlesex Sessions of the Peace Register (1608–13)
MJ/SBR/2 Middlesex Sessions of the Peace Register (1613–18)
MJ/SBR/4 Middlesex Sessions of the Peace Register (1623–9)
MJ/SBR/6 Middlesex Sessions of the Peace Register (1634–9)
MJ/SBR/7 Middlesex Sessions of the Peace Register (1639–41)
Remembrancia Books 1-8 COL/RMD/PA/01/001-008
Repertories of the Court of Aldermen 11–45 COL/CA/01/01/016-049
WJ/SR/NS/36 Westminster Sessions Rolls
524/1 St. Michael Wood Street Churchwardens Accounts (1619–1718) P69/MIC7/B/003/MS00524/001
593/2 St. Stephen Walbrook Churchwardens Accounts (1549–1637) P69/STE2/B/008/MS00593/002
645/1 St. Peter Westcheap Churchwardens Accounts (1441–1601) P69/PET4/B/006/MS00645/001
818/1 All Hallows the Great Churchwardens Accounts (1616–1708) P69/ALH7/B/013/MS00818/001
878/1 St. Benet Paul's Wharf Churchwardens Accounts (1605–57) P69/BEN3/B/007/MS00878/001
942/1 St. Botolph Billinsgate Churchwardens Accounts (1603–74) P69/BOT3/B/007/MS00942/001

943/1 St. Botolph Billinsgate Vestry Minutes (1592–1673) P69/BOT3/B/001/MS00943/001
1124/1 St. Katherine Coleman Street Churchwardens Accounts (1609–71) P69/KAT1/B/011/MS01124/001
1176/1 St. Margaret New Fish Street Churchwardens Accounts (1576–1678) P69/MGT3/B/014/MS01176/001
1240/1 St. Mary-at-the-Hill Vestry Minutes (1609–1752) P69/MRY4/B/001/MS1240/001
1303/1 St. Benet Fink Churchwardens Accounts (1610–99) P69/BEN1/B/005/MS01303/001
1432/3 St. Alphage London Wall Churchwardens Accounts (1580–1631) P69/ALP1/B/009/MS01432/003
1568 St. Benet Gracechurch Churchwardens Accounts (1548–1724) P69/BEN2/B/012/MS01568/001
2088/1 St. Andrew-by-the-Wardrobe Churchwardens Accounts (1570–1688) P69/AND1/B/009/MS02088/001
2895/2 St. Michael le Querne Churchwardens Accounts (1605–1717) P69/MIC4/B/005/MS02895/002
2968/2 St. Dunstan-in-the-West Churchwardens Accounts (1608–28) P69/DUN2/B/011/MS02968/002
3016/1 St. Dunstan-in-the-West Vestry Minutes (1588–1663) P69/DUN2/B/001/MS03016/001
3146/1 St. Sepulchre (Holborn)-Without-Newgate Churchwardens Accounts (1648–64) P69/SEP/B/01/MS03146/001
3570/2 St. Mary Aldermanbury Vestry Minutes (1610–1763) P69/MRY2/B/001/MS03570/002
3908/1 St. Lawrence Pountney Vestry Minutes (1614–73) P69/LAW2/B/001/MS03908/001
4051/1 All Hallows Lombard Street Churchwardens Accounts (1614–84) P69/ALH4/B/010/MS04051/001
4071/2 St. Michael Cornhill Churchwardens Accounts (1608–1702) P69/MIC2/B/006/MS04071/002
4072/1 St. Michael Cornhill Vestry Minutes (1563–1697) P69/MIC2/B/001/MS04072/001/001
4165/1 St. Peter Cornhill Vestry Minutes (1574–1717) P69/PET1/B/001/MS04165/001
4180/1 St. James Garlickhithe Churchwardens Accounts (1555–1627) P69/JS2/B/005/MS04810/001
4180/2 St. James Garlickhithe Churchwardens Accounts (1627–99) P69/JS2/B/005/MS04810/002
4214/1 St. Benet Gracechurch Vestry Minutes (1607–1758) P69/BEN2/B/001/MS04214/001
4457/2 St. Stephen Coleman Street Churchwardens Accounts (1586–1640) P69/STE1/B/012/MS04457/002
4524/1 St. Botolph-without-Bishopgate Churchwardens Accounts (1567–1632) P69/BOT4/B/008/MS04524/001
4956/3 All Hallows Staining Churchwardens Accounts (1645–1679) P69/ALH6/B/008/MS04956/003/0 01
5018/1 St. Pancras Soper Lane Churchwardens Accounts (1616–1740) P69/PAN/B/014/MS05018/001
5090/2 All Hallows London Wall Churchwardens Accounts (1566–1681) P69/ALH5/B/003/MS05090/002
6544/1 St. Brides Vestry Minutes (1644–65) P69/BRI/B/001/MS06554/001
7706 St. Katherine Overseers Accounts (1638–42) P69/KAT2//B/025//MSO7706

9057/1 Archdeaconry of London General Examination and Deposition Book (1632–8)
9235/2 St. Botolph Aldgate Churchwardens' Accounts (1586–1691) P69/BOT2/B/012/MS09235/002/002
9236/1 St. Botolph Aldgate Vestry Minutes and Memoranda Book (1622–78) P69/BOT2/B/001/MS09236
9680 St. Katherine-by-the-Tower Constables' Accounts (1598–1706) CLC/199/TC/024/MS09680
12806/2 Christ's Hospital Court Minutes (1562–92) CLC/210/B/001/MS12806/002

Norfolk Record Office

Aylsham MS
Norwich Assembly Book 5 (1613–42)
Norwich Assembly Book 6 (1642–68)
Norwich Bridewell Treasurers Accounts I
Norwich Bridewell Treasurers Accounts II
Norwich Chamberlains Accounts (1580–9)
Norwich Chamberlains Accounts (1589–1602)
Norwich Chamberlains Accounts (1603–1625)
Norwich Chamberlain's Accounts (1625–48)
Norwich City Informations and Examinations (1690–9)
Norwich Clavors Book 1 (1555–1646)
Norwich Mayor's Court Courtbooks 3–25
Norwich Mayor's Court Interrogatories and Depositions (1549–54)
Norwich Mayor's Court Interrogatories and Depositions (1561–7)
Norwich Mayor's Court Interrogatories and Depositions Book 1A
Norwich River and Street Accounts (1598–1605)
Norwich St. George's Guild Courtbook (1452–1602)
Norwich St. George's Guild Minute Book (1602–1729)
Norwich Sessions Book (1571–81)
Norwich Sessions Book (1581–91)
Norwich Sessions Book (1630–8)
Norwich Sessions Book (1639–54)
Norwich Sessions Book (1671–91)
Norwich Sessions Book (1691–1702)
Norwich Sessions Files
T/C1/1 Thetford Assembly Book (1577–86)
T/C1/2 Thetford Assembly Book (1574/75–1581/1601)
T/C1/6 Thetford 'The Town Booke' (1598–1627)
T/C1/9 Thetford Sessions Book (1620–6)
T/QS/1 Thetford Sessions Book (1633–9)
Y/C/19/1 Great Yarmouth Assembly Book (1550–9)
Y/C/19/3 Great Yarmouth Assembly Book (1570–9)
Y/C/19/4 Great Yarmouth Assembly Book (1579–98)
Y/C/19/5 Great Yarmouth Assembly Book (1598–1625)
Y/C/19/6 Great Yarmouth Assembly Book (1625–42)
YD41/104 Thomas Damet, 'The Foundation and Antiquitye of Great Yarmouth'

Northamptonshire Archives: Northampton

3/1 Northampton Assembly Book (1553–1629)

3/2 Northampton Assembly Book (1629–1744)
4/1 Northampton Mayor's Courtbook (1694–1752)
NQS/1 Northamptonshire Quarter Sessions Minute Book (1668–78)
NQS/2 Northamptonshire Quarter Sessions Minute Book (1679–90)
NQS/3 Northamptonshire Quarter Sessions Minute Book (1690–1708)
NQS/4 Northamptonshire Quarter Sessions Minute Book (1708–27)
NSP1 Northamptonshire Quarter Sessions Presentments Book

North Devon Record Office: Barnstaple

1064Q/SO1 Bideford Sessions Book (1659–1709)
1190A/B1 South Molton Orders and Ordinances (1627–1737)
1190A/Q1 South Molton Sessions Order Book (1670–84)
1190A/Q2 South Molton Sessions Order Book (1684–1703)
2558A/11/8 Petition of John Evans to be keeper of Torrington Bridewell, *c.*1660.
3058add7/44/1–2 Agreement for Humphrey Buckingham to Become Master of South Molton Bridewell
B1 Barnstaple Town Miscellaneous documents (Seventeenth Century)
B1/3792 Barnstaple Receivers Accounts (1389–1649)

Nottinghamshire Archives: Nottingham

DD/4P/68/23 Extracts from London Bridewell Letter Patent
C/QSM/1/12 Nottinghamshire Quarter Sessions Minute Book (1641–2, 1652–4)
C/QSM/1/13 Nottinghamshire Quarter Sessions Minute Book (1654–9)

Oxfordshire History Centre: Oxford

C/FC/1/A1/O1 Oxford Council Act Book A (1520–92)
C/FC/1/A1/02 Oxford Council Act Book B (1591–1628)
C/FC/1/A1/03 Oxford Council Act Book C (1629–63)
C/FC/1/A1/O4 Oxford Council Act Book D (1663–1701)
QS/C/A1/O1 Oxford Sessions Minute Book (1687–1701)

St Bartholomew's Hospital Archive, London

Governors' Journal 2 (1567–86)
Governors' Journal 3 (1586–1607)

Shropshire Archives: Shrewsbury

3365 Shrewsbury Bailiffs Accounts 489–549 (1560–1608)
3356/2430 Shrewsbury Sessions Order Book (1680–1740)
BB/C/2/2/3 Bridgnorth Submissions to bailiffs (1659–73)
LB/11/4 Ludlow Sessions Rolls

Southampton Archives

6/1 Southampton Court Leet Books (1565–1617)
SC9/2/1 Southampton Sessions Book (1609–35)

Suffolk Archives: Ipswich

B/105/2/1 Suffolk Sessions Order Book (1639–51)
B/105/2/3 Suffolk Sessions Minute Book (1652–6)
B/105/2/4 Suffolk Sessions Minute Book (1656–62)

B/105/2/6 Suffolk Sessions Minute Book (1662–7)
B/105/2/8 Suffolk Sessions Minute Book (1674–9)
C/3/4/1/2 Ipswich Treasurers accounts 1–41 (1557–1616)
C/4/3/1/1/3 Ipswich Assembly Book (1589–1608)

The National Archives

SP12 State Papers Domestic: Elizabeth I
SP14 State Papers Domestic: James I
SP16 State Papers Domestic: Charles I
SP29 State Papers Domestic: Charles II
STAC8 Star Chamber: James I

Warwickshire Record Office: Warwick

CR103 William Bromley Justicing Book
QS0040/1/1 Warwickshire Sessions Order Book (1625–37)

Westminster Archive Centre

F2001 St. Martin-in-the-Fields Vestry Minutes (1574–1640)
F2003 St. Martin-in-the-Fields Vestry Minutes (1651–66)
WCB/1 Westminster Court of Burgesses Courtbook (1610–13)
WCB/2 Westminster Court of Burgesses Courtbook (1613–16)

Wiltshire and Swindon History Centre: Chippenham

A1/150/10 Wiltshire Sessions Entry Book (1648–53)
A1/150/11 Wiltshire Sessions Entry Book (1654–60)
A1/160/1 Wiltshire Sessions Order Book (1642–54)
G22/1/107 Marlborough Clerk of the Peace Notebooks (1585–1624)
G/22/1/205/2 Marlborough General Account Book (1572–1727)
G23/1/3 Salisbury Ledger C (1571–1640)

York City Archives

F7 York Sessions Book (1638–62)
Y/HTG/15 Holy Trinity Goodramgate, constables accounts (1636–1735)

Early Printed Books (before 1850)

A List of the Conventicles or Unlawful Meetings Within the City of London and Bills of Mortality (1683).
A Statute for Swearers and Drunkards or Forsake Now Your Follies (1624).
A View of the Penal Laws Concerning Trade and Traffick (1681).
An Account of the Proceeding to Judgement Against Thomas Saxton... upon a Conviction of Willful Perjury (1685).
An Ease for Overseers of the Poore (1601).
An Humble Address Offer'd to the Consideration of the Lords and Commons Touching a Law Concerning Perjury (1695).
Brief Reflections Upon the Inconveniences Attending Wilful Malitious Forgery and Perjury with Some Reasons Why Such Crimes Ought to be Made Felony (1685).

By the King. A Proclamation for Reformation of Great Abuses in Measures, Published by the Kings Commandement. Whereas for the Avoiding of Varietie and Deceits of Weights and Measures, Diuers Statutes, Acts and Good Ordinances Haue Heretofore Beene Made, That One Weight, and One Measure Should Bee Used Throughout the Realme (1603).
By the King. A Proclamation for Reformation of the Great Abuses in Weights and Measures, and For the Due Execution of the Office of Clerke of the Market of Our Houshold, and Throughout Our Realme of England (1619).
By the King. A Proclamation for Reliefe of the Subject that Might be Otherwise Damnified by the Late Burning of Records in the Sixe Clarkes Office (1622).
By the Queene. A Proclamation Against Sundry Abuses Practised by Diuers Lewd and Audacious Persons Falsely Naming Themselues Messengers of Her Maiesties Chamber (1596).
Considerations Humbly Offered to the Honourable the Knights, Citizens and Burgesses in Parliaments Assembled shewing the Necessity and Benefitt of Act of Parliament to Incorporate a Certain select Number of Persons for the More Beautiful and Useful Paving and Cleansing the Streets in the Cities of London and Westminster (1700?).
Diuers Lewd and Audacious Persons Falsly Naming Themselues Messengers of Her Maiesties Chamber, Trauelling From Place to Place with Writings Counterfeited in Forme of Warrants as Also Against Another Sort of Vagabond Persons That Carrie Counterfeit Pasports Wherewith to Begge and Gather Almes (1596).
Greevous Groans for the Poore (1621).
Perjury, the National Sin, or An Account of the Abuses and Violations of Oaths Among Us of This Nation Humbly Offered to the Consideration of the High Court of Parliament (1690).
The Assize of Bread (1600).
The Boke for a Justice of Peace (1544).
The Counterfeit Constable, Or the Wicked Watch (1674).
The Cucking of a Scould to the Tune of The Merchant of [?] (c. 1630).
The Model of a Design to Reprint Stow's Survey (1694).
The Office of the Clerk of Assize Containing the Form and Method of the Proceedings at the Assizes, and General Gaol-Delivery… Together with the Office of the Clerk of the Peace (1676).
The Proceedings Against Mr J. Reading who Being Found Guilty of High Misdemeanours, was Fined to the King in One Thousand Pounds, to Suffer One Years Imprisonment, and to Stand Three Several Days in the Pillory, at Three Several Places (1679).
The Rates of the Custom House Reduced into a Much Better Order for the Redier Finding of Any Thing Therin Contained Then at Any Time Heretofore Hath Been (1582).
The Third Commandment: An Essay Tending to Prove that Perjury Deserves Not Only the Pillory but a Much Severer Punishment (1685).
The Thirty-Second Report of the Charity Commissioners of England and Wales. Per Acts 38 Geo.3.c.91 and Geo.3.c.8.81, part IV, 1840 (219).
The Whole Examination of the Birth of the Pretended Prince of Wales and the True Mother of that Notorious Counterfeit and Impostor Fully Discovered and Proved, before the Lords and Commons of England, For the Publick Satisfaction of the Whole Kingdom (1689).

Abbot, R., *A Christian Family Builded by God* (1653).
Agard, A., *The Repertorie of Records Remaining in the 4 Treasuries on the Receipt Side at Westminster* (1631).
Agas, R., *A Preparative to Platting of Landes and Tenements for Surueigh Shewing the Diuersitie of Sundrie Instruments Applyed Thereunto* (1596).

Allen, J., *Of Perjury, A Sermon Preached at the Assizes Held at Chester April the 4th 1682* (1682).
Aray, M., *The Discoverie and Confutation of a Tragical Fiction Devised and Played by Edward Squyer Yeoman Soldiar Hanged at Tyburne the 23. of November 1598* (1599).
Ayres, J., *Arithmetick a Treatise Fitted for the Use and Benefit of Such Trades-men as Are Ignorant in That Art* (1693).
B.E., *A New Dictionary of the Canting Crew in its Several Tribes of Gypsies, Beggers, Thieves, Cheats &c* (1699).
B.G., *The Joyfull Receyuing of the Queenes Most Excellent Maiestie into Hir Highnesse Citie of Norvvich the Things Done in the Time of Hir Abode There: and the Dolor of the Citie at Hir Departure* (1578).
B.P., *A Help to Magistrates and Ministers of Justice, Also, A Guide to Parish and Ward-Officers* (1700).
B.W., *A Touch-stone For Gold and Silver Wares, Or A Manual for Goldsmiths and All Other Persons, Whether Buyers, Sellers, or Wearers of Any Manner of Goldsmiths Work* (1677).
Barker, J., *Measurer's Guide or the Whole Art of Measuring Made Short, Plain, and Easie* (1692).
Bill, J., *Accompts Cast Up With an Addition of Measuring Timber, Boord, Waynscot, Glasse, and Land* (1632).
Blount, T., *Nomo-lexikon, A Law-Dictionary* (1691).
Brian, T., *The Pisse-Prophet, Or Certain Pisse-Pot Lectures. Wherein are Newly Discovered the Old Fallacies, Deceit, and Jugling of the Piss-Pot Science, Used by All Those (Whether Quacks, and Empiricks, or Other Methodical Physicians) Who Pretend Knowledge of Diseases, by the Urine* (1679).
Brome, J., *Travels Over England, Scotland, and Wales Giving a True and Exact Description of the Chiefest Cities, Towns, and Corporations* (1700).
Browning, T., *Prison Thoughts* (1682).
Burton, H., *A Narration of the Life of Mr Henry Burton* (1643).
Bush, R., *The Poor Man's Friend, or Narrative of What Progresse Many Worthy Citizens of London Have Made in that Godly Work of Providing for the Poor* (1649).
Butcher, R., *The Survey and Antiquitue of the Towne of Stamford* (1646).
Carew, R., *The Survey of Cornwall* (1602).
Carpenter, J., *A Most Excellent Instruction for the Exact and Perfect Keeping Merchants Bookes of Accounts* (1632).
Cary, J., *An Essay on the State of England in Relation to its Trade, its Poor, and its Taxes for Carrying on the Present War Against France* (1695).
Catley, S. R., ed., *A Treatise or Letter Written by Dr Ridley Instead of His Last Farewell to All His True and Faithful Friends in God*, in *The Acts and Monuments of John Foxe* (1841).
Cawdrey, D., *Family Reformation Promoted* (1656).
Cawdrey, R., *A Table Alphabeticall Conteyning and Teaching the True Writing and Understanding of Hard Usuall English Wordes* (1604).
Chamberlain, R., *The Complete Justice Being a Compendious and Exact Collection Out of All Such Statutes and Authors as May Any Way Concern the Office of a Justice of Peace* (1681).

Churchyard, T., *A Discourse of the Queenes Majesties Entertainment in Suffolk and Norfolk With a Description of Many Things Then Presently Seene* (1578).
Cocker, E., *Cockers Arithmetick Being a Plain and Familiar Method Suitable to the Meanest Capacity...* (1678).
Cockeram, H., *The English Dictionarie: Or An Interpreter of Hard English Words* (1623).
Coke, E., *Institutes of the Lawes of England* (1644).
Coles, E., *An English Dictionary* (1676).
Cressy, E., *Spiritual Directions for Hospitals, Houses of Correction and Prisons* (1675).
Crofton, Z., *Perjury the Proof of Forgery: Or Mr Crofton's Civilitie Justified by Cadman's Falsitie* (1657).
Crouch, H., *London's Vacation and the Countries Tearme* (1637).
Dafforne, R., *The Merchants Mirrour, Or Directions for the Perfect Ordering and Keeping of His Accounts* (1684).
Dalton, M., *The Country Justice*, first published in 1618 (1661).
Davenant, C., *The Political and Commercial Works*, ed. Sir C. Whitworth, 5 vols (1771).
Dawson, R., *The Humble Addresse and Remonstrance of Richard Dawson Gentleman Now Prisoner in the Fleet* (1661).
De Chassanion, J., *The Merchandises of Popish Priests Laying Open to the World, How Cunningly They Cheate and Abuse Poore People, With Theyr False, Deceitfull, and Counterfeit Wares* (1604).
Dingley, R., *Divine Opticks or A Treatise of the Eye Discovering the Vices and Virtues Thereof; As Also How That Organ May be Tuned* (1655).
Dorney, J., *Certain Speeches Made Upon the Day of the Yearly Election of Officers in the City of Gloucester* (1653).
Dugdale, W., *Origines, Juridiaries, or Historical Memorials of the English Laws, Courts of Justice, Forms of Tryall, Punishment in Cases of Criminal Law ....* (1666).
Dunning, R., *A Plaine and Easie Method Shewing How the Office of Overseer of the Poor May be Managed* (1686).
Dunton, J., *Dunton's Whipping-Post, Or a Satyr Upon Every Body* (1706).
Echard, L., *An Exact Description of Ireland Chorographically Surveying All its Provinces and Counties* (1691).
Ellison, N., *The Magistrates Obligation to Punish Vice* (1700).
Every, J., *Speculum Mercativum, Or The Young Merchants Glass Wherein are Exact Rules of All Weights, Coins, Measures, Exchanges, and Other Matters Necessary Used in Commerce* (1674).
Firmin, T., *Some Proposals for the Imploying of the Poor* (1678).
Fitzherbert, A., *The Newe Boke of Justices of* Peace (1544).
Forster, T., *The Lay-mans Lawyer: Or the Second Part of the Practice of Law* (1654).
Foster, S., *The Art of Measuring Containing the Description of the Carpenters New Rule* (1677).
Freart, R., *A Parallel of the Antient Architecture With the Modern*, trans. J. Evelyn, 2nd edition (1707).
Fuller, T., *Words to Give the Young Man Knowledge and Discretion* (1653).
Garey, S., *Lentaculum Iudicum: or A Breake-fast for the Bench Prepared, Presented, and Preached in Two Sacred Seruices, or Sermons, the Morning Sacrifice Before the Two Assises: at Thetford, at Norwich 1619* (1623).

Gent, I. C., *A Most Excellent Instruction for the Exact and Perfect Keeping [of] Merchants Bookes of Accounts* (1632).

Goodman, G., *The Fall of Man, Or the Corruption of Nature Proved by the Light of Natural Reason* (Cambridge, 1616).

Gouge, W., *Of Domesticall Duties* (1622).

Graunt, J., *Natural and Political Observations... Made Upon the Bills of Mortality* (1662).

Gray, W., *Chorographia, Or A Survey of Newcastle upon Tyne* (1649).

Griffith, M., *Bethel, Or a Forme for Families* (1634).

Haines, R., *Provision for the Poor, Or Reasons for the Erecting of a Working-Hospital in Every County* (1678).

Hall, T., *Comarum Askomia: The Loathsomenesse of Long* Haire (1654).

[Hare, H.,] *A Charge Given at the General Quarter Sessions of the Peace for the County of Surrey Holden at Dorking on Tuesday the 5th Day of April 1692* (1692).

Harpur, J., *The Jewell of Arithmetick: or, The Explanation of a New Invented Arithmeticall Table, Whose Portraiture is Here Demonstrated Pleasant to Reade, and Profitable to be Practised by all Degrees of Men, at All Times, and in All Places* (1617).

Hartlib, S., *London's Charity Inlarged Stilling the Orphans Cry* (1650).

Hill, J., *The Exact Dealer Being an Useful Companion for All Traders* (1689).

[Hooker, J.,] *The Discription of the Cittie of Excester, Collected and Gathered by John Vowell Alias Hooker, Gentleman and Chamberlain of the Same Cittie* (1575).

Howell, J., *Londinopolis: An Historical Discourse or Perlustration of the City of London, the Imperial Chamber and the Chief Emporium of Great Britain* (1657).

Howes, E., *Annales, Or A Generall Chronicle of England Begun by John Stow: Continued and Augmented With Matters Forraigne and Domestique, Ancient and Moderne, Unto the End of the Present Year, 1631* (1631).

Hylles, T., *The Arte of Vulgar Arithmeticke* (1600).

Ingram, W., *The Secrets of Numbers According to Theologicall, Arithmeticall, Geometricall, and Harmonicall Computation* (1624).

Jenison, R., *The Cities Safetie: Or a Fruitfull Treatise (and Usefull for These Dangerous Times) on Psalm 127* (1630).

Jenkins, D., *Pacis Consultum... Describing the Court Leet* (1657).

Johnson, M., *Ludgate, What It Is, Not What It Was, Or A Full and Clear Discovery and Description of... That Prison* (1659).

Johnson, R., *The Pleasant Walkes of Moore-fields* (1607).

Kitchin, J., *The Grand Statute: Or the Law of Death Unalterable, Opened and Applied in a Sermon Preached May 11 1660* (1660).

Lambarde, W. *The Duties of Constables, Borsholders, Tythingmen and Such other Law and Lay Ministers of the Peace*, first published in 1584 (1602).

Layer, J., *The Office and Dutie of Constables, Churchwardens and Other the Overseers of the Poore* (1641).

Leadbetter, A., *Arithmetical Rules, Digested and Contracted for the Help and Benefit of Memory Very Necessary and Useful, as Well for Gentlemen and Tradesmen, as for Youth and Apprentices, in Mercantile Affairs* (1691).

Leigh, E., *A Phililogicall Commentary Or an Illustration of the Most Obvious and Useful Words in the Law* (2nd edition, 1658).

Leybourn, W., *The Art of Numbering* (1667).

Leybourn, W., *The Art of Dialling Performed Geometrically by Scale and Compasses* (1669).
Leybourn, W., *The Art of Measuring Containing the Description and Explanation of the Carpenters New Rule* (1669).
Lithgow, W., *The Present Surveigh of London and England's State* (1643).
Lowe, J., *Geodaesia Or The Art of Surveying and Measuring of Land* (1688).
Malynes, G., *England's View, in the Unmasking of Two Paradoxes* (1603).
Meriton, G., *A Guide for Constables, Churchwardens, Overseers of the Poor, Surveyors of the Highways, Treasurers of the County Stock, masters of the House of Correction, Bayliffs of Mannours, Toll-takers in Fairs &c* (1674).
Mill, H., *A Night's Search Discovering the Nature and Condition of All Sorts of Nightwalkers With Their Associates* (1640).
More, R., *The Carpenters Rule or a Booke Shewing Many Plain Ways Truly to Measure Ordinarie Timber and Other Extraordinarie Solids* (1602).
Mynshul, G., *Characters of Prisons and Prisoners* (1638).
Newcomen, M., *The All-Seeing Unseen Eye of God Discovered in a Sermon Preached Before the Honourable House of Commons at St. Margarets Westminster, December 30, 1646* (1647).
Nichols, T., *Arcula Gemmea: Or A Cabinet of Jewels. Discovering the Nature, Vertue, Value of Pretious Stones, With Infallible Rules to Escape the Deceit of All Such as Are Adulterate and Counterfeit* (1653).
Norden, J., *England an Intended Guyde for English Travailers* (1625).
Norden, J., *The Surveiors Dialogue* (1610).
Ogilby, J., *The Traveller's Guide, Or A Most Exact Description of the Roads of England* (1699).
Oldcastle, H., *A Briefe Instruction and Maner Hovv to Keepe Bookes of Acompts After the Order of Debitor and Creditor & As Well for Proper Accompts Partible, &c* (1588).
P.W., *The Prentise's Practice in Godlinesse and His True Freedome* (1613).
Payne, E., *Antichrist in Spirit Unmasked: Or Quakerism a Great Delusion* (1692).
Peacham, H., *A Discourse Between the Crosse in Cheap and Charring Crosse* (1641).
Petit, P., *A Discourse of the Growth of England in Populousness and Trade Since the Reformation* (1689).
Petri, N., *The Pathway to Knowledge* (1596).
Phillips, Edward, *The New World of Words, Or a General English Dictionary* (4th edition, 1678).
Powell, T., *Directions for Search of Records Remaining in the Chancerie, Tower [and] Exchequer* (1622).
Powell, T., *The Beauty, Vigour, and Strength of Youth Bespoke for God* (1676).
Prynne, W., *The Unlovelinesse of Love-Lockes. Or a Summarie Discourse, Proving the Wearing and Nourishing of a Locke or Love-Locke to be Altogether Unseemely and Unlawfull Unto Christians* (1628).
Pulton, F., *An Abstract of All the Penal Statutes Which Be General, in Force and Use Wherein is Conteyned the Effect of All Those Statutes Which do Threaten to the Offenders Thereof the Losse of Life, Member, Landes, Goods, or Other Punishment or Forfaiture Whatsoeuer...* (1577).
R.F., *A Collection of English Proverbs* (Cambridge, 1670).
R.M., *Micrologia. Characters, Or Essayes, of Persons, Trades, and Places, Offered to the City and Country* (1629).

Raleigh, W., *Maxims of State* (1650).
Record, R., *The Whetstone of Witte Whiche is the Seconde Parte of Arithmetike* (1557).
Record, R., *The Ground of Arts. Teaching the Perfect Worke and Practise of Arithmeticke... Augmented by Mr John Dee* (1640 edition).
Richardson, C., *A Sermon Concerning the Punishment of Malefactors* (1616).
Rid, S., *The Art of Jugling Or Legerdemaine VVherein is Deciphered, All the Conueyances of Legerdemaine and Jugling... Cautions to Beware of Cheating at Cardes and Dice* (1612).
Ridley, G., *The Life of Dr Nicholas Ridley, Sometime Bishop of London Shewing the Plan and Progress of the Reformation* (1763).
Sanderson, T., *Of Romanizing Recusants, and Dissembling Catholicks. A Countermaund of a Counterfeit Embassage* (1611).
Seller, J., *Practical Navigation* (1669).
Seller, J., *A Description of the Sands, Shoals, Buoyes, Beacons, Roads, Channels, and Sea Marks on the Coast of England From the Southforeland to Flamborough Head* (1671?).
Seller, J., *The English Pilot* (1671).
Seller, J., *The Coasting Pilot Describing the Sea Coasts, Chanells, Sounding Sands, Shoals, Rocks, and Dangers, the Bayes, Roads, Harbors, Rivers and Ports, with the Buoyes, Beacons, and sea marks upon ye coasts of England, Holland, Flanders, & France* (1673).
Seller, J., *Atlas Caelestiss, Containing the Systems and Theoryes of the Planets, the Constellations of the Starrs, and Other Phenomina's of the Heavens* (1677?).
Seller, J., *A Coelestiall Planisphere* (1678?).
Seller, J., *Proposals for the Carrying on an Actual Survey of All the Counties in the Kingdom of England and Principality of Wales* (1679?).
Seller, J., *A New Systeme of Geography* (1690).
Seller, J., *A Moderate Computation of the Expences in Provisions, Spent in the Cities of London and Westminster, and the Places Within the Weekly Bills of Mortality, for a Year, Month, Week, Day, Hour and Minute* (1691).
Seller, J., *Anglia Contracta, Or A Description of the Kingdom of England and Principality of Wales in Several New Mapps of All the Countyes Therein Contained* (1695).
Shelford, R., *Lectures Or Readings Upon the 8 Verse of the 22 Chapter of Proverbs, Concerning the Vertuous Education of Youth* (1606).
Sheppard, W., *A New Survey of the Justice of Peace His Office* (1659).
Sheppard, W., *Of the Office of the Clerk of the Market, of Weights and Measures, and the Laws Provision for Man and Beast, for Bread, Wine, Beer, Meal, &c* (1665).
Shower, J., *Seasonable Advice to Youth* (1692).
Smith, Sir T., *De Republica Anglorum: The Maner of Governement or Policie of the Realme of England* (1584).
[Smith, W.,] *The Charge Given by Sir William Smith, Bart, at the Quarter-Sessions of the Peace Held for the County of Middlesex at Westminster on Monday the 24th of April, 1682* (1682).
Squire, J., *A Thankes-giving for the Decreasing and Hope of Removing of the Plague* (1637).
Strype, J., *A Survey of the Cities of London and Westminster... Written at First in the Year MDXCVIII by John Stow... Corrected, Improved, and Very Much Enlarged: and the Survey Brought Downe From the Year 1633*, 5 books in 2 vols (1720).

Thorndike, H., *Just Weights and Measures That is the Present State of Religion Weighed in the Balance and Measured by the Standard of the Sanctuary* (1662).

Turner, F., *Letter to the Clergy of the Diocese of Ely From the Bishop of Ely Before and Preparatory to His Visitation* (Cambridge, 1686).

Van Langeren, J., *A Direction for the English Traviller By Which He Shal be Inabled to Coast About All England and Wales* (1636).

Vaughan, W., *The Golden-Grove* (1600).

W.R., *A True Relation of His Majesties Coming to the Town of Shrewsbury on the 20 of This Instant September and His Passage From Thence the 23 Day to the City of Chester With the Manner of His Entertainment There* (1642).

Wall, T., *Spiritual Armour to Defend the Head From the Superfluity of Naughtiness Being a Loving and Christian Tender* (1688).

Warwick, Sir P., *A Discourse of Government as Examined by Reason, Scripture, and Law of the Land, Or True Weights and Measures Between Soveraignty and Liberty Written in the Year 1678* (1694).

White, C., *Of Oathese, Their Object, Forme, and Bond: The Punishment of Perjuries and the Impietie of Papal Dispensation* (1627).

Wingate, E., *Justice Revived being the Whole Office of a Countrey Justice of the Peace* (1661).

Wingate, E., *The Exact Constable With His Origin and Power in All Cases Belonging to His Office* (1677).

Wormock, L., *Billa Vera, Or The Arraignment of Ignoramus* (1682).

Yearwood, R., *The Penitent Murderer* (1659).

Editions of Early Books and Manuscripts

A Calendar to the Records of the Borough of Doncaster, 4 vols (Doncaster, 1899–1902).

Allen, D. H., ed., *Essex Quarter Sessions Order Book, 1652–1661*, Essex Record Office Publications, 65 (Chelmsford, 1974).

Atkinson, J. C., ed., *North Riding Quarter Sessions Records*, 9 vols, North Riding Record Society 1–9 (1884–92).

Axon, E., ed., *Manchester Sessions: Notes of Proceedings Before Oswald Mosley (1616–1630), Nicholas Mosley (1661–1672), and Sir Oswald Mosley (1734–1739)… Volume 1, 1616–1623*, Lancashire and Cheshire Record Society, 42 (1901).

Bacon, F., *Francis Bacon: Major Works*, ed. B. Vickers (Oxford, 1996).

Bacon, N., *The Annalls of Ipswiche. The Lawes, Customes, and Government of the Same* (1654), ed. W. H. Richardson (Ipswich, 1884–5).

Bailey, F. A., ed., *A Selection from the Prescot Court Leet and Other Records, 1447–1600*, The Record Society of Lancashire and Cheshire, 89 (Chester. 1937).

Barron, C., Coleman, C., and Gobb, C., eds., 'The London Journal of Alessandro Magno 1562', *London Journal* (1983).

Bates, E. H., ed., *Quarter Sessions Records for the County of Somerset*, 4 vols, Somerset Record Society (1907–19).

Bennett, H. E., and Dewhurst, J. C., eds., *Quarter Session Records With Other Records of the Justices of the Peace for the County Palatine of Chester, 1559–1760*, The Record Society of Lancashire and Cheshire, 94 (Chester, 1940).

Bennett, M., ed., *A Nottinghamshire Village in War and Peace: The Accounts of the Constables of Upton, 1640–1666*, Thoroton Society, 39 (Nottingham, 1995).

Blades, R., ed., *Oxford Quarter Sessions Order Book 1614–1637*, Oxford Historical Society, NS, 29 (Woodbridge, 2009).

Bolton, E., *The Cities Advocate* (first published in 1629), facsimile copy, The English Experience, 715 (Amsterdam and Norwood, NJ, 1975).

Brinkworth, E. R. C., ed., *South Newington Churchwardens' Accounts 1553–1684*, Banbury Historical Society, 6 (1964).

Burne, S. A. H., ed., *Staffordshire Quarter Sessions Rolls. Vol II, 1590–1593* (Kendal, 1932).

Burnet, G., *The History of the Reformation of the Church of England*, 1679, ed. N. Pocock (Oxford, 1865).

Chapman, G., Jonson, B., and Marston, J., *Eastward Hoe*, first published in 1605, Tudor Facsimile Texts (New York, 1970).

Cockburn, J. C., ed., *Calendar of Assize Records. Hertfordshire Indictments. James I* (HMSO, 1975).

Cox, J. C., ed., *Churchwardens' Accounts from the Fourteenth Century to the Close of the Seventeenth Century* (1913).

Cunnington, B. H., ed., *Some Annals of the Borough of Devizes*, 2 vols (Devizes, 1925–6).

Cunnington, B. H., ed., *Records of the County of Wiltshire* (Devizes, 1932).

Day, W., ed., *Oswestry Parish Church: The Churchwardens' Accounts for 1579–1613* (Oswestry, 1970).

de Beccaria, C., *On Crimes and Punishments*, first published in 1764, ed. H. Paolucci (New York, 1963), 57.

Dekker, T., *Lanthrone and Candle-Light*, first published in 1608, The English Experience, 585 (Amsterdam and New York, 1973).

Drew, C., ed., *Lambeth Churchwardens' Accounts 1504–1645 and Vestry Book 1610*, Surrey Record Society, 3 vols., 60 and 63–4 (1940, 1941, 1943).

Dyer, A., and Palliser, D., eds., *The Diocesan Population Returns for 1563 and 1603*, British Academy Records of Social and Economic History, NS, 31 (Oxford, 2005).

Earwaker, J. E., ed., *The Court Leet Records of the Manor of Manchester, From the Year 1552 to the Year 1686, and From the Year 1731 to the Year 1846*, 12 vols (Manchester, 1884–90).

Earwaker, J. E., ed., *The Constables' Accounts of the Manor of Manchester From the Year 1612 to the Year 1647 and From the Year 1743 to the Year 1776*, 3 vols (Manchester 1891–1902).

Emmison, F. G., ed., *Early Essex Town Meetings: Braintree, 1619–1636; Finchingfield, 1626–1634* (London and Chichester, 1970).

Evelyn, J., *The Diary of John Evelyn*, ed. E. S. Beer, 6 vols (Oxford, 1955).

Eyre, A., 'A Diurnall or Catalogue of All My Accions and Expences from the 1st of January 1647', in C. Jackson, ed., *Yorkshire Diaries and Autobiographies in the Seventeenth and Eighteenth Centuries*, Vol. I, Surtees Society Publications, 65 (Durham, 1886).

Foster, J. E., ed., *The Diary of Samuel Newton Alderman of Cambridge (1662–1717)* (Cambridge, 1890).

Fraser, C. M., ed., *Durham Quarter Sessions Rolls 1471–1625*, Surtees Society, 1 99 (Newcastle-upon-Tyne, 1991).

Fussell, G. E., ed., *Robert Loder's Farm Accounts 1610–1620*, Camden Record Society, 3rd series, 53 (1936).

Gibson, J. S. W., and Brinkworth, E. R. C., eds., *Banbury Corporation Records: Tudor and Stuart*, Banbury Historical Society, 15 (1977).

Guilding, J. M., ed., *Reading Records: Diary of the Corporation*, 4 vols (Oxford, 1886).

Harman, T., 'A Caveat or Warning for Common Cursetors', first published in 1567 in A. F. Kinney, ed., *Rogues, Vagabonds, and Sturdy Beggars: A New Gallery of Tudor and Early Stuart Rogue Literature* (Amherst, MA, 1990).

Hearing, T., and Bridges, S., eds., *Dorset Quarter Sessions Order Book 1635–1638: A Calendar*, Dorset Record Society, 14 (Dorchester, 2006).

Hill, R., and Holley, G., eds., *A Miscellany Comprising the Correspondence of Thomas Corie, Town Clerk of Norwich, 1664–1687 and Observations and Comments on the Visitation of Norfolk, 1664*, Norfolk Record Society, 27 (1956).

Horrocks, J. W., ed., *The Assembly Book of Southampton*, 4 vols, Southampton Record Society, 9 (Southampton, 1917–25).

Howell, J., *Familiar Letters or Epistolae Ho-Elianae*, 3 vols (1903).

Howes, John *MS, 1582, Being a Brief Note of the Order and Manner of the Proceedings in the First Erection of the Three Royal Hospitals of Christs, Bridewell, and St. Thomas the Apostle*, ed. W. Lemprière (1904).

Lambarde, W., *Eirenarcha, Or the Office of the Justice of the Peace*, first published in 1581, facsimile copy, The English Experience, 273 (Amsterdam and New York, 1970).

Le Hardy, W., ed., *Hertford County Records: Notes and Extracts from the Sessions Rolls 1581 to 1698*, 9 vols (1905–39).

Machyn, H., *The Diary of Henry Machyn Citizen and Merchant Taylor of London From A.D. 1550 to A.D. 1563*, ed. J. Gough Nichols, Camden Society, 42 (1848).

Mandley, de J. G. T., ed., *The Portmote or Court Leet Records of the Borough or Town and Royal Manor of Salford*, 2 vols, Chetham Society Publications, 46 (Manchester, 1902).

Manship, H., *The History of Great Yarmouth*, completed in manuscript in 1619, ed. C. J. Palmer, Kessinger Legacy Reprints (1854).

Masters, B. E., ed., *Chamber Accounts of the Sixteenth Century*, London Record Society, 20 (1984).

Mclure, N. E., ed., *The Letters of John Chamberlain*, 2 vols., The American Philosophical Society (Philadelphia, PA, 1939).

Melling, E., ed., *Kentish Sources VI: Crime and Punishment* (Maidstone, 1969).

Pound, J. F., ed., *The Norwich Census of the Poor, 1570*, Norfolk Record Society 40 (1971).

Power, M., ed., *Liverpool Town Books, 1649–1671*, The Records Society of Lancashire and Cheshire, 136 (Dorchester, 1999).

Quintrell, B. W., ed., *Proceedings of the Lancashire Justices of the Peace at the Sheriff's Table During Assizes Week, 1578–1694*, Lancashire and Cheshire Record Society, 121 (1981).

Ralph, E., and Williams, M. E., eds., *The Inhabitants of Bristol in 1696*, Bristol Record Society, 25 (Bristol, 1968).

Ramsay, E. M. E., and Maddock, A. J., eds., *The Churchwardens' Accounts of Walton-on-the-Hill, Lancashire, 1627–1667*, Lancashire and Cheshire Record Society, 151 (2005).

Ratcliff, S.C. and Johnson, H. C., eds., *Warwick County Records*, 9 vols. (Warwick, 1935–64).

Rev. Oliver Heywood, B.A., 1630–1702; His Autobiography, Diaries, and Anecdote Books, ed. J. Horsfall Turner (4 vols.; Brighouse, Bingley, 1881–85).

Salter, H. E., ed., *Oxford Council Acts, 1626–1665*, Oxford Historical Society, 95 (Oxford, 1933).

Scouloudi, I., ed., *Returns of Strangers in the Metropolis 1593, 1627, 1635, 1639: A Study of an Active Minority*, Huguenot Society of London Publications, 57 (1985).

Sharpe, F. R., ed., 'The Order Book of Ormskirk, 1613–1721', in *A Lancashire Miscellany*, Lancashire and Cheshire Record Society, 109 (1965).

Shaw, J., 'The life of Master John Shaw', in C. Jackson, ed., *Yorkshire Diaries and Autobiographies in the Seventeenth and Eighteenth Centuries*, Surtees Society, 65 (Durham, 1877).

Slack, P., ed., *Poverty in Early-Stuart Salisbury*, Wiltshire Record Society, 31 (Devizes, 1975).

Spicksley, J., ed., *The Business and Household Accounts of Joyce Jeffreys, Spinster of Hereford, 1638–1648*, Records of Economic and Social History, NS, 41 (Oxford, 2012).

Steel, T., ed., *Prescot Churchwardens' Accounts, 1635–1663*, Record Society of Lancashire and Cheshire, 137 (2002).

The Casebook of Francis Ashley JP, Recorder of Dorchester, 1614–35, ed. J. H. Bettey, Dorset Record Society, 7 (1981).

The Diary of Thomas Isham, ed. Sir G. Isham, trans. N. Marlow (Farnborough, 1971).

The Diary of Ralph Josselin, ed. A. Macfarlane, British Academy Records of Social and Economic History, NS, III (Oxford, 1976).

The Diary of Roger Lowe of Ashton-in-Makerfield, Lancashire, 1663–74, ed. W. L. Sachse (New Haven, 1938).

The Diary of the Rev. Henry Newcome From September 30, 1661, to September 29, 1663, ed. T. Heywood, Chetham Society, 18 (Manchester, 1849).

The Diary of Samuel Pepys, ed. R. Latham and W. Matthews, 11 vols (1970–83).

The Letters of John Chamberlain, ed. N. E. McClure, American Philosophy Society, 2 vols (Philadelphia, 1939).

The Notebook of Robert Doughty, 1662–1665, ed. J. Rosenheim, Norfolk Record Society, 54 (Norwich, 1989).

The Vestry Minute Book of the Parish of Stratford-on-Avon (1899).

Twemlow, J. A., ed., *Liverpool Town Books, Proceedings of Assemblies, Common Councils, Portmoot Courts etc. 1550–1862*, 2 vols (Liverpool, 1918–35).

Webb, J., ed., *Poor Relief in Elizabethan Ipswich*, Suffolk Records Society, 9 (Ipswich, 1966).

Weinstock, M., ed., *Weymouth and Melcombe Regis Minute Book 1625 to 1660*, Dorset Record Society, 1 (Dorchester, 1964).

William Whiteway of Dorchester, His Diary 1618 to 1635, Dorset Record Society, 12 (1991).
Willis, A. J., and Hoad, M. J., eds., *Portsmouth Record Series: Borough Sessions Papers 1653–1688* (Chichester, 1971).
Willis-Bund, J. W., ed., *Worcester County Records; The Quarter Sessions Rolls* (Worcester, 1899).
Wilson, T., *The State of England anno. Dom. 1600*, ed. F. J. Fisher, Camden Miscellany (1936).
Wright, T., ed., *Queen Elizabeth and Her Times*, 2 vols (1838).

Secondary Work

Ahnert, R., and Ahnert, S. E., 'Metadata, surveillance, and the Tudor state', *HWJ*, 87 (2019).
Alexander, A., *Geometrical Landscapes: The Voyages of Discovery and the Transformation of Mathematical Practice* (Stanford, CA, 2002).
Allison, K. J, 'An Elizabethan village "census"', *Bulletin of the Institute of Historical Research*, 36 (1963).
Almeroth-Williams, T., *City of Beasts: How Animals Shaped Georgian London* (Manchester, 2019).
Anderson, C., *Inigo Jones: The Architect of Kings* (New Haven and London, 2011).
Andrews, J., Briggs, A., Porter, R., Tucker, P., and Waddington, K., *The History of Bethlem* (London and New York, 1997).
Archer, I. W., 'The arts and acts of memorialization in early modern London', in J. F. Merritt, ed., *Imagining Early Modern London: Perceptions and Portrayals of the City from Stow to Strype* (Cambridge, 2001).
Arkell, T., 'Illuminations and distortions: Gregory King's scheme calculated for the year 1688 and the social structure of later Stuart England', *ECHR*, 59 (2006).
Ash, E. H., *Power, Knowledge, and Expertise in Elizabethan England* (Baltimore, MD, 2004).
Barber, C. L., *Shakespeare's Festive Comedy: A Study of Dramatic Form and Its Relation to Social Custom* (Princeton, NJ, 2012).
Bayman, A., *Thomas Dekker and the Culture of Pamphleteering in Early Modern London* (Farnham, 2014).
Beattie, J. M., *Policing and Punishment in London 1660–1750: Urban Crime and the Limits of Terror* (Oxford, 2001).
Beattie, J. M., *Crime and the Courts in England, 1660–1800* (Oxford. 1986).
Beier, A. L., *Masterless Men: The Vagrancy Problem in England, 1560–1640* (1985).
Beier, A. L., 'On the boundaries of new and old historicisms: Thomas Harman and the literature of roguery', *English Literary Renaissance*, 33 (2003).
Beier, A. L., 'Foucault Redux?: The roles of humanism, Protestantism, and an urban elite in creating the London Bridewell, 1500–1560', *Criminal Justice History*, 17 (2002).

Beier, A. L., 'Anti-language or jargon? Canting in the English underworld in the sixteenth and seventeenth centuries', in P. Burke and R. Porter, eds., *Languages and Jargons: Contributions to a Social History of Language* (Cambridge, 1995).

Ben-Amos, I. K., *The Culture of Giving: Informal Support and Gift-Exchange in Early Modern England* (Cambridge, 2008).

Ben-Chaim, M., 'The value of facts in Boyle's experimental philosophy', *History of Science*, 38 (2000).

Bidwell, J., 'The study of paper as evidence, artifact, and commodity', in P. Davidson, ed., *The Book Encompassed: Studies in Twentieth-Century Bibliography* (Cambridge, 1992).

Borsay, P., *The English Urban Renaissance: Culture and Society in the Provincial Town 1660–1770* (Oxford, 1989).

Borsay, P., '"All the town's a stage": urban ritual and ceremony, 1660–1800', in P. Clark, ed., *The Transformation of English Provincial Towns, 1600–1800* (1984).

Boswell, C., *Disaffection and Everyday Life in Interregnum England* (Woodbridge, 2017).

Boulton, J., 'The poor among the rich: a long-term view of pauperism in London's west end', in P. Griffiths and M. S. R. Jenner, eds., *Londinopolis: Essays in the Cultural and Social History of Early Modern London* (Manchester, 2000).

Boulton, J., 'The Marriage Duty Act and parochial registration in London, 1695–1706', in K. Shurer and T. Arkell, eds., *Surveying the People: The Interpretation and Use of Document Sources for the Study of Population in the Later Seventeenth Century* (Matlock, 1992).

Boulton, J., 'The limits of formal religion: the administration of holy communion in late Elizabethan and early Stuart London', *London Journal*, 10 (1984).

Braddick, M. J., *State Formation in Early Modern England, c.1550–1700* (Cambridge, 2000).

Brett-James, N. G., *The Growth of Stuart London* (1935).

Broadway, J., *'No Historie so Meete': Gentry Culture and the Development of Local History in Elizabethan and Early Stuart England* (Manchester, 2006).

Brooks, C., 'Projecting, political arithmetic and the Act of 1695', *English Historical Review*, 97 (1982).

Brushfield, T. N., 'The financial diary of a citizen of Exeter', 1631–43', *Reports and Transactions of the Devonshire Association for the Advancement of Science, Literature, and Art*, 33 (Exeter, 1901).

Burke, P., *A Social History of Knowledge from Gutenberg to Diderot* (Oxford, 2000).

Burke, P., 'Perceiving a counter-culture', in his *The Historical Anthropology of Early Modern Italy: Essays on Perception and Communication* (Cambridge, 1987).

Cain, P., 'Robert Smith and the reform of the archives of the city of London, 1580–1623', *London Journal*, 13 (1987–8).

Cannadine, D., 'The transformation of ritual in modern Britain: the Colchester Oyster Feast', *P&P*, 94 (1982).

Capp, B., 'Arson, fear of arson, and incivility in early modern England', in P. Burke et al., eds., *Civil Histories* (Oxford, 2000).

Carrel, H., 'The ideology of punishment in late medieval English towns', *SH*, 34 (2009).

Cassedy, J. H., *Demography in Early America: Beginnings of the Statistical Mind, 1600–1800* (Cambridge, MA, 1969).

Chapman, C. R., *Pre-1841 Census and Population Listings in the British Isles* (Dursley, 1999).
Clark, P., *British Clubs and Societies 1500–1800: The Origins of an Associational World* (Oxford, 2000).
Clark, P., and Clark, J., 'The social economy of the Canterbury suburbs; the evidence of the census of 1564', in A. Detsicas and N. Yates, eds., *Studies in Modern Kentish History* (Maidstone, 1983).
Clark, S., *Thinking with Demons: The Idea of Witchcraft in Early Modern Europe* (Oxford, 1997).
Clay, C., 'Landlords and estate management', in J. Thirsk, ed., *Agrarian History of England and Wales, VII, 1640–1750: Agricultural Change* (Cambridge, 1985).
Cockayne, E., *Hubbub: Filth, Noise, and Stench in England* (New Haven and London, 2007).
Cockburn, J. S., *A History of English Assizes, 1558–1714* (Cambridge, 1972).
Cohen, E., 'The animated pain of the body', *AHR*, 105 (2000).
Coleman, D. C., *The British Paper Industry, 1495–1860: A Study in Industrial Growth* (Oxford, 1958).
Coleman, O., 'What figures? Some thoughts on the use of information by medieval governments', in D. C. Coleman and A. H. John, eds., *Trade, Government, and Economy in Pre-Industrial England* (1976).
Cooper, T., *Citizen Portrait: Portrait Painting and the Urban Elite of Tudor and Jacobean England and Wales* (London and Newhaven, 2012).
Corbin, A., *The Foul and the Fragrant: Odour and the Social Imagination* (1996).
Cormack, L., 'The commerce of utility: teaching mathematical geography in early modern England', *Science and Education*, 15 (2006).
Covington, S., 'Cutting, branding, whipping, burning: the performance of judicial wounding in early modern England', in J. R. Allard and M. R. Martin, eds., *Staging Pain, 1580–1800: Violence and Trauma in British Theatre* (Farnham, 2009).
Cressy, D., *Gypsies: An English History* (Oxford, 2018).
Cressy, D., 'Literacy in context: meaning and measurement in early modern England', in J. Brewer and R. Porter, eds., *Consumption and the World of Goods* (Abingdon, 1993).
Cummins, T., and Rappaport, J., 'The reconfiguration of civic and sacred space: architecture, image, and writing in the colonial northern Andes', *Latin American Literary Review*, 26 (1998).
Dabhoiwala, F., *The Origins of Sex: A History of the First Sexual Revolution* (2012).
Dawson, A. B., and Yachnin. P., *The Culture of Playgoing in Shakespeare's England* (Cambridge, 2001).
Dawson, M. S., 'Histories and texts: refiguring the diary of Samuel Pepys', *HJ*, 41 (2000).
De Vivo, F., *Information and Communication in Venice: Rethinking Early Modern Politics* (Oxford, 2007).
De Vivo, F., Guidi A., and Silvestri, A., eds., 'Archival transformations in early modern European history', special edition, *European History Quarterly*, 46 (2016).

Dolan, Frances E., *True Relations: Reading, Literature, and Evidence in Seventeenth-Century England* (Philadelphia, PA, 2013).

Dooley, B., and Baron, S. A., eds., *The Politics of Information in Early Modern Europe* (Abingdon, 2001).

Dyer, A., 'The Bishops' Census of 1563: its significance and accuracy', *Local Population Studies*, 49 (1992).

Eckstein, N. A., 'Florence on foot: an eye-level mapping of the early modern city in time of plague', *Renaissance Studies*, 30 (2015).

Eliav-Feldman, M., *Renaissance Imposters and Proofs of Identity* (Basingstoke, 2012).

Farrell, M., *Counting Bodies: Population in Colonial American Writing* (Oxford, 2016).

Feingold, M., *The Mathematicians' Apprenticeship: Science, Universities, and Society in England, 1560–1640* (Cambridge, 1984).

Feingold, M., 'Gresham College and London practitioners: the nature of the English mathematical community', in F. Ames-Lewis, ed., *Sir Thomas Gresham and Gresham College: Studies in the Intellectual History of London in the Sixteenth and Seventeenth Centuries* (Aldershot, 1999).

Forster, G. C. F., 'Civic government in Chester, 1642–1660', *Northern History*, 37 (2000).

Fox, A., *Oral and Literate Cultures in England, 1500–1700* (Oxford, 2000).

Freear, J., 'Robert Loder, Jacobean management accountant', in R. H. Parker and B. S. Yarney, eds., *Accounting History: Some British Contributions* (Oxford, 1994).

Freeman, M., '"Splendid display, pompous spectacle': historical pageants in twentieth-century Britain', *SH*, 38 (2010).

French, H., *The Middle Sort of People in Provincial England 1600–1750* (Oxford, 2007).

French, H., '"Ingenious and learned gentlemen": social perceptions and self-fashioning among parish elites in Essex, 1680–1740', *SH*, 25 (2000).

French, H., 'Social status, localism, and the "middle sort of people" in England 1620–1720', *P&P*, 166 (2000).

Fuller, M. C., *Voyages in Print: English Travel to America, 1576–1624* (Cambridge, 1995).

Fumerton, P., *Unsettled: The Culture of Mobility and the Working Poor in Early Modern England* (Chicago, IL, 2006).

Gaskill, M., 'Witchcraft and evidence in early modern England', *P&P*, 198 (2008).

Gatrell, V. A. C., *The Hanging Tree: Execution and the English People, 1770–1868* (Oxford, 1994).

Glaisyer, N., *The Culture of Commerce in England, 1660–1720* (Martlesham, 2006).

Glaisyer, N., 'Calculating credibility: print culture, trust, and economic figures in early eighteenth-century England', *ECHR*, 60 (2007).

Goose, N., 'The bishops' census of 1563: a re-examination of its reliability', *Local Population Studies*, 56 (1996).

Goose, N., 'Household size and structure in early Stuart Cambridge', *SH*, 5 (1980).

Grafton, A., and Jardine, L., '"Studied for action": How Gabriel Harvey read his Livy', *P&P*, 129 (1990).

Grassby, R., *The Business Community in Seventeenth-Century England* (Cambridge, 1995).

Griffiths, P., *Lost Londons: Change, Crime, and Control in the Capital City, 1550–1660* (Cambridge, 2008).

Griffiths, P., *Youth and Authority: Formative Experiences in England, 1560–1640* (Oxford, 1996).
Griffiths, P., 'Surveying the people', in K. Wrightson, ed., *A Social History of England, c.1500–c.1750* (Cambridge, 2016).
Griffiths, P., 'Local arithmetic: information cultures in early modern England', in S. Hindle, A. Shepard, and J. Walter, eds., *Remaking English Society: Social Relations and Change in Early Modern England* (Woodbridge, 2013).
Griffiths, P., 'Punishing words: insults and injuries, 1525–1700', in A. McShane and G. Walker, eds., *The Extraordinary and the Everyday in Early Modern England: Essays in Celebration of the Work of Bernard Capp* (Basingstoke, 2010).
Griffiths, P., 'Bodies and souls in Norwich: punishing petty crime, 1540–1700', in S. Devereaux and P. Griffiths, eds., *Penal Practice and Culture, 1500–1900: Punishing the English* (Basingstoke, 2004).
Griffiths, P., 'Introduction: punishing the English', in S. Devereaux and P. Griffiths, eds., *Penal Practice and Culture, 1500–1900: Punishing the English* (Basingstoke, 2004).
Griffiths, P., 'Inhabitants', in C. Rawcliffe and R. Wilson, eds., *Norwich Since 1550* (2004).
Griffiths, P., 'Politics made visible: order, residence, and uniformity in Cheapside, 1600–45', in P. Griffiths and M. S. R. Jenner, eds., *Londinopolis: Essays in the Cultural and Social History of Early Modern London* (Manchester, 2000).
Griffiths, P., 'Overlapping circles: imagining criminal communities in early modern London', in A. Shepard and P. Withington, eds., *Communities in Early Modern England* (Manchester, 2000).
Griffiths, P., 'Secrecy and authority in late sixteenth- and seventeenth-century London', *HJ*, 40 (1997).
Griffiths, P., 'Masterless young people in Norwich, 1560–1645', in Griffiths, A. Fox, and S. Hindle, eds., *The Experience of Authority in Early Modern England* (Basingstoke, 1996).
Groebner, V., *Who Are You? Identification, Deceptions, and Surveillance in Early Modern Europe*, trans. M. Kyburz and J. Peck (New York, 2007).
Hackel, B., *Reading Material in Early Modern England* (Cambridge, 2005).
Halliday, P., 'Authority in the archives', *Critical Analysis of Law*, 1 (2014).
Harkness, D. E., *The Jewel-House: Elizabethan London and the Scientific Revolution* (New Haven and London, 2007).
Harkness, D. E., 'Accounting for science: how a merchant kept his books in Elizabethan London', in M. C. Jacob, ed., *The Self-Perception of Early Modern Capitalists* (Basingstoke, 2008).
Hart, V., *Inigo Jones: The Architect of Kings* (New Haven and London, 2011).
Head, R., ed., 'Archival knowledge cultures in Europe, 1400–1900', special issue, *Archival Science*, 10 (2010).
Headrick, D. R., *When Information Came of Age: Technologies of Knowledge in the Age of Reason and Revolution, 1700–1850* (Oxford and New York, 2000).
Heal, F., *The Power of Gifts: Gift Exchange in Early Modern England* (Oxford, 2015).
Healy, M., *Fictions of Disease in Early Modern England: Bodies, Plagues and Politics* (Basingstoke, 2001).

Henderson, J., *Florence Under Siege: Surviving Plague in an Early Modern City* (New Haven, CT, and London, 2019).

Higgs, E., *The Information State in England: The Central Collection of Information on Citizens Since 1500* (Basingstoke, 2004).

Hindle, S., *On the Parish: The Micro-Politics of Poor Relief in Rural England, c. 1550–1750* (Oxford, 2004).

Hindle, S., *The State and Social Change in Early Modern England, c.1550–1640* (Basingstoke, 2000).

Hindle, S., 'Dependency, shame, and belonging: badging the deserving poor, c.1550–1750', *Cultural and Social History*, 1 (2004).

Holly, M., 'King Lear: the disguised and deceived', *Shakespeare Quarterly*, 24 (1973).

Hopper, A., 'Social mobility during the English Revolution: the case of Adam Eyre', *SH*, 38 (2013).

Hug, T. B., *Impostures in Early Modern England: Misrepresentations and Perceptions of Fraudulent Identities* (Manchester, 2009).

Hulme, T., 'A nation of town criers': civic publicity and historical pageantry in inter-war Britain', *Urban History*, 44 (2017).

Hunter, M., 'New light on the "Drummer of Tedworth": conflicting narratives of witchcraft in Restoration England', *Historical Research*, 78 (2005).

Hurl-Eamon, J., 'The Westminster imposters: impersonating law enforcement in early eighteenth-century London', *Eighteenth-Century Studies*, 38 (2005).

Hyland, P., *Disguise on the Early Modern English Stage* (Farnham, 2011).

Ingram, M., *Carnal Knowledge: Regulating Sex in England, 1470–1600* (Cambridge, 2017).

Ingram, M., 'Shame and pain: themes and variations in Tudor punishments', in S. Devereaux and P. Griffiths, eds., *Penal Practice and Culture, 1500–1900: Punishing the English* (Basingstoke, 2004).

Ingram, M., 'Sexual manners: the other face of civility in early modern England', in P. Burke, B. Harrison, and P. Slack, eds., *Civil Histories: Essays Presented to Sir Keith Thomas* (Oxford, 2000).

Ingram, M., 'Juridical folklore in England illustrated by rough music', in C. Brooks and M. Lobban, eds., *Communities and Courts in Britain, 1150–1900* (1997).

Innes, J., *Inferior Politics: Social Problems and Social Policies in Eighteenth-Century Britain* (Oxford, 2008).

Innes, J., 'Prisons for the poor: English bridewells 1555–1800', in F. Snyder and D. Hay, eds., *Labour, Law, and Crime: A Historical Perspective* (Oxford, 1987).

James, M., 'Ritual drama and the social body in late medieval England', *P&P*, 98 (1983).

Jenner, M. S. R., 'Civilization and deodorization? Smell in early modern English culture', in P. Burke, B. Harrison, and P. Slack, eds., *Civil Histories* (Oxford, 2000).

Jenner, M. S. R., 'The great dog massacre', in W. G. Naphy and P. Roberts, eds., *Fear in Early Modern Society* (Manchester, 1997).

Jobe, T. H., 'The Devil in Restoration science: the Glanvill-Webster witchcraft debate', *Isis*, 72 (1981).

John, A., *The Nature of the Book: Print and Knowledge in the Making* (Chicago, IL, 1998).

Jones, A. R., and Stallybrass, P., *Renaissance Clothing and the Materials of Memory* (Cambridge, 2000).

Jones, N., *The English Reformation: Religion and Cultural Adaptation* (Oxford, 2002).

Jutte, R., *Poverty and Deviance in Early Modern Europe* (Cambridge, 1994).

Karim-Cooper, F., 'Disguise and identity in the plays of Middleton', in S. Gossett, ed., *Thomas Middleton in Context* (Cambridge, 2011).

Kent, J., *The English Village Constable, 1580–1642: A Social and Administrative Study* (Oxford, 1986).

Kent, J., 'The rural 'middling sort' in early modern England circa 1640–1740: some economic, political, and socio-cultural characteristics', *Rural History*, 10 (1999).

Kent, J., 'State formation and parish government in England circa 1640–1740', *HJ*, 38 (1995).

Kesselring, K. J., 'Law, status, and the lash: judicial whipping in early modern England', *JBS*, 60 (2021).

King, P., *Crime, Law, and Discretion in England, 1740–1820* (Oxford, 2000).

King, P., *Crime and Law in England, 1750–1840: Remaking Justice from the Margins* (Cambridge, 2006).

King, S., 'Locating and characterizing poor households in late seventeenth century Bolton: sources and interpretations', *Local Population Studies*, 68 (2002).

King, W. J., 'How high is too high? Disposing of dung in seventeenth-century Prescot', *Sixteenth Century Journal*, 23 (1992).

Kishlansky, M. A., 'Martyr's tales', *JBS*, 53 (2014).

Kishlansky, M. A., 'A whipper whipped: the sedition of William Prynne', *HJ*, 56 (2013).

Klein, B., '"Between the bellies and the bums of the multitude": civic pageantry and the problem of audience in late Stuart London', *London Journal*, 17 (1992).

Klein, B., *Maps and the Writing of Space in Early Modern England and Ireland* (Basingstoke, 2001).

Kreager, P., 'New light on Graunt', *Population Studies*, 42 (1988).

Kyle, C., 'Monarchs and marketplace: proclamations as news in early modern England', *Huntington Library Quarterly*, 78 (2015).

Landau, N., 'The laws of settlement and the surveillance of immigration in eighteenth-century Kent', *C&C*, 3 (1988).

Laqueur, T., 'Crowds, carnival, and the state in English executions, 1604–1868', in A. L. Beier, D. Cannadine, and J. Rosenheim, eds., *The First Modern Society* (Cambridge, 1989).

Laslett, P., and Wall, R., eds., *Household and Family in Past Time* (Cambridge, 1972).

Leonard, E. M., *The Early History of English Poor Relief* (Cambridge, 1900).

Liappi, L., *Roguery in Print: Crime and Culture in Early Modern London* (Woodbridge, 2019).

Lockwood, M., *The Conquest of Death: Violence and the Birth of the Modern English State* (New Haven and London, 2017).

Luu, L. B., '"Taking the bread out of our mouths": xenophobia in early modern London', *Immigrants and Minorities*, 19 (2000).

McCarthy, H., 'The league of nations, public ritual and national identity in Britain, c.1919–56', *HWJ*, 70 (2010).

McCormick, T., *Human Empire: Mobility and Demographic Thought in the British-Atlantic World, 1500–1800* (Cambridge, 2022).
McCormick, T., *William Petty and the Ambitions of Political Arithmetic* (Oxford, 2009).
McGowen, R., 'From pillory to gallows: the punishment of forgery in the age of the financial revolution', *P&P*, 165 (1999).
Mackenney, R., *Tradesmen and Traders: The World of the Guilds in Venice and Europe, c. 1250–c. 1650* (London and Sydney, 1987).
McRae, A., *Literature and Domestic Travel in Early Modern England* (Cambridge, 2009).
McRae, A., *God Speed the Plough: The Representation of Rural England, 1500–1660* (Cambridge, 1996).
Mandelbrote, S., 'William Petty and Anne Greene: medical and political reform in Commonwealth Oxford', in M. Pelling and S. Mandelbrote, eds., *The Practice of Reform in Health, Medicine, and Science, 1500–2000: Essays for Charles Webster* (Aldershot, 2005).
Merritt, J. F., 'Contested legitimacy and the ambiguous rise of vestries in early modern London', *HJ*, 54 (2011).
Millstone, N., 'Seeing like a statesman in early Stuart England', *P&P*, 223 (2014).
Minson, S., 'Public punishment and urban space in early Tudor London', *London Topographical Record*, 30 (2010).
Morgan, G., and Rushton, P., *Rogues, Thieves, and the Rule of Law: The Problem of Law Enforcement in North-East England, 1718–1800* (1998.).
Mowl, T., and Earnshaw, B., *Architecture Without Kings: The Rise of Puritan Classicism Under Cromwell* (Manchester, 1995).
Munro, I., *The Figure of the Crowd in Early Modern London: The City and its Double* (Basingstoke, 2005).
Newman, J., Inigo Jones and the politics of architecture', in K. Sharpe and P. Lake, eds., *Culture and Politics in Early Stuart England* (Basingstoke, 1994).
Orgel, S., *Impersonations: The Performance of Gender in Shakespeare's England* (Cambridge, 1996).
Orlin, Cowen, L., *Locating Privacy in Tudor London* (Oxford, 2007).
Overton, M., *Agricultural Revolution in England: The Transformation of the Agrarian Economy 1500–1850* (Cambridge, 1996).
Overton, M., Whittle, J., Dean, D., and Hann, A., eds., *Production and Consumption in English Households, 1600–1750* (Abingdon, 2004).
Pearl, V., 'Change and stability in seventeenth-century London', *London Journal*, 5 (1979).
Pelling, M., *The Common Lot: Sickness, Medical Occupations and the Urban Poor in Early Modern England* (Harlow, 1998).
Phythian-Adams, C., 'Ceremony and the citizen: the communal year at Coventry, 1450–1500', in P. Clark and P. Slack, eds., *Crisis and Order in English Towns, 1500–1700: Essays in Urban History* (Toronto, 1972).
Pitman, J., 'Tradition and exclusion: parochial officeholding in early modern England, a case study from North Norfolk 1580–1640', *Rural History*, 15 (2004).
Poovey, M., *A History of the Modern Fact* (Chicago, IL, 1998).
Popper, N., 'An information state for Elizabethan England', *Journal of Modern History*, 90 (2018).

Porter, R., The rise of physical examination', in W. F. Bynum and R. Porter, eds., *Medicine and the Five Senses* (Cambridge, 1993).
Postles, D., 'Penance and the market place: a Reformation dialogue with the Medieval Church (c.1250–c.1600)', *Journal of Ecclesiastical History*, 54 (2003).
Pugh, R., *Imprisonment in Medieval England* (Cambridge, 1968).
Randall, A., *Riotous Assemblies: Popular Protest in Hanoverian England* (Oxford, 2006).
Rawcliffe, C., *Medicine for the Soul: The Life, Death and Resurrection of an English Medieval Hospital* (Stroud, 1999).
Rawcliffe, C., 'Town tykes and butchers' hounds: urban dogs at work in the later Medieval Ages', *Medieval Prosography*, 33 (2018).
Richeson, A. W., *English Land Measuring to 1800: Instruments and Practices* (Cambridge, MA, 1966).
Roberts, B., 'Entertaining the community: the evolution of civic ritual and public celebration, 1860–1953', *UH*, 44 (2017).
Robertson, J.C., 'Reckoning with London: interpreting the Bills of mortality before John Graunt', *UH*, 23 (1996).
Rogers, A., 'An early seventeenth-century listing: Wollaston, Notts', *Midland History*, 5 (1980).
Rudolph, J., 'Gender and the development of forensic science: a case study', *EHR*, 123 (2008).
Rule, J., and Trotter B., *A World of Paper: Louis XIV, Colbert de Torcy and the Rise of the Information State* (Montreal, 2014).
Rushton, P., 'Texts of authority: witchcraft accusations and the demonstration of truth in early modern England', in S. Clark, ed., *Languages of Witchcraft: Narrative, Ideology, and Meaning in Early Modern Culture* (Basingstoke, 2001).
Rushton, P., 'Idiocy, the family, and the community in early modern north-east England', in D. Wright and A. Digby, eds., *From Idiocy to Mental Deficiency: Historical Perspectives on People with Learning Disabilities* (London and New York, 1996).
Rushton, P., 'Lunatics and idiots: mental disability, the community, and the Poor Law in north-east England, 1600–1800', *Medical History*, 32 (1988).
Rusnock, A. A., *Vital Accounts: Quantifying Health and Population in Eighteenth-Century England and France* (Cambridge, 2002).
Rutledge, P., 'Archival management at Great Yarmouth since 1540', *Journal of the Society of Archivists*, 3 (1965).
Rutledge, P., 'Thomas Damet and the historiography of Great Yarmouth', *Norfolk Archaeology*, 33 (1965).
Sargent, R., 'Scientific experiment and legal expertise: the way of experience in seventeenth-century England', *Studies in History and Philosophy of Science Part A*, 20 (1989).
Schurer, K., and Arkell, T., eds., *Surveying the People: The Interpretation and Use of Document Sources for the Study of Population in the Later Seventeenth Century* (Oxford, 1992).
Scott, J. C., *Seeing Like a State: How Certain Schemes to Improve the Human Condition Have Failed* (New Haven and London, 1998).
Scott-Warren, J., *Shakespeare's First Reader: The Paper Trails of Richard Stonley* (Philadelphia, PA, 2019).

Serjantson, R. W., 'Testimony and proof in early modern England', *Studies in History and Philosophy of Science*, 30 (1999).

Shapin, S., *A Social History of Truth: Civility and Science in Seventeenth-Century England* (Chicago, IL, 1994).

Shapin, S., and Shaffer, S., *Leviathan and the Air-Pump: Hobbes, Boyle, and the Experimental Life* (Princeton, NJ, 1985).

Shapiro, B. J., *A Culture of Fact: England, 1550–1720* (Ithaca, NY, 2000).

Shapiro, B. J., *Probability and Certainty in Seventeenth-Century England: A Study of the Relationships Between Natural Science, Religion, History, Law, and Literature* (Princeton, NJ, 1983).

Shapiro, B. J., 'Religion and the law: evidence, proof and "matter of fact", 1660–1700', in N. Landau, ed., *Law, Crime, and English Society, 1660–1830* (Cambridge, 2002).

Sharpe, J. A., *Judicial Punishment in England* (1990).

Sharpe, J. A., '"Last dying speeches": religion, ideology, and public execution in seventeenth-century England', *P&P*, 107 (1985).

Sharpe, J. A., 'Enforcing the law in the seventeenth-century English village', in V.A.C. Gatrell, B. Lenman, and G. Parker, eds., *Crime and the Law: The Social History of Crime in Western Europe Since 1500* (1980).

Shoemaker, R. S., *The London Mob: Violence and Disorder in Eighteenth-Century England* (2004).

Shoemaker, R. S., *Prosecution and Punishment: Petty Crime and the Law in London and Rural Middlesex c.1660–1725* (Cambridge, 1991).

Shoemaker, R. S., 'Streets of Shame? The crowd and public punishments in London, 1700–1820', in S. Devereaux and P. Griffiths, eds., *Penal Practice and Culture* (Basingstoke, 2004).

Skelton, L. J., *Sanitation in Urban Britain, 1560–1700* (Abingdon, 2015).

Slack, P., *The Invention of Improvement: Information and Material Progress in Seventeenth-Century England* (Oxford, 2015).

Slack, P., *Perceptions of Population in Early Modern England*, (Stenton Lecture, 2010, University of Reading 2011).

Slack, P., *Poverty and Policy in Tudor and Stuart* England (Harlow,1988).

Slack, P., 'Counting people in early modern England: registers, registrars, and political arithmetic', *EHR*, 137 (2022).

Slack, P., 'Government and information in seventeenth-century England', *P&P*, 184 (2004).

Slack, P., 'Measuring the national wealth in seventeenth-century England', *ECHR*, NS, 57 (2004).

Slack, P., 'Great and good towns 1540–1700', in P. Clark, ed., *The Cambridge Urban history of Britain, Volume II, 1540–1840* (Cambridge, 2000).

Slack, P., 'Hospitals, workhouses, and the relief of the poor in early modern London', in O. P. Grell and A. Cunningham, eds., *Health Care and Poor Relief in Protestant Europe, 1500–1700* (1997).

Slack, P., 'Books of Orders: the making of English social policy, 1577–1631', *TRHS*, 5th series, 30 (1980).

Slack, P., 'Poverty and politics in Salisbury, 1597–1666', in P. Clark and P. Slack, eds., *Crisis and Order in English Towns, 1550–1700: Essays in Urban History* (Toronto, 1972).

Smith, G. T., 'Civilized people don't want to see that sort of thing: the decline of public physical punishment in London, 1760–1840', in C. Strange, ed., *Qualities of Mercy: Justice, Punishment, and Discretion* (Vancouver, BC, 1996).

Smyth, A., *Autobiography in Early Modern England* (Cambridge, 2010).

Soll, J., *The Information Master: Jean-Baptiste Colbert's Secret State Intelligence System* (Ann Arbor, MI, 2009).

Spierenburg, P., *The Prison Experience: Disciplinary Institutions and Their Inmates in Early Modern Europe* (New Brunswick, NJ, and London, 1991).

Steinberg, P. E., 'Calculating similitude and difference: John Seller and the "placing" of English subjects in a global community of nations', *Social and Cultural Geography*, 7 (2006).

Stephens, W. B., *Sources for English Local History* (Cambridge, 1981).

Stewart, L., *The Rise of Public Science: Rhetoric, Technology, and Natural Philosophy in Newtonian Britain, 1660–1750* (Cambridge, 1992).

Stewart, L., 'Philosophers in the counting-house: commerce, coffee-houses and experiment in early modern London', in P. O'Brien, ed., *Urban Achievement in Early Modern Europe: Golden Ages in Antwerp, Amsterdam, and London* (Cambridge, 2001).

Stuart, K., *Defiled Trades and Social Outcasts: Honour and Ritual Pollution in Early Modern Germany* (Cambridge, 1999).

Styles, P., 'A census of a Warwickshire village in 1698', *University of Birmingham Historical Journal*, 3 (1951).

Tadmor, N., 'The settlement of the poor and the rise of the form in England, c.1662–1780', *P&P*, 236 (2017).

Tate, W. E., *The Parish Chest: A Study of the Records of Parochial Administration* (3rd edition, Cambridge, 1969).

Thirsk, J., 'Plough and pen: agricultural writers in the seventeenth century', in T. Aston, P. Coss, C. Dyer, and J. Thirsk, eds., *Social Relations and Ideas: Essays in Honour of R. H. Hilton* (Cambridge, 1983).

Thomas, K., *Religion and the Decline of Magic: Studies in Popular Beliefs in Sixteenth- and Seventeenth-Century England* (1971).

Thomas, K., 'Numeracy in early modern England', *TRHS*, 5th series, 37 (1987).

Thomas, K., 'The meaning of literacy in early modern England', in G. Baumann, ed., *The Written Word: Literacy in Transition* (Oxford, 1986).

Thorsheim, P., *Waste into Weapons: Recycling in Britain During the Second World War* (Cambridge, 2015).

Tittler, R., *Portraits, Painters, and Publics in Provincial England 1540–1640* (Oxford, 2012).

Tittler, R., *The Face of the City: Civic Portraiture and Civic Identity in Early Modern England* (Manchester, 2007).

Tittler, R., *Townspeople and Nation: English Urban Experiences 1540–1640* (Stanford, CA, 2001).

Tittler, R., *The Reformation and the Towns in England: Politics and Political Culture, c.1540–1640* (Oxford, 1998).

Tittler, R., *Architecture and Power: The Town Hall and the English Urban Community c.1500–1640* (Oxford, 1991).

Tittler, R., 'Portraiture, precedence, and politics amongst the London liveries, 1540–1640', *UH*, 35 (2008).

Twyning, J., *London Dispossessed: Literature and Social Space in the Early Modern City* (Basingstoke, 1998).

Underdown, D., *Fire from Heaven: Life in an English Town in the Seventeenth Century* (1992).

Underdown, D., '"But the shows of their street": civic pageantry and charivari in a Somerset town, 1607', *JBS*, 50 (2011).

Ungerer, G., 'Prostitution in late Elizabethan London: the case of Mary Newborough', *Medieval and Renaissance Drama in England*, 15 (2003).

Ungerer, G., 'Mary Frith, alias Moll Cutpurse, in life and literature', *Shakespeare Studies*, 28 (2000).

Unsworth, C. R., 'Witchcraft beliefs and criminal procedure in early modern England', in T. G. Watkin, ed., *Legal Record and Historical Reality* (1989).

Verner, C., 'John Seller and the chart trade in seventeenth century England', in N. J. W. Thrower, ed., *The Compleat Plattmaker: Essays on Chart, Map, and Globe Making in England in the Seventeenth and Eighteenth Centuries* (Berkeley, CA, 1978).

Vigarello, G., *Concepts of Cleanliness: Changing Attitudes in France since the Middle Ages*, trans. J. Birrel, (Cambridge, 1988).

Waddell, B., 'Writing history from below: chronicling and record-keeping in early modern England', *HWJ*, 85 (2018).

Wales, T., '"Living at their own hands": policing poor people and the young in early modern England', *Agricultural History Review*, 6 (2013).

Wales, T., 'Poverty, poor relief, and the life-cycle: some evidence from seventeenth-century Norfolk', in R. Smith, ed., *Land, Kinship and Life-Cycle* (Cambridge, 1984).

Wall, R., 'English population statistics before 1800', *History of the Family*, 9 (2004).

Walter, J., *Covenanting Citizens; The Protestation Oath and Popular Culture in the English Revolution* (Oxford, 2017).

Walter, J., *Crowds and Popular Politics in Early Modern England* (Manchester, 2006).

Webster, C., *The Great Instauration: Science, Medicine, and Reform 1626–1660* (New York, 1975).

Wheeler, H., 'The invention of modern empiricism: juridical foundations of Francis Bacon's philosophy of science', *Law Library Journal*, 76 (1983).

Whiteman, A., 'The Compton census of 1676', in K. Shurer and T. Arkell, eds., *Surveying the People: The Interpretation and Use of Document Sources for the Study of Population in the Later Seventeenth Century* (Matlock, 1992).

Whitney, C., '"Usually in the werking daies": playgoing, journeymen, apprentices, and servants in guild records, 1582–92', *Shakespeare Quarterly*, 50 (1999).

Whittle, J., and Griffiths, E., *Consumption and Gender in the Early Seventeenth-Century Household: The World of Alice Le Strange* (Oxford, 2012).

Williams, L., '"To recreate and refresh their dulled spirites in the sweet and wholesome ayre": green space and the growth of the city', in J. Merritt, ed., *Imagining Early Modern London: Perceptions and Portrayals of the City from Stow to Strype* (Cambridge, 2001).

Williamson, F., *Social Relations and Urban Space: Norwich 1600–1700* (Woodbridge, 2014).

Withington, P., *The Politics of Commonwealth: Citizens and Freemen in Early Modern England* (Cambridge, 2005).
Wood, A., *The Memory of the People: Custom and Popular Senses of the Past in Early Modern England* Cambridge, 2013).
Wood, A., *The 1549 Rebellions and the Making of Early Modern England* (Cambridge, 2007).
Wood, A., 'Tales from the "Yarmouth Hutch": civic identities and hidden histories in an urban archive', in *P&P*, supplement 11, *The Social History of the Archive: Record-Keeping in Early Modern Europe* (2016).
Woolf, D., *The Social Circulation of the Past: English Historical Culture, 1500–1730* (Oxford, 2003).
Wrightson, K., *Earthly Necessities: Economic Lives in Early Modern Britain* (New Haven and London, 2000).
Wrightson, K., *English Society, 1580–1680* (1982).
Wrightson, K., 'The decline of neighbourliness revisited', in N. Jones and D. Woolf, eds., *Local Identities in Late Medieval and Early Modern England* (Houndmills, 2007).
Wrightson, K., '"Sorts of people" in Tudor and Stuart England', in J. Barry and C. Brooks, eds., *The Middling Sort of People: Culture, Society, and Politics in England, 1550–1800* (Basingstoke, 1994).
Wrightson, K., 'Two concepts of order: justices, constables, and jurymen in seventeenth-century England', in J. Brewer and J. Styles, eds., *An Ungovernable People: The English and Their Law in the Seventeenth and Eighteenth Centuries* (1980).
Wrightson, K., and Levine, D., *Poverty and Piety in an English Village: Terling 1525–1700* (New York, 1979)—reprinted by Clarendon Press in 1995 with a new 'postscript' written by Wrightson.

Theses

Carrel, H., 'Civic Government and Identity in the Provincial Towns of Late Medieval England, c. 1370–c. 1500' (PhD thesis, University of Cambridge, 2007).
Hitchcock, T., 'The English Workhouse: A Study in Institutional Poor Relief in Selected Counties 1696–1750' (DPhil thesis, University of Oxford, 1985).
Jenner, M. S. R., 'Early modern English Conceptions of "Cleanliness" and "Dirt" as Reflected in the Environmental Regulation of London, c.1530–c.1700' (DPhil thesis, University of Oxford, 1991).
Minson, S, 'Political Culture and Urban Space in Early Tudor England' (DPhil thesis, University of Oxford, 2013).
Skelton, L. J., 'Environmental Regulation in Edinburgh and York, c.1560–c.1700' (PhD thesis, University of Durham, 2012).
White, M. T., 'Ordering the Mob: London's Public Punishments, c. 1783–1868' (PhD thesis, University of Hertfordshire, 2009).
Winter, C., 'Prisons and Punishments in Late Medieval London' (PhD thesis, University of London, 2012).

Index

For the benefit of readers, indexed terms that span two pages (e.g., 52–53) may, on occasion, appear on only one of those pages.